AF064090

The Social Archaeology of Australian Indigenous Societies

Edited by Bruno David, Bryce Barker and Ian J McNiven

Aboriginal Studies Press

First published in 2006
by Aboriginal Studies Press

© Bruno David, Bryce Barker and Ian J McNiven
© in individual chapters remains with the authors

Reprinted 2008

All rights reserved. No part of this book may be reproduced or transmitted in any form or by any means, electronic or mechanical, including photocopying, recording or by any information storage and retrieval system, without prior permission in writing from the publisher. The *Australian Copyright Act 1968* (the Act) allows a maximum of one chapter or 10 per cent of this book, whichever is the greater, to be photocopied by any educational institution for its education purposes provided that the educational institution (or body that administers it) has given a remuneration notice to Copyright Agency Limited (CAL) under the Act.

Aboriginal Studies Press
is the publishing arm of the
Australian Institute of Aboriginal
and Torres Strait Islander Studies.
GPO Box 553, Canberra, ACT 2601
Phone: (61 2) 6246 1183
Fax: (61 2) 6261 4288
Email: asp@aiatsis.gov.au
Web: www.aiatsis.gov.au/asp

National Library of Australia Cataloguing-In-Publication data:

David, Bruno, 1962– .

The social archaeology of Australian indigenous societies.

Bibliography.
Includes index.
ISBN 0 85575 499 0.

1. Aboriginal Australians/Social life and customs. 2. Social archaeology/Australia. 3. Australia/Antiquities. I. Barker, Bryce. II. McNiven, Ian. III. Title.

305.89915

Printed in Australia by Ligare Pty Ltd

Front cover photograph: Cygnet Repu of Mabuyag island, Zenadh Kes (Torres Strait), painting a Kaigas (shovelnosed shark), his maternal totem (awgadh), at Puluw Kod in 2001. Kind permission from Cygnet Repu to reproduce the photo. Photo courtesy of Ian J McNiven.

Cover design by Phil Scamp, Arts Imaging, Monash University

*This book is dedicated to Harry Lourandos,
who paved the way to a social archaeology of Indigenous Australia.*

Contents

Figures and tables   vii
Acknowledgements   ix
Contributors   x

Part 1 The emergence of social archaeology in Australia

1. The social archaeology of Indigenous Australia *Ian J McNiven, Bruno David and Bryce Barker*   2
2. An interview with Harry Lourandos *Harry Lourandos, Bruno David, Bryce Barker and Ian J McNiven*   20
3. Harry Lourandos' life and work: an Australian archaeological odyssey *Sandra Bowdler*   40

Part 2 Tyranny of text

4. Unpacking Australian prehistory *Bruno David and Tim Denham*   52
5. Hierarchies of knowledge and the tyranny of text: archaeology, ethnohistory and oral traditions in Australian archaeological interpretation *Bryce Barker*   72
6. Colonial diffusionism and the archaeology of external influences on Aboriginal culture *Ian J McNiven*   85
7. Harry Lourandos, the 'Great Intensification Debate', and the representation of Indigenous pasts *Deborah Brian*   107

Part 3 Anthropological approaches

8. Footprints of the ancestors: the convergence of anthropological and archaeological perspectives in contemporary Aboriginal heritage studies *Luke Godwin and James F Weiner*   124
9. Earth, wind, fire, water: the social and spiritual construction of water in Aboriginal societies *Marcia Langton*   139

10. The social, economic and historical construction of cycad palms among the Yanyuwa   *John J Bradley*   161
11. Landscapes with shadows of once living people: the *Kundawira* challenge   *Amanda Kearney and John J Bradley*   182
12. Towards an experiential archaeology of place: from location to situation through the body   *Franca Tamisari and James Wallace*   204

Part 4   Late-Holocene change
13. Hunter-gatherer social complexity at Roonka, South Australia   *F Donald Pate*   226
14. Social dynamism in the archaeology of the Western Desert   *Peter Veth*   242
15. Environmental change and variability in south-western Victoria: changing constraints and opportunities for occupation and land use   *John Tibby, A Peter Kershaw, Heather Builth, Aline Philibert and Christopher White*   254
16. Landscapes in western Torres Strait history   *Cassandra Rowe*   270
17. North of the Cape and south of the Fly: discovering the archaeology of social complexity in Torres Strait   *Melissa Carter*   287

Part 5   Extending the boundaries
18. Destablising how we view the past: Harry Lourandos and the archaeology of Bodmin Moor, south-west England   *Barbara Bender*   306

Publications by Harry Lourandos   319
References   322
Index   368

Figures and tables

Figures

Chapter 2   An interview with Harry Lourandos
Figure 1. Harry Lourandos (right) and Rhys Jones (left) excavating at Rocky Cape South cave in 1965 (photo courtesy of Harry Lourandos) — 21

Chapter 3   Harry Lourandos' life and work: an Australian archaeological odyssey
Figure 1. Harry Lourandos at Mount Cameron West in 1969 (photo courtesy of Harry Lourandos). — 42

Chapter 10   The social, economic and historical construction of cycad palms among the Yanyuwa
Figure 1. The study area — 163

Chapter 13   Hunter-gatherer social complexity at Roonka, South Australia
Figure 1. Map showing location of the Roonka Flat archaeological site, lower Murray River, South Australia — 227
Figure 2. Map showing location of larger Aboriginal burial sites (more than twenty individuals) in the Murray-Darling river system, south-eastern Australia (after Littleton 1999) — 230

Chapter 14   Social dynamism in the archaeology of the Western Desert
Figure 1. Location of key sites discussed in the text lying within the Western Desert and arid margins — 243

Chapter 15   Environmental change and variability in south-western Victoria
Figure 1. Lake Surprise and its immediate catchment — 258

Figure 2. Location of Lake Surprise, Mt Eccles — 258
Figure 3. Age–depth curve for the Lake Surprise sediments — 260
Figure 4. Lake Surprise environmental sequences — 268

Chapter 16 Landscapes in western Torres Strait history
Figure 1. Torres Strait showing major island groups — 273
Figure 2. Badu 15 — 274
Figure 3. Archaeological site Badu 15 pollen percentage diagram plotted against depth and age — 277
Figure 4. Multi-dimensional Scaling (MDS) ordination in two dimensions for combined pollen and spore presence/absence data set (stress = 0.2) — 281

Chapter 17 North of the Cape and south of the Fly
Figure 1. The Torres Strait with, inset, the eastern islands of Mer, Dauar and Waier (after McNiven & Feldman 2003) — 289
Figure 2. Ethnohistorically recorded clan divisions on Mer Island and the location of stone walled fish traps (after Haddon 1908, p. 170) — 299

Tables

Chapter 4 Unpacking Australian prehistory
Table 1. Prejudicial homologues used in the interpretation of Australian Aboriginal and New Guinean cultures — 60
Table 2. Gradients of prejudice often implicit to the interpretation of hunter-gatherers in Australia and agriculturalists in New Guinea, reflecting nineteenth-century evolutionary thinking — 63
Table 3. Geographical and historical prejudices implicit to the interpretation of Australian and New Guinean places and peoples — 67

Chapter 14 Social dynamism in the archaeology of the Western Desert
Table 1: Occupation phases and language movements (after Veth 2000) and likely art correlates — 252

Chapter 16 Landscapes in western Torres Strait history
Table 1. Badu 15 radiocarbon dating results (adapted from David *et al.* 2004b) — 276

Acknowledgements

First and foremost, warmest thanks to Harry Lourandos for the inspirations that led to this book. Thanks also to Gary Swinton of the School of Geography and Environmental Science at Monash University for drafting the figures. And a big thank you to the publishing team at Aboriginal Studies Press at the Australian Institute of Aboriginal and Torres Strait Islander Studies in Canberra, in particular Gabrielle Lhuede and Rhonda Black for their continued support.

Contributors

Bryce Barker is a senior lecturer in anthropology at the University of Southern Queensland, and is currently Head of Anthropology. He is a Fellow of the Australian Anthropology Society and is an editor of *Australian Archaeology*.
barker@usq.edu.au

Barbara Bender teaches at the Department of Anthropology, University College London. She has spent the last twenty years working on the social construction of landscape — the prehistoric, historic, and contemporary — with a particular interest in contested landscapes and landscapes of movement and exile. She is also concerned with finding ways to involve non-academics in discussions and presentations of their variable and changing notions of being in or out of place.

Sandra Bowdler graduated from The University of Sydney with an honours degree in anthropology in 1971, and from the Australian National University with a PhD in prehistory in 1979. She has taught archaeology at the University of Papua New Guinea, the University of New England and the University of Western Australia, where she has been professor of archaeology since 1983. She has carried out research into the archaeology of NSW, Tasmania, Victoria and Western Australia, as well as the Papuan Gulf and South-East Asia.
sbowdler@cyllene.uwa.edu.au

John J Bradley has worked for over two decades with the Yanyuwa people of the south-west Gulf of Carpentaria. An anthropologist, he has concentrated on issues of land and kin relationships as well as issues of memory as the point of emotional engagement with country. He has produced an Indigenous atlas of Yanyuwa country and is presently working on new understandings of song lines.
John.bradley@arts.monash.edu.au

Deborah Brian is a researcher and doctoral candidate at the University of Queensland in Brisbane, Australia. Her early research work, under the supervision of Harry Lourandos, explored the potential of taphonomic methodologies to provide more detailed readings of evidence for past cultural change. Her current research is an interrogation of the logical and discursive aspects of explanations of past cultural change in the Australian context, in the context of broader interests in Australian historiography, the politics of identity and the social construction of the past.

Heather Builth has spent over ten years researching Gunditjmara aquaculture in south-western Victoria. She is currently an ARC Research Fellow in the School of Geography and Environmental Science, Monash University. She is a landscape archaeologist specialising in past Indigenous land management, and also works with Indigenous communities on applying this knowledge to current ecological and cultural heritage issues. Heather is a director on the board of the Glenelg–Hopkins Catchment Management Authority.
heather.builth@arts.monash.edu.au

Melissa Carter's PhD thesis represents the first investigation into the pre-European archaeology of the Murray Islands, eastern Torres Strait. Her major interests are island colonisation and subsistence history, and she is currently developing new research on the ethnoarchaeology of the Solomon Islands. Melissa is presently employed as an archaeological consultant for the Australian Museum Business Services in Sydney, NSW.
melissac@austmus.gov.au

Bruno David is QEII Fellow with the Programme for Australian Indigenous Archaeology, School of Geography and Environmental Science at Monash University. He has undertaken cultural historical research in Australia, Vanuatu, Papua New Guinea and the USA. He has published widely on social aspects of archaeology, and is currently researching the archaeology of village life, oral tradition and rituals with local community groups in Torres Strait.
bruno.david@arts.monash.edu.au

Tim Denham is based at the Programme for Australian Indigenous Archaeology, School of Geography and Environmental Science at Monash University. His research focuses on early-to-mid–Holocene plant exploitation and early agriculture in the Highlands of Papua New Guinea.
tim.denham@arts.monash.edu.au

Contributors

Luke Godwin is Director of Central Queensland Cultural Heritage Management. He has been active in cultural heritage management in Queensland and NSW for more than twenty years, with particular reference to resource extraction and large-scale infrastructure development. A significant component of his practice is the provision of strategic advice on project design and management to a wide range of Aboriginal organisations and development proponents.
lgodwin@irock.com.au

Amanda Kearney has carried out fieldwork in the south-west Gulf of Carpentaria with the Yanyuwa people, and has more recently held a research position in Jinbunken, the Institute of Research and Human Studies at Kyoto University in Japan. Her work is inter-disciplinary and moves between anthropology, archaeology, cultural geography, ethnography and ethnohistory.

Peter Kershaw is Professor of Geography and Environmental Science and Director of the Centre for Palynology and Palaeoecology at Monash University. He has researched and published extensively, over the last thirty-five years on the history of vegetation in the Australasian–South-East Asian region and its applications to the elucidation of past climate change, biomass burning and human-environment relationships.
peter.kershaw@arts.monash.edu.au

Marcia Langton is Chair of Australian Indigenous Studies, University of Melbourne, and lectures at the School of Anthropology, Geography and Environmental Studies at the University of Melbourne. Marcia has published extensively on Aboriginal affairs, including land, resource, and social impact issues; Indigenous dispute processing; policing and substance abuse; gender; identity processing; art, film, and cultural studies.
marciall@unimelb.edu.au

Harry Lourandos, formally of the University of Queensland (Anthropology and Archaeology), has published extensively on Australian Aboriginal archaeology and ethnography, emphasising social perspectives, in international publications such as *World Archaeology, Quarternary International, Proceedings of the Prehistoric Society* and with Cambridge University Press.

Ian J McNiven is Senior Lecturer and Co-director of the Programme for Australian Indigenous Archaeology, Monash University. His research focuses on the archaeology of Australian Indigenous maritime cultures and the colonial history of archaeology.
Ian.McNiven@arts.monash.edu.au

Contributors

Donald Pate is Associate Professor of Archaeology at Flinders University and Editor-in-chief of *Australian Archaeology*. Pate received graduate and post-doctoral training in anthropological archaeology at Brown and Harvard universities, and was an Australian Institute of Aboriginal and Torres Strait Islander Studies Post-Doctoral Fellow at the Australian National University. He commenced research in Australia in 1983 with a focus on bio-archaeology.
donald.pate@flinders.edu.au

Aline Philibert obtained two masters degrees from France and Switzerland on ecological dimensions of environmental health, specialising in terrestrial and aquatic population dynamics and environmental toxicity. She obtained a PhD in palaeoecology at the University of Quebec in Montreal, Canada, after having worked on the long-term impact of forest cutting and wildfire on biogeochemical dynamics in boreal lakes and in arctic ponds. Her recent work in Australia explored long-term human-environmental interactions (measured over millennia) in south-western Victoria. She is currently based in Quebec, where her present work focuses on human impacts on the environment and environmental health (cardiovascular status), especially by aquatic proxy records in Canadian native populations and in the Brazilian Amazon.
philibert.aline@courrier.uqam.ca

Cassandra Rowe is a recent graduate of the Centre for Palynology and Palaeoecology within the School of Geography and Environmental Science, Monash University. Her doctoral research explored the environmental history of western Torres Strait, documenting natural and human causes for vegetation change. Her research focuses on how palynology, fire history and environmental change in the seasonal tropics can inform on people–land relations through history. She is based in the Department of Archaeology and Natural History at the Australian National University, and at the School of Geography and Environmental Science, Monash University.
cassandra.rowe@arts.monash.edu.au

Franca Tamisari, a sociocultural anthropologist, has carried out research work in north-east Arnhem Land since 1990. Her main research interests are often inter-disciplinary in nature, focusing on art, aesthetics, performance, and bicultural education, with a particular attention to dance and Australian Indigenous law. Since 2002 she has taught and conducted research at the School of Social Science, University of Queensland. She also taught at The University of Sydney (1996–2001) and at the Dipartimento Studi Storici, University Ca'Foscari of Venice, where she is currently seconded until the end of 2006. She has published nationally and internationally.
tamisari@unive.it or f.tamisari@uq.edu.au

Contributors

John Tibby is an Australian Post-Doctoral Fellow at the University of Adelaide, whose main interest is in reconstructing human impacts on the environment and past climate regimes using diatoms. He has worked on lakes in Australia, Turkey, Kenya and Indonesia on timescales ranging from less than 100 to over 20 000 years.
john.tibby@adelaide.edu.au

Peter Veth is Director of Research at the Australian Institute of Aboriginal and Torres Strait Islander Studies in Canberra. He has carried out long-term research on the evolution of desert societies in Australia and globally. He has also carried out collaborative multi-disciplinary work in Torres Strait, the Aru Islands, East Timor and the remote Pacific. Peter also holds an Adjunct Senior Research Fellowship at the Australian National University.
peter.veth@aiatsis.gov.au

James Wallace is a PhD candidate in the School of Social Science, Anthropology, Archaeology, Criminology and Sociology, at the University of Queensland His research interests are interdisciplinary and include issues associated with archaeological theory, ethnography, relationships of people with place, experience, perception and intentionality.

James F Weiner is a consultant anthropologist based in Canberra and is Visiting Fellow in Resource Management in the Asia–Pacific Program at the Australian National University. Formerly Lecturer in Anthropology at the Australian National University and University of Manchester, he has conducted fieldwork since 1979 in the Southern Highlands of Papua New Guinea, and since 1998 in eastern Queensland.
james.weiner@anu.edu.au

Christopher White is based at the School of Geography and Environmental Science, Monash University. He is completing his doctoral research on environmental change and variability in south-western Victoria, exploring its implications for the history of Indigenous regional occupation and land use.

Part 1
The emergence of social archaeology in Australia

Bevel-edged tool dating to the last 1000 years. It was used by an Aboriginal woman in southeast Queensland to process the starchy rhizome of Bungwall fern (a local staple plant food).

1.
The social archaeology of Indigenous Australia

Ian J McNiven, Bruno David and Bryce Barker

December 1978

A large group of volunteers is helping record and excavate Aboriginal cultural sites during an archaeology field summer school at Wood Wood, near Swan Hill in northern Victoria. The days are exciting, dirty and dusty but rich in the promise of better understanding through archaeological research the local Aboriginal past. The afternoons are abuzz with the day's discoveries, the seventy-odd people sharing ideas and interpretations with a communal sense of research achievement. Each evening the day is capped by a lecture by one of the distinguished staff attending the school.

One evening made a particularly profound impact on the audience. The director of the field program had delivered his daily 'sermon', this time a lecture on the late British archaeologist David Clarke's influential characterisation of what archaeology is all about: understanding how environmental 'subsystems' (the fauna, climate, geology and flora) interact with various cultural 'subsystems' (the economic, religious, psychological, social and material culture). On the blackboard these subsystems are depicted as a set of circles each interlinked by arrows (Clarke 1978, figure 23). Archaeology, it is claimed, concerns these subsystems; it tries to reveal information about each of them, and to understand the past means to understand the nature of their interactions.

Question time. One man stepped forward — a local Koorie man, a stranger to most present — with one deeply simple statement that reached to the heart of the matter. He said: 'This is all very well, but you forgot one thing'. With chalk in hand he reached to the blackboard, drew a large circle over the subsystems diagram, and inscribed the word 'people' into our hearts and souls.

Towards a social archaeology

If archaeology concerns human history, then by definition archaeology is about people both past and present. For most, this statement seems simple and self-evident. Think of the archaeology of ancient Egypt and we think of Pharaohs, the worship of animal gods, and the millions of hours worked by people building those same pyramids that continue to entertain our imaginations today. Think of the archaeology of ancient Rome and we think of the Colosseum and gladiators fighting to the death, or perhaps of Roman legions battling it out on some far-flung frontier. In each of these cases the past is filled with people and with forms of social interaction far removed from the daily activities we see in modern Egypt or Italy.

Now think of ancient Australia, the Australia of, say, 2000 years ago, or 5000 or 40 000 years ago. Who do we see? What are they doing? Are these ancient Indigenous Australians hunting and gathering for food in a dry land? Perhaps a man, spear in hand and kangaroo over one shoulder, or a small group of women gathering birds' eggs or digging for goannas?

In what ways do our images of those distant times differ from what we know of Indigenous Australians of the last 200 years? After thousands of journal articles — academic and popular — and hundreds of books written about the archaeology of Indigenous Australia over the last fifty years, why is it so difficult to imagine ancient Indigenous Australians (sometimes many thousands of years past) as anything more than ethnographically known peoples wandering across a timeless landscape in search of food?

In some respects lack of relevant imagery for what ancient Indigenous Australians did in the past reflects a general ignorance of the fruits of archaeological research and poor public education (Balme & Wilson 2004). But we also suggest that the problem lies elsewhere. We contend that the issue is not so much about selling the 'product' of archaeological research as about the nature of the 'product' being produced by archaeologists. We cannot expect the public to easily imagine the rich and varied lives of Aboriginal peoples living 1000, 5000, 10 000 or even 40 000 years ago if archaeology always focuses on diet and stone tools and changing adaptations to different environments through time and across space. The history of 'hunter-gatherer' societies is like the history of any society. It concerns the ways that people interacted with each other in the past, and about ways people structured — and were structured by — their social and ecological settings.

This 'social' archaeology is an explicit attempt to access a peopled past through the material remains of that past. This book explores such social archaeologies and the varied ways of understanding the history of Indigenous Australians through archaeological practice. In doing so, it honours the work of Harry Lourandos who, for some thirty years, has been pivotal to the establishment of a social archaeology in Australia (see Bowdler, this volume).

A different social archaeology for Indigenous societies?

In their influential book *Archaeology* Colin Renfrew and Paul Bahn (2000, p. 173) note that social archaeology is 'about people and about relations between people, about the exercise of power and about the nature of organisation'. They present two major approaches to social archaeology. The first, a 'top-down' approach, focuses on inter- and intra-group organisation. The second, a 'bottom-up' approach, focuses on the individual as the smallest unit of social organisation and investigates inter-individual dynamics and issues such as identity, gender and status. But is the social archaeology of Indigenous peoples any different to the social archaeology of any other group of people? According to Renfrew and Bahn (2000, p. 173), the answer is yes:

> Different kinds of society need different kinds of question. For example, if we are dealing with a mobile group of hunter-gatherers, there is unlikely to be a complex centralized organization. And the techniques of investigation will need to vary radically with the nature of the evidence. One cannot tackle an early hunter-gatherer camp in Australia in the same way as the capital city of a province in China during the Shang Dynasty. Thus, the questions we put, and the methods for answering them, must be tailored to the sort of community we are dealing with. So it is all the more necessary to be clear at the outset about the general nature of that community, which is why the basic social questions are the first ones to ask.

While in some respects we agree with these claims, exactly how and why the study of identity, gender, and status for 'hunter-gatherers' should be fundamentally different to state societies is not clear. Nor is it clear how different questions and methods for different types of societies allow for cross-cultural comparisons. Despite these problems, however, we agree with Renfrew and Bahn for the distinctiveness of 'hunter-gatherer' (and by extension Indigenous) social archaeology, but for different reasons to those given by their explanation.

Indigenous peoples around the world have had their societies and power bases transformed in the last two to five hundred years as a result of European colonialism. In settler-colonial contexts, Indigenous peoples have had to contend with a broad range of onslaughts: the expropriation of land, genocide, assimilation, oppression and neglect. Colonialism has constructed a view of Indigenous societies, and of hunter-gatherer societies in particular, that has fundamentally and uniquely shaped archaeological approaches to their pasts. In the context of this book, a social archaeology of Indigenous societies must therefore incorporate three key dimensions: understanding social interactions in the past; understanding the contemporary social contexts of researching Indigenous pasts; and understanding contemporary social impacts of archaeological representations of Indigenous pasts.

Immediately apparent is that two of these three dimensions relate to people in the *present*. Social archaeology engages with and interrogates, often with reflexive discursiveness, our opening point that 'archaeology is about people both past and present'. The critical point here is that most archaeological research on Indigenous societies is undertaken in settler-colonial contexts where Indigenous peoples represent a colonised, and numerically a minority, culture (e.g. North America and Australia). In contrast, most archaeologists are inheritors of that hegemonic, colonising, majority culture.

Yet such a power differential is only part of the issue. It is generally accepted that the development of archaeology in colonial contexts such as Australia, North America and Africa, has been (and in some ways continues to be) tied intimately to the colonising project. That is, conceptual frameworks — such as social evolutionism, diffusionism and migrationism — produced archaeologies that represent Indigenous peoples and their pasts in an inferior light (Trigger 1984; McNiven & Russell 2005). Far from simply presenting distorted representations of Indigenous pasts, such archaeologies have helped legitimise the colonial appropriation of Indigenous lands by representing Indigenous peoples as unevolved savages with rudimentary culture tied closely to the environment. William Sollas' (1911, p. 383) extraordinary conclusion, in his famous 1911 book *Ancient hunters,* illustrates the point well:

> What part is to be assigned to justice in the government of human affairs? So far as the facts are clear they teach in no equivocal terms that there is no right which is not founded on might. Justice belongs to the strong, and has been meted out to each race according to its strength; each has received as much justice as it deserved. What perhaps is most impressive in each of the cases we have discussed is this, that the dispossession by a new-comer of a race already in occupation of the soil has marked an upward step in the intellectual progress of mankind. It is not priority of occupation, but the power to utilise, which establishes a claim to the land.

In this sense, the link between archaeology and contemporary Indigenous peoples is not new, and the political and social implications of archaeological historicism become abundantly apparent and integral to the birth of 'pre-historic' archaeology, as is equally well demonstrated by the title of prehistoric archaeology's foundational text, John Lubbock's 1865 *Pre-historic times, as illustrated by ancient remains, and the manners and customs of modern savages.*

Beyond ecology: socialising Indigenous pasts

While archaeology has produced many negative images of Indigenous peoples and their pasts, attention also needs to be given to what archaeologists have neglected to say. For example, there has been a lack of research into social processes. The archaeology of Indigenous peoples has traditionally been the archaeology of hunter-gatherers, with an analytical focus on subsistence, settlement and human-environmental interaction. This focus became entrenched during the mid-twentieth century as anthropologists produced sophisticated conceptual frameworks that appeared to support the view that the form and structure of hunter-gatherer societies was conditional on the form and structure of the environment. When this spatialised framework was transposed into archaeology, chronological changes in the form and structure of these societies were linked somewhat mechanistically — and in many cases deterministically — to chronological changes in the form and structure of the environment. Within the Australian context, this environmentally deterministic view is best represented by the work of Joseph Birdsell (1953) and his attempt to link Aboriginal population density to rainfall levels. At least as influential in the English-speaking world was Julian Steward's theory of cultural ecology, which developed out of his work with Shoshonean groups in the Great Basin, USA. Indeed, Richard Lee and Irven DeVore (1968b, p. 5), in their introductory chapter to the classic *Man the hunter*, state that Steward largely founded modern 'hunter-gatherer' studies. Cultural ecology was keenly taken up by processual archaeologists (of the 'New Archaeology' movement) in the 1960s and 1970s, with Brian Fagan (1995, p. 51) suggesting that it 'was, perhaps, the most important theoretical development in North American archaeology in a century'. The key dimension of cultural ecology adopted by archaeologists was the notion of the 'cultural core'. According to Steward (1955, p. 37), this cultural core should be seen as:

> [the] constellation of features which are most closely related to subsistence activities and economic arrangements. The core includes such social, political, and religious patterns as are empirically determined to be closely connected with these arrangements. Innumerable other features may have great potential variability because they are less strongly tied to the core. These latter, or secondary features, are determined to a greater extent by purely cultural-historical factors — by random innovations or by diffusion — and they give the appearance of outward distinctiveness to cultures with similar cores.

Cultural ecology pays primary attention to those features which empirical analysis shows to be most closely involved in the utilization of environment in culturally prescribed ways.

Steward (1955, p. 89) emphasised that the cultural core concept was simply a 'heuristic' device to facilitate 'cross-cultural' comparisons. The reality for most archaeologists was that subsistence not only became a simple proxy for Steward's cultural core but, along with environmental interaction, an end in itself when researching single cultural groups or small regions. In this sense, most archaeologists employed an abstract version of cultural ecology. However, as Daniel Myers pointed out (2004, p. 185), the fact remains that 'Religion, ritual and much of the social order were dismissed or completely abandoned in Steward's work'.

Australia, the continent of paradigmatic hunter-gatherers, developed a tradition of environmentally based 'prehistoric' archaeology that was closely tied to the American theoretical traditions of cultural ecology (Steward 1955) and its derivative, cultural materialism (M Harris 1979). While both theoretical approaches focus on environmental adaptation, cultural materialism also places emphasis on the deterministic properties of technology and demography. Bernard Huchet (1991) found that cultural materialist approaches dominated Australian archaeology during the 1960s, Seventies and Eighties. Although Huchet considered cultural ecology *per se* to have been an insignificant theoretical framework for Australian archaeology during this period, he did note that in many ways cultural ecology is subsumed within cultural materialism. Ecologically based archaeological studies have made significant contributions to understanding Australia's Aboriginal past. As with all societies, Aboriginal peoples have had to contend with a broad range of spatial and chronological changes in environment and resource availability through the course of their long history (see overview by Veth *et al.* 2000). But the success of the archaeological studies that have attempted to investigate those *cultural* histories through environmental and resource-based explanations belies a series of deep-seated theoretical problems.

The early 1980s marked an epistemological and theoretical revolution in Australian archaeology, a revolution that had parallels with the post-processual movement in English archaeology (e.g. Hodder 1985). Nicholas Thomas (1981) delivered a broadside on the discipline, focusing on the misguided use of empiricism and environmental determinism to epistemologically and theoretically frame and constrain research approaches and agendas. Rhys Jones' (1978) Tasmanian research was singled out for critique, particularly the characterisation of the cessation of fish eating around 3500 years ago as 'strange' and maladaptive. Thomas pointed out that those critics of Jones who attempted to argue that removal of fish from the diet was somehow 'adaptive' were in fact employing the same form of 'vulgar [cultural] materialism which reduces economy to ecology' (Allen 1979; Horton 1979; Parry 1981). Drawing on Marxist and neo-Marxist theoretical frameworks and the work of Tim Ingold (1980), Thomas (1981, p. 171) concluded that 'It is clearly the case that subsistence practices have both a social and an ecological dimension'. He recommended that 'serious consideration needs to be given to the formation of social approaches in [Australian] archaeology' (Thomas 1981, p. 172).

However, the most far-reaching and piercing critique of the discipline came from Harry Lourandos (1980b, 1983b). Like Thomas (1981), Lourandos advocated a historical materialist (neo-Marxist) approach (*cf.* Friedman 1974) whereby social change is better understood and explained by examining the dialectical relationship between the forces of production (e.g. technology) and social relations of production. Ultimately, Lourandos argued that causality is centred on social relations of production for they 'set the limits on the development and stability of the system as a whole' (Friedman 1974, p. 448). Under the label of 'intensification', Lourandos showed by example the way towards a socially oriented archaeology for Australia's Aboriginal past. At key was his epistemological and theoretical critique of the environmental focus of Australian archaeology and his plea for archaeologists to analyse and represent the Aboriginal past as socially dynamic, Aboriginal environments as socially constructed, Aboriginal landscapes as socially inscribed, and Aboriginal history as social agency. For Lourandos, and often in contrast to his predecessors, the land was inscribed with social relations (see Langton, this volume), and the archaeologist's task was to figure out the changing configurations and dynamics of such relations over time. Out of this critique, Lourandos offered an alternative way of constructing and interpreting Australia's Aboriginal past, particularly with regard to historical transformations of the last 4000 years. Significantly, and as Deborah Brian (this volume) elaborates, debate about 'intensification' has focused narrowly (and in some cases trivially) on the nature of the archaeological record and the empirical basis of Lourandos' new synthesis of Australian 'prehistory'. Missing has been explicit appreciation of the new epistemological and theoretical arena established by Lourandos. This new arena is the true legacy of Lourandos and one that both frames the structure of the chapters in this volume and sets the foundations for social archaeologies of Aboriginal history into the future.

The Aboriginal past as socially dynamic

Lourandos (1980b, 1983b, 1985b) saw the environmental focus of Australian archaeology as (re)presenting a 'static' view of Aboriginal society and history.

That is, by analysing and (re)presenting cultural change simply in terms of adaptive responses to environmental change, Aboriginal history is seen to be at the mercy of external agents of change (in this case the environment). Such a view was not unique to Australian studies but part of a paradigmatic view of hunter-gatherers that had its origins with nineteenth-century social evolutionism and colonialist representations of Indigenous peoples. Steward (1955, p. 40) thus remarked that 'The simpler societies [i.e. 'hunter-gatherers'] are more directly conditioned by the environment than advanced ones'. *Internally* generated (social) changes were, under such logic, seen to have little role to play in understanding the Aboriginal past. As McNiven (this volume) points out, archaeology and anthropology's obsession to analyse *externally* driven change in Aboriginal societies can also be extended to diffusionism. Indeed, both environmental determinism and diffusionism were long-established colonial tropes that aided the (mis)representation of Aboriginal peoples as ahistorical, non-inventive 'savages' time-locked to a Stone Age past. Thus, Lourandos' critique was not about denying the potential effects of environmental change on Aboriginal history, but about an epistemological and theoretical rupture to the deterministic role of environmental change underpinning (and hence explaining) historical change.

One of the most important epistemological and theoretical implications of Lourandos' attempts to break the simplistic causative nexus between environmental and cultural change was reconceptualising hunter-gatherer archaeological records, and subsistence remains in particular, as more than the simple by-products of environmental adaptations. Subsistence remains were recast as the left-over materials of a society working to feed itself — not simply feeding the individuals, but also the social mechanisms which gave each group its particular character, and in the process creating self-generating social dynamisms. While environmental conditions affected individuals and groups, it was the social system that was now seen to make particular demands on the environment through the resourcing strategies employed. Changes in these social conditions were in turn generated by the social dynamics resulting from the way people related with each other, with their technologies, and with their broader environments: in this sense the social forces employed by people were now seen to regulate change. Change and stability became two sides of the same social coin. For example, Lourandos argued that in south-western Victoria Aboriginal people began to construct complex fish-trapping devices, not to maximise productivity as such but to ensure continual, year-round production to meet existing social needs in the face of an unpredictable environment (e.g. Lourandos 1980b). Once in place, the fish traps generated demands of maintenance and operation, as well as new means of representing corporate identities linking people with country, and a new configuration of inter-personal dynamics involving place, people and resources ensued (see Lourandos 1980b, 1988a).

Since the resource requirements of a society reflect both its internal structure and relationships (based on age, status, gender and so forth), and external structures and relationships (with other societies), the form and patterning of subsistence and other resourcing strategies that remain will by definition reflect these internal and external social structures and relationships (see also Bender 1978, 1981; Ingold 1979, 1980). To reduce subsistence remains simply to their collective energy function not only denies their social embeddedness but ultimately silences their cultural meaning and values. It renders the study of subsistence as ethology, not anthropology or archaeology. Again, Lourandos (1980b) illustrated this key point by reference to certain Aboriginal societies of south-western Victoria; these societies developed technological and land-management strategies for enhanced production of eels to support intergroup social gatherings. Lourandos also documented analogous ethnographically known examples of Aboriginal societies that placed extra-production/productivity demands on the economy to support inter-regional gatherings from across Australia and Papua New Guinea (Lourandos 1988a). With these examples, Lourandos demonstrated that Aboriginal societies could radically alter their subsistence activities and 'levels of energy harnessing' in response to relative changes in population density (in this case inter-regional gatherings) instigated by internally generated changes in social organisation and relations.

It is significant that both Jones (1977a, 1977b, 1978) and Lourandos (1980b) documented subsistence practices (both associated with fishing) among Aboriginal Australians that were unorthodox in terms of the paradigmatic ecological constructions of 'hunter-gatherers'. Yet while Jones interpreted his data as evidence of maladaptation and the result of failed hunter-gatherer strategies, Lourandos interpreted his data as evidence of the inadequacy of then-prevalent archaeological approaches to the past, and in doing so questioned the validity of simplistic, ecologically based constructions of 'hunter-gatherers'. While both made reference to social explanations, Jones used his taboo-based interpretation to illustrate the negative consequences should hunter-gatherers allow social practices to impinge on ecological relations. This interpretation reinforced the orthodox view that hunter-gatherers were fundamentally ecological peoples who could not let epiphenomenal (social) practices impact upon their cultural core, lest they suffer the 'maladaptive' consequences. Jones' view was further elaborated in his classic paper 'Tasmanian paradox', in which he stated that 'the balance between man and land which is so deeply embedded within Aboriginal behaviour and lore, and which was the prime feature of his prehistory for three hundred centuries' (Jones 1977b, p. 202). He further argued that technological innovations — such as the introduction of the so-called Small Tool Tradition across mainland Australia during the late Holocene — should be seen as epiphenomenal, as these had little or no impact on demography (Jones 1977b). Assumed increases in subsistence efficiency from the new technology were seen (by Jones) to produce extra available time that was invested into extra (ephemeral) social gatherings and ceremonies. 'Positive feedback' and demographic expansion were considered to be 'at best anarchic to the social order and, at worst, disastrous for the long-term balance of the community to its resources' and the maintenance of ecological 'homeostasy' (Jones 1977b, p. 202). In this sense, Ian Lilley (2001) missed the point when he argued that the social approaches of Jones and Lourandos had 'important areas of common ground' (see also Brian, this volume).

In many respects, Lourandos (1980b) shattered the colonial myth of Aboriginal demography as being deterministically shaped by the environment, and in the process destabilised the notion of 'hunter-gatherer' (see also Bender, this volume). In a pivotal shift, Lourandos demonstrated that Aboriginal societies were capable of demographic change for *social* reasons, with concomitant changes in subsistence and in ecological relations. Thus, it is worth asking the question as to whether or not archaeological studies that do little more than focus on subsistence practices to understand Aboriginal ecological relationships are not only profoundly inadequate, but also colonialist in approach.

Aboriginal environments as socially constructed

Lourandos (1980b) went further still with his social archaeology approach by revealing how Aboriginal societies could dramatically manipulate the so-called 'natural' environment, in this case by increasing the habitat of eels to accommodate social needs. Certainly Jones (1969) had already transformed our understanding of purposeful manipulation of the environment by Aboriginal people through his concept of 'fire-stick farming'. The conceptual advance of Lourandos (1980b, p. 246) was his argument that 'These environmental manipulations are not seen as attempts to increase environmental productivity, but to regularize (stabilize) the availability of resources'. Thus, 'by relaxing pressures on other neighbouring resource areas' (Lourandos 1980b, p. 256), Aboriginal communities could decrease mobility, increase the degree of sedentism, and be in a better position to contribute to the extra-productive demands of increased ceremonial and intergroup alliances and gatherings. Such changes have considerable potential for self-amplification and lay the foundations for possible demographic expansion.

These insights had major implications for Australian archaeology, given that it was then generally accepted that most aspects of society adapt to the environment, either in a functional or evolutionary sense (see Head 1986).

Whether aimed at increasing production, productivity or regularity, environmental manipulations reveal that hunter-gatherers — and Aboriginal peoples in particular — were not simply adapting their society to the environment but also actively and intentionally adapting the environment to their society.

John Tibby et al. and Cassandra Rowe (both this volume) each explore environmental change in Australia through this lens, specifically asking how we can investigate social history through environmental impacts. By looking at environmental change this way, they invert the classic 'hunter-gather' formula. No longer is a people's physical surroundings seen simply as dictating social behaviour; it is the actions of people in and on place that are now seen as affecting environmental processes, be they vegetation succession, hydrologic processes or sedimentation regimes. Given this dynamic interplay between people and their engaged worlds, it has become possible to investigate social history through environmental impacts, and it is towards this new possibility that Tibby et al. and Rowe (respectively) explore south-western Victorian and Torres Strait history.

Perhaps the most important outcome of Lourandos' theorising on Aboriginal environmental manipulation was a blurring of the conceptual boundary between 'hunter-gatherers' and 'agriculturalists'. His 1980 *World Archaeology* paper described how the highest population densities for Aboriginal Australia overlapped with certain New Guinea agriculturalists. In an instant, Lourandos shattered the myth that agriculture automatically supports higher population densities. Furthermore, it helped explain why Aboriginal hunter-gatherers 'resisted the direct imposition of food producing techniques', as their own subsistence strategies produced 'commensurable levels of energy harnessing' (Lourandos 1980b, pp. 258–9). Lourandos' blurring not only asked us to question the validity and heuristic utility of the 'hunter-gatherer' and 'agriculturalist' conceptual *categories*, but also to interrogate the 'prejudicial homologues used in the interpretation of Australian Aboriginal and New Guinean cultures' (David & Denham, this volume). As John Terrell et al. (2003, p. 323) recently argued, rather than attempting to straightjacket cultural practice into either of these two opposed normative categories, one should investigate the particular skills involved with the harvesting of individual or sets of species along with 'the circumstances under which they are being taken'. Melissa Carter (this volume) uses a similar logic to destabilise the notion of the 'agricultural frontier' in Torres Strait, and instead aims to track — archaeologically — the history of intergroup dynamics and the emergence of specific ethnographically documented cultural practices through time, thereby better allowing an understanding of the historical trajectories engendered. One of the key contributions of a social archaeology is this tracing of ethnography — that is, the observed cultural practices of living peoples — through archaeology to create a history that extends seamlessly from the present or near-present into the deeper past. In this sense a social archaeology enables us to create a material understanding of the ethnographic present by which to trace its historical emergence.

In recent years, Lourandos' concept of socially constructed environments has been extended to spiritscapes and to sites associated with what McNiven and Feldman (2003) refer to as the 'ritual orchestration' of landscapes and seascapes. Whereas previous investigations of environmental manipulation investigated technological *facilities* — eel traps/canals (e.g. Lourandos 1980b) and fire-managed resource zones (e.g. Godfrey 1983; Head 1988; Jones 1969) — ritual orchestration focuses on ritual *sites* — stone arrangements (e.g. David et al. 2004c; McNiven 2003), bone arrangements (e.g. McNiven & Feldman 2003) and general areas of ceremonial agglomeration (e.g. David 2002) — and the ways in which these were used to spiritually alter the elements (tides, wind and so forth), animal behaviour and availability. While traditional ecological approaches tended to relegate such behaviours as epiphenomenal to understanding hunter-gatherer environmental interactions, it is now clear that rituals of orchestration not only mediated peoples' interactions with their environment, but also dramatically impacted on the nature of subsistence sites, such as middens. As others in this volume point out (see Langton; Bradley; Kearney & Bradley), individual features of the landscape, including water, are each imbued with meaning, and it is this meaningfulness that guides people's environmental engagements. Because this meaningfulness is socially circumscribed — involving a present that is already historicised through memory and through ancestral connections — its material expressions are never random and always ordered in social engagement. Social landscapes, through their already-meaningful material patterning, are thus amenable to archaeological enquiry.

Aboriginal landscapes as socially inscribed

As noted above, an ecological view of the Aboriginal past constructs Aboriginal landscapes as little more than assemblages of subsistence sites whose patterning reflects environmental interaction and adaptation. Symbolic and ceremonial sites, while acknowledged, are seen to have little analytical value as they are transformed into epiphenomena peripheral to a sociocultural core consisting of settlement-subsistence strategies. This approach, the cornerstone of the processual archaeology of the 1960s and 1970s, marginalised and silenced considerable dimensions of the archaeological record. For example, one of the paradigmatic studies of processual archaeology has been Lewis Binford's 1980 *American Antiquity* paper 'Willow smoke and dogs' tails: hunter-gatherer settlement systems and archaeological site formation'. Junko Habu and Ben Fitzhugh (2002, p. 1) rightly note that this ethnoarchaeological study of the Nunamiut of Alaska 'revolutionized the study of hunter-gatherer settlement and land use'. Binford focused his research on Anaktuvuk Pass and documented complex mobility patterns associated with a broad range of site types such as kill sites, butchering sites, hunting stands and storage sites. We are presented with a secular landscape where ecological relationships are materially manifested in settlement patterns and different site types. But as Insoll (2004, p. 48) pointed out, this secular view is at odds with Nunamiut cosmology and shamanism. Binford stripped Nunamiut landscapes of their cosmological, symbolic and spiritual meaning and failed to mention 'shrines' and 'sacred sites' that clearly structured and mediated ecological relationships. This is an archaeology of place devoid of meaningful place and of meaningful emplacement, just as it is devoid of social experience and salience.

Within the Australian context, the spiritual and symbolic aspects of Aboriginal landscapes were well appreciated by anthropologists and many archaeologists long before Lourandos' voice entered archaeological discourse. While archaeologists had systematically documented rock art, stone arrangements and burials since the early twentieth century at least, the apparent non-ecological dimension of such sites resulted in their marginalised (epiphenomenal) status as far as the grand narratives of Australian prehistory were concerned. For example, prior to the 1980s, burial sites were only considered archaeologically significant if they contributed to understanding the antiquity of colonisation (e.g. Lake Mungo burials) or evolutionary relationships (e.g. Kow Swamp burials), and rock-art sites only became important to Australian archaeology after they became subject to radiocarbon dating, hereby positioning the art in more secure chronological contexts. Yet as Veth (this volume) shows, archaeological studies of rock art, social gatherings and emplacement are now at the forefront of our understanding of Aboriginal history. It is therefore even more remarkable that little theorising has been undertaken on the social significance (beyond issues of repatriation) of the Lake Mungo burials, given that they are among the world's oldest known burials, and the fact that Kow Swamp may well be the world's oldest known cemetery (*cf.* Pardoe 1988; Stone & Cupper 2003). One exception to this is the large cemetery at Roonka, South Australia. Here, researchers have explored in some detail more than just biological relationships to also consider patterns of sedentism, intergroup competition, territoriality, gendered patterns of authority, and social ranking in the past (Pate, this volume).

Perhaps the key contribution of Lourandos — at least in terms of seeing Aboriginal landscapes as socially inscribed — concerns the theorising of the emergence of mound sites in western Victoria. Such anthropogenic mounds tend to have a diameter of 5–10 m with a height range of 0.5–1 m, although some are more than 100 m long and 3 m high. Most contain subsistence remains, stone artefacts, and a matrix dominated by ground-oven materials such as burnt earth and charcoal. While some mounds contain burials, for the most part these sites have been treated by archaeologists as secular facilities that had the added advantage of providing elevated and dry camping locations during floods (e.g. Coutts *et al.* 1979). Lourandos (1993) pointed out that mound sites were a distinctive manifestation of broader social changes taking place in south-eastern Australia during the last 3000 years (see also E Williams, 1988). He also pointed out that if such sites were an adaptation to allow use of the swampy and flooding landscapes of the region (i.e. the creation of elevated and dry campsites), evidence for such sites should also occur during the early Holocene (when climatic conditions were wetter than during the late Holocene), but it does not. Clearly, mound sites had extra layers of social meaning beyond their secular and utilitarian value as wetland camping/cooking facilities.

This question of extra layers of social meaning for mounds was taken up by Nathan Wolski (1995). Noting that many mounds are located away from swampy areas (some even on top of granite outcrops), Wolski recast the mound question to ask why Aboriginal people during the last 3000 years used campsite remains to construct 'protuberances' (up to 6 m in height according to one nineteenth-century observer) across their landscapes? The subtle phenomenological move of Wolski was to consider mound sites as deliberately built and 'imposing' landscape 'structures' (i.e. 'monuments') as part of a constructed 'social landscape'. Wolski noted the intriguing spatial 'overlap' between the distribution of mounds and the distribution of greenstone axes within the Kulinic language group of western and central Victoria (e.g. McBryde 1978). Informed by McBryde's argument that greenstone-axe trade relationships were an expression of social relationships, Wolski (1995, p. 64) concluded that mounds were employed as a form of landscape 'social marker' that were 'connected with a more intricate web of social, economic and linguistic factors'. Wolski encouraged extension of his 'interactional phenomena' model to the Weipa shell mounds of north-eastern Australia. In doing so, and by applying the notion of 'monument' to Aboriginal inscriptions of place, he helped to further break down the erroneous yet popular notion that Aboriginal relations to place were subject to environmental agency, with negligible social inscription from Aboriginal people as agents themselves. Like rock art, the presence of monuments helps illustrate to a public that expects material evidence that Aboriginal people did indeed actively engage in social discourse with the land. These processes of engagement, like the mounds themselves, generated cumulative responses by Aboriginal people as historically positioned agents, with those mounds embodying the ancestors as they embody the present-past for their Aboriginal owners and custodians. This approach to material expressions of history acknowledges an embodied presence of the past on the land that is much more akin to Indigenous approaches to ancestral presences than more conventional forms of archaeology allow. Archaeological 'sites' and objects are now no longer so distant from the Indigenous present and presence. And through such rapprochements, new doors are opened towards archaeologies of experience — where 'sites' are no longer abstract archaeological places, but locations of social and personal experience, where the past is engaged in the present, where the ancestors live and breathe — not yesterday, but today and on to tomorrow. It is with such logic in mind that Franca Tamisari and James Wallace (this volume) develop a new sense of archaeological place where archaeology itself is extended, newly overlapping with Aboriginal meaningfulness as it reaches out to *ancestral* pasts, through the notion of *place*. It is in this logic also that John Bradley (this volume) and Amanda Kearney and John Bradley (this volume) newly conceptualise and subjectify an archaeology of the everyday objects, such as cycads and stone markers, that archaeologists have for so long made the objects of their enquiries.

Aboriginal history as social agency

In *Continent of hunter-gatherers*, Lourandos (1997, p. xv) made explicit the proposition that archaeology is about people past and present:

> Traditionally, prehistory, like its data, was considered as yet another resource for scientific investigation; as there for the taking. With some notable exceptions, little consideration was given to the descendants of that past — the Australian and Tasmanian Aboriginal people — let alone their viewpoints. This attitude has now changed considerably. Australian prehistoric archaeology is now a highly politicized, complex arena of negotiation . . . Today, it is becoming increasingly common for anthropologists and also archaeologists to work on behalf of particular Aboriginal communities who employ them as specialists and direct their research. Archaeology and its findings on the prehistoric past are part of the consciousness of Aboriginal communities, to use in whatever way suits them.

Lourandos was well aware that Aboriginal people were now engaging archaeologists to research aspects of their own history, for their own reasons. Yet Lourandos was also keenly aware that the theoretical frameworks employed by archaeologists also played into the hands of colonialist discourses of Aboriginality (Lourandos 1997, p. xvi):

> The inheritance of colonialism includes the ways indigenous people's history and 'prehistory' was presented and interpreted, often

to the disadvantage of the people themselves; often as a means of social control. The story of Aboriginal Australia and Tasmania is much the same. Unilinear evolutionary models of the nineteenth and early twentieth century, for example, presented by anthropologists and archaeologists, which placed these peoples on the lowest rungs of the socio-cultural evolutionary 'ladder', have largely served to preserve the status quo; to keep Aboriginal Australians and Tasmanians in their place — as dependent, 'conquered' peoples, largely divorced from land, society, economy and their past. The traditional models of Australian prehistory, discussed above, with their emphasis upon the dominance of the natural environment over Aboriginal society — assigning to the latter a passive role — producing long-term stability and lack of change, have, in their own way, also reinforced these conditions.

For some two decades Australian archaeologists have been attempting to decolonise work practices and to embrace the rights of Indigenous Australians to own and control their heritage and their past. While all archaeologists acknowledge and understand the inherent colonialist and racist fabric of nineteenth century theoretical constructs such as social evolutionism, little theorising has been undertaken on the more subtle but no less colonial aspects of modern archaeological research (see McNiven & Russell 2005). For most of his career, Lourandos was troubled by the colonialist overtones of the ecological focus of Australian archaeology. How could we expect the general public to engage with and appreciate archaeological characterisations of Australia's Aboriginal past when ecological relationships and stone-implement typologies continued to masquerade as history? And, more pertinently, how could we expect Aboriginal people to engage with and accept this past; a past in which their most complex religious and spiritual knowledge systems are reduced to mere subsistence and settlement patterns and statistical characterisations of stone tools (of which the most significant implements such as microliths were said to be 'external diffusions')?

With Lourandos' concept of 'intensification' came the possibility of a social archaeology and of an ancient history of Indigenous Australians. Perhaps most significantly of all, Lourandos dared us to realise that a social archaeology by definition implicates *people*; and in doing so he introduced 'people' into discourses of Australian Indigenous archaeology; the people of the past, the people of the present whose ancestors and history we write about, and the people of the present who participate in this history writing and history reading. The New Archaeology's emphasis on cultural processes abstracted the past actions of people to composite 'human behaviour'. Social archaeology explicitly focuses on social relations and people–people relationships. In this formulation, people make decisions that alter both their lives and the lives of those around them, near and far. Thus, the past — and cultural change — are imbued with social agency. The social archaeology of Indigenous Australians moves away from passive ecological relationships to people actively engaging with and constructing their social and ecological worlds. It also considers archaeology as interpersonal engagement, and the archaeologist as *author*, replete with his or her own social, cultural and personal prejudices. This is what philosopher Hans-Georg Gadamer (1988) meant when he coined the word 'preunderstanding', a notion which is founded on the philosophy of hermeneutics.

A past filled with people and social agency is *history*, rendering the term 'prehistory' a redundant relic of the colonial culture of archaeology (see David & Denham, this volume). In the context of Australia, such an archaeological construction is much more appealing to Aboriginal people because a past with people is a past with ancestors, and a past with ancestors is history. All Aboriginal people — and most archaeologists — appreciate the phenomenological difference in describing an exposed Aboriginal burial as 'a person' as opposed to the scientising label of 'skeletal remains'. This is not simply a basic issue of respect. If archaeologists acknowledge a past with Aboriginal people and Aboriginal ancestors it is obvious that contemporary Aboriginal people have a right to engage with and control that, their own, past. Furthermore, such acknowledgement presents a challenge for Australian archaeology to develop epistemological strategies to accommodate Aboriginal historiographical traditions such as oral history, particularly when oral history questions the veracity and authority of archival records (see Barker this volume). It is salutary to remember that the writing of history is always about people choosing to historicise a past; the question is, which past, and under whose power to determine the nature of evidential strengths and the validity of approaches?

Finally, Luke Godwin and Jimmy Weiner (this volume) remind us that Aboriginal people have their own reflexive 'archaeological' traditions of reading the material traces of their past — 'footprints of the ancestors' — when they walk across their ancestral lands. In this sense, Aboriginal people have always had their own traditions of social archaeologies that recognise the inherent social, historical and spiritual properties of material remains. Epistemologically and ontologically these traditions recognise the inherent and pervasive links between people past and present, a dimension of social archaeology that we in the West are slowly coming to understand and appreciate. As Aboriginal people and Torres Strait Islanders constantly remind us, understanding the past requires more than epistemological refinements; it necessitates a heightened awareness of ontological differences as well as meeting points. Indigenous people have always used falsification in going about their everyday life, and the epistemology of archaeological practice — including methodological principles of falsification — is nothing new. What *is* different is how we filter our epistemological approaches ontologically, through our world views. We can thus have the same evidential bases for different understandings, not because of epistemological differences (i.e. not because of differences as to the methods of enquiry and how knowledge can be validated), but because of different understanding of how the world works. Here, then, is a meeting point: if social archaeology is anything, then surely it is a remembrance of people past in present social practice; with chalk in hand, to inscribe 'people' onto history, in the present and into the past.

2.
An interview with Harry Lourandos

Harry Lourandos, Bruno David, Bryce Barker and Ian J McNiven

Harry Lourandos is a gentle man. He has always presented his academic ideas in a polite manner; it is thus that we imagine him entering and leaving the classroom, the seminar or conference. Yet despite this gentle and polite demeanour, Harry Lourandos' writings rocked the very foundations of Australian archaeology in the 1980s and continue to echo far and deep in the recesses of Australian archaeology today. His is a message of politics, of the way we think and of the way we do things in archaeology, a message that concerns how we perceive the Aboriginal past through variously tinted eyes, but most particularly about the *sociality* of historical trajectories and of Aboriginal lives past and present.

In Australia, Lourandos' approach to Aboriginal archaeology has generated more heated debate than any other in the discipline. Yet over the years many of his ideas about the Aboriginal past have come to merge into conventional wisdom, while his role in changing academic and popular perceptions has remained largely unacknowledged. Here we three — archaeology students of the 1980s, and now colleagues — interrogate Harry through a series of emailed questions and answers about the place of his own ideas, and of archaeology in general, in a post-colonial Australia.

Two of the interviewers (Bruno David and Bryce Barker) have had extensive discussions with Lourandos over a number of years as his doctoral students at the University of Queensland; Ian McNiven remained Lourandos' colleague during his own undergraduate and then PhD studies at that same university.

BD, BB, IM: How did you get into archaeology?
HL: As a child I was fascinated by Aboriginal people's culture, and in high school I loved history — especially ancient history with its focus on the Greek world. Coming from a Greek–Australian family, it empowered me. So, while enrolled in an arts–law degree at the University of Sydney, I took up archaeology as an extra option and, as it happened, never left. But this was classical and Near Eastern archaeology, with its strong historical emphasis. I drifted towards the Anthropology Department, where 'prehistoric' archaeology and the teaching of Rhys

Jones, newly arrived from Cambridge, was being taught. Here, a new brand of archaeology was starting up that emphasised 'economy' and was closely tied to the natural sciences. I was selected to go on Rhys' second, inspirational expedition to north-western Tasmania for the entire summer of 1964–65 (Figure 1). I was hooked. A whole second summer was spent with Wilfred Shawcross and his students on the northern tip of New Zealand. Straight after my honours year, I took up my first professional position as research archaeologist at the Tasmanian Museum. I deeply felt that as I lived in Australia, I needed to concentrate on the (pre)history of this region and its Indigenous people.

BD, BB, IM: Most Australian archaeologists practicing in the late 1960s into the 1970s — including your own teachers and many of your contemporaries — were Cambridge trained, as we're reminded by Tim Murray and Peter White's (1981) essay 'Cambridge in the Bush'. Yet you were one of the first who was not: you were Australian trained. How do you think this influenced your own perspectives on Australian archaeology? Did it have any impact, or do you think this local training and early experience is largely irrelevant to your early and subsequent perspectives?

Figure 1. Harry Lourandos (right) and Rhys Jones (left) excavating at Rocky Cape South cave in 1965 (photo courtesy of Harry Lourandos).

HL: Being an Australian archaeologist, rather than overseas trained, bonded together a new generation of archaeologists with common ideals. This was instrumental in forging a new archaeological culture in Australia during the 1960s and 1970s. This expanding profession, branching into public archaeology, was led by a generation of largely Cambridge-trained people who controlled key academic positions, in a handful of institutions, and key academic journals. They largely set the research agenda and influenced knowledge creation through control of research and publication. My approach and ideas were influenced by this emerging archaeological culture, my undergraduate training, my engagement with the data (archaeological and ethnohistorical) and the changing world around me. It was a time of change. As the discipline was new and largely untested, there were opportunities here to introduce new approaches and also new interpretations. In some cases, this proved to be more difficult than I ever imagined.

BD, BB, IM: Your Marxist approaches to Australian archaeology leave a very distinctive mark on the discipline and on our understanding of the Aboriginal past, one that dares us to think of social relations — relations of production — as generating social dynamism. It also allows us to think of social conditions as forces that regulate change. Yet, more traditionally, Australian archaeologists — and archaeologists around the world generally — have considered Aboriginal Australia as a rather neat and stereotypical example of *the* 'hunter-gatherer' largely at the mercy of environmental forces; *Homo sapiens sapiens* the biological being in Nature, so to speak. How do you see, and engage with, the relationships between social and environmental forces within Aboriginal societies — and small-scale societies more generally — of the present and the past?

HL: Yes, the traditional model for Australian archaeology is ecologically based, where the natural world largely shapes or controls Aboriginal demography, culture and society. Forces within society itself are quite secondary: epiphenomena. I worked within this paradigm employing also a 'landscape' approach. My results, however, indicated that while much could be explained by the traditional model, by environmental/ecological factors, *other issues could not* (Lourandos 1977a, 1980a, 1980b). So I turned *also* to sociocultural theory to expand upon these explanations; to social forces as a dynamic in their own right. Marxist approaches in anthropology flourished anew during the 1970s and provided theory and data to both critique and augment the dominant ecological approach. I saw strong parallels between my south-western

Victorian case study of intensification, eels and large-scale ceremonial occasions and examples of resource intensification from Papua New Guinea. Here, in 'agricultural' societies, production was increased to meet the demands of inter-group feasts and ceremonies that regulated social interaction between largely autonomous groups. Classic ecological explanations of these studies saw such 'regulation' as a form of demographic control, or linked predominantly to control of diet. On the other hand, Marxist explanations pointed out that 'regulation' was largely a sociopolitical 'tool' and that the commodities themselves (yams, pigs etc.) were items of exchange whose value far outweighed their dietary worth. I felt that similar explanations could be applied to the Australian (Victorian) example, that ecological factors such as demography and diet had to be seen in a broader sociopolitical context. Here, the eels and their ecology (including reproduction) were being manipulated, for example through control of their aquatic habitats by artificial drainage systems, with largely sociopolitical ends in mind. In these ways, there seemed to be essentially little difference between the Australian 'hunter-gatherer' and 'agricultural' New Guinean examples (Lourandos 1988a). I saw these key variables — environment, demography, sociopolitical and the like — as *interdependent*, but I placed emphasis upon the *social relations* as here all cultural *choices* were made, including reactions to environmental factors. People, therefore, can be seen to react to changing *opportunities*; as agents of choice rather than passive victims of circumstance.

BD, BB, IM: In the 1960s, when you first entered the archaeological scene, the 'New Archaeology' — championed by Lewis Binford, Michael Schiffer, David Clarke and many others — took a strong hold in Australia. How were you influenced by this movement, and how did you respond to it?

HL: I leapt upon the New Archaeology bandwagon — more a life raft of survival — in the late 1960s, to explain the results from my Tasmanian (and later Victorian) research. It offered fertile new perspectives, especially regarding spatio-geographical and ecological frameworks, as well as a strong middle-range focus. It was also particularly helpful for planning research design. But it proved less helpful in *explaining* change through time; oddly, it was *a*historical in many ways. And sociocultural factors were largely seen as secondary appendages. The 'systems theory' model worked better for explaining the ecological realm than the sociocultural, where it appeared quite mechanistic. One problem here is that human social systems are largely open and not closed. How then to try and define or separate 'systems' and 'sub-systems', especially when *time* is involved? I overcame this by focusing on the *interrelationships* between social units or groups, that is, the *social relations*. To do so, I had to move from the theory of the natural sciences to that of the social sciences. Sociocultural theory, in many ways, has a strong neo-Marxist base, while the natural science base is, of course, neo-Darwinian. While there is some overlap, essentially the data and logic are different.

BD, BB, IM: Closely tied to the New Archaeology was the 1966 'Man the Hunter' symposium. You were obviously influenced by it — your own writing has always been strongly set *within* a hunter-gatherer framework, arguably even more so than many of those who presented at the symposium itself, in the sense that gathering and hunting for you has always been more than an evolutionary stage preceding sedentism or agriculture. Yet at the same time you have, more than most, destabilised the concept of 'hunter-gatherer' by arguing, first, that gatherer-hunters do not represent a single, homogeneous concept and, second, by suggesting that peoples who gather and hunt can be structurally complex and dynamic, in many ways much akin to farmers or fishers. For example, rather than contrasting hunter-gatherers against agriculturalists, you pointed out in your 1980 *World Archaeology* paper that 'population levels reached in high-density [Aboriginal] hunter-gatherer societies equalled, or were only marginally lower than, those of shifting agriculturalists in New Guinea. This similarity in population density between the two regions suggests comparable levels of energy harnessing, and raises the problem of explaining functional differences between these two socioeconomic systems: . . . the hunter-gatherer system, like that of the food-producer, involves the artificial manipulation and expansion of ecological niches' (Lourandos 1980b, p. 259). The implication is that it is these particular manners of artificial manipulation and expansion that needed to be understood, not the overarching labels 'hunter-gatherer' versus 'agriculturalist'. In light of the influential advances of the 1960s, and your own destabilisation of the concept of hunter-gatherer as a cultural type, where do you see the theoretical notion of 'hunter-gatherer' going today? Does the concept of hunter-gatherer still have currency in anthropology and archaeology?

HL: I think it still has currency, and maybe always will in some ways. By destabilising the term 'hunter-gatherer' it became a contested arena of debate, rather than a safe haven or defined, bounded and boxed category. It now serves, therefore, as a reference point or shibboleth; a starting point for debate and one easily identifiable. Merely to deconstruct it and attempt to replace it (with what?) robs the very debate of power. It dissolves only to re-emerge elsewhere. Yes, it is a *colonial artefact* serving to control Indigenous people and the ways to view them now and in the past. And yes, hunter-gatherers overlap with a very wide range of societies, including hunter-horticulturalists, agriculturalists and some stratified societies; which destroys some of the old stereotypes. But doesn't this also make the debate more complex, more interesting? Whatever label is used may be seen as biased (loaded) or oppressive in some way. Better that labels be linked to *context*. The colonial tag 'hunter-gatherer' can then be readily identifiable and distinguished from all other labels (see also McNiven, this volume, on diffusion). This will allow new ways to explore. The concept of 'hunter-gatherer' — the original human society — seems to be deeply embedded in the Western psyche, its culture and literature. It lies at the core of the Darwinian and Marxist models of human society — the bases for the natural and social sciences. And it has always been constructed as 'other': as contrasted, different. Obviously we need the *other* more than they need us!

BD, BB, IM: There is a popular saying that is often repeated today within undergraduate classes that states that archaeology is considered anthropology in the US, whereas it is considered history in the UK. Yet you — perhaps through your Marxist orientations — have shied away from such dichotomies, even shown the futility of such divisions without ever writing explicitly about it. Your writings have always been intimately anthropological *and* historical. How do you see this supposed divide (and relationship) between archaeology as anthropology and archaeology as history as affording opportunities for, and/or constraining, archaeological practice and social discourses about the Aboriginal past.

HL: It's interesting to see how the division came about — in America through the tie to their Indigenous cultures with little written history, as opposed to the UK where archaeology was closely bound to 'literate' Eurasian societies of the Bronze Age and the like. Australia, in effect, inherited both strands, and this has always been reflected in the archaeology. It's just that the dominant paradigm developed in the American anthropological form via Birdsell (1953, 1957), in the main, then reinforced by the Cambridge connection, with its close ties to the natural sciences. My own training, in Australia, was in both camps and I consciously maintained this as a strong point. In today's globalised and decentralised academic climate, it's possible to move more easily between schools of thought; indeed, we are encouraged to be *interdisciplinary*. Given the obvious advantages flexibility brings, it's difficult to see how the old boundaries, once imposed around the discipline, can be maintained. An anthropological/historical approach opens up a powerful window into the Aboriginal past, at the same time mindful of the present, its problems and solutions. Multiple debating grounds can easily be accommodated within such an approach.

BD, BB, IM: Most Australian archaeologists have targeted Pleistocene origins (the earliest traces of people) and the antiquity of later, newer traits, for their own sake: the origins of the Australians, the arrival of people and the demise of the megafauna, the origins of backed artefacts, the origins of the dingo. What archaeologists in general saw in Australia was not a continent of people with social histories, but a continent of original settlers who, through time, accumulated a series of new cultural traits. But not you. You seem to have never truly engaged with notions of origin as a research agenda, rather focusing on social process as a means of understanding the past. Where do you see the need for a social archaeology of *origins* **(rather than of the differential retention or rejection of particular cultural traits) — the first appearance of traits. For example, we can't remember reading a social archaeology of migration or movement, one that would lead people to leaving their ancestral homelands to colonise Australia, yet questions of origins have long predominated in Australian archaeology.**

HL: Colonisation and its aftermath, and emphasis on the Pleistocene, sit well within the biological model, concerning origins. In contrast, in my approach and work, I focused on the sociocultural realm, on transformation, which comes from another world model and paradigm (see below). This is why I approached origins somewhat differently. I feel that your suggestion works well in some contexts, such as the colonisation of the Pacific where the dominant biological model can be augmented by the sociocultural. But as regards Australian colonisation, there is little data on the timing of events, let alone any associated sociocultural aspects. This places major constraints on modelling and the like. I did make a few suggestions myself as regards the dynamics of more open social networks in fuelling migration (Lourandos 1997); and I can also see fertile ground here using modelling based, for example, on ethnographic, ecological as well as comparative archaeological data drawn from other parts of the world.

BD, BB, IM: You wrote influentially in the 1980s, and into the 1990s, of 'intensification' in Aboriginal Australian history, which for you was never just about food or food production. If you were to revisit your 1983 intensification arguments today, what would you have to say — what remains the same, what changes, and why?

HL: I think the core of the 1983 'intensification' arguments still holds up well today and helps illuminate current debate. This is after some twenty-five years or more of information collection and interpretation. For me, the intensification debate emerged out of an engagement with the ethnohistorical data from south-western Victoria and some limited archaeological data. Most of the archaeological information — trends et cetera — came later. The underlying theory, therefore, with its strong sociocultural slant and emphasis on social relations was also linked to this ethnohistorical information. These arguments still hold today, in fact have emerged internationally as part of a dominant 'post-processual' paradigm. In Australia, they have also been absorbed, in various ways, within the more traditional paradigm. The wider debate can be linked to that of complexity and relates to *all* periods of Australian (pre)history, including the Pleistocene (Lourandos 1997). It's just that the complexity/intensification trends are more pronounced in the late Holocene. The archaeological trend data show this even when taphonomic and 'decay-curve' factors are considered (Lourandos & David 2002). The archaeological trends also run contrary to the palaeoenvironmental trends in the late Holocene. As to details, most key Australian environments are represented — including the arid zone — thus removing an emphasis upon coastal Holocene processes which clouded the earlier debate (for details see Lourandos 1997). But islands, such as the tropical Whitsundays, also clearly show the general trends and distinguish these from environmental trends (Barker 2004). Regarding resource intensification, change and expanding social networks, clear recent data came from the arid zone linked to seed use and new languages (Pama–Nyungan/Western Desert) which spread through-out the region during the late Holocene (Veth, this volume). The late-Holocene intensification of grass-seed use had been predicted by the 'intensification' model (Lourandos 1980a, 1980b). We (David & Lourandos 1998) tried to more clearly model these sociodemographic processes in terms of an 'open/closed' dynamic (Lourandos 1997; David & Lourandos 1998), focusing especially on Cape York's emphasis on more closed/bounded social formations and painted rock art in the late Holocene. Biological dimensions — only a suggestion (and poorly phrased) in the original model — have been strongly identified and modelled by Pardoe (1995) for the Murray basin; and pointed to larger, more complex and more numerous cemeteries and territorial behaviour (also Pate, this volume, for Roonka; Webb 1995). A broad range of phenomena, therefore, including archaeological sites and trends, linguistics, rock art, skeletal data and cemeteries thus can be interrelated and explained by these general models. On the other hand, they confound the traditional environmental model.

BD, BB, IM: You once concluded a paper with the words: 'Intensification of social and economic relations would appear to have been increasingly taking place during the Holocene period on the Australian mainland, the process being nipped in the bud by the coming of the Europeans' (Lourandos 1983b, p. 92). Many Australian archaeologists interpreted you to mean that Aboriginal peoples were moving along a unilineal evolutionary trajectory leading to agriculture (e.g. Cosgrove 1995; Head 2000, pp. 103–4) or that you have left no room for changes continuing into the last 200 years (Allen 1997). However, such interpretations appear contradictory to everything else you have written on the subject — contradictory to your very approach against progressionist evolutionism. What did you mean by these words?

HL: This was a tag line to a long paper, but it emerged directly from the arguments advanced from the start. It viewed Aboriginal Australia as a dynamic landscape — an interplay of changing relationships, including socioeconomic relations among others. The data pointed to sociocultural changes during the late Holocene, at perhaps an increasing rate. From this perspective, European colonisation entered a dynamic Aboriginal world with its own momentum — not some time capsule as the traditional model suggested. The model I was advancing was not one of unilinear, progressive change— towards agriculture. In fact, it was a critique of that evolutionary model. Change was viewed here as intrinsic to all societies — and not necessarily environmentally driven — and could lead to myriad sociocultural variation; in this case, including more 'complex' features of 'hunter-gatherer' society. It seems as if the whole debate on hunter-gatherer sociocultural variation, including complexity, was either misunderstood or overlooked by some critics. I sometimes wondered whether some had read much more than the paper's last line.

BD, BB, IM: Three of your most vocal critics are John Beaton (1983), and Caroline Bird and David Frankel (1991a). How have their critical commentaries enabled you to refine your views of Australian Aboriginal history?

HL: Both papers avoided or misunderstood the core debate — concerning changing paradigms — and remained well positioned within the traditional environmental/biological paradigm (see also last answer). Sociocultural factors were again relegated a secondary role. Bird and Frankel's data — long-term chronological trends (using radiocarbon dates based on Rick's (1987) method) — was a novel introduction. The trends themselves lent clear support to similar archaeological trends from the same region (south-western Victoria), obtained earlier by myself and others based upon smaller data sets. But unfortunately these authors failed to acknowledge this. Their archaeological trends also did not fit any general palaeoenvironmental trend. In another paper, similar methods — also based on Rick's method — were used to explain south-western Tasmanian archaeological trends — spanning some 25 000 years — and to link the archaeological trends to long-term environmental oscillations (Holdaway & Porch 1995). Why then was the same method applicable and informative in relation to Pleistocene data but not so for the Holocene? Obviously this could not be the case. Subsequently, David and I employed similar methods in a range of papers concerning comparison between Pleistocene and Holocene archaeological trends throughout Australia (David & Lourandos 1997; Lourandos & David 1998, 2002). A further paper, by Cosgrove, Allen and Marshall (1990), argued that it was not only in the mid-to-late Holocene that features of complexity took place. They pointed to their data from southwestern Tasmania where, they argued, more sedentary patterns emerged and were sustained in the uplands of interior Tasmania throughout the Pleistocene for some 25 000 years. This interpretation, however, appears to have been replaced by more recent research and interpretation (see critique in Lourandos 1993, 1997, pp. 247–54).

BD, BB, IM: Australian archaeologists have reacted strongly to — often against — your ideas of intensification. Yet today many of your once-loudest critics have silently adopted ideas central to your intensification arguments. How has this come about, and what made you so controversial in the first place?

HL: My ideas and approach were welcomed warmly and enthusiastically overseas, in Britain and the United States, as is reflected in invitations to present papers at important conferences and publish key articles in signature volumes and journals. There was change in the air and hunter-gatherers and their (pre)history were being deconstructed and revised (e.g. Price & Brown 1985; Ingold *et al.* 1988). Old paradigms were giving way to new, and the post-processual movement (although barely named at the time) had arrived boots and all! There was a thirst for new approaches and new case studies; participating was an exhilarating experience. At home, in Australia, the reaction was more complex. And this needs to be seen in its historical context and as it played out over the years. I see it as a case of inter- and intra-generational competition — the battle for control of a key debate.

To put this in context there are, of course, two great debates in world archaeology: human biological evolution; and sociocultural transformation. Australian Aboriginal archaeology, and hunter-gatherers in general, were constructed largely within the human biological debate in which culture and society are subordinated to environmental and ecological forces. The second debate focuses on the origins of agriculture and sociocultural complexity. The archaeology of Papua New Guinea, for example, was firmly constructed within the second, 'towards agriculture', debate. There was a clear divide, therefore, between the ways 'Australian Aborigines' and 'Papuans' — and their respective archaeologies — had been constructed: the classic 'hunter' versus 'agriculturalist' split. Now, the Australian intensification debate of the 1980s also drew from this *second* debate, rather than the *first* biological/environmental debate where 'hunter-gatherers' were traditionally housed. It thus challenged the basic paradigms of 'Australian Aborigines as hunter-gatherers' — stretched it to its limits — and introduced, if you like, a *new* paradigm. As the Australian debate began to attract significant international interest from 1980 onwards, it became the prized object to control. At the time, one key academic department had dominated Australian archaeology throughout the 1970s, and by 1980 one key academic journal was beginning to assert its predominance. As well, there was a generation of aspiring archaeologists still climbing the academic ladder, some with professorial ambitions, who sought their place in or control of the debate. My own role and success, both here and overseas, only frustrated their ambitions. Many strategies were employed to assert control over the debate: managing the production, wording and accreditation of papers in journals, or by labelling the very debate as misguided while at the same time absorbing its ideas, data and significance. By de-powering and sanitising the debate in these ways, attempts were made (and still are in some cases) to appropriate it and rework it into the prior dominant paradigm. As it turned out, the power of the debate and its ideas, together with the shift in paradigm overseas, finally left their mark. The 'intensification and complexity' of 'hunter-gatherers' now stands as a chapter in its own right, even in the most conservative of textbooks on world archaeology.

BD, BB, IM: What have been some of the key ways you believe your work has been misrepresented by other archaeologists?
HL: Firstly, the underlying debate — that was a critique of the traditional ecological/biological paradigm — was most often not acknowledged. This debate was well established in the international anthropological and archaeological literature by 1980 and clearly addressed in my work (Lourandos 1980a, 1980b, 1983b). My arguments were drawn from this debate and applied to hunter-gatherers and also to the Australian material that was firmly set within the traditional paradigm. Essentially, it was a re-examination of hunter-gatherers. The arguments, therefore, were primarily *anthropological*, concerned with theory and ethnography and *then* applied to archaeology and its data. My approach was still framed within the ecological data, not outside of it or against it, as was often suggested. To critique the ecological model was not a rejection of ecology itself, which is an important plank of anthropology and archaeology. A new paradigm, if you like, was emerging and this seemed either to be challenged or, as I suspect, to be largely misunderstood. Hunter-gatherers could now be viewed as having the potential to *transform*, like all other societies, and this included features of complexity and intensification. This was not a unilinear or progressionist trajectory, but it allowed them a *history* like everybody else. The mistake was to confuse 'intensification' and 'complexity' with 'agriculture' or its imminence. This may have been because this new paradigm was set within the world debate concerning sociocultural transformation and complexity, a debate that traditionally related to agriculturalists and more complex societies and *not* to hunter-gatherers. It permitted Australia, traditionally constructed as 'hunter-gatherer', to be considered in new and different ways and to be compared to other small-scale societies, such as those of Papua New Guinea, traditionally constructed as 'agricultural'. There was also misunderstanding regarding the archaeological data and trends and the question of *scale* (see below).

BD, BB, IM: Your earlier writings were influenced by the works of Barbara Bender, Phil Hughes and Ron Lampert, to name a few. But what of more recent influences? What archaeological work in Australia over the past twenty years has been influential in helping you redefine your own views of Australia's Aboriginal past?

HL: In truth, I probably learnt as much from my critics — by needing to react to them — as from others and their work. You can scan my commentary here for references from both sides of the fence. But, in my work, I've always tried to make reference to the work of others — the more the better — and to *interact*, if you like, with their ideas and results.

BD, BB, IM: In your later writings you began to write more of increasing complexity than of intensification as such — what some theorists in other fields have called 'complexification'; the way social dynamics lead to increasing structural complexity — in a way that is neither linear nor entirely predictable but historically situated. This is perhaps most evident in your 1988 'Palaeopolitics' paper in which you argued that competitive social relations in Aboriginal Australia led to surplus production that fed large, communal rituals and formalised exchanges, which in turn led to enhanced status or prestige, polygyny and an expansion of social networks, feeding back to further intensify competitive social relations and so on (Lourandos 1988a). In this paper you outlined, for the first time and in considerable detail, social mechanisms for the archaeological changes observed in late-Holocene south-eastern Australia. How do you now see the relationship between 'intensification' and 'complexification', theoretically, and in the Australian Aboriginal past.

HL: I *began* my research with the question of complexity (complexification) within hunter-gatherer society, and chose a case study from southwestern Victoria — its ethnohistory and Holocene archaeology. The focus on intensification came with the eel-drains example which was a clear fit — it couldn't be explained adequately as a product of local-group economics (but at the wider *inter-group* level). It therefore defied explanation by traditional ecological explanations (that is, optimal foraging theory) and needed a broader — including social — approach. I later widened the term 'intensification' as so many other variables also appeared to be associated. The term 'intensification' also seemed to ground the more general question of complexity and direct it theoretically. I began with the work of Yengoyan (1968, 1976) who considered Australian *social networks* from an ecological perspective and Godelier

(1975) from a sociopolitical. It was at the inter-group level, therefore, beyond the local group or band, that more complex relationships both *social* and *ecological* were *managed*. My more recent work has suggested that throughout Australian (pre)history social networks have moved from more open, fluid and flexible formations towards more closed, territorially bounded and formalised networks, and that this general trend was most evident in the late Holocene. This assessment, drawn from both archaeological and ethnohistorical information, indicates that complexity is more clearly linked to more closed social networks. It is here that relationships, both social and ecological, are more complex and therefore costly. This is not to say that aspects of more closed networks and complexity had not occurred earlier on in Australian (pre)history, such as during the terminal Pleistocene where archaeological signs exist; but that they were demonstrably *more pronounced* during the late Holocene (Lourandos 1997; David & Lourandos 1997, 1998, 1999; Lourandos & David 2002). As to the question of the *expanding* social network acting as a *dynamic* and fuelling change (focused upon in my earlier work); this can occur at all levels both more open and closed. It is, however, with more closed formations that expanding networks involve more complex and costly relationships, and are thus more dynamic. This is clearly demonstrated ethnohistorically by the vast, expanded networks of south-eastern Australia (Victoria in particular), which incorporated territorially bounded (or 'closed') social units.

BD, BB, IM: A few years ago you said to one of us (BD) that we should move beyond intensification; that knowledge has moved on, that we are now at a different period of understanding Aboriginal history. What did you mean by that, given that aspects of your intensification writing now forms a basic cornerstone of much of what we know of temporal trends in late-Holocene Australian Aboriginal history? (Unlike post-modernism, and post-positivist archaeologies, it is arguable that there is not yet a 'post-intensification' period of Australian archaeology.) What should a 'post-intensification' Australian archaeology look like?

HL: I was referring to issues raised in my last answer (above) — that in some ways the debate has moved on. As you say, many of the ideas have now become part of the mainstream dialogue; but as we have acknowledged here, it was also a much broader debate, involving new paradigms. It became in effect the 'post-processual' forum for Australian archaeology abreast, and in some ways ahead, of its overseas counterpart. The Australian debate had a strong influence on the overseas debate, especially concerning hunter-gatherer studies. What has followed, if you like, is a continuation of the post-processual movement or paradigm in Australia. This is clearly demonstrated by this book, with its emphasis upon reflexivity, interpretation, the questioning of 'text' and keeping a respectful distance from positivist stances. It is also reflected presently in a lot of Australian literature, especially concerning Indigenous issues and public archaeology. I see it as a way to critique the more traditional ecological/processual approach. At the same time it provides a forum for a much wider range of approaches and issues, which just cannot be accommodated by the traditional approach. In other words, there is room for both, for they still overlap considerably and people move between approaches for a variety of reasons. The days of a monolithic and centrally controlled archaeology are well and truly over.

BD, BB, IM: What do you see as the strengths and limitations of a Marxist archaeology for understanding the Australian Aboriginal past today? Is there a role for a Marxist archaeology, or for Marxist archaeologies, in Australia and elsewhere today?

HL: As I've tried to explain above, Marxist approaches can be used either to augment other approaches or can serve in their own right, for a variety of reasons. In many ways Marxist or neo-Marxist theory lies at the base or core of sociocultural theory (even when this is not made explicitly clear) and so it cannot go away. Archaeology itself has been strongly influenced by Marxist approaches (as has anthropology), again, sometimes not explicitly. This is particularly so in the recent post-processual literature.

BD, BB, IM: In your later work you began to stress more the role of analytical scale both to the setting of research questions and agendas, and to how these may pattern or prejudice our results. This appears to signal an increasing concern with methodology, perhaps in response to the way others responded to your earlier writings and a call for more fine-grained and reliable data by which to investigate past historical trajectories. How do methodological advances, including concerns over temporal and geographical scales of analysis, affect how you now view the late Holocene and intensification in Aboriginal Australia?

HL: The question of *scale* is central to questions of intensification and complexity, and opens up so many doors. Also, understanding scale helps to overcome some of the stumbling blocks in the earlier intensification debate. The debate kept slipping between scalar levels (both theoretical and archaeological): between *large*-scale, big picture, to more nitty-gritty *middle* range. This was so for all data and theory. It was a case of comparing apples to oranges. The two levels need to be kept separate as they have different *logic* and data. But they can be compared through a *bridging* logic. For example, the long-term archaeological trends were often criticised as not including enough middle-range information; as if finer-grained analysis would reveal further variation in the general trend itself. But the two sets of data are quite different. Finer-grained data would not necessarily alter the *general* trend, but just provide more information; in this case, at finer temporal levels. It's a bit like saying, for example, that while population in Great Britain *generally* has continued to increase over the past 150 years or since the Industrial Revolution, when one looks at *finer-grained* regional British data the patterns are varied. Both may be correct, and data from one level doesn't necessarily alter the information or pattern from the other. But arguments comparing finer-grained data (trends, sites, artefacts and their technologies etc.) were often used to discredit the *general trends* observed in the Holocene (e.g. Bird & Frankel 1991a; Lourandos 1996). In my more recent research, therefore, I tried to demonstrate that by using a consistent methodology these archaeological temporal trends were valid and also, as it turned out, visible in most major Australian environments during the mid-to-late Holocene. The Holocene trends were then compared with long-term Pleistocene archaeological trends and indicated that, since about 25 000 years ago, only during the late Holocene did the trends run *contrary* to the general long-term palaeoenvironmental trends (Lourandos & David 1998, 2002; David & Lourandos 1997). This was just another way to approach the intensification debate — anew and without all the other accompanying baggage.

BD, BB, IM: Your work has long been deeply political, even if not always overtly so. For instance, your writings have always destabilised conventional western thinking about the Australian Aboriginal past, and by implication about the Australian Aboriginal (and our own) present. Yet you have rarely explicitly written about politics and the politics of archaeology. Is there a tension between your academic writing and your political views? The way you wrote about archaeology certainly changed our thinking about the Aboriginal past and present, but were your academic messages intended to have a social reach beyond academia? Do you see a role, or a line of influence, from academia to the public?

HL: I don't see politics and academic work as separate, as some more conservative people would argue. There is no neutral, objective position and such a stance invariably supports the *status quo* at any point in time. I felt no problem, therefore, in attempting to 'humanise' the past and, in Australia's case, the Aboriginal past. In doing so, a sociocultural perspective allowed me to act as observer, participant or critic, as long as the arguments used were logical and consistent. Working within any institution, such as a university, and a community, such as academia, imposes restrictions and hence the tension in perspective you point to. I see the *ways* we (archaeologists, academics, non-Indigenous Australians) *construct* 'Aboriginal' history as entirely political and therefore needing to be examined (reflexively) in their own right. I would hope my work has wider appeal and it's really up to me now to open myself up to a wider audience, don't you think?

BD, BB, IM: When you first came to the Department of Anthropology and Sociology at the University of Queensland you made an immediate intellectual impact on students by showing many of us the enormous potential of an explicitly social archaeology that moved beyond 'humans' and 'things' and into the realm of 'people' and 'society'. For many of us, here at last was an archaeological praxis that was not constrained by a narrow empiricism, but was more reflective of what many of us had already sensed related, in a real way, to the complexity of human groups and the theoretical tools necessary to explain them. How important for you was teaching in propagating and developing your ideas about Australian prehistory, and were you ever conscious through your teaching of instilling a legacy of theoretical continuity in your students?

HL: Teaching and students were all-important to me and helped me clarify and expand my ideas. I valued students' reactions and insights, which stimulated me to go further in my work. I often tried out new ideas and new ways to approach material and problems in class. The debates, or dialogues, really first took place there, before being let loose on the world outside. I was interested in opening up students' perceptions to new and different ways of seeing things — a continuity of ideas and enquiry — but not a legacy for its own sake.

BD, BB, IM: After teaching undergraduate students for nearly thirty years, what do you see as the most important message(s) to pass on to archaeology students?

HL: A simple message: to always keep an open mind. Answers are few and facts fewer still. But if you do intend to express an opinion of your own, make sure you do your homework first.

BD, BB, IM: You once told one of us (BD), when commenting on a PhD thesis draft, that when writing of the past it is not 'humans' that we write about but 'people'. You pointed out that 'humans' is a biological notion; ironically that the very term 'human' is a non-humanistic concept devoid of the people who are those real, living and sensual individuals whose ancestors we try to write about. How do you see the role of (archaeological) science in understanding this very real and living Aboriginal history?

HL: Here you also enter the realms of anthropology, history and politics and therefore 'science', in some ways, may have to be put to one side. It's a matter of differing paradigms, as discussed above. But given the greater flexibility today of being able to move between paradigms, of facing contrasting viewpoints, I cannot see a great problem.

BD, BB, IM: In 1998, one of us (IM) commented that writing about the history of others 'is more than a clash of belief systems — it is a clash of powers to control constructions of identity' (McNiven 1998, p. 47). How can archaeological practice avoid such problematic academic colonialism?

HL: I think the only solution to this pervasive problem of control of others' histories and identities is to create a truly *reflexive* disciple; an arena of debate that continually looks back upon itself and the ways it goes about doing things. Reflexivity involves responsibility and the effect one has on others. In this way, it's quite different to the defensive stance often taken when one feels challenged; different to the ways some archaeologists have reacted in the past when their authority and control over the discipline appeared to be threatened.

BD, BB, IM: Do you see Australian archaeology realistically going beyond these problematic issues?

HL: The last answer, I feel, points to positive directions. I really cannot see much point to Australian archaeology if it doesn't try to transcend these problems — to problematise them and embrace them as praxis. Anthropology, for example, is already acting in this way and the seeds have been planted in archaeology, especially by its public face.

BD, BB, IM: Looking back, what has Australian archaeology achieved, academically, socially, politically?

HL: It has provided data but also ideas and, at times, has shown the way, as we have discussed here, by illuminating overseas debate. This is so for debates on human, as well as Aboriginal, origins and the history and nature of hunter-gatherers. And, perhaps most important of all, it has assisted Indigenous people's concerns — including their history and links to land, as well as human and social rights. In many ways Australian archaeologists have acknowledged the Indigenous position in Australian society as one of 'first among equals'. But these are ongoing concerns and need to be continually fought for.

BD, BB, IM: Do you see Australian archaeology capable of engaging more deeply than it has with society in general, and in doing so is it capable of helping redress some of the social prejudices and social injustices so prevalent in Australian society today? Can archaeology participate in social debates in Australia? Does it have a responsibility to do so, and are Australian archaeologists likely to? Do they already?

HL: As I've indicated, Australia archaeologists have already achieved a lot, especially through the Australian Archaeological Association and public archaeology — the interface between the academic, public and governmental. But by addressing these issues of social injustice and participating in as well as creating debate — by building it into the disciple in this way — a politicised and action archaeology can face and handle these issues and problems. Archaeologists, as anthropologists have already done, need to be better schooled in these ways, to have these practices built into curricula. Archaeology cannot stand apart from these social issues as a 'neutral science'. In this regard, it has a responsibility to engage with and assist Indigenous communities and their concerns. Many archaeologists, including myself, already operate in this way, but this now needs to be formalised more extensively and legitimised through university courses, sessions at conferences and in the literature. Post-processual archaeology has already shown that archaeology cannot simply model itself on the natural sciences; it has much in common with anthropology and the social sciences that already operate in these ways.

BD, BB, IM: What do you see as the big issues in Australian archaeology today, those that you think will guide Australia into the future? And how do these differ from those you would like to see Australian archaeology address in the near future?

HL: I think the big issues are those we've already identified above, the big three that also form the core of world archaeology: biological evolution and origins; sociocultural transformation (including complexity and intensification), and also historical archaeology; and Indigenous perspectives. Public archaeology, of course, forms a fourth related area. How we approach these issues, however, depends upon our particular perspectives.

BD, BB, IM: If you had an opportunity to start up a new research project in Australian archaeology, what would be the issue(s) you would address and where would you like to undertake fieldwork?

HL: Many possibilities come to mind here, for example working more closely with Indigenous communities and their perspectives on the past and how they interact with the present. Or the construction of Indigenous history as a contested arena; an entangled complex of relationships — including Indigenous voices, legal issues and such like. This construction would benefit from more textured and multi-vocal information. But I would also like to return to south-western Victoria and complete my original field project there, using a broad-based perspective; landscape/social (also phenomenological) as well as ecological.

Acknowledgements

Thanks to Peter Hiscock for digitising Figure 1.

3.

Harry Lourandos' life and work: an Australian archaeological odyssey

Sandra Bowdler

'To strive, to seek, to find, and not to yield.'
Tennyson, *Ulysses*

Harry Lourandos was born in Sydney in 1945. His father came to Australia from the rocky isle of Ithaca in western Greece, as had his mother's family in the 1890s. The Lourandos family was involved in business (including restaurants) and the professions, Harry's uncle being Sydney's second Greek solicitor. He grew up in the eastern suburbs, enjoying a typical Sydney childhood, with beach excursions, and attended Sydney Grammar School, an independent non-denominational institution with a reputation for academic excellence. While this might appear to be a typical comfortable academic's background, bear in mind that Australia in the 1950s was not the multicultural society it is now, and indeed the last vestiges of the White Australia policy were not swept away until the 1970s. Imagine, therefore, growing up in a bilingual home, and one can begin to understand the roots of Harry Lourandos' empathy for the social underdog.

Harry Lourandos enrolled at the University of Sydney in 1963, eventually taking an honours degree in archaeology. Almost immediately he was appointed to a position as Research Archaeologist at the Tasmanian Museum and Art Gallery in Hobart, the first such appointment of a professional archaeologist. If Sydney in the early 1960s was not exactly the centre of metropolitan diversity and sophistication it is (or thinks it is) now, imagine Hobart. Bemused by the milieu in which he found himself, Harry nevertheless embarked on a program of research in eastern Tasmania.

Modern archaeological research in Tasmania began with Rhys Jones who, as a young Welsh migrant with a Cambridge degree, had been appointed to an academic post at the University of Sydney in 1963. He began fieldwork in Tasmania in the summer of 1963–4. On his second season that summer he was accompanied by Lourandos (Jones 1971, p. 61), still at the time an undergraduate at the university. Lourandos had, therefore, a first-hand acquaintance with Tasmanian archaeology when he began his job in Hobart. Almost immediately after taking up this post he was told of the discovery of an 'enclosed chamber' at the Rocky Cape South cave site, which he had helped excavate in 1965. This was a 'midden surface which had been sealed off by outside deposits already dated to more than 5000 years old ... Lourandos recognised the importance of the site' and contacted Jones (Jones 1971, p. 64). Jones and Lourandos together carried out a detailed survey and excavation of this undisturbed surface, a particularly important discovery in Tasmanian archaeology (although, several decades later, it still awaits detailed publication).

Lourandos' first independent excavations in Tasmania took place in January 1968 (Little Swanport) and February 1968 (Crown Lagoon) (Lourandos 1970, pp. 30, 61). By 1968, Jones had established himself as the pioneer of Tasmanian archaeology, with several publications describing his fieldwork and results (Jones 1965a, 1965b, 1966, 1967) and a paper giving an overview of his work in the wider Australian context (Jones 1968). Harry was, to a large extent, working under Jones' aegis; the latter had inspected and sounded middens at Little Swanport on his first field trip in 1964 (Jones 1971, p. 59) and had also identified the lunette site at Crown Lagoon in 1967, and shown it to Lourandos (Jones 1971, p. 64; Lourandos 1970, p. 60). Also working under Jones' supervision was Betty Hiatt (as she was then, later Betty Meehan), who had produced an honours thesis in 1965 analysing what was known from ethnohistorical sources of the traditional Tasmanian diet and economy (Hiatt 1967). This had been much facilitated by the availability at the Mitchell Library in Sydney of the papers of George Augustus Robinson, published in 1966 by NJB Plomley. There was thus, in the mid-to-late 1960s, a considerable ferment in the air about research into the Tasmanian Aboriginal past.

In December 1968 Lourandos' first publication, 'Dispersal of activities — the east Tasmanian Aboriginal sites', was published in the *Papers and Proceedings of the Royal Society of Tasmania*. This was not just a summary of his field work, the 'what I did on my holidays' of most first publications, but a bold attack, in the best scholarly traditions, a Trojan horse dragged into the citadel of his mentors. Lourandos argued that previous formulations — which saw no difference in the diet and economy of the Aborigines of the west coast and those of the east — were flawed by a failure to correctly distinguish the relevant ecological biomes, and instead simply drew a line down the middle of the island. This theme was elaborated in his Master's thesis (for the Australian National University), his critique extending to the use of ethnohistoric sources and arguing that previous work had not sufficiently distinguished sources related to the undisrupted period before settlement from those relating to the later period (Lourandos 1970, p. 95). This work, however, was not primarily a negative critique of previous work, but a substantial and positive contribution to the unfolding story of Tasmanian archaeology and signaled many of the concerns which were to signify Lourandos' work throughout his career.

'Coast and hinterland: the archaeological sites of eastern Tasmania' was the title of Lourandos' MA thesis, embodying the results, analysis and interpretation of field and archival work he had carried out in Tasmania between 1967 and 1970 (Figure 1). As well as the two excavated sites in eastern Tasmania already mentioned, the fieldwork also comprised survey work in western Tasmania. Lourandos also explored the ethnohistoric record in detail, according to his own stringent criteria, to elucidate the patterns of life led by Tasmanian Aborigines in the recent past. The basic argument of the thesis was that there were indeed economic and settlement patterns which distinguished eastern and western Tasmania. In western Tasmania — as demonstrated by Jones' research, as well as his own observations — people had led a semi-sedentary lifestyle, with their activities concentrated within the relatively narrow coastal strip. In the east, however, their activities were more dispersed across the much broader coastal plain, with a concomitant more nomadic settlement pattern, thus anticipating by a decade Binford's model of residential and logistic patterns (Binford 1980).

Figure 1. Harry Lourandos at Mount Cameron West in 1969 (photo courtesy of Harry Lourandos).

In his thesis we see many of the hallmarks of Lourandos' work: a dedication to meticulous field work; an interest in sites in their wider landscape settings and the relationship between people and environment; a perception of the need to consult ethnographic or ethnohistoric sources and interrogate them scrupulously; and a commitment to the proper use of theory as a structural underpinning of sound work. There are several references to the early work of the 'New Archaeology', which is generally considered to have made its mark with the publication of *New perspectives in archaeology* in 1968 (Binford & Binford 1968), particularly to the work on assemblage variability by the Binfords (e.g. Binford 1968).

After submitting his thesis and leaving the position in Hobart, Lourandos spent some time travelling in Europe, including a visit to his ancestral homeland. Fortunately for Australian archaeology (and possibly himself), his plans to open a restaurant on Ithaca selling Vegemite sandwiches came to naught, and he returned to take up a position as Teaching Fellow at the University of Sydney in 1973. He then began a new research project in south-west Victoria.

Archaeology in Victoria in the 1970s was subject to an interesting government regime. The statutory authority for archaeological site protection interpreted its responsibilities as best fulfilled by carrying out the maximum amount of research and excavations possible. Interlopers were not particularly welcome but, confronted with these bureaucratic Laestrygonians, Lourandos persevered and carried out the research for which he is probably best known, again combining field and archival research with the strong cement of a new theoretical position.

His initial results and interpretations appeared in three published articles (Lourandos 1976, 1977b, 1980a) and were described in detail in his PhD thesis, 'Forces of change: Aboriginal technology and population in south-western Victoria'. Two specific entities linked his work in Victoria with that in Tasmania: the similarities of coastal sites such as Seal Point in the Otways to those of the west coast of Tasmania; and the writings of George Augustus Robinson.

Robinson had moved amongst the Tasmanian Aborigines in the 1830s and persuaded them to enjoy the benefits of European civilisation; for these efforts he was known as the 'Conciliator of the Aborigines' and became the Protector of Aborigines in Victoria in 1830 (the amount of irony which one brings to bear on these titles is a matter of personal perception). In both places he kept voluminous diaries of great ethnohistorical significance, but while his Tasmanian journals were well known through their publication by Plomley (1966, 1987), those of his Victorian sojourn were effectively unknown until brought to light by Lourandos.

Lourandos continued his interest in using ethnohistorical records, not as a source of analogies for interpreting the archaeological record, but as an extension of it, fleshing out our understanding of the recent life of Aboriginal people. He also developed his interest in an ecological approach, but in the course of his Victorian research came to the position that environmental forces — as significant as they might be — did not entirely determine the course of human cultural change.

The first fruits of this new direction were evident in a short but significant article published in 1976 (Lourandos 1976). The article drew attention to the archaeological and ethnohistorical evidence for sophisticated water controls in western Victoria in the form of extensive and elaborate drainage systems, along with evidence for high population densities in the region, large seasonal concentrations of people, and a semi-sedentary lifestyle. Such concepts were a direct challenge to traditional ideas about hunter-gatherers in general, and the life of Australian Aborigines in particular. They also directly challenged the models of some archaeologists who, while avoiding the simplistic conclusions of earlier scholars, were nonetheless moving in rather different directions. Lourandos was arguing that, in western Victoria, Aboriginal people of the recent past were managing resources such as eels in ways not consistent with ideas of hunter-gatherers as passive exploiters of natural resources, nor with the idea that their populations grew 'naturally' to reach a certain level dictated by the 'carrying capacity' of the natural environment. Lourandos was also arguing for much higher population densities than were generally accepted for non-tropical areas.

In his article 'Aboriginal spatial organisation and population: south western Victoria reconsidered' (Lourandos 1977b), a detailed reading of Robinson's Victorian journals and other ethnohistorical sources was used to construct a model of Aboriginal demography in the region different to that thought possible for south-eastern Australia. Population size and density and settlement patterns were considered in the light of ecological factors. In contrasting this evidence with that from Tasmania, Lourandos observed that 'as differences in population density between the two latter areas would be difficult to explain as due to environmental factors alone, we should also turn to cultural factors for an explanation'. In addressing this issue, Lourandos used a fine-grained anthropological model to look at the distribution of identifiable social groups in the Victorian landscape.

A further development of ideas was evident in his 1980 paper 'Change or stability? Hydraulics, hunter-gatherers and population in temperate Australia' (Lourandos 1980b). Here again he tackled the view that Aboriginal populations were essentially stable from the time of colonisation onwards, and argued that changes in energy-harnessing techniques led to population density increases in certain environments. He invoked his detailed sociogeographical modelling for Victoria, and presented data showing that population densities in some parts of Australia overlapped those of horticultural communities in New Guinea, another serious challenge to traditional views about hunter-gatherers.

These themes underpin Lourandos' PhD thesis, 'Forces of change: Aboriginal technology and population in south-western Victoria' (Lourandos 1980a). This magisterial work embodies the detailed results of his Victorian research — both field and archival — supported, as with all his work, by a solid and consistent theoretical structure. In this thesis we find, for the first time, the idea of 'intensification', in this instance derived from the work of David Harris (1977a), used to indicate five 'avenues of economic exploitation' (Lourandos 1980a, p. 13). The overall conclusion of the thesis was to suggest a model of 'dynamic equilibrium' for the socioeconomic past of Aboriginal societies, allowing for change in both technology and demography (Lourandos 1980a, p. 416).

In 1979, Harry was appointed to a lectureship at the University of New England, where I was delighted to welcome him as a colleague, hoping like Calypso that he would remain (he outstayed me, as it turned out). While resident in the remote fastness of the tablelands, he was able to pursue the theoretical paths indicated in his thesis, and also turn his attention to his old stamping ground, Tasmania. This may have been triggered in part by a joint paper we gave at a conference in 1980 (Bowdler & Lourandos 1982), comparing aspects of the archaeological record of northwest Tasmania with that of coastal south-west Victoria. In any case, Lourandos returned to Tasmania in early 1982, and excavated at Warragarra rock shelter in the upper Mersey Valley region of central Tasmania (Lourandos 1983a). Here he revealed a sequence of *c.* 10 000 years, from the early deglaciation period to the beginning of the establishment of rainforest in the region. Lourandos here is emphatic that while climatic change may have provided an incentive for change, 'environmental factors should not be viewed as *determining* cultural change' (Lourandos 1983a, p. 43).

He also describes a period of more extensive occupation from *c.* 3400 years BP which, while connected with the cessation of fishing across Tasmania, also represents a period of economic *expansion* (Lourandos 1983a, p. 44; see also Lourandos 1988b). This is extremely relevant to debates about the Tasmanian past, debates that are even more current now than at the time of Lourandos' publication (Windschuttle 2002; Manne 2003). Indeed, Lourandos merits the honour of a serve from Windschuttle for daring to think his work might in some way benefit Aboriginal people (Windschuttle 2001).

However, it is the concept of 'intensification' among hunter-gatherers, and its application to the Aboriginal Australian past, with which Harry Lourandos' name is most closely associated. His 'Intensification: a late Pleistocene–Holocene archaeological sequence from south-western Victoria' (Lourandos 1983b) is one of the most influential archaeological papers ever published in Australia.

It, and its argument, are surely too well known to necessitate repeating here, but can be seen as the natural outcome of Lourandos' evident intellectual trajectory to this time. Lourandos himself makes no claims for originality in the concept of socioeconomic intensification as such, and drew heavily on the works of Barbara Bender (e.g. Bender 1978), as well as the previously mentioned David Harris, in its formulation. The concept in their work was developed primarily to identify a pathway from hunter-gatherer to agriculturalist; novelty lay in the application of such models to people who always remained hunter-gatherers. The significant point was to show that hunter-gatherers could indeed intensify their economic activities *without* becoming agriculturalists and that, eschewing environmental determinism, such intensification could be related to developing social complexity.

The significance for Australian archaeology, apart from the theoretical implications, was in finding an elegant way of both identifying and interpreting a very evident trend in the archaeological data of the Holocene period. The trend towards increasing numbers of sites, increasing density of occupational debris in sites, and increasing technological complexity from the mid-Holocene, had been noted by others in the mainland Australian archaeological record (including me, Bowdler 1981). However, it remained for Lourandos to provide a useful shorthand title by which to refer to it (not to be sneezed at), an action that did more than just name it. Too often in archaeology (and other disciplines) the act of naming a phenomenon comes to be seen as somehow explaining it (see Amis 1983, p. 12 for an amusing description of this habit). 'Intensification' for Lourandos involved a clear and specific theory of socially driven economic and settlement change. Naturally there were Cyclopean critics, some of whom flatly denied the existence of the phenomenon observed, some who ascribed it to the 'natural' ravages of time, others wanting to somehow attribute it to some sort of 'natural' increase in evidence. Only Beaton (1985) put forward anything that even looked like an alternative explanatory theory. Whatever most Australian archaeologists working on Aboriginal material thought of it, few have not used at least the name, and generally the concept, of 'intensification' in their work.

In a series of succeeding publications, Lourandos refined his model and expanded its range to encompass the whole of Australia during the Holocene. He also addressed international conferences on the subject, and publications in international journals and edited collections soon followed (Lourandos 1985a, 1987a, 1988a, 1993). The last-cited article was chosen to appear in the first issue of an important new organ, the *Journal of Archaeological Research*. This paper also explored the question of scales of inquiry, a significant factor in considering cultural change, and particularly directional change through time (see also Lourandos 1996). In 1987, Lourandos summarised his Victorian research in one of the volumes published to mark the bicentennial of European Australian settlement, bringing his ideas and findings to a wider audience: 'the people of southwestern Victoria and their neighbours were more numerous, more sedentary and far more ingenious than we ever imagined' (Lourandos 1987b, p. 307).

In 1986, Lourandos moved from Armidale to lotus-eating Brisbane, and a position at the University of Queensland. This brought him into contact with one of the scholars who had made most effective use of his intensification argument, Anne Ross. Together they published a paper titled 'The great "intensification debate": its history and place in Australian archaeology' (Lourandos & Ross 1994). Not only does this article revisit the original concept, it also considers evidence recovered by archaeologists subsequent to the original publication and tests it against the theory. More interestingly, the authors reflect on the impact of the concept, not just on scholarly work and debate, but in the wider world. They consider that the intensification debate 'democratised the discipline', as it shifted the focus of research in Aboriginal archaeology away from the Pleistocene sites that had tended to monopolise debate. They also argued that it represented a more sophisticated phase of archaeological research, moving away from the '"cowboy era" of data collection, where theory played a minor role, and linked the discipline with the contemporary discourses of anthropology' (Lourandos & Ross 1994, p. 59). Finally, they suggest that the debate provided a framework for 'understanding the continuing dynamics of modern indigenous culture', with recent changes in the archaeological record showing that more recent post-European changes are 'simply a continuation of a tradition which goes back thousands of years' (Lourandos & Ross 1994, p. 60): the final nail in the coffin of any idea of Aboriginal people as having been unchanging people in an unchanging land.

A career as a teacher as well as a researcher has its drawbacks, but also its rewards. After teaching courses in Australian Aboriginal archaeology for over twenty years, Lourandos was well situated to gather his extensive experience in and vision of the subject into a single volume, *Continent of hunter-gatherers: new perspectives in Australian prehistory,* published by Cambridge University Press in 1997. This book was intended to present a fresh look at Australian Aboriginal archaeology, contrasting 'traditional approaches' with 'more recent viewpoints' (Lourandos 1997, p. xiv). It is a wide-ranging exercise, basically testing Lourandos' particular theoretical position against all the evidence available at the time it was written. It was not, on the face of it, written as a textbook, but in fact it serves very well for that purpose.

There are good reasons why textbooks are not generally compatible with works in good scholarly standing. A textbook must be organised into topics which can be taught as 'packages' on a weekly basis, be extremely well-referenced so that students can find for themselves the primary material for each topic, and above all be clearly written and immediately comprehensible. There is of course no good reason why research monographs should not be like this too, but usually they are not. There is the further problem that monographs written to support a particular theory are not usually sufficiently expansive to stand as a textbook. *Continent of hunter-gatherers,* however, fulfills all these requirements, in particular because — while it does embody a particular theoretical standpoint — this leads to a tidy organisation and a flow in the narrative. Furthermore, Lourandos is scrupulous in presenting alternative viewpoints, allowing the reader to assess the merits of different arguments, and to pursue them through the original sources. As a text for teaching Australian Aboriginal archaeology, it easily sees off all rivals.

One of the other advantages of teaching is the opportunity to foster postgraduate students, that is, the potential to produce your own new colleagues. Lourandos has been particularly fortunate in this regard, as can be seen by the Telemachean editors of and contributors to this volume. In recent years, he has fruitfully worked in collaboration with, in particular, Bruno David (David *et al.* 1996, 1997, 1999; David & Lourandos 1997, 1998, 1999; Lourandos & David 1998, 2002). This work brings the Lourandos theoretical perspective to bear more closely on a new geographical area — north Queensland — and a new area of investigation, that of rock art. Lourandos's particular interest in the epistemology and nature of long-term trends is also evident, particularly in Lourandos and David (1998, 2002).

Lourandos' scholarly contribution will surely continue in his retirement from a full-time academic position, but his significant role in the history of Australian Aboriginal archaeology is well secured. His concept of socioeconomic intensification among Aboriginal people in the Holocene has been one of the most significant contributions made by an archaeologist, not just to his own discipline, but to our understanding of Aboriginal society generally. This involved not merely the naming and description of an observable phenomenon or group of phenomena, but also a clearly developed theory to support it. The further significance of this theory was that it rejected the idea of Aboriginal people as helpless victims of environmental forces, and claimed instead a role for them as actors in an ongoing cultural context. It also brought into focus the idea of Aboriginal society as dynamic and changing, rather than a nomadic but culturally static entity, and as complex and ingenious.

Lourandos was able to achieve this vision by his appreciation of the proper role of theory in archaeological analysis and interpretation, and by his understanding of the place of ethnohistoric research. Australian archaeologists (and not only Australian ones) are often uneasy with the role of theory in archaeology, on the one hand regarding it as not necessary in empirical enquiry and thus delivering themselves into the hands of some long-dead ecologist (to paraphrase Maynard Keynes), or on the other seeing it as something needing to be specifically addressed, but again outside the common pursuit of substantive work. Lourandos almost uniquely understood from the beginning of his career that an archaeologist must have a specific theoretical position underpinning his or her practical research, and that any argument about the past must proceed from a definite theoretical basis. Every example of his work demonstrates theory at work without any parading of a theoretical discourse beyond what is necessary to illuminate the problem at hand.

For Lourandos, the ethnohistorical literature was not a 'quarry' for clues and analogies (in the memorable words of McBryde 1979), but a resource as significant as the archaeological data base itself, capable of yielding up a coherent view of past Aboriginal lives. His work demonstrates the value of this source of information as representing the final phase of the Australian substantive archaeological record. It is for this reason that his research is focused on people as people, not as just some species of animal in the landscape driven by biological imperatives and environmental dictates. By concentrating on the recent archaeological past, as represented by the Holocene archaeological record and the more recent historical record, Harry Lourandos has made a unique contribution to our understanding of Aboriginal society and culture as a living entity past and present.

Acknowledgements

I would like to thank Jacques Bierling for his help in preparing this chapter, and especially I thank Harry himself for being a great colleague over the years.

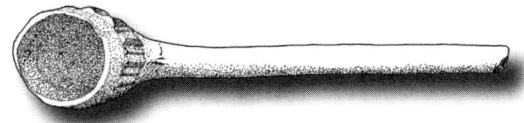

Part 2
Tyranny of text

*Clay tobacco pipe from a shell midden on Fraser Island, obtained by
Aboriginal people from European timber-getters in the late 19th century.*

4.

Unpacking Australian prehistory

Bruno David and Tim Denham

Unpacking our library, unpacking our thinking

Shortly before 1931, Walter Benjamin unpacks his library (Benjamin 1969). He opens innumerable crates crammed with books, retrieving them from two years' hibernation in their dark spaces. He takes each book and places it on new shelves not yet acquainted with their worth. Before the library was packed away, each volume had previously been aligned on those older shelves, not singly but like a file of soldiers ordered to attention, or musicians orchestrated into an ensemble. For a library is more than a set of books: it is a symphony of titles and concepts, an arrangement conducted in paper and cloth. It is made up of the short and the long; of poetry, history and mathematics; or, for those of us interested in Australian archaeology, by the stranded categories — hunting and gathering, Australian prehistory, Pacific archaeology, the origins of agriculture, the Middle East and so on. We expect to see, and we do see, Mulvaney and Kamminga next to Flood and to White and O'Connell; these are not random associations.

Like Benjamin, let us pack up our library and then set it out again. Let us put it on new shelves. And let us dare be informed anew by an archaeologist who, over a period of some thirty years, challenged our perceptions of Aboriginal and — to a lesser extent — New Guinean history. In this library we will rearrange our books, we will rethink how and why we have hitherto assembled various disparate concepts about Indigenous pasts in those certain, particular and peculiar, associations. In rearranging our books we can rearrange our minds, clearing them of certain preconceptions, but to do so will not be easy. And since no arrangement is neutral, undoubtedly along the way we will introduce new preconceptions that will themselves need to be revisited.

But before packing our books, we should inspect what we have, for our memories wander and we are not sure what we will find when we again open the boxes. We cannot visit every volume now for there are too many, so we will restrict ourselves to one shelf. On the left we have the Australian books, those that deal with Aboriginal prehistory. On the right we have those of New Guinea and the Pacific islands. But that is not strictly correct, for the shelf is not really ordered geographically; there is, on this and on neighbouring shelves, a conceptual progression. Comfortably tucked beside, and accustomed to creep among the Australian books, we find others: Richard Lee and Irven DeVore's *Man the hunter*, Douglas Price and James Brown's *Prehistoric hunter-gatherers*, Lewis Binford's *Constructing frames of reference*, MG Bicchieri's *Hunters and gatherers today*, Betty Meehan and Neville White's *Hunter-gatherer demography*, Bruce Winterhalder and Eric Alden Smith's *Hunter-gatherer foraging strategies*, and Tim Ingold, David Riches and James Woodburn's *Hunters and gatherers*. At some distance away, separated by the Pacific books, are David Harris and Gordon Hillman's *Foraging and farming: the evolution of plant exploitation*, Peter Ucko and Geoffrey Dimbleby's *The domestication and exploitation of plants and animals*, Charles Reed's *Origins of agriculture*, and David Rindos' similarly titled *Origins of agriculture: an evolutionary perspective*. These last books rub shoulders with others on China and the Near East, and their 'high civilisations'; but these are on the next shelf so we return to the 'Australian' and 'Pacific' sections, the shelf that on this day captures our attention.

And one by one briefly we open each book, lest we forget. Again we find that we transgress regional borders in what is already becoming a familiar logic: those books eyeing Aboriginal Australia speak of hunter-gatherers, prehistory, mobility, transient camps, environmental adaptations. Those Pacific stories tend to speak of agriculture, villages, complexity, social processes, human impacts on the environment. Along this shelf we find repeated themes, and repeated associations. Why is this? What informs these associations, these alignments of books and concepts? Are these simple and logical categories with which we pack our library, sets of classifications based on qualitatively different social conditions among disparate social forms and cultural groups, or is there something more besides?

It is the task of this essay to unpack familiar associations to see where we stand within the discipline of archaeology. Like the peoples and cultures of its enquiries, archaeology is itself very much an historical and social practice. Its classificatory schemas impregnate and inform how we come to know the place of other peoples and other cultures in the world, and in the process how we come to know ourselves through our own discipline. We shall return later to the more explicitly political dimensions of our concerns.

Approaching the past: a concern with prejudice

As social scientists of various ilks have long come to realise, interpretations of the past are as much conditioned by historiographic trends — by the prejudice of authors — as they are by patterns and signatures within the material culture and texts studied. Australian archaeological understandings of the past are only partially rooted in evidential concerns. Those different lines of evidence are woven together with preconceptions about the past in two regions (Australia and New Guinea), in the terms we use, in particular how various words and concepts are banded together when discussing the archaeological history of certain peoples, while other sets of terms are used for other peoples.

Our view of prejudice follows Hans-Georg Gadamer:

> Prejudices are not necessarily unjustified and erroneous, so that they inevitably distort the truth. In fact, the historicity of our existence entails that prejudices, in the literal sense of the word, constitute the initial directedness of our whole ability to experience. Prejudices are biases of our openness to the world. They are simply conditions whereby we experience something — whereby what we encounter says something to us. (Gadamer 1976, p. 9)

Grand narratives about the past, like all narratives, are rich in symbols, metaphors and assumptions — prejudices — about how the world is ordered. They draw on and selectively weight different concepts and lines of material evidence to construct notions — in this case, notions of 'history' and 'prehistory', and disparate pasts of 'hunting and gathering' in Australia and 'agriculture' in New Guinea. Each classification is defined by two things: similarities, or 'what something is'; and dissimilarities, or 'what something is not'.

Definitions are drawn in order to stabilise the meaning of words, but meanings are not fixed and immutable. Take a minute to reflect on how the different concepts of 'an Aborigine', 'an Australian' and 'unAustralian' have been applied in different contexts at various points in time (for example, Attwood 2003; Gelder & Jacobs 1998; Langton & David 2003). In archaeology, we use categories to construct the subjects of our discourse. These categories represent people, as well as their actions, beliefs and cultures. No matter how we define these subjects, something on the margin begins to emerge (Spivak in Winant 1990; *cf.* Spivak 1988). There is always a tension between the subjects we delineate in academic, official and public discourses and those about whom nothing is said, the excluded. Australia was termed a *terra nullius*; yet it was evidently populated by peoples with land. Aborigines did not automatically hold Australian citizenship before 1967; yet they were certainly Australian. The construction in public discourse of inadequate recognition, identification and representation is an act — or rather, a motion — of institutional replacement that silences and leaves people and cultural practices 'neither One nor the Other, but *something else besides*' (Bhabha 1994, p. 219).

In light of these exclusions, we examine the relevance and consequences of terminology used to characterise Australian Aborigines in the distant and recent past. The terms 'prehistory' and 'hunter-gatherer' are used more widely than others to characterise the Aboriginal past and its legacy in the Aboriginal present. In particular, we focus on the binary couplets of similarity–dissimilarity for 'prehistory'/'history' and 'hunting and gathering'/'agriculture', and consider the continuing influence of these terms on contemporary debates about Australia's past and present.

Prehistory

The word 'prehistory' is applied to societies that have in common an absence of writing, and distinguishes them from purportedly dissimilar societies that are literate. Or so it seems. The word 'prehistory' is a useful place to start unpacking our library.

Christopher Chippindale (1989, p. 305) noted that the concept of *pre*history 'was not a single invention, but an idea, variously formulated and usually vague, in which one element, the idea of some primeval age of stone before those of metal, goes right back to Greek philosophers and historians'. Within the English and French languages, the terms prehistory/*préhistoire* and prehistoric/*préhistorique* emerged from earlier cognate terms. A parrallel term *anté-historique* had earlier been coined by Paul Tournal (1833, p. 175) to refer to an early period of human history akin to, but not adequately covered by, the concept of the *anté-diluvienne* which preceded the biblical flood; Tournal argued that there was no sedimentary evidence of this universal flood where he looked. He therefore called that ancient period before Thebes the '*période anté-historique*' rather than the '*période anté-diluvienne*', as he and others previously had. Tournal's major contribution to our modern discipline, argues Chippindale (1989), is that he broke away from biblical notions of time, from a biblical temporal frame of reference based on a universal flood (see also Daniel 1962). But it was Daniel Wilson (1851) who first used the term 'prehistoric' in 1851 in his treatment of *The archaeology and prehistoric annals of Scotland*. Others soon followed, including John Lubbock (1865) in his most influential *Pre-historic times* (see also Grayson 1983).

Within the discipline of archaeology generally, the term 'prehistory' is conventionally used to distinguish a period of time without writing from a subsequent progressionist phase of 'history', that is, the period of writing. In this sense its usefulness is predicated on a two-fold division of historical time and, by implication, on a linear historical trajectory. But as Chippindale (1989, p. 311) notes:

> [The] coining of a word and the passing of the word into general circulation are important markers of an idea's intellectual progress, especially useful in the case of prehistory ... Neither the three-age system, invented in the Nordic region in the 1820s and 1830s, nor the

antiquity of man, demonstrated in France and England at the same time, sufficed alone to create an empirical prehistoric science: it was the combination of the two, thirty years later and in the evolutionary fashion of the 1860s, which constituted the invention of a real prehistory and forced the lasting creation of a word by which to call it.

As Chippindale rightly identifies, the words 'prehistory' and 'history' do not merely demarcate a division between, respectively, 'a time without' and 'a time with' writing. The prefix 'pre' shows that one state will advance to the other. The very definition is itself evolutionary in character, imbued with the notion that cultures will move forward from a lower to a higher state. While Daniel Wilson (1851) may have originally been concerned with Scottish antiquities in coining the term that we ourselves have come so readily to use, 'prehistory' and its progressionist overtones were never distant — nor separate — from the perception that *living peoples* were themselves ordered along those same evolutionary lines. Europeans of today and of the recent past, as people with writing, were placed at the top of the evolutionary ladder (see Trigger 1989). Hence, the full title of Lubbock's 1865 book is indeed apt: *Pre-historic times, as illustrated by ancient remains and the manners and customs of modern savages*.

Like others before and since, Lubbock was ready to directly link the fossil record to living peoples. Having coined the terms Palaeolithic and Neolithic to refer to the periods of, first, hunting and gathering and, then, of agriculture evident in Europe's distant past, Lubbock also sought living examples of this past in the geographically distant peoples at the ends of the earth. Since none of them had writing, they belonged in the first era, of 'pre-historic times'. Like Edward Tylor (e.g. 1871), the founding Professor of Anthropology at Oxford University, Lubbock's presumption was that the globe was originally peopled by savages at an early stage of evolution. In some parts of the world — notably Europe — cultural and intellectual developments eventually led to the emergence of 'high' civilisation, the most advanced progressionary stage hitherto known to humankind. Elsewhere, earlier evolutionary stages could still be found in the distant colonies. As Lubbock (1870, p. v) made clear in the preface of *The origin of civilisation and the primitive condition of man: mental and social condition of savages*:

> In my work on 'Prehistoric Times' I have devoted several chapters to the description of modern savages, because the weapons and implements now used by the lower races of men throw much light on the signification and use of those discovered in ancient tumuli, or in the drift gravels; and because a knowledge of modern savages and their modes of life enables us more accurately to picture, and more

vividly to conceive, the manners and customs of our ancestors in bygone ages.

Lubbock's *Pre-historic times* is perhaps the most important and influential archaeology book ever published; it demonstrates that the notion of 'prehistory' was never just a reference to peoples without writing. It was a *social evolutionary* concept from the onset, prioritising Old World history, and imposing Old World historical trajectories onto the rest of the world. The absence of those cultural traits among living peoples elsewhere in the world placed them in an evolutionary backwater. For 'prehistory' and 'prehistoric' were not only used to order ancient cultural relics into a temporal framework, but also to identify living peoples themselves as relics of ancient times. Living prehistoric peoples were not simply peoples without forms of writing; they were peoples at an early evolutionary stage — they represented the state of human affairs in the pre-writing west, the deep ancestors of the Romans, Greeks and Egyptians.

To what purpose do we use the word 'prehistory' today when addressing Australian Aboriginal pasts, distant or more recent? If talking of Indigenous pasts from an archaeological perspective, why not just say Aboriginal 'history'? To be sure there are periods of time we may wish to distinguish in Australia, such as those times before and after the period of early European influence, but then why do we not say precisely that, the 'pre-European contact' and 'post-early European contact' periods or the like. The Aboriginal past — the Aboriginal history we wish to understand — stands outside the Old World evolutionary hierarchies outlined by Lubbock and so many others. As twenty-first century scholars, do we still want to be beholden to nineteenth century terms, with their ethnocentric, progressionist, and often racist overtones? Having coined and used the term, it is now our responsibility as historians — archaeological ones at that, but historians nonetheless — to shed our discipline from the sociolinguistic shackles of 'prehistory'.

Symbolic ways of Being: hunting and gathering versus agriculture

Aboriginal lifestyles until, and often into, the arrival of Europeans in Australia are traditionally characterised as 'hunting and gathering', and are often differentiated from their 'agricultural' equivalents in New Guinea (e.g. Harris 1995; White & O'Connell 1982; Yen 1995; *cf.* Hynes & Chase 1982; Lourandos, 1988a). Hunting and gathering is defined as those food-extraction strategies that concern the foraging of plants and animals from supposedly 'wild' environments, in contrast to exploitation strategies reliant on 'domesticated' animals or resources whose reproductive cycles are anthropogenically manipulated. David Harris (1995, p. 849) sees plant-food exploitation as making an evolutionary continuum that can be:

distinguished according to how the plants are exploited and how much energy people invest in the process . . . This allows an initial distinction to be made between plant-food *procurement* and plant-food *production*. The former is restricted to the gathering and protective tending of wild plants; the latter encompasses production from wild plants *and* domesticated crops.

The evolutionary bar in our region has both a temporal and a spatial element: after the flooding of the Torres Strait separated New Guinea from Australia, one region advanced to agriculture, while the other was marooned in hunting and gathering. Several questions concerning this regional dichotomy of 'hunting and gathering' versus 'agriculture' come to mind. How accurately does this terminology represent actual subsistence practices in Australia and New Guinea? Can the terms be accurately defined? What symbolic meanings adhere to them in academic and public discourses? Each question is addressed below.

Materiality of subsistence practices

Authors have sought to justify the veracity or artificiality of the hunter-gatherer–agriculturalist dichotomy with reference to the materiality of subsistence practices, that is, through archaeological reconstructions and ethnographic accounts of how people obtained food and the effects of those practices on specific animals, plants and their conditioning environments. Yet subsistence practices within the two regions were not homogenous, but varied widely.

What we have come to know as mobile 'hunting and gathering' in Australia includes a broad range of practices conflated under the label 'hunter-gatherer'. Some of these widely varying practices include:

- The management of extensive yam fields across alluvial plains in south-western Western Australia (e.g. Hallam 1975).
- The casual but repeated planting of yams and other useful plants, such as baobab seeds, sometimes beyond their natural distributions, in northern Australia (e.g. Bruno David, personal observation 1989; Jones & Meehan 1989).
- The promotion of cycad groves through repeated burning (Beaton 1982).
- Burning favoured hunting grounds to promote young shoots to attract grazing fauna in much of Australia (e.g. Flannery 1994; Jones & Bowler 1980).
- The reaping of grass seeds across the arid and semi-arid zone, and the promotion of grasslands through fire (e.g. Cane 1989; Kimber & Smith 1987).
- The construction of artificial channels diverting natural waterways to capture eels in south-western Victoria (Lourandos 1980b).
- Prolonged occupation of villages in riverside clearings in north Queensland rainforests (e.g. Horsfall 1987).

In New Guinea, the diversity of practices in the recent and distant past similarly prevents a universal application of the term 'agriculture'. In the Highlands, a general reliance on garden horticulture is based on the propagation of vegetables and root crops, supplemented by the rearing of pigs and hunting. However, horticultural practices in the Highlands are variable in type and intensity, and include:
- intensive cultivation of artificially drained wetlands on the floors of intermontane valleys (e.g. Ballard, 2001)
- intensive short-fallow, mounded and raised-bed cultivation on valley slopes (e.g. Waddell, 1972)
- extensive long-fallow, swidden cultivation in montane rain forests (e.g. Clarke 1971).

In the Lowlands, a greater reliance on managed stands of trees — such as sago palms — is supplemented by hunting, fishing, foraging and garden horticulture in some diverse practices not readily classified as agricultural or hunting and gathering (Dwyer & Minnegal 1991; Roscoe 2002; Specht 2003), but 'ambiguous' in the traditional terminology (Terrell 2002).

From a different perspective, and depending upon where the analytic focus is placed, modes of horticultural production in the Highlands of New Guinea were or were not qualitatively different to plant exploitation practices in Australia. A formal comparison of practices reveals that horticultural plots in the Highlands (Powell *et al.* 1975), as well as swidden plots along the Highland fringes (Clarke 1971), were cleared, burned, (sometimes) fenced, and variously tilled and planted, whereas heavily utilised areas in Australia generally were not. In contrast, a behavioural comparison of practices points out that the use and the advertent and inadvertent translocation of plants may not have been, at least until the mid Holocene, of a qualitatively different kind, but had different emphases within and between the two regions (see Denham & Barton in press, for a consideration of New Guinea).

From the first paper he wrote, 'Dispersal of activities', Lourandos (1968) conceptualised as dynamic the interrelated systems of logic that govern everyday human existence. In that paper he argued that Tasmanians were not simply creatures of their environment but managed resources in a determined way. This was a revolutionary thought in the 1960s. From here on Lourandos (1977b, 1983b) sought to move beyond economic and technological comparisons to develop more socially oriented interpretations. He drew on ethnography to show similarities between Australia and New Guinea in the past and the present, and to bring attention to dynamism and social change in Aboriginal history. Lourandos turned to examples from New Guinea in his discussions of the Australian Aboriginal past because researchers until then had talked of Australian hunting and gathering peoples and New Guinean agriculturalists in terms of qualitatively different social processes. The traditional, progressionist framework assumed that hunting and gathering (read Australian Aborigines) was an ancestral (read primitive) cultural trait that, through time, gave way to more complex forms of hunting and gathering and eventually to agriculture (read New Guinea agriculturalists) (see Table 1). Following the framework so clearly set out in Sollas' *Ancient hunters* of 1911, the distinctive feature of Aboriginal Australians had been their failure to 'evolve' or advance towards that higher state.

Lourandos found within Australian Aboriginal hunting and gathering societies the same kinds of social processes known among New Guinean agriculturalists. In particular, he argued that 'Change in social relations should be viewed not merely as a solution to problems caused by environmental or demographic conditions. Competitive political relations can generate a dynamic which may lead to economic intensification in both hunter-gatherer and farming societies, among others. This process tends to be amplified at the intergroup level' (Lourandos 1988a, p. 160). For Lourandos (1988a, p. 149), 'competitive relations between groups may have led to increases in production (including surpluses), and also to increases in environmental productivity'.

Table 1. Prejudicial homologues used in the interpretation of Australian Aboriginal and New Guinean cultures. The horizontal correspondences and vertical contrasts are not exact, but are interpretative tendencies. Note how material relationships have social equivalents. Table 3 illustrates the gradients of difference which have been used to bridge the vertical contrasts.

Place	Mode of subsistence	Relative chronology		Environmental associations		
Australia	Hunter-gatherer	Prehistory	Earlier	In nature	Adapted to environment	Wild
↕	↕	↕	↕	↕	↕	↕
New Guinea	Agricultural	History/ archaeology	Later	In culture	Technological mastery of environment	Domesticated

Lourandos' solution was to destabilise and reshape the concept of 'hunter-gatherer', to distance it from the traditional 'hunter-gatherer to agriculture' frame of reference. As he (1988a, p. 259) noted:

> population levels reached in high density [Aboriginal] hunter-gatherer societies equalled, or were only marginally lower than, those of shifting agriculturalists in New Guinea. This similarity in population density between the two regions suggests comparable levels of energy harnessing, and raises the problem of explaining functional differences between these two socio-economic systems . . . the hunter-gatherer system, like that of the food-producer, involves the artificial manipulation and expansion of ecological niches.

There is change — complexification — in Lourandos' thinking. Many scientists in the physical and social sciences (see in particular the work of the Santa Fe institute, e.g. Casti 1995; Gell-Mann 1994) have explored the notion that, through time, history builds on itself in such a way that a system's organisational dynamics lead to increasing structural complexity. The same approach

Social practices and forms					
More primitive	Mobile	Static (outside history)	Change through internal (environmental) adaptation and diffusion	Simple, smaller, unstructured societies	Lower population density
↕	↕	↕	↕	↕	↕
More advanced	Sedentary	Dynamic (in history)	Change through internal (cultural/evolutionary) processes and external interaction	Complex, larger, structured societies	Higher population density

underlies Lourandos' writings. For Lourandos there had to be a strong connection between the past and the present, in the sense that people always had the capacity in time and space to make choices about their life condition, and those choices could not simply depend on the natural world but more on the social arrangements that enabled one choice or the other to gain economic, political and religious sanction. In other words, the key to change was social relations and these were, by their nature, dynamic. Within the Australian version of this dynamic logic, as outlined by Lourandos, competitive social relations engender surplus–production feeding rituals and formalised exchange; these lead to enhanced status or prestige, polygyny and an expansion of social networks; those feed back to intensify further competitive social relations; and so forth (Lourandos 1988a). Change is not random, and the particular forms of social transformation neither predictable nor linear. Social, religious, economic and political circumstances are always historically conditioned so that, at any point in time and through time, the trajectory of any culture is unique.

Aspects of Lourandos' thinking are evolutionary, but these aspects are not progressionist, contrary to what some have said about his work (e.g. Cosgrove 1995; Head 2000). A key issue for Lourandos is that each area, each group, each people, can only be understood in its own terms, for each has emerged historically from a unique set of historical circumstances. His turn to New Guinea to understand the Australian Aboriginal past was a heuristic device aimed at transcending the hunter-gatherer–agriculturalist dichotomy underwritten by often unstated, unilineal and simplistic progressionist presumptions (see Table 2). Indigenous (agricultural) communities in New Guinea were well understood to undergo social change as a result of interpersonal dynamics, but Australian Aboriginal peoples and their histories were not considered in this way by archaeologists.

Following his investigations of the archaeological record in one part of Australia, Lourandos' (1983b, p. 92) parting sentence, to probably his most influential paper yet, ended thus: 'Intensification of social and economic relations would appear to have been increasingly taking place during the Holocene period on the Australian mainland, the process being nipped in the bud by the coming of the Europeans'.

This wording has been taken to mean a progressionist passing of hunting and gathering to agriculture (by Head 2000, pp. 103–4, among others). It does not. His 'nipped in the bud' presented another view, a questioning of the very notion of predetermination, set in the conviction that Aboriginal cultures were moving in their own directions, untethered to the other modes of production documented by anthropologists elsewhere in the world (Lourandos, personal communication 1998). Hence the irony of his subsequent book, *Continent of hunter-gatherers* (Lourandos 1997): who could say where Aboriginal futures

Table 2. *Gradients of prejudice often implicit to the interpretation of hunter-gatherers in Australia and agriculturalists in New Guinea, reflecting nineteenth-century evolutionary thinking. Note how changes in mode of subsistence have evolutionary implications.*

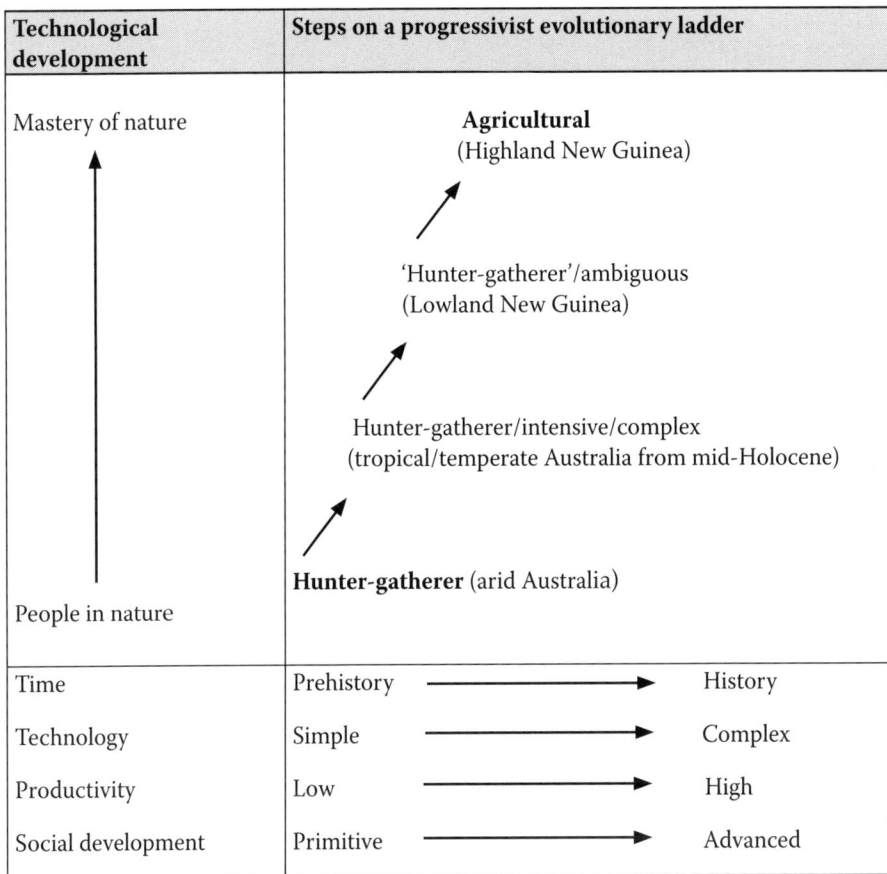

might have lain, had Europeans not intervened, for Aboriginal histories have their own momentum.

One thing was certain: Aboriginal cultures and societies were changing, and had always been in a process of change, as is amply evident in the late Holocene archaeological record in particular (where historical data were most detailed). And this change showed no evidence of abating. Here lay Lourandos' twist, at once encapsulating the unique position of Australian Aboriginal cultures and histories, while at the same time recognising that Aboriginal peoples — like all other peoples around the world — also underwent internally driven processes of change as a result of their own, historically positioned social dynamics. Change, he argued, was regulated by social conditions and political hegemonies, yet forever transcendant as a result of internal and inter-group social dynamics.

Definitions

As is true of all familiar terms, we initially think it is obvious what we mean by the terms 'hunting and gathering' and by 'agriculture'. It is only when we come to define these names precisely, either individually or in relation to each other, that we encounter problems. What we thought was obvious is no longer clear: it loses its sharpness of focus.

People have tried to clarify, or overcome, this definitional problem for 'agriculture' in three different ways. Firstly, diagnostics have been proposed which do clearly define agriculture and differentiate it from hunting and gathering, or forager, activities. These have tended to focus on macrobotanical, microbotanical or genetic evidence of animal and plant domestication (e.g. Harris 1989). In the last decade, less specific social definitions have been proposed for agricultural practices, including practices which do not lead to the creation of morphogenetically identifiable domesticates (Spriggs 1996).

Secondly, numerous concepts have been proposed to account for the often ambiguous practices that bridge the gap separating hunting and gathering from agriculture: complex hunting and gathering (Zvelebil 1986), hunter-horticulturalism (Guddemi 1992), incipient agriculture (Ford 1985), low-level food production (Smith 2001), transitional and proto-agriculture (Yen 1989). Although illuminating, these studies become trapped by the same categorial and definitional disputes, as the debate moves to distinguishing hunting and gathering from an intermediate concept, and that intermediate concept from agriculture.

Thirdly, some have advocated the abandonment of the traditional terminology altogether. Terrell *et al.* (2003) advocate a subsistence-ecology approach based on the twin concepts of domesticated landscapes (how people manage the landscape) and of the provisions spreadsheet (how people use particular resources within the landscape). But issues of classification remain, such as distinguishing activities that are intentional behaviours targeted on resources from more casual and predetermined environmental manipulations.

Most writing on the subject does not explicitly define the terms 'agriculture' or 'hunting and gathering'. Yet, ever since the 1966 *Man the Hunter* conference in Chicago, hunting and gathering has been identified, more or less explicitly, as an 'economic system . . . based on several core features including a home base or camp, a division of labor — with males hunting and females gathering — and, most important, a pattern of sharing out the collected food resources' (Lee & DeVore 1968b, p. 11). These are the commonly assumed properties of a more or less unified — if somewhat heterogeneous — pre-agricultural and ancient mode of subsistance.

There are other categories and qualifications of the term: David Harris (e.g. 1995, see above) recognises an evolutionary continuum from hunting and gathering to agriculture involving differential energy expenditures and yields, and categorically differential engagements with and control over environmental resources. But here too the implication is an essentially inevitable lineal evolutionary path from hunting and gathering to agriculture. A rare alternative view — one more in line with the authors' own views of social process — was presented by Ross Hynes and Athol Chase (1982), who do not engage so much with the abstract concept of 'hunting and gathering', or with a trajectory from hunter-gatherer to agriculture, preferring instead to think of food production as 'the outcome of strategies which include not only physical resource exploitation, but as well systems of locality and territoriality that recognize ties between particular individuals and groups and particular home environments' (Hynes & Chase 1982, p. 38).

Hynes and Chase (1982) also employed the term 'domus' to describe the geographically delimited space in which people operate on a daily basis. The domus consists of the hearth-centred life-space of daily activity; it is an area 'where selective environmental knowledge and resource strategies are applied at a specific time. We may consider each of these hearth-based parcels of knowledge, strategies and actions applied to each domus as a *domiculture*' (Hynes & Chase 1982, p. 38). Like all residential spaces, the domus is socially constructed, social interaction resulting 'in a series of hearth-based areas of exploitation (domuses), each carrying with it a package of resource locations, restrictions upon open-ended exploitation (religious prohibitions, strategic planning for delayed harvesting, etc.), and localized technologies to fit particular domuses' (Chase 1989a, p. 43).

Hynes and Chase's domus and domiculture are alternatives to the progressionism of hunting and gathering versus agriculture; they are concepts explicitly coined in recognition of the inadequacy of confining Australian Aboriginal gathering-hunting as an economic or social category 'ecologically passive in a supposedly "natural" landscape simply because they did not engage in a pattern of behaviour usually subsumed under the concept of agriculture' (Chase 1989a, p. 42).

In this paper, we do not attempt to see whether the terms 'hunting and gathering' and 'agriculture' are accurate representations of archaeologically visible practices in Australian and New Guinean pasts, respectively. We are, rather, concerned with the prejudices and implications of these categories, powerfully if often subliminally used in archaeological and public discourses in Australia and beyond. Irrespective of their veracity or otherwise, concepts such as 'hunting and gathering' and 'agriculture' are used by anthropologists, archaeologists, historians and the general public. Rather than immediately rejecting the terminology as too hard to define, we wish to consider questions such as 'Why are these terms used?' and 'What types of meaning do they convey?'. We seek to uncover the symbolic nature of the terms 'agriculturalist' and 'hunting and gathering'. From the beginning these terms have represented more than just subsistence practices; they are ciphers, markers, or symbols of distinctive ways of life (Table 2). Only after we see these terms in their fullness, and begin to see the conceptual baggage that accompanies their usage, can we begin to evaluate their usefulness and, if need be, consider alternatives.

Symbolic meanings

Take a moment to reflect upon what the terms 'hunter-gatherer' and 'agriculturalist' connote. Do they refer solely to something material, a matter just of subsistence? Do they not signify, or point towards, something else? Are not the terminology — as well as the similarities and gradients of difference, or prejudice, they spawn — born of nineteenth-century evolutionary perspectives, including variously those of Lubbock, Morgan and Spencer? Do they not signify steps on an evolutionary ladder (after Golson 1977), with latent correspondences between the evolution of subsistence practices and social forms? From these perspectives, 'hunting and gathering' and 'agriculture' are keys to a broader social world; a social world that can be referred to in a general way without actually being understood in terms of *hunting* and *gathering* or *agriculture*.

The use of the terms 'hunting and gathering' and 'agriculture' to denote subsistence practices in Australia and New Guinea during the recent and distant pasts illustrates tendencies whereby the terms are used as symbols of different ways of being. These different ways of life, as well as the places themselves, can be characterised, or caricatured, as follows (Tables 2 and 3).

Australia is portrayed as the land of hunter-gatherers. Aboriginal histories tend to emphasise vertical, people–environment relations and 'humans in nature', views that underlie many ecological and economic interpretations of Aboriginal prehistory. Consider most behavioural, ecological and foraging-based interpretations that focus on more-or-less mechanistic resource optimisation, mobility, stone tool use and so on (e.g. Binford 2001). Societies are generally viewed as static, with change arising internally through realignments of people's relationship to geophysical and biological environments and resources.

New Guinea, by contrast, is portrayed as an island of horticultural gardeners. Portrayals of New Guinean history tend to emphasise horizontal, people–

Table 3. Geographical and historical prejudices implicit to the interpretation of Australian and New Guinean places and peoples. Note how First Contact perceptions are maintained in historical and contemporary discourses about Australian Aborigines and New Guinean people.

Location	Climate	People	Time of 'discovery'	Initial historical view	Culture	Social landscape
Australia	The arid continent	Hunter-gatherers	1770	*Terra nullius*	Without	The empty place
↕	↕	↕	↕	↕	↕	↕
New Guinea (Highlands)	The humid tropics	Stone age horti-culturalists	1933	'The land that time forgot'	With	Out of place

people interactions, as well as vertical, people–environment relations (Golson & Gardner 1990). Perspectives vary but include 'humans as social beings' as much as 'humans in nature' (after Modjeska 1982 and Gorecki 1986). Societies are viewed as dynamic, with change originating through social transformation and external interaction, as well as through changing relationships between people and place.

Agriculture, which is bound to concepts of the Neolithic across Europe and Asia, is an Enlightenment symbol of historical change, dynamism, advancement, mastery and civilisation. Perhaps this explains an enduring fascination with understanding the origins and diffusion of the European Neolithic throughout twentieth-century debates in archaeology from 'culture-history' (Childe 1925), through 'processualism' (Renfrew 1973), and to 'post-processual' (Thomas 1999). Conversely, hunter-gatherers are the Other, the non-agricultural and all that that connotes: historical stasisism; lack of cultural, economic and social development; lack of control; and lack of civilisation. The Australian Aboriginal past and recent present allows us to have 'Palaeolithic reflections' (Hayden 1977). In as much as agriculture has positive connotations, hunting and gathering signifies a 'lack'.

Here we literally see the interconnection of academic (knowledge) and political (power) spheres, and we need to ask whether or not, as archaeologists, we want to react to this, reminding ourselves that *we are already caught in this sphere of discourse and power*. How best to react? Do we subvert or change the language which has become so binding and burdensome? Do we destabilise the language, as Lourandos attempted? Do we still want to construct Aboriginal subjects of archaeological discourses through the established and progressionistic label 'hunter-gatherer', knowing what we know about the associated meanings of this term? Do we actively take responsibility for the way we represent (which we do whether we keep the language or not)? Doing nothing is still actively making a choice.

We conclude with a recent example of the pervasiveness of these problematic concerns in Australian political and civic life.

Continuing Lourandos' project

The divergent interpretations of Aboriginal and New Guinean culture and history characterised above are evident in public narratives — academic, political and civic — but they are not rigid and mutually exclusive spheres of thought and discourse. Nevertheless, these tendencies have long ethnocentric and progressive-evolutionary traditions which pervade academic discourse as much as they pervade contemporary public debate. For example, 'hunter-gatherers' have been characterised as 'primitive', static and a 'people without history' since the nineteenth century; these same authors view agriculture as a primary motor, and even a precondition of change in pre-industrial societies. Similar ethnocentric and primitivist/progressionist biases confront us in contemporary public debate on Aboriginality.

Perhaps the clearest public demonstration of this pervasiveness of thought took place during the first year of the twenty-first century (for full details see David *et al.* 2002). On 1 September 2000, as the world's media focused on Australia on the eve of the 27th Olympiad, the French newspaper *Le Monde* reported an interview with Philip Ruddock, then the Federal Minister for Immigration and Multicultural Affairs and the Minister Assisting the Prime Minister for Reconciliation. The topic of the interview concerned Aboriginal disadvantage and what has come to be known as 'sorry business' and the Stolen Generation. *'Pourquoi les Aborigènes restent-ils la minorité la plus désavantagée d'Australie?'* ('Why are Aboriginal people still the most disadvantaged minority group in Australia?'), asked Bruno Philip (2000), *Le Monde*'s correspondent. Ruddock's response was more revealing of western preconceptions and attitudes towards race and land than it was of Aboriginal history or Aboriginal disadvantage:

> De tout les peuples indigènes de la planète, si on les compare avec les Indiens du Canada ou des Etats-Unis, les Aborigènes d'Australie ont été les peuples qui sont entrés en contact le plus tardivement avec des civilisations développées. Les Aborigènes étaient des chasseurs collecteurs. Ils ne connaissaient pas la roue. Ils ont survécu grâce à leur ingéniosité dans un environnement très difficile. Les Indiens d'Amérique, eux, vivaient au sein d'une société plus structurée. Je ne

veux pas dire par là qu'ils étaient supérieurs en cela aux Aborigènes mais certainement ils vivaient au sein d'un environnement plus convivial. Exemple, ils maîtrisaient les techniques de l'agriculture, ce qui n'était pas le cas des Aborigènes d'Australie. Pour ces derniers, le processus d'ajustement à la civilisation occidentale s'est fait de manière plus lente.

(Of all the indigenous peoples of the world, if we compare them with Canadian or American Indians, the Australian Aborigines were the peoples who came into contact with developed civilizations the latest. The Aborigines were hunter-gatherers. They did not know the wheel. They survived because of their ingenuity in a harsh environment. The American Indians lived in a more structured society. I don't want to imply that the American Indians were more advanced than the Australian Aborigines, but certainly they lived in a less harsh environment. For example, they had agriculture, which Australian Aborigines did not have. For the latter, the process of adjustment to Western civilization was slower.)[1]

Ruddock's comments were soon reported in the Australian press, inciting widespread anger, and many community groups reported losing faith in the government's ability to move towards a process of reconciliation (e.g. ABC 2000; Taylor 2000). Ruddock defended his statement to *Le Monde* with the view that his comments about technological developments such as the wheel, and late contact with European civilisation, were taken out of context by the broader media. His statement to this effect was reported in *The Age* (Taylor 2000):

> When people write about some comments that you make and they take some of them and not the whole, there can be, in such an approach, matters that are taken out of context . . . In no way then or now did I intend to reflect adversely on indigenous culture . . . My comments need to be seen in the context of a wide-ranging discussion on the reasons for Aboriginal disadvantage.

But, it also came to be revealed, Ruddock had earlier made similar comments to *The Washington Post*:

> 'We are putting in an enormous amount of work to improve the conditions of our indigenous people,' Ruddock said. 'But we are starting from a very low base. We're dealing with an indigenous population that had little contact with the rest of the world. We're dealing with people who were essentially hunter-gatherers. They didn't have

chariots. I don't think they invented the wheel.' (Chandrasekaran 2000, A01)

How has it come to be that two of the world's most respected newspapers similarly reported 'matters that are taken out of context', as expounded in two different interviews a few months apart? Democrats Senator Aden Ridgeway was subsequently reported in *The Age* to have:

> ... renewed the Democrats' call for Mr. Ruddock to be removed from the reconciliation portfolio. 'It raises questions about the suitability of the minister for the position, given his role is to advocate reconciliation,' he said. It appeared Mr Ruddock was appealing to prejudices held by some people. (Taylor 2000)

Do the views of the minister, and his conjuring of a cultural *nullius* for peoples without agriculture — that is, for Aboriginal people defined (by him) through a series of absences rather than through their own being — imply an inherent supremacy and right to rule of 'agricultural', western, progressive and (implicitly) white colonists and immigrants over pre-existing 'hunting and gathering', Aboriginal, backward and (implicitly) black inhabitants of Australia? Are these *a priori* or *a posteriori* views? Indeed, could not the merging of two Commonwealth government departments in November 2001 (formerly the Department of Immigration and Multicultural Affairs and the Department of Reconciliation and Aboriginal and Torres Strait Islander Affairs) to form the Department of Immigration and Multicultural and Aboriginal Affairs be seen as an example of ethnocentrism? If Aborigines are grouped with 'new immigrants', are they not also being consigned to a position outside 'mainstream Australian' society? And further, that at the same time that they are conceptually united with newly arrived citizens with newly acquired civil rights, Aboriginal people are stripped of any privileged rights they may have, or may have claim to, as *the* indigenous peoples of the land? 'Indigenous Affairs' are placed after 'Immigration' in the new minister's title: an afterthought, a floating (non)issue that does not deserve to be addressed in its own right yet that cannot entirely be ommitted from official concern. Are Mr Ruddock's statements and the merging of ministries giving voice to a quasi-official view of Aboriginality?

These are questions to which our reflection on the differential use of the terms 'prehistory', 'history', 'hunting and gathering' and 'agriculture' lead. Philip Ruddock's comments clearly perpetuate nineteenth-century frames of reference. However, the sensitivity is — as Ian McNiven (1998a, p. 47) has so cogently noted — that the power to write Indigenous history is the power to control constructions of identity. And if the process of identifying

Aboriginality through the label 'hunter-gatherer' comes with the proviso that Aboriginality is in the first instance non-agricultural rather than its own thing (*without* chariots, *without* the wheel, *without* agriculture) we are left with a scenario that Lourandos long ago fought to overcome: a concept of an 'unchanging people' and a contemporary social scape stuck in First Contact; a world, to borrow his phrase, forever 'nipped in the bud'.

When Walter Benjamin put his books away in crates for two years, he put them away in dark coffins, for they were the death of a structure. Following Emmanuel Levinas (e.g. 1987), what makes archaeology exciting is our ability to unravel history — not just a history that is supposedly 'out there', but one that imbues our very discipline as a forever-unfolding, transcendent social practice. We continually pack and unpack our libraries, and in doing so the world changes. When Benjamin unpacked his library, the books may have been the same, but the new shelves had no memory of what had gone before. Lourandos, like Benjamin, made a new library, a new order by which to live.

Acknowledgements

Foremost we thank Harry Lourandos for inspiration, for Bruno David as a university teacher and subsequently as colleague and friend, always a teacher. Many thanks also to Ian McNiven, Jacques Bierling, Christopher Chippindale and Marcia Langton for useful comments and discussions on earlier drafts of this paper.

Note

1. This is a translation of the French newspaper statement; it is not the original English text, to which the authors do not have access.

5.
Hierarchies of knowledge and the tyranny of text: archaeology, ethnohistory and oral traditions in Australian archaeological interpretation

Bryce Barker

Introduction

This paper examines how different ways of knowing about the past are used in the formulation of archaeological models. It uses a case study from the Whitsunday Islands off the central Queensland coast.

Various ways of constructing knowledge about the region can be made, based upon the ethnographic records of Norman Tindale and Walter Roth, historical and archaeological records, and oral traditions of contemporary local Aboriginal communities. The resultant re-evaluation of a western, science-based construction of the past, heavily influenced — as it often is in Australia — on the written historical record, questions the primacy of the written record in interpretation over that of indigenous oral traditions.

The practice of pre–European archaeology during the last decade in Australia has become increasingly entwined with a recognition that archaeology is more than about the past but is, as McNiven (1998a) states, about the power to construct notions of identity. It is therefore no surprise to learn that the archaeology of Aboriginal Australia has come under a greater degree of control by those Aboriginal peoples whose cultural heritage is being investigated. This has by definition resulted in a politicisation and, in some cases, radicalisation of issues relating to the past. As Lourandos states:

> Australian prehistoric archaeology is now a highly politicised, complex arena of negotiation. The recent renaissance in Aboriginal society and culture throughout Australia has drawn upon, and been empowered by, knowledge of the distant and more recent past; and

is embedded in a reassertion of Aboriginal identity and its association with the land. (Lourandos 1997, p. iv)

In spite of a recognition — from some quarters, at least — of this as an important aspect of 'doing archaeology' in Australia, archaeologists have to a considerable extent been slow in coming to terms with the greater degree of sociocultural and political empowerment the Indigenous peoples of this country exert over matters concerning their own heritage. The issue centres around the perceived dichotomy between, on the one hand, a western science (archaeology) and, on the other, Indigenous knowledge of the past (oral traditions mediated by Indigenous ontologies). At the heart of this issue is the power to control notions of Indigenous pasts as an ongoing legacy of colonialism, a problem not unique to Australia (Layton 1989, 1994; Meskell 1998; Hodder 1991).

Australian archaeology has responded to this challenge by a philosophical shift emphasising the contrast between specialist and positivist research paradigms, and more community-based approaches. The former generally tackles the past as a universal entity, free of cultural proprietary rights, whereby the prehistory of humans rather than the history of Aboriginal culture is the subject of study (see David & Denham, this volume, for a discussion of 'prehistory' versus 'history'). In contrast, community-based approaches by definition generate research questions from within Aboriginal communities, combining community needs with academic research. As Harry Lourandos once said (Bruno David, personal communication 2000), the difference concerns an abstract, scientific and biological approach that deals with *humans*, and a more humanistic (yet still scientific) approach that deals with *people*. This latter approach incorporates degrees of traditional knowledge as it relates to the past, and recognises the past as culturally specific in which a degree of ownership and control rests within culturally distinct groups with clear links to that past. A key component of this issue, then, is how archaeologists construct and use knowledge, and the relative positions of oral traditions, texts and archaeological data in such constructions.

The construction of scientific evidence

In general, Australian archaeology places great emphasis on ethnographic/historical analogy at the level of interpretation; especially direct historical analogies rather than general comparative ones (Murray 1988). Much of the debate about the use of ethnography in archaeology revolves around how it is applied scientifically in the context of inference, analogy, context and scale rather than around notions of authenticity or accuracy. In this contextual view the historical and ethnographic record interprets archaeological data in terms of human behaviour, which involves some form of analogy and inference set within a contemporary cultural contextual framework. These analogous inferences involve an assumption of broad behavioural uniformitarianism and the attribution of specific historical and cultural links with the ethnographic record. However, like all historical enquiries, the ethnographic/historic record should be carefully assessed if it is to be used. Further, the hermeneutic process needs to be recognised in reading and writing, especially of ethnographies such as those of Roth, set as they are during the late–nineteenth century colonial period. Although there is a considerable body of archaeological writing that questions the use of the ethnographic/historical records in interpretation (e.g. Galloway 1992; Simms 1992), it is still the case that all interpretations are hermeneutic in nature; that is, the author is always implicated in interpretation, shaping concepts of the past (see David 2002 for an extended discussion of the hermeneutic nature of Australian archaeological historicism). Furthermore, because of the particular deficiency of the archaeological record, it is essential that all possible avenues of evidence be utilised when interrogating the past if we are to do anything that gets us beyond data lists and dates.

Historicising the Whitsunday's past

In the past, academics reconstructed pre-European lifeways in the Whitsunday Islands region of the central Queensland coast (and tropical mainland coastal peoples generally) from ethnographic, ethnohistorical and archaeological records (Barker 2004). However, it became apparent that disparities existed between certain Aboriginal views of their past and European versions, especially those relating to the make-up and extent of group boundaries, as well as a range of other sociocultural practices. Prior to the Commonwealth *Native Title Act* of 1993, differing models or interpretations of Aboriginal pasts would often have been academic in nature, rarely achieving broader social debate. Currently, however, archaeological research relating to such factors as cultural boundaries and cultural continuity can have ramifications under the Native Title Act as part of the formal legal process of legislative recognition of Indigenous rights. This means that archaeological interpretation is now very much a part of the contemporary legal landscape, confirming the notion of archaeology as contemporary socio/political practice. The legislative recognition of Indigenous rights to place also means a legislative recognition of Indigenous practice *in* place; that is, those social activities that took place in a particular location in the past are now not just overtly recognised as the province of historical researchers, but also of Indigenous rights. While this is nothing new to Indigenous peoples themselves, who have always recognised their own cultural attachments and rights to their own traditional lands, it has resulted in a greater degree of public and professional awareness that archaeological practice is indeed from the onset a social practice. Consequently, the way we write Aboriginal history has become increasingly reflective, taking care to consider the evidential bases of knowledge and how these may contain different levels of bias and reliability. It is this evidential base — the nature of the data — that I explore in this chapter.

The historical record

The ethnographic and historical data here focus mainly on the work of Tindale (1974) and, to a lesser degree, Roth (1901–06 and 1908–10) (see also Barker 2004 and in press). These sources remain the most important and comprehensive for the region.

Norman B Tindale

Although working in different eras and with different objectives, Tindale and Roth have each deeply influenced how we view Aboriginal pasts for the region. Tindale's study of Aboriginal society spanned five decades and covered a wide range of interests and areas of research. It is, however, for his participation in the Harvard–Adelaide Universities Anthropological Expedition of 1938–39, and the subsequent publication of a preliminary edition of his Australian 'Tribal map' (that culminated in his seminal 1974 *Aboriginal tribes of Australia*) that he is most recognised. Having visited many areas in Australia to gather primary data for these works, he often relied — out of necessity — on secondary and tertiary historical sources, and in the case of the Whitsunday Islands on unpublished oral information. The three main sources for his boundary reconstructions in the Whitsunday region are: two informants from Curr's 1886 book *The Australian race*; a 1938 reference from his journal of the Harvard–Adelaide universities expedition; and a 1940 manuscript entry referenced as coming from an earlier field survey which formed the basis of his 1974 publication. It appears, however, that Tindale himself never visited the Whitsunday region, but recorded an oral account on Palm Island — the closest he got to the Whitsundays and a place to which Whitsunday Islanders were sent from the late-nineteenth century onwards. In his *Aboriginal tribes of Australia* Tindale identifies the Whitsunday people as the 'Ngaro', whose territory is described as covering an area including:

> Whitsunday Island; ranging over Cumberland Islands; also to mainland at Cape Conway and on mountains east of Proserpine. Sewn ironbark canoes, called 'winta' were used for journeying between the islands — all reefs between St. Bees and Hayman Islands were known intimately and searched for food. (Tindale 1974, p. 182)

A search of primary sources reveals that neither of Curr's informants made any reference to the Ngaro; thus it can only be assumed that this identification came from Tindale's 1938–39 journal entry or from his field notes and relates to an oral account recorded while on Palm Island (Tindale 1940). Despite the uncertainty concerning the sources and validity of Tindale's Ngaro tribal boundaries, it is worth noting that all subsequent boundary reconstructions refer solely and exclusively to Tindale. Tindale's Ngaro entity is used extensively in archaeology and anthropology and is identified as a linguistic boundary in, for example, Oates and Oates' (1970) linguistic survey of Australia, based on Tindale's boundary reconstruction.

In many respects the contemporary Aboriginal community in the wider region has been uncomfortable with the Ngaro physical and linguistic boundaries as defined by Tindale, Oates and Oates and others (Whitley 1936). The Ngaro are variously seen as part of a much larger socio/cultural entity defined by coastal regional communities as a linguistic entity incorporating all of Tindale's Ngaro, Gia, Juru and Bindal 'tribes'. These groups are viewed as part of a wider mainland group ranging from just south of Townsville down to just north of Mackay and extending west as far as Collinsville. A senior Birri Gubba Elder, Peter Pryor, often stated to his children that the entire coastal region — including the islands of the Whitsundays — belonged to 'all one mob' and that they all spoke a single language (Pat Pryor, personal communication 2000). This is given some support from the linguistic evidence relating to peoples to the west of the Clarke Range who were 'Biria' speakers. Although not stating that the coastal people all spoke the same language, Terrill (1998) does state that the coastal groups — Bindal, Yuru (Juru) and Gia languages — are not related to Birri and thus it is possible that they may form a single linguistic grouping.

Walter E Roth

Between 1901 and 1910, Walter Roth published eighteen ethnographic bulletins on various aspects of Aboriginal culture based on his official reports as Protector of Aborigines. The data for these bulletins largely came from his own observations of, and discussions with, Aboriginal people in Normanton in 1894 and Cooktown in 1898. However, as far as can be ascertained, Roth only visited the Whitsundays briefly — possibly in 1900 and again in 1901. Roth's bulletins are considered especially important in Queensland archaeology because they are seen as capturing an element of uncontaminated 'traditional' life analogous to pre-European society and thus of direct relevance to the archaeological record. Extensive research on Roth's field notes and original manuscripts have, however, raised serious issues about important aspects of his data and how they were collected (see Barker, in press). These range from minor issues relating to omissions and transcription errors to outright errors of fact. One example is Roth's statement that the South Molle Island quarry was a site used for the manufacture and trade of stone axes: 'Quarries whence these Celts were originally obtained are none too common, there is one on Molle Island in the Whitsunday Passage' (Roth 1904, p. 19). It is clear from the descriptions, photographs and line drawings, that 'Celt' is Roth's term for edge-ground axes, yet extensive and intensive archaeological research on South Molle Island, focusing on its famous stone quarry, has failed to reveal any evidence of axe quarrying or axe making. Although Roth is considered to have been an accurate and, even by contemporary standards, an objective and scientific observer, the archaeological evidence clearly demonstrates that his identification of the quarry as an axe workshop was incorrect. Ongoing research relating specifically to the quarry itself has failed to identify a single axe, axe blank or anything resembling any stage of axe manufacture (Barker & Schon 1994; Lamb 1996). It is significant that Roth's accounts have become embedded as historical truth and are repeated as fact by subsequent historians and researchers. Evidently once a 'fact' is established the context of its production and historical reference to the social and contextual conditions of its construction is lost (Gero 1995, p. 175). We thus get numerous other published accounts of the South Molle Island quarry as being principally used for axe manufacture. These include Bauer (1958), Lamond (1960), Rowland (1986), Colfelt (1995) and the South Molle Island Resort website, to name just a few. Colfelt refers to Rowland's 1986 paper, which references Roth, as the source and the South Molle Island Resort website references Colfelt. The earlier references of Bauer and Lamond are attributed to Roth as his was the earliest and only record of the South Molle quarry before Bauer's 1958 account, and both are similar to each other and to Roth's description. The power of text and the belief in Roth as a careful scientific ethnographic observer is such that this error continues to be perpetuated to this day. It appears, however, that Roth never actually went to South Molle Island himself but was relating a secondary source — yet this is never made clear by commentators of his work.

The archaeological record

The direct archaeological evidence relates to the spatial distribution of a unique stone-artefact raw material sourced to the South Molle Island quarry. This raw material initially appeared to be adjoining them, and the mainland coastal fringe directly adjacent to the Whitsunday Islands — but it was never found in archaeological sites of the coastal hinterland — thus ostensibly supporting the ethnographic and ethnohistorical accounts and thus contrary to what might be expected according to oral accounts. A range of factors — such as sampling size, taphonomy and collection strategies — were subsequently found to account for the apparent lack of black tuff artefacts on the mainland; more recent intensive surveys have now located this raw material 100 km north of its source on the coast, crossing three of Tindale's boundary delineations incorporating Ngaro, Gia and Juru lands. Although this does not prove either Tindale or the archaeological model wrong, as this distribution could be interpreted as due to trade or cross-'tribal' ceremonial interactions, it does closely fit the north–south coastal limits of the larger 'tribal' grouping known by contemporary Aboriginal communities as belonging to a single language group.

Similarly, ongoing research on rock art distributions indicate a homogenous body of art consistent with contemporary oral traditions of cultural boundaries, and incorporating the area delineated as separate tribal entities (comprising Ngaro, Gia, Juru and Bindal) by Tindale. The cultural blocs identified through rock art and oral tradition also bear little resemblance to the historical or ethnographic accounts of Roth and Tindale.

Discussion

The fact that Roth wrongly describes a site he never visited, and Tindale uses two tertiary sources (Curr's informants, one a police sergeant and the other a missionary, neither of whom it appears had a good understanding of Aboriginal societies or cultures, and an unnamed oral source of his own; Tindale 1974), illustrates how tenuous some historical reconstructions of aspects of Aboriginal society can be.

Considering the influence these early ethnographers have had in shaping past and present Aboriginal cultural, political and linguistic landscapes in Queensland and Australia, and considering also the important part these authors continue to play in archaeological interpretation today, it may seem surprising that they have not sooner come under greater scrutiny. However, because of the embededness of text and the perception that rigid scientific methods have been applied, European models of Aboriginal pasts are often accepted as truth and so are rarely scrutinised. Thus, text-based studies — archaeological, historical and ethnographic — combine to provide a powerful 'reality' in which contemporary Aboriginal peoples are often excluded. This new reality can be a creation of selective use of an ethnographic/historical record — usually encapsulating a brief moment of time but viewed, at least in the context of direct historical analogy — as having the authenticity of tradition. This is particularly the case if the ethnography dates to the nineteenth century as it incorporates the weight of authenticity reserved for what is considered to be uncontaminated cultural practice. This historical record is then extensively used to flesh out the archaeological record at the level of interpretation, which necessarily constitutes a highly selective, socioculturally derived story. As Preucel and Hodder (1996, p. 15) state, writing can close down and restrict reinterpretation by stressing the authority and unimpeachable scholarship of the writer, or by emphasising the authority and scrutiny of an apparently objective science. These factors are implicit in the use of the ethnographies of both Roth and Tindale and are often linked in the production of texts, which expect the reader to be a passive consumer of the facts as stated. Because they often lack a recognised authority of scholarship and objective science such as that enjoyed by texts, Indigenous versions of the past are usually subject to rigid scrutiny and criticism (and sometimes they are ignored outright).

That this has been the general experience of Australian Aboriginal people is illustrated by the Mabo judgement in the High Court in which prior ownership of land was finally recognised, but only in part because of the presence of written records from the colonial land court dealing with disputes between traditional owners in regard to garden plots. These records outlined a system of kin-based ownership of land which closely paralleled oral traditions. Ironically, the Mer Islanders were principally a marine-oriented society with the same kin-based rights and ownership over sea, fringing reefs and marine resources as occurred on land, but because there were no written records of customary marine tenure — only oral traditions — this was not even presented as part of their case and thus not considered in the *Native Title Act* (Beckett 1995). Although not an archaeological example, it is reflective of the power of text and the position of oral histories in the hierarchy of western knowledge. They are invariably seen as not relating to 'tradition' or having been 'reinvented' from fragmentary remains, including non-Indigenous ethnographies, or intrinsically enmeshed in contemporary political aspirations and ambitions. And yet in reality the historical construction of the past as outlined above can often be an uncritical, selectively mined and fragmentary history imposed on an archaeological record which is itself an often deficient reflection of past lifeways. It is little wonder when seen in this light that Aboriginal communities might be sceptical of the so-called scientific basis for reconstruction of their past over their own oral traditions.

An integrative model?

How then do we resolve the issue of what can amount to two widely differing versions of the past? To some extent it depends on how we view the past: either as rigid, homogeneous, monolithic and directly retrievable; or that there is no finite truth about the past, that it is always entwined with contemporary social process. If we accept the latter view — which acknowledges that there are various pasts, which are often contradictory and inferred — then it is at the level of interpretation that Indigenous versions of their past can be accommodated into archaeological models. As Hodder *et al.* (1995, p. 5) state, interpretation in archaeology should be an ongoing process, in which there is no final and definitive account of the past; that it is a creative process which, although critically constrained within certain parameters, nonetheless is predicated on the interests, needs and desires of different constituencies.

If we can accept, then, that archaeological interpretation is a creative process culminating in a 'story' of the past — albeit based on data and certain uniformitarian principles relating to human behaviour — is it not also possible to incorporate aspects of Indigenous pasts within this framework? In this context Indigenous knowledge of the past can contribute to and reinforce archaeological models.

One of the major problems with this, however, is the difficulty of reconciling Aboriginal versions of the past with our own, not only because the Aboriginal version sits outside the western scientific canon — and therefore outside what constitutes disciplinary expectation and acceptability — but also because of the very different ways in which temporalities are themselves constructed. For example, Aboriginal notions of time often interlace pasts and present, mutually constituting the one in the other in daily life; there is no simple and overarching opposition of (western) past and present. In western constructs the past is considered to be an objective record of what happened during periods of time more or less remote from the present, whereas Aboriginal historical knowledge is never readily separated from space and revolves around cyclical and imminent — rather than linear and progressive — time. Thus, as Preucel and Hodder (1996, p. 604) state, 'the contrast between a dead and living past underlies many of the responses of indigenous peoples to archaeology. Almost by definition, archaeology separates people from their past'.

Although it is clear that an Indigenous cyclical view of the past cannot easily be reconciled with a western linear view — the latter being crucial to archaeology — Williams and Mununggurr (1989) provide a possible point of entry by dismantling the implacable dichotomies between the two. They point out that:

> interpretations of culturally different systems of time and time use that are based on dichotomies, binary oppositions or continua, obscure the fact that all cultural systems have or use aspects of what are often presented as opposing or mutually exclusive features.
> (Williams & Mununggurr 1989, p. 73)

They state that the most common features in such interpretations are viewed as timeless, cyclic, changeless and concrete on the one hand, and time-based, linear, changing and abstract on the other, yet in every society each of these features is likely to be present to varying degrees, recognising that different emphases are placed on various aspects of how time is constructed and perceived. Thus, the representation of western versus Aboriginal temporalities as dichotomous — linear versus cyclical — is overly simplistic (Williams & Mununggurr 1989, p. 73).

Chase (1989b) for example sees Lockhart River Aboriginal groups as perceiving the past through the continuous 'framework of episodic periods, each representing a transformation in the relationships with other indigenous people of the region and with Europeans' (Chase 1989b, p. 172). In this scenario it is generally agreed that most Aboriginal societies have categories of past events often but variously including the historical period. In this context then we do not necessarily have to grapple with a vastly different concept of how the past is constituted, but can focus on those aspects meaningful to archaeology but also incorporative of other versions of that past.

Along the central Queensland coast these 'episodes' relate to relatively recent historical periods and events, such as nineteenth-century employment in the logging industry, or residence on Palm Island. The most recent historical marker has been the passing of the Native Title Act, the oldest being the recognition of a time before Europeans, as signified by sites in the landscape. Chase (1989b) has been able to categorise a form of linear historical knowledge relating to the past in much greater detail for the Kuuku Ya'u people of Cape York Peninsula. His study describes periods of time 'before people'; 'beginning period', a past generally denoting the Dreaming or period of creation; followed by a period known as 'long time before', a post-creation period in which there are now no eyewitness accounts, or any remembered first-hand experience of eyewitness accounts among living people. This period is remembered through stories, songs and sites in the landscape. According to Chase this period is viewed as a classical period before alien intrusion, and is marked on the landscape by physical sites remembered through important events (Chase 1989b, p. 172). Chase then describes several other periods of time within the more recent European-contact era. The importance of distinguishing between categories relating to the remote pre–European contact past and the period of European contact is, as Chase states, of obvious importance to archaeology, especially as it can be constructed into a generalised linear sequence (although not necessarily viewed in this way by Kuuku Ya'u). So what is important here is that we can restructure events of Kuuku Ya'u pasts, using their knowledge and their version of events, into an archaeologically meaningful temporal framework.

In the Whitsunday region, for example, Ngaro knowledge of settlement and subsistence practice as it relates to the past is no longer as detailed as it once was. The archaeological evidence concerning the descendants of the contemporary population ceases around 100 years ago as massacre and forcible displacement of peoples occurred from the 1870s onward; today none of the community lives on the islands. And yet, even in these highly fragmented cultural circumstances, a broad level of knowledge relating to their own experiences of a pre-European past exists, which has subsequently been borne out by the archaeological record. For instance, Ngaro know that turtle and dugong were important major resources in the past, as they continue to be today. They identified the core islands of Whitsunday, Hook, and South Molle as being at the centre of marine activity, with islands outside of this being peripheral and visited infrequently. Ngaro representatives also talk about a major camping area on the western side of Whitsunday Island, where one Elder's grandmother was born, as well as relating other events from the historical period (Irene Butterworth, personal communication 2000). Similarly, they never once stated that the South Molle Island quarry was used for axe manufacture. These are all oral traditions relating to the past that have been subsequently supported by the archaeological research, often in contrast to the (western, written) historical accounts.

Yet what of statements of the Aboriginal past which cannot be corroborated archaeologically? For example, Ngaro state that people regularly visited the Great Barrier Reef to a distance of approximately 70 km from the mainland and 40 km from the eastern-most island. Are we then in a position of having to take on board unsubstantiated, untestable claims? How do we deal with oral accounts which on the surface appear to be in direct contradiction of the archaeological evidence? What if, for example, Ngaro stated that turtle was not a major component of their diet when the archaeological record clearly shows large quantities of turtle bone and shell in excavated sites?

In regard to the first example, an absence of evidence of a kind constructed in a western sense is not proof that people did not travel to the reef. The fact that the reef is an important component of local Dreaming-based understandings of the region demonstrates knowledge of the Great Barrier Reef as a physical entity, which implies visitation. Furthermore, it is entirely plausible that people *did* indeed travel to the reef, as they were certainly technologically capable of this.

As for the second example, there is not necessarily a contradiction in these accounts. The archaeology just tells us that turtle was hunted; it does not tell us by whom. It is just as plausible to place oral accounts at the same level as text-based historical ones on our hierarchy of knowledge which could state, hypothetically speaking, that turtle hunting and consumption was carried out by non-Ngaro peoples who visited on a seasonal basis.

Conclusion

Although the Ngaro are on the whole interested in the substance of archaeological research, as it is seen to validate their presence in the landscape, in the eyes of European managers and users Ngaro are not as interested in dates relating to the excavated sites in the region, possibly reflecting their rejection of a linear form of the past. As Creamer states (1990, p. 131), sites have intrinsic value as symbols of identity. They are seen as ends in themselves, their meaning central to their very existence as a people and reflective of an emotional commitment and spirituality. It is apparent from their knowledge of events outlined above, however, that certain groups do have temporal categories which could be broadly defined as historical and pre-European, which we can arrange in a linear fashion meaningful to conventional archaeological practice.

And even in the case of the Ngaro who do not generally define events of the past in a strictly linear historical framework it is possible to take on board the oral information and allow the archaeology to provide the temporal component. Of course this approach could be seen as another form of cultural imperialism, contextually separating Indigenous knowledge into the dominant cultural paradigm. Although this is true to a certain extent, we cannot, however, abandon scientific methods in archaeology, and nor am I advocating such a path. Indeed, in one respect I am advocating a more rigorous and critical examination of text-based historical and ethnographic records. What archaeology can do is attempt to engage Indigenous groups and adopt a more holistic approach incorporating as much as possible the Indigenous versions of the past at the level of interpretation, as well as taking into account and recognising the position and aspirations of contemporary Indigenous communities. For the Ngaro people, inclusiveness in the interpretative process — rather than how the substance might necessarily be arranged — is of prime importance. It is interesting from the case study presented here to reflect on how little the regional pre-European history of the Whitsunday region would have differed if I had used the oral traditions as the starting point of my research, perhaps even testing oral traditions archaeologically.

It could be argued from what has been outlined here that the textual/ethnographic as well as the oral traditions relating to the past are just too problematic to use in any meaningful scientific way, and this is often the view of the hard-science approach to archaeology in which archaeological interpretation is sometimes restricted to a narrow empiricism. I can only reiterate the point that it is essential that we use whatever data there is — whether qualitative or quantitative — to make sense of the complexities of past societies. In this context the use of the textual/ethnographic record remains a powerful tool, and indeed in this context I argue that Indigenous oral histories should be no less important as a source of meaningful data for interpretation in archaeology.

My intention is not to deconstruct what remains a primary tool of research into the past, but to demonstrate how European textual histories often have privileged authority over how Indigenous pasts are written. This is especially so when the textual/ethnographic record is used in support of the archaeological record, when archaeologists may be less than critical in their examination of the accuracy of the ethnographic material they incorporate, or in their attempts to encompass contemporary Indigenous views of the past into their models. Thus, archaeology can potentially assume an unwarranted position relative to Indigenous knowledge. Although wary of some of the obvious limitations of postmodern theory as it applies to archaeology, notions of textured knowledge — so central to postmodernism — are an important theoretical advance in regard to the role of archaeology and contemporary indigenous cultures. This is not necessarily because it validates all knowledge as meaningful but because, if nothing else it makes us critically scrutinise the position of our own knowledge system relative to those of others.

Acknowledgements

I wish to thank the 'Ngaro'/Birri peoples of the central Queensland coast for their input into this research and to Bruno David and Lara Lamb for helpful additions and comments relating to this paper.

# 6.
Colonial diffusionism and the archaeology of external influences on Aboriginal culture

Ian J McNiven

Introduction

This paper explores the changing face of archaeological approaches to the impact of external influences on Aboriginal culture during the Holocene. My approach is epistemological, empirical and focuses on the origins of the so-called Australian Small Tool Tradition (ASTT). Despite near-abandonment of the issue by the younger generation of archaeologists, senior members of the discipline have kept the external-influences flame alive. One of these torch bearers is Harry Lourandos who, in the final two pages of his 1997 *magnum opus*, *Continent of hunter-gatherers*, stated that to understand the 'prehistory' of Australia we need 'to look beyond regional prehistories to those of the wider cultural area or sphere of social interaction' (1997, pp. 334–5). However, Lourandos was quick to point out that he was not suggesting that 'cultural changes of the late Holocene in Australia were due solely to external influences, but rather to an interplay of internal and external forces' (1997, pp. 334–5). Here I concur with Ian Lilley (2000, p. 39) who noted that Lourandos 'is to be applauded for revisiting the question of external connections [between New Guinea and Australia] during the Holocene'. Yet in this 'post-colonial' (or, more accurately, decolonising) era, Lourandos sets a challenge: to redefine and revitalise investigations of external influences without encouraging anachronistic diffusionist studies underwritten by colonial tenets (*cf.* Bradshaw rock art debate: see McNiven & Russell 1997 for discussion).

In this paper I engage with that challenge. In doing so I take a historical approach to reveal how external-influences studies in Australian archaeology developed their colonialist underpinnings, and subsequently maintained relevance linked to the known introduction of the dingo. In the wake of this postcolonial critique I argue that an external-influences research agenda for ASTT origins collapses, thus opening the way for the development of new models to account for the introduction of the dingo. In this connection, the final section of the paper refocuses and redefines an external-influences research agenda for Australian archaeology based on new information supporting the hypothesis that the dingo was introduced to mainland Australia from New Guinea via Torres Strait around 3500 years ago.

Changing relevancy of an 'unresolved debate'

In 1993 Sandra Bowdler wrote: 'There is a standard and unresolved debate amongst Australian archaeologists as to whether the Australian Small Tool Tradition represents an introduction or an "independent invention"' (1993, pp. 133–4). However, recent reviews of stone artefact research in Australia by younger generation archaeologists make no mention of this 'unresolved debate' (e.g. Fullagar 1994; Hiscock & Clarkson 2000; Holdaway 1995). Furthermore, it is difficult to find any papers in *Australian Archaeology, Archaeology in Oceania, Queensland Archaeological Research* or *The Artefact* from the last two decades that mention, let alone engage with, the issue of external influences and the origins of the ASTT.

Alternatively, major syntheses of Australian Indigenous archaeology written in the last fifteen years, all by older members of the discipline (Flood 1999; Lourandos 1997; Mulvaney & Kamminga 1999), engage with the issue of Australian Small Tool Tradition origins and discuss the possible impact (or non-impact) of external influences for understanding late-Holocene changes in Aboriginal Australia. Thus, on the one hand we have older members of the discipline saying the issue remains relevant and worth resolving, and on the other hand a younger generation of scholars who appear to regard the issue as redundant — or at least no longer on the research agenda.

What has happened in Australian archaeology to create this classic Kuhnian case of a generationally based paradigmatic change? Why is it that younger generation archaeologists show little interest in exploring ancient Aboriginal engagements with the outside world? We know Indonesians have been part of an Old World maritime trade system for over 2000 years (Lansing *et al.* 2004). We also know that Torres Strait Islanders have been part of wide-ranging Melanesian maritime trade systems for at least 2000 years (Carter 2002a, 2002b, this volume). Did not Aboriginal people participate at least peripherally in these ancient maritime interchanges? The introduction of the dingo provides compelling evidence that Aboriginal Australians engaged directly with people beyond our continental shores sometime between 3000 and 4000 years ago. So why has the question of external influences fallen out of favour in recent decades?

According to Bowdler (1993, p. 134), the lack of interest in external influences is a form of archaeological xenophobia, 'perhaps mirroring wider contemporary Australian attitudes: protectionist and isolationist'. A few years later, Bowdler put the blame on political correctness, speculating that the:

> reluctance [of archaeologists] to look outside Australia for antecedents of aspects of the archaeological record [e.g. the Australian Small Tool Tradition] may be due to perceived Aboriginal sensitivities. As is now widely recognised, traditional Aboriginal cosmologies do not allow of such external antecedents, and many contemporary Aboriginal people are unhappy with such ideas. (1997, p. 25)

Alternatively, Mike Rowland (1987, pp. 38–9) posited that 'environmental models and those that include elements of outside influences appear to have taken a hammering in recent years at the expense of newer models of intensification' (1987, pp. 38–9). As is well known among the archaeological community, 'newer models of intensification' is an implicit reference to the work of Harry Lourandos. Rowland (1999b, pp. 13, 33) repeats this stand, explicitly referencing the work of Lourandos that he labels 'internalist' due to its neo-Marxist emphasis on social relations and structural change. While this representation is true to a certain extent, Lourandos (e.g. 1985b, 1997) makes it clear that he considers the question of external influences as neither antithetical to intensification nor a redundant question (see below).

In contrast to Bowdler and Rowland, I believe that two key developments within Australian archaeology over the past twenty years are responsible for driving younger generations of archaeologists away from the question of external influences. The first development is the ascendancy of technological investigations over typological analyses (see Fullagar 1994; Hiscock & Clarkson 2000); the second is a rejection of scholarship underwritten by colonialist tenets and negative stereotyping of Aboriginal people.

The impacts of the first development are threefold. First, 'disassembling' the integrity of the ASTT by pointing out that its key components — tula adzes, backed blades (e.g. geometric microliths) and points (bifacial and unifacial) — have different histories in different parts of the continent, and even within individual sites (Hiscock 1994a, p. 275). The ASTT is no longer seen by most people as being a 'package' available for diffusion into Australia. Second, breaking down the notion that implement 'types' represent standardised predetermined forms with inherent meaning as intentionalised end products of reduction and tool manufacture. Technological approaches have identified morphological/reduction continuums reflecting a range of processes including different degrees of both edge rejuvenation and core reduction (e.g. Hiscock 1994b, 1998; Hiscock & Attenbrow 2002). Third, the antiquity of backing, a key feature of the ASTT, is now seen as an ancient feature of Australian technology (Flenniken & White 1985), with examples of backed flakes known from the early Holocene (Hiscock & Attenbrow 1998) and the late Pleistocene (Campbell 1984, pp. 176–8; McNiven 2000; Slack *et al.* 2004). As such, artefact assemblages once grouped under the banner of the ASTT are seen more as locally generated (adaptive) responses to changing social and environmental circumstances (Hiscock 1994a). In terms of dismantling the conceptual integrity of the ASTT as an imported 'package', I find these technological critiques compelling.

The second development — the rejection of colonialist scholarship — is more elusive, as little research has been devoted to documenting either the colonial foundations of Australian Indigenous archaeology or recent decolonising attempts within the discipline (*cf.* McNiven & Russell 1997, 2005, in press; Russell & McNiven 1998). In terms of stone artefact studies, Veth *et al.* (1998) provide the most recent critique of the redundancy of diffusionist/evolutionist models within Australian archaeology, noting that such models are products of nineteenth-century social evolutionism (see also Mulvaney 1977). In *Continent of hunter-gatherers*, Lourandos similarly draws our attention to colonialist tenets that have underwritten much previous scholarship on Aboriginal Australians:

> The inheritance of colonialism includes the ways indigenous people's history and 'prehistory' was presented and interpreted, often to the disadvantage of the people themselves; often as a means of social control. The story of Aboriginal Australia and Tasmania is much the same. Unilinear evolutionary models of the nineteenth and early twentieth century, for example, presented by anthropologists and archaeologists, which placed these peoples on the lowest rungs of the socio-cultural evolutionary 'ladder', have largely served to preserve the status quo; to keep Aboriginal Australians and Tasmanians in their place — as dependent, 'conquered' peoples, largely divorced from land, society, economy and their past. (Lourandos 1997, p. xvi)

Rejection of diffusionist/evolutionist models by younger generation archaeologists is important for understanding the abandonment of external-influence studies. Yet this association raises the question of how Lourandos could take an anti-colonialist stance while at the same time supporting external-influences studies. The answer is that instead of simply dropping external influences questions, Lourandos has made a conceptual and epistemological separation (at least implicitly) between appropriate and relevant (non-colonialist) and inappropriate and redundant (colonialist) approaches to diffusionism. This latter form of diffusionism is what McNiven and Russell (2005) refer to as 'colonial diffusionism'. I believe younger generation archaeologists have failed to make this separation and have simply 'thrown the baby out with the bathwater' when it comes to external-influences questions.

But what *is* colonial diffusionism, and how has it shaped external influences research in Australian archaeology?

Colonial diffusionism

The prevailing view of nineteenth century scholars was that 'savages' remained in a 'primitive state' because they had been 'prevented from advancing by exposure to adverse or less stimulating conditions' (Bowler 1992, p. 722). This view was a cornerstone of social evolutionism and part of a long-standing European colonial ontology that divided the world into two major cultural domains: an *Inside* (European) domain representing the world's 'cultural hearth' characterised by innovation and progress; and an *Outside* domain that was stagnant and unchanging ('traditional') (Blaut 1993). Within this Inside–Outside schema, Europe is 'humanistic' and 'historical' while the Outside world of 'savages' is 'natural' and 'ahistorical'.

One of the earliest and most explicit statements on the Inside–Outside schema was by German philosopher Georg Hegel. In his *Lectures on the philosophy of world history* published between 1822 and 1828, Hegel elaborated on how Europe, particularly in the vicinity of the Mediterranean Sea, '*is* the focus of the whole of world history'. Furthermore, the 'lands which lie beyond Syria constitute the beginning of world history, and this beginning itself lies suspended, as it were, outside the historical process'. For most of Africa, 'history is in fact out of the question', while history only began in the New World (the Americas and Australia) with European colonisation (cited in Eze 1997, pp. 113, 121, 126).

The Inside–Outside schema was born out of colonialism and European attempts to justify and legitimate colonisation of lands and peoples far from Europe. Within nineteenth century anthropology and archaeology, the Inside-Outside schema was most clearly expressed and elaborated through the theoretical frameworks of social evolutionism and diffusionism. Social evolutionism is a colonial ontology founded upon the assumption of staged progressivism, as developed by the ancient Greeks and elaborated by Enlightenment scholars (Adams 1998; McNiven & Russell 2005). While it is beyond the scope of this paper to elaborate upon the colonial foundations of social evolutionism (see McNiven & Russell 2005 for detailed discussion), suffice to say that this theoretical framework represented Aboriginal Australians (particularly Tasmanians) in a very negative light as unevolved 'savages' and exemplars of primordial 'man' ('living fossils') time-locked to a Stone Age past (e.g. Lubbock 1865, 1870; Morgan 1877; Tylor 1865).

Colonial diffusionism operationalises the Inside-Outside schema by modelling material-culture trait movements from one area/group to another area/group such that the source area/group is essentialised as dynamic and inventive and the recipient area/group is essentialised as static and uninventive (Blaut 1993; McNiven & Russell 2005). But the challenge for nineteenth century anthropologists and archaeologists was differentiating between internally generated change (independent invention) and externally stimulated change (diffusion). Tylor (1884, p. 547) described this issue of differentiation as the 'great problem, the solution of which will alone bring the study of civilization into its full development as a science'. It is in this context that Aboriginal Australians presented nineteenth century anthropologists and prehistoric archaeologists with a conundrum. Tylor, in his *Researches into the early history of mankind* (1865), remarked that the idea of Aboriginal Australians as a 'pure' race untouched by 'external conditions' is to some extent challenged by their use of a range of artefacts too advanced for a people at the bottom of the evolutionary ladder. For example, how was it possible that some Aboriginal groups possessed polished stone axes — one of the 'highest' tool types of the Stone Age (Neolithic) — when as a general rule Aboriginal Australians had an 'extremely low' (Palaeolithic) technology?

The issue of Australian stone-tool technologies representing a mixture of European Palaeolithic and Neolithic stone artefact types did not escape the attention of Australian researchers of the late nineteenth century (e.g. Mathew 1889, p. 35). While early twentieth century Australian researchers put the admixture down to the technical limits of raw materials (e.g. Howchin 1934, p. 91; Kenyon & Mahony 1914, p. 4; Spencer 1901, pp. 78–9), such a view came about following critiques of the local applicability and usefulness of European social evolutionary models (e.g. Smyth 1878, I, pp. iv, lv–lvi).

Tylor, much more keenly aware of the far-reaching implications of this Australian anomaly, made the extraordinary admission that this mixture of so-called advanced and primitive technology actually had the potential to question the validity of using stone tools 'as a test of culture anywhere'. Clearly the stakes were high, for unless a good argument could be formulated to explain the diversity of Aboriginal technology, a fundamental flaw was to be exposed in social evolutionism and anthropological theories on staged progressivism and the development of humanity. 'Fortunately', Tylor stated, 'there is an easier way out of the difficulty'. The advanced polished axes had been added to the primitive core of Aboriginal technology following contact with more advanced peoples such as 'Malay or Polynesian' axe makers (Tylor 1865, pp. 200–1). Thus, colonial diffusionism was not only essential to maintain the integrity of social evolutionism, but also necessary to keep Aboriginal Australians in their primordial place to help justify and legitimate European colonisation of Australia. Social evolutionism and diffusionism allowed representation of nineteenth century European colonialisation of Australia as a process that not only assisted Aboriginal societies to advance, but also initiated cultural change and *gave them a history* (McNiven & Russell 2005).

In this context it is no surprise that diffusionism has been central to discussions of the origins of Aboriginal culture ever since Europeans began speculating on the subject during the early years of the colony (McNiven & Russell 1997, 2005; Russell & McNiven 1998). In every case, explanations involving external (non-Aboriginal) origins only concern cultural traits considered sophisticated or advanced (i.e. those cultural traits that would challenge the social evolutionary assumption that Aboriginal Australians are simple 'savages' and Palaeolithic survivals). Perhaps the most famous example is Kimberley rock art which continues to attract colonialist interpretative frameworks and controversy (see McNiven & Russell 1997, 2005; Redmond 2002).

On a broader stage, twentieth century diffusionist explanations for the external origins of certain Aboriginal cultural traits are best associated with the works of Grafton Elliot Smith, William Perry, Daniel Davidson and Fred McCarthy. The 1910s and 1920s saw a resurgence of diffusionist theories to explain the global spread of so-called 'megalithic' cultures. This new hyper-diffusionist school — headed by Elliot Smith and Perry — held that advanced cultural traits (such as megaliths, agriculture, polished stone axes and mummification) became grafted onto the primitive cultural base of the peoples of Oceania, including Aboriginal Australians (e.g. Elliot Smith 1930; Perry, 1923). Following a nineteenth century agenda, Elliot Smith (1930 p. 126) sought to explain what he called the 'incongruity' of the 'mixture of primitive and highly developed customs' within Aboriginal society (for a more extended discussion see Russell & McNiven 1998). Elliot Smith was blunt with his lowly opinion of Aboriginal Australians. He clearly believed Aboriginal Australians were incapable of claiming credit for the 'superior traits'. 'Of constructive efforts of originality there is little or no trace. Apart from implements of stone, bone, and wood, *they invented nothing*' (Elliot Smith 1930, p. 262, emphasis added). Furthermore, '[t]he Food-Gatherers have survived since the birth of mankind without learning much, certainly not originating much' (Elliot Smith, 1930 p. 261). As such, '[i]t is clear that the Australians have received practically every element of their culture from abroad in relatively recent times' (Elliot Smith, 1930, p. 129). However, Robert Lowie (1937, p. 15) aptly expressed a commonly held view among anthropologists that 'the contributions... of Elliot Smith and Perry are probably nil'.

The role of colonial diffusionism in denying Australian Indigenous agency in the manufacture of so-called advanced technological traits is revealed by stone-headed clubs of Torres Strait (see McNiven 1998b for details). During the nineteenth century, Europeans observers (including explorers and anthropologists) identified New Guinea as the source of stone-headed clubs used by Torres Strait Islanders. For example, Alfred Haddon (1900, p. 244, see also 1890, p. 341) stated categorically that 'most of the clubs from Torres Strait were imported from the Fly River District and Daudai [i.e. south-west Papua New Guinea]'. This interpretation persisted despite the incongruous facts that southwest Papua New Guinea is essentially devoid of stone, while the Torres Strait abounds in stone suitable for club-head manufacture. Raw-material sourcing of Torres Strait stone-headed clubs in museums confirms that most club heads are indeed made from Torres Strait stone (see also Hitchcock 2004 and McNiven & von Gnielinski 2004 for further confirmation of this inference). McNiven (1998b) concluded that such misunderstanding on Torres Strait club-head origins reflected in part diffusionist assumptions that so-called advanced cultural traits such as polished-stone club heads must have been made by relatively more advanced neighbours in New Guinea.

External influences and small tools

Following visits to Australia in 1930–31 and 1938–39, American anthropologist Daniel Davidson produced a series of papers on the distribution and likely dispersal (diffusion) of various classes of Aboriginal material culture across the continent. Davidson concluded that most Aboriginal material culture items were of local origin based on the simple and conservative assumption that lack of presence of these items in the surrounding regions of South-East Asia or Oceania ruled out external diffusion. Alternatively, continuous distribution of items from Australia into New Guinea revealed diffusion from the latter to the former via Torres Strait (e.g. outrigger canoes, see Davidson 1935).

Fred McCarthy laid down the paradigmatic foundations of his long career in two of his earliest publications (McCarthy 1936, 1938). His 1936 *Mankind* paper 'The geographical distribution theory and Australian material culture' endorses the approach of Davidson, but is critical of his results as many were based on incomplete distributional data. Towards the end of his career, McCarthy acknowledged that Davidson's research was a 'landmark in the study of change in Aboriginal culture' and that his 'own studies of culture change in Australia have really been an extension of Davidson's work' (McCarthy 1970, pp. 142, 150).

McCarthy's (1938) paper is historically important as it sets the diffusionist framework for the next half century of archaeological research into the origins of 'prehistoric' Aboriginal material culture. In this paper, technological and typological similarities (and diffusionist links) were examined for stone- and bone-artefact industries between Australia and various parts of South-East Asia. Comparisons were based on available publications and museum collections in Australia and Indonesia (McCarthy visited Indonesia in 1937–38). McCarthy (1938, p. 40) suggested that serrated points found both in the Kimberley (north-west Australia) and Toalian industry of the Celebes (Sulawesi) 'can only be explained by the conclusion that the technique was introduced into north-west Australia from Malaya, and its restricted distribution indicates a comparatively recent introduction'. However, due to scant data, the question of '[w]hether or not the [geometric] microlithic industry came to Australia from India *via* Sumatra and Java, or *via* Philippine Island from south Asia, cannot as yet be decided' (McCarthy 1938, p. 39). McCarthy (1938, p. 47) concluded that '[d]iffusion of traits due to contact of peoples must have played a most important part in Australian prehistory just as it has done in the material culture'.

McCarthy (1940) lists more than ninety Aboriginal artefact and site types as having a probable external origin. That McCarthy was well aware of the stigma attached to diffusionist studies in the wake of Elliot Smith and Perry is revealed in the opening paragraph of his paper: 'one hesitates to write upon a controversial subject' (1940, p. 241). Similarly, McCarthy (1940, p. 243; 1953, p. 245; 1974, p. 214) repeatedly made it clear that his diffusionist stance was in opposition to Spencer's (1921, p. 89) view that Australian Aboriginal culture developed 'without any outside influence'. While McCarthy elaborated notions of external influences, his key advance on Davidson (and enduring legacy) was in providing a plausible mechanism for the diffusion of traits across Australia in the form of trade networks (see McCarthy 1939–40). Unfortunately, McCarthy's external-diffusionist arguments are founded upon a subjective and spurious assumption:

> An interesting point to note is that there is a progression of culture advances in Australia extending from the south-western portion of the continent northwards and north-eastwards, and also from the south-eastern portion northwards and north-westwards. The south-west and south-east regions are the most distant points on the continent from contacts with neighbouring island culture. Outstanding deficiencies in south-west Australia comprise canoes, netting techniques, reed-spears, fish-nets and hooks, platform burial, knobbed and bladed clubs. Similarly, in south-east Australia, the use of one-piece bark canoes and containers, simple loop netting, coiling and hammer-dressed round-axes, indicates an earlier stage of

development than the use in Queensland of the more advanced sewn multiple-piece bark canoes and containers, loop and twist and hourglass netting techniques, polished lenticular axes and tanged axes, and especially of the many Papuan traits in Cape York. (McCarthy 1940, p. 261)

Predictably, McCarthy then proceeded to identify essentially all of the so-called complex cultural traits of northern Australia as 'external influences' from either Melanesia or South-East Asia.

Ironically, McCarthy (1953, p. 244; 1957, p. 186) argues that diffusionism demonstrates that Aboriginal culture was not as simple and static as once thought because it 'has been considerably enriched by external influences'. During the late Holocene this 'constant enrichment of Aboriginal material culture centred on three main areas — Cape York, Arnhem Land and the Kimberley coasts' (McCarthy 1974, p. 223). In a further backhanded compliment, he states that 'the Aborigines [sic] is not an isolated culture which developed independently as is commonly supposed, it is one that has thrived, in a limited manner, on the continuous progress of Oceanic cultures with their roots in Asia' (1953, pp. 252–3). More extraordinarily, McCarthy (1963, p. 181) wrote: '[w]hile Aboriginal culture, however, is not a local Australian phenomenon, neither is its development due solely to outside influences'. Yet hindsight can nourish churlishness, and we must be mindful of McCarthy's (1940, p. 242) revolutionary stance that 'the material culture of the aborigines has not remained static . . . The aborigines have experimented with many aspects of their culture, and in the adaptation to their environment have brought into play a great deal of ingenuity, resource and skill'. As John Mulvaney (1993, p. 22) reminds us, McCarthy made these comments at a time when '[i]n the negative opinion of those times, Aboriginal culture was dismissed as unchanging and uncreative'. Yet McCarthy (1953, p. 257; 1957, p. 191) stated that '[i]nvention, as such, is not a feature of aboriginal culture'. Furthermore, 'Aboriginal culture has advanced principally through outside influences' (McCarthy 1963, p. 182). As late as 1977, McCarthy restated both his external-influence hypothesis and his essentialised and lowly view of Aboriginal people:

> There is not a great deal of evidence to support invention as a prominent principle of Aboriginal culture, as Davidson has pointed out in his various papers, while the vital importance of diffusion within Australia has been proved beyond doubt. The ease with which artefacts could be obtained by barter and gift exchange militated somewhat against a cultural climate in which invention was necessary or actively encouraged. (McCarthy 1977, pp. 260–1)

In 1940, McCarthy hypothesised that unifacial and bifacial points (including serrated Kimberley points) were 'Malayan' introductions through 'northwest Australia' (1940, p. 309). In contrast, Davidson (1938, p. 69) held that Kimberley points were 'of local origin'. As late as 1977, McCarthy maintained that 'One would expect the northern Kimberleys to have been the entry point for the symmetrical points as this is the area in which they reached their highest development' (1977, p. 256). Although Casey (1938, cited in Mulvaney 1961) thought the microlith industry was introduced, McCarthy (1943, p. 151) was more ambivalent towards the origin of 'microliths' (geometric microliths and 'end or thumb-nail' scrapers): 'The possibility of the microlithic culture being an independent development in Australia must be considered, and it is not known whether it is historically related to Asiatic cultures of the same nature, especially in India'. Expressing views sympathetic to hyper-diffusionism, McCarthy (1953, p. 249) stated that the 'ultimate origin [of 'geometrical microliths'] appears to have been in the Mediterranean region, whence they spread to many parts of the world during Mesolithic and Neolithic times'. Despite these views, in his major text on Aboriginal stone tools (co-authored with Elsie Bramell and Herbert Noone, 1946), McCarthy sidestepped the origins question altogether. Perhaps this omission reflected the authors' different views on the issue as Noone (1943, p. 279) rejected external origins for Aboriginal stone technology, speaking instead of the 'inventive genius' of Aboriginal Australians. And on a more sardonic note: 'So much evidence has been put forward to indicate that the Australian aboriginal has brought, or borrowed, many traits of his culture from overseas sources, that one is led to look for anything of his that is left' (Noone 1943, p. 279).

It is clear from the discussion above that Aboriginal stone tools, particularly ground stone axes, have played a key role in the representation of Aboriginal Australians as Palaeolithic survivals. More significant, in terms of this paper, such representation was founded upon an arbitrary and spurious categorisation of Aboriginal tool technology into locally invented ('simpler') and externally diffused ('sophisticated') elements. In this connection, speculation continued on the external diffusion of ground stone axes and associated manufacturing techniques such as 'hammer-dressing' into Australia (e.g. McCarthy 1940, pp. 249, 268; 1953, p. 250), until the notion was crushed by the excavation of some of the oldest ground stone axes in the world from Arnhem Land by Carmel Schrire (then White) (White 1967). For most of the twentieth century, however, speculation on external influences on Aboriginal stone tool technology focused on small retouched implements such as backed blades (geometric microliths), points and adzes that were seen eventually to form part of what Richard Gould (1969a) termed the 'Australian Small Tool Tradition'.

In many respects McCarthy, as a museum-based archaeologist, represents the first era of scientific archaeology in Australia and the beginning of the next (Moser 1994). However, his strong and successful advocacy for professionalisation of the discipline saw a new generation of university-based archaeologists in the 1960s and 1970s armed with a broader range of paradigms emphasising 'ecology' and 'adaptation' with vague links to processualism, yet maintaining strong links to culture history and normative views of the past (*cf.* Bowdler 1993, p. 123; McBryde 1986; Mulvaney 1962). This curious paradigmatic admixture saw continued courting of diffusionism but increasing ambivalence towards external origin hypotheses. The 1960s and 1970s also represent a period where a definite chronological framework for human introduction of the dingo emerges, and archaeologists slowly associate this new line of evidence with the issue of the introduction of the ASTT.

External influences, small tools and the dingo

In 1958–60 John Mulvaney wrote a paper, 'The Stone Age of Australia', which was published in the *Proceedings of the Prehistoric Society* in 1961 (Mulvaney 1990, p. 1). In that paper, he suggested that pirri (unifacial) points have 'affinities' with 'incipient pirris' of the Toalian assemblages of Sulawesi (Mulvaney 1961, p. 79). In terms of microliths, the 'evidence from Indonesia is suggestive of diffusion, but only systematic excavation in that area can contribute reliable data' (Mulavney 1961, p. 81). As for 'edge-ground axes', Mulvaney (1961, p. 93) posited that 'it seems probable that the technique, the sole "neolithic" component of aboriginal culture, diffused to Australia from New Guinea or other islands to the north of Australia'. Behind Mulvaney's external origin hypotheses was a belief that '[d]iffusion and local adaptation of diffused techniques are more likely to have been operative [during Australia's prehistoric past] than is local invention' (Mulvaney 1963, p. 36). Like McCarthy, Mulvaney (1963, p. 36) juxtaposed his position to Spencer's isolationist approach, which he labelled 'nationalist'.

Mulvaney's attitude to external influences changed by the time he finished analysing materials excavated from Kenniff Cave in central Queensland. In the excavation report, Mulvaney and Joyce (1965) divided the stone artefact assemblage into a 'Non-Hafted Phase' and 'Hafted Phase'; the latter dating to within the last 5000 years and associated with implements consistent with the ASTT. Significantly, Mulvaney and Joyce (1965, p. 209) did not follow McCarthy's diffusionist/external origins paradigm, but rather made a passing, ambivalent reference to 'the arrival, or local invention of hafting in Australia . . . followed by its rapid diffusion, particularly during the 3rd millennium B.C.' In the final sentence of their paper, Mulvaney and Joyce (1965, p. 21) reveal their leanings:

Are we then on the threshold of uncovering a massive diffusion of ideas, or are we documenting one of those surging 'waves' of 'folk', so dear to the hearts of earlier prehistorians and so distrusted today, because of their mechanistic and racial implications?

A year later, Mulvaney (1966) made no mention of external origins for 'hafted phase' implements despite a reference to the '3000-year-old' dingo skeleton he had excavated from Fromm's Landing (Mulvaney et al. 1964). Acknowledged at the time as the 'earliest authenticated occurrence of the dingo in Australia' (1966, p. 93), these remains mark the entry of the dingo into modern Australian archaeological discourse. Although the dingo had been long recognised by zoologists as a 'prehistoric' import (Barker & Macintosh 1979), Mulvaney (1966) drew no link between the external origin of the dingo and introduction of the 'hafted phase'.

In his 1969 book *The prehistory of Australia* Mulvaney posited that the new tool types of the last 'six thousand years or so' represented a 'single industrial complex' he termed the 'Inventive Phase' in preference to his earlier 'Hafted Phase' (1969, pp. 107, 110). This time he tentatively supported McCarthy's diffusionist/external origins ideas, noting that it was a 'speculative hypothesis that both point and microlithic blade industries had differentiated before reaching Australia, although diversification continued here, and while Arnhem Land was the likely beachhead for the former technology, north-western Australia was the possible entry for the latter' (1969, p. 127). Although McCarthy (1966, p. 8; 1967, p. 93) posited that tula adzes were 'an Australian invention', Mulvaney felt that the 'possibility remains, however, that future field work in tropical Australia and Island South-East Asia may yet rob the Aborigines of their presumed indigenous invention' (1969, p. 116). Mulvaney (1969, p. 65) mentioned the newly available (now discredited) dates of 'between 7000 and 8000 years ago' for dingo bones at Mount Burr in South Australia, but again no link was made between the introduction of the 'Inventive Phase' and the dingo.

The question of possible outside origins for Australian microlithic assemblages led to a joint Australian-Indonesian archaeological expedition to Sulawesi Selatan in 1969 (Mulvaney & Soejono 1971; *cf.* Chapman 1986; Presland 1980). Despite the explicit external influences agenda of the expedition, its approach was cautious and self-reflective. For example, Mulvaney and Soejono (1971, p. 32) stated that 'it is premature to leap from morphological comparison to diffusionist inference'. On a more anti-colonial note:

> Diffusionist and evolutionary hypotheses are therefore implicit, with the inbuilt preconception that nothing significant developed locally and that as far as Australian contacts were concerned, traffic was

one-way: Australia absorbed traits but exported nothing in return. (Mulvaney & Soejono 1971, p. 29)

In an important and thought provoking paper, Peter White (1971, pp. 191–2) took the critical step of linking the introduction of the dingo with the introduction of what Mulvaney and Joyce (1965) referred to as 'Phase II' (i.e. ASTT) stone-artefact technologies. White (1971, p. 191) mentioned that the unconfirmed dates of 'around 7,000 BP' for dingo bones at Mount Burr 'conform closely to the earliest dates for the beginning of Phase II' — a reference to recently dated points from Arnhem Land (White 1967, 1971). Using the same evidence, Thorne (1971b, p. 322) similarly observed that 'typological changes and the introduction of the dingo are related'. According to White (1971, p. 192), the 'striking temporal correlation between the probable beginnings of agriculture in Melanesia and Indonesia and the start of Phase II in Australia's technological history, which may be associated with the introduction of the dingo', was 'too marked to be simply coincidental'. Pre-empting aspects of Lourandos' intensification approach by more than a decade (see below), here White articulates Holocene cultural changes in Australia with broader cultural changes and dynamics in Melanesia and South-East Asia.

In the revised 1975 edition of *The prehistory of Australia*, Mulvaney continued his openness to an external origin for the ASTT:

> How valid is 'Australian', in the Australian Small-Tool Tradition? The tula adze is the oldest known tool of this tradition and best claimant to a 'made in Australia' label (unless grinding technology and boomerangs are also included). Chronology currently fits an Australian origin for backed blades, but distribution and typology both make diffusion from overseas (Sulawesi, India, Ceylon?) possible, and Kimberley excavations may provide the answer. The earliest projectile points are in the northern Oenpelli area, so that an introduction from Indonesia is possible, as undated analogues occur there, particularly in Java. (Mulvaney 1975, p. 236)

This time, however, Mulvaney (1975, p. 211) hypothesised explicit links between the introduction of the dingo and the introduction of the ASTT: 'the fact that species [dingo] traversed the wide post-glacial ocean implies that it was brought here by a migrant group . . . [and] may explain the introduction of new technological concepts'. While Pearce (1974, p. 307) posited that New South Wales might have been 'a centre of [backed-blade] innovation', given that it had the earliest-dated backed blades in Australia, Mulvaney (1975, p. 230) preferred to see these dates simply indicating 'the region where microlithic techniques matured'.

In contrast to Mulvaney, McCarthy (1976, p. 99) stated the case for external origins boldly:

> From 7000 to 5000 years ago . . . there took place the introduction into Australia of backed blades (geometric microliths and *Bondi* points) in northwestern Australia, and of uniface and biface points in the Kimberley area, in particular the probable development within Australia of the highly specialised *tula* chisel and *leilira* blade in the Northern Territory–Central Australian region, and the *juan* knife in Queensland.

McCarthy only made a link between the introduction of the dingo and the ASTT in his last stone-artefact paper (McCarthy 1977, p. 154).

Peter White and Jim O'Connell (1979, p. 21; see also White & O'Connell 1982, p. 219) had equally strong views on external diffusion hypotheses. Yet the significance of their 1979 review article on 'Australian prehistory' in *Science* stems from its anti-external origins stance (contra White 1971). The paper opens with the statement: 'Interpretations of Australian prehistory have generally emphasized the foreign origin of many aspects of Aboriginal culture, as of Aborigines themselves'. After reviewing available archaeological data for items generally thought to have been foreign influences (e.g. backed blades, ground-edge axes, boomerangs), they conclude 'by stressing that the local development of many aspects of Aboriginal technology is increasingly supported by the data' (1979, p. 26). This conclusion is based on the simple and compelling fact that the earliest examples of all these items come from Australia and not so-called diffusion sources in New Guinea and South-East Asia.

Since White and O'Connell's strong anti-diffusion/local invention stand, opinion has increasingly become polarised on the question of external influences and origins of the ASTT. Charlie Dortch, a strong advocate of external origins for the ASTT (e.g. Dortch 1977, pp. 130–1), reacted strongly against White and O'Connell's (1979) critique. He stated that their 'simple approach' was 'misleading' as it had gone too far and had subsequently 'exaggerated' the notion of 'indigenous development' (Dortch 1981, pp. 27, 29). Dortch made the interesting observation that:

> Strangely enough White and O'Connell (1979) do not mention the dingo, even though this animal's presence on the continent offers one of the most interesting clues to the timing and nature of events in the

evolution of continental cultures, as White (1971) once recognised. (Dortch 1981, p. 27)

In *Archaeology of the Dreamtime*, Josephine Flood (1983, p. 186) acknowledged that while the issue of external influences was 'debatable', the consensus among 'most archaeologists' was 'that some new tools and technology were brought into Australia by diffusion of ideas and possibly migration of people from outside'. While she acknowledged that 'adze flakes' of the tula and burren forms, 'may be an Australian invention', a range of evidence was marshalled to support an external origin for backed blades and points (1983, pp. 191, 198). In the revised editions of her book from 1989 to 1999, Flood changed her tune and made no mention of the consensus (Flood 1989, p. 196; 1995, p. 221; 1999, p. 221). Yet Flood maintained her strong position on external origins and similarly made the link between the introduction of the dingo and ASTT. The following quote appears in the chapter 'Arrival of the dingo' in Flood (1983, p. 198; 1989, p. 208; 1995, pp. 235–6 and 1999, pp. 235–6):

> The different distribution of backed blade and point industries in Australia can be neatly explained by two main migration routes: one through Australia's north in the region of Arnhem Land by people using stone projectile points, and the other via the north-west coast by people using backed blades. The latter would be a natural landfall for people coming from the Indian Ocean, so the Indian subcontinent may have been the original homeland of both Australian backed blades and the dingo. The point industries could derive from the same source, or could have filtered down from Japan and northeast Asia, where projectile points were widespread in late Pleistocene times.

The last major focused discussion of microlith origins in Australia was at the 1978 IndoPacific Prehistory Association (IPPA) conference held in India (see Misra & Bellwood 1985). Glover and Presland (1985, p. 194) concluded that the 'present evidence favours a diffusionist answer, but the question is by no means a dead one'. On a stronger note, Bellwood (1985, p. 198) concluded that similarities in the dating of the 'Australian small tool tradition' with 'industries of the flake and blade technocomplex' in South-East Asia 'seem unlikely to be purely coincidental'. Significantly, Mulvaney (1985, p. 215) questioned the usefulness of the dingo for understanding ASTT origins: 'while Australian prehistorians link dogs [dingoes] and microliths directly', such a link was questionable given that dingoes arrived in Australia 'between 3000 and 4000 years ago' but backed blades date back 'over 5000 years ago'. Hallam (1985, p. 219) stated somewhat profoundly that perhaps the 'problem' of backed-blade origins was an illusion as the category of 'microlithic backed blades' encapsulated 'a variety of possibly unrelated phenomena'.

Throughout the 1990s the strongest advocate of the significance of the dingo introduction for understanding the exotic origins of the ASTT was Bowdler (e.g. 1993, pp. 128, 134; 1994; 1997, p. 26; Bowdler & O'Connor 1991, p. 61; see also Allen & Kershaw 1996, p. 188). Other archaeologists during the late 1980s and 1990s simply stated their sympathies for external-origin hypotheses in relation to the ASTT (or aspects of it) (e.g. Allen & Barton 1989, p. 135; Allen & Kershaw 1996, p. 187; Attenbrow et al. 1995; Morwood & Hobbs 1995, p. 753).

But not all archaeologists agree with this pro–external-influence position. The strongest and most explicit stance supporting local origins of the ASTT since White and O'Connell (1979, 1982) is made by John Mulvaney and Jo Kamminga in *Prehistory of Australia*: '[w]e see no reason to infer that any of the innovations in stone technology derive from overseas' (Mulvaney & Kamminga 1999, p. 257). Significantly, in terms of Lourandos' work, Mulvaney and Kamminga (1999, p. 267) state:

> [The] appearance of Small Tool Phase implement types in different parts of Australia is cited as evidence of social and economic 'intensification', particularly increased productivity and efficiency, which we reject as the total explanation . . . We believe that a number of different factors are probably responsible for the appearance of new implement types and for their particular distributions in Australia, not least technological and social ones.

What these 'technological and social' factors might be, and how these implements have been linked with 'intensification', is not made clear. With such ambiguity, and Rowland's (1987, 1999a) claim of the incompatibility of external influences ideas with 'intensification', I turn now to examine what Lourandos actually says about the origins of the ASTT and notions of external influences.

External influences and intensification

Overall, Lourandos had little to say on the role of diffusion and 'external influences' on Aboriginal society. Indeed, prior to his book *Continent of hunter-gatherers* (1997), Lourandos used McCarthy's work very little, citing only one of his publications (McCarthy 1964 in Lourandos 1983b, p. 87; 1985b, p. 393). Yet in his writings Lourandos neither embraced, rejected nor sidestepped the issue of external influences, with a number of publications making clear statements on the issue. For example, Lourandos (1985a, p. 38) supported Beaton's

(1985) argument that late-Holocene changes in the use of Princess Charlotte Bay (especially the use of offshore islands) may be linked to 'the introduction of more efficient marine technology (outrigger canoe) which would have allowed a wider range of marine exploitation'. This support is at odds with Rowland's (1987) claim that intensification has been responsible in part for sidelining research on external influences. Rowland's claim is all the more puzzling given that his paper focused on the possible impact of outrigger canoe diffusion down the Queensland coast. Lourandos (1985b, p. 413) further elaborated his sympathetic views towards external influences:

> I have so far avoided discussing influences from outside Australia as explanations of change. Contact appears to have existed between northern Australia, New Guinea, and Southeast Asia, especially in recent times, and to have resulted in cultural borrowings (Flood 1983; Mulvaney 1975; White & O'Connell 1982). Status items, involving ritual, art, and the like, were also involved. Exchanges such as these should be viewed as part of intensification processes taking place outside as well as within Australia during the late Holocene. Diffusion alone, however, is not an acceptable explanation for the late Holocene cultural changes in Australia, inasmuch as evidence of the most dynamic processes has come from southeastern Australia, the region farthest removed from the source. Recent Tasmanian prehistory, as well, indicates that change does not require an external cultural stimulus.

In *Continent of hunter-gatherers*, Lourandos indirectly implies his openness to external influences in terms of ASTT origins. He begins by stating:

> The issue of whether the new tools were introduced to Australia from external sources or developed within the continent is also the subject of some debate (White 1971; McCarthy 1977, pp. 254–6; Mulvaney 1977, p. 211). Backed blades and points have been reported from Southeast Asia — the Macassar area of Sulawesi — during the mid-late Holocene period (Mulvaney & Soejono 197[1]; Glover 1976, 1978), but are absent from regions closer to Australia, such as Timor and New Guinea. (Lourandos 1997, p. 295)

Furthermore, Lourandos (1997, p. 295) observed that '[m]any have associated the appearance of the Australian Small Tool Tradition with the roughly synchronous arrival of the dingo on the Australian continent during the late Holocene'. Lourandos neither disputes this association nor explicitly criticises previously suggested diffusionist links between Australia and South-East Asia. While Lourandos has not engaged explicitly with the technological literature 'disassembling' the integrity of the analytical/conceptual category of the ASTT, a bigger issue is at play here. Echoing White (1971), Lourandos notes that both Australia and New Guinea 'have experienced an economic expansion or intensification in the late Holocene' and that 'the cultural contexts in which the late Holocene changes occurred in northern coastal Australia are associated, in some ways, with those of coastal New Guinea' (1997, p. 334). Most significantly, Lourandos (1997, pp. 334–5) posited that:

> In some ways this scenario implies a 'destablisation' of prior Australian hunter-gatherer relations, with Australia beginning to merge with a broader Australasian system, one increasingly influenced by socio-economic and demographic changes. Such an explanation asks us to look beyond regional prehistories to those of the wider cultural area or sphere of social interaction. I am not suggesting, however, that the cultural changes of the late Holocene in Australia were due solely to external influences, but rather to an interplay of internal and external forces.

External influences, the dingo and Torres Strait

Lourandos links Australia and New Guinea through common processes of intensification that included geographical expansions in social networks that facilitated or hindered the movement of particular cultural traits. The point to emphasise here is that diffusion is not a one-way process, as colonial diffusionists posit. Ideas, like material culture in exchange systems, move between groups in reciprocal arrangements. In order to develop a decolonised external-influences agenda involving Australia and New Guinea, we must move beyond *diffusionism* and examine *interchanges*. This reconceptualisation acknowledges the fact that 'diffusion is not a process per se, but the result of a complex set of interactive events' (McNiven 1993, p. 27). As Barker (2004, p. 148) notes for the central Queensland coast, any possible northern influences need to be seen within the context of 'regional *interaction*, in which the flow of ideas and materials was probably mutual'. A focus on interchanges also acknowledges that we need to examine processes controlling the movement of ideas and material items from New Guinea into Australia as much as we examine such movements from Australia into New Guinea. This new agenda places the focus of attention firmly upon Torres Strait. But our intellectual gaze must move beyond the old diffusionist agenda of seeing Torres Strait simply as a 'bridge and barrier' to the movement of cultural traits (*cf.* Walker 1972; see also Carter, this volume; Harris 1995). Our challenge is to understand how over thousands of years Torres Strait Islanders constructed, negotiated and managed a *nexus* between their immediate mainland neighbours to the north (New Guinea Melanesians) and south (Aboriginal Australians).

As a result of colonial diffusionist thought, external-influences research involving Torres Strait has focused on movements of Papuan and Torres Strait cultural traits into Australia. Recent archaeological approaches to this issue have focused on outrigger canoes (e.g. Beaton 1985; Lourandos 1997, p. 47; Rowland 1987) and fishhooks (e.g. Lourandos 1997, pp. 48, 210–11; Walters 1988). It has been argued that Papuan/Melanesian technologies were responsible in part for intensified Aboriginal use of the Queensland coast during the late Holocene (Beaton 1985; Rowland 1986, p. 83, 1987).

Yet recent archaeological research in Torres Strait challenges the diffusionist assumptions and empirical basis of these so-called introductions. David *et al.* (2004b) and McNiven *et al.* (2005) present evidence for a major expansion across Torres Strait by maritime peoples some 3500–4000 years ago. This chronology provides a likely maximum date for the diffusion of Papuan marine technologies into Australia since formation of the Torres Strait some 8000 years ago. While it remains possible that outrigger canoe technology diffused down the Queensland coast, it is clear that this technology was not necessary for Aboriginal offshore island use as some of these islands were used prior to 5000 years ago (e.g. Barker 2004; McNiven unpublished data; see also Rowland 1996, p. 198). Similarly, no evidence of shell fishhooks has been recovered from any archaeological context in Torres Strait despite considerable midden research over the past 20 years (e.g. Barham *et al.*, 2004). As such, how could the idea of shell fishhooks have diffused into Australia through Torres Strait when no evidence exists for use of these items by Torres Strait Islanders?

The counter argument that Torres Strait could be a source area because of the known ethnographic use of perishable (turtle-shell) fishhooks is invalid as the same argument can be used to support the central Queensland coast (also with ethnographically known turtle-shell fishhooks) as the source area. Thus, the new Torres Strait research indicates that archaeologists need to focus on modelling internal cultural changes within Aboriginal societies to understand late-Holocene maritime intensification along the east coast of Australia, at least in terms of offshore island use and use of seagoing canoes and fishhooks.

It would be naïve to consider that cultural changes along the east coast of Queensland took place without influences from newly established peoples in Torres Strait within the last 3500–4000 years. However, we need to keep in mind that uptake of new ideas and traits are far from a passive exercise (Barker 2004, p. 148). Indeed, it is entirely possible that outrigger canoes were actively taken up along various parts of the Queensland coast to assist Aboriginal peoples in their need to intensify use of land and seascapes due to the increased productivity demands of larger populations brought on by internally generated social changes in the last 3000–4000 years (see Barker 2004; Border 1999). In this sense, uptake of outrigger canoes can be seen as the strategic employment of a risk-minimisation strategy to enable safer and regular use of a dangerous, albeit resource-rich, domain.

The new colonisation dates for the Torres Strait islands also have implications for understanding the origins of the dingo in Australia. Available evidence strongly supports the view that the dingo was introduced into Australia around 3500 years ago (Gollan 1984, p. 924; 1985, p. 439; see also Corbett 1995, p. 17; McBryde 1982, p. 33; Mulvaney *et al.* 1964). This date is based on the oldest-known dingo remains in Australia: dingo bones from 75–90 cm below the surface of Madura Cave (south-east Western Australia) associated with a radiocarbon date of 3450±95 years BP (Milham & Thompson 1976, p. 176). Synchronicity in the earliest dates for a major demographic expansion across Torres Strait and introduction of the dingo to Australia is not coincidental. It is highly likely that the dingo was introduced into Australia not directly from South-East Asia but from New Guinea via Torres Strait (McNiven & Hitchcock 2004; Mulvaney & Kamminga 1999, p. 260). While the antiquity of the dingo in Torres Strait has not been established directly, the presence of dogs (dingoes) in New Guinea by 5500 years ago (Brisbin *et al.* 1994; Bulmer 2001) is consistent with this hypothesis. Furthermore, near-synchronicity in the introduction of the dingo at Cape York (north-east Australia) and earliest dingo remains at Madura Cave (south-west Australia) is not surprising given that the European-introduced red fox spread across Australia in less than a century (Mulvaney & Kamminga 1999, p. 260).

Thus, the dingo continues to provide a rationale and focus for exploring ancient maritime interchanges between Australia and the outside world, in this case with New Guinea and Melanesia more broadly. Yet, ironically, in the quest to document high-impacts such as the ASTT, most archaeologists have overlooked what may have been the biggest impacts of them all: the dingo. From an ecological perspective, introduction of this new carnivore had considerable impact on the mainland Australian environment, not the least of which was extinction of two other carnivores: the Tasmanian Tiger and the Tasmanian Devil. In this connection, Dodson *et al.* (1992, p. 131) rightly note that 'the direct competition effect of the dingo was profound'. Flannery (1994, p. 276) notes that dingoes are 'efficient hunters of the larger marsupials and feral populations may have actually reduced the numbers of these important prey species that were available to Aborigines'. Within Aboriginal societies, dingoes took on a wide range of hunting, domestic, emotional, cosmological, totemic and ritual roles (Meehan *et al.* 1999).

What other changes took place in Australia and New Guinea following 3500–4000 years of interchanges operating through Torres Strait? The dingo alerts us to the possibility that, as a result of colonial diffusionism, too much emphasis has been placed on looking for technological diffusions between New Guinea and Australia. Perhaps the biggest impacts were ecological in terms of plant and animal introductions (see Low 2002, pp. 13–15). In this connection, McNiven and Hitchcock (2004) discuss the implications of terrestrial animal translocations across Torres Strait. How different would late-Holocene Aboriginal societies and the Australian environment have been if Torres Strait Islanders had blocked introduction of the dingo and facilitated introduction of the pig? And what of the implications of possible disease transmissions (e.g. Blainey 1983, p. 104; Groube 1993) and known gene flow (e.g. Birdsell 1993, p. 43; Larnach 1978, pp. 76–7) across the Strait? Whatever the case may be, the new wave of research in Torres Strait has provided an opportunity to redefine, decolonise and revitalise an 'external-influences' research agenda within Australian archaeology.

Acknowledgements

Helpful comments on an earlier version of this paper were kindly provided by Lynette Russell.

7.
Harry Lourandos, the 'Great Intensification Debate', and the representation of Indigenous pasts

Deborah Brian

For a generation of Australian archaeologists, Harry Lourandos is synonymous with 'intensification', the concept he invoked to explain patterns of socioeconomic change among Aboriginal communities of the mid-to-late Holocene. While Lourandos' ideas and influences have clearly strayed far beyond this concept — amply illustrated by the diversity of this volume — intensification is a good place to begin this retrospective for two reasons. First, Lourandos' intensification concept is appropriately indicative of his broader commitment to a social archaeology of Aboriginal Australia, and so it embodies the kind of representational shifts that Lourandos championed throughout his career. Second, the debates over intensification have been a major turning point in the history of Australian archaeology and its discursive representation of Indigenous peoples.

Lourandos' intensification arguments were outlined in a succession of hotly debated publications during the early 1980s (Lourandos 1983b, 1984, 1985a, 1985b) and derived much of their impetus from his earlier doctoral research in south-western Victoria (Lourandos 1980a). They became the catalyst for a prolonged and intense series of debates on the nature of cultural change in hunter-gatherer Australia. Though never clearly resolved (see, for example, Murray 1998, p. 5), these exchanges transformed archaeological thinking about the Indigenous past to such an extent that Lourandos' case for a Holocene intensification of social and economic relations has become an accepted element of the 'long-term history' (Lourandos 1997, p. xiv) of Aboriginal Australia.

However, recent overviews (e.g. Fullagar 2004; Gosden & Head 1999; Lilley 2001; Mulvaney & Kamminga 1999, pp. 267–72; Ulm in press; Williamson 1998) indicate that while the intensification argument currently enjoys a degree of orthodoxy, it has also fallen victim to a kind of creeping ambiguity, raising the question as to whether the complexities of Lourandos' own formulations have been fully appreciated. In this chapter I explore some of the enduring themes of the intensification debate in order to better understand the nature of ongoing dissent, and to gauge the extent of Lourandos' influence on contemporary Australian archaeology. The intensification debate has, of course, been reviewed on many previous occasions, and I refer the reader to these accounts for details of the history of the debate (see especially Lourandos & Ross 1994; also David 2002; David & Chant 1995; Frankel 1995; Lourandos 1997; Ulm in press; Williamson 1998). In contrast to earlier treatments of this subject, however, my chief concern lies not with the evaluation of the explanatory potential of the intensification concept but with the broader discursive undercurrents that flow from Lourandos' innovative approach to Aboriginal history.

Lourandos' intensification arguments changed the way that Australian archaeologists view Aboriginal history, not only through the provision of a new 'continental narrative' (Frankel 1993, p. 31; Ulm in press), but in a much more fundamental way (see also Frankel 1995, p. 652). Where prior essentialist approaches had tended to regard Aboriginal cultures as inherently static and conservative, Lourandos' interpretations portrayed Aboriginal people as dynamic, innovative, and resourceful. Where earlier approaches favoured explanations for cultural change based on relatively passive adaptation to a changing environment, Lourandos' explanations described Aboriginal people as actively managing their social and natural environments, and envisioned cultural change as first and foremost a response to culturally defined social and political imperatives. These conceptual shifts — promoted by Lourandos's intensification arguments, and since adopted more widely throughout the discipline — amount to nothing less than a paradigm shift within Australian archaeology: a veritable revolution in representation.

'Intensification' revisited

'Intensification', as employed by Lourandos in the Australian context, refers in general to an acceleration of a set of historical processes by which social, economic and political relations become more intensive and structurally complex. More specifically, it is taken to refer to historical processes of this kind as evidenced in Australian archaeological deposits from the mid-to-late Holocene. The intensification process includes changes in the ways that people relate to one another and to their lands and resources, the nature and effects of which can be investigated archaeologically. The archaeological markers of intensification typically include increases in the number of living sites occupied within a region (including sites that were never previously occupied), increases in the density of cultural deposits in sites, changes in technology and subsistence practices (especially the addition of new foods to the diet, or changes in the proportions of different foods in the diet), and perhaps the use or occupation of new areas (although the latter may be more accurately described as 'extensification').

Although some of these archaeological patterns had been noted previously (see Beaton 1977; Hallam 1977; Hughes & Lampert 1982 for earlier variants of 'intensification'), Lourandos was the first to unite them within an explanatory framework that permitted speculation about the nature of the social processes behind such changes. Prior approaches tended to emphasise environmental forces as the cause of changes in settlement patterns or subsistence practices; people moved about the landscape differently, or changed their resource consumption habits because alterations in the landscape or the climate *required* them to 'adapt'. More sophisticated alternatives implicated population pressure, demographic restructuring or technological innovation — or combinations of such factors — but were all-too-frequently reducible to 'environment' as the ultimate cause of cultural change. Furthermore, such explanations failed to specify a *mechanism* by which change might occur beyond the rather simplistic expectation that humans, like other animals, would simply adapt or perish.

In the absence of a suitable theoretical framework for explaining such systemic cultural change among hunting and gathering peoples, Lourandos borrowed the concept of 'intensification' from the earlier international debates on the emergence of agriculture (Boserup 1965). Significantly, however, rather than seeking to place Australian hunter-gatherers within an Old World evolutionary schema for the development of agriculture, Lourandos adapted the concept for use in the local context, and in ways that were better suited to the social and economic structures of hunter-gatherer societies (see Lourandos 1985b, pp. 389–91). Thus, his interest in intensification was not vested in those *products* of intensification emphasised in the Old World debates, or in the cultural evolutionary paradigm within which these debates were frequently cast, but in the *process* of intensification: the cumulative, contingent, historical process that might aptly describe what had happened among the Aboriginal communities of south-western Victoria in the Holocene.

Will the 'real' intensification please step forward?

Although 'intensification' is now something of a household word among Australian archaeologists, it is by no means certain that we all mean the same thing when we employ the concept. Perhaps because of this very familiarity — and its consequent use in the service of a range of different approaches, by supporters and detractors alike — intensification seems to have become a rather flattened, two-dimensional version of Lourandos' original concept. In particular, there seems now to be scant appreciation for the inherently *dual* character of the concept. We tend to forget that, when Lourandos first explicitly set out his approach to this issue, he discussed intensification in terms of a pair of 'models' (Lourandos, 1983b p. 81; see also Lourandos 1984). There was the *theoretical* (or 'explanatory') model of intensification which explained the *process* of intensification; this drew upon ethnographic records of the complexity of social, economic and political structures among the Indigenous peoples of south-western Victoria during the early colonial period. Then there was the *empirical* (or 'descriptive') model of intensification; this set out the evidential *pattern*, the archaeological 'signature' which might be expected to mark the occurrence of the process. The two models of intensification were complementary, each informing the other, and together constituting an ambitious and innovative approach aimed at uniting detailed observations on the structure of the archaeological record with sophisticated theoretical interpretation.

More often than not, 'intensification' is used to refer to only one or the other of the two original components: the theoretical model *or* the empirical model. Frequently it is the latter, perhaps because the empirical model for intensification can more readily be made to fit into existing explanatory frameworks; that is, the data generated by traditional processualist regional studies can be 'tested' against the archaeological signature extrapolated from Lourandos' explanation. The theoretical model of intensification, on the other hand, tends to be regarded as only one among many potential explanations for the pattern specified in the empirical model. Both models have been to some extent modified, or even 'corrupted', in the service of a variety of different approaches. The empirical model is frequently expected to provide a more definitive or prescriptive set of cultural attributes or chronological parameters than is strictly required by the nature of the intensification process; the theoretical model has been simplified to the extent that it has sometimes been made to stand for some abstract and absolute notion of cultural 'complexity', or for an exclusively social account of causality, again at the expense of an understanding of the more sophisticated and nuanced concept that 'intensification' was intended to describe.

Over the years since it was first advanced, the intensification argument has gained currency to the extent that it could now be considered an orthodox position within Australian archaeology. The ambiguity inherent in the concept of intensification, however, has permitted the development of a rather confusing scenario. Inasmuch as 'intensification' is taken to mean the empirical pattern of cultural change — the 'something' that happened in the Australian Holocene (White 1994, p. 225) — it has been widely accepted and assimilated into mainstream archaeological narratives of the Aboriginal past. However, when taken to mean the highly developed social archaeological approach applied by Lourandos to that empirical evidence, it would seem that those who find themselves in opposing theoretical camps are unlikely to ever reach a consensus on intensification. It is this deep and fundamental division at a theoretical level that ensures that the primary source of contention in the intensification debate remains hopelessly unresolved.

The 'Great Intensification Debate'

Dubbed the 'Great Intensification Debate' (Lourandos & Ross 1994; Lilley 2001) as much for its notoriety as a spectacle at times verging on the gladiatorial as for its genuine significance in the history of the discipline, the debate over intensification has been one of the most engaging and controversial episodes in the history of the discipline in Australia. The debate gave Australian archaeologists the opportunity to closely examine some of their most fundamental beliefs about hunter-gatherer societies and those societies' potential for cultural change, and about the interpretative potential of the Australian archaeological record. The debates on intensification questioned the perceived 'uniqueness' of the Australian situation, forcing local practitioners to engage with the kind of explanatory frameworks then being popularised through international debates on cultural change, particularly those concerning the emergence of hunter-gatherer complexity (see Price & Brown 1985). On the local stage, it gave form to the broader conflict between the established processualist paradigm and a nascent post-processualism (Lourandos & Ross 1994, p. 55), and fostered the development of more densely theorised approaches to the archaeology of Aboriginal Australia.

Although there were some who questioned the empirical veracity of the intensification phenomenon (particularly the strength of the site-occupation trends: see Bird & Frankel 1991a, 1991b) and the taphonomic integrity of the dataset as a whole (Frankel 1995, p. 654; Godfrey 1989; Head 1983) the bulk of the debate concerned the interpretation of the *causes* of cultural change (see especially the early exchanges between Lourandos and Beaton, in Beaton 1983, 1985; Lourandos 1984, 1985b; see also Lourandos & Ross 1994; David & Chant 1995).

Generally, participants divided neatly along lines of causality largely predetermined by their commitment to specific theoretical approaches. The dynamics of the debate thus became linked to an intractable, although somewhat simplistic, theoretical opposition between 'ecological' and 'social' approaches (Fullagar 2004, p. 13; *cf.* Bird & Frankel 1991a, p.10; Lourandos 1997, pp. 10–11; Lourandos & Ross 1994, p.58). In reality, however, adherents of the ecological approaches tended to allow that social factors constituted part of the intensification 'package', but that they had little causal agency, while advocates for more social approaches saw the environment as *less directly* responsible for cultural change, but as setting parameters for human action in the form of opportunities and constraints (Lourandos 1997, p. 2; see also Tibby *et al.*, this volume).

Lourandos' approach to explanation was based in Marxist-influenced social theory, which privileged social and political forces over other potential determinants of human behaviour such as natural environmental productivity or purely economic motivations. While theoretical perspectives such as those employed by Lourandos were becoming increasingly popular in Britain and parts of continental Europe, they constituted a radical departure from what Lourandos has called the 'traditional' approaches then prevalent in Australia. 'Traditional', in this sense, refers to the uneasy combination of traditional culture history, cultural ecology and New Archaeology 'processualism' — the blend of which was heavily laced with environmental determinism — which held sway in Australia prior to and during the period of the earliest intensification debates (see Lourandos 1984, p.29; 1997 pp. xvi , 2, 308–9).

While such approaches continue to strongly influence archaeological discourse in this country, there seems also to be a growing tolerance for a plurality of approaches that may be collectively branded 'social archaeology'. Even among those who reject what they see as the excesses of post-processualist, post-structuralist, or postmodern approaches there has been a move away from the heavily scientific or environmentally deterministic extremes of the processualist era. It is no longer uncommon, for example, to encounter Australian archaeologists of diverse theoretical persuasions who speak in terms of social dynamics or of cultural decision-making processes as meaningful forces to be taken into account in the explanation of Aboriginal history. In light of these developments, Lourandos' early insights — as articulated in the intensification arguments — can be seen as a significant force in the evolution of those contemporary approaches to the archaeology of Aboriginal Australia which demonstrate a greater sensitivity to the social aspects of cultural change.

Outcomes

Broadly speaking, Lourandos's approach to the explanation of late-Holocene Aboriginal history has been influential in Australian archaeology on three key fronts: the empirical, the theoretical and the representational.

The first influence, the empirical, provided a narrative of historical process that not only offered an intelligent and satisfying 'reading' of the ethnographic and archaeological records of south-western Victoria, but could also be seen to have explanatory potential beyond its original geographical and temporal contexts.

The second influence, the theoretical, was achieved via the introduction of theoretical frameworks capable of articulating the social dimensions of Aboriginal history, thus setting a new benchmark for the level of theoretical sophistication expected of archaeological understandings of the Aboriginal past.

The third (and in my view most important) influence, the representational, promoted a new vision of Australian 'prehistory', helping to dismantle some of the stereotypical images of Aboriginal peoples which had seemingly become entrenched in the discourse of Australian archaeology. These three key aspects of Lourandos' argument — the empirical, theoretical, and representational — have received differential notice in the debates that flourished around intensification during the 1980s and early 1990s, and in the critiques and reviews that have appeared in the intervening years.

The third key element of Lourandos' intensification argument (which might for the sake of clarity be understood as the 'representational' model of intensification) is an element which Lourandos has repeatedly emphasised, but which again is regarded as an optional layer of interpretation rather than an integral part of his approach. In Lourandos' original concept of intensification the representational model rests alongside the empirical and theoretical aspects of the intensification argument, making the link between the theoretical input and the narrative product clear and necessary. This representational dimension of intensification is a bold step away from earlier ways of seeing past Aboriginal culture. It holds that, rather than understanding Aboriginal culture *a priori* as a generally stable and conservative way of life governed by the dictates of a harsh environment, much can be gained by envisioning a more active, more dynamic way of being that incorporates the exercise of cultural choice in determining relations to the land, to its resources, and to other people.

Lourandos' argument for the priority of social forces not only constituted a different way of explaining past cultural change, it also entailed an entirely different view of Australian 'hunter-gatherers'. Ecological models, regardless of the intentions of their makers, tend to construct hunter-gatherers as more or less 'passive' participants in their own histories — natural exploiters of a natural environment. In this traditional view, cultural change all too often becomes mere 'adaptation': alterations in human behaviour are perceived as automatic responses made to accommodate changes in climate or in resource availability, and motivated simply by the need to survive. In contrast, Lourandos' socially oriented approach invests past Aboriginal people with the individual and collective agency to make cultural choices based on a range of social and political imperatives. The result is a generally richer, more social, construction of Aboriginal history.

According to Lourandos' interpretations, the past few thousand years of Aboriginal history were characterised by increasing levels of social, economic and political complexity. While Australian hunting and gathering peoples and their cultures have traditionally been regarded as exceptionally 'simple', 'homogeneous', 'generalised' and 'egalitarian', Lourandos saw them as inherently complex and diverse, with economic and sociopolitical structures to match. Moreover, he imbued past Aboriginal cultures with the kind of fundamental 'historicity' that is taken for granted with respect to other kinds of cultures. Where traditional views held that Aboriginal cultures were relatively static and timeless, Lourandos argued they were instead innovative and dynamic. These differences in representation are key to Lourandos' ongoing influence, and have been an explicit element of his theoretical approach from the outset; however, they have also been the source of considerable discord.

Lourandos' challenge to the old frameworks, and the debate it provoked within the discipline, created an unprecedented opportunity for Australian archaeologists to re-examine their assumptions about the nature of the Aboriginal past. As a result of this process, and spurred on by parallel developments in the politics of Australian race relations, there were significant changes in the way that Aboriginal cultures were conceptualised and represented by archaeologists and by others in the social sciences. In turn, the features of the old frameworks to which Lourandos most objected — environmental determinism, adaptationism, social evolutionism — have since become the subject of almost universal contempt within the discipline. Today, the archaeology of Aboriginal Australia is predicated on an accepted pattern of genuine historical change, and a previously unrecognised complexity of social relations among communities, and between community and country. Moreover, what might be termed the 'core values' of the intensification approach — complexity, dynamism, agency, historicity — seem to have been steadily assimilated into the discourse of Australian archaeology.

Reactions

Because of its unorthodox theoretical origins, and the radically different way in which it represented the Aboriginal past, Lourandos' approach attracted sustained and often trenchant criticism. In addition to arguments over the causality of change, and reservations about the limitations of the methods used to identify and measure evidence for cultural change, there were also objections to Lourandos' allegedly 'political' motivations (*cf.* Lilley 2001, p. 85). Such comments functioned rhetorically to cast Lourandos' arguments as illegitimate and unwarranted, incapable of conforming to the idealised objectivity of a processualist archaeology trying very hard to be 'scientific'. At the heart of this argument was the notion that *some* constructions of the past were 'political', while others were not (*cf.* Yoffee & Sherratt 1993, p.1), a notion that now assumes a certain naivety in light of contemporary understandings of the construction of the past (and especially of others' pasts) as inherently political (see, for example, contributions to Bond & Gilliam 1994). In this sense, Lourandos' revision of Aboriginal 'prehistory' was indeed 'political', but no more so than the traditional approaches that he challenged.

A more concrete variant of the critique of Lourandos' motives came in the form of a recurring complaint that Lourandos was attempting to 'make' Australian hunter-gatherers 'look like' farmers (e.g. Gosden & Head 1999 p. 238, 240; Frankel 1995, p. 653; *cf.* Horton 1982, p. 248). It may be that these concerns originated in Lourandos' association with international discourses on the origins of agriculture in the Old World (from which context the concept of 'intensification' was derived) and the emergence of 'cultural complexity' among New World hunter-gatherers (Lourandos 1985a; see also other contributions to Price & Brown 1985). Elements of both literatures drew, to varying extents, on normative frameworks of cultural evolution, within which the eventual development of agriculture seemed almost inevitable. It was implied that in emphasising parallels with such processes, Lourandos must also have been adopting these evolutionary ideas, seeking to place Australian hunter-gatherers within some kind of global evolutionary framework.

However, these international literatures were notable also for their emphasis on the role of social and political forces in stimulating economic and cultural change, a feature lacking among traditional theoretical approaches to hunter-gatherers, in Australia or elsewhere. Lourandos selected, from among the international theoretical debates, concepts and structures capable of delivering access to the social dimension of the Aboriginal past, and of illuminating those aspects of cultural change which existing frameworks were ill-equipped to explain. In the process, he effectively redefined what it meant to be a 'hunter-gatherer' in the Australian context — but rather than making hunter-gatherers look like farmers, he simply made them look like a very different kind of hunter-gatherer (Huchet 1991; Thomas 1981). Drawing on fresh theoretical perspectives, Lourandos stretched the concept 'hunter-gatherer' to incorporate economic, political, social and behavioural complexities once assumed to be the exclusive province of gardeners, herders and farmers (see also David & Denham, this volume; Bender, this volume).

Despite repeated efforts at clarification (e.g. Lourandos 1997, pp. 2–4; Lourandos & Ross 1994), there remains some uncertainty about just how Lourandos' arguments about cultural change and complexity related to issues of evolution and agriculture. Contemporary commentators who pursue this style of critique contend that Lourandos' model necessarily invokes a unilinear evolutionary pathway from hunting and gathering to farming (e.g. Williamson 1998, p. 145). Yet the simplistic equation of 'intensification' with a 'towards agriculture' grand narrative is something Lourandos has repeatedly and explicitly rejected (e.g. Lourandos 1980b, p. 258; 1997, pp. xvi, 4, 9; see Lourandos et al. this volume). Though they are seldom expressed in much detail, these criticisms seem reminiscent of earlier speculation about the likely end point of Aboriginal historical trajectories truncated or deflected by European invasion (e.g. Davidson 1989; Frankel 1995, p. 653; Horton 1993, p. 11; Lourandos 1983b, p. 92; Williamson 1998, p. 142; see also Rowley-Conwy 2001). Importantly, and in spite of the rhetoric, there was never any good reason to suppose that agriculture ought to have been the logical outcome of pre-invasion Aboriginal historical trajectories, nor that the intensification approach implied such a thing.

All in all, given that progressivist epithets were traded liberally on both sides of the debate (e.g. Williamson 1998, p. 145; Lourandos 1997, p. xvi; see also Lilley 2001, p. 86), it seems to me that these comments say less about the theoretical limitations of any single approach than they do about the perennial insecurities of Australian archaeology as a whole. While certain general concerns, such as that regarding our ability to articulate narratives of cultural change without brushing up against the ghosts of outdated evolutionary ideas (*cf.* Murray 1992, p. 6; 1998, p. 3; Shanks & Tilley 1987b, p. 138; see also McNiven, this volume), are comparatively well-founded, this is not always the case. Criticisms such as those discussed above signal deep-seated anxieties about representation and the maintenance of traditional anthropological categories and frameworks. Despite the current level of scepticism that attaches to evolutionary approaches, many archaeologists find it very difficult, for instance, to imagine cultural change which does not result in an (evolutionary) shift from one narrowly defined cultural 'type' to another, and so the notion of hunter-gatherers undergoing meaningful change and yet remaining hunter-gatherers seems to fly in the face of our received logic. Lourandos' 'intensification' arguments made many people uncomfortable because his construction of Holocene Aboriginal societies deviated substantially from traditional notions of hunter-gatherer cultures, and because his explanation of the dynamics of cultural change among those societies effectively transcended the representational repertoire of the traditional paradigm.

Revisions

In the years since Lourandos first outlined his vision for a social archaeology of the Aboriginal past, Australian archaeology has undergone significant transformation — particularly with respect to its dealings with Indigenous peoples as both heritage owners and as a critical audience for archaeological histories of the Indigenous past. Some of the changes that have taken place within the discourse of archaeology have been in response to external political events, or to developments in the related disciplines of anthropology and history. Other reforms have come about as a result of internal tensions within the discipline itself. The intensification debate was a highly significant moment in the history of the discipline in that it provided an arena wherein disparate theoretical perspectives and long-held assumptions might be examined anew, resulting in lasting changes to the culture of the discipline. Lourandos' ideas on intensification, and the responses they drew from colleagues and critics alike, became, in effect, a site of resistance to traditional notions of Australian hunter-gatherer cultures as inherently stable, simple, passive and conservative.

While the intensification debate proper was a rather brash, noisy affair, the gradual adoption of the changes in representation championed by Lourandos has been by comparison something of a quiet revolution. The transformations apparent in the representation of Indigenous peoples within Australian archaeological discourse have received little explicit attention, and the link between these shifts in understanding and the debate in which those issues came to prominence remains largely unexplored (*cf.* Murray 1992, 1998). That such changes have occurred almost by stealth is hardly problematic, except that it makes these less tangible gains of the intensification era that much more vulnerable to future erosion. Particularly germane to this discussion are recent reviews of the intensification debate which not only ignore these representational changes but which implicitly deny their salience.

Of special concern in this regard is Lilley's review of the intensification era debates in the *festschrift* for the late Rhys Jones (Anderson *et al.* 2001). Writing in an explicitly revisionist vein, Lilley (2001) argued that the differences between the 'traditional' stance on cultural change, as represented by Jones, and Lourandos' intensification approach have been grossly exaggerated. While apparently approving of much of the content of the intensification argument, Lilley claims that these views were in fact prefigured in the earlier work of Jones. In his efforts to emphasise the similarities between the ideas of Jones and Lourandos, however, Lilley traces only rather superficial parallels, relying on the ambiguity implicit in many of the generic concepts utilised in these debates. For instance, in arguing that both Jones and Lourandos believed 'change' was a significant aspect of the Holocene archaeological record, Lilley (2001, p. 80) effectively conflates 'technological innovation' and 'temporal diversity' with the kind of genuine social change advocated by Lourandos. Furthermore, it is clear that Jones and Lourandos had very different ideas about the kind of cultural change that might have occurred. Jones saw cultural change as subordinated to an essential homeostasy governing the relationship between 'man' and 'environment' (essentially following Birdsell

1957, 1977; see Jones 1973, 1977a, 1977b, 1979); his one concession to the kind of cultural agency emphasised by Lourandos was to allow that this homeostasy was 'skilfully regulated' (see Lilley 2001, p. 82–3). Jones' views on homeostasy were in turn underwritten by the then-common belief in the inherent conservatism of Aboriginal cultures (e.g. White 1971; Mulvaney 1971; Lilley 2001, p. 86; *cf.* Lourandos 1980b, p.245), a notion few Australian archaeologists would find acceptable today.

In seeking to emphasise the similarities at the expense of the differences, Lilley ignores the fact that archaeologists at the time *did* find these two points of view incongruent, and that these were the very sorts of differences, spread throughout the Australian archaeological community, that fostered the development of the intensification debate. Lourandos was in part reacting to what he saw as the inadequacies of the 'traditional' approach; the ideas of Jones and others surely did help to 'inspire' Lourandos' new vision of Aboriginal history, but perhaps not in the way that Lilley (2001, p. 79) envisions. Indeed, if Australian archaeologists had not disagreed so violently over much of the content of the intensification debates it is doubtful they would have been sufficiently interesting for us to still be discussing them almost a quarter of a century later. Presumably the point of such revisionism is to recommend the 'traditional' approaches, or those to which they are ancestral, to a contemporary audience. However, in selectively emphasising those aspects of opposing views which most resemble one another, we risk losing what was meaningful in that initial discursive rupture.

On the face of it, Lilley's attempt to elide the views of Lourandos with those of relative traditionalists like Jones is a measure of the popularity and intellectual respectability of intensification today. It could, perhaps, be viewed as a kind of 'parallax error': a tendency to project back in time the recent rapprochement between mainstream and pro-intensification views. While such revisionist versions of the history of archaeological thought in this country are of concern as they risk distorting our understanding of the discourse, there is much more at stake here than mere historical accuracy or the politics of an intra-disciplinary debate. First, there is the injustice of such cynical attempts to silence or appropriate the hard-won gains of past conflicts now that they are relatively well accepted. Second, critics like Lilley— in attempting to overwrite this phase of disciplinary history — do not merely add an alternate narrative to our understanding of that time, they risk compromising our capacity to build on those past gains. Third – and of most concern – in revising our understandings of the debate itself we render vulnerable to revision the discursive consequences of those debates, the new ways in which we have learnt to understand and to represent past Indigenous cultures.

Discussion: the politics and poetics of an archaeological debate

Clearly, the traditional views of Jones and others and the intensification approach of Lourandos have very different implications for the way that Aboriginal cultures are portrayed in archaeological accounts of the past. Lilley's analysis not only fails to consider this aspect of their difference, but explicitly excludes it by refusing to discuss anything which might be considered merely 'rhetorical'. In fact, Lilley takes the view that to understand Jones' work more clearly it needs to be pared back, 'stripped of its rhetorical flourishes and its distracting speculation about cognitive devolution' (Lilley 2001, p. 81). It could be suggested that this sort of rhetorical content is actually a powerful force in the production of meaning in scholarly texts, and that our representations of past peoples flow much more readily from our employment of rhetorical devices, abstract description and narrative reconstruction than from the presentation of the data on which they are based. What is more, these representations come ready-sanctioned with the imprimatur of 'science', and thus go on to carry considerable weight not only within our discipline but more broadly in non-academic discourses.

Over the past couple of decades archaeologists have begun to acknowledge the inherent textuality of our knowledge, realising that the way that we think about and write about the past is in part directed by our own culturally derived preconceptions, and that in writing as we do we inevitably participate in their reproduction (Bond & Gilliam 1994; Shanks & Tilley 1987b; Shennan 1989; Graves-Brown *et al.* 1996; Meskell 2002; see also David 2002 on the notion of 'preunderstanding'). It behoves us then to recognise that in publicly communicating our research findings we are also inevitably participating in the production of authoritative accounts of the past. These are taken up by other archaeologists and by those outside the discipline, and since histories are such an important element of identity construction they are influential in the development of representations of contemporary Indigenous peoples as well. While Australian anthropology has widely acknowledged the embeddedness of its own knowledge production, and of its representation of Indigenous peoples, within the politics of the colonial — and emergent post-colonial — world (e.g. Attwood & Arnold 1992; Beckett 1988; Finlayson 2001; see also Thomas 1990, 1994; Wolfe 1999; and more generally, Asad 1973; Fabian 1983; Stocking 1987), archaeologists have been less inclined to involve themselves in such debates (but see, for example, Byrne 1996; McNiven & Russell 1997, 2005; Russell & McNiven 1998, in addition to those cited above). Meskell (2002) has suggested that this reluctance derives from a largely unquestioned presumption that archaeology's subjects are 'dead and buried', and that the representation of living peoples is therefore no business of ours.

Australian archaeology's ambivalence regarding the representation of Indigenous pasts is apparent today in ways that echo the spirit of the arguments mobilised against Lourandos during the 1980s. These trends appear to have their origins in two distinct phenomena. The first is a tendency within Australian archaeology to take for granted the advances of the intensification era. This kind of complacency sees the intricacies of Lourandos' theoretical position virtually forgotten in favour of a more nonchalant incorporation of the empirical dimensions of intensification. The second factor — which is not necessarily causally related to the first — is a return to conservative values on Aboriginal issues more generally within the Australian nation, a growing trend in recent years to which the academy is unfortunately not immune. This right-wing critique is particularly vitriolic in its condemnation of recent liberal interpretations of post-invasion Aboriginal history. The ideological conflagration known colloquially as the 'history wars' has raged on both academic and popular fronts, fanned by the popularity of the revisionist backlash against the so-called 'black armband' history.

One recent episode has special salience for the archaeological community. Keith Windschuttle's (2002) ambitious and much criticised volume questioning the magnitude of colonial massacres of Indigenous Tasmanians draws on archaeological accounts in an attempt to portray the Aboriginal cultures of Tasmania as overwhelmingly simple, anarchic and inherently maladapted. In doing so, he relies heavily on the preliminary constructions of Rhys Jones (e.g. 1977b) and on some of the earlier histories on which Jones himself had based his reconstructions of Tasmanian Aboriginal society. While it has been repeatedly demonstrated (Murray & Williamson 2003; see also Breen 2003) that Windschuttle's use of the archaeological data is seriously flawed (to the extent that some details appear to be invented or transposed from unrelated contexts), it seems likely that he has at least drawn some comfort from the spirit in which Indigenous peoples were represented in some early archaeological writings. Although when confronted with the likes of Windschuttle's study our only real recourse is to subsequent critique and clarification, we ought perhaps to consider whether we do not also bear some responsibility for the creation and perpetuation of these kinds of representations of Indigenous peoples.

Representations beget representations. Once articulated, scholarly representations seem to have a life of their own, and may go on to be reproduced in discursive contexts far beyond their discipline of origin. Those that appeal to the popular imagination can become entrenched in 'commonsense' understandings of both the ancient past and contemporary Indigenous identities. Once established in popular discourse, such representations tend to generate considerable intellectual inertia, resisting revision long after they have passed from favour in their original context. We have only to reflect on the longevity of some of the most common popular tropes of the 'prehistoric' past — the shambling figure of the Neanderthal, perhaps, cast as the archetypal 'caveman', or the familiar notion of Aboriginal people as 'nomads', aimlessly wandering the harsh Australian landscape — to appreciate how this process operates. While it is unrealistic to believe that we can predetermine or control all the uses of the pasts we generate, we may choose to take an active, or even activist, role in disseminating or promoting within popular arenas those views of the Indigenous past which are considered more appropriate (Jones & Graves-Brown 1996, p. 19).

The representation of Indigenous 'others' is not merely incidental to archaeology. We *think* with such representations, they are theoretically embedded in the way we approach our subject matter; and we *write* with those representations, we produce and reproduce images of Indigenous peoples that have meaning both within and beyond the discipline. Only relatively recently have we begun to explore the implications of these understandings for archaeological practice, and the implications of our practice for Indigenous peoples (most notably in the 'One World Archaeology' series: see especially Bond & Gilliam 1994; Gathercole & Lowenthal 1990; Layton 1989, 1994; Shennan 1989; Torrence & Clarke 2000). Thus, we begin to recognise that the archaeological construction of the past is an inherently political act (Hodder, 1991; Shanks & Tilley 1987a, 1987b), and one which is never more potent than in the representation of Indigenous peoples and their histories in the context of colonial — and imminently post-colonial — nations (see Fabian 1983).

Conclusion

Harry Lourandos' intensification arguments, part of his broader commitment to a social archaeology of Aboriginal Australia, have had a profound impact on Australian archaeology. This is perhaps most readily apparent in the advent of a dedicated research agenda, based on these same theoretical principles, and having as its aim the further exploration of the processes responsible for the emergence of distinctive regional traditions and identities (see, for example, Barker 2004; David 2002; David & Chant 1995; McNiven 1999; Ross 1985; Williams 1987; see also David & Lourandos 1997, 1998, 1999). More broadly within Australian archaeology, however, there has been a tendency to engage differentially with each of the component parts of Lourandos' approach. While the empirical aspects of intensification have been widely accepted, forming the basis of the current 'continental narrative' of Aboriginal 'prehistory', the fate of its theoretical and representational counterparts has been less straightforward. Lourandos' theoretical explanation for intensification has received mixed responses, dictated for the most part by the pre-existing theoretical commitments of the Australian archaeological community. Notably, there have also been attempts to accommodate aspects of Lourandos' theoretical approach, particularly his emphasis on social dynamics, in the reformulation of more traditional models of cultural change based on environment, population increase and technology.

While the theoretical aspects of intensification are perhaps as contentious as they ever were, it seems that the language and concepts in which they were set forth have long since been quietly absorbed into the 'wordstream' of the discipline. The manifest ubiquity of the representational aspects of intensification gives the impression of a greater degree of consensus on past cultural change than is perhaps warranted. It seems that even those who do not agree with Lourandos tend to express themselves in ways that are largely in accord with his vision of Aboriginal peoples as dynamic, historical, diverse, complex, and so on — and often strangely at odds with the kind of traditional theoretical and explanatory structures to which many Australian archaeologists still cling. While the prevalence of Lourandos' style of representation is to be welcomed, since it is generally productive of more 'appropriate' constructions of the Aboriginal past, it is also indicative of a weakening of the overall structure of the intensification approach; it seems that the empirical and representational aspects of intensification have slipped their theoretical moorings.

The genius of Lourandos' intensification approach was its comprehensiveness; it encompassed methods for the identification and measurement of evidence for change, a sophisticated and densely theorised explanatory model that articulated well with the archaeological and ethnographic records, and resulted in a richer, more realistic and more respectful construction of Holocene Aboriginal history. Australian archaeology has benefited greatly from Lourandos' contribution, both in terms of its immediate applications and as a role model for more refined explanations of the archaeological past. However, there has also been a tendency to engage very selectively with this approach, and this has potentially problematic implications for its future integrity. Only with a renewed appreciation of the complexities of the entire intensification approach are we able to recognise the value of Lourandos' contribution, build on its solid foundation, and thus bring about richer, more satisfying representations of Aboriginal history.

Acknowledgements

I wish to thank the editors and two anonymous reviewers for reading and commenting on this paper; special thanks to Bryce Barker for editing above and beyond the call of duty. Thanks also to Kate Quirk and Angela Holden for lengthy discussions of some of the issues covered in this paper and for feedback on various draft versions. Errors of fact or judgement are entirely my own.

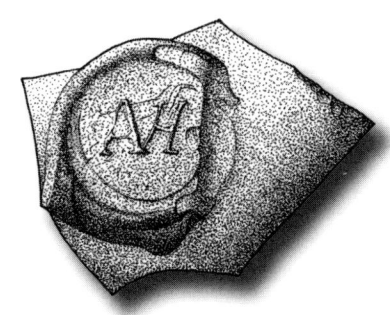

Part 3
Anthropological approaches

Glass scraper from a shell midden on Fraser Island, made from a fragment of Dutch gin bottle in the late 19th century.

8.
Footprints of the ancestors: the convergence of anthropological and archaeological perspectives in contemporary Aboriginal heritage studies

Luke Godwin and James F Weiner

Introduction: archaeology *contra* anthropology

Recent directions in archaeology indicate that a long overdue rapprochement between prehistory and social anthropology is vigorously underway. In the recent volume *Inscribed landscapes*, archaeologists Bruno David and Meredith Wilson begin with the tenet that the material marking of the earth occurs as a social practice. Landscapes are not simply inert backdrops or containers for the arrangement of human artefacts but are a product of a complex interaction between a symbolically and historically constituted human social world and a material environment (David & Wilson 2002, p. vii): 'Both people and place are co-defined in a process of engagement that involves inscription'. Places are not only marked through the physical act of marking but also — as part of the same process — 'through kin and *Story* ties that inscribe the self in place and place in the self' (Langton 2002b, p. 255).

This is not just a matter of the convergence of anthropology and archaeology in a new and more powerful materialism. Archaeologists themselves now acknowledge that they work in situations where they must take regard of the social and political dimensions of their interpretative tasks. They are being asked to comment not just on the material properties of artefacts and sites, but also on the social and political conditions under which the research was conducted in the first place. Exemplary among these is the work of Jones and White in examining the significance of the Ngilipitji quarry in eastern Arnhem Land, depicted in the film *Spear in the stone* (McKenzie 1983). The quarry was (and is) widely known throughout this region as the source of spear points prized for the power inhering in them, and material from the quarry was a vital element of the region's vibrant exchange network. Donald Thomson visited the quarry in the 1930s and collected numerous specimens of the fine points made there. Jones and White (1988) made special arrangements to visit the quarry with its traditional owners and to visually record them quarrying and knapping the material. The arrangements for this filming required extensive negotiations because there was real concern that *balanda* (non-Aboriginal people) could unwittingly disturb the spiritual essence of the site and perhaps capture some of its *mali* ('shade' or 'power') in the course of filming it. This would have had dire consequences for Yolngu and White people alike.[1]

In other words, the organization of the research itself is a social, political and cultural act that frames the archaeological inquiry as such. It is not limited to the accretion of our understanding of the stylistic or categorical features of the artefacts. The value that Aboriginal people place on material culture is likely to be very different than that of the archaeologist, and this fact must become a part of the survey rather than an adventitious comment upon it. It is noteworthy, however, that few archaeological reports prepared as part of academic research or as part of the environmental impact studies process have included any significant methodological acknowledgement of this contemporary sociopolitical act of framing.

The material dimension of Aboriginal social life

The subject matter and theorising of archaeology and anthropology have the opportunity to converge in Australia more thoroughly than anywhere else. At the heart of the classical Aboriginal world view is a concern with interpreting the material conditions and composition of the land.[2] The world was set down by the actions of ancestral creator beings whose actions, bodily substances, and tools forged the landscape and its features as current Aboriginal people inhabit it. Life, at once both religio-mythological and practico-economic, is a matter of reading marks and objects on the earth. These marks inform Aboriginal actors as to the nature of their food source and its environmental determinants, and the mythico-cosmological framework within which food-getting activities are defined.

Therefore, the conceptual life of Aboriginal people is always indexed by some material mark, sign or impression on the environment from which it is possible to infer the actions of beings — whether they be animals, humans, or creator beings. This most archaeological of premises thus becomes at the outset the anthropologist's subject matter.

At the level of ideology, Aboriginal people often maintain that the world was set down in its present form for all time:

> Every plant and animal of any economic value whatever forms a separate totem. Accordingly, if the myths gathered in the Northern Aranda area are treated collectively, a full and very detailed account will be found of all the occupations which are still being practised in Central Australia. In his myths we see the native at his daily task of hunting, fishing, gathering vegetable food, cooking, and fashioning his implements (Strehlow 1947, p.35).

However, the instrumental exigencies of following and hunting fauna, being attentive to the appearance of other edible species, and in general inferring the actions of people through the marks they leave on the earth, means that such a premise serves as a background against which the contemporary world of events takes place. Each act of food gathering in the present, each journey across the land, is a unique event in the life of a person, however much it is seen as 'following' the tracks laid down by the ancestors.

Moreover, writers such as Berndt (1970), and more recently Rumsey (1994), Myers (1986b), Merlan (1998) and Weiner *et al.* (2002), have shown that the historical events of contact history take their place within the mythico-cosmological recreation of the landscape. Ronald Berndt supervised some of his Margu and Gunwinggu informants of western Arnhem Land, Northern Territory, in the drawing of maps of sites on Croker Island, adjacent islands and the mainland. There had already been a mission on Croker Island and as Berndt says, 'all of these [Aboriginal] people are relatively sophisticated in European terms and have had intensive mission and other contact' (1970, p. 13). The people Berndt interviewed were asked to draw their own maps of sites in this area. On one sheet (No. 1, p. 16) a man inserted the following sites in succession:

> 1. Indjinaidj, Point David: waterhole. Sacred site of *jurwa*, the greenbacked turtle, metamorphosed in stone; 2. Djinan. Or 'Djmngan' Point; 115. Wunuri or Gwunjuri: camp and hunting centre; 116. Gadjungunjan camp; 117. Wagiwagaid camp; 118. Wurul camp.; 147. Water runs down from the 'the nine Mile' to Warilidj, which is a good area for hunting possum and collecting wild honey; 151. A tall stone or rock which is Chickenpox Dreaming, *miamia*. It is strictly tabu; 152. Maramara, on a small creek: good hunting area; 153. Aragadji, where Alfred Brown, a Customs official whose depot was at Bowen Strait, kept his goats; he also collected trepang here. (Berndt 1970, p.15)

The striking thing about this sequence of sites is how, literally side-by-side, there reside a sacred mythological creature, camping site, hunting place, an obvious post-settlement Dreaming site (e.g. 'Chickenpox Dreaming') and the site of European settlement and subsistence (Mr Brown's goat herd and trepang-collecting place). These places do not exist separately from each other — they are linked along the same pathway of movement, experience and memory for the Aboriginal persons who follow them, know them, carry out tasks along them, and describe them to others. The 'new' sites must have emerged almost immediately in Aboriginal people's experience of these tracks and were promptly incorporated into the sequence.

Cultural continuity

One of the major dilemmas facing Aboriginal people today in Australia is this: although there is now in place legislation that affords them a means of protecting their material heritage and recognising their native title, the interpretations of Aboriginal law, custom, social organisation and cultural activity under this legislation takes place squarely within the Euro-Australian cultural and legal framework. Significantly, there is no nationally encompassing legal recognition of Aboriginal customary law.

Under the Commonwealth *Native Title Act 1993*, Aboriginal claimants are required to demonstrate that they have maintained continuity of connection to country, and continuity of their traditional law and custom. Unless these continuities are demonstrated, their relations to and activities on their ancestral lands will not be accepted as evidence of the maintenance of their native title rights and interests. Although recent interpretations — for example in the High Court cases of *Yorta Yorta* and *Ward* — have in theory at least accepted that culture and tradition undergo transformation through time, Aboriginal people still bear the burden of having to demonstrate continuity of contemporary cultural practices with those inferred to have been regnant at the time of sovereignty.

In this chapter, we describe two examples of contemporary Aboriginal interpretation of tracks, artefacts and other material traces on the earth. We demonstrate that this interpretative practice has emerged without substantive conceptual interruption from the classic mythico-cosmological practices of reading tracks and traces, and that events in historical time continue to be read as instantiations of ancestral power, even among those Aboriginal groups for whom the colonial experience appears to have had the most profoundly altering effect on their traditional life. In so doing, we argue that the apparent differential time frames that distinguish anthropological analysis from archaeological analysis are illusory, and that both modes of interpreting material life must take account of the historical world of event and cultural transformation.

Interpreting actions on Country

The evidence presented in the *Yorta Yorta* native title claim demonstrated that Aboriginal people throughout settled Australia interpret richness of artefactual remains — and the consequent evidence of high-density settlement sites — as significant in and of themselves. They reason that any site so rich in resources as to afford repeated occupation must have been special and sacred, in the sense that evidence of fecundity is everywhere interpreted as religiously and totemically significant. They go on to reason, not altogether groundlessly, that such settlement sites must also have had ceremonial grounds nearby. They seek to protect and maintain the residue of such human and natural fecundity by acknowledging the importance and sacred qualities of such sites — much as they would judge a site sacred by the implied presence of ancestral spirits described above.

In the *Yorta Yorta* decision[3], Justice Howard Olney discussed what he called the 'main thrust of contemporary activity' by members of the native title claim group (at 122). At 128 he stated:

> Preservation of Aboriginal heritage and conservation of the natural environment are worthy objectives the achievement of which may lead to a more ready understanding and recognition of the importance of the culture of . . . indigenous people but in the context of a native title claim the absence of a continuous link back to the laws and customs of the original inhabitants deprives those activities of the character of traditional laws acknowledged and traditional customs observed in relation to land and waters which is a necessary element of both the statutory and the common law concept of native title rights and interests.

These judgements are made from a peculiar view of 'contemporary' Aboriginal 'tradition'. Aboriginal people, it appears, can only have an interest in artefactual remains from an exclusively 'archaeological' perspective. They are not free to interpret and re-interpret their prehistorical record in line with changing conditions of the present (as westerners have continuously re-interpreted Egyptian sites, the Dead Sea Scrolls, Olduvai Gorge, and so forth). Native title rights and interests, on the other hand, must relate decisively to a pre-colonial Aboriginal tradition, even though it has been accepted since the *Mabo 2* decision that tradition does change and has changed over time. Contemporary interest by Aboriginal people in the archaeological record of their forebears is, therefore, by definition *not* part of pre-colonial tradition. No matter how strenuously or seriously the activity of heritage protection is carried out by an Aboriginal community, and no matter how central such activities are to the community's self-identity and its social and normative functioning, they cannot support a case for the continuity of Aboriginal law and custom over time. Although this judgement does not do justice to the real dimensions of contemporary Aboriginal interpretations of their past, it has not yet been successfully challenged in court.

Justice Olney's judgement refuses the historical dimension of 'emplacement' in human life, and in particular, Aboriginal life. It does not sufficiently focus on the *temporal* significance of place: that is, how places serve as foci or anchor points of activities and patterns of habitation over time. It is from these habitual activities that we construe the patterns of action, customs and laws that substantively comprise a local Aboriginal cultural and social community. In this anthropological view, places are accorded significance insofar as they are sites of repetitive and culturally patterned *actions* and *behaviours* that support and maintain the discreteness of the community and their attachment to a particular country.

In an important sense Justice Olney's judgement concerning the difference between archaeological and Aboriginal significance parallels what we identify as the previous incommensurability between anthropological and archaeological interpretations of artefactual remains. For in both cases, his judgement attempts to insulate our knowledge of the past from any meaningful insight achieved in the present. It denies that the meaning of past events and their material remains is always a process occurring in the present. In this paper, we therefore construe a present-oriented view of the past that illuminates and preserves the cultural framework within which Aboriginal people are emplaced in the present, and use this as both a model and product of a successful fusion of anthropology and archaeology.

Aboriginal interpretations of artefactual remains

We now turn to a description of the topics and methods that would comprise an anthropological archaeology in which the perception of persistence and longevity is a genuine social articulation in a contemporary community. To repeat our premise, we assume that archaeological and historical time frames are everywhere instaurated in 'customs and practices' in the present, and previous events and artefacts, no matter how ancient, must be perceived to have had an effect on social practices in the present. In contemporary Australian Aboriginal communities, some of these practices include the birthplace, burial sites, footprints, and massacre sites.

Birthplace

The 'cosmological time' of the Dreaming was always experienced through the 'historical' events of any human society — birth, death, coming of age and so forth. These punctuations of the human life span continue to be key structural points for the construction of historical and cultural narratives in Aboriginal society. In pre-colonial times the most important of these 'historical' events was the place of one's birth — the propinquity of the totemic ancestor is thought to have caused the woman's pregnancy:

> It is true that the totemic clans from which the individual owners spring exert certain rights over the local *tjurunga* of which no accident of 'conception' can deprive them . . . But the conception site occupies by far the most important place in all the complex arguments which centre around the possession of the myths, chants, ceremonies, and sacred objects owned by a large local totemic clan. (Strehlow 1947, p.87)

These days, the place of one's birth, or the birth of one's ancestors, is taken as a primary indication of one's affiliation to country.

Burial sites

Known burial places of Aboriginal people are among the most significant contemporary sites that Aboriginal people in settled Australia recognise and desire to protect today. Uniformly among Indigenous communities of settled Australia, the presence of burial sites implies the presence of ancestral spirits. Ancestral spirits play an important role in the exercise of traditional law and custom, and in particular in the maintenance of publicly acknowledged rights in country; a person will be very reluctant to travel onto land he or she knows to be the abode of ancestral spirits not their own, without asking permission from the living relatives of the spirits or being accompanied by them. To do otherwise might invite supernatural punishment, such as illness or misfortune.

Likewise, the possibility that burial sites might be damaged or interfered with by development activities is taken most seriously by Aboriginal custodians. Damage to human remains are seen to have adverse effects on the well-being of spirits and the nature of their predisposition towards the living.

Footprints

The known places of habitation of ancestors, and the traces of their life activity that they left behind — whether these actions took place in mythical or historical time — constitute a record of occupation of country for any Aboriginal local community. Dreaming sites are sites in the landscape where the actions of Dreaming beings were permanently inscribed into the landscape. Usually this results in some notable or unusual formation, and the formation is often thought to resemble the incident, action, or object that created the site itself. What we identify as 'footprints of the ancestors' bears some similarity, but is not identical to the more conventionally understood Aboriginal concept of the 'Dreaming track'.

'Footprints of the ancestors' is how many contemporary Aboriginal people characterise these material remains of deceased ancestors. The presence of such material remains makes a very important contribution towards humanising and historicising the landscape for virtually all Aboriginal communities, particularly in settled Australia.

Massacre sites

Places where Aboriginal ancestors were killed as a result of frontier violence constitute one of the most important and impassioned categories of contemporary 'sacred' places for all Indigenous communities in Australia. Firstly, such places are heavily populated by the spirits of the people killed there. These spirits are considered by the Koori and Murri peoples of the east and south-east to be very sensitive, and still bear the grief and terror of their passing. These spirits remain extremely sensitive to disturbances and improper or disrespectful behaviour at such places. They often seek to communicate their sorrow to living people who visit the place. Secondly, we suggest there is often a perception of consubstantiality between shed blood and the earth, such that the earth has been hallowed by the shedding of ancestors' blood and the mingling of their flesh with the earth itself. This perception would be analogous and quite possibly related to the consubstantial dimension of the traditional process — that by which sacred sites were commonly brought into being by the shedding of bodily substance by ancestral creator beings. Thirdly, as is the case with sites of significant human death throughout human cultures, there is the contemporary determination to not allow such events to erode in human memory. Indigenous people's desire to acknowledge, mark and record such sites are actions taken against the possibility of forgetting, and to protect such sites from profanation, inadvertent or otherwise, by other people.

One of the differences between the footprints of the ancestors and the Dreaming sites along an ancestral track is in regard to selectivity. Nowhere in the literature on conventional Dreaming tracks is it suggested that every spot along the track is equally sacred or significant, or that every action in which the ancestor was engaged was thought to have resulted in the creation of a sacred site. However, with respect to contemporary interpretations of artefactual remains in settled Australia where such detailed myth complexes are no longer part of the cultural repertoire, it is clear that each and every piece of stone and remain associated with human activity — from the stone implements themselves to the waste flakes and chips, to casually manuported stones — all are imbued with significance. These material remains—stone artefacts of all sorts, rock-art sites, carved and scarred trees, etc. — are thought to have sacred or spiritual qualities. Interfering with these remains in an inappropriate way is tantamount to sacrilege or desecration of the artefacts and, through them, the ancestors themselves.

Case 1: Waanyi and Gangalidda, Gulf of Carpentaria

The first case study draws on work undertaken with the Waanyi people and involved a survey of a proposed optic-fibre cable route from the Century Mine to Doomadgee in Queensland. Although ostensibly undertaken under the provisions of the *Cultural Record (Landscapes Queensland and Queensland Estate) Act 1987* — with its focus on material culture meeting the narrow definition of Items of the Queensland Estate — the survey did not restrict itself purely to the archaeological. Rather, a broad definition of cultural heritage was adopted wherein we were to record any cultural places or values of archaeological, anthropological, historical or contemporary significance to the relevant Aboriginal people.

A communications infrastructure company negotiated directly with the Waanyi and Gangalidda people regarding the conduct of the necessary cultural heritage investigations. The critical points to emerge from these negotiations were: a formal agreement that provided for the groups to conduct the studies under culturally appropriate governance structures; selection of people to be involved in the studies in accordance with that governance structure; selection of the technical advisers they wished to work with them in documenting the cultural places and values; and appropriate control of the information generated from this study, i.e. that it would remain the property of the Waanyi and Gangalidda and could only be used as agreed between themselves and the company for management purposes.

Aboriginal personnel chosen for the survey met one major criterion: they were seen by the larger group as having the necessary links to the country by birth, totemic association and knowledge of country. Crew membership changed not on the basis of equity of distance, number of days or amount of pay, but primarily on who were the appropriate people to be conducting the work and making decisions about that piece of country. Rates of pay were linked to a person's ritual status. A team varying from four to six people inspected almost the entire route. This number is not to be taken as an indication of the number of people traditionally responsible for sections of country, nor of the Traditional Owners' preferred level of participation. Rather, it represented a reluctant compromise based upon commercial considerations, the narrowness of the infrastructure corridor and the fact that site avoidance was the preferred management strategy.

Predictably, stone artefact scatters dominated finds, while two substantial quarries were also recorded. Numerous excellent examples of intact knapping floors were also seen. There also were concentrations of cultural material that included middens, hearths, artefact scatters (which included grinding equipment), and scarred trees that suggested distinct habitation areas where a range of activities were carried out.

Of course, the cultural landscape not only has a material dimension, but is alive as a mythico-religious one as well. A dominant figure is Budjimala — the rainbow serpent who inhabits Lawn Hill Creek — who can, if one acts inappropriately, be easily disturbed, leading to unforeseeable consequences. There were also several places associated with important dreamings, notably including Barngalinyi (a place where there are eggs of the catfish in the creek), and another ceremonial place associated with the Catfish Dreaming. Dangerous places associated with malevolent beings that have to be avoided by those who are not suitably knowledgeable were also recorded. Provisions were set in the management plan to restrict activities in the vicinity of such places so as to protect the developer's personnel: a form of Aboriginal occupational health and safety, as it were, for those on their country.

The individuals on the survey were well aware of the limits of their authority. At several points they chose to not make decisions about the desirability of the route and the acceptable limits of change along it, preferring to defer to those they saw as having a stronger right, competence or authority in such cases. Thus, a case in which the route passed close to part of a major Dreaming site required a second visit by more senior people. Importantly, deferment was also the preferred decision of the field team in relation to some places where occurrences of cultural material were encountered. In these cases, the issues revolved around the impact of the proposed development on places or items associated with the 'old people' and it is on some of these instances we now wish to focus. So, for instance, an extended section of the route included a huge quarry, artefact scatters, middens and hearths running down to Lawn Hill Creek. The field team decided that the clear evidence of the importance of the area to the 'old people' was reason enough to refer the matter on to their own senior people for adjudication.

One of the quarries we found turned out to be in extremely close proximity to a place where one of the field team had experienced *bari bari*, a ball of light travelling through the air. One of the features of the *bari bari* is that it can be controlled by 'clever' men (i.e. men holding a high level of knowledge of

Aboriginal Law) and can be 'sung' (or directed) deep into a person's body creating a physical sensation of burning. It can then only be removed by another clever man. Given the proximity of the member's experience to the quarry, there was a view that senior people should visit the location to pass judgement, as it was considered that there may have been a clever man associated with the quarry who was attempting to protect it by use of *bari bari*.

Later in the survey, and following a change in the field team, one new member (the generally recognised *jungai*, or manager, for the area) related a story about a particular Waanyi person who had become sick, and subsequently died, after collecting stone artefacts and carrying them away from that country. The generally accepted cause of sickness and death, or alternatively insanity, was that the 'old people' can sing artefacts, and that this singing can continue to reside in the artefacts long after the physical passing of the 'old people'. This event was told in the context of examining a single snapped blade beside a station track. Critically, the point being made did not have any reference to the size or complexity of a site or site complex, only to the apparently mundane artefacts themselves.

Case 2: Ghungalu and Kangoulu, central Queensland

Our second case study is from Central Queensland, an area of great contact violence towards, and dispossession and displacement of, the Aboriginal people of that country. Here, the authors undertook extensive cultural heritage investigations prior to the development of new coal reserves in the Blackwater area. The work was undertaken in conjunction with the Ghungalu and Kangoulu people, claimants for that area. The study area has the single greatest concentration of cultural material, and has the greatest diversity of cultural remains, observed anywhere in the entire Bowen Basin, an area of over 80 000 km^2.

The survey of the area proceeded with six representatives of the involved claimant groups. On its conclusion these representatives reported to their elders at general meetings on the results of the survey, noting the large amounts and diverse nature of the material. The elders then concluded that this was an extremely significant area for their people. Following this, a general inspection of the area was arranged. On arrival the nest of a native bee was observed, and the bees buzzed around people for the duration of the visit. This was interpreted in the following fashion: the native bee is the *yuri* (totem) of a Ghungalu person who is one of the acknowledged apical ancestors for their claim. Now, being long deceased, he is one of the 'old people'. The presence of the nest and the bees was a demonstration that he was present — watching over the area and watching the behaviour of his descendants — and served to reinforce the conclusion already reached about the area, namely that it was of great cultural significance.

In another example, a non-Ghungalu person behaved in a way that was seen as disrespectful at another artefact scatter. It was necessary to cleanse him by 'smoking', not just as a punishment but also to ensure that the 'old people' did not pursue and torment him. We have documented several cases in which people sickened and even died as a result of inappropriate handling or otherwise dealing with cultural material, or because people undertook survey work on country that was not theirs. In all cases it was seen as retribution from the 'old people' for the disrespect shown to them by such actions.

Discussion

As we have shown, there is considerable consistency between the Waanyi and Ghungalu in regard to their attitudes and beliefs about the material remains of past activities of those they call the 'old people'. But who are these 'old people'? They are the spirits of the Waanyi and Ghungalu ancestors that continue to inhabit their countries. The cultural sites found in their 'country' are, to Waanyi and Ghungalu people, a physical demonstration that their 'old people' have been there, and continue to be there: in this respect, the sites are their footprint. This is a widely shared view in many parts of Queensland and New South Wales. These material objects are not only a tangible link to their past; they are directly situated within the currently extant cosmology of these people and must be handled within a distinctly cultural context that has clear continuity with classical cosmological practices. Thus, we suggest that while the current interest and involvement in the management of cultural heritage places and values is undoubtedly undertaken within current legal and technical parameters, it is a contemporary manifestation of traditional practices and conventions of cultural custodianship.

The picture we have painted in relation to these apparently mundane materials is by no means restricted to these two groups. Thus, comments made by Cribb (no date) about the huge shell middens found in western Cape York bear attention. He suggests that the process of piling shells into these massive mounds appears in part at least to be driven by cultural factors. Thus, to scatter shell is to create an untidy country that shows little respect for oneself, one's ancestors and those to come. Moreover, to scatter shell around in such a fashion would be to invite 'spearing by the traditional people', that is, those who have gone before and are now dead but resident as spirits. The middens also serve as an increase site not just for shellfish, but for the people themselves. To damage such sites is to directly affect the spiritual, emotional and physical health of the people who own those places.

In both the above cases, the Aboriginal people were involved in work associated with what we can loosely call the 'EIS process'. The question to be asked is this: is the interest in these cultural places and values, and the method of management, part of a corpus of customary practices that is consistent with the maintenance of native title?

In considering this question we must squarely face the challenge posed by observations made in the *Yorta Yorta* case. In his published decision Justice Olney noted in the first Federal Court judgement that, while taking a strong interest in the protection of certain categories of cultural places was admirable, it did not constitute a proof of the maintenance of traditional custodial roles. This was because, in the past, the types of places now being protected and managed were not of importance to Aboriginal people, and therefore the current interest was a recent invention that had no links to traditional law and custom. Following this line of reasoning, in the cases we have cited it could then be suggested that — while damaging similar sites without appropriate mitigation might be proscribed by state law — it does not constitute an issue for arbitration in native title because these sites and places are not part of that native title. Thus, any impact on them is not a matter for consideration beyond the need to operate within the context of existing state cultural heritage legislation. It is our view that this overly reduces and misrepresents what is a far more complex issue.

In Aboriginal society there is no static list of places that are deemed to be culturally important. People regularly have special experiences on their country, and regularly dream about places and things on that country. These experiences and dreams are then offered or described to older, knowledgeable people for their reflection and interpretation. In this context, pre-existing knowledge of cultural places beforehand does not exhaust the potential for cosmologically significant events in the present regarding country. Dependent on the outcome of that adjudication, places and events associated with them can then be added to a corpus of places that are seen as important, demanding special attention and response from people: that is, those places must be managed. For example, there are along the proposed fibre-optic route in Waanyi country an exceptional range of cultural places and values, material or otherwise. The Aboriginal researchers duly reported this to ritually senior individuals who gave the matter considerable thought and direct attention through field inspection. While other aspects of the mythico-religious landscape have certainly drawn their attention, so too has the duty of care they owe to the material culture (as a manifestation of the 'old people') been to the forefront in their deliberations.

Why does it appear only now that this association or linkage to these 'archaeological' sites emerged? We think there are three factors at play. The first harks back to the disciplinary divide we touched on earlier, in which archaeologists were not necessarily well informed from an anthropological perspective, and anthropologists likewise had interests that did not necessarily focus on the material dimension of human behaviour that is the natural domain of archaeologists. Thus, there was only limited cross-fertilisation, as it were. The second factor concerns the focus on the material dimension of cultural heritage legislation, certainly as it was developed and applied in the eastern states. This is the preserve of archaeologists, who took the running in EIS-related cultural heritage management. It is still largely the case in Queensland, New South Wales and Victoria that such work has an almost exclusively archaeological focus. In other states and territories, where the archaeological paradigm did not reign supreme in heritage legislation, the disciplinary divide still remained: archaeologists dealing with the material dimension and anthropologists the metaphysical, although this is starting to break down. The final factor concerns the way in which Aboriginal people, even where they might have been involved in fieldwork, have been marginal to the larger process of documenting and devising management strategies, at least until the recent past. It is only since the mid-1990s that they have assumed a more prominent role in the process, affording them the opportunity to see what is going on, situate it within their own cultural beliefs, and seek to influence management based on that knowledge and those beliefs.

We would now like to turn briefly to some implications of the above argument. Clearly, the ostensibly mundane archaeological material dismissed as rubbish or discard — and thus perceived to be of little significance to most people other than archaeologists — occupies quite a different place in the world view of Aboriginal people. In various ways, places where such materials occur are integrated into the cosmology of Aboriginal people: that is, there is some sacred dimension to them. The Queensland Government has passed legislation through the parliament: the *Aboriginal Cultural Heritage Act 2003*. This legislation uses the clumsy and simplistic device of separating cultural places and information into two categories: the secret/sacred domain, and the open/unrestricted domain. If places or information reside in the former, it does not have to be disclosed, but where it sits in the open domain it must be released to the government, which in turn can release it to others it deems have an interest by virtue of wanting to use the land in question for some purpose. Clearly, there is some view that large amounts of data will be open, and that only a small body will fall in the category of secret/sacred. But the relation between public and restricted in contemporary Indigenous communities is not a fixed and static category: it is a dimension of a still vital and functioning cosmological system of perception and action. From this perspective, the Queensland legislation fails statutorily to capture and protect the living and progressive nature of this system and its living human adherents.

Acknowledgements

Portions of this paper were presented at the 2002 Australian Archaeological Association annual meeting and the 2003 Australian Anthropological Society annual meeting. We thank Peter Veth for comments on an earlier draft of this paper.

Notes

1. Aboriginal references to the rock at the quarry are described in terms of human kidney fat, but with the additional inside or restricted meaning of 'power'. It is this power that makes the points from this quarry so good, because it is this property that confers the great killing power of the points as they sap the life from the target. Even knapping the stone can be dangerous: people are at risk of cutting themselves and drawing blood, and this is attributed to the inherent power in the rock. Rock from other quarries does not have this fat, and, as a consequence, those quarries are considered inferior sources.
2. The classic accounts of the Aboriginal myth-ritual-land complex include, for example, Strehlow (1947), Berndt (1970), Spencer and Gillen (1904, 1938), Munn (1973).
3. The Members of the Yorta Yorta Aboriginal Community v The State of Victoria & Ors 1606 FAC.

9.
Earth, wind, fire and water: the social and spiritual construction of water in Aboriginal societies

Marcia Langton

Introduction

In the cosmologies of Australian Aboriginal peoples, water is a sacred and elemental source and symbol of life. Throughout the continent we find Aboriginal people observing, studying, naming and attributing meanings and significance to large and small phenomena inherent in water bodies and forms (Buku-Larrngay Mulka Centre 1999; Langton 2002a; McNiven 2003; Rose 2004; Sharp 1996, 1997, 2000, 2002; Williams & Baines 1993). That most elusive of substances — water — is the focus of this account of present-day Aboriginal stewardship of their coastal and river-basin landscapes, transformed during the nineteenth and twentieth centuries from the Holocene homelands of several Australian language groups to post-colonial cattle-grazing rangelands (Strang 1997).

In this chapter I discuss some of the Aboriginal traditions practiced in relation to water bodies, the ontology of waterscapes that is revealed in these practices, and the social nature of water with respect to some Aboriginal tenure relations in the Laura Basin on the Cape York Peninsula. The traditional Aboriginal knowledge of both water and fire that is entailed in these management practices is expressed in a variety of ways, not all of which can be discussed here. By focusing on particular social constructs of people-water relations in the Laura Basin, and the agency of the Aboriginal protagonists who explained these traditions, I hope to reveal the more subtle social elements of present-day Aboriginal landscape management in the area. Three powerful characteristics of the Aboriginal relationships with their environments emerge from the humanistic approach (Ingold 1993, p. 172) of my ethnographic efforts: cognition, sociality and temporality.

Water

Water is manifest in several obvious ways, and human engagements with these forms are amenable to observation and measurement: the flow of rivers, the surge of tides, precipitation. Less easily observable incidents involve the daily and hourly prediction of dewfall — and its exploitation as an inhibitor of the cool anthropogenic fire fronts — or the seasonally changing water content of grasses. The use of water bodies (rivers, lakes and lagoons) as firebreaks may not at first seem to be deliberate and planned; nor would the use of the predictable late-afternoon lapse in the wind in the dry season as a fire inhibitor be seen as intentional. Yet these inconspicuous events involving the application of traditional knowledge to large-scale landscape management are profoundly important for the ethnographic record. They tell us about cognitive engagements of people with physical environments that would escape the attention of archaeologists and scientists relying solely on measurable physical evidence. Even less discernible to the scientific gaze are the social and temporal (including religious and spiritual) aspects of such engagements and practices.

Economic approaches to pre–European contact history have evolved from an initial view of prehistoric Australians as simple foragers to a greater understanding of the complex connections between the social and physical dimensions of resource exploitation in hunting and gathering societies. Several archaeologists have used ecologically and economically rationalist models — such as optimality models — to ascertain the range of strategies used in food production. Others have studied the degree of intensification of food production contributing to accumulated social wealth, changes in settlement patterns, and increased site usage (Lourandos 1997, pp. 296–305); population growth (Beaton 1983, p. 96); and social complexity and diversification of tool and other material culture and human environmental impacts (e.g. Bowman 1998) to explain temporal trends in Australia's long Aboriginal history.

As anthropologist Tim Ingold (1993, p. 172) asked: 'What is archaeology the study *of*?' His answer: 'I believe there is no better answer than "the temporality of landscape"'. Ingold proposed 'the perspective of dwelling' as a discovery procedure to ascertain meaning in landscape by recognising its temporality:

> Only through such recognition by temporalizing the landscape can we move beyond the division that has afflicted most inquiries up to now, between the 'scientific' study of an atemporalized nature, and the 'humanistic' study of a dematerialized history. And no discipline is better placed to take this step than archaeology. (Ingold 1993, p. 172)

Ethnographic and ethnohistorical studies have enriched archaeological analysis of the evidentiary record. For instance, Terrell (2002) regards 'inherited friendships' and social networks across large-scale landscapes as a critical factor in the agro-forestry of coastal Papua New Guinea. Thomson (1939) identified differential resource use in both the temporal and spatial scales. His observations of seasonality as a characteristic of Aboriginal people's resource use in Cape York Peninsula, and his observations of their movements from coastal to interior areas, alerted archaeologists to a greater complexity in Australian economic life than was previously assumed.

Among the several Australian archaeologists who recognised the social dimensions of such changes in the archaeological record, Harry Lourandos has been an eminently influential exponent of several important ideas. For Lourandos, discovery of greatly increased density and intensity of human occupation, social relations and ceremonial life in the Holocene sparked a re-examination of the evidence (Lourandos 1983b, p. 91). Lourandos (1997, pp. 20–21) was also concerned with the distribution of groups of people across landscapes, rethinking assumptions about residence and logistical food-harvesting strategies, thus building on previous studies in Australian societies. Lourandos' work on eel irrigation and swamp management in western Victoria (Lourandos 1987b; 1997, pp. 216–22) led to a new understanding of Aboriginal exploitation and management of water resources which is pertinent to the history of people's engagement with, and stewardship of, the coastal plains and valleys of coastal eastern Cape York Peninsula. The environmental changes that came about in the Princess Charlotte Bay area during the mid-to-late Holocene critically altered coastlines, waterways and rainfall patterns, and these must have also been fundamental in shaping the way that the local societies institutionalised their land and water tenure and property relationships. In presenting an anthropological view of Aboriginal understandings of water and waterscapes, as informed by local indigenous Elders and other individuals from local Aboriginal communities in the late twentieth century, my aim is to introduce into the ethnographic record their own accounts of their engagement with waterscapes to enrich the archaeological historicization of Australian landscapes as human domains (see David *et al.* 1994).

The people and environments of Princess Charlotte Bay

Within the Laura Basin region are the homelands of several Aboriginal language-speaking groups — the Guugu Yimithirr, the Lamalama, the Alu Aya (or Kuku Thaypan), the so-called 'Koko Warra', and the people of Barrow Point, among others[1] — that once flourished before the colonial encounter. Rigsby (1992, p. 354) states that:

> In the Aboriginal view, the landscape consists of hundreds of 'countries', named tracts or sites, including streams, swamps, lagoons, certain saltpans and sand ridges, islands and reefs. Country names often label focal sites as well as their surrounding areas.

In the late twentieth century these societies were represented by named family groupings, their members residing in small communities located in an arc around the region and asserting their connections to homelands both through descent from named ancestors and language affiliation.

These social traditions are practiced in a particular type of environment, a dry-adapted tropical savanna with rich and complex environments in the riverine areas of the hinterland and along the coastlines. Anthropologists Athol Chase and Peter Sutton, in their studies of the ecological processes of coastal peoples of eastern Cape York Peninsula, observed 'the considerable range of interactions across a variety of coastal habitats' (Chase & Sutton 1981, p. 1819):

> Due to its length and progressive narrowness, the Peninsula provides an extraordinary length of coastline in proportion to its area. In its central area north of Princess Charlotte Bay, the most remote inland location is only some seventy miles from either coastline, and the large western sea inlets at the mouths of such rivers such as the Archer and the Wenlock reduce the distance from saltwater even further. Because of this geography, the great majority of Aboriginal populations inhabited the coastal margins.

This vast, broad triangular peninsula landform was shaped during a time 'well within the presumed span of human occupation of the area' (Beaton 1985, p. 1; see also Beaton 1979) when the late-Pleistocene/early-Holocene sea-level rise flooded the broad peri-coastal continental shelf and changed it from a terrestrial plain to a shallow and rich marine ecosystem, now part of the Great Barrier Reef province. The sea level rose (and eventually stabilised some 5–6000 years BP) to a level close to that of today, separating what is now the Flinders Island group from its parent landform, the Bathurst Range. Nothing is known of the social impact of this 'event' on the Aboriginal population(s) of the area, although something of the alterations to their environments are now understood (Beaton 1985; Grindrod et al. 1999; Crowley et al. 1994; Woodroffe & Grindrod 1991).

Cape York Peninsula has a distinctive annual climatic pattern of a wet monsoonal season followed by a dry season (see Ridpath & Corbett 1985; Williams et al., 2002 p. 13). The heaviest rainfalls are from January to late March/early April, ranging from an annual average of 800 mm in the south to 2400 mm along parts of the coast. The plains of Cape York are frequently inundated. The native vegetation includes eucalypt forest but eucalypt, melaleuca and acacia woodlands are the most extensive vegetation types (Williams *et al.* 2002, p. 13).

Several Elders explained to me that Aboriginal groups in the region recognise six seasons, in contrast to the common understanding of a 'wet' and a 'dry' season. (I shall, however, use the commonly understood terms 'wet' and 'dry' in my descriptions below.) Rigsby and Williams (1991) report climatic conditions in relation to their discussion of Aboriginal seasonal burning practices:

> The yearly cycle is not uniform with respect to rainfall and temperature. A pronounced monsoon or wet season generally lasts from January through April, when the prevailing wind is from the northwest and the mornings often are calm and clear — good times to hunt dugongs and turtles safely and easily. By June the dry season is well under way and the prevailing winds — the southeast trade winds — can blow for days at a time at 30 knots or more. By late June and July, the nights are quite cool. By August the weather warms up; temperatures and humidity are at their most uncomfortable levels. By late November into January, the storms build up before the monsoon sets in again. The wet season is a good time to camp at the beach because food and fresh water are plentiful and easy to procure.
>
> The wet season also sees great vegetational growth; the grasses grow tall and rank on the savanna and plains areas as well as in the fringes of the scrubs. When the wet season ends and particular areas dry out, the men begin to set them alight. (Rigsby & Williams 1991, pp. 12–13).

The south-eastern coast of the peninsula is a rain catchment area, a result of the Great Dividing Range which runs like a spine from the northeast central area of the peninsula and onwards down the south-eastern coast, forming a long series of ranges and foothills that extend to the southernmost part of the Australian continent. The south-eastern area of the Peninsula has the highest rainfall in the region and supports areas of tropical rainforest. A poor or early end to the wet season can lead to difficult conditions late in the dry season. Rivers that run east tend to be shorter and fall more steeply to the coast, whereas those flowing west are longer and fall more slowly. The land becomes less undulating the further west one travels from the Great Dividing Range until one reaches the almost-flat depositional plains of the west coast. In addition to the river catchments, plains predominate; there are also extensive rolling and hilly lands and some mountains (Williams *et al.* 2002, p. 13). River systems are formed by the water flows in the upper reaches of the ranges and traverse both the eastern and western coastal plains (Frith & Frith 1995, pp. 32–3).

In the Great Dividing Range the headwaters of the rivers in the area of study begin on a large sandstone plateau known by some as 'the Desert'. The Desert forms a hub from which five rivers flow: the King, Alice and Coleman rivers flow south-west and west into the Gulf of Carpentaria; the Hann and Morehead rivers flow northeast into Princess Charlotte Bay (Trezise 1993, p. 86). The coastal plains include vast tidal wetlands, including mudflats, brackish estuaries and inlets, saline claypans and saltflats, and brackish lakes with varying degrees of access to the open sea. These estuarine wetlands might be immersed by the daily tide, and during spring tides or high spring tides they combined with seasonal freshwater flooding.

Aboriginal ontologies of waterscapes

Bodies of water are constituted by Aboriginal people as being more than just a physical domain. They are construed spiritually, socially and jurally, according to the same fundamental principles as affiliations to terrestrial places in the land; the dialogic relationship in Indigenous thought between the ancestral past and its effect on human existence derives from the Aboriginal understanding of the transformative powers of the spiritual beings that inhabit those places, whether a landscape, waterscape or skyscape. For Aboriginal people, the distinctions between land and water are not absolute; rather, they are constituted as a cultural space that includes both land and water bodies that may be viewed as a unitary cultural phenomenon, such as a traditional estate in a littoral riparian or marine area, or a water body believed to be the resting place of an ancestral being and deemed to be a sacred site. In eastern Cape York Peninsula, where this distinctly Aboriginal ontology remains the basis of people-environment relations, there is a pattern of particular social relations with significant cultural places in wetlands and around water sources. Indigenous resource use is guided by water availability — that is, the types of waterscapes and their locations — whose location, bounty, dangers and other characteristics are understood as being predetermined by the sacred past.

Pama (or Murri), as the people of this region generically refer to themselves, reckon their affiliations with land through their descent from ancestral beings, and so too do they reckon such affiliations with water places. That is, relations with water are always social relations, but so too are they always ontological — relating to how the world is known and understood — and spiritual relations. In order to understand local cultural perceptions of place and environment — in this case, water places — it is necessary to understand the local traditions of performative engagement with water places and local accounts of those engagements (*cf.* Morphy 1991).

Just as much as the simple economic goal — use of water — is the purpose of engaging with a water place, so too are their contingent outcomes of encounters with waterscapes. Relationships with water places are steeped in social and religious traditions, from which spring power, knowledge, well-being, good fortune (e.g. in food harvesting or fecundity), and even extraordinary misfortune, often the consequence of the punitive wrath of an ancestral being disturbed by human malfeasance.

Two sacred stories: water forms, ancestral beings and places

The following stories recounted by Elders of the Laura Basin area are exemplary narratives from this world of places peopled by the human descendants of extraordinary spiritual beings whose creative and transformative powers remain present in the land and waterscapes where their deeds are memorialised (Langton 2001).

The Hammerhead and Groper waterhole

The first account is the record of my discussion with a Lamalama Elder who described to me the desecration of a sacred waterhole by the white pastoral lessee, as we stood on its banks. The waterhole is a sacred place, and the religious explanation of the source of its sacredness related by the Elder was in typically cryptic style:

> Old hammerhead shark and one on the left hand side of me; by the pool over there, that's a groper . . . They great mates . . . they tie him before when they be a human being before, walking around together. And that's how the story goes. (Langton 2001)

The Elder explained that he remembered Lamalama people using the waterhole when he was a child, and lamented the changes that had occurred since the waterhole was dynamited by a local grazier to make the waterhole accessible to his cattle. The waterhole was especially important because it was a permanent source of water: 'Must be one here, some time later in the year when there's no water around' (Langton 2001). At the end of the dry season it became necessary for the Elder's people to visit this water source because elsewhere the waterholes had dried up. He remembered affectionately the permanence of the water and how people would collect drinking water in a bucket:

> There's a lot of water up here behind my back, never go dry that we can remember. Got water there all the time. It doesn't matter if we camp down near the beach, where we had lunch today, old people

> used to come up with a canoe. Just tie the canoe down there, quietly, come up and get a bucket of water, take it back. Well some old lady might be walking up this way, old man come over with the canoe, fill up the drum and take it back there. (Langton 2001)

He also described how the very fine white sand that once edged the waterhole had disappeared:

> From that time 'til today we keep coming down here. And a lot of sand area, this is all rock now. You know, used to be a lot of sand, real fine sand. Like that over there, just on the side there. Good water up there, that water never dry. Stay like that, yeah. (Langton 2001)

The Elder had not personally witnessed the incident of the desecration of the site, but had heard about it from the Aboriginal employees of the grazier. The Elder remained aggrieved and emotionally affected by the alteration to this lovely place caused by the grazier; so affected, in fact, that he could not utter the name of the sacred being, referring only to 'what's-a-name':

> I didn't see him blow it up, but that's what I heard from the workers . . . Them boys now, they told me that [name of grazier] blow thing up . . . [Name of grazier] blowed that bit of rock up for cattle to go down because there was fresh water in there. I don't know why he want to blow that, what's-a-name, down there. (Langton 2001)

The consequence of this discretion, according to this Elder, was that the grazier became crippled.

> I don't know why you want to break it down. And when somebody told me that issue, the next time I saw old [name of grazier], real cripple, 'cause he shouldn't do that. I do that, I'll be the same. I'm tribal owner for this country and I can't just can't do it. Or even the old bloke over here, Paddy — or Albert — can't do it. Because it's our land we just can't say, 'Oh, this is our land, we can do this'. You know. Break this, go on. Go for your life, but you can't tell anybody to do that 'cause we will get crippled. We'd be get crippled more faster than old [name of grazier], you know. It might just kill us straight away or it might just damage us properly, we won't walk any more. (Langton 2001)

The swimming dog story

The following story, by a Kuku Thaypan Elder, recounts a mass drowning in an incident involving people described as 'police' (but perhaps vigilantes) who attempted to force Aboriginal people into a river when chasing them (Langton 2001). The 'old people' — the deceased forebears of the Elder — were collecting medicine plants in the grass plains, which they traversed with care — hiding from the parties that constantly hunted them — under the cover of the high grass. He speculated that the police hunted his forebears because those 'old people' were 'wild Murris', regarded by the settlers as vermin, although the people themselves had no idea why they were being hunted: 'And that's why they . . . [came for them] because they're wild Murri; they don't know why they used the police chase him' (Langton 2001).

The Elder had told this story to me in the context of my questions about their practice of burning landscapes seasonally. However, he explained that they did not burn the grass plains at this time because of the shelter that they provided, enabling their passage unseen by the police:

> They never burn the grass, see, they let him go. Because . . . police go by and they got the medicine there. So [while collecting medicine they hid in the grass] and police go past, that's why they don't like to burn the grass. They keep the grass and they don't [burn it]. They know the firestick, they make a bit of a firestick for cooking and after push them in the water [the fire sticks]. Keep the grass. No letting it go [burn and disappear]. Grass really high like a tree, same like in the plains, this no tree, this is grass grow, cane grass, go high and high. (Langton 2001)

The fire regime of their forebears is remembered as one that was interrupted by the frontier harassment and violence of Aboriginal people. The Kuku Thaypan Elder recounted to me a story (with similarities to that of the Lamalama Elder, above) about the old people travelling in the tall grass to avoid white men. During the early phase of colonisation, as he explained, Aboriginal people were afraid to burn the long grass on the plains that concealed them during their travels across the country and allowed them to evade the troopers, the native police, and vigilantes:

> my father used to say, 'Oh what do you want to burn the grass for?' . . . 'Cause we worrying about the soldiers . . . And they used to keep the grass all the time . . . What the grass for? [To] hide people [in the] olden days. [Soldiers] shooting them. [Aboriginal people] duck and fall in the grass. [Soldiers] can't see their tracks. And they dodging the police, the police the ones [who] don't see their tracks. . . . You might see the cattle track but you won't see the man track. (Langton 2001)

An important Kuku Thaypan Elder had related this story to a young Aboriginal man, who, in an interview with me in 2001, explained that fire was also used to backfire, that is, to create a wall of fire moving away from the people lighting the fire, and a weapon to turn back the settlers:

> And yeah, and so he also said other stories, like in the time when there were settlers . . . Old people used to hold backfire burning traditionally so they could use grass to hide from people too, who was chasing them, and they also used to turn around and use it for a weapon to burn it in certain areas where fire would grow. (Langton 2001)

However, in the story in which the ancestors were chased by the police or vigilantes, many people drowned as they attempted to swim across the river course. It is believed that those who drowned were caught in the whirlpool of an ancestral being, a black dog with a white tail and a white face, which swam around in circles in this part of the river:

> That's the time start that they get drowned near the plain . . . Black dog with a white tail, white face, and black dog just swimming around and around and everybody down. All the Murri just swim the course. The people die. (Langton 2001)

To emphasise the truth of the story, the Elder explained that he had taken people in a boat to show them where the incident had occurred, because they would not believe him: 'And they wouldn't believe me and I took them over went just for little a tour in the boat there. And they said "Oh yeah, what's in there?" and [I] said dog used to swim in the course' (Langton 2001).

Waterscapes, water bodies and social institutions

The sociality of land tenure

The Aboriginal conceptions of land tenure, property and the nature of the landscape in which these societies live (which includes what we would call the 'natural' and 'supernatural', or spiritscapes) are intimately interwoven. In societies such as those in Princess Charlotte Bay, amongst which customary laws of land inheritance and tenure continue to operate, Aboriginal people are born with inchoate, inherited and transmissible rights in an estate of land and waters, whether marine or riparian. These rights are held in common with other members of clans or local kin-based groups which, together, form the customary land-holding organisations. Such a customary land-tenure system is expressed in social action, including rituals and etiquette, language and discourse strategies, and kinship reckoning. The investment of territory — including water — with social, religious and other symbolic meanings produces a perception of landscape as a series of places that are constituted by the living drama of history, sacred meaning, memory and social obligation (see also Casey 1996).

Traditions concerning the knowledge required to negotiate the egress, occupation and right of residency, and resource use in places (such as estates proper, favoured hunting grounds or fishing sites, or sacred places such as 'baby' sites usually located in water places, burial places, or rock-art sites where ancestors camped), are the preserve of men and women of senior years. Such Elders usually spent much of their lives acquiring the relevant knowledge and authority and have done so at the relevant places in these landscapes. Their genealogies and personal histories are implicated in particular places, and they often communicate directly with the ancestral beings and ancestors that are said to reside in such places (Langton 2002b; see also Morphy 1996). Such knowledge is shared by both senior and junior traditional owners who ascribe to these local customs and traditions, although senior people exercise authority and invoke spiritual protection for their junior charges and visitors. Their history of prior presence at such places is a powerful factor in their authority. They exercise a commanding body of rights and responsibilities with respect to their fellow traditional owners of such places, providing authorisation for access and use of places and resources, which I describe as traditions of property and governance (see Langton 2002b; Rigsby 1998).

Entering a spiritual landscape is potentially dangerous. Protection from the spiritual dangers is offered by the Elders who know the land and its spiritual inhabitants best. They call out to the ancestors announcing their presence, and introduce their less well-known relations and guests, including strangers. In some areas of Cape York Peninsula, including the peoples of the Laura Basin, the Wik and the Kaanju, Elders 'give smell': they take their underarm perspiration and touch the visitors hair and shoulders so that the essential spiritual smell of a knowledgeable landowner is transferred to the guest, thus bringing that person into the local social group as one who 'smells' — that is, spiritually — like the locals (Langton 2002b).

At Kowanyama, in western Cape York Peninsula, Aboriginal Ranger John Clarke explained that a demonstration of respect by the traditional owners and all who visit and use the land is required. In accordance with Aboriginal cosmology, this respect includes the riverscapes and seascapes. He explained the custom of:

> 'baptizing' newcomers to land with water so that the country knows them; how treating the land respectfully and with a good feeling is reciprocated by the ancestral spirits there who provide for their kin, 'This is your tucker'; what you've got to know about the land, where the story places are, what clan comes from each country. (Sharp 1997, p. 12)

A similar tradition exists among the Yir Yiront's neighbours near Kowanyama, as Bruno David (David & Cordell 1993) recounts from his fieldwork experience in the early 1990s:

> Walter Greenwool, the senior Kin Kopl man of the Kawn Yorrvm clan called out to two old ('spirit') men who live in a hole under the river bank (below the water line) to not hurt or 'steal' a new visitor's reason and resources when visiting his country: 'No-good old men', he called out. 'Old men, old men, down here, old men'. 'I got to put a smell on you' said Walter to the visitor. Walter then called out in language. 'That mean I got sing out la you. That they not look so I baptise you. "There . . . there . . . there that . . . No, old men no good, old men"'.

This act of baptism is performed whenever Walter introduces a new visitor to his country. The Story Beings he calls out to here have their home in the river. The 'powers' of the land are as much 'powers' of the water, and it is on the water's edge, calling to the beings in the river, that the appropriate 'baptism' took place. (Bruno David personal communication 2000)

The right of a group to hunt, fish, camp and reside in an area depends in ideal circumstances on their having among their members some person or persons with a connection based on descent from an ancestor, preferably at the grandparental generation. While it is rare for an individual to seek to enter someone else's country, even if only to fish, that person is welcomed either as a 'relation' (or relative in standard English) or as a stranger. If the former, then that person would be no imposition on the normal social life of the host group. If a stranger, that person would soon become an imposition, unless some commitment to a longer-term relationship was made for a specific reason. This is because their spiritual wellbeing must be watched out for. If they do not know about the spiritual and physical dangers of the territory, their presence is a strain on the patience of the Elders whose responsibility it is to ensure their wellbeing (Langton 2002b).

Sharing freshwater and saltwater

There is a tradition of sharing freshwater locales and saltwater locales which is a significant organising principle of regional land-based relationships among coastal groups in Princess Charlotte Bay. Like the Yolngu (see Williams 1982), Pama hold that asking and obtaining permission of senior landowners is a fundamental jural principle of land tenure relations (Langton 2002b). Also like the Yolngu, 'a boundary is to cross' (Williams 1982, p. 1), and this applies especially to the regional categorisation of landscapes into this binary opposition of freshwater and saltwater — the terms used by the Aboriginal landowners themselves as an organising principle for social and economic institutions of sharing resources and cooperation in their management and harvesting (see also Williams & Hunn 1982). The inland Kuku Thaypan and Ayapathu, and the coastal Lamalama, Yiithuwarra, Guugu Yimithirr, Barrow Point and Red Point peoples, are bound by kinship bonds that oblige them to share according to these traditions.

Such regional social networks across these two natural systems permit spatial relationships on a large scale, the enhanced prospects of compliance with the relevant social rules and regulations, and optimal food and resource harvesting opportunities. How these resources are used and managed requires an understanding of the relatedness of neighbouring groups and their traditions of sharing. The territories of these groups are not simply the length of river systems but wedges of differential ecological resource locales, including specific stretches of river systems, combined in a patchwork effect. Such a land-owning pattern assists in the exploitation and management of basic necessary resources for the sustenance of the regional land-using and land-owning groups. Access by these groups to resources outside of their own territorial or estate locale is achieved by compliance with jural principles governing permission for various kinds of social intercourse and exchange with their neighbours.

Such social involvement necessarily involves relationships of marriage and cognatic descent, or reckoning descent from both parents (Rigsby & Hafner 1994; see also Hafner 1999; Rigsby 1980, 1981, 1992, 1995; Rigsby & Hafner 1992) and the bonds of kinship that result from marriages between members of neighbouring groups in previous generations. If members of land-owning groups move away to marry elsewhere, they are remembered, and their rights in land preserved. This entitles their children to return to their lands — with the permission, implicit or explicit, of those Elders who live on or near that land — to hunt, fish, camp and visit. People in such situations are spoken of as 'having a share' in the 'country' — the estate or territory. Sometimes people say 'they come in there'. What is being referred to is a set of rights based on descent and alliance principles, not simply arbitrary sharing of resources. However, a prerequisite to exercising rights to land is some primary knowledge of the terrain, its fauna and flora and, most importantly, of the spiritual landscape.

In his New Guinean studies, Terrell (2002, p. 17) refers to 'inherited friendships', as indicated earlier, which constitute a vast network of human relationships, uniting people and local communities from sixty language groups into larger human associations (or 'regional systems'; see Terrell 1993), and extending for many hundreds of kilometres along the Sepik coastline. This social institution is extraordinarily similar to the relations between Elders of the Cape York Peninsula groups whose practices of land and resource management are outlined here. He observes that these relationships extend 'well beyond the level of economic and socio-cultural integration represented by what anthropologists conventionally refer to as "face-to-face" communities', and that 'This commonality of material and social culture is nurtured by a fascinating local social institution: inherited friendship' (Terrell 2002, p. 17). Customs and traditions concerning how people ought to behave toward one another as friends, and of having friendships between individuals and families, are deep-rooted trans-generational phenomena: they have been handed down from one generation to the next suggesting, I would add, considerable antiquity. Terrell elegantly explains the multiple social and economic dimensions of these traditions:

> inherited friendships maintain ties of mutual advantage between generations on the coast that are directly analogous to the inter-generational responsibilities that are so essential to the success of agroforestry as an economic institution on the coast. And both of these institutions hint at what 'community' means in this part of New Guinea. It seems evident that people here have ties to the past and obligations to the future that are intimate and enduring. (Terrell 2002, p. 17)

'Boundaries': ownership as management responsibility

If we examine the ways in which people speak about their country we find that the natural features of particular locations in the landscape — most particularly the riverine, estuarine and marine features — are both the focal references for boundary markers and the religious references which are inferred in these places by the mythologies. The economic resources — water, fish, game and plant foods of such places — are regarded, and spoken of, as characteristics of these places, equally determined by spiritual and biogeographical factors.

Anthropologists Bruce Rigsby and Nancy Williams have explained patterns of resource use in the freshwater domain of the Lamalama people:

> People also fish in the interior. Above the estuaries, most streams run only in the wet season, but there are permanent pools and waterholes in and away from the streambeds. Many streams are fringed by gallery rain forest that includes desirable fruiting trees and plant species. People dig and gather several yam species that grow in the sandy soils found in the scrubs behind the beach dunes and along the streams, and hunt ducks, geese, and other birds in the large freshwater swamps and wetlands that are home to many species, some migratory and others present year round. They also hunt feral pigs near swamps and waterholes, and use .22-caliber rifles and single-

barrel 12-gauge shotguns for hunting pigs, wallabies, kangaroos, and birds. People utilize a more restricted range of plant foods, however, than in the past; flour replaced tubers, seeds, and edible mangrove pods, all of which require labor-intensive preparation. Older people have intimate knowledge of places and bush resources and the techniques to gather and process them. (Rigsby & Williams 1991, p. 13)

On these rich coastal plains and their hinterlands, the Kuku Thaypan, Lamalama, Guugu Yimithirr and their neighbours describe their territorial domains and estates by referring to river-system locales, in particular the focal areas for exploitation of riverine, estuarine or marine resources along stretches of rivers and other features associated with river systems — creeks, lagoons, junctions, mouths, and bays.

It is typical of the older generation to describe their country in terms of rivers, creeks and waterholes. For instance, when questioned about the extent of his traditional estate by Bruce Rigsby during the Lakefield National Park land claim (Aboriginal Land Tribunal 1994, pp. 461–2), a Kuku Thaypan Elder did so by referring to creeks:

> Bruce Rigsby: Country belong to you mob?
> Kuku Thaypan elder: Well, really, Saltwater Creek from there to right up to the Hann River . . . Come right down to right near the; you know where the Possum Hole go.

An Olkolo Elder, whose traditional estate neighbours the one referred to above, also described the boundary in terms of a water body (Aboriginal Land Tribunal 1994, p. 647):

> Boundary runs down — when you leave Musgrave, it's on the jump-up, you've got climb a range there and the range runs right through the Nevabina Swamp, them people — that's boundary.

A senior Kaanju Elder described his understanding of the boundaries between Kaanju land and Lamalama land as being the Archer River Crossing, a major river crossing on the Development Road that traverses Cape York from south to north (Aboriginal Land Tribunal 1994, p. 608).

The Lamalama strictly observe rules that apply to fishing, use of bait and preparation of fish in both freshwater and saltwater areas respectively. At the Cape York Land Summit held in 1993 at the Port Stewart River, a Lamalama Elder called Sunlight explained the local customs and laws to the visiting participants, and politely asked everyone to comply with them. He was explicit about the spiritual retribution for breaching these rules — 'we might be get flattened again' — referring to the cyclonic winds that rush off the sea and flatten their camps and camping areas in retribution:

> [And] another thing I like to say about fishing, everybody looking at fishing here. I know everybody wishing to go down to the beach and I hope everybody use the right bait. Not dugong baits or . . . not turtle baits or not bullock baits, if you blokes come along an' ask me for a net, just use the mullets . . . baits. And that's the law belong to this place. So if you happen to use something wrong . . . we might be get flattened again. So use the right baits. Don't use them White man baits, use the Aboriginal baits if you wouldn't mind, please. Thank you. (Langton 1993)

Elsewhere in Cape York, water and water bodies hold cultural significance pertaining to the power of ancestral beings and the responsibility of Traditional Owners to mediate between the mundane and the spiritual worlds. Other Aboriginal groups in Australia share, if not the specifics of such performative engagements with water bodies, then at least similarly rich belief systems that imbue the personal and social approaches to water places with a reverence shaped by religious interpretations of such places as being pregnant with ancestral power. The identification of specific water locations — waterholes, parts of rivers with frequent water eddies, particularly deep-water places within creeks or rivers and so forth — with fecundity is common across Australia. Personal identities, as well as a number of shared group identities from extremely localised to regionalised, are constructed around the idea of ancestral origins expressed in terms of precious water sources (Williams 1986, pp. 66–8).

For coastal groups and those who live in the semi-arid regions where there are saline water sources, the distinction between 'freshwater' and 'saltwater' is a critical one in the cultural construction of places in the environment and environmental and economic knowledge of place. Freshwater and saltwater domains are distinct and separate, and rules that apply to the use of resources in each domain emphasise that distinctiveness in daily life. The estuarine zone is further differentiated as another spiritual and biophysical domain. Along with other features of the natural world, the estuarine zone is not just a biophysical feature, but a metaphorical reference to knowledge (Marika *et al.* 1989, pp. 13–14).

For some clan-based groups, riverscapes are constructed as complexes of places, each a localised spiritual source of an ancestral being of local groups. The estates of these groups are located along river systems, and are linked to each other by stories about the activities of ancestral beings — in some areas called Dreaming tracks — or the pathways of ancestral beings, and thence by economic and social exchange links. This intensely localised identification with water sources, especially springs, contrasts with basin-wide sociogeographic identities of cultural groups in other parts of the world. In Aboriginal social geographies, the river basin or catchment may rather form a region with permeable boundaries across which particular forms of social and economic exchange may take place.

The social dimensions of a single water body, then, might encompass religious beliefs, observances and rituals concerning water and waterscapes, naming practices specific to water bodies, principles of kinship and descent, the social organisation of estate-owning groups, regional sharing practices, and the allocation and distribution of rights and responsibilities in places.

Some aspects of an Aboriginal biogeography of water

The traditional use of dew as an inhibitor of a fire front

Water comes in many forms and dew, as Pama know, is not the least significant of them. Knowledge of dewfalls, the ability to predict whether they will be heavy or light, and their impact on a fire front, are a key aspect of this postcolonial approach to managing vast landscapes in the prevailing conditions of frequent wildfire.

There are two coeval Aboriginal fire management traditions in the Laura Basin region: one that was inherited from the forebears of their grandparental generation who were engaged in the frontier conflicts of the period from the late nineteenth to the early twentieth century; and one that the local Aboriginal people developed, following that period, as they became employed tending the large herds of cattle that came with the frontiersmen, applying their traditional environmental knowledge to the new challenge of feeding and managing livestock. To afford these large, hard-hoofed grazing animals the grasslands that they required, a new burning regime transformed the wooded plains into grasslands across which the stock spread, becoming the dominant faunal presence. The result was a mixed fire use regime incorporating ancestral and 'stockman' practices.

I interviewed an Olkolo leader at Laura in 2001, about this second 'stockman' way of burning, and the importance of dew emerged in this discussion, as in many others:

> Olkolo Elder: [I]t's around about June, a little after May, June and July — in those three months are the perfect time . . . And you gotta make sure that the grass are lit at the right time. At the same time ... soon as it gets to afternoon, like now, before the fire gradually dies away, and there's no wind. And you get feed on the other side of it.

> [I]n the morning, 'round about as soon as, after the heavy dew, as soon as the grass dries, you know, you start burning. And 'round about after lunch, you know, before lunch or after lunch, you're getting a good fire. It might spread for a while, it spreads all right for a while . . . You know, it's all grass. But as it goes on, like this time of the afternoon, then when the wind dies down, and the fire just sort of almost dies away itself, and finish. If it's by any chance caught on to, caught on to a dead tree or something, and if it's, and if it's fell down and burnt, and maybe about, maybe sometimes it's about, sometimes about two or three weeks, that fire gets on to the old grass. The tree must fall over the old dry grass and suddenly it just carries on again . . . It just goes for maybe a day or so and that's it. (Langton 2001)

A knowledgeable Lamalama Elder explained the distance and duration of burns that resulted from exploiting the fall and evaporation of the dew on the grass during the dry months from July to November:

> [I]f I burn down the grass, say at about 8 o'clock in the morning, and that fire will go a long way. You know, it might 30 kilometre, or more, 40 kilometre, from this way, in the west. And good idea to stop that fire from burning that far, 40 kilometre, that's a long way. Might be 20 kilometre wide, or 40 kilometre that way, or 60, that's a long way, you know . . . We burn down here about 2 o'clock, the fire might go about 25 kilometre up here, by 5 o'clock, stop. The whole afternoon . . . We know we've got to burn it. About midday might burn a little bit, a little bit long way, but by 3 o'clock in the afternoon it might do about 20 kilometres up here. It'll stop about 5 or 6 and that's the way. (Langton 2001)

Early dry season burning, or 'burn grass', is held to be the correct burning period by some Aboriginal Elders, while others hold that early wet season burning, or 'storm burn', is the correct period. Another explanation is that these two different views on seasonal burning have been coexistent for a number of decades, and indeed continual burning throughout the dry may have been the case prior to European invasion (see Whitehead *et al.* 2003; see also Langton 1998; Russell-Smith *et al.* 2003). Burning in different seasons is implemented with respect to different types of vegetation, and with different purposes. By example, early wet-season burning, or 'storm burn', is practiced to control salt grass. As one senior Lamalama Elder pointed out, 'Some place you burn them, some place you save the grass for storm time.' (Langton 2001). Other grass types are best burnt in the dry. Seasonal burning, then, depends on the type of vegetation in the landscape: salt grass, ti-tree, grasses for cattle feed — each requires burning during the season that best suits its economic purpose, that is, when it should be regenerated for the animals dependent on it for food.

The key, as the Elders explained, is that the risk of 'hot' fires, and especially uncontrollable wildfires, must be avoided by commencing the annual burning in the early dry season when the landscape and vegetation still retain high levels of water. Elders uniformly report that areas that have not been burned for some years pose a high risk, and must be burnt in the late wet season.

Local Aboriginal knowledge of the type of vegetation, and of the marked wet and dry forests that predominate in the east and west respectively, are critical to fire management. So too is knowledge of rivers, creeks and other waterways, as they are used as fire breaks. The presence of water bodies also increases the growth of the highly flammable grasses of the region and therefore, while offering firebreaks, waterways also encourage dangerous levels of fuel. At the end of the wet season, however, the grasses contain high levels of water and are less flammable. It is not until they become desiccated during the dry season that they become flammable. As with the hourly effect of dew, the seasonal water content of grasses is also predicted and ascertained with great accuracy and attention to detail.

Waterways as firebreaks

I discussed with a knowledgeable Lamalama Elder a particular area burnt during the previous season: reading the signs in the blackened landscape, he pointed out that the fire was lit when the prevailing wind direction would carry the fire towards a nearby lake, and that it had been extinguished at the water's edge.

A young man I interviewed in the Laura area had focused on learning the ways of the Elders in using fire. He, too, referred to waterways as firebreaks:

> So we burn around them places a lot at that time of year. But then that doesn't go very far because of the Brakeman Rivers, there's a lot of rivers out that way, creek beds, so there's heaps of fire breaks. So natural... (Langton 2001)

A Kuku Thaypan Elder described the lapse of wind in the afternoon in the following way:

> And you sort of, well in those, in those times of the north, soon as it gets to afternoon, like now, before the fire gradually dies away, and

there's no wind. And you get [fresh grass suitable for cattle] feed on the other side of it. (Langton 2001)

One of the Lamalama Elders also referred to water bodies as firebreaks:

Oh, about early in the morning. Except you just go down bit to the creek and you just stop, you can't go any further. A big lake down the end. (Langton 2001)

While gauging wind direction is a straightforward exercise, predicting the wind's pattern and its strength throughout the day requires traditional knowledge of local climate inherited from forebears. For Aboriginal people a sound knowledge of daily and seasonal wind patterns and characteristics is an essential tool in fire management and, more generally, in choosing where to camp, when to travel, and when to conduct other affairs in these landscapes. The daily wind pattern in this northern wet-dry climate involves a lapse of wind in the afternoon. This is a critical factor in Aboriginal fire control, as a young Aboriginal man living in the Laura area explained:

[T]hey don't burn at all around the town this time of year [June] when it's too windy ... So they wait [until] the wind drops ... they'll burn when there's no wind at all. At this time of year, so sort of pick the right day. (Langton 2001)

This skilful control of fire by exploitation of wind strength and direction, water bodies and dew is the core practical knowledge of fire use and management that Aboriginal men learn from a young age. The ability of Elders to read landscapes in intimate detail depends on long experience in those landscapes, and a body of knowledge concerning topography, climate, and seasonal and daily alterations in the climate, and the animacy of flora and fauna.

Discussion

What emerges consistently from Pama knowledge of water and fire, and their disciplined stewardship of the resources of their estates, is anthropologist Tim Ingold's (1993) notion of 'the temporality of landscape'. This includes the 'temporal rhythms' (Ingold 1993, p. 168) of the sun and the moon; the tides; the monsoon and the six Aboriginal seasons; the 'resonance' of human activity with the 'natural rhythmic phenomena' (Ingold 1993, p, 163); Aboriginal 'stockmen' burning grass in the early dry season when the water content of the vegetation is still high; the gentle desiccation of dew during the course of the day and its precipitation again in the afternoon; the seasonality of wind and its lapse in the late afternoon in the dry season; the burst of growth in the vegetation throughout the wet season until the grass is taller than a man, and its dehydration over the course of the dry season; the scheduled 'storm burn' in the early wet.

I have discussed Australian Aboriginal relationships with water and water places to draw attention to a critical dimension common to all mainland Aboriginal groups: that water and water places are constructed socially through the experiences of the knowledgeable men and women who live in these landscapes as tenure systems and spiritscapes; and that these waterscapes can be better understood through indigenous worldviews. For this reason, historicising relationships between Aboriginal people and country must begin with the notion that landscapes, including water and water places, are meaningfully entangled in social relations.

Lourandos initiated an archaeology of waterworlds when he investigated water management systems in south-western Victoria (*cf.* Tibby *et al.*, this volume). He regarded the network of manufactured channels and eel-holding ponds as social and political phenomena, not just narrow, economic events. Their origin late in the Holocene was startling evidence of Aboriginal manipulation of environments, including large-scale social constructions of water technology and water places. The new comprehension that such an approach initiated led to theoretical and methodological innovation in Australian history and studies of Aboriginal society. By going beyond the standard archaeological approaches of the time — ecologically and economically rationalist as they then often were — Lourandos oriented historical research towards people and their places.

The distinctly Aboriginal investment of deeply held religious beliefs in places and estates (see David *et al.* 1994; Taçon *et al.* 1996), including the territorial, marine and riparian constituents, have become a legitimate area of inquiry in archaeology, So too has the possibility of historicising Aboriginal relations with water places in new ways, as windows into the history of Aboriginal engagements with the world (see David 2002 for such an approach to archaeological historicism). In the result, our investigation of the social dimensions of waterscapes — and of a social archaeology of ontology and spirituality — is not limited by narrow disciplinary concerns. Rather, the wide scope now available for the framing of questions and methodological approaches includes the imperceptible, but not insubstantial, transformative power of Aboriginal knowledge and belief systems, their forms of sociality and apprehension of the temporality in the landscapes they dwell in and animate.

Acknowledgements

I am grateful to the Elders of the Guugu Yimithirr, the Lamalama, the Alu Aya or Kuku Thaypan, the so-called 'Koko Warra', and the people of Barrow Point, whose encyclopaedic knowledge of their homelands is represented in a faint manifestation here.

I acknowledge the foundational anthropology of my mentors: Bruce Rigsby, Diane Hafner, Nancy M Williams, and Richie Howitt, and Bruno David. I thank them for their scholarship and generosity. I also acknowledge and thank Peter Cooke and Michael Storrs of the Caring for Country Unit of the Northern Land Council for their contribution to my work on this paper over the last decade.

Note

1. I worked in the Princess Charlotte Bay region in 1993 and 1994 as an anthropologist employed by the Cape York Land Council, although I had visited in 1990 and 1991 when I was employed in the Queensland Public Service. I came to know many of the Elders of the region and visited their homelands with them, camping at times for up to three weeks.

10.
The social, economic and historical construction of cycad palms among the Yanyuwa

John J Bradley

Within archaeological debates on prehistoric Australia, much discussion is given to resource use. Central to many of these discussions has been the concept of 'intensification', conceived and popularised by Lourandos as an increase in resource management and use during the late Holocene (Lourandos 1983b, pp. 81–2). For Lourandos, these late Holocene processes of resource intensification were linked to social network growth 'and their related ceremonies . . . [promoting] . . . reciprocity and the benefits accrued by it' (Lourandos 1983b, p. 88).

The following ethnographic descriptions and reconstructions of cycad (sometimes referred to in historical texts as 'cycas') use among the Yanyuwa people of the southwestern Gulf of Carpentaria, Australia, provides first-hand evidence for Lourandos' notions of intensive resource use, given that, among the Yanyuwa, intense religious and practical use of cycad seeds can be documented up until the present time. I also highlight the fact that such resource use is not just about food, but at their core concern also worldviews and how people organise themselves, among themselves and on the ground.

Cycad palms are peculiar plants. Their seeds are highly toxic and carcinogenic, and yet Indigenous peoples in parts of Australia have long used some species — predominately *Cycas angulata*, *C. media* and *Macrozamia* spp. — as sources of food (Beaton 1977, 1982; Flood 1983; Hooper 1978; Lourandos 1997; Smith 1982; Whiting 1963). The meticulous, labour-intensive methods necessary to make cycad seeds edible gives them a special place in the annals of the culturally curious, as much as affording them a special place in Indigenous sociology.

Much existing research on cycad use in Aboriginal Australia comes from north-eastern Arnhem Land (Beck *et al.* 1988; Meehan & Jones 1977; Thomson 1949; Watson 1989), Groote Eylandt (Levitt 1981) and northern Queensland (Beaton 1977, 1982). A common theme of enquiry has revolved around the nutritional quality of the food; in the case of *C. media* carbohydrates account for 44–65% of the cooked flesh (Beaton 1982; Beck *et al.* 1988). But among the Yanyuwa people it is not such nutritional or economic observations that hold primary significance, but the way cycads help construct notions of place, social affinity and personhood. Cycads reference the social order and, in this sense, actively partake in the construction of social relations, relations between people and land, and relations between people and the cosmological order in which they dwell. The social entanglement of cycads in Yanyuwa thought is well demonstrated by their inspiration as a source of meaning and metaphor, revealing in the process not so much a network of rationalist economic signs, a symbolic order that makes cultural demands in the process of social dwelling and that reveals the world as a varied and historically contingent realm of ontological possibilities. In the process, and rather than offering the archaeologist little hope of historicising a cultural logic, it is precisely this open symbolism, economic indeterminacy and historical specificity of meaning that allows for an archaeology of cultural landscapes and meaningful worldly engagement. This, then, is the main message of this chapter: that cycads reveal their cultural significance not simply as items of food, but more critically as sources of meaning and metaphor in Yanyuwa cosmology. More generally, it is precisely this dimension of human behaviour with the material world that enables the possibility of an archaeology of cultural landscapes to take place.

The Yanyuwa and Garrwa

The information presented in this chapter has been gathered over a period of twenty years' working with the Yanyuwa and Garrwa peoples of the southwest Gulf of Carpentaria, tropical northern Australia. The Yanyuwa people define their country as the delta regions of the McArthur River, the saltwater limits of the McArthur and Wearyan rivers, and the Sir Edward Pellew islands (Figure 1). They describe themselves as *li-Anthawirryarra*, or 'those people whose spiritual and cultural origins are from the sea'; this phrase is generally abbreviated as 'people of the sea'. It is a term widely used by individuals of all ages, even those who have grown up in an urban environment and who have little, if anything, to do with the sea. People use the Yanyuwa or English phrase to emphasise feelings of distinct identity as sea people, as opposed to mainland or 'scrub' people. Thus, the landscape — or more accurately the seascape — is an important dimension in discussions and constructions of identity.

The neighbouring Garrwa see themselves as inland freshwater people; their country is associated with the Robinson River and Calvert River systems to the east of Yanyuwa country. While the Yanyuwa and Garrwa peoples keep a sense of identity that is strong and distinctive, there is a long history of intermarriage

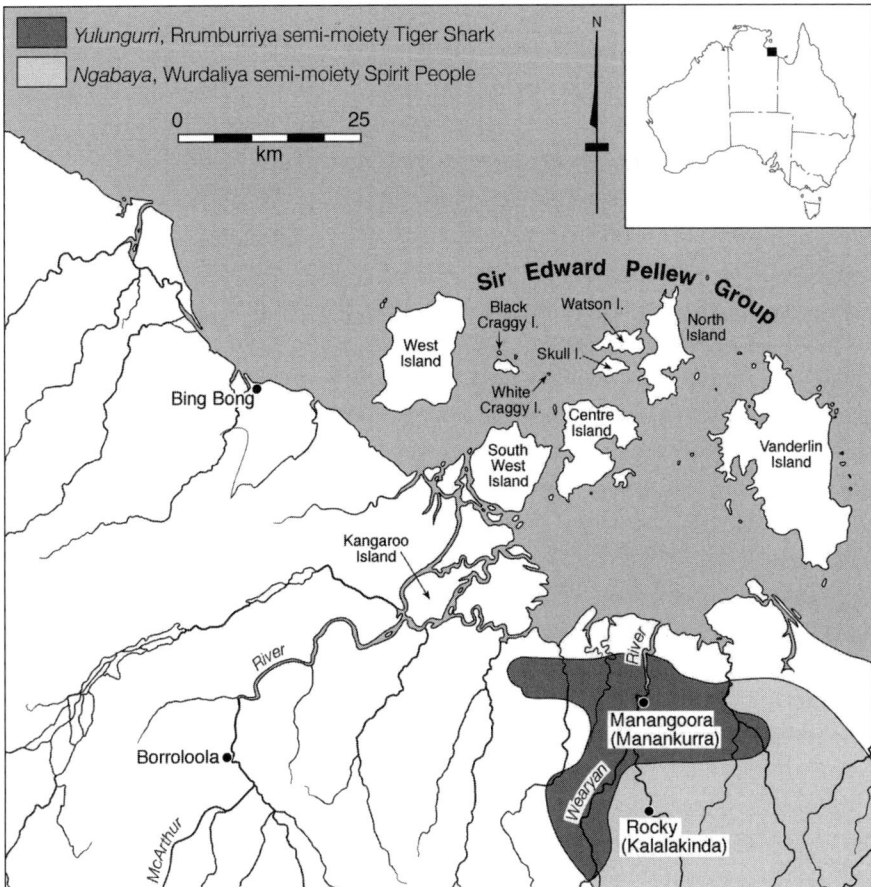

Figure 1. The study area.

and intergroup alignment through economic ties and shared religious traditions, themes that are well demonstrated by the cycad palm.

Yanyuwa and Garrwa perceptions of their land and seascapes are multifaceted. They see their environment as a universe whose ecology consists of many diverse forms that include spirit beings or spirit essences, people, and 'natural' phenomena such as rocks, trees and stars, all of which are intricately interrelated through kinship ties mediated by the Dreaming. The complexity of this environment is highlighted when the Yanyuwa and Garrwa speak of life and land, invariably themes that unite in the spirit essences of the Dreaming. In many respects the Yanyuwa and Garrwa peoples do not see themselves as managers of their environment, but rather as peoples who are in constant apprehension and negotiation with it, following the Law established during the formative activities of the Dreaming. It is this Law that set the ongoing kinship links between people and between people and their surroundings.

The Yanyuwa and Garrwa system of kinship is characterised by four terminological lines of descent that are distinguished at grandparental level. Thus an individual may be perceived as being descended from each and all of four distinct patrilineages of his or her father's father, mother's father, father's mother (brother) and mother's mother (brother). Each of these lines of descent has a set of rights and responsibilities with the ownership of land/sea, resources, rituals and ceremonies. Each is associated with a named semi-moiety. The Rrumburriya and Mambaliya-Wawukarriya semi-moieties comprise one un-named patri-moiety, and the Wurdaliya and Wuyaliya semi-moieties comprise another unnamed patrimoiety (for a detailed discussion see Bradley 1997 and Trigger 1989).

In the Yanyuwa language there are three food sources classified as *wurrama* or 'being of authority': dugong, sea turtle and the kernel of the cycad palm. (I have discussed elsewhere the importance of dugong and sea turtle to the Yanyuwa, see Bradley 1991, 1997.) While the cycad palm is a terrestrial food source, it has both economic and religious links to the sea and to the marine environment. These links determine relationships between people and plant, and between people and land as relations of belonging and ownership (Bradley 1988).

An important point to consider in the following discussion is that, for the Yanyuwa and other nearby groups, landscape and identity are integrally related. One could also say that in some instances it is the living things inhabiting the landscape that are the foci of relationships between groups of people, and between people, the spirits and the land/water. In the instance of the cycad palm, the kernel and history of its use are an important part of who people feel they are, and of notions and experiences of the landscape they inhabit. The knowledge of the cycad palm is not just knowledge of botany and plant use; it is a knowledge embedded within systems of thought, belief and belonging. People draw on all of these factors to give meaning and significance to their lives. Groups such as the Yanyuwa, through their fine-grained knowledge of resources, religion and history, identify strongly with culturally and socially important species such as the cycad palm. The names they give to and the geographical features by which they describe their country are also important. Cycad groves become entwined with notions of individual and group identity. The naming and ordering of any given landscape means that it is transformed from a purely physical and geographic environment to a place biographically embedded as a history of lived experiences, and among the Yanyuwa cycads have an important role to play in this transformation.

The Manankurra cycad groves

Some 100 km east of the present-day township of Borroloola flows the Wearyan River, and on its banks is the locality known as Manangoora or Manankurra. This is the central nucleus of an area that spreads north, south, east and west for some kilometres and which contains many large groves and scattered cycad palms of the species *C. angulata* (Brock 1988). Within the area (Figure 1) there are cycad palms that grow to 10 m in height, some reaching higher. The average height ranges between 2 m and 5 m.

According to Yanyuwa belief, the cycad palms that spread out from the central focal site of Manankurra were deposited there by a Tiger Shark spirit ancestor (Yulungurri) who travelled from the southern Gulf of Carpentaria in the formative period popularly known in the west as the Dreaming (Bradley 1988). This Tiger Shark is associated with the Yanyuwa Rrumburriya semi-moiety. Some 10 km upstream, on the Foelsche River, is the equally important site of Kalalakinda. This site is associated with the Garrwa Wurdaliya semi-moiety. For the Garrwa people the distribution of the cycad palm over their country is the result of the activities of a group of human-like spirit beings (*ngabaya*). This Garrwa Wurdaliya estate abuts the southeastern edge of Yanyuwa country. It is as if the saltwater-island orientated Yanyuwa people and the freshwater-riverine Garrwa people had deliberately divided this important food source among themselves. Rituals and socially, individuals from both groups cooperated with each other and here, among the vast cycad groves, the Yanyuwa and Garrwa interacted through ritual, economic knowledge, symbolism, and ownership of various songs associated with the cycad palms, at once symbolising and activating a complementary opposition (Avery 1985).

The first European to visit the Manankurra area and note the importance of the cycad kernel as a food source was Ludwig Leichhardt. Leichhardt passed through Yanyuwa and Garrwa countries during his westward travels in 1845. In his journals he noted the large size of the cycad palms, describing them as 'Cycas palms from thirty to fifty feet high, thick at the butt, and tapering gradually towards the crown' (Leichhardt 1847, p. 403). Leichhardt (1847, pp. 407–10) also described the many 'groves' which were linked together by anthropogenic pathways and observed in some detail the stages by which the cycad kernel were prepared by local Indigenous people:

> I also observed that the seed of the cycas were cut into very thin slices about the size of a shilling and these were spread out carefully on the ground to dry after which slices are put for several days in water, and, after a good soaking, are closely tied up in tea-tree bark to undergo a peculiar process of fermentation.

> . . . large packets contained soaked cycas seed which seemed to be undergoing fermentation. They were of a mealy substance, and harmless; but had a musty taste and a smell resembling that of common German cheese.

Although Leichhardt never actually went to Manankurra, he did pass through the Kalalakinda area, which is also known as Rocky. In 1876 the explorer George de Latour subsequently published an article of this general area in the *Brisbane Courier*. He mistakenly called the cycad palms 'tree ferns', noting that (de Latour 1876, no page numbers):

> On the Wearing [sic], Foelsche and Scott Rivers the vegetation, as stated above, is most luxuriant, and literally awe-inspiring. Immense groves of tree fern . . . from two to three feet in diameter at their base and rising straight as possible to a height of from 60–80 feet without and excrescence, cover the banks of those rivers, and present the grand appearance of so many hundreds of columns supporting a vast edifice of tropical verdure.

Details of the cycad palms and the use of their kernel were also recorded by Bill Harney (senior). Harney was the first European to realise the importance of the Manankurra area to the local Yanyuwa and Garrwa peoples. He saw the significance of cycads not just as items of food, but also in relation to ritual and trade cycles. Harney wrote (1971, p. 122):

> The Cycas palms brought ritual, and with the rituals came also the trading Aborigines. The Anulas [Yanyuwa] with their 'mutta-mutta' possum fur aprons. The 'Gadanjes [Gudanji] came with boomerangs beaked and plain. From the east and west they gathered to this 'this place of food', and great were the fights they had over past grievances.

Harney (1953, p. 44) also documented the little-known but common practice of European settlers in this area of the Gulf who became dependent upon the cycad as an important staple when more normal foodstuff became hard to obtain:

The white setters of the Borroloola area soon realized the value of munja-[cycad]palm when food became short owing to a delay in the Darwin or Burketown boat service, or through a lack of funds to carry on. When this happened the 'paperbark and greenhide sqatters' came down to Manangoora and, emulating the aboriginals, gathered, sliced and dried the cycas pods, filled up the empty flour and sugar bags, carted these back to their cattle station humpies, and rode out the food famine till relief or better days arrived.

During the early 1940s Alison Harvey, the wife of one of the welfare administrators at Borroloola, visited the region and she too realised the economic and religious importance of the cycad palm to the area. She (Harvey 1945, p. 191) commented:

> The tribes of this area have an increase centre for the Cycad Palm at Manangura, some seven miles from the mouth of the MacArthur River, which is the scene of corroborees and where much *nagwiama* and *Mundja* [cycad food] is brought for practical purposes and for exchange between approved tribal relations.

Harvey described the methods used to treat the cycad nuts so that they could be eaten. These correspond well with the descriptions of contemporary senior Yanyuwa women and men, some of which are reproduced below.[1]

The country and its harvest

The broad area of land that encompasses the central focal site of Manankurra (and the greatest stand of cycad palms), is called Ma-wirla by the Yanyuwa. The term defies word-for-word translation; rather, it carries meanings of a place with abundant vegetable food, a place where many people could come together for ceremonies and for other important events. The name, especially for older Yanyuwa people, entwines memory, emotion and ceremony into place-identity through the special food that is located there, and its special needs in terms of its preparation. The following quote from a senior owner of the Manankurra area directly addresses the cycad palm as a site of social signification that at once includes and transcends its value as a food item:

> This is a good food, we grew up on this food, we ate this food. The Marra people would come from the west, the Garrwa people would come from the east, they would all come here to eat this food . . . This is a food of strength, this food of great importance and power, all the people used to gather here, coming from the north, from the islands. They would gather here for this cycad food . . . This food is for us [Yanyuwa people]. It is a food of great importance, of great power, it is for those who came from a long way away. They used to come here for the fighting grounds which are nearby on the plains to the north. They would fight with boomerangs, those who used to eat this food. This food is my senior paternal grandfather, it is my kin. My senior father's sister, she used to grind this food, her name was a-Manankurrmara, just like mine, just like the name of this country, these cycad palms, this food is for us. (Eileen McDinny a-Manankurrmara 1988, in Bradley 1980–98)

Similar sentiments have been voiced by other members of the Yanyuwa community, and the personal testimonies of Indigenous people I have worked with who have eaten cycad-derived foods embody a repeated theme: how filling and substantial a foodstuff it was (I say 'was' because cycad as a source of food has been replaced nutritionally during the last fifty years by commercial wheat flour). Contrary to popular anthropological notions, cycads were not seen as 'starvation tucker' by the Yanyuwa, Garrwa and Marra. As Yanyuwa woman Minnie Wulbulinimara comments:

> That cycad food, that is the food that reared me from the time I was a baby to my womanhood. Truly it is good food, when one eats that food one becomes replete, not like the bread of white men it does not fill you. The cycad food on the other hand fills people, they grow strong and they are healthy, I was reared on that food, all of us old people we yearn for that food, truly it is a food with a quality of excellence. (Minnie Wulbulinimara 1980, in Bradley 1980–98)

Among the many old people I spoke to about the use of cycad food, the above comment represents a standard response. The food was seen to give strength and vitality. Some speakers also attribute this to the fact that the food source, in their area at least, is associated with a sense of the past, 'old people' long dead, important regional ceremonies and spirit ancestors.

Across Yanyuwa territory there are a number of localities that are known by the term *wirriwangkuma* — a term that can be applied to Manankurra and its surrounding area. *Wirriwangkuma* is a term given to country where people can come together on a seasonal basis and expect to share in the resources that are abundant there. It is not a word that is widely used among the Yanyuwa, in fact the term is applied only to three places: Manankurra for its abundance of cycad food; the southern point of Centre Island; and the coastal area known as Bing Bong, both these latter areas being sites of renown for hunting dugong and sea turtle (Bradley 1997).

The term *wirriwangkuma* is voiced in reference to kinship groups. People describe *wirriwangkuma* as meaning a locality where, regardless of one's kin relationships to the country and to the owners of that country, people are free to come and utilise the resource. In effect, however, there are some restrictions with such uses, but these vary with time and event, and generally at a day-to-day level such a place is free for people to use. Any social control to be given over such an area is under the direction of a group of people called, in Yanyuwa, *li-wilanguwarra*. This term is usually translated as 'the bosses for country', but more specifically refers to acknowledged senior men and women who are associated with the land in question by paternal and maternal descent. Examples of the kinds of control they could and still exercise are given below. For now it is enough to say that social control over the land and resources indicates that a resource such as the cycad palm and kernel is not seen to be free, that it is perceived as property that can be shared with people, but in the past when dependence on cycads was greater these 'bosses' could refuse or restrict its use.

Cycads as social and cosmological signifiers

In Yanyuwa there is a rich vocabulary describing the cycad palm and the various stages of preparation of the kernel. Many of these terms begin with the Yanyuwa *ma-* noun prefix used for non-meat and/or vegetable foods. An analysis of these terms provides information on how the food is perceived culturally.

Ma-arnbaka: generic term for the cycad palm (*C. angulata*). The term *ma-ardakantha* is given to a grove of very tall cycad palms, while *ma-kaykalkaykal* is used to describe a cycad palm of exceptional height. The tall palms are usually seen as proof of the power of the creative force associated with this palm species, often referred to in local Aboriginal English as 'properly Dreaming'.

Nu-warda: literally 'its hair', the fronds of the cycad palm. This is the only kind of tree whose foliage is described as such, the usual term being *wanjirr*. This term references human characteristics that relate to the Dreaming significance of the palm. Harney (1953) describes Yanyuwa and Garrwa people eating the soft central fronds of this palm, but no Yanyuwa or Garrwa person I have worked with has confirmed this observation.

Ma-widiwidi: the cone that appears on male plants. The term *wididwidi* is usually associated with the action of holding a baby.

Ma-yijan: literally 'Dreaming food', the term is used to describe the tessellated diamond texture of the trunk of the cycad palm. These marks are said to be evidence of cuts and other wounds sustained by the Tiger Shark Dreaming when he fought the other sharks, rays and fish for the possession of the food (Bradley 1988).

Ma-ngakuya: cycad nut. The best time to gather this food is seen to be the later part of the dry season, from about July through to November.

Ma-mudi: cycad nut, but the term literally translates as 'sacred food' and again highlights the importance of this food's mythological origins.

Ma-wurlyurr: literally 'the eyeball that is food'. This is the term given to the cycad kernel when removed from the hard outer shell, called *nu-waba*, literally, 'its outer covering'.

Ma-budanja: a cycad kernel in peak condition. It falls easily from the outer shell when cracked open and does not have any of the thin, brown inside layer of the outer shell adhering to it. The root word of the term, *budanja*, means 'messmate tree' (*Eucalyptus tetradonta*), but I have not been able to find any reason for this.

Ma-lirrka: nut that has fallen from the palm naturally and may be only a few weeks or few months old. Such nuts still require full treatment before being eaten.

Ma-mangkilangu: old cycad nuts that have fallen to the ground, with kernels that are old and either white or black, sometimes powdery. The term has as its root *mangkil*, which is used to describe dried nasal secretions and dried or congealed blood. These old cycad nuts are gathered, shelled and then sorted; those that have begun to sprout and those that have been attacked by worms are discarded. Once sorted, women will feel them between their fingers and then smell them or put a small piece on the tongue (see also Beck *et al.* 1988, pp. 141–2 for similar observations among the Yolngu of northeast Arnhem Land). The cycad kernels are then classified into *ma-yabingalki* or 'food of a good essence', or *ma-wardingalki* or 'food of a bad essence'. Those that are classed as good can be eaten and prepared for eating without further treatment as their age means that the toxins have naturally leached out of them. Women I have worked with say it is only two older women who know how to differentiate between the two. The process was described in Yanyuwa in the following way:

> *Ngayamantharra nganu li-bardibardi li-mirdan muwu-ja ma-wulungu yamulhu namba ju-wurrungkayi yabi, junganu-wuburrmanji kulu junganu-ngalkiwunjayarra, nungka ma-yabi yamulhu anmaya nganuwa, nungka ma-wardi junganu-walimaya.*
>
> Only we old ladies are knowledgeable for this kind of old cycad nut, yes if it smells good, then we rub it, then we taste it [literally: test its essence], alright, if it is good food it stays with us, if it is not good food we throw it away. (Dinah Norman Marrngawi 1987, in Bradley 1980–98)

These old, dried cycad nuts are usually crumbled into a container of water until the mixture is a thick paste, light grey in colour. The food can then be eaten directly and is described as being like porridge; or it can be cooked by wrapping in paperbark and placing in the ashes of a fire; or it can be poured directly onto some clean hot ashes, be cooked on one side, and then flipped over and cooked on the other. Older Yanyuwa people often describe this cycad food as being for old people and children because it is easy to prepare. As long as they are kept dry, the gathered old cycad nuts keep for an indefinite period.

Ma-nhandurangu: a heap of freshly shelled cycad nut kernels ready for further treatment. Such cycad nuts will keep for a few days before they have to be used.

Ma-wirimbul: sliced cycad nut kernels. The nuts were originally sliced using the shoulder blade of the Agile wallaby (*Macropus agilis*) whose thin inner part provided an ideal blade. In later years the tops of tins that had been opened with a can opener were and are occasionally still used. The tops of the lids are folded over and this provides a blunt edge from which to hold the lid and push the sharp round edge through the kernel. The term can be used for both fresh slices that are called *ma-yilbiyilbi* 'moist', and *ma-ruku* 'dry' if they have been dried for the required number of days. After slicing, people speak of the need to be very careful to wash their hands and any object that may have been contaminated by the fresh toxic cycad kernels. The slices of cycad kernel are laid out on large sheets of paperbark to dry in the sun. At the end of each day they are rolled up and then placed back out in the sun the next day. The rolling up prevents the sliced nuts from being dampened by the dew, or made wet by a fall of rain. Children are kept well away from these drying areas, as people are well aware of the toxic nature of the cycad food.

Ma-rabarrarra: cycad nut slices that have been soaking in water for one or two days but are not yet safe to eat or grind. The cycad nuts were soaked in dishes (*na-kulkarra*) made from paperbark or the bark of the messmate tree (*E. tetradonta*), and in more recent times flour drums and buckets. The water was changed daily. After four days the nuts were considered safe to eat.

Ma-ngalkinkarra: soaked cycad nut slices that are ready to eat, grind and cook or re-dry for storage. The term literally means 'being of good essence'. Paperbark bundles of re-dried, fully treated cycad slices were carried long distances by various Indigenous groups in this area. For the Yanyuwa and Garrwa peoples they constituted an important item of trade. The Yanyuwa also took them to the islands off the northern coastline in large packages as they represented an important and readily available food source. A number of older Yanyuwa men and women spoke of storing packages of these cycad slices in dry caves and rock shelters for future use.

Munmun: the froth that gathers on top of the water in which cycad nuts are being soaked.

Ngurlangurla: water in which cycad nuts have been soaking. It is considered very dangerous.

Ma-mawirl: cycad nuts that are either sliced in half or crushed whole using a grinding stone and then laid in long trenches lined with the leaves of the *a-marrabala* (*Grevillea pteridifolia*) tree. The halved or crushed nuts were thrown on top of these leaves. When the required amount of nuts had been placed in the grevillea leaves, more leaves were placed on top, then a layer of dried grass, a layer of paperbark, and then a covering of earth. The nuts were left for one to three months to ferment underground. This method of preparing cycads was used when people knew a ceremony would be happening and sufficient cycad food could be stored to feed the extra number of people. At such times it has been said that old men would sing power songs (*narnu-nyiri*) over some of the trenches. These songs were said to cause the cycad kernels to ferment quickly, but they also had the added effect of making certain cycad-filled trenches available only to the men for their use on the ceremonial ground, even though it was the women who prepared the resulting dampers before handing them over to the men. This method of preparation was usually done prior to the first wet-season storms. It is likely that the rain expected soon after would leach through the ground and help detoxify the cycads in the trenches.

De Latour (1876, no page numbers) described in some detail an area of land used for the ground fermentation of the halved cycad kernels:

> In certain localities hundreds of these mounds may be seen close together, giving the place (especially by moonlight) a most ghostly appearance, and forcibly calls to mind an old village graveyard in the old country.

Ma-yabarlarla: fully fermented halved cycad kernels/crushed kernels that on removal from the trenches have a powerful smell and are black in colour. They are washed and then ground up into paste and baked into dampers or eaten straight after being washed. The root of this word, *yabalarlarla*, literally means 'turtle hatchling'; the figure of speech seems to equate the turtle hatchling, which comes up through the sand, and the cycad nut, which is brought from the earth. The term is not used for any other vegetable food (such as yams which also come from the earth), and as such is probably a symbolic referent to the notion that they are both classed as a food of importance.

Ma-wurrbiyal: ground cycad kernels that resemble a thick paste or dough. The term has as its root *wurrbi,* which means something that is correct and proper in relation to the Law, or its original source or origins. Again this term marks the food as having significance beyond food, and relates cycads directly to the Law whose source lies in the Dreaming.

Ma-lhandawarr/ma-wurlukurlu: dampers/bread made from the ground cycad kernels. The paste is folded into a paperbark container and cooked in the ashes from a fire. When properly cooked the resulting loaf can be sliced. It keeps for about a week.

Ma-wanjirl: large dampers, sometimes up to 50 cm in length, prepared by women but taken by men for use in large secret and sacred ceremonies. Such food could not be eaten by women or children. It is during such ceremonies that cycads became a 'communion food' bread, as suggested by Beaton (1982, p. 57). During these times loaves could be seen publicly and were often placed on specially constructed platforms (*ma-alakala*) for the purpose of payment to senior men after rituals had concluded. These damper pastes were wrapped in paperbark sheets and cooked in hot ashes.

Ma-rdabalarri: small dinner-plate sized dampers cooked in a ground oven. The cycad paste was ground thickly, transferred to a bark dish, and then placed in a pit that contained wood burnt down to hot ashes: dollops of paste were tipped onto the coals. When sufficient paste had been used, hot coals were then placed directly on top of the paste and then the whole ground oven was sealed with paperbark and earth and left to cook for one to two hours. These smaller dampers were specifically made for men who were bringing young circumcision initiates with them for their ceremony. The food was given to the men and could be consumed publicly. Once the men had received it they were free to give it to whom they chose, so both women and children would eventually receive some.

Na-bakinda: notches cut into the trunks of tall cycad palms to facilitate climbing. Large numbers of cycad palms in the Manankurra area show evidence of such notches. It was usually only men and boys who climbed the tall palms to gather the kernel. The very tall palms were usually not climbed due to their associations with the power of the Dreaming said to reside in them.

It should also be noted that after Yanyuwa men and women had been exposed to western gardening methods by white settlers at Borroloola and Manankurra, a number of older Yanyuwa men attempted to transplant cycad palm seedlings on the offshore islands to the immediate north of the mainland. One grove on South West Island grew quite well but was destroyed by Cyclone Kathy in 1984 (Steve Johnson personal communication 1997).

Grindstones and memory

The main tools needed to prepare cycad foods were (as mentioned above) wallaby-bone blades or tin slicers, and grindstones. The grindstones used to prepare the cycad food can still be found *in situ* across the whole area where the cycad palms grow. There is no local stone source in this area for the preparation of the cycad food, and procurement of suitable stone involved negotiation between men and women. The most suitable and most favoured base and top (hand-held) grinding stones came from the Sir Edward Pellew islands; a fine-grained sandstone is found on the northern reaches of Vanderlin Island, Centre Island and North Island (Figure 1).

When a woman wanted to procure a base stone, she would approach her mother's brother, who would then negotiate on her behalf with the men who were owners of the source islands. Most of the grinding-stone plates that still exist in the area today are large and heavy. The men would obtain what they considered to be a suitable stone, sometimes roughly shaping it on the islands before they brought it to the mainland where it was given to the woman who required it. The women also sometimes pecked the stone into a more suitable shape. The simple description given above, however, obscures the effort that was required to get the stone to the places where the women wanted them. For example, if the woman was of an estate that abutted the Wearyan or Foelsche rivers, in the general area of Manankurra, the stone was easily deposited near the desired cycad stands. However, sometimes the stone had to be carried far inland to the west of Manankurra to the lagoon systems that supported large stands of cycad palms. This was especially the case if the women were from the Wawukarriya semi-moiety associated with the vast savanna plains west of Manankurra. The estates in the area of Manankurra are Rrumburriya, Wurdaliya and Wuyaliya, so women of these groups lived near the rivers. Some of these stones have been weighed in the field. A number of them were in excess of 24 kg; the average weight for the ten that were sampled was 19 kg. Some of these stones were carried up to 10 km inland before being deposited at the desired location. From oral histories given by both men and women, it was the men who carried these stones to their locations for the women. Such grinding stone bases are called *rra-walma* in Yanyuwa. The term *walma* is usually a term given to large, flat submerged rocks that surround parts of the coast of the Sir Edward Pellew islands. The prefix *rra-* is a feminine prefix that is added to denote the association of the stone to the activity of women. The term *walma* is used, I suspect, to signify the maritime origins of the base stones and perhaps their similarity of appearance, though on a much reduced scale.

The smaller, round or oval top stone that is held during the grinding process was also sometimes brought from the islands, but equally could be derived from river beds where smooth, water-washed cobbles could be found. Some of these stone have also been weighed, and the ten sampled ranged from 500 g to 1.16 kg. Once the stone was given to the woman it became her property and the property of her matrilineal descendants (see also Hamilton 1980), though any other individual within the appropriate matriline could also procure their own grindstones. The first food prepared on the grindstones was always given to the men who had obtained the grindstone for the woman. The mother's brother of the woman who negotiated the obtaining of the stone could, during times of ceremony, order that the stone only be used for the production of food for ceremonies, and then on completion of the ceremony release it for secular use.

When women moved away from the area where their grindstones were located they often buried them; older Yanyuwa women who were alive in the early 1980s could speak of locations where they or their mother had buried their grindstones (see also Levitt 1981, p. 50). People said that the stones were buried so that individuals who may have wished to exercise sorcery against their families would not be able to ensorcel their grindstones, which would result in any food prepared on them causing sickness or death. Other people stressed their private ownership of the stones and that burying them was a way of avoiding conflict over the rights of other individuals to use the stones. In Yanyuwa the base and top stones are together called *warranthangu*, or 'those things for grinding'.

Today, grindstones are a source of emotional attachment to place and to the past; they have ceased to be used for grinding, as readily available, commercial wheat flour has replaced the once-laboriously produced cycad flour. Occasionally an old grindstone at a still well-used campsite might be used for sharpening a dugong harpoon point, crushing pandanus nuts, or pounding dugong meat to make it soft, but generally speaking they are said to be the property of the 'old people' or the spirits of deceased Yanyuwa people, who still inhabit the landscape and hunt and move over it and still care about the stones (Bradley 1997). Some people believe that to move or tamper with such objects would result in sickness or worse. People become quite emotional about such objects still being present in the landscape. The speaker below located a grindstone that belonged to his father's sister. As he recited the following statement he gently stroked the stone. The text also speaks of the presence of old people in the country and how they guided the speaker to the stone:

> This grindstone is for the old people, our ancestors, they carried it here, from the north, from the sea. It was brought to this placed named Aluwanja so that they could break open and grind the cycad food, also lily corms and *Pandanus* nuts but really cycad food. This stone had been here from times past, it has been here with the senior people, those who are now deceased. When I was small I saw this stone, my father's sister, her name was a-Wambadurna, I saw her here grinding. Now today the old people have allowed[2] me to see it again, I have grown up and for all that time it was hidden from me, but now I am here an old man and I can see it. This grindstone belongs to my father's sister, it makes me sad. (Old Pyro Dirdiyalma 1998, in Bradley 1980–98)

Older people also sustain an enduring and emotional relationship with the area of Manankurra. They maintain a close knowledge of the area, even though they are no longer dependent on it for food. Younger Yanyuwa people who have no knowledge of cycads as a food source also maintain a strong emotional attachment to the locality and to the cycad palms. Partly this relationship is based on the ongoing knowledge of the Dreaming entities associated with the place, but it is also based on stories from the oral tradition of their parents and grandparents who have reminded their descendants of the social and cosmological importance of the place.

Part 3 • Anthropological approaches

Ritual and healing

Some of the public esoteric knowledge associated with Manankurra has a strong cosmological charter. An example of this is the song used to heal a person poisoned by eating untreated cycad kernel. Cosmologically the cycad palm and its kernel are associated with the Yanyuwa Rrumburriya semi-moiety, but the special songs of healing and poisoning associated with the kernel are associated with the Garrwa Wurdaliya semi-moiety. The reasons for this are explained in the following section of the Tiger Shark Dreaming narrative:

> And there was to the south a Spirit Man at *Kalalakinda* [Rocky on the Foelsche River]. He spoke to the Tiger Shark saying, 'Hey! Give me the power songs for the poison that the cycad fruit contains, you live in the water, you are an inhabitant of the sea, while I am a man, a fully initiated man, give the things I ask for to me!' It was in this way the Spirit Man spoke and the power songs belonging to the cycad fruit came to belong to the Wurdaliya people. (Bradley 1988, p. 14)

These songs are now the possession of Garrwa Wurdaliya men and their maternal kinsmen. The songs are jealously guarded and provide a point of tension between the Yanyuwa Rrumburriya men and Garrwa Wurdaliya men and people associated with the cycad palm through their mothers who came from those estates. An example of such a song is given below. The speaker was careful not to sing the song as it is the tune that gives the song its power, but he was quite happy to speak the words and provide glosses and translations for them. This is a healing song for someone who may have eaten untreated cycad kernel, or drunk the water in which still-toxic cycad nuts had been soaking. The person presumed to have been poisoned was sat in a shallow pit lined with cycad palm fronds and a layer of earth. They were seated on the earth-covered cycad palm fronds and the healer placed his mouth over the top of the sick person's head and forcefully sang the song. The recording, of Dinny McDinny Nyilba and made in 1986 (in Bradley 1980–98), was said to drive the poison from the body and back into the cycad fronds and the earth:

> Driving you out!
> Blocking your progress!
> Driving you out!
> Poison of the cycad fruit!
> Go back to your source!
> Poison of the cycad fruit
> Go back to the hair of you head [literally: cycad palm fronds]

Such a song highlights the issues of trying to come to a holistic understanding of ownership of resources in an Indigenous setting. It is a situation that is mediated by religion, kinship and rights to knowledge. No single group can be considered to know everything, so there is also a sense of mutual engagement with each other that is at the same time seen as a partnership but also a source of tension. The rights to own resources and associated information in situations such as the cycad palm and kernel are complex and multi-faceted.

Manankurra is also an increase centre for the cycad palm, a place where its reproductive power is located and that can be stimulated by the correctly affiliated and knowledgeable people.[3] In past times, the control of increase sites and associated knowledge was of considerably more importance than it is now. There was once a high degree of prestige attached to the authority and knowledge to perform the necessary increase rituals at a particular site. People are no longer dependent on the resources associated with increase sites, such as cycad palms at Manankurra, and the knowledge concerning most of them brings little social power and prestige to those who still possess the necessary knowledge. In the pre-contact period up until probably the 1950s, just prior to the permanent settlement of the Yanyuwa people at the township of Borroloola, the knowledge and associated actions concerning the maintenance of species appears to have been much more impressive. Those individuals who were called upon to perform the rites had a degree of prestige and negotiating power which they used with individuals in the society who were seeking the rituals to be performed, as the following highlights:

> They would be asking him my brother, his name was Jayungkurri, they would ask him, 'Make the cycad nuts come out in abundance, so next year there will be more, make it so there will be much food so we will not starve.' He would say, 'Mmm. Alright but you will get a sea turtle for me.' They would say yes to that. Then he would go and get a stick, a small one, he would put his sweat from under his armpit on it, he would strike a cycad nut kernel and then he would throw it into the palm fronds, one here, another over there, yet another further away, all the way like that. When he threw the cycad kernel he would call out in the following manner, 'Cycad kernel! Cycad kernel! May you become many! May there be an abundance!' That was it, he would come back and they would give him a turtle, maybe a kangaroo, alright they would wait and next year there would be too many cycad nuts, nobody would go hungry ... Nobody does that today ... I can do it if I want to. (Ida Ninganga 1988, in Bradley 1980–98)

The final comment, 'if I want to' is of interest, as it reflects the contemporary setting in relation to the cycad palms at Manankurra and to increase sites general. The above speaker could have indeed performed the rituals, but she has no need to. The Yanyuwa community, now centred in the township of Borroloola, is no longer economically dependent on the kernel of the cycad palm; the speaker had no way of getting to Manankurra to perform the rituals; and why perform the rituals when there is no need to?

While this ritual may no longer be performed, Yanyuwa people are still insistent about the annual burning of the country around Manankurra. There are a number of reasons for this. Primarily it is perceived as a requirement under Indigenous Law and it seems to be beneficial to the country (Bradley et al. 1997), and secondly the Yanyuwa believe that regular burning of cycad country will help keep the palms 'healthy', that is they will produce abundant nuts and they will ripen at the same time (see also Beaton 1982). Such an understanding raises issues of the anthropogenic nature of the cycad stands in the Manankurra region. A question that needs to be discussed (though it is beyond the scope of this chapter) is the relationship of the numerous cycad stands in the area, and whether their formation is also due in part to a background of long-term human activity. Older Yanyuwa men and women believe that the country is not as productive as it once was because they are not moving through the country, burning it and using the cycad nut as an annual resource:

> This country is a little bit low, it is a sad place, they have all gone, all the old people who hunted and sang and danced many ceremonies here. The children have gone, those who used to laugh and play here, they have gone, the land is silent. The woman have gone those who used to hunt and dance they have gone. There is only me here, this country is weak. In times when I was a child this country would move with people, this food, this cycad food was everywhere in abundance, there is nothing now, the old people have gone the country is weak, we cannot hear it. (Johnson Timothy Rakawurlma 1990)

This emotive comment speaks of what it is that keeps the land healthy. Primarily it is use: if the land is used it will become an abundant place. The last comment is also interesting. The ability to hear country is a process of quiet observation and introspection where an individual will quietly absorb all that country is, in terms of its historical, economic and religious wealth. Today people say that there are too many movements in the country — tourists, travellers, pastoralists — and this, combined with the sad death of kin, are all things that cloud the process of listening.

Conclusion

In Yanyuwa and Garrwa life, cycads are more than sources of food. They invite particular sets of relationships between genders, between kin groups, between individuals who trace their ancestry to particular Dreamings, between landowners and land managers. The meanings of cycads in Indigenous life are also located in particular metaphoric relations that link the plant to other elements in the landscape, such as the Tiger Shark. The grindstones used to process cycads are themselves entangled in complex gender, kinship and broader intergroup relations. Cycads are thus a source of Yanyuwa and Garrwa identity, participating in the social construction of being through its engagement in day-to-day practice. Cycads are meaningful, and as such changes in their human engagement imply changes in their meaningfulness and in the way they contribute to social identity. Given their strongly gendered position in Indigenous life, the emergence of cycad use also implies a change in the gendering of the social and cultural landscape, along with the complex social processes and contradictions that this may entail. While no archaeological research has yet been undertaken in Yanyuwa and Garrwa country, cycads offer an opportunity to investigate long-term cultural dynamics and the emergence of the ethnographically known cultural landscape. What is at stake is the historical emergence of the ethnographically documented ways people interact with place, with each other, and of how metaphoric relations are referenced in the creation of distinctively Yanyuwa and Garrwa worldviews. Like other aspects of the material record, it is more than the material object that is at stake when considering the archaeological record, but the history of how objects articulate in everyday life, historicising notions of being, and in the process of social identity.

A Yanyuwa approach to an environment — such as that embodied by a single place like Manankurra — is not simple. It is firmly based on esoteric, mystical and practical utilitarian knowledge, such as through the use of fire or the technology to treat toxic cycad palm food. Ultimately, the 'practical' too has a profound significance. The land and people are firmly bound together. Speech, use of resources, fire and ritual may not seem particularly important to an outside observer, but they are aspects of continual engagement and negotiation with country and with people, which to the internal workings of a community are very important. Ultimately all events are related to each other: they are a synthesis. These are principles that the Yanyuwa well understand. Through constant negotiation with the past and present, with self and the community, it is this requirement of 'balance' that they hope to achieve with the 'big places' on their country, such as Manankurra. In this sense, the cycad kernel itself offers us evidence for Yanyuwa notions of responsibility to country and therefore its significance. And yet despite its place as a source of food — or maybe because of it — cycads cannot adequately be perceived simply in dietary terms. Cycads are located in a meaningfully structured world, a world of cosmological signification, of social and spiritual order. It is metaphorically associated with other aspects of Yanyuwa life, such as the Tiger Shark, and it references notions of belonging, helping to construct social relationships and territorial relations in the process. The cycad food was once eaten, but it requires correct preparation before it can provide sustenance; conversely, if it is used incorrectly it causes illness and ultimately death. This perhaps is the metaphor for Indigenous perceptions of land use in general.[4]

Individuals and groups today still claim rights and responsibilities to cycad groves such as those at Manankurra. These rights and responsibilities are in the form of ceremonial knowledge, in the responsibility to burn the country regularly, to generally see that the land and associated cycad palms are not damaged, and to ensure that the food is used properly and not wasted if it is to be used by anyone. These are also the birthrights of children born into the appropriate land-owning groups, and are deemed a part of the ongoing relationships with place. Each of these continuing interests positions cycads not merely as an item of food, but as a source of social power and sentiment that articulate relations between people, between people and the land, and between people, the land and the spirits who give the former their identity. The ongoing use of cycads in social process heralds their involvement in the construction of social and personal identity, through a process of social dwelling that implicates all engaged 'objects'. Because of this, tracing the history of human engagement with cycads, through archaeological research, has implications for the history of Yanyuwa signification of place and being, sociality, territoriality, gender relations, and Yanyuwa identity. It is this ontological embeddedness of cycads that I have tried to unfold in this chapter.

Acknowledgements

This paper would not have been possible without the support and enthusiasm of the following Yanyuwa people: Annie Karrakayn, Dinah Norman, Jemima Miller, Don Miller, Pyro Dirdiyalma, Dinny McDinny, Steve Johnston, Johnson Timothy, Old Tim Rakawurlma and Leo Yulungurri.

Bruce Rigsby, Harry Lourandos, Elizabeth Mackinlay and Steven Johnson made valuable comments on an earlier draft. Tony Roberts assisted with a number of hard-to-locate articles.

Notes

1. Statements from informants used throughout this paper come from two sources. Short statements were written down as heard in the language given: Kriol, Yanyuwa or Aboriginal English. The longer texts are from field tape recordings, the majority of which were in Yanyuwa. A few of the statements were recorded after a particular event had occurred and I was interested in the content of the speech and I asked the speaker to restate the information for me on tape.
2. In the original Yanyuwa version of the text the term I translate as 'have allowed' is the Yanyuwa phrase *kalu-ngunda ngarna-mi* which literally means 'they have given me eyes'. The same term is used when young men and women have restricted knowledge revealed to them for the first time by senior men and women.
3. The people who are seen to be able activate the creative energy at such sites are senior men and women whose mothers have come from that country.
4. I am indebted to Steve Johnson who drew this analogy for me.

11.

Landscapes with shadows of once-living people: the *kundawira* challenge

Amanda Kearney and John J Bradley

This chapter concerns the explication of sociality for the human past. It represents a commitment to social archaeologies and sees the coming together of archaeological, ethnographic and ethnoarchaeological observations in a study of material culture. The latter discipline, ethnoarchaeology is a research strategy that embodies a range of approaches to understanding people in the past (Nicholas & Kramer 2001). The significance of its contribution to archaeology has traditionally come from the perceived value of mapping contemporary Aboriginal behaviour onto the archaeological record, enabling actualistic studies, and providing a range of possibilities to explain human action in the past (Nicholas &Kramer 2001). Ethnoarchaeology is commonly described as a branch of archaeology that uses ethnographic data to inform the examination and interpretation of the archaeological record. In some cases this involves the study of living communities by selectively looking at the archaeologically recoverable material culture: a sort of living archaeology. Ethnoarchaeologists carry out a kind of ethnography to examine and document the relationships between human behaviour and the resultant patterns of artefacts and food remains (Darvill 2002, p.136).

In the context of this study, we argue — in line with Robins and Trigger (1989, p. 42) — that ethnoarchaeology's significance to archaeology comes not from the value of mapping contemporary Aboriginal behaviour onto the archaeological record, but rather comes from the challenge it presents to archaeologists, who need to be aware of relationships between objects and human behaviour that challenge old notions and perhaps prompt the search for alternative explanations. One setting in which these points come together and illuminate the complex social engagements that people have with the world is within the context of Yanyuwa culture.

The Yanyuwa are the Indigenous owners of land and sea in the south-west Gulf of Carpentaria, Northern Territory, Australia. Their country includes the delta regions of the McArthur River and the saltwater limits of the McArthur and Wearyan rivers and the Sir Edward Pellew Islands. The offshore islands and immediate coastal areas represent the foundation of Yanyuwa thought and existence, thus for the Yanyuwa their identity is grounded in the expression *li-anthawirriyarra*, 'those people whose spiritual and cultural origins are from the sea' (Bradley 1997, 12). They are people of the sea.

Yanyuwa country represents a vast and complex social and physical world that has the character of a contested land and seascape. Both today and in the past, Yanyuwa people have asserted their group identity and place in the world by anchoring this identity to the land, sea, animals, elements, phenomena, ancestral spirits and objects. The relationships that people activate with all elements of the physical, cognitive and ideational world are inherently social and necessarily linked to the actions of those people and spirit beings who came before.

Working in the context of Yanyuwa country demands an approach to the human past that is culturally relative and socially aware. Hence, archaeological work in this country is framed by the principles of a post-structural social archaeology, abandoning conventional approaches to the human past in preference of an approach that tackles sociality and emotion in understandings of the past and embraces multiplicities of meaning to explain the tangible heritage of human groups. This type of approach allows for flexibility in the techniques of analysis and interpretation that are employed in studies of material culture. A post-structural and socially oriented climate in archaeology has seen the discipline extend its range of research concerns as far and wide as landscapes and sociality; bereavement and commemoration; the social role of material culture; the individual, personhood and identity; the relationship between archaeology and anthropology; the history of archaeological thought; and post-structural, phenomenological and feminist approaches to the past (see Bapty & Yates 1990; Barrett 2001; Conkey & Spector 1984; Gilchrist 1994; Gosden 1994; Shanks & Tilley 1987b; Sorenson 2000; Tarlow 1999, 2000; Thomas 1996, 2001; Tilley 1994). We draw on several of these themes in attempting to understand Yanyuwa material culture.

Material culture, as part of the social archaeology project, is understood as a point of engagement, entanglement and experience among human groups. This in itself is nothing new, as postmodern, post-structuralist, interpretive and social archaeologies have been with us for the better part of two decades, during which concepts of sociality and humanity have been debated and reconfigured. Post-modern archaeological approaches are closely aligned with the principles of post-structuralism, which is the guiding theoretical paradigm of social archaeologies. As Walsh (1990, p. 279) notes, 'the philosophical roots of what is seen to be the post-modern world . . . lay with post-structuralism and its implicit denial of the possibility of discussing absolute "truths" and "values"'. A postmodern approach, as adopted here, is one that attempts to theorise the 'social' with conscious abandonment of the 'metanarratives' or 'guiding principles' (long upheld in archaeological practice) that imply a rigid objectivism and thorough, authoritative, analysis of the world. This requires 'broad critical concern with a number of issues' (Smart 1996, p. 399). These include: the crisis of representation and associated instability of meaning; the absence of secure foundations for knowledge (Smart 1996, p. 399); and a general mistrust of grand theories, and any notion of 'truth' (Pearsall & Trumble 1996, p. 1132). What presents itself as the point of departure from orthodox archaeological investigations is this study's preoccupation with the social networks surrounding people and the objects of their daily and sacred lives and the emotions that come into being with people's recollections of objects of and in the past.

Social archaeologies are often seen to breach the disciplinary boundaries of orthodox method and practice, increasingly blurring the line between anthropology and archaeology — disciplines long held to be separate. Continuing this tradition, and in an effort to illustrate the methods and merits of a socially informed approach to the human past and its residing expressions, this work presents an ethnographic account of one element of the tangible record of the Yanyuwa people's past. By reflecting on 'stone markers' — or what the Yanyuwa people term *kundawira* — we aim to highlight the complex relationships people have with place and with objects, particularly those objects that are entangled in the past and present, with little hope of ever belonging exclusively to one or the other.[1]

The *kundawira* are part of a system of complex engagement that Yanyuwa people have with aspects of material culture and the world around them. The use of stone markers in the past, and the continued significance that surrounds the *kundawira* today, are testament to the embedded nature of material culture and the extent to which material culture elements have the capacity to constitute and self-regulate culture itself (see Hodder 1989, 1991). This chapter focuses on a discussion of the link between objects and people and the ability of a standing piece of sandstone to carry or embody layers of meaning and significance, something that can be incorporated into reconstructions of sociality, engagement and emotion in the human past. As such, we indirectly seek to address the manner in which anthropology and archaeology has long sought to define items of material culture in rather limited terms and to categorise them according to classes of non-utilitarian and utilitarian. The *kundawira* are utilitarian but, in ways that run much deeper than every day practical use, they reflect the enduring relationships between people, spirit beings, landscape and memory. The stones also embody some of the sentiment behind the term 'sacred' and demonstrate that, for the Yanyuwa people at least, the term is intimately linked to places, people and objects and adheres to both the sacred and profane in an incredibly complex system of meaning and constitution.

Rethinking material culture

In dealing with these concerns, we adopt the view that material culture is more than simply reflective of culture but in many ways goes to constitute it (see Hodder 1982, 1989, 1991; Tilley 1990). In many instances humans have a cognitive and symbolic intimacy with the construction and actualisation of material culture items, and it is these items that potentially become the objects of concern for archaeologists. As Jordan (2001, p. 25) writes, the formation of both human and material culture biographies is recursively linked to the spatial, temporal and social organisation of ritual and daily activities across the landscape. In a discussion of the *kundawira*, a working definition of material culture is applied that extends beyond the conventional realm of the physical remains of humanly made traces of past societies to include a more holistic and socially constructed view of material culture. The physicality of material culture is not central to the definition employed here.

Although the *kundawira* are tangible expressions of past engagements with place, the knowledge associated with the stones is not. In an effort to capture something of this knowledge and understand the *kundawira* as constituted in tangible and intangible form, as a socially embedded and living object, we have opted for a view of material culture that incorporates the constructedness of culture and elements of cultural expression that surround the material object. *Kundawira* are created and socially located as part of an overall process of cultural construction and place making. All of this is built from knowledge of the Yanyuwa past and present, ancestors and Law. People's engagements with *kundawira*, as one part of the material culture of Yanyuwa people, reflect and manifest an accumulated body of knowledge or enculturated *habitus*. Knowledge of the *kundawira*, the history of these stones and the embedded meaning they instill in the land is part of the accumulated body of cultural traditions held by Yanyuwa people. This knowledge is as much a cultural artefact as the stone itself, with both being creations of Yanyuwa being that have been maintained through time, to persist in the present.

A discussion of stone markers must be set within a cultural framework, in which systems of meaning and material culture are understood in terms of causal loops in human action. For the Yanyuwa people, the *kundawira* are located in one part of a system of interdependence of action and meaning whereby the existence of the stones creates the possibility of their meaning and some of the sociality inherent in human engagements with the spiritual and physical worlds. As such, these stones, and their continued place in Yanyuwa oral histories and individual narratives, present us with a wonderful — and unique — opportunity to generate a different type of account of material culture. We take the position that, in the context of Yanyuwa country, the politicising of place, people and objects throughout a history of colonial incursion — and the historically embedded nature of Yanyuwa engagements with the world — it is necessary to generate an account of *kundawira* that is of a different scale to that which is typically generated in orthodox archaeological accounts of material culture. A culturally attuned approach is one that locates these stones within a lived and living 'countryscape'[2], emphasising the value of incorporating sociality into our disciplinary focus and confidently drawing links between the time frames of the recent and distant pasts and the present.

The stones of great men

On lonely islets, windswept beaches, rocky headlands, lodged in caves and crevices, scattered along the sandy banks of freshwater rivers and creeks among stands of cypress pines, cycad palms and eucalyptus, occasionally forgotten on the edge of a lonely lagoon, stand and lie — sometimes half buried — sandstone obelisks. These stones, few of which exceed 60 cm in height, are silent sentinels of the past lives of important men. In December of 1802, while travelling on North Island, Matthew Flinders observed these stones and recorded the occasion in his diary *Voyage to Terra Australis*, writing (1814, p. 172):

> Under a shed of bark were two cylindrical pieces of stone about 18 inches long; which seem to have been made smooth from rolling in the surf, and formed into a shape something like a nine pin. Round each of them were drawn two black circles, one towards each end; and between them were four oval black patches at equal distances around the stone, made apparently with charcoal. The spaces between the oval marks were covered with white down and feathers, stuck on with the yolk of a turtle's egg, as I judged by the gluten and by the shell lying near the place. Of the intention in setting up these stones under a shed, no person could form a reasonable conjecture; the first idea was, that it had some relation to the dead, and we dug underneath to satisfy our curiosity; but nothing was found.

The obelisks that Flinders describes are classified by archaeologists as cylcons (see Cundy 1985, p. 1), and have been recorded in parts of eastern and central northern Australia (see Black 1942; Etheridge 1916; Kamminga & Allen 1973, p. 11; McCarthy 1976, p. 66; McCourt 1975, pp. 149–52). In the archaeological literature they are given relatively minor consideration and granted the term 'cylcon' as a generic classification given to 'cyclidro-conical stones, cylindrical in shape, tapering to a pointed or distal end' (McCarthy 1976, p. 66). While some acknowledge a symbolic function, other archaeologists have sought to identify a strictly utilitarian function for such stones, as extrapolated from the use-wear patterns observed in some recorded cases. The most obvious utilitarian purpose attributed thus far has pertained to food preparation, pounding hollows and mortar and pestle arrangements.

Cundy (1985) sought to amalgamate both utilitarian and symbolic lines of thinking in a study of cylcons from the Northern Territory. In his work he attempted to ascribe a utilitarian use for the stones and discussed research by Peterson (1969), Warner (1958) and Levitt (1981), each of whom record ethnographic observations of the stones being used in the preparation of foodstuffs. Cundy (1985, p. 1) took the discussion of the cylcons to another level, however, when he suggested that over the life history of the cylcon they underwent complex functional shifts between cultural subsystems: from an initial ritual use to later incorporation in preparation technology. He sought to test this proposition archaeologically, by examining use-wear patterns on the cylcons and reduction sequences.

Having examined the use-wear and identified patterns of battering, flaking and surface smoothing, Cundy moved towards three hypotheses of functional change. He (1985, p. 6) prefaced a discussion of these hypotheses by noting that 'much of the use-wear observed on these forms can be attributed to recent food production, rather than ritual behaviour', but acknowledged that a lack of ethnographic literature to shed light on the likely food production methods and techniques presents challenges to this view. To overcome this incongruity he (1985, p. 8) proposed the following hypotheses to account for a functional change:

1. That the transference of forms from one subsystem to another was maintained as a method of disposing of sacred stone objects. This would have the advantage of freeing potentially usable stone resources for use in the technological system, in an area where such resources were not readily available.

2. That cylcons represent not the final user's solution to disposal, but that of a neighbour. This implies that sacred objects, and those associated with them, were often incorporated into an exchange system once the appropriate ceremonies were over. The cylcons' systems switch could therefore be a product of exchange of this sort.

3. That the functional shift occurred through local cultural change. In this case diachronic change in the socio-ideological subsystem would have made previously captured stone resources available at a later time for utilisation in the preparation technology.

Cundy's (1985) attempts to locate the cylcons within the dual worlds of sacred and non-sacred functionality gave only a partial account of the potential sacred functions performed by the stone markers. His initial claims that much of the use-wear identified on the cylcons was attributable to food preparation underpinned his hypotheses. His preference is to treat the cylcons as liminal objects teetering on the brink of ceremonial and technological worlds. The potentials for sacred meaning are not treated explicitly and it is assumed that objects once at home in socio-ideological subsystems can necessarily be released from this category and their sociality diluted through the act of exchange and re-inscription.

Amateur ethnographers and anthropologists have attempted to identify and record the social function of these objects. Having described the stones at length, McCarthy (1976, pp. 63–4) writes:

> The simple line motifs on the cylcons represent the earliest art of the Australian Aborigines . . . Cylcons were in use probably from a very early period of occupation . . . Unfortunately, no information about their meaning or function has been obtained from the Aborigines . . . it is generally believed that they had a ritual significance.

Among the earliest interpretations for the cylcons that were gathered from Aboriginal informants in the nineteenth century were claims that the stones were used in rain-making, in ceremonies 'for the purpose of increasing the supply of snakes', 'in ceremonial observances connected with the assembling of people at the time the mardoo seed was ripe', 'in incantations for causing the supply of game and other food to increase', and for other 'secret ceremonies' (Black 1942, pp. 20–24). Authors such as Harney (1959) attributed the stones to fertility rituals and sorcery and both Warner (1958) and Berndt and Berndt (1964) speak of stone sacred objects in the general western Arnhem Land area. Given the range of possible functions for 'cylcons' it would seem that a generic and purely utilitarian and technological classification does not do justice to the range of form or nature of these objects. Certainly, reflecting on these points within the context of Yanyuwa epistemology and culture reveals that 'stone markers' are embedded in a world of social meaning and shrouded in a sociality that gives altogether new meanings to notions of material culture and embedded artefacts. By examining and reconstructing the place-based nature of stone markers it is possible to consciously incorporate symbolism and meaning into archaeological understandings of the human and material record and re-inscribe these meaningful objects in a much more complex category than the simple term 'cylcon'.

In the case of Yanyuwa stone markers, Flinders' belief — that these stones could possibly be related to burial practices — is not far from the truth. They have long been associated with the memory of deceased kin, at times taking the physical place of the deceased's body in cases where it could not be retrieved.

They were also placed on country in instances where the *jungkayi* ('manager' of country) and *ngimirringki* ('owner' of country: see Bradley *et al.* 1992, pp. 159–60) of the site desired to revivify decaying log coffins by leaving a stone marker in their place (McLaughlin, 1977 p. 1280). In Yanyuwa language these *kundawira* are given the more specific name of *wurlulu* (Bradley 1992, p. 312). The stones were transformed into sacred *kundawira* through the process of ceremony — a ceremony that carries the same name, i.e. *Kundawira*.

The *kundawira* stones are imbued with a sociality from their initial entry into the 'socio-material' world of Yanyuwa culture. This sociality originates in the location where the stones were found. In the past they were obtained from locations classed as *yijan*, places created in the ancestral, Creative past at a time when ancestral spirits or Dreaming beings travelled across the land and sea. These are places where the spirit ancestors now reside; *yijan* places are of the Dreaming. The stones were removed from *yijan* places with the intent of bringing into being the memories of deceased kin. The potency of *yijan* places is what renders the stones appropriate to be *kundawira* and, once acquired, the stones were not altered in any way, other than with the placement of designs in a ritual context.[3] Through the act of adding designs the stone was transformed to symbolically represent the individual, thus anchoring people's memory to the object and the object's place of resting. In the case of *kundawira*, the objects were enlivened by virtue of where they came from and how Yanyuwa people subsequently engaged them with. In many cases, these stones represent metamorphosed elements of the Dreaming.

The places where the stones were obtained are manifestations of the spirit ancestors, their bodies and their travels. It is at these points on country that the ancestors are still seen to reside and it is to these places that Yanyuwa social memory is anchored. Muluwa, Cape Vanderlin, is one such location. Muluwa is rich in an ancestral history that is dominated by a huge sand dune that is the body of the Wave Spirit Ancestor and also the mark of the Sea Snake Spirit Ancestor. Below the sand dune, standing in the sea, is Ngangangayu — an elderly ancestral Dugong Hunter who remained behind as his kinsmen travelled on into the west. The Tiger Shark Yulungurri passed through the area, as did Mananjana the Hammerhead Shark, accompanied by his two stingray companions. Scattered along a section of the intertidal zone lie many egg-shaped stones deposited by the *a-Kuwaykuwayk* bird. This bird is large but invisible, described as being like a bustard. She pulled a string (*yurrwa*) through the air, on which were attached sorcery stones that are called *wukurdu* or *wayku*. Where this ancestral bird rested she left the sorcery stones. The stones deposited at Muluwa by the *a-Kuwaykuwayk* are also *kundawira*: the stones that could be transformed, through ritual, into the memory of deceased men.

The *wayku* stones of the *a-Kuwaykuwayk*, while respected, are not overly feared.[4] If one were to be removed — with the intent to bring forth the memory of a deceased kinsmen — then that stone would begin the process to becoming *kundawira* and, during its transformation, it would be granted the enduring status of *kurdukurdu*, meaning that it would become secret and sacred (these terms are not, however, fixed categories in Yanyuwa cosmology). *Muluwa* is classified *yijan awara* by Yanyuwa people. It is a place where the spirit ancestors found their final home and where others left behind some of their possessions and their *ngalki* — the essence or quality which all things carry in Yanyuwa worldview, and with which the spirit ancestors created and named the country.

When one looks west across the sea from Muluwa, the cliffs of Red Bluff, Wulibirra rear up. In Yanyuwa tradition Muluwa is the older brother and Wulibirra the younger brother. Collectively these two places are called by the kin term *nyinkarra*: younger and older brother. The Yanyuwa say that Muluwa and Wulibirra are *nyinkarra jawulamba-wunkananji yurrngumantha kariya baki karakarra*: 'the younger brother and the older brother who are continually looking at each other from the west and east'. Wulibirra is the final resting place of the White-bellied Sea Eagle Spirit Ancestor (*a-Wurrwilhi*); she stands there today as a huge monolith looking at her nest of disturbed eggs below her on the shoreline. This place is known as Kandanbarrawujbi: 'her eggs fell down'. Wulibirra and Kandanbarrawujbi are also *yijan awara*, the final resting place of this sea bird. The whole area is held to be *kurdukurdu*: secret and sacred. There are two reasons for this. Firstly the White-bellied Sea Eagle spirit ancestor is the creator of, and major being celebrated in, the *Kundawira* rituals during which the *wayku* stones from Muluwa or the eggs from Wulibirra become stone markers: objects of memory and remembering. Secondly, Wulibirra is also the final resting place for the bones of deceased kin from this country, either wrapped firmly in bundles of paperbark or interred in hollow log coffins. Many *kundawira* have also been returned to Wulibirra and stand and lie in various locations. Wulibirra may be the younger brother, but he is considered by the Yanyuwa to be the most potent.

As illustrated by the stone markers 'coming into being' and *yijan* associations, these objects were not merely incorporated into the repertoire of Yanyuwa people's material life. They exist by virtue of the ancestral past and underwent a journey to become objects of such magnitude. This magnitude is ultimately expressed in the object's power to embody deceased kin, to transform the meaning attached to place, and to subsequently set the parameters of interaction — and demand certain behaviours and actions on the part of Yanyuwa people — in their relationships to one another, points across the landscape and objects. Once placed in the country of the deceased individual the *kundawira* could imbue a status of *kurdukurdu* or *nganjira* on the land, as in the case of Wulibirra and Kandanbarrawujbi. *Kurdukurdu* places are points on the land that are restricted zones, often located within a wider restricted area. That is, trespass on the land was forbidden to all but the most senior and appropriate men.[5] The concepts involved in such terms as *kurdukurdu* or *nganjirra* can be applied to places, to times (such as during the performance of certain ceremonies), to objects and to procedures. It is often conceived as a physical force that can pass from one object to another and have potentially dangerous power. The rules governing *kurdukurdu* places and objects were such that only people under control of the *jungkayi* could view the *kundawira* and only *jungkayi* — and those with permission from the *jungkayi* — could visit *kurdukurdu* places.

The terms *kurdukurdu* and *nganjirra* carry connotations of prestige and power, an understanding that is encompassed by the Kriol term 'dear'. In Kriol the word 'dear' is applied to those things that are considered sacred and of great value. The term does not always mean absolute restriction, in terms of access and viewing, as long as specific procedures are followed; for example, certain public funeral rituals are classified as *kurdukurdu*. However, where Yanyuwa Law sanctioned significant restrictions, disregard for the procedures that were in place to govern human engagement and action — whether intentional or otherwise — was seen as a desecration that may lead to disastrous results. Procedures or rules of engagement and action are addressed to the whole community, not just individuals or groups of individuals. As such, the *kundawira* is given the power of agency, and acts to ascribe meaning to country, mediating the interaction of Law, the spirit ancestors, *Yijan*, the deceased individual and living Yanyuwa people. The power and prestige contained in the object and the land of its placement brought a distinct status to that land, taking on the additional and unmistakable connotations of symbolic and spiritual wealth. Places imbued with this status are called *wurrama awara* (a place of authority) or *wirrimalaru awara* (a place of great power).

The making of meaning

The power and status to transform the *kundawira* was achieved through undertaking the *Kundawira* ceremony. The ceremony provided the channels to make the *kundawira* a stone marker for the deceased person. It was the *Kundawira* ceremony that provided the pathway by which the stones were transformed into the memory of people. Once having been placed in a ritual context, designs were worked onto the stone using bird's down (*yirriny*) coloured with red and white ochre, with blood being used as a fixative.[6] These designs represented the major spirit ancestor of the person concerned, or sometimes the spirit ancestor of the deceased persons mother. Thus the stone became a symbolic representation of the person and patterns of kinship, as they exist within Yanyuwa society.

The ceremony has not been performed since the mid-1930s, and the last of the old men and women who were familiar with this ceremony died in the 1990s.[7] Why the ceremony is no longer performed is not a necessary part of this discussion, suffice to say that the last group of performers and owners suggested to Bradley that the world had become 'too busy' for such things, and that the world now 'moved too fast' (Johnson Timothy 1985, personal communication). Amid such discussion there were also suggestions that the cattle industry, which came with the arrival of non-Indigenous land ownership in the region, and its need for a labour force, removed the young men from the community, resulting in many of them travelling hundreds of kilometres away from the coast. Increased mobility and settlement beyond the Gulf country also occurred as part of an overall process of 'coming in', which saw the old people from the islands move in to Borroloola, and with this came the development of a more sedentary life and town-based lifestyle (see Baker 1989a, 1989b, 1990, 1999). These developments created a distance between the locations of the stones needed for the ceremony and the old men of knowledge, a distance that became too great for these men to traverse. Gradually, the ceremony fell into abeyance, but the significance of the remaining stones did not — as evidenced by the continued importance of these stones and the rich social memory attached to the *kundawira* in present times.

Prior to the undertaking of the *Kundawira* ceremony, the process of acquiring the stones was in itself a socially structured affair. Reflective of the pivotal role of kinship in structuring Yanyuwa people's lives and individual histories, the stones were most often acquired by the sons of the deceased person's sister. The role of nephews in their mother's brother's funeral rites or commemorative rites reflects a close personal relationship which was, and still is, indicative of relatives in the category of maternal uncle and nephew. The articulation of this relationship is linked closely to Yanyuwa bride bestowal, whereby the mother's brother is credited with providing his sister to his nephew's father. Thus, the role of the nephew in preparing the *kundawira* was critical and functioned in a varied framework of negotiated relationships that includes this affinal (i.e. close family, blood relations) dimension. Men who wished to obtain *kundawira* stones as symbols of remembrance and memory had to provide gifts to the senior *ngimarringki* and *jungkayi* for the rights to obtain and possess a stone. Only the men concerned with the ownership of the stones' source locality had the capacity to carry out the transformative ceremony of *Kundawira*. Furthermore, those wishing to acquire a *kundawira* also had to pay for the performance of the correct rituals, rituals which could transform the stones.

While it is difficult to reconstruct the nature of 'payment' that was issued for the acquisition or transformation of the *kundawira*, older Yanyuwa men and women suggest that payment meant in the first instance foodstuffs of authority, such as dugong, sea turtle and cycad dampers. Material goods also used in the exchange included items such as human-hair string belts, pubic tassels of spun possum fur, harpoon ropes, boomerangs and women.

As reflected in the processes of acquiring, creating and maintaining the *kundawira*, Yanyuwa kinship is vital to structuring the world and the place of Yanyuwa people within that world of meaning. Understanding something of the relationships between people is imperative to understanding the sociality of *kundawira* as embodiments of kinship classification, Yanyuwa people, *ngalki* and Law.

Four terminological lines of descent characterise the system, each distinguished at a grandparental level. Thus, an individual may be perceived as being descended from all four distinct patrilineages of his or her father's father (*wirriyarra*), mother's father (*nyankarra*), father's mother (*mankarraninja*) and mother's mother (*wutharraninja*). Each of these lines of descent has a set of rights and responsibilities linked to ownership and kinship, and is associated with spirit ancestors for certain tracts of land. The four lines of descent can be matched to a moiety and semi-moiety. The semi-moiety system divides people, land and animals, plants and phenomena into four named types: *Wurdaliya, Wuyaliya, Rrumburriya* and *Mambaliya-Wawukarriya*.

Recruitment of people to semi-moieties is patrilineal, in that a person belongs to the same semi-moiety as his or her father. The children of a marriage belong to the semi-moiety of their father, but they also have important rights and responsibilities to the semi-moiety of their mother. Marriage ideally should be exogamous, whereby partners are found in the opposite semi-moiety. At their most basic semi-moieties are categories that codify relationships of kin and relationships of importance in land and ritual activities. The semi-moiety also provides a framework for inter-group alignment. Each semi-moiety is described as having direct paternal kinship with certain spirit ancestors and owning a set of rituals, designs, sacred objects and songs which then gives them pivotal rights to land and sea ownership. If a Yanyuwa individual is asked who owns a particular portion of land and sea, the answer is inevitably a semi-moiety category. In more contemporary times, a family surname is often given as a link to a semi-moiety. These surnames are often referred to obliquely as, for example, the 'Friday mob' or 'the Timothy mob'. While semi-moiety categories are used to express general notions of land ownership, there are within each semi-moiety a number of smaller patrilineal clans or patriclans.

In the context of this paper the *kundawira* stones are associated with the *Rrumburriya* semi-moiety. Both the White-bellied Sea Eagle and the *a-Kuwaykuwayk* 'bird' are *Rrumburriya*, thus the ceremony of *Kundawira* was seen to be the exclusive possession of the *Rrumburriya* semi-moiety, and in particular with the patriclans of North and Vanderlin islands. Rights to use the stones and have them placed on country belonging to the other semi-moieties could be negotiated, and this was often achieved through the development of kin ties structured on gift giving and patterns of bride bestowal. Thus, while it is most common to find these stones on *Rrumburriya* country, there are also large numbers on *Mambaliya-Wawukarriya* country and a few on both *Wuyaliya* and *Wurdaliya* country. Therefore, these stones stand as important indicators of inter-group relationships over many years.

Kundawira as the embodiment of Yanyuwa Law and ways of being is a persistent theme in ethnographic observations and contemporary social memories attached to these objects. It is clear that the *kundawira*, both in the past and present, are associated with prestige and power. The process of acquiring these stone markers imbued the memory of the deceased person and the people obtaining the stone with prestige. The act of obtaining a stone conferred symbolic power on the *Rrumburriya* groups of Vanderlin Island and North Island and, one suspects, there would have been intense negotiations as to what island the stone came from. Indeed it would also appear that the stones were strongly male gendered and linked to men's Law and only ever celebrated *wirdi*: 'big men'. The classification of *kundawira* as markers celebrating the lives of great men was based on the ritual knowledge held by the deceased individuals, such as the mastery of singing song cycles and the skill of the deceased man as a *maranja*, that is, a dugong and sea-turtle hunter of excellence.

Memories of emotion and warmth

The relationship of people to *kundawira* reflects an emotional engagement with the world and a way of being that embodies Yanyuwa Law, and the experiences of Yanyuwa people and their spirit ancestors. This relationship is articulated in the following account, given by one of the last senior men associated with the placement of *kundawira* stones on country:

> The old men they would speak in the following manner. Let that stone be standing in the country of the deceased one. Let his nephew obtain that stone and place it there. The nephew of the deceased one will place designs on the stone and he will take it and stand in the home of the deceased one, he will talk to the stone saying, 'Remain here for ever, stay here and be warm in your country, let the country warm you'. It was in this way now that these stone of importance were taken and stood up in country (Old Tim Rakawurlma 1986, in Bradley 1980–98)

What is of interest in Rakawurlma's comments is his reference to the stones being warm and the country warming the individual. Warmth in this context is part of the act of nurturing the individual and the land of that person. Placing the stone in country warms and maintains the health of the spirit of the deceased kin and other spirit entities who inhabit that place. The country is kept warm (i.e. healthy), and in a state that allows it to respond to both the living and deceased kin who move across the land. Yanyuwa country is an animated landscape that contains living people and the sprits of the dead. These living people must find ways to relate to the spirits so that humans and deceased kin can co-exist within one countryscape. The stones positioned the metaphoric body and memory of the deceased person on the land. The physicality that the stone presented, coupled with the ideological anchor that the object created, provided Yanyuwa people with a means to negotiate and understand the spirits of the dead and the spiritual world they came to occupy. Each stone that was placed in country represented a named individual and the stone itself took on the name of the individual that it stood to represent. This is expressed beautifully in the following statement made by a senior *jungkayi* when he visited an area where a number of stone markers stand:

> Oh I am too sorry for this place, here they are still standing. My mother's kin they stand here, here [indicating to stone] this is Mangayi, that old man who was a rainmaker, and close by this tall stone this is Mamudibarrku a big man, a ceremony man who knew the song cycles. This smaller one there in the north is Narnuwungkuwungku and that smaller one I don't know. He is old, he has stood there from before me, he belongs to the old people. There is another here and it is broken, who broke this one? I don't know, they have broken the back of the old man who is this stone, it is no good I am sorry he has stood here for a long time (Jerry Brown Ngarnawakajarra 1985, in Bradley 1980–98).

This quotation gives a clear indication of the way in which the stones represent named individuals. There are also those stones that are no longer named and this, because of the death of senior men and subsequent loss of social memory, is fast becoming far more common. It does not, however, destroy or reduce the power and symbolic value of these objects. In many respects as the old people die and the political value of the past, the land and the sea become a part of the present day Indigenous political reality, such objects are revalued and reinterpreted and remain powerful objects worthy of reverence.

The words of these old men also demonstrate the understanding that things within the country create and sustain social and personal relationships, and that memory and the sustaining of memory is the binding agent. There is a sense of reciprocity between people and place, and of an emotional relationship between the speaker, the objects, and the country: there is a recursive relationship between people, place, objects, time and memory. *Kundawira* have the power to construct and maintain place and a potency of meaning that shapes human engagements with the world and this prompts people to recall times past. All of this is called upon in secular and sacred contexts, when people move across the land and sea, and when navigating one's place in a world of ancestral spirits. In the old man's statements, he expresses great concern that the stone has been broken and that he cannot recall the name of the individual belonging to the stone. The disjuncture in knowledge is, for the old man, symptomatic of the trajectory of time and the change that this brings, and ultimately this saddens and concerns him. Social memory becomes the crucial pivot of people's negotiations with the world; through memory, history is tracked and through narrative people and place are remembered. Memory connections are what bind people to each other, to place and to objects. For as DeLyser (2001, p. 36) writes 'social memory is not merely a process of calling up the past but [is] an active process of engaging with it, of making meaning for the past in the present'. Part of the act of finding and voicing these social memories is about re-inscribing country and anchoring Yanyuwa identity to places of importance, a move that at once ascribes power to places of the past, and bridges people in the present to their ancestors in the spirit world (see Van Dyke & Alcock 2003).

For the Yanyuwa there remains a strong social memory of the importance of the *kundawira,* the knowledge system associated with their creation and placement in country and the power of *kurdukurdu* places. Elders attest to realising the potency that placement of stone markers gives to place, they acknowledge the prestige and power associated with *kundawira,* and have long tailored their interactions with place to adhere to the laws associated with *kurdukurdu* locations as instilled by Law and the spirit ancestors. Knowledge associated with the *kundawira* and *kurdukurdu* locations remains but is understood in terms of the present, in that a temporal shift has seen the memory of Law associated with these objects and places persist while a memory of the individuals once represented by the *kundawira* often lost. What this indicates is continuity in the knowledge systems associated with engagement, and a continued apprehension of the Law associated with certain objects and locations.

Stones occasionally reappear after being buried for a long period of time. This is especially the case on beach areas on the smaller islands in the Pellew group. In 1984 a large cyclone ravaged the islands, and in its wake many beaches were stripped bare of vegetation and sand dunes were moved. In 1992 Bradley travelled to one of these small islands with a group of Yanyuwa men and women and found a lone *kundawira* stone exposed where the dune that once covered it had been washed. Upon seeing the stone, the men and women stood in silent contemplatation. Communication was reduced to eye contact and body language. That night around a campfire one of the older women said:

> That stone over there that is the big law for old people, old men like my uncle, they are really *kurdukurdu* you know, women shouldn't see them. They are all over this country really *kurdukurdu*, *nganjirra* [forbidden], but maybe we can look at this one it is *warruki*, *warruki* that means half sacred, little bit free, we can all look the *kurdukurdu* is old. It will never be *lhamarnda* [secular, not sacred] never, it is a big law, it makes me sad, this stone is somebody, it had a name, but we don't know now, we will never know. (Annie Karrakayn 1992, in Bradley 1980–98)

Karrakayn went further, stating that some *kurdukurdu* places remain sacred forever, while others shift in status. Both Karrakayn and Dinah Norman Marrngawi give the Yanyuwa place of Wudalwanga Plain as an example of an area that was once *kurdukurdu*, but is now freed from restriction. They state that: '*jungkayi* and *ngimirringki* all gone now, so freed up now' (Kearney 2003). To express that *kurdukurdu* places are 'freed up', and the '*jungkayi* and *ngimirringki* all gone' does not mean that the land is without owners and managers and does not remove the power of place. What Karrakayn and Marrngawi's comments indicate is that the old people, who set the parameters of engagement by making Wudalwanga Plain a *kurdukurdu* place, are no longer alive; they have since passed away and moved into the ancestral world. While there are both young and old Yanyuwa people who keenly assert their status as *jungkayi* and *ngimirringki* for this stretch of country, the act of placing *kundawira* on country is no longer practiced and therefore the status of *kurdukurdu* is not as strictly maintained in the present. In today's world Yanyuwa people, through desire and necessity, enact their roles and responsibilities to place differently.

Karrakayn's statement gives a socially constructed view of the stones which is relative to the Yanyuwa world as it is today, and also provides an insight into the flexible usage and meaning applied to terms that, in English, we equate with 'secret' and 'sacred'. The term *warruki* is used to refer to places that were once guarded by total restriction due to the objects housed there or the activities that took place there. It is a term that is used to describe places or objects of value whose original potency has passed due to the age of the objects or the time that has lapsed since events considered sacred and dangerous were performed there. The term is used for old bone-bundle burials scattered over the islands, for log-coffin burials where the sacred designs can no longer be seen, and in cases where the coffins themselves are decaying. It is used for ceremony grounds where natural forces have all but obliterated the evidence of their existence. However, people are still wary; they will not touch the objects and walk quickly and quietly past areas where they know such objects are located. Terms such as *warruki* are dense with meaning and are used in ways that defy easy translation. For example, on one occasion Bradley asked a senior Yanyuwa man, on behalf of the local school principal, if he could come and see the performance of a public post-funeral ceremony. The response was 'Yes that is fine, it is *lhamarnda* but still *kurdukurdu*' (Kearney 2000). Thus even in this context the terms are seen to be totally negotiable.

The negotiation of shifting status, or the actual 'freeing up' of *kurdukurdu* places, has — according to Yanyuwa elder Pyro Dirdiyalma — increasingly occurred in the post-contact period, particularly with the arrival of tourists throughout Yanyuwa country. As Dirdiyalma notes, traditionally the breaking of laws associated with *kurdukurdu* places resulted in death for those people who saw fit to travel across and hunt in restricted areas. To enforce or police such Law at a time when countless tourists travel through and around Yanyuwa country oblivious of the *ngalki* and Law of the land or the placement of *kundawira* across country would be an impossible task for Yanyuwa people today. Historical and recent events have shaped a context in which Yanyuwa Law, knowledge and engagements with place are understood in relation to historical and contemporary social and physical arrangements on country. Overall there is an understanding that some parts of country have had to become more open, and thus are considered *warruki* for reasons that relate to the specifics of recent history.

Despite the shift in *kurdukurdu* status and recollections of who the stone markers represent it is clear that the knowledge systems attached to country and the stones are vital and continue to be negotiated among Yanyuwa elders. It is this knowledge of 'appropriate' and enculturated engagement that has a place in social archaeologies. It has the potential to be modelled and channelled into an ethnoarchaeology of engagement in which human agents are granted states of emotion and volition in their engagements with places and objects. An ethnoarchaeology of engagement keenly looks to the nature of present and historical engagements with place to unlock or illuminate the potential sociality and complex meaning structures in the human past.

Material culture in the lived cultural domain: a recursive intimacy

The *kundawira's* transformative journey from *yijan* places into the lives and landscapes of Yanyuwa people reflects the complexities that can be present in interactions and meanings associated with material culture, and both the temporal and 'legislative' power of the secret and sacred within Yanyuwa culture. For Yanyuwa elders today there is a strong memory of the *kundawira* and *kurdukurdu* locations, with the stones embodying memory and relationships to the sea and land. In an archaeological and heritage survey of land around the Yanyuwa place of Manankurra during the mid-1970s, McLaughlin and a number of senior Yanyuwa men recorded several locations that were home to *kundawira*. These places, at the time, were considered *kurdukurdu* and consultants expressed concern about the presence of deceased sprits in the area and adopted appropriate behaviour whilst present on country. McLaughlin (1977, p. 1280) notes that the sites where *kundawira* stood on country were guarded and defined by strict conditions of access.

The presence of such locations around Manankurra and in association with large cycad forests throughout the area is testament to the significance of Manankurra as a Yanyuwa place. The presence of stone markers as monuments to the old people adds considerably to the time depth of people's visitation and occupation of the area. It also informs a great deal on the extent to which the region was socialised by the ancestral spirits and people actively engaging with it in the past. McLaughlin (with Dirdiyalma 1974) records that the 'ceremonial burial stones "stone *gundibirras*" [are] very old, beyond living memory in the area'. It is clear, however, from ethnographic accounts provided here, that the *kundawira* were not and are not beyond living memory, as McLaughlin has suggested. For it is the case that detailed knowledge of the objects, their status and power, the individuals represented by the stone markers, and people's emotional engagements with these objects were recorded by Bradley over a decade later.

McLaughlin's assertion that the *kundawira* he recorded were beyond living memory gives added meaning to the stone markers and reflects something of the importance of the *kundawira* as symbolic objects, and the rules governing the associated knowledge and sharing of oral testimony. The knowledge associated with *kundawira* is equated with symbolic and intellectual power. As such, it is likely that people's willingness to share sacred knowledge with others (particularly researchers) is measured by the individual's kinship and right to speak of these stones and the relationship that has been fostered between individuals and the act of 'earning' rights to knowledge. It is time that allows any researcher to find the threads of connection that exist between places and objects and people. Information relating to such objects as *kundawira* is regarded as powerful and therefore is guarded and shared only where appropriate, often in the most intimate and unlikely settings: while sitting around a campfire or while travelling in the back of a Toyota. It is often what would appear to be 'throwaway' comments that are in actual fact the lexical codes that create the structure of meaning and allow the information to come together to reflect complex systems of meaning. Simply because McLaughlin was not told of the social memories associated with the stone markers does not mean they were beyond living memory but, rather, may reflect the vitality of power associated with the stones, Yanyuwa Law concerning the sharing of sacred oral traditions[8], or individual and group relationships.

As time passes and older Yanyuwa men and women die, objects such as the memorial stones become important symbols of powerful men who knew and upheld a strong Law. In recent times, these stones have come to obtain a depth and richness that builds upon their original meaning. They have become suffused with additional layers of emotion, memory and remembrance. The stones increasingly have qualities attributed or ascribed to them that relinquish them to a point of emotion, engagement, physicality and mediation between what is now and what once was. With this it becomes increasingly difficult to distinguish between what is felt and what is perceived. For Yanyuwa elders, these stones are perceived to be kin; that is, the stones represent the bodies of deceased family still standing in country. Just as living kin are addressed, so too the stones are spoken to and their names recalled, and thus the past lives of the men they represent are remembered because, though stone, they are granted the position of perceiving and knowing bodies. One is left with an understanding that people are involved in a process of meaning and knowledge construction where people animate country through experiences, emotions and knowledge. The *kundawira* are also reciprocating by animating and defining people through their own particular attributes, attributes that are associated with important rituals and notions of power, authority and the sacred. These stones, standing and lying throughout Yanyuwa country, are inseparable from the culture that first imbued them and shaped their particular relationship to country, and this is irrespective of time's passing. In a Yanyuwa worldview stone markers bring about the cultural transformation of a place and prompt memories of people, place and past; they are objects that transcend simplistic utilitarian classification; they are objects of enrichment for both people and the land that sustains them.

Investigating the *kundawira* — and also the associated bodies of knowledge, social memory, engagement and narrative as forms of material culture — illuminates the recursive intimacy that occurs between people and objects. Each of these elements of Yanyuwa life are at once tangible and intangible, they are humanly made traces or constructions that have emerged from past and present interactions with country and negotiations of the ancestral spiritscape. The 'constructedness' of culture and elements of cultural expression are the vital components to understanding the complex meanings associated with material-culture items that propel through both secular and sacred worlds.

In a discussion of Yanyuwa *kundawira* as material culture, we have prompted an examination of the cognitive, ideational and emotional aspects of people's relationships with one part of the tangible heritage of Yanyuwa culture. Orthodox archaeological treatments of material culture, as seen in Cundy's attempts to understand the cylcons, would have been inadequate to unlock the sociality that is embodied by an object such as *kundawira*. A growing appreciation for research into symbolism, agency and emotion in the past creates the inspiration for the approach to material culture that is adopted here.

The social world is primary in shaping the nature of people's understanding of the *kundawira* and *kurdukurdu* places, and this in turn has shaped the relationships held between people and between people and place. The sociality that is captured by the memory of the stone markers creates an intimacy in past and present time frames, and in many regards reflects a continuity of Yanyuwa engagement with the world. Through time a uniquely Yanyuwa way of interacting with the world has come about, shaped by language, social organisation and ancestral myths, and this is reflected in the accounts of *kundawira* and the laws governing engagements with *kurdukurdu* locations. This has an antiquity that Yanyuwa people trace to the Creative past, the time of the ancestral spirits and the times of the 'old people'. Understanding material culture as being both reflective of and constituting this past signals a new chapter in archaeology and material culture studies.

Part of this new chapter is realising that oral histories are testament to that which cannot always be revealed by the archaeological record. As illustrated throughout this work, oral testimony is a record of the past and speaks volumes of the way Yanyuwa people engaged with and experienced their country in that past and the extent to which this has shaped more contemporary interactions with place. As direct statements by Yanyuwa elders reveal, the *kundawira* were located within a world of meaning that ultimately involved emotion and commemoration, and generated the means to navigate a world that contains both living people and the sprits of the dead. In many respects the *kundawira* represent the attempts of the living to relate to the spirits of the dead, so that humans and deceased kin can co-exist within one countryscape. This is part of the Yanyuwa people's habitual situation-in-the-world, and it is governed by life, Law, language, country, kinship and history.

It is the engaged *habitus*, built up over the individual and group's lifecourse, that defines stone markers as deceased kin, shrouds with meaning the land in which the stone is placed, and prompts rules of engagement. The way Yanyuwa people engage with *kundawira* is fundamentally different to how archaeology has long modelled people's construction and interaction with material culture.

As illustrated here, an ethnographic and ethnoarchaeological approach to tangible and intangible heritage unlocks the immediate sociality that can be contained by material culture items. The temporal legacy of the actions of ancestral spirits in creating the *kundawira* stones is apparent in today's recollections of the stone markers and *kurdukurdu* locations.

All human engagement is social, and the elements of life are formulated within the cultural realm, shaped and given meaning by this realm. The world is necessarily linked to the ancestral spirits, and this is entangled in all elements of life for Yanyuwa elders — as is witnessed in accounts of the *kundawira*. This has shaped the manner in which people engage with country and how they apprehend objects embedded in the physical and spiritual landscape. People apprehend the world in a manner that enacts ancestral Law and *ngalki*, the essence and substance of its and their being. Knowing this complicates orthodox archaeological investigations of the past and material culture, but helps us to problematise the study of material culture and the lived cultural domain in archaeology. Without this complication we could not begin to see the shadows in the landscape and seek to understand or illuminate emotion and warmth in the lives of past peoples.

Notes

1. Initially we adopted the term 'standing stone' to describe the stone obelisks that are found throughout Yanyuwa country. We have, however, subsequently chosen to avoid using such an expression and have adopted the descriptor 'stone marker'. The category of 'standing stone' has a long history of definition and investigation in archaeology, particularly in Europe, Britain, Ireland and the Near East (see Darvill & Malone 2003; Mohen 1990, 1999a, 1999b; Service & Bradbery 1997; Williams, 1988). The term carries connotations of monumental stone structures or megaliths, dolmen, capstones, pillars and henges. None of these definitions or categories captures the form of neither stone markers found throughout Yanyuwa country nor the meanings generally associated with stone markers in Australian Aboriginal material culture.
2. In this chapter the term 'countryscape' is often used. We adopt this term as a means for expressing both land and seascapes at once. It is drawn from experience working with Yanyuwa people and the repeated assertion, on the behalf of cultural consultants, that the land and sea are not separate, as Dinah Norman Marrngawi (personal communication) said, 'country is all country'. As such 'countryscape' seems a more fitting term to use when speaking collectively of Yanyuwa country.
3. The designs were coloured with red and white ochre and blood was used as a fixative. Few of the still known stones show evidence of their decoration, although those that have been placed in sheltered environments sometimes carry traces of red ochre.
4. The a-Kuwaykuwayk travelled from the mainland across the country of the Yanyuwa people's eastern neighbours, the Garrwa. The sites associated with this bird in Garrwa country are dangerous places and are feared. One of the reasons

for this can be traced to sorcery songs, the power of which is said to reside in the actual stones, were used to kill people. These songs are associated with mainland Garrwa sites while the songs of healing associated with the stones belong to the Yanyuwa and sites on the Pellew Islands.

5. Many Yanyuwa speakers suggest that the terms *kurdukurdu* and *nganjirra* are synonymous and equally interchangeable. From reviewing a number of translated texts it appears, however, that *nganjirra* is actually a much more forceful word, referring to ultimate restrictions or the sacred nature of an object. *Nganjirra* is a word that conveys much authority.

6. People who have viewed the illustration by Flinders and have heard the description of the designs on the two stones he found believe that they were a secondary reworking of the design on the stones. This was often done in situ as a process of revivifying the stones and the memory of the deceased individual. People point to the use of the egg as a fixative and the use of charcoal markings as being indicative of this kind of measure.

7. Some of the sacred objects associated with this ceremony are located in the South Australian Museum. Older Yanyuwa men familiar with the ceremony did not, and still do not want them returned. They belong to a ceremony that is considered dangerous and one that no one has the authority to perform anymore. Senior Yanyuwa men with whom Bradley worked in the 1980s in regard to these objects were even more pragmatic about the fate of the objects and suggested that among other things, 'maybe they sold the ceremony for tobacco'.

8. The late Olga Miller provides a brief but interesting commentary on oral tradition and the process of sharing sacred information among Aboriginal groups and outsiders. Miller was an elder of the Butchulla (Badtjala) people whose country is Fraser Island, off the east coast of Australia. She (1998, p. 28) discusses the parameters for sharing knowledge and oral histories, among Indigenous and non-Indigenous people. In a very personalised account of Fraser Island history, Miller explains how this knowledge came to be shared, giving insight into the highly negotiated process Aboriginal people enact in the sharing of knowledge and oral histories (see also Brady *et al.* 2003; David *et al.* 2004a; Ricks 1999).

12.

Towards an experiential archaeology of place: from location to situation through the body

Franca Tamisari and James Wallace

Introduction

Following the lead of other disciplines — such as anthropology, philosophy and sociology — archaeology has recently started to question the assumptions underlying the notion of 'space' employed in the interpretation of the past, and also field practice. In reflecting on and acknowledging Harry Lourandos' contribution to archaeology, and more specifically to the interpretation of Australian prehistory, we focus on changing conceptualisations of spatiality in the discipline and highlight, albeit in broad terms, the major theoretical shifts in this development. In tracing the ways in which Lourandos' theoretical and methodological approach introduced a sophisticated social interpretative framework for explaining the past, we argue that his conceptualisation of spatiality constitutes his most innovative contribution and most enduring legacy.[1] The critical trajectory we follow aligns itself with emerging archaeological approaches which — in deconstructing the 'humanist tradition' of western modernity and its consequent social, moral and political implications in the production of knowledge (Thomas 2002, p. 30) — have recently turned their attention to explore notions of place (David 2002), embodiment (Fisher & Loren 2003), perception and experience (Hamilakis *et al.* 2002).

Thus we have three interrelated aims. Firstly, we suggest that in contrast to the processual notions of space as static, uniform and inert (*cf.* Binford 1962, 1968), Lourandos' critique rests on an understanding of space as an arena of interaction and involvement between people and land constituting regional dynamics that have been central to understanding social change in Australian prehistory. Secondly, we discuss the ways in which Lourandos' shift from 'location' to 'situation' — in particular the notions of 'activity areas' and 'intensity of occupation' — can be seen to set the basis for notions of 'taskscape', 'dwelling' and 'place' developed in recent post-processual approaches (*cf.* Bradley 2003; Ingold 2000; Thomas 1996; Tilley 1994). Finally, drawing from some Australian

Indigenous images in the construction and experience of place emerging from recent ethnography, we propose that theorising notions of dwelling, engagement and emplacement for understanding the past in Australia cannot avoid the living body, and the ways in which it inhabits and constitutes space. In challenging the disciplinary boundaries of archaeology and social anthropology, this essay proposes an ambitious move towards an 'archaeology of bodily experience and perception' aimed to allow the formulation of new questions in the exploration and interpretation of archaeological evidence.

Three factors in Lourandos' conceptualisation of spatiality: activity areas, large-scale data, and ethnohistory

Social relationships and activity areas: the influence of Marxist theory

During the period in which Lourandos (1977a, 1977b, 1980a, 1980b) produced his doctoral dissertation and early papers, archaeological approaches in Australia were influenced by environmentally adaptive perspectives of processual archaeology. Such perspectives often drew on Marvin Harris' (1968) cultural materialism, and were introduced to the discipline through two influential papers by Lewis Binford (1962, 1968). In contrast to such approaches, many archaeologists and other scholars in Britain and Europe — such as Bender (1978, 1981), Faris (1975) and Godelier (1977) — were inspired by the writings of Marx to produce a more socially orientated yet economically driven approach to understanding the past. While processual perspectives explained change by concentrating on 'external influences' — such as environmental factors and demography — Marxist approaches usually emphasised 'internal dynamics', or what could be described as sociocultural relationships of cultural groups (Lourandos 1997, p. 10). Thus, by examining patterns and dynamics of economic systems, any fluctuation in the size and density of populations could be determined as evidence of modifications in sociocultural relationships (Lourandos 1980a, pp. 12–13). However, Lourandos (1997, p. 11) became critical of what he termed the 'techno-environmental hue' of Marxist theory, and proposed a more structuralist approach in which 'social dynamics' were the primary (rather than just a necessary) factor for any cultural change. In addition, while Lourandos (1997, p. 11) recognised the influence that environmental and biological constraints exercised on cultural groups, he also stressed that these ecological factors were not the guiding influence for human behaviour, but needed to be considered through what he termed the 'cultural filter' of locally and historically specific social relationships. In other words, whereas environment, demography and biology were all important elements impacting on human behaviour, responses to changing ecological conditions could only be understood through a contextual understanding of social practices. Thus, it is through the kaleidoscopic complexity of intense and continually evolving social relationships that Lourandos approached people's engagements with land, territory and resources.

This emphasis on 'interaction' and 'interrelatedness' led Lourandos to re-evaluate the importance of understanding social relationships for interpreting archaeological material in Australia. While most processual archaeologists aimed, like Binford (1962, 1982), to produce a universal, adaptive and uniform conceptualisation of spatiality, Lourandos focused on gaining a contextual understanding of people's behaviour in relation to land and territory through ethnohistorical and historical information. This shift towards a more social archaeology had an important effect on Lourandos' conceptualisation of spatiality as it allowed him to move from the processual concept of 'location' — a geographical coordinate — to the notion of 'situation', which is centred on specific group activities in their social, cultural and historical contexts. For Lourandos (1996) the past world was composed of many different 'situations' (including the hunting and butchering of marine and terrestrial animals, the use of quarries, the enactment of ceremonies and the establishment of permanent and temporary camps) and each of these situations constitutes specific areas of activity integrated in a complex territorial system where economic productivity was maintained and/or modified according to cultural regulations and needs. Space was no longer constructed as a series of autonomous sites but as an interrelated and interdependent series of 'activity areas' that could only be analysed in relation to each other, always within a context of interpersonal social relationships. Thereby, in conceptualising spatiality in terms of continual inter- and intra-group sociocultural interactions, contestations and negotiations over ownership and authority, Lourandos not only questioned the limitations of processual conceptualisations of space — as site and location — but brought to the fore the 'relationality' of people and land, thus heralding the notion of place as 'event' or 'happening' (Casey 1993, 1996; see below). As such, Lourandos' emphasis on situation preludes the concept of social dwelling as an embodied experiential process, a concept that characterised recent theoretical approaches in the archaeological interpretation of the past in Australia (*cf.* David 2002; David & Wilson 1999) and elsewhere (cf. Bradley 2003; Hamilakis *et al.* 2002).

Large-scale data

A second element that distinguished Lourandos' approach to spatiality was his employment of large-scale data sets for archaeological interpretation. Large-scale approaches allow the researcher to explore 'the big picture' and produce interpretations that cover cultural changes over long time periods and large regional areas (Lourandos 1996, p. 16). By employing this methodology, Lourandos (1996, p. 15) was able to compare archaeological evidence from many different areas, note general trends in archaeological patterning, and produce regional and continental interpretations of Australian prehistory. In contrast to the processual emphasis on 'finer-grained' levels of analysis — i.e. focusing on smaller sections of these larger data sets to identify so-called 'adaptive' moves — Lourandos produced a 'general model' that aimed to develop and theorise a macro-level understanding of Australian prehistory.

It is important to note at this point that there has been much debate over the value and implications of 'scale' analysis for interpretation in Australian archaeology (*cf.* Bird & Frankel 1991a, 1991b; Lourandos 1996; David & Lourandos 1999). Much of this debate has been in regard to what Lourandos (1996, p. 15) termed 'a confusion in scale' in which researchers have drawn general-level conclusions from fine-grain data or vice versa. In contrast, Lourandos maintains that researchers must 'compare like with like' and coordinate both the level of data (large-scale or fine-grained) with the scale of interpretation (general or fine-grained models respectively) to ensure an effective and consistent argument.

Lourandos (1993) interpreted both diachronic and spatial trends and patterns in this large-scale data set and, through the existence of consistencies in archaeological patterning (such as the increase in density of artefacts combined with an amplification of site use during the late Holocene) he was able to note changing patterns of human behaviour and also intensification and complexity in relationships between people and land. This research has two important implications for understanding people–land relationships in the past: it provides a large amount of information about the dimensionality of the spatial unit, and it also supplies valuable information for understanding temporal variations in people's relationships with land. In the first instance, the spatial data suggests that the dimensions of the spatial unit were varied, and were influenced by the social practices, activities, regulations and diplomatic relationships of the dwelling Indigenous groups. These relationships of people and land were not static or uniform but were generally intense within one's own territorial area and less intense with the territorial areas of other groups (Lourandos 1977b, pp. 204–10, 1980a, pp. 56–64). Furthermore, these relationships were not limited to a group's territory but were deeply affected by intra- and inter-group interaction — such as kinship, trade and ceremony — and could often cover extensive distances. Secondly, the diachronic evidence indicates that people's relationships with land were not static or consistent but evolved and changed according to variables such as modification of the social practices of the group, contestation between groups and also in response to environmental and biological changes (Lourandos 1977b). For Lourandos, large-scale archaeological data produced a conceptualisation of spatiality with the inherent characteristic of 'fluidity', where boundaries and interactions with land were constantly redefined by the changing social practices of Indigenous groups.

Ethnohistory

From early on in his career, the application of ethnohistorical evidence was probably the most important factor informing Lourandos' conceptualisation of spatiality, allowing him to meld his theoretical approach with the archaeological data. Through a detailed analysis of sources — such as George Augustus Robinson (1839 to 1849), Dawson (1881), and Howitt (1904) — Lourandos explored the breadth and complexity of sociocultural relationships between Indigenous people and land. Much of the ethnographic evidence — and in particular Robinson's accounts — suggested that people and land were involved in intense political relationships where land was associated with specific groups in south-western Victoria, and that access and use of this land was governed by complex processes of negotiations between groups and individuals (Lourandos 1977b, pp. 204–8). This ethnohistorical knowledge allowed Lourandos to develop a structural Marxist approach for research in Australia. While the Marxists and neo-Marxists had directed their analyses towards the industrialised societies of Europe, there had been very little attempt to adapt these frameworks for hunter-gatherer groups and, in this case, Australian prehistory.

For Lourandos the historical data called into question the emphasis of the Marxist researchers on social variables — such as technology — as a dominant medium for cultural change. Rather, Lourandos argued that economics was the more important factor for hunter-gatherer groups, not only for instigating cultural change but also for stabilising and managing resources. However, archaeological data in support of Lourandos' (1983b, p. 81) theories was limited as material in Australia is generally restricted to either stone or bone, which provides only partial information about social practices.[2]

By employing an interdisciplinary approach, drawing from historical and ethnographic information, Lourandos was able to view archaeological assemblages more in terms of representations of social activities or 'situations', and the crucial role these played in the economic system. Although Lourandos' emphasis remained on economics, his research highlighted that place was intertwined in the social relationships and practices of Indigenous groups: in areas like ceremony, kinship, cosmology and trade. For Lourandos place, people and groups were no longer viewed as separate elements but were conceptualised as relational and co-dependent phenomena.

New directions in archaeological research: 'activity areas' and 'intensity of occupation'

The significance of Lourandos' contribution can be more precisely highlighted by a conceptualisation of spatiality in specific social contexts defined in terms of 'relationality' and 'fluidity'. In net contrast to Binford's notion of spatiality as universal, adverse and hostile (*cf.* Wallace 2002, pp. 23–34), Lourandos' interpretation of archaeological material through historical and ethnographic accounts led him to view people, groups and land as interrelated through emerging patterns of interaction in continuous flux. It is from this perspective that Lourandos (1980a) examined the relational dynamics of the semi-sedentary settlement of Seal Point, and later in northern Queensland, and used the heuristic concepts of 'activity areas' and 'intensity of occupation'[3] for exploring the different relationships of people, social practices and land. By viewing spatial and temporal archaeological data as complimentary, Lourandos was able to explore change in both the vertical (diachronic) and horizontal (spatial) levels.

Activity areas

The concept of 'activity areas' has long been a part of the archaeological analyses of past people both in Australia and also overseas. Early reference can be found in Binford's work (1983, pp.146–7) where activity areas were viewed as 'places where particular functions relevant to the life of the social unit present are carried out'.[4] In other words, an area where particular activities were conducted and which can be recognised through the existence of specific 'tool kits' (Binford 1983,p. 147) or groupings of artefactual materials. This notion is taken up by Whallon (1971, 1973) in his study of variability among Palaeolithic artefact assemblages at a site, and also by Schiffer (1976, 1987) in both his works on 'behavioural archaeology' and on the effects of formation processes in the interpretation of archaeological material. Despite the diversity of the above theoretical approaches, there are clear similarities in the way the concept of activity areas is conceptualised. While Binford (1983, p. 148) defines activity areas as 'places where technological, social, or ritual activities occur' Schiffer (1976, p. 45) identifies them as 'a specified unit of space' where activities are repeatedly performed. It is in this way that the concept of activity areas becomes a method of demarcating groupings of artefacts and their suspected use and function from other particular artefact assemblages. Furthermore, in drawing from a positivist framework, these archaeologists limit the activities defined in these areas to only subsistence and adaptation (*cf.* Binford 1983, Chapter 7; Schiffer 1976, pp.149–52) and in doing so produce a largely functional and systemic understanding of activity areas.

For Lourandos the concept of activity areas represented a way of understanding the different 'situations' that existed between people, groups and land (Lourandos, 1980a, pp. 297–300). In contrast to the Processual and behavioural archaeologists who saw activity areas in light of adaptive techniques, methods of subsistence (*cf.* Binford 1968; Whallon 1971, 1973), and behavioural laws (Schiffer 1976), Lourandos viewed them in terms of maintenance and modification of the Indigenous economy. For Lourandos people, groups and land were economically interrelated and, through explorations of archaeological material, he was able to piece together the economy of the residing group. Thus, while archaeological material offered evidence of subsistence, trade, and developments in technology, it also represented fragments of economic relationships between people and groups within a study area. By collating both vertical and horizontal data, Lourandos aimed to piece together fragments of the economic history of people, groups and land.

The case study of Seal Point is an excellent example. Seal Point is located about 2 km east of Cape Otway in south-western Victoria and consists of a large and extensive shell midden surrounded by a number of smaller, less-dense middens (Lourandos 1980a, Chapter 12). The artefactual material uncovered at Seal Point was varied, and Lourandos (1980a, pp. 222–6) noted the archaeological signatures of seven specific activity areas: hut pits; hearths and hearth complexes; living areas; midden dumps; butchering areas; stone tool manufacturing areas; and areas for preparing vegetal foodstuffs. Of these, stone manufacturing areas present the most interesting example as people had to rely on access to imported material due to the poor quality of local quartz, flint and quartzite. Drawing on Dawson's (1881) ethnohistory — from the area near Noorat, north of Seal Point — Lourandos (1980a, pp. 174–5) outlined two ways of acquiring the necessary stone resources: 'great' trade meetings incorporating many Indigenous groups, and smaller meetings between neighbouring groups. In the case of the 'great' meetings, groups came from all over the general area and were involved in the trade of various resources, including stone. During these meetings trade was only one aspect of proceedings, which included other activities such as the performance of ceremonies, diplomatic exchanges, politics and the settlement of disputes (*cf.* Lourandos 1980a, Chapter 8). Smaller trade meetings were also held between neighbouring groups who would gather with the sole intent of accessing required material. In focusing on the smaller meetings, Lourandos concluded that the limited properties of the localised stone resources at Seal Point were a significant factor for influencing and promoting internal and external social relationships, such as interactions between the trader and buyer, owners of the resource, traders in stone, stone craftsmen and everyday users. Therefore, the specific economic properties of the place were an important factor for guiding the social dynamics of both the intra- and inter-group relationships of the people who dwelt and traded at Seal Point, thus renewing and altering existing relationships with place, and also promoting new relationships with places outside the territorial area.

The evidence of the economic interrelationships in these activity areas at Seal Point highlighted that archaeological materials (artefacts) represent more than evidence of adaptation to, or subsistence in, a particular environment, and instead are capable of being perceived as 'fragmentary evidence' of social relationships. In other words, each artefact can be viewed as a manifestation both of social practices and people's relationship to place. From this perspective archaeological material represents a small piece of a much larger puzzle for understanding past worlds. This type of approach goes beyond functional conceptualisations of artefacts, which concentrate on morphological characteristics (indicating use and function), instead viewing artefactual material as partial evidence of intra- and inter-group social relationships for the people dwelling at Seal Point. As such, the provenance of each artefact can reveal the dynamism of past social practices, the properties of activity areas in terms of exchange and trade, kinship relations and rights and ownership of areas of land. In this way, artefacts allow not only for an understanding of adaptive practices of past people but — when correlated with place, other artefacts, and anthropological knowledge — they become a window for seeing and understanding social practices in past worlds.

Intensity of occupation

Another important concept that Lourandos (1980a, p. 303) employed to explore people–land relationships in Australian prehistory is 'intensity of occupation' (see also Hughes & Djohadze 1980; Hughes & Lampert 1982). 'Intensity of occupation' can be described as the degree of interaction between people and activity areas, and has been investigated through the study of changes in spatial and temporal patterning of archaeological material. Two influential aspects of this concept are the notions of 'correlation' and 'difference', which Lourandos and David (1998, p. 105) used to explore correspondences between artefactual material, activity areas, period of deposition and environmental data. By comparing the correlation of the archaeological material with the external environmental data it is possible to explore causal factors for change. In analysing the data from northern Queensland, Lourandos and David (1998) noticed that there is an apparent correlation of environmental and archaeological trends from approximately 17 000 years ago to about 4000 years ago in all semi-arid, arid and tropical zones. From about 4000 years ago this patterning changed dramatically and the correlation ceased between environmental and archaeological trends.

For Lourandos the notion of 'difference' becomes very important for determining the role of sociocultural factors in promoting change in the prehistory of northern Queensland. While there is a clearly defined relationship between general archaeological and environmental trends over the period between 17 000 to 4000 years ago, this correlation of data promotes an interpretation of long-term archaeological trends in terms of environmental factors at this scale of analysis. This explanation may or may not be the case, but due to the close association of environmental and archaeological data it limits the argument for an interpretation grounded on social factors. However, in the case of the last 4000-year period, there is a marked difference between environmental and archaeological trends, and this data supports the argument that social elements were important factors for change. From this position Lourandos and David argued that by focusing on finer-grained data it is possible to explore causal factors: such as population growth, sedentism, intra- and inter-group social relationships, seasonality of resources and subsistence strategies.

Drawing from Lourandos: moving towards the concept of place

Lourandos' research into activity areas and intensity of occupation signalled a preliminary movement away from the concept of space to the notion of place. While this shift from space to place was not directly suggested by Lourandos, it was implied in his emphasis on, and attention to, the complex dynamics of social and economic relationships to land. Here we would like to draw attention to Lourandos' insistence on conceptualising spatiality not in terms of the meanings that particular activities might confer to an area but in terms of the interrelatedness or 'interanimation' (*cf.* Basso 1996) of environmental factors and cultural activity, location and situation. Activity areas are not considered as cultural configurations which transform or inscribe a pre-existing empty space (*cf.* Casey 1996, p. 14) — in other words a sociocultural geography overlaying and adapting to essential and constraining natural factors — but as emergent elements of places which were lived and experienced in the ever-evolving processes of change. It is from this position that we see Lourandos' research preluding Ingold's notion of the 'taskscape' and David's concept of 'regionalisation'.

The 'taskscape'

The research of Ingold follows Lourandos in adopting Marxist theory for analysing past worlds, and views economics as the dominant force for social development. Ingold's (2000, p. 516) conceptualisation of spatiality rests on the concepts of 'landscape' that is defined as 'an array of related features' and 'taskscape' which is 'an array of related activities'. Moreover, Ingold (2000, p. 521) elaborates that 'landscape seems to be what we see around us whereas the taskscape is what we hear', and by this he means that while landscape represents the things we see — mountains, buildings, trees — the taskscape corresponds to people's activities and actions. Both the taskscape and the landscape can only be conceptualised in relation to people, and Ingold (2000, p. 520) argues that these 'scapes' only come into being through 'a process of incorporation, not of inscription'. Thereby, taskscape and landscape are symbiotic and are governed by what Ingold (2000, p. 517) terms 'the temporality of the taskscape', which he describes as the network of natural rhythms or cycles that define the dwelling group's economy.

This type of conceptualisation bears an uncanny resemblance to Lourandos' concept of spatiality, and enforces a similar economic perspective. Both Lourandos and Ingold construct the past world as a multitude of interlocking tasks or activity areas which combine together to form an economic system of labour. Each of the particular activity areas has a specific role in ensuring the continuation, modification and further development of the group's economy. Furthermore, both perspectives view the archaeological material as fragmentary evidence of economic interactions between people and activity areas. However, while Lourandos emphasised sociocultural and political aspects of the economic system, Ingold reduced the taskscape to activities of subsistence. Myers (2002, p. 104) expressed concern with the primacy Ingold gave to the economic activities in gathering and hunting societies, and argued that there is a 'hint of primitivism' in this type of approach. Lourandos avoided this limitation by drawing extensively from ethnographic and ethnohistoric sources, and in doing so he developed a highly complex understanding of Australian Indigenous people's social practices in Australia.

Regionalisation

Bruno David has also built on Lourandos' perspective, but shifted attention from economics to sociodemographic and political elements as crucial factors in the study of change in Australian prehistory. By examining alterations in rock art conventions and comparing their relationships to certain geographical areas, David and Lourandos (1998, p. 213) explored what David terms the 'increased compartmentalisation of relationships between people and the land', or in other words social and territorial 'regionalisation' during the late Holocene period. For David *et al.* (1998, pp. 194–7) regionalisation reveals the different nature of people's relationships with each other and with land, and also uncovers general sociocultural and demographic changes which are linked to such factors as inter-group dynamics, population growth, climatic adaptation to group size and structure. In examining the distribution and aggregation of specific forms of rock art, David argues that it is possible to note contexts of social closure and openness, where 'open' signifies flexible and fluid social practices and formations (characterised by homogenous art forms) and 'closed' refers to more territorially bound practices and formations (dense levels of stylistically differentiated art). When this information is correlated with other forms of archaeological data — such as increased use of sites, development of new stone-tool technology, adoption of marginal foods and increased intensities of regional land use — David is able to support arguments for the intensification of land-use strategies, intra- and extra-group social relationships, demography, territoriality and increased development of closed social systems (*cf.* David *et al.* 1999; Lourandos & David 1998).[5]

One particular argument that David focuses on is tracing change over time in the relationships of Indigenous people to country: that is, a move towards a 'spatial history'. David argues that through an analysis of rock art and archaeological material it is possible to explore modifications and interruptions to the way Indigenous people conceptualised and perceived their territorial region (David *et al.* 1999). For northern Australia, he examines the long-term (large-scale) correlation of archaeological material (increased deposition rates, number of sites, type and use of stone artefacts, rate of site establishment and sedimentation rates) with the increased use of ochre, amplification of pigment art, stylistic differences, and proximity of new paintings to old paintings (painted over the top). For instance, in drawing from fine-grained data from Ngarrabullgan — an important place for the Djungan people — David explores archaeological patternings in light of processes of occupation and abandonment of sites. In suggesting that occupation was occasional from about 32 000 to 5400 years BP, and increased until about 900 years ago (when the site was abruptly abandoned), David (*cf.* David *et al.* 1999, p. 107) argues that the clear process of intensification in this period was interrelated to changes in the conceptualisation of people–land relationships. Recently, David (2002, p. 46) has proposed that changes in the archaeological evidence at Ngarrabullgan corresponds to the emergence of 'a new system of signification' which ethnohistorical accounts described as the Dreaming, including 'religion, morality, law, geographical mapping, social mapping, time, ontology . . .' (David 2002, p. 18). In doing this David examines change not only in terms of economy, demography or adaptation, but also in terms of ontology and epistemology. Drawing from the work of Gadamer, David approaches (2002, p. 3) the Dreaming as a way of 'pre-understanding' that signs and 'topographises' the land, providing 'a culturally conditioned conceptual framework' within which people create new meanings. In other words, 'pre-understanding' becomes a template for positioning 'people in meaningful space' and characterising their social engagement with place (*cf.* David 2002, p. 207).

Place, embodiment and experience: posing new questions

While David, in strongly reacting against the dominant positivist approaches in archaeology, rightly stresses ontology and epistemology as essential guiding forces in determining social change over time[6], his contribution is hampered by an intellectualist framework which privileges cognition over perception, meaning and symbols over experience and event. For the purpose of our present discussion, this bias is evident in the redefinition of place which is argued to coincide with the emergence of the Dreaming as a new ontological framework between the middle- and late-Holocene period. If David (2002, p. 29 and following), on the one hand, clearly rejects the primacy of space as a neutral pre-given medium onto which culture and history come to be inscribed (Casey 1996, p. 14), and insists, on the other, on the place of the Dreaming as a 'world . . . already formed while forming' through continuously negotiated social engagement, he downplays the experiential nature of such emplacement in continuous historical becoming. If place is not made out of space, and if culture — David's symbolic order or 'pre-understanding' — does not transform empty space into meaningful place, or land into owned and sacred country, what does it mean to be in place? How are places inhabited and experienced? What is the nature of this experiential engagement with place both in the past and the present?

In order to answer these questions we must return not to the objective body, but to the living, knowing or phenomenal body entwining with the world (Merleau-Ponty 1962, p. 98 and following) and (more specifically, in the context of Australian Indigenous relationships to land) to the moving and perceiving (ancestral and human) body and its participation — or, more correctly, collusion — with place (*cf.* Tamisari 1998, p. 263). As Casey (1996, p. 21) forcefully argues: ' . . . the body is *essentially*, and not just contingently, involved in matters of emplacement' (emphasis in original). The primacy of place constructed as a body, and the integration of the body with place, comes to the fore if we consider and give attention to the images which dominate how the world, as Indigenous peoples know it today, came into being and how the logic of its existence has been maintained and reproduced in ritual and everyday practices. Here we propose to stress the movement in interpretation from the present to the past, from people's lifeworlds to archaeological material, and how constructions and experience of place can inform the interpretation of available archaeological evidence. In other words, we propose that contemporary Indigenous constructions of place, as an 'interanimation' of place and bodies (*cf.* Basso 1996, p. 55), could, if given due attention, inform and guide an exploration of people's experiential relationship to place in the past. With the only aim, at this stage, to suggest how this perspective could pose different questions in approaching the past, we now turn to the image of the ancestral journey and the ways it not only underpins and articulates the construction and experience of place in Indigenous lifeworlds, but also reveals ontological dimensions. In turning to the contribution social and cultural anthropology has to offer in understanding the 'essential' involvement of the body in relation to place, we draw on some telling ethnographic examples from north-east Arnhem Land.

'A teeming place-world': events and connections

If there is a trait that Indigenous cosmogonic stories have in common across the whole of Australia, both as reported in early and more recent ethnographic accounts, it is the image of the journey of ancestral beings who shaped and named each place along their trajectory by transforming their bodies into landscape features and 'natural' phenomena such as plants. Wherever they stopped, ancestral beings also gave life to people, bestowed those places upon them and taught them the correct manner of looking after and inhabiting them: from foraging and hunting, processing of food, and the making of tools to the performance of paintings, songs and dances. Indeed these cosmogonic events constitute the unique knowledge of these places, a knowledge which needs to be reproduced both in ritual and in everyday life to sustain all aspects of biological, social and political life. The significance of these journeys does not reside as much in the content of the narrative but, for the purpose of this discussion, in the repetition of their rhythm: ancestral beings' incessant arriving and departing, resting and moving again, being-in-place yet being continuously between places.

The 'site-path flow' of these journeys, as Munn (1973, p. 137) termed it, is crucial as it conveys and articulates connections between land, people and ancestral events in terms of different yet interdependent modalities of relatedness: a corporeal intentionality in which the body, combining with and belonging to space and time, 'has its world, or understands its world, without having to make use of [the] "symbolic" of "objectifying function"' (Merleau-Ponty 1962, pp. 140–1). Running the risk of simplifying complex images and expressions of relatedness in Australian Indigenous cosmologies and everyday practices, let's say that these journeys establish at once two interdependent dimensions of connections. Firstly, each ancestral event at any given place establishes a corporeal connection between the ancestral bodily transformation and the person or group owning that place. Secondly, the journey also establishes a connection between the places and the groups who are positioned along any ancestral trajectory. Thus, the journey articulates two interrelated dimensions of relatedness through the body in its actions and movements: a unique consubstantial identification in and with any given place, and a spatio-temporal connection between places and associated groups. The point here is the dynamics of groups and individual identities, the tension between the uniqueness of each place and its people yet their association and connection; in other words, the interplay of similarity and difference in terms of identity, identification and ownership rests on the construction of a 'teeming place-world' (Casey 1996, p. 17) which is experienced and can be (re)navigated in the journey.

In transforming their bodies into visible manifestations, such as landscape features and all other natural phenomenon at any given location, each cosmogonic action establishes a consubstantial relationship between place, ancestral beings and human bodies who were given life at these sites. As ancestral beings' bodies become place and place acquires the perceiving qualities of a body, so people's bodies partake of this substance. As Stanner (1979, p. 35) noted, the 'kind of oneness' which includes 'notions of the body, spirit, ghost, shadow, name, spirit-site and totem' entails the sharing of a unique common substance, form, smell and behaviour which relate all natural elements, human and animal presence constituting a place. This 'corporeal connection' (Stanner 1979, p. 135) is powerfully expressed by Yolngu people of north-east Arnhem Land in terms of sharing the same bony substance. As the bones of the ancestral beings turn place into a body by resting there, Yolngu talk about one's patrilineally owned land as 'bone country' (*ngarraka*, literally 'bones') — the place one's ancestral substance (or 'bone-soul', *birrinbirr*) comes from before birth and returns to after death (*cf.* Tamisari 1998, p. 255). The bond of ancestral and human bodies and place is further elaborated in language, and especially in toponyms and proper names of groups and individuals. Among other proper names, 'bone names' (*likan* and *bundurr*, literally 'elbow' and 'knee' names), may be seen at once reiterating the sharing of a common bony substance, as well as establishing and affirming a specific corporeal connection between a place and a person bearing, or more correctly embodying that name. As knees and elbows are the main joints which give movement to a body, so knee and elbow names articulate specific individual and groups' emotional responses with relationships of identification, authority, and ownership of places (Tamisari 2002; *cf.* Keen 1995, pp. 509–12).

This process of the interanimation of human and ancestral bodies is evident in the lived relationships people have with places. While the relationships an individual establishes with a specific place vary according to one's kinship link, gender, age, purpose and degree of knowledge, many places are perceived as alive: sentient and knowing. They sense people in the same way they are sensed by people: they recognise strangers by smelling their body odour and, conversely, they recognise and heed to their own peoples' voices asking for food or protection (Povinelli 1993), and they are potentially dangerous if they are not approached with due respect and precaution (*cf.* Biernoff 1974). Similarly, people's behaviour and actions — such as the ceremonial re-enactment of ancestral cosmogonic events, infringements of the Law and the death of an individual — can equally be sensed by and affect specific places. It is in this way that, following Casey (1996, p. 27), 'a given place takes on the qualities of its occupants, reflecting these qualities in its own constitution and description and expressing them in its occurrence as an event: places not only *are*, they happen' through a reciprocal interaction: bodily transformations, ritual enactments, just being there — hunting, visiting, camping, walking (Povinelli 1993, pp. 133–67), witnessing an event (Sansom 1980, p. 79 and following), remembering and feeling. To paraphrase Feld (1996, p. 91), the meaning of place — that is, 'how places make sense and senses make place' — can only be approached through an understanding of how 'places are sensed and senses are placed'.

As mentioned above, the image of the journey conveys two complementary aspects of relatedness: a consubstantial or corporeal connection in place and a spatio-temporal connection between places. In Indigenous cosmogonies all ancestral beings, human, animal and natural phenomena, trace a path from one place to the next, from east to west, from north to south, from the inland to the coast, from inside to outside, from above to below or vice versa. Indigenous cosmogonies are replete with images of bodies in movement, stars crossing the skies, water flowing, sea and land creatures walking, running and swimming over long distances, and ancestral body parts travelling separate paths to different countries. In their perpetual motion across the land they also changed their language as they bestow particular tracts of land and specific names upon people. The point here is that places are not only perceived as different and unique — due to the embodiment of particular cosmogonic actions (*cf.* Munn 1996, p. 457) — but are also experienced as connected through movement as they are positioned along the same ancestral route. It is in this way that the places reached, shaped, named and bestowed upon people by any one ancestral being are perceived as distinct yet connected, different yet similar, and each individual or group along the journey — or 'string' (Keen 1994, p. 73 and following; Rudder 1993, pp. 30–1) — jointly share the same events but specifically own particular features and are responsible for the enactment and reproduction of the specific knowledge associated with them.

Thus, the performance of songs, dances and paintings associated with different groups along the same ancestral route differ in location, tune, language, narrative details, music structure, dance movement and choreography (Keen 1994, p. 149; Morphy 1984, p. 20 and following). It is by emphasising the uniqueness of each cosmogonic action or, conversely, effacing them, stressing the association established by the unity of any given ancestral journey and the shared common knowledge associated with it, that Yolngu and other Indigenous people remark 'we are the same', or 'we are on the same line, share the same Law — songs and dances and the same sacred objects — yet we are different' (*cf.* Taylor 1996). As Yolngu people succinctly put it: 'we are one and many', 'together and alone', 'close and far apart' (*wanggany ga dharrwa, rrambangi ga ga:na* and *galki ga barrkuwatj* respectively).

The image of the footprint: fragment and agent of space

If the image of the ancestral journey reveals that the body is crucial in emplacement or social dwelling, both in terms of the constitution of group and individual identities and their negotiation. It also conveys an ontology rather than a phenomenology of perception: a being-of and being-with place (Casey 1996, p. 19). This ontological dimension clearly emerges through the notion of *djalkiri*, 'footprint'. As Tamisari (1998) discussed in greater detail elsewhere, in Yolngu languages the words *luku* or *djalkiri* (literally 'foot' and, by extension, 'footprint' and 'step'), is used to refer to all visible manifestations of the Law derived from ancestral journeys. Here the term 'manifestation' should be considered in its primary sense of 'palpable'. The footprint refers to everything that was produced through bodily transformation and connected through movement: named places and landscape features, kinship relationships between places and groups derived from their positioning along the same ancestral journey, language and narratives of ancestral shape-giving events, personal and groups names. In addition *djalkiri* also refers to the correct manner of doing things, taught to humans for hunting, foraging, processing of food, the making of tools, or the performance of the paintings, songs and dances associated with these practices. Therefore, *djalkiri* not only fuses place and body but marks connections between places and relationships between people, visualises movement, unravels narratives, embodies names and reveals the itineraries to be retraced in songs, and the actions to be performed in dances. *Djalkiri*, as the foundation of Yolngu Law, is simultaneously a way of moving through life, coming and going out of being, visiting the same camping places, sitting around the ashes of a hearth which has been used by family members long gone, reproducing or reperforming everyday activities in the right way, and following the way taught and the footprints left by the ancestors (Tamisari 1998, pp. 250–1).[7] However, the notion of the footprint cannot be entirely understood in terms of analogy — following the Law in the same way as following the track of an animal (*cf.* Wagner 1986, p. 21) — nor as a production, objectification or inscription of ancestral and human experience on the landscape. The visibility of the footprint goes beyond the prosaic and profane sense of vision and speaks of people's bodily participation in the world. In phenomenological terms, the footprint is a 'living body' and a 'knowing body', an embodied consciousness/ perception of-the-world and in-the-world, simultaneously a fragment and agent of space, a product and actor of social relations, a subject and object of action and experience (Tamisari 1998, p. 263). The question here is that place in Indigenous thought and practice is not only considered as a sentient subject or 'quasi-subject' — and as such is approached through behaviours which usually characterise interpersonal relations between kin — but it also possesses its own essential individuality, its own way of being, mainly determined by the consubstantial connections it shares with people and other natural manifestations. It is in this sense that the ontological dimension of place is deeper than subjectivity. Place is not simply constructed as a centre of agency and will but has its own individuality. The ontological significance of the footprint is revealed in condensing dimensions of experience such as stasis and movement, singularity and similarity, permanence and transience, meaning and agency. If, as a static spatial referent, the footprint speaks of the depth of experience in the singularity, autonomy and difference of the interanimation of emplacement in a specific instant, the permanence of these dimensions of identity depend on the flow of connections established through movement. As footprints cannot be considered in isolation but in relation to the path they visualise by following one another and to the social and emotional bonds they establish, so place is about permanence and flow, fixity and change, site and situation, localised and regional identities.

Body, experience and archaeology: getting into place through the body

In approaching the end of our discussion we are in a position to raise more questions than offer answers for a phenomenological archaeology of space, especially in light of Indigenous constructions of place from the socio-cultural perspective offered by an anthropological approach. If it is apparent that archaeological approaches have shifted towards the primacy of place, they have done so bypassing the living body which is essential to inhabiting, perceiving and being-in and being-with place. This theoretical shortcoming or oversight contributes to maintain three grand narratives in archaeological interpretation and field practice.

Firstly, it has promoted a perspective where the relationships of people and place are always reconstructed in light of geometric models of space and western notions of time. It is in this way that archaeological understandings of time and space instantly promote the idea of a geometric grid where the vertical or diachronic data is mapped in relation to the horizontal or spatial data. Therefore, the vertical data highlights time and the horizontal data fixes a location in space, and by coordinating the two data sets archaeologists continue to plot human behaviour at a certain point in western time. In other words, a deconstruction of archaeological conceptualisations of vertical and horizontal data reveals the limitations of the concept of location, and exposes the social vacuum such a narrative generates: a concept of space devoid of any 'placial' characteristics (*cf.* Casey 1993, pp. 15–17).

Secondly, by downplaying the nature of the 'relationality' of people and place — so powerfully conveyed in the image of the body in movement through ancestral journeys and, in the Yolgnu case, the notion of *djalkiri* — archaeological approaches offer a limited understanding of past human behaviour. While Lourandos' insistence on complex relational dynamics with place characterising all Indigenous social practices is well hidden under the theoretical emphasis of his structural Marxist approach, a deeper reading uncovers the deep, complex and reciprocal relationship of people and place which was implied in his use of the notion of activity areas. Here, place is not made or constructed from space but was and is always there: embedded in the lifeworlds of past people. It is thus in restricting or constraining the 'power of place' to particular aspects of cultural formations and constructions, such as economics and the symbolic, that bodily experience and perception of place is ignored in regard to past human behaviour.

Thirdly, in cases where perception is given attention in archaeologcal approaches to place the sense of vision is usually privileged (*cf.* Boado & Vasquez 2000; Llobera 2001). Recently, for instance, Richard Bradley (2003) has begun to explore the implications of bodily experience for assisting in the analysis of surface remains. Bradley (2003, p. 156) describes this process as 'learning to see': the process where archaeologists over time gradually accumulate a perceptual understanding of the forms of archaeological sites. To this end Bradley (2003, p. 156) draws from his work on the cemetery of massive cairns in Balnauran of Clava, in Scotland, where his perception of place — the colour of the stones, the angle of light beaming through the rock opening — greatly contributed to his understanding, and as a result produced an alternative interpretation of the use and function of these archaeological formations. Elsewhere, Rainbird (2002), Watson and Keating (1999) and Dams (1985) focused on the place of sound in rock art production and a social dwelling that resulted in the formation of spatially patterned archaeological deposits.[8] The point here is that the shift towards an understanding of place through perception and bodily experience should 'liberate itself from the tyranny of vision and sight, and reclaim the other sensory devices through which human agents comprehend their world, generate remembering and forgetting, and construct social relationships, including relationships of power' (Hamilakis 2002, p. 101)

In drawing inspiration from Lourandos' insights into the priority of place over space in the past world we thus stress the essential involvement of the body and sensual experience for interpreting social dwelling and emplacement in the past. To this end it is necessary to cross-discipline boundaries and, following Lourandos, to explore the implications of an approach encompassing archaeology, anthropology, oral history and western and Indigenous philosophies. When the body in its interanimation in and with place is taken into account, the past world can be best approached in terms of situations: movement, memory, social relationships, relatedness, reciprocity, performance and event. 'Place' as an event or happening moves beyond the generic notions of meaning, practice or even agency and expresses a specific individuality or 'idiolocality' (Casey 1996, p. 26) as it constitutes itself through the negotiation of events and memories, thoughts and actions, symbols and practices. It can only be through this mutual interanimation that it is possible to explore the nature of emplacement. Every time we talk about past people, place and experience we cannot avoid the body. It is through the body that people inhabit place and through bodily dimensions that we 'reach in place'. Experience of place is first and foremost corporeal, the senses and perception are the origin of place. Dwelling is the body inhabiting place (*cf.* Casey 1993, 1996; Merleau-Ponty 1962).

Archaeological approaches to understanding space in terms of measurements, demographics, location, environmental use and taskscapes will not suffice to understand how past and present people — both the Indigenous owners and the learning analysts — inhabit and construct place. Therefore, while acknowledging Lourandos' conceptualisation of artefacts as fragments of social relationships, we propose to broaden his approach and highlight that archaeological and ethnographic material are also fragmented evidence of people's experiential involvement and bodily participation in the world. It is in turning to the living, sensing and knowing body that we propose that common archaeological notions such as locality, artefact, phase and system could be more productively rethought and developed in terms of the new heuristic concepts of situation, event, perception, sensual experience and idiolocality. If notions of place, body and experience are not critically reviewed in light of Indigenous epistemological and ontological frameworks, archaeological research will continue to be dominated by theoretical biases and grand narratives reproducing the very humanist traditions that they aim to deconstruct. This implies that, in exploring the power and possibilities of place in the past, we need to give theoretical and methodological attention to notions of embodiment, perception and experience.

Notes

1. Isabel McBryde also proposed a social approach to archaeological interpretation which, like Lourandos, highlighted the importance of notions of spatiality for understanding the material remains of Indigenous people.
2. Lourandos (1980a, chapter 14, 1980b) also explored water management installations in the Toolondo region in western Victoria as evidence of intensified relationships of people and land.
3. On this subject Lourandos partly followed the earlier works of Hughes and Djohadze (1980); Hughes and Lampert (1982) and Bowdler (1981). It is not our aim to give a complete history of the concepts of 'activity areas' or 'intensity of occupation' but to highlight the way in which it was conceptualised and applied by Lourandos.
4. Binford (1983 p. 147) cites earlier research into activity areas but doesn't give a specific reference to this work. A clue may be found in footnote 10 in chapter 7 in which he outlines discussions held with students as a precursor to the development of the concept of activity areas.
5. Here David's approach to the archaeological record stems from yet another intellectual foundation that Lourandos has laid (David, personal communication, August 2004).
6. To be sure, while writing his book focusing on an archaeology of ontology David realized the limitations of his approach – his focus on ontology was a step towards and 'archaeology of experience'. But before attempting such a programme, which at the time he considered more difficult especially in light of contemporary archeological theory and practice, David decided to explore ontology as 'preunderstanding', partly as a way of transcending the positivist archaeologies that for so long have held a more or less strong stranglehold on Australian archaeology (David, personal communication, August 2004).
7. The Yolngu term for 'fire ashes' (*ganu*) is often used to stress the fact of belonging to a certain family group whose deceased and living members have shared and keep on sharing life around the same hearth. See Stockton (1981) and Tamisari (2006).
8. Other researchers, such as Houston and Taube (2000) and MacGregor (1999), have argued against the dominance of vision in archaeological analyses and have explored other areas of sensory experience.

Part 4
Late-Holocene change

Small thumbnail scraper dating to last 2000 years. This tool was used by Aboriginal people camping on the edge of Lake Colac in western Victoria.

13.
Hunter-gatherer social complexity at Roonka Flat, South Australia

F Donald Pate

Introduction

The two phenomena of the appearance of cemeteries and the presence of mortuary differentiation within those cemeteries have been used as indicators of increased sedentism and organisational complexity in past societies. Thus, the analysis of cemetery sites has played a central role in the examination of past social complexity in hunter-gatherer and agricultural societies. As there have been a limited number of well-controlled excavations of pre-European contact cemetery sites in Australia in comparison to other regions of the world, a few key burial sites have emerged as important databases for the study of Aboriginal social change. These include the Willandra Lakes sites in New South Wales (Bowler *et al*. 1970, 1972; Thorne *et al*. 1999; Webb 1989), Kow Swamp in Victoria (Thorne 1971; Thorne & Macumber 1972), Roonka in South Australia (Pretty 1977), and Broadbeach in Queensland (Haglund 1976).

Rescue excavations conducted by the South Australian Museum at the Roonka Flat archaeological site between 1968 and 1977 produced one of the largest, best provenanced pre–European contact Aboriginal burial populations in Australia. The excavations along the eroding sandy banks of the lower Murray River near Blanchetown, South Australia (Figure 1) resulted in the recovery of over 150 interments dated from *ca*. 10 000 BP to 1840 CE (Pretty 1977, 1986), i.e. spanning most of the Holocene. The mortuary variability and elaborate grave goods observed at this hunter-gatherer site suggested the possibility of a non-egalitarian social organisation (Pretty 1977; Pate 1984). Because of the worldwide focus on hunter-gatherer diversity and social complexity at the time, the Roonka Flat site received a great deal of attention from archaeologists and anthropologists in Australia and abroad.

Aboriginal societies were generally regarded as egalitarian by social anthropologists (see review by Hiatt 1986). Meggitt (1964) argued that Aboriginal society was intensely egalitarian and had no enduring hierarchy of authority for the administration of public affairs. In contrast, Myers (1980a, 1980b)

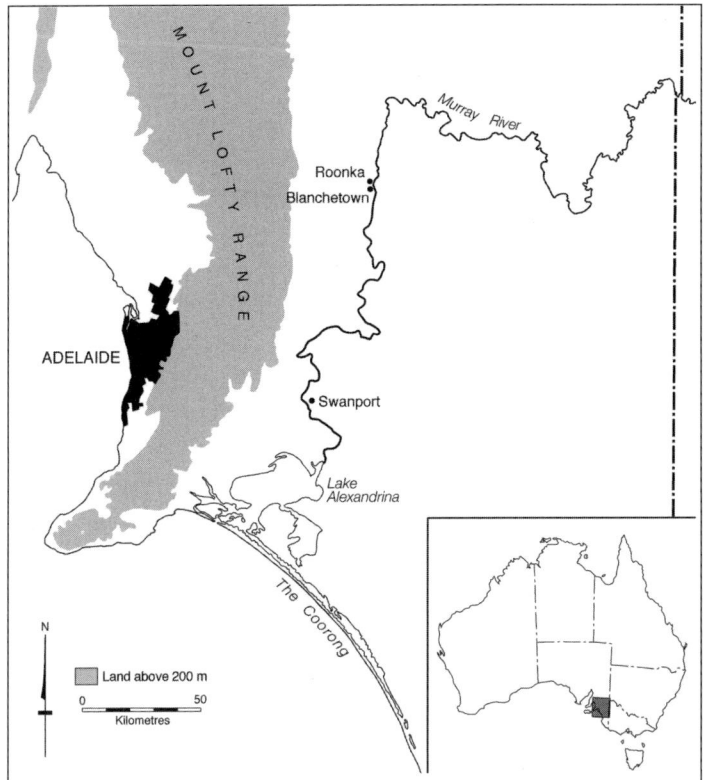

Figure 1. Map showing location of the Roonka Flat archaeological site, lower Murray River, South Australia.

argued that Pintupi political life in central Australia involved a co-existence of hierarchy and egalitarianism. Religious authoritarianism as expressed in male cult-lodges existed alongside an egalitarian secular life. Strehlow (1970) supported this latter view in relation to the monopoly of cult-based power held by male ceremonial leaders and old men of authority among the Arrernte of central Australia.

Prior to the early 1980s, the traditional Australian archaeological paradigm depicted Aboriginal culture as relatively homogenous and unchanging. Long-term socioeconomic and demographic stability were inferred from a simple, generalised, conservative stone-tool technology and stable population estimates. Aboriginal people were seen as recent migrants to Australia who adapted to the new continent by achieving a rapid homeostasis or equilibrium with various natural environments (see reviews by Mulvaney 1975; White & O'Connell 1982; Beaton 1983, 1990; Lourandos 1985b, 1997; Williams 1987, 1988; Mulvaney & Kamminga 1999). Thus, technology and social forces were not regarded as major catalysts for social dynamics and change.

Following the first international conference on hunter-gatherers (the *Man the Hunter* conference) in 1966, it was widely recognised that hunter-gatherers showed extreme diversity in relation to subsistence practices, technology, and social organisation. Sedentary and semisedentary hunter-gatherer societies with specialised food procurement and storage technologies and stratified social systems were reported for various regions of the world (Lee & DeVore 1968).

In regions of the world where there were reliable water sources associated with abundant wild plant and animal foods, hunter-gatherers could live a settled village life without the use of agriculture. The development of new food extraction techniques, or the intensification of existing subsistence strategies to improve the yields of wild foods combined with food preservation and storage methods allowed hunter-gatherers to accumulate food surpluses. These surpluses were used to even out the distribution of wild foods over the year, thus providing a reliable long-term food source that allowed the development of permanent and semipermanent villages. Social networks and exchange systems provided additional mechanisms to reduce risks associated with long-term variability in food production.

Following an analysis of differential mortuary practices at hunter-gatherer cemeteries in central California in the mid-1970s, Tom King argued that many of the traits previously associated with intensive agriculturalists could also be attributed to sedentary hunter-gatherers. King (1978, p. 228) stated:

> Much of California was occupied by hunter-gatherers living under the administration of fairly powerful chiefs who each stood at the apex of an hereditary hierarchy. Economic systems utilizing shell bead currencies and validated by ritual exchange obligations facilitated sharing of subsistence resources over broad areas while maintaining ruling lineages in positions of authority. Rulers were often fed and housed by the ruled and in turn might support specialists in various non-subsistence trades . . . California societies largely approximate 'chiefdoms' or 'ranked societies' rather than 'bands'.

Archaeological research in Australia was influenced significantly by these developments overseas. In the late 1960s Graeme Pretty, Senior Curator of Archaeology at the South Australian Museum, commenced excavations at a large pre–European contact Aboriginal burial ground on the lower Murray River near Blanchetown, South Australia, in order to address hunter-gatherer social complexity via an analysis of variability in mortuary practices. Pretty's research at the Roonka Flat site was modeled after Stuart Struever's (1968) analyses of pre-European contact hunter-gatherer cemetery populations at the Koster site in Illinois, USA. As the central and lower Murray River regions of

Australia were one of the most densely populated areas of Aboriginal Australia, they provided an ideal landscape to address social complexity in hunter-gatherer societies.

Harry Lourandos conducted research in south-eastern Australia to address the impacts of technological and social forces on sedentism and social complexity in late-Holocene Aboriginal Australia (Lourandos 1977b, 1980a, 1980b, 1983b, 1985a). Following Bender (1978, 1981), Lourandos argued that the economic, settlement, and wider cultural changes observed in the late-Holocene archaeological record in Australia were influenced strongly by the development of more intensive and competitive social networks.

The changes are described as closely associated with a restructuring of social relations that placed increasing demands on economy and production. Such processes appear to have resulted in increases in the complexity of social relations and economic growth, semisedentism and, by inference, population sizes (Lourandos 1985a, p. 386).

In more recent work, Lourandos (1988a, 1993) focused on the key role of intergroup social relations in establishing the context for change within hunter-gatherer societies. He argued that competitive relations between various residential groups associated with access to food resources, raw materials, spouses, exchange partners, and information necessitated the employment of intergroup meetings and ritual ceremonies that functioned to validate, maintain, and enhance the status of local groups within the larger social system (*cf.* Mulvaney & Joyce 1965; McBryde 1984, 1987; David & Chant 1995; Hayden 1996a, 1996b; David & Wilson 1999; McNiven 1999; Builth 2002). Intensive harvesting and land management practices were required to produce surpluses of key food resources (e.g. eels, fish, yams, cereals) that could be used to support these large intergroup meetings and ceremonies. The social dynamics generated by intergroup competitive relations provided a catalyst for further changes or 'complexification' in hunter-gatherer societies, including the establishment of extensive exchange and alliance networks, craft specialists, ritual leaders, polygyny, more complex economic strategies and facilities, territorial boundaries, and semisedentism.

Lourandos' research addressing 'intensification' and 'complexification' has made a major contribution to the evolution of archaeological theory and method in Australian archaeology, culminating with the publication of his book *Continent of hunter-gatherers* in 1997. Research at Roonka Flat provides additional archaeological evidence that supports the development of more complex social relations in late Holocene Aboriginal Australia associated with increased sedentism, greater intergroup competition, and the maintenance of territorial boundaries.

Part 4 • Late-Holocene change

Social complexity in the Murray–Darling river system

Large cemeteries are generally associated with semi-permanent or permanent settlements (Rothschild 1979; Chapman *et al.* 1981; O'Shea 1984; Price & Brown 1985; Chatters 1987; Bird & Monahan 1995; Beck 1995). Aboriginal burial grounds are common in the soft Holocene sand dunes, flats and lunettes bordering the Murray–Darling river system in south-eastern Australia (Figure 2). Large cemeteries are concentrated in the lower and central Murray regions, whereas the upper Murray and lower Darling River regions are dominated by smaller burial grounds consisting of clusters of between two to twenty individuals (Littleton 1999). Cemetery sites in the riverine region become larger and denser after 5000 BP (Pardoe 1988, 1994, 1995). The occurrence of these large cemeteries in the lower and central Murray provides archaeological evidence for the presence of semisedentary and sedentary hunter-gatherer settlement systems.

In his paper 'The cemetery as symbol' Pardoe (1988, p. 14) argues that the social organisation of the Murray River people 'was clearly designed at least

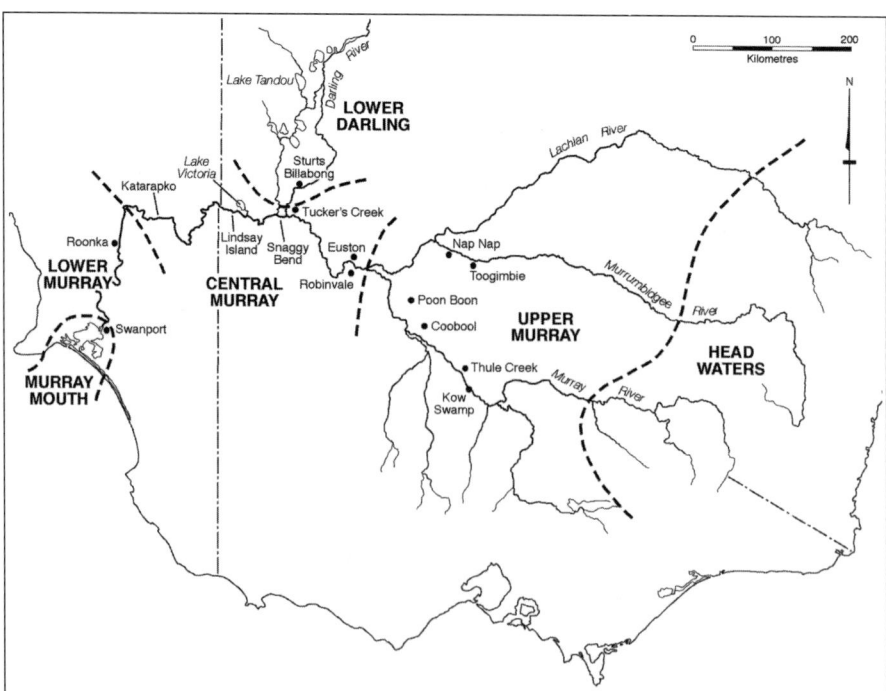

Figure 2. Map showing location of larger Aboriginal burial sites (more than twenty individuals) in the Murray-Darling river system, south-eastern Australia (after Littleton 1999).

partly around some form of corporate descent group.' These corporate descent groups are regarded as territorially based, and their burial grounds provide one of the symbols validating corporate ownership of that territory. Thus, in the late Holocene, large well-defined cemeteries along the banks of the lower and central Murray River provide a mechanism of boundary maintenance for various Aboriginal territorial groups occupying the region.

Stable isotope, palaeopathological, and cranial non-metric analyses of human skeletons recovered from the riverine zone provide additional evidence for increased sedentism and territoriality in this region during the Late Holocene (Prokopec 1979; Hobson & Collier 1984; Pretty & Kricun 1989; Pate 1995, 1997, 2000; Webb 1995; Pardoe 1994, 1995).

Stable isotope analysis

Stable carbon- and nitrogen-isotope analysis of collagen derived from small 0.5–1 g pieces of bone provides an indication of geographic source of dietary protein and access to foods from various habitats from the coast to inland regions. Analyses of human bone samples from the coastal Coorong and Murray-mouth regions, the riverine Swanport area, and the riverine Roonka area provide strong evidence for the existence of sedentary, territorial social organisations along the lower Murray River and adjacent southern coastal regions of South Australia during the late Holocene. Stable isotope results indicate that neither significant amounts of foods nor people were moving across the various boundaries of the corridor stretching from the coastal Coorong and Murray River mouth in the south to the inland riverine Swanport and Roonka sites toward the north (Pate 1998a, 1998b; Pate et al. 2002).

Stable carbon- and nitrogen-isotope analysis of bone collagen from late-Holocene human remains recovered from various cemeteries in south-eastern South Australia provide isotopic signatures that distinguish the following geographic regions: the coastal Coorong; the coastal Murray River mouth, Adelaide–lower Murray River; and the upper Murray River.

The first regional group, the coastal Coorong, has the most positive $\delta^{13}C$ and $\delta^{15}N$ values in relation to high levels of seafood intake. The second group, from the Murray River mouth, shows intermediate $\delta^{13}C$ and $\delta^{15}N$ values due to consumption of marine and terrestrial foods. The third and fourth groups, the Adelaide–lower Murray River and upper Murray River regions, have the most negative $\delta^{13}C$ values reflecting a predominantly terrestrial diet based on C_3 plant foods and animals that fed on C_3 plants. However, $\delta^{15}N$ values are more positive in the inland semi-arid Roonka population than they are in the temperate Adelaide–lower Murray region (Pate et al. 2002). These distinct regional isotopic signatures, which are related to long-term dietary intake, provide strong evidence for the limited movement of foods and people between the various environmental zones and associated social territories throughout the late Holocene.

In addition, stable-isotope data from the Roonka Flat population indicate that adult males had diets that were significantly different from those of adult females and subadults (individuals less than fifteen years of age). In comparison to adult males, adult females and children included greater amounts of δ^{13}C-depleted foods such as aquatic and terrestrial plants and freshwater shellfish in their diets (Pate 1998a, 1998b).

Palaeopathology

Webb (1995) provides an overview of the distribution of human pathological conditions in middle-late Holocene Aboriginal Australia. The study examined six ecological zones: South Coast; East and Southwest Coasts; Central Murray; Rufus River; Desert and Arid Area; and Tropical Area. The pathological conditions assessed include chronic and acute stress (cribra orbitalia, dental enamel hypoplasia, Harris lines); infectious disease; osteoarthritis; and trauma.

Aboriginal populations that occupied the Desert Arid continental interior were generally the healthiest, whereas those from the Central Murray region were the least healthy. Arid-land inhabitants had the lowest incidence of cribra orbitalia (anaemia), dental enamel hypoplasia, and Harris lines. Thus, chronic malnutrition, parasitic infection, and population aggregation would have been minimal in the arid zone. In contrast, the Central Murray shows a high incidence of cribra orbitalia and dental enamel hypoplasia in children and adults, but a low incidence of Harris lines. This pathological profile indicates that Central Murray populations were subject to chronic stress. Harris line formation was most likely suppressed by this persistent stress. After considering the archaeological evidence relating to the dense occurrence of large oven mounds in the Central Murray, Webb argues that the health pattern for this region reflects that of large, sedentary populations with high frequencies of malnutrition, parasitism, non-specific infection, endemic (non-venereal) treponematoses, and mechanical stress associated with increased workload. Thus, the Central Murray populations provide a health pattern similar to that of settled agriculturalists (*cf.* Cohen & Armelagos 1984a, 1984b).

Cranial non-metric traits

Analyses of thirty-five cranial non-metric traits (Pardoe 1994) at a large number of burial sites along the Murray River also support the existence of 'exclusive' social relations and territoriality during the late Holocene. Non-metric traits are minor features of skeletal morphology that are classed as attributes rather than measurements, i.e. they are recorded as either absent or present. Multivariate analyses of these traits provide patterns of variation associated with different geographic populations. Differences between geographic populations are calculated and provide a matrix of biological differences or distances. On the basis of biological distance, as determined by cranial non-metric traits, biological diversity is much greater along the Murray River than elsewhere, and gene flow between territorial groups along the river was minimal during the late Holocene. These data suggest that there were well-defined boundaries between various territories along the riverine zone that were maintained by social practices of exclusion (Pardoe 1994, p. 188).

Mortuary practices

The use of a range of skeletal orientations in the burials at Roonka provided one means of differentiation of the various individuals interred there. Furthermore, the burials at Roonka contained a range of grave goods suggesting the use of material culture as an additional means of signalling differences in social status during life. Some burials included a large number of grave goods and elaborate ornamentation that suggested the possibility of social roles during a past life that required greater economic input at time of death. Prior to the Roonka excavations there was only limited evidence for extreme mortuary differentiation on the basis of burial mode and the association of grave goods in pre–European contact Aboriginal Australia.

Lower Darling River burial sites

A number of Aboriginal burials were found eroding from an aeolian lunette at Lake Nitchie along the lower Darling River anabranch north-east of Lake Victoria (Macintosh et al. 1970; Mulvaney & Kamminga 1999, p. 37). The best-preserved burial was excavated and it produced the first evidence for the presence of elaborate grave goods with pre-European contact Aboriginal inhumations in Australia. The Lake Nitchie burial consisted of an adult male skeleton crammed into a narrow circular pit in a contracted position. A long necklace constructed from the pierced teeth of an extinct marsupial carnivore *Sacrophilus* (Tasmanian Devil) was found around the neck of the skeleton and draped over the chest. Additional grave goods included pieces of pearl shell and a tektite (fused silica related to meteor impact). The skeleton had been covered with red ochre and the remains of a small fire were adjacent to the burial. Pretty stated that 'This discovery cast a completely new light on Australian mortuary practice as it was understood' (1977, p. 324). The skeleton was later radiocarbon dated to 6820 ± 200 BP (Macintosh 1971).

Central Murray River burial sites

Blackwood and Simpson (1973) reported the use of a range of burial orientations at seven late-Holocene Aboriginal burial sites along the central Murray River between Mildura, Victoria, and the South Australian border and at one site at Lake Victoria, New South Wales. Of the seventy-two skeletons recovered, sixty-seven retained enough burial integrity to determine orientation of the skeleton. Of these sixty-seven burials, twenty-seven were extended supine, one extended prone, two extended on side, ten flexed prone, fourteen flexed on right side, four flexed on left side, and eight squatting. No artefacts or personal possessions were reported as associated with the burials. The skull of one skeleton from the Lake Victoria site was adorned with a gypsum 'widow's cap'.

In contrast, grave goods including plaster 'widow's caps', bone awls, stone scrapers, and freshwater shellfish had been recorded previously in the region during the recovery of over 800 Aboriginal burials from sand dunes along the central Murray River by the pastoralist George Murray Black from 1943–50. Unfortunately, the Murray Black Collection was removed without the use of the detailed recording practices associated with professional archaeology. Thus, there is limited information regarding spatial relationships between buried skeletons and associations of grave goods with individual burials (Sunderland & Ray 1959).

Lower Murray River burial sites

A large late-Holocene Aboriginal burial ground was discovered at Swanport near Murray Bridge, South Australia, by Crown Lands Department workers in 1911 during swampland reclamation (Stirling 1911; Pate et al. 2003). Over 135 individuals were recovered from the site. Unfortunately, the portion of the site that contained the majority of the burials had been disturbed by the workers prior to the arrival of Mr FR Zeitz from the South Australian Museum. The bones had been indiscriminately placed in a large hole or shovelled into the trucks with sediment. Consequently, the individual identity of each skeleton and its position in the burial ground were lost. Bones of dingoes, kangaroos, possums, bustards, pelicans, turtles, and fish were also found heaped with the human material. The faunal bones may have been associated with either the burials or the kitchen middens.

Zeitz recorded the stratigraphic positions, burial postures, and associations of grave goods for sixteen skeletons following his arrival at the site. Most of the inhumations consisted of single adults placed in a sitting position with knees drawn up to the chest. Some had been placed in this position on their sides. None of the burials were extended. Group burials contained only two individuals and usually consisted of an adult and a child. Crania and the small bones of the hands and feet were often missing from the grave pit. Grave goods consisted of two kangaroo fibulae awls, one quartzite graver, stone flakes, hammerstones, and oven/hearth stones. Several of the graves included large oval slabs of a composite material consisting of sand, white earth, small fragments of limestone, burnt clay, broken mussel shell, and pieces of charcoal. The largest slab measured 53 cm x 38 cm and was 13 cm thick.

In addition, five bone points were associated with one of three Aboriginal burials recovered at Tartanga along the lower Murray River south of Roonka, but grave goods were absent with three burials at the nearby Devon Downs site (Hale & Tindale 1930). The skeleton of a six-month-old dingo and vegetal mats were associated with three burials at Fromms Landing (Mulvaney 1960; Mulvaney *et al.* 1964).

Social complexity at Roonka Flat

Archaeological excavations

The Roonka Flat archaeological sites are located on a 350 ha sand flat on the western bank of the Murray River 7 km north of Blanchetown, South Australia (Pretty 1977; Pate 1998c, pp. 204–5). Pretty excavated four 15 m x 30 m units (Trenches A, 1A, B, 1B) and six smaller trenches (0A, 0A1, 0B, 2A, 3A, 3B) at various localities on the Roonka Flat. Lenses of ash, charcoal, and freshwater mussel shells are the dominant cultural components at these open-air sites. Limestone oven stones are the predominant stone artefacts. Bone and stone tools and faunal remains are not well represented. The most common features are the remains of fireplaces. Radiocarbon dates on occupation debris indicate that the first Aboriginal use of Roonka Flat was at approximately 18 000 years BP.

In addition to cooking refuse, Roonka Flat Dune Trench A exposed an extensive Aboriginal burial ground. Trench A was divided into eighteen 5 m x 5 m units and excavated vertically at 3 cm levels until basement clays were encountered at approximately 6–7 m. Most of the human skeletons were concentrated in a 15 m x 30 m x 2 m area of the trench. The absence of refuse in the lower levels of the trench suggests that the dune was used exclusively as a burial ground from *ca.* 10 000–7000 years BP. Thereafter, camp debris occurred in burial pit fill and in sediments adjacent to the burials.

The Trench A subsample consisted of 147 skeletons with the following temporal distribution: 10 000–7000 years BP (23); 6000–4000 years BP (16); 3000 BP–1840 CE (82); and undetermined (26). Many of the late-Holocene burials were lost to aeolian erosion at the surface of the dune.

Mortuary variability

Approximately 60% (53/90) of the Trench A adults that could be sexed were male (Prokopec 1979). When subadults were present, they often accompanied adults. Forty percent (20/50) of the subadults were placed in group burials with single adults. Over 80% of these adults (10/12) were male. Thirteen of these subadults were infants with a mean age of 2.2 years. These group burials also contain the most elaborate grave furnishings, including ornaments (animal bone and teeth pendants, necklaces, and chaplets), animal skeletons, ochre, bone cloak pins, and stone and bone tools. Six of the remaining subadults occurred in two group burials, while the other twenty-four were buried singly. These latter individuals had a mean age of 7.0 years. New modes of burial were added to existing forms throughout the temporal sequence. Orientation of the body in relation to compass points and location of interment within the burial ground also varied with time (Pretty 1977, 1986; Pate 1984).

Three basic types of burial pits were excavated in the loose sands of the Roonka Flat dune. Shallow longitudinal pits and deep circular shaft pits were used in the early and late Holocene. The shallow pits averaged 114 cm x 36 cm x 21 cm and mostly contained fully extended dorsal burials. Several extended prone burials dated to the late Holocene. The shaft pits averaged 75 cm x 62 cm x 74 cm. It appears that Aboriginal bodies were placed in a vertical, standing position in these deep pits and were then allowed to slump down. Circular-to-oval pits averaging 107 cm x 47 cm x 22 cm were confined to the late Holocene. The bodies buried in these pits had been placed on their sides, and the upper and lower limbs were contracted so that the knees approached the chest and the arms hugged the lower body. Because of aeolian reworking of the sands, little horizontal stratification occurred in the adjacent layers of sand (Pretty 1977, 1986).

In summary, a majority of the early-Holocene burials consisted of adult males associated with a distinct cemetery, whereas late-Holocene interments included an entire age/sex cross-section of the population associated with habitation remains. Modes of burial also changed through time. Early-Holocene burial was dominated by individuals who were placed fully extended in shallow pits or slumped in deep, vertical shafts. Late-Holocene interments occurred in shallow pits in either a fully extended, recumbent-contracted or fully contracted (flexed) position, with approximately 38% of individuals included in group burials consisting of two to five persons per grave pit.

Grave goods were associated with most of the burials. These included a range of stone and bone tools, animal-bone and tooth headbands, necklaces and pendants, animal-bone clothing pins, animal skeletons, freshwater mussel and snail shells, vegetable mats, hearthstones and associated ash and burnt nuts, seeds, clay and bone, and various ochres. Contact-period burials included items of European origin, such as pearl and metal buttons and clay and metal pipe fragments (Pretty 1977, Pate 1984).

Due to the increased representation of females in the late-Holocene sample, mortuary differentiation on the basis of role or division of labor was addressed. The types of artefacts included as grave goods varied with sex. Ochre, bone projectile points, and stone tools were associated primarily with males, whereas vegetable mats placed beneath the bodies were confined to female and subadult burials. Animal bones and mussel shells were associated with both males and females. The association of bone projectile points and stone tools with the male activities of hunting and tool manufacture/maintenance and vegetable mats with the gathering activities of females and subadults is suggested by these differences in grave goods. In addition, there is differentiation based on quantity of grave goods. The majority of the more elaborate graves with greater amounts of grave goods are those of older males.

Historical accounts

According to historical accounts, the lower Murray region was one of the most densely settled Aboriginal areas of Australia (Eyre 1845, II, p. 317; Taplin 1874, 1879; Lawrence 1968). The artist George French Angas commented:

> In this district the natives were very numerous, their encampments being scattered along the narrow strip of ground between the limestone cliffs and the water's edge: there they find plenty of food from the fish, mussels, crayfish, bulrush-root and other products of this large river.

Conflict developed between European pastoralists and Aboriginal hunters from 1838 as the pastoralists drove herds of stock down the lower Murray River corridor. EJ Eyre was appointed as resident magistrate and occupied a government station from October 1841 to November 1844. The station was located at Moorunde, 11 km south of the Roonka Flat. Eyre's journals provide an invaluable source of information about Aboriginal lifeways during this tumultuous period of contact. Eyre (1845, II, pp. 251–89) provides data regarding Aboriginal subsistence and settlement practices. Aboriginal gatherings as large as 400–500 occurred at Moorunde. He noted that settlement sizes changed from season to season according to the abundance of food. During the summer, the river flooded and increased the wetland habitat size for mussels, crayfish, and fish. Summer camps were quite large and consisted of simple brush windbreaks on the banks of the river. In the winter, the populations dispersed into smaller camps consisting of rockshelters or solid log huts covered with grass and vegetation in response to cold, wet weather and reduced river levels.

The riverine populations exploited a wide range of resources. Fish were netted, speared, captured in weirs and dams placed across smaller streams, and caught with seines made from rush string. Turtles and mussels were obtained by diving; the mussels being placed in a net worn around the neck. Large crayfish — weighing up to 1.8 kg — were speared from canoes or were captured by divers at night. Small crayfish and frogs were taken by waders. Waterfowl were netted and both their eggs and nestlings eaten. The bulrush root was roasted year-round and leaves and stems of other river plants were steamed in stone-earth ovens.

Both animal and vegetable foods were also obtained from the surrounding mallee plains. Emus and kangaroos were speared, netted, or caught in pitfalls. Emu and mallee hen eggs were popular. Other animal foods included stick-nest rats, possums, snakes, lizards, moths, grubs, and white ants. Berries, fleshy fruits, roots, and fungi were gathered from plants. Honey was extracted from banksia cones and beehives. Eyre reports three methods used to prepare foods: broiling on hot coals; baking in hot ashes; and roasting or steaming in ovens.

Furthermore, Eyre provides some information regarding social differentiation on the basis of sex and age and gender-specific subsistence roles. Old men were privileged members of society, and they received the best and largest share of everything (Eyre 1845):

> Males generally are generous and liberal to each other in sharing what food they have, but it is not often that females participate in the division. I have seen the men after an hour or two's fishing with the nets, sit down and devour all they had caught, without saving anything for their family or wives, and then hurry about noon to the camps to share in what had been procured by the women, who usually begin to return at that hour, with what they have been able to collect.

In relation to Aboriginal political organisation in the lower Murray River region of South Australia, ethnohistoric accounts report the existence of two separate formal offices of territorial headman (secular) and cult-lodge leader or spirit medium (religious) within local landowning groups. Both of these offices were occupied by dominant, older men (Howitt 1904, Elkin 1938–40, 1945; Berndt & Berndt 1993).

There are a number of detailed historic and ethnographic accounts relating to the socioeconomically complex Ngarrindjeri people, whose country included the area downriver from the Roonka Flat. The Ngarrindjeri peoples consisted of a number of territorial clans that occupied a large triangular area of coastal and riverine land stretching from just above Murray Bridge in the north to Encounter Bay in the south-west and Kingston in the south-east. This region includes the coastal Coorong, the Murray River mouth, and the lower Murray River in the vicinity of Swanport. The written records include the journals of the missionary George Taplin (1874, 1879); ethnographic accounts of the anthropologists Norman Tindale (1974) and Ronald and Catherine Berndt (1993); and more recent overviews by Graham Jenkin (1979), Steve Hemming, Philip Jones and Philip Clarke (1989), Steve Hemming (1994, 2000), Barbara Salgado (1994), Diane Bell (1998, 2001), Brian Marshall (2003), and Tim Owen (2004).

Taplin (1879, p. 34) estimates that there were eighteen territorial clans or *Lakalinyeri* that constituted the Ngarrindjeri 'confederacy' or 'nation'. Each territorial clan was administered by a group of ten to twelve men or elders, referred to as the *Tendi*. The *Tendi* from each clan collectively elected the *Rupulli* or the head of the entire Ngarrindjeri confederacy. Religion and the powers of supernatural forces played a major role in the maintenance of social order by the *Tendi* and *Rupulli*. Thus, the Ngarrindjeri were landowners who had a centralised and hierarchical government to administer the laws of the confederacy and its eighteen independent territories.

Thus, historical documents provide additional support for increased sedentism and social complexity in the resource-rich region along the lower Murray River. On the basis of these accounts it can be hypothesised that some older men (e.g. headmen, or cult-lodge leaders: the *Tendi*) may have been treated differently in death than other members of the society. Archaeology provides the time depth that allows the testing of this hypothesis over various periods of time, e.g. the early Holocene (10 000–5000 years BP) versus the late Holocene (5000 years BP to the present). For example, at Roonka Flat the majority of the more elaborate graves are those of older males throughout the Holocene period. Thus, mortuary differentiation at Roonka can be employed as one line of evidence to support increased Aboriginal social complexity in the lower Murray River region of South Australia.

Discussion

Several independent forms of data suggest increased territoriality and social complexity in the lower Murray region in the vicinity of Roonka Flat during the late Holocene. Mortuary practices at Roonka also suggest some differential treatment of older men in the early Holocene.

At Roonka Flat, mortuary practices provide indicators of social differentiation in three areas: gender roles related to subsistence activities; some specialised hieracrchical role for older men; and differential treatment of older men not being extended to their wives or children.

In addition, stable-isotope analysis indicates that adult males had diets that were distinctly different from those of adult females and children. Thus, distinctions in diet and mortuary practice appear to be restricted to the variables of age and sex and are not extended to individuals based on their social or family relationships to higher status persons. This suggests that a highly stratified non-egalitarian system of social differentiation like that associated with hereditary chiefdoms was not employed at Roonka (see Binford 1971, pp. 19–20; Saxe 1970, 1971; Peebles & Kus 1977). However, some form of ranking based on sex and age was clearly operating at Roonka. The greater mortuary attention associated with older males at Roonka throughout the Holocene provides archaeological evidence for the possible existence of male authoritarian roles such as headman, law-man, cult-lodge leader, or sorcerer.

The limited number of well-provenanced excavated burial sites in the lower Murray region places major limitations on analyses of social complexity employing mortuary practices and biological anthropology. Because a majority of the Roonka Flat burials were excavated from a single 15 m x 30 m unit (Trench A), intra-site spatial variability is difficult to assess. Furthermore, as Roonka Flat is the only well-documented prehistoric mortuary site in the region, inter-site variability cannot be assessed. In other words, the Roonka Flat burial ground may not represent the total range of mortuary behavior associated with past local and/or regional social systems. Consequently, analyses of prehistoric mortuary differentiation in the lower Murray River valley are currently restricted to a limited number of variables relating to intra-site behavior at Roonka Flat, e.g. age, sex, pathology, genetic variability, diet, treatment of body, mortuary facility, and grave furnishings (Pate 1997, p. 111).

Nevertheless, research at Roonka Flat provides valuable data that contribute to ongoing debates regarding the context, timing, and causes of the development of more complex hunter-gatherer social relations in Australia and other regions of the world.

Evidence from Roonka for increased sedentism, greater intergroup competition, the maintenance of territorial boundaries, and social ranking based on sex and age complement archaeological research from other regions of Australia in relation to complexification during the late Holocene. Furthermore, mortuary evidence for differential treatment of older men in the early Holocene suggests that the emergence of male authoritarian roles in the lower Murray region may have preceded the development of intense territoriality and boundary maintenance.

Finally, the Roonka research challenges traditional perceptions regarding the long-term survival of an egalitarian, nomadic, culturally homogenous, and static Aboriginal society. It complements a growing body of research addressing complexification in Aboriginal Australia that is providing valuable data to deconstruct these resilient European myths. Such research has important implications for our views of past cultural diversity in Aboriginal Australia and their relation to ongoing negotiations regarding the roles of Aboriginal peoples in contemporary Australian societies.

Acknowledgements

I am grateful to the late Colin Cook, former chairman, Gerard Reserve Council, and the late Graeme Pretty, former senior curator of archaeology, South Australian Museum, for their long-term efforts associated with the development of an inclusive archaeological research in South Australia. Richard Gould and Doug Anderson (Anthropology, Brown University), Margaret Schoeninger (Anthropology, University of California, San Diego), Keith Norrish and the late John Hutton (CSIRO Soils, Adelaide), Ken Brown (Dentistry, University of Adelaide), Jack Golson and the late Rhys Jones (Prehistory, Australian National University), and Donald Munns (Land, Air and Water Resources, University of California, Davis) played key roles in my MA, PhD, and postdoctoral research at Roonka Flat. Bruno David provided valuable comments regarding the development of the manuscript. My research at Roonka has been funded by various institutions, including the South Australian Museum, the Australian Institute of Aboriginal and Torres Strait Islander Studies, the Australian Research Council, the Wenner-Gren Foundation for Anthropological Research, the Sigma Xi Scientific Research Society, the Australian Institute for Nuclear Science and Engineering (AINSE), Brown University, Harvard University, the University of Wisconsin (Madison), the University of Adelaide, the Australian National University, and Flinders University.

14.
Social dynamism in the archaeology of the Western Desert

Peter Veth

Introduction

Some of the most persuasive evidence for dynamism in Aboriginal ritual and ceremonial transmission and economic and demographic behaviour has arguably come from Australia's Western Desert (*cf.* Gibbs & Veth 2002; Myers 1986a, 1986b; Tonkinson 1991; Veth in press; Widlok in press). It is curious, therefore, that against this backdrop of social complexity some archaeologists have persisted in characterising Western Desert groups as conservative and essentially risk-minimising (e.g. Gould 1977). A review of sites from the Western Desert covering the last 30 000 years, and those components of their cultural assemblages likely to inform on social process and change (rather than stasis), inevitably leads to the conclusion that these societies have been anything but conservative and unchanging (see Figure 1 for key sites described in the text). Indeed, when a socially informed archaeology is employed, as advocated by Lourandos (1997), understandings of the undoubtedly ecological imperative of Western Desert existence expand to embrace ideational, sociodemographic and political dimensions of these demonstrably dynamic societies.

New data and models focusing on territorial boundaries, exchange and distribution networks, levels of residential mobility, language dispersion and artgraphic systems highlight the degree to which the configurations of these desert groups have changed through time (e.g. McDonald in press; Rosenfeld & Smith 2002; Smith *et al.* 1998; Veth 2000; Veth & McDonald 2002). In this paper particular focus will be made on aggregation locales during the Holocene and the probable role these had in renegotiating and perpetuating peoples' associations with their totemic and domestic landscapes.

The size and nature of data sets for occupation of the central and Western Deserts dating to before the late Holocene is still relatively small for this vast area, with some twenty-five sites and an estimated 120 m² excavated (*cf.* Gould *et al* 2002). The sample sizes of the most recent assemblages dating to the Holocene are considered large enough, however, to make first-stage observations about social dynamism and the likely material signals of this.

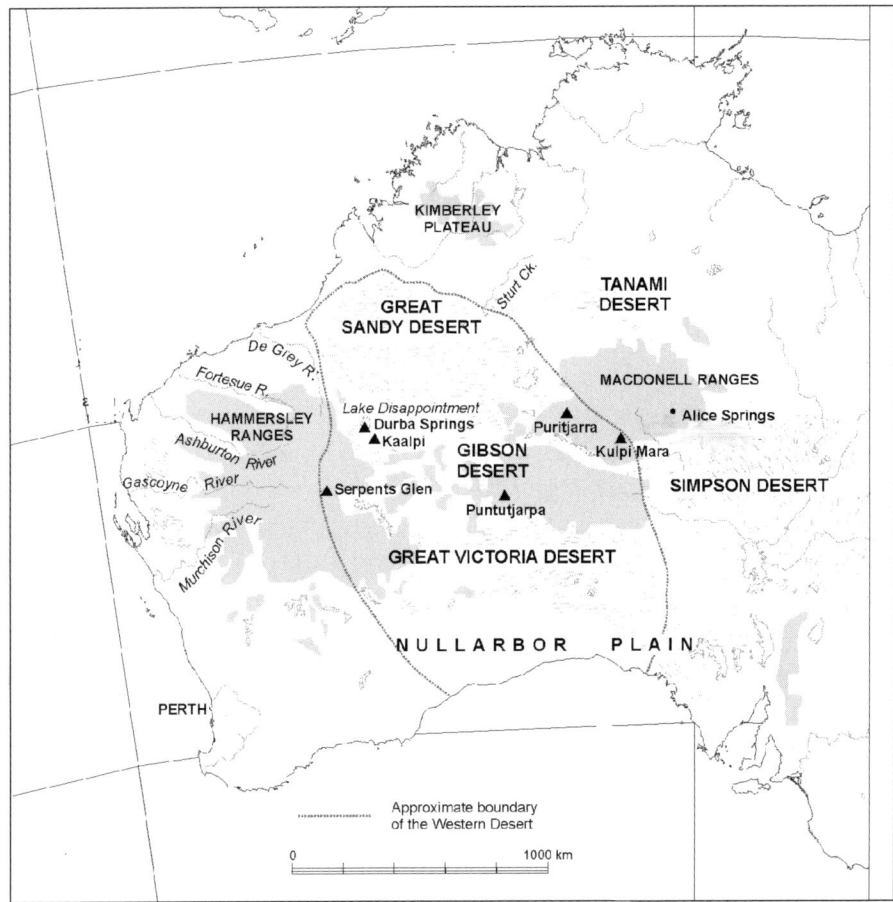

Figure 1. Location of key sites discussed in the text lying within the Western Desert and arid margins.

Dynamism within a conservative society?

Earlier work in the Western Desert by Richard Gould (e.g. 1969a, 1969b, 1977, 1980) portrayed a uniform and conservative desert culture — the 'Australian Desert Culture' — analogous to the American Great Basin. This was thought to be Holocene in age, similar to the ethnographic pattern, and having great uniformity in material culture, economy and settlement patterns. The type-site of Puntutjarpa was argued to have evidence over the last 10 000 years for the continuous presence of hafting in the form of micro- and macro-tula adzes, similar spatial configurations in hearth/activity areas and similarities in discard patterns of formal implements (Gould 1977). Most of these apparent continuities have now been overturned and are seen to be more the products of the analytical frameworks employed by Gould (e.g. Hiscock & Veth 1991).

During the mid-1980s there was a convergence in interpretations by three researchers working in different areas of the arid zone, with Mike Smith focusing on the ranges of central Australia (Smith 1989), Peter Hiscock on gorge refugia of north-eastern Australia (Hiscock 1988) and myself, working within the Western Desert and Pilbara regions (Veth 1989).

Hiscock (1988) described the retraction of groups' ranges towards Lawn Hill Gorge following peak aridity at 18 000 years BP, with persistence of occupation in this well-watered and richly resourced refugia between 17 500 and 13 500 years BP, after which time, by 13 000 years BP, a more humid climate is registered. Groups then appear to have expanded their range once again.

Smith established an early human presence in the well-watered but remote Cleland Hills rock-shelter site of Puritjarra, lying to the west of the Central Australian Ranges (Smith 1989). Extensive dating by Smith and colleagues provides a date for occupation at approximately 30 000 years BP (Smith *et al.* 1997). The demographic modelling of Smith (1989) for the Last Glacial Maximum (LGM) suggested changes in territory, residential mobility and possibly trade/redistribution networks as a result of changes in climate. Many of the predictions have been substantiated by central Australian studies focusing on lithics, ochre distributional studies, vegetation reconstructions and rock art phases (Smith *et al.* 1995, 1997, 1998; Rosenfeld & Smith 2002).

Our work in the Western Desert has provided Pleistocene dates from the interior of the Western Desert as well as rich mid-to-late Holocene sequences (O'Connor *et al.* 1999; O'Connor & Veth 1996; Veth 1989, 1993, 1995, 1999, 2000, 2001; Veth *et al.* 2001). Dates coinciding with the LGM — even the older dates for the global LGM now recognised (e.g. Lambeck & Chappell 2001) — have, however, been largely absent from the Western Desert. My own long-term collaborative desert research has aimed to link archaeological, linguistic, rock art and settlement-pattern data: some of the latter based on detailed ethno-economic studies carried out with the last viable nomadic groups to leave the Australian deserts in the 1960s. These studies have been conducted by Bob Tonkinson, Fiona Walsh, Arpad Kalotas, Nick Thieberger, Douglas Bird and Rebecca Bliege Bird (e.g. Bird & Bliege Bird in press; Tonkinson 1991).

Various studies have now demonstrated that, firstly, initial occupation of the Australian arid zone is Pleistocene in age (O'Connor *et al.* 1998; Smith 1989); secondly, that there have been changes in the size of the territory of groups in response to increased aridity during the LGM (Marwick 2002; Smith *et al.* 1998; Veth 1989) and, lastly, that significant economic and presumed social changes took place in the late Holocene (Smith 1989; Veth 2000). This represents a very different scenario to the picture of a conservative, Holocene-age, 'Desert Culture' popularised by Gould (1977).

Late-Holocene mobility patterns, territoriality and art, language diffusion and aggregation locales

Residential mobility

It is now widely argued that patterns of residential mobility during the Pleistocene were higher than in the Holocene (*cf.* Lourandos & David 2002). A case for decreased mobility has especially been made for the last 1500 years in the Western Desert and adjacent arid lands. During the late Holocene a range of open and stratified sites from the Western Desert and adjacent arid uplands illustrate increased rates of cultural discard, increasing proportions of exotics, higher intensity of stone artefact reduction, higher values for implement curation, higher diversity of implements, increased numbers of wet-milling grindstones and more broadly-based dietary suites (Andrefsky 1998; Marwick 2002; O'Connor *et al.* 1998; MA Smith 1989; Thorley 1998; Veth 1993, in press; Veth & O'Connor 1996; and see Law 2003). While some of these apparent trends must be tempered by considerations of taphonomy, sample size effect and visibility, their presence in a number of adjacent arid lands (e.g. David 2002) suggests they are real.

While composite implements — such as the tula adze and geometric microlith — enter assemblages from after approximately 3600 years BP (*cf.* Marwick 2002; Veth 1993) it is the appearance of significant numbers of formal millstones after 1600 years BP, and the inferred ability of these grinding 'stations' to support larger aggregations of people, which is of interest. More intensive use of aggregation locales (implying some degree of sedentism) must be underpinned by access to, and the processing of, a ubiquitous resource. These are almost certainly seed stands — described as a major staple group for the Western Desert (*cf.* Veth & Walsh 1988).

At the Western Desert site of Kaalpi (Veth *et al.* 2001) there is a noticeable increase in the quantity of grinding material above Spit 10 (approximately 1300 years BP). Classification of the grinding material (McNamara 2000) indicates that all of the formal millstones, whole and fragmented, have been manufactured from arenaceous sandstone. All of these occur from after 1300 years BP. All of the grindstones prior to that date are of the informal basal grindstone type and are predominately manufactured from coarser sandstones and quartzites. Smith (1989), Marwick (2002) and Veth (1993) all note the efflorescence of formal grindstones of this kind during the late Holocene — the caveats being that sample size effect, site function and the use-lives of these implements need to be adequately accounted for (*cf.* Gorecki *et al.* 1997). In a recent review of the social entanglement and antiquity of systematic seed grinding across the Australian arid zone, David (2002, p. 175) concluded that:

What changed with the emergence of systematic seed grinding during the late Holocene was the *domus*, the experienced landscape that incorporated the entire network of social relations and relations to place, and the framework of understanding, sentiment and experience through which personal and social identity are built. The emergence of grass seeds as a source of staple food affected dietary habits, together with an understanding and experience of the world in social practice. It signalled the emergence of new environmental knowledge, social strategies and actions. What came about were new domicultural relations and practices. The beginning of seed grinding at a definable point in the past motioned the emergence of new ways of being, new systems of social relations and personal identity, and in the process new world views.

These conclusions are consistent with my own and others' work in the Western Desert.

While groups may be expected to have switched their residential mobility strategies through time in response to such factors as regional drought (Gould 1991), the overall impression from the Western Desert is one of decreasing residential mobility and greater embeddedness in scheduling resource use (e.g. lithic and ochre quarries) during the late Holocene — in contrast to earlier patterns of land use.

Territoriality and art

Patterning in art has been used by a range of researchers to indicate aggregation and dispersion patterns resting largely on interpretations of inside/outside (exclusive/inclusive) access to information networks (Conkey 1980; Galt-Smith 1997; Gould 1980; McDonald in press). The lower residential mobility scenario of the late Holocene would predict for higher stylistic diversity and the predominant use of inside/exclusive symbols. We can predict for an increase in the use of art to demarcate territory and to highlight inter-group differences. The occurrence of behaviours resulting in 'emblatic' signalling is expected at aggregation locales.

Both the Serpents Glen site (at the southern end of the Carnarvon Ranges) and the sites of Kaalpi and Durba Springs (to the north in the Little Sandy Desert), have extensive rock art galleries comprising both petroglyphs and pictographs. Although dating the rock art is in the early stages, the majority of paintings are thought to date to the late Holocene. Ochre specimens were recovered from occupation deposits from the site of Kaalpi dating from 1300 years BP and essentially absent from before this time (Veth *et al.* 2001).

In contrast, a large number of the engravings occur on quartz sandstone panels which have been significantly weathered, chemically altered, and in some cases covered in very thick coatings of natural varnish and other crusts. It seems quite likely that many of these engraved motifs may date to the Pleistocene.

Ongoing recording of motifs at three of these art complexes suggests there are significant differences in the style, spatial patterning and frequency of different classes of motifs between the engravings and the paintings (McDonald in press; Veth *et al.* 2001). The engravings include a range of tracks, circles, concentric circles and arcs in addition to a range of naturalistic motifs including macropods, marsupials and various birds. Noticeable are some very large anthropomorphs which have extensive infilling and the so-called 'archaic faces': disembodied faces which have a distribution through the arid zone from the coastal Pilbara to the Cleland Hills of central Australia, where Puritjarra is located (David *et al.* 1992; Dix 1977; McDonald in press). The geometric motifs, archaic faces and large anthropomorphs can be found in differing proportions at Kaalpi and Durba Hills.

In contrast the paintings display greater assemblage diversity and contain a higher proportion of complex designs, although many of the fundamental geometric and figurative motifs are also present. Numerous anthropomorphs are depicted with ornate expanded headdresses, these only being recorded from this specific locality of the Western Desert. As such they may be signifiers of corporate identity. The use of inside/outside symbols is consistent with the increasing role of these sites for aggregation, rather than dispersion (*cf.* Galt-Smith 1997). Anthropomorphs with ornate headdresses are not common in comparison to the higher frequency and distribution of geometric and simple figurative categories (and indeed clusters of 'non-elaborated' anthropomorphs) which occur more widely within different landscape units. The highest proportions and greatest diversity of ornate headdress figures appear to correlate with circumscribed and resource-rich locales which are interpreted as aggregation locales on the basis of different lines of evidence in addition to the art (such as grindstone counts and the like).

Recent rock art research in the Australian arid zone (e.g. Frederick 1997, 1999, 2000; Galt-Smith 1997; Gunn 1995; McDonald in press; Rosenfeld 1993, 2002) has revealed an interesting trend towards heightened localised stylistic variability, particularly in the recent past. This had not been systematically documented before and, like early views of Aboriginal occupation of this continent, it had been assumed that there was a broad continuity and unchanging nature across the arid zone.

In terms of how rock art is thought to have functioned in Aboriginal peoples' lives, art production took place in a number of contexts, from secular and casual to sacred and ceremonial (Gunn 2000). Following the theoretical lead of Wobst (1977), Conkey (1990) and others (e.g. Hodder 1982; Wiessner 1983), Ursula Frederick (1997, 1999, 2000) notes that in the Australian arid zone art is an important tool for promoting and controlling the exchange of information, functioning at multiple levels to identify and integrate, as well as to demarcate, social boundaries (see also Gould 1969; McDonald 1994, 1999; Galt-Smith 1997).

Brett Galt-Smith's (1997) work was aimed at investigating aggregation locales in central Australian painted and engraved rock art. His results showed distinct patterning in regional assemblages, which fitted with the ethnography. The patterning among the pictograph sites (in particular) correlated well with the documented totemic clan-based social system. Galt-Smith argued that the pigment art demonstrated a control of information in the *local* context. This was in contrast with the patterning shown by pecked engraving (petroglyph) sites, which he found to be homogenous over vast areas of arid Australia. This fitted well with the original findings of Edwards (1966), Maynard (1976) and, more recently, Andree Rosenfeld (2002) (but see Franklin 1991).

McDonald and Veth (in press) have recently argued that the different rock-art media in the arid zone present independent lines of evidence in that they have a dual signalling capacity to demonstrate both localised group and broad scale group cohesions (see McDonald 1994 for elaboration of this argument). A shift is observed at approximately 1500 years BP when there appears to be a major increase in site numbers and artefact densities. This timing coincides with the proposed timing for the influx of the Western Desert language, which currently is distributed across an area one-sixth the size of the continent (see below). The timing of the spread of the Western Desert language is thought to coincide with major increases in intensities of regional and site occupation, accelerated ritual and ceremonial cycles and an expansion of long distance exchange networks (see dates for baler shell at rainmaking sites in Smith & Veth in press). The model assumes that the ramified social networks described by current anthropological research have functioned for at least the last 1000–1500 years.

McDonald and Veth (in press) have suggested that social and territorial organisation became increasingly localised at the time of the LGM, following a long phase of high mobility and multivalent art. Groups could have become more tethered to uplands like the Calvert and Carnarvon ranges (e.g. the Serpents Glen site) due to intensified aridity and lowered accessibility to resources, including water. Large tracts of plains and inter-dunal corridors may have been dropped from normal scheduling. A likely consequence of this would have been an inevitable intensifying process if some continuity of occupation were maintained. This is the classic scenario proposed for retraction to an LGM refuge in north-eastern Australia at Lawn Hill Gorge by Peter Hiscock (1988). Using this model — and information-exchange theory (e.g. Wobst 1977) — one would expect that art being used as a form of negotiated identity could have played varying roles throughout this time frame.

McDonald and Veth (in press) and McDonald (in press) argue that initial occupation of the region may well have been accompanied by the creation and corporate use of rock art. Low intensity, sporadic art production at this time would have demonstrated widespread group cohesion. The engraved art fits within this schema, supported by dates around the continent (e.g. Watchman 1992, 1993). As Veth (2000) has suggested elsewhere, Pleistocene networks across the arid zone were probably more open and far-reaching than has previously been argued in reflecting an extreme form of mobility (although see Lourandos & David 2002).

With the LGM and changes in residential patterning (between 22 000 and 13 000 years BP), regional behaviour appears to have become more localised and tethered to shorter-spaced territories. Perhaps it was at this time that the large decorative infilled motifs — the embodiments of the Cleland Hills faces into people — were developed. As indicated above, these appear to be geologically old with the tops of the heads of one panel having weathered away. In the Calvert Range at the site of Kaalpi, this style appears at least as old as the classic Panaramitee-style art (on the basis of patination and weathering).

Prior to the arrival of the Western Desert language during the late Holocene, regional social networks, which are thought to be the antecedents to current social organisation, developed. Art would again have been used to negotiate both broad-scale and local group identity. It would still be expected to have been relatively homogeneous because of the need to maintain long-distance alliance networks and ramified kinship networks, although there should have been an increased use of art to negotiate local group identity with distinctive localised style regions evolving.

This pattern would have continued during the spread of the Western Desert languages in the period between 1500 and 500 years BP, and one might expect that the development of regionally specific art provinces developed at this time to an unprecedented level. Archaeological and anthropological evidence would suggest that artistic influences from the east and further afield would have been introduced into the graphic system during the last 500 years. Diachronic change is clearly evidenced in the Calvert Range — but so too is evidence of impressive stylistic heterogeneity in the art, which is arguably recent.

In their recent paper examining the history of occupation and rock art at Puritjarra Rockshelter, Rosenfeld and Smith (2002) also highlight significant changes in the graphic vocabulary during the last millennium. There is evidence for a significant increase in the use of the shelter after 800 years BP. Changes in the provenance of recovered ochre also indicate realignments of contacts, suggesting connections towards the central Australian ranges rather than the desert to the west. Rosenfeld and Smith (2002, p. 121) note that 'In the rock art, changes in style and composition evident in the surviving frieze of paintings at Puritjarra record fundamental changes in graphic vocabulary over the last millennia'. They argue that shifts in the rock-art (abandonment of composite lines and arc motifs towards large, bichrome single emu tracks) reflect changes in either the totemic referent of the site or the identity of the people who occupied it. Rosenfeld and Smith (2002, p. 122) conclude that 'as Puritjarra's place in the social geography changed, the motifs appropriate for the site also changed'. Clearly, during the last thousand years a complex interplay between graphic systems, social relations and site use took place; the dynamics of one are bound to the others.

So how do we explain this level of diversity in the late-Holocene art of the arid zone?

The model needs to take into consideration not only residential mobility of particular groups at any one time, but also likely aggregation cycles that would have had great importance in terms of cultural/genetic/ritual flows. The 'aggregation locale' concept originally proposed for Palaeolithic Spain by Meg Conkey (1980) is good for describing art sites/provinces where groups from many disparate social groupings get together. This concept aims to describe the dynamic social relations at play at these resource-rich locales, given the social imperatives for groups to coalesce and the ecological pressure for groups to disperse. As discussed by Veth (1993) and Gibbs and Veth (2002), such locales are central to the (re)negotiation of regional alliance networks (i.e. so-called 'ritual engines').

The high degree of stylistic variability displayed in the abundant engraved and painted motifs within the well-watered gorges of the Calvert Range strongly suggest that this place has acted as an aggregation locale over a considerable period of time. Such aggregation sites are believed to have served as important centres for ritual production, in addition facilitating the rapid exchange of linguistic elements, material goods and genes. The paradox of arid-zone settlement behaviour is that groups must coalesce in order to effectively negotiate the social contracts and relations of reciprocity that set the necessary conditions for subsequent dispersal (*cf.* Veth 1993). In resource-poor areas aggregation locales are essentially the 'engines' for information exchange and, in such localities, art will exhibit high stylistic diversity as an expression of contested group identities, rather than bounded territoriality (see also Gibbs & Veth 2002).

Language diffusion

Western Desert speakers now occupy a vast area of Australia. McConvell (1996) has argued that the high degree of internal homogeneity of the language testifies to its relatively recent establishment and expansion (within the last 1500 years). In summary, McConvell (1996) argued that initial Pama–Nyungan expansion occurred approximately 5000 years BP. The Nyungic language is thought to have spread from north-west Queensland across arid northern Australia between approximately 3500 to 3000 years BP. The homeland of the Wati subgroup (to which the Western Desert language belongs) was in the southern Pilbara–Gascoyne region, with the homeland of the Western Desert language modelled to be in the vicinity of Durba Springs, now located on the Canning Stock Route. The movement of proto-Wati into the desert is thought to date to just before 2000 years BP, with the Western Desert language in place by 1500 years BP. I have previously reviewed a range of archaeological data from the Western Desert, including changes in assemblage composition, occupational intensity, technology, mythology, symbolic schema and exchange systems, and concluded that the most likely donor area is indeed the Pilbara and that a date of approximately 2000 to 1500 years BP sits well with the timing of a major cultural shift and the emergence of a new cultural system (*cf.* Veth 2000; see also Marwick 2002). Veth (2000) and McDonald and Veth (in press) have provided syntheses of Western Desert archaeology, linguistics and art that allow a phased occupational model to be constructed (see Table 1).

Of relevance to the present paper are phases 5 and 6. During phase 5, from approximately 1500 years BP, the Western Desert language is seen to have spread. Loan words are discernable from northern languages, and evidence for some contact with Arandic languages to the east occurs by approximately 500 years BP (Veth 2000). There is increased evidence in intensities of occupation at excavated sites within the Western Desert (e.g. Smith 1989, 1996; Thorley 1998; Veth 1993, 1996) along with an increase in the diversity of trade/exchange items, such as exotic, fine-grained lithic materials and ochres, and the presence of marine shell in the remote interior (Smith & Veth in press; Thorley & Gunn 1996). It is suggested that art is increasingly used to negotiate broad-scale and local group identity, with distinctive, localised style regions emerging. This is seen to be a direct reflection of 'corporate' signalling behaviour during a phase of increasing territoriality; a process also highlighted through mapping of ochre supply zones around the eastern Western Desert site of Puritjarra over the last 20 000 years (*cf.* Smith *et al.* 1998). This late-Holocene trend is much akin to what David (1991) and McNiven (1999) have coined 'regionalisation' elsewhere in Australia, further indication that what was taking place in the Western Desert was somehow tied to broadly contemporaneous innovations

Table 1. Occupation phases and language movements (after Veth 2000) and likely art correlates.

Occupation phase	Years BP	Linguistic correlations	Occupation model	Likely art correlate
6	500 to contact	Western Desert speakers encroach into central Australia.	Increased interaction with social networks in central Australia.	Art influences also appear from the east and further afield.
5	1500–500	Spread of Western Desert language; loan words from northern languages; some evidence of Arandic contact.	Increased intensity of site occupation; accelerated ritual and ceremonial cycle; increase in long distance exchange.	Increased use of art to negotiate broad-scale and local group identity with distinctive localised style regions evolving; art influences at this time come from the north.
4	5000–1500	Pama–Nyungan occupation of Western Desert.	Occupation of all desert ecosystems; re-establishment of regional exchange/information networks.	Art used to negotiate broad-scale and local group identity.
3	13 000–5000	Pama–Nyungan occupation of Western Desert.	Climatic amelioration; marginal lands used more systematically.	Art used to negotiate broad-scale and local group identity.
2	22 000–13 000	Pama–Nyungan occupation of Western Desert.	Changes in residential patterns; shifts in demography (LGM); lowlands used more opportunistically.	Broad scale social cohesion with perhaps increased localised identifying behaviour; territorial tethering.
1	>22 000	Non-Pama–Nyungan speakers.	Early colonisation; all land systems in use; broadly based economy.	Sporadic art production; widespread group cohesion.

and transformations in other parts of Australia. During phase 6 (the last 500 years) the Western Desert language moved to the margins of central Australia and the margins of the southwest. The development of distinctive localised art style regions continues, however there is some evidence that the symbolic schema from central Australia and possibly other 'frontiers' begin to be incorporated in Western Desert iconography.

As argued by Gibbs and Veth (2002, p. 14), 'Territorial "ascendancy" might be seen as a natural condition of arid zone foragers, essentially being a social solution to resource stress, rather than a functional solution bound up with technological innovation and the like'. They argue that where landscapes are occupied and periodic resource stress occurs, then rights of access to neighbouring groups' lands are crucial and are only made possible by kinship ties and other social links such as histories of residence and the like. An intensification of social and ritual networks at aggregation locales (where noviates from adjacent fertile areas are 'recruited' and their corresponding kin are incorporated into local networks; see Yengoyan's (1976) views on the adaptive efficiency of the eight-class kin system) provides the ultimate risk-minimising strategy and provides a persuasive explanation for the efflorescence and expansion of the Western Desert culture noted at contact (and more recently).

Conclusion

In concluding his landmark volume on Australian hunter-gatherers, Lourandos (1997, p. 335) notes that the cultural changes he identifies during the late Holocene in Australia were likely due to 'an interplay of internal and external forces'. These forces are likely to have included biogeographic processes, the formation of alliances and sociodemographic factors. In my current discussion of aggregation locales within the Western Desert I have reflected on changes in mobility patterns, territoriality and art, language diffusion, and exchange systems during the late Holocene. While undoubtedly relationships between these nascent data sets are complex, and subject to differential temporal and spatial scales of analysis, there is little doubt in my mind that they can be held together by an explanatory framework that owes much to the socially informed approaches projected onto the arid landscapes of Australia by Harry Lourandos.

Ecological factors alone do not explain the apparent duality and diversity in artistic graphic systems at aggregation sites through time. Ideational frameworks alone are not persuasive as a prime mover for changes in residential mobility during the last thirty millennia. Equally, demographic considerations on their own do little to explain emergent territoriality or the extraordinarily recent and expansive uptake of the Western Desert language. It is the appreciation of nuanced social and political actions, set against a transforming set of ecological circumstances, that provides for a more persuasive and satisfactory view of Indigenous history within the Western Desert of Australia.

15.

Environmental change and variability in south-western Victoria: changing constraints and opportunities for occupation and land use

John Tibby, A Peter Kershaw, Heather Builth, Aline Philibert and Christopher White

Climate change and its associated impacts have been seen as a trigger to human migration and changing settlement and land-use patterns throughout the world. Initial global colonisation from the original home of *Homo sapiens* has been linked to the removal of the 'Sahara barrier' during wetter conditions of the last interglacial period, while migration of *Homo sapiens* into the 'New World' has a strong link to global climate. Glacially induced low sea levels apparently facilitated movement into Australia during the last glacial period, and the development of an ice-free corridor allowed overland travel from Siberia to the Americas with climatic warming at the end of this glacial period.

Dry conditions during the last glacial period are considered to have limited populations and established new environmental constraints and opportunities. This led to cultural change in many parts of the world, with population increases and associated innovations (such as the origins of agriculture) occurring around the glacial-Holocene transition, as both precipitation and temperature increased (Wright 1976; Haberle & Chepstow-Lusty 2000). Within the Holocene the onset or intensification of climatic variability within approximately the last 5000 years, generally linked to the El Niño-Southern Oscillation (McGlone *et al.* 1992; Rodbell *et al.* 1999), has recently been advocated as a major driver of social change and population increase, precipitating the onset of the Sumarian and Egyptian civilisations and expansions in agriculture in South-East Asia, New Guinea and north-west Europe (Fagan 1999).

However, the view of climate as an overriding influence on human society is by no means universal. For example, in Australia, although population levels appear to have increased continent-wide in a humid phase during the early to mid Holocene, there is little apparent relationship between occupation patterns and lake levels through most of the late Quaternary (Lourandos & David 2002). Where population increased in the early-to-mid Holocene there is debate over whether this was accompanied by social or technological developments (O'Connell & Allen 1995). Evidence for a further marked increase in population within the last few thousand years is explained as largely due to sociocultural developments influenced, but not determined, by climate change (Lourandos 1983b; Lourandos & David 2002). Elsewhere, Lourandos (1987b), Lourandos and David (2002) and Haberle and David (2004) have argued that it is following the early-Holocene wet period, with an already rapidly growing population, that the social transformations of the mid-to-late Holocene took place. These social responses included a regionalisation of territorial networks, followed by increased diet breadths to include systematic grass seed grinding and the commencement of toxic plant processing (e.g. cycads) (Lourandos & David 2002).

Complicating any assessment of the effects of climate change on human activities is the impact that people may have had on the environment that could precipitate alteration in climate or induce environmental change that could equally be interpreted in climatic terms. Johnson et al. (1999) consider that burning by Indigenous people, on their arrival on the Australian continent, altered the vegetation to such a degree that it reduced the degree of penetration of monsoon rainfall into the interior resulting in drier conditions. Increased burning recorded within both New Guinea (Haberle et al., 2001) and Australia (McGlone et al. 1992; Shulmeister & Lees 1995) within the last 5000 years could be attributable to human activity or climate variability, or to a combination of the two.

Haberle and Chepstow-Lusty (2000) review a variety of evidence for the influence of physical environmental change on human society and note that comparisons of archaeological and environmental evidence are often difficult because such data have different spatial and temporal characteristics. Central to any evaluation of the relative influence of environmental and sociocultural influences on human population levels and impact is the degree of resolution of past records. In a comparison of temporal human population trends and climate change in Australia, Lourandos and David (2002) used regional compilations of radiocarbon dates from available archaeological caves and rockshelters as one proxy for intensity of occupation; other proxies — such as deposition rates of various cultural materials and sedimentation rates within cultural sites — were also used in comparison, and Lourandos and David argued that multi-proxies should be used when such modelling is attempted. Proxies derived from available sedimentary sequences (*cf.* Ross et al. 1992) were used to provide generalised regional climate constructions. Although providing a broad spatial picture, temporal resolution was, by necessity, limited and generalised.

The acquisition of temporally refined archaeological data is difficult, but a few sedimentary deposits are amenable to detailed analysis of at least a substantial part of the period of human occupation.

Here we present preliminary but fine-grained results of a study from Lake Surprise within the Mount Eccles lava flow of south-western Victoria that covers the period from the Last Glacial Maximum to present. The site is well located to address human settlement questions, being situated within the region of archaeological research by Lourandos that gave rise to his 'intensification' writings of Aboriginal occupation in the mid-late Holocene based, in part, on evidence for extensive eel harvesting (Lourandos 1983b). This is also a region where considerable archaeological details have already been obtained, and where fine-grained palaeoenvironmental data have long been required to better contextualise the well-documented archaeological patterns.

Lake Surprise is situated within an area that provides evidence for the development of a sophisticated and largely sedentary society based on eel aquaculture (Builth 2004). Although there has been extensive research into the palaeoenvironmental history of the western plains of south-western Victoria (see Kershaw et al. 2004), no other site has yet revealed a continuous sedimentary record that allows comparative analysis through the period from the last glacial to the present. Evidence of terrestrial environments is provided by pollen and charcoal while information on the lake environment is provided by diatoms. It was felt that comparison of these two environments might provide some means of separating climate and human influences as, in this relatively deep lake, human impact is likely to be more evident in dryland vegetation. Rate-of-change (ROC) analysis is employed to provide a measure of environmental variability, a feature that is generally overlooked in palaeoenvironmental studies but is considered critical to the assessment of the degree of landscape stability, including the timing and intensity of the operation of El Niño cycles and any other abrupt changes in the climate record, as well as a potential measure of human impact. In particular, we focus on any evidence for Holocene climatic variability, as it is during this period that the greatest apparent divergence between environmental conditions and occupation patterns has been noted (Lourandos & David 2002). By better understanding the environmental conditions in which people lived, we also position ourselves to better understand *contexts* of social dwelling and change.

ROC analysis has, for the most part, been utilized to assess the effect of climate on various proxies (Grimm & Jacobsen 1992; Lotter 1998). However, Dodson and Mooney (2002) have applied the technique to assessing European impact on environments in south-east Australia in the context of Holocene proxy records. Haberle (2003) has applied the technique to determine the likely commencement of agricultural land use within the New Guinea highlands. In this latter example, rate of change in regional and globally significant proxy data were compared to rate of change for vegetation derived from pollen records. A late-Holocene increase in vegetation rate of change in the absence of an obvious climate forcing was taken to indicate the likely imprint of people on the landscape. Here we apply ROC analysis to both pollen and diatom data from Lake Surprise in an effort to identify periods of heightened climate variability, and thereby provide a context for observed changes in the regional archaeology.

The study area

Lake Surprise (90 m above sea level) formed in the vent of the Mount Eccles volcano (Figure 1). It is about 700 m long, 180 m wide and the maximum depth, in the centre of the lake, is presently around 12 m. Slopes around the crater are steep so there is little catchment, with no evidence of inflow or outflow streams. Crater slopes are dominated by species-poor *Eucalyptus viminalis* woodland with abundant trees of *Acacia melanoxylum* and a ground cover composed largely of bracken (*Pteridium esculentum*), with grasses on drier slopes. *Cassinia longifolia* and *Bursaria spinosa* form a scattered shrub layer. The margins of the lake support a variable width of emergent aquatic vegetation that includes *Carex appressa*, *Triglochin procera*, *Rumex brownii*, *R. bidens* and *Urtica incisa*, with the floating aquatics *Lemna* sp. and *Azolla filiculoides* in sheltered shallow water.

A similar vegetation type to that around Lake Surprise dominates most of the Mount Eccles lava flow (Figure 2). Prior to clearance for agriculture with the arrival of Europeans, Tertiary sediments surrounding the flow also supported woodland whose canopy included *E. ovata* and *E. obliqua* as well as *E. viminalis*, with an understorey predominantly composed of grasses with sedges prominent in more swampy areas. *Leptospermum* scrub was a major component of swamp areas, created by drainage disruption with the extrusion of the Mount Eccles lava flow, dated to about 30 000 years BP (Head *et al.* 1991; Stone *et al.* 1997).

The area experiences a winter rainfall regime with rainfall derived largely from the passage of westerly depressions. Strong winds often accompany these depressions. Climatic estimates derived from the BIOCLIM bioclimatic prediction system for Lake Surprise (Busby 1991) indicate a mean annual rainfall of 746 mm, with 256 mm falling in the winter and 112 mm in the summer. Mean annual temperature is 13°C, mean summer temperature is 17.1°C, and mean winter temperature of 9.2°C.

Part 4 • Late-Holocene change

Figure 1. Lake Surprise and its immediate catchment.

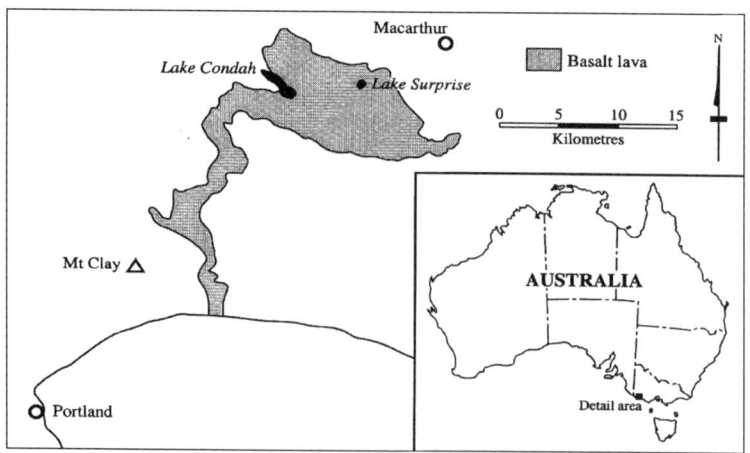

Figure 2. Location of Lake Surprise, Mt Eccles.

Methods

Fieldwork was undertaken in July 2002. A sediment core was extracted from close to the centre of the lake using a modified stainless steel Livingstone piston sampler guided into the sediment by PVC casing attached to a connected pair of inflatable dinghies. Coring continued to 13 m below the sediment surface where the compact nature of the sediment prevented further penetration. The unconsolidated nature of the topmost 1 m of sediment prevented conventional collection with the stainless steel Livingstone sampler. This sediment was carefully recovered using a clear polycarbonate Livingstone sampler. Upon return to the shore the upper metre of core was sampled in contiguous 1 cm slices, while the other Livingstone cores were wrapped in PVC and plastic before all sediment collected was taken back to the laboratory and kept in a cool store at 4°C until processed.

The Livingstone cores were described according to the modified Troels-Smith system of Kershaw (1997) before sampling. One centimetre slices were taken at 10 cm intervals from the whole core sequence, and 1 cm^3 subsamples were extracted for pollen and diatom analyses. Pollen preparation involved sediment dispersal in 10% sodium pyrophosphate for twenty-four hours, treatment with hydrochloric acid to remove carbonates, sieving through mesh sizes of 180 μm and 7 μm to remove unwanted large and small fragments respectively, acetolysis to reduce cellulose matter and darken grains for ease of identification, and heavy liquid (specific gravity 2.0) separation of mineral matter from the pollen residue using sodium polytungstate. Prepared samples were mounted on microscope slides for analysis and calculation of pollen and charcoal concentrations. Pollen counts were undertaken using a Zeiss Axioscope microscope at x 750 magnification, with initial identification of grains at x 1875. Sample counts were continued until a total of 150 grains from predominantly dryland taxa had been recorded. Clark's (1982) point count method was used to provide a measure of charcoal concentration.

Samples for diatom analysis were initially dried and then each sample was placed in a solution of hydrochloric acid to dissolve carbonates. A mixture of nitric and sulphuric acid was then added to digest organic matter. The residue was dried on a coverslip and then mounted on slides within the resin Naphrax. A minimum of 300 diatom valves were identified and counted under x 1500 magnification on a Zeiss Axioscope microscope.

Four radiocarbon dates and the first appearance of non-Australian, exotic pollen formed the basis of the chronology. Radiocarbon determinations were undertaken at The University of Waikato radiocarbon facility (for sample depth 1342–1350 cm) on bulk sediment, and at the ANTARES facility at the Australian Nuclear Science and Technology Organisation (for sample depths 360–361 cm, 754–755 cm and 1069–1070 cm) on samples prepared in a similar manner to pollen but excluding acetolysis to prevent contamination with modern carbon.

Radiocarbon dates were calibrated to calendar ages using the INTCAL98 data set (Stuiver et al. 1998) in Calib 4.4 (Stuiver & Reimer 1993). The median of the 2 sigma of the probability distribution with the greatest relative area (minimum 83%) was taken as the calibrated age. Calibrated ages were linearly interpolated above and below dated levels (Figure 3), with the upper boundary of this interpolation being the first appearance of exotic pollen at 75 cm in the core (ascribed an age of 1850 CE, or 100 cal. BP).

ROC analysis was undertaken separately on pollen and diatom data. With pollen data, all dryland pollen sum taxa (following D'Costa & Kershaw 1997) were included, while for the diatom data, all taxa which exceeded 1% in at least one sample were used. In order to reduce the influence of factors such as counting errors and short-term spikes in pollen and diatom production and sedimentation, the fossil pollen and diatom values were first smoothed (using a sample smoothing of between five and nine samples, (Grimm & Jacobson 1992). The data were then standardised to equal-time intervals of 200 years to ensure comparability between time periods. Chord distance was the similarity measure used to calculate the degree of change between samples, although Euclidean distance produced a similar outcome (Tibby unpublished data).

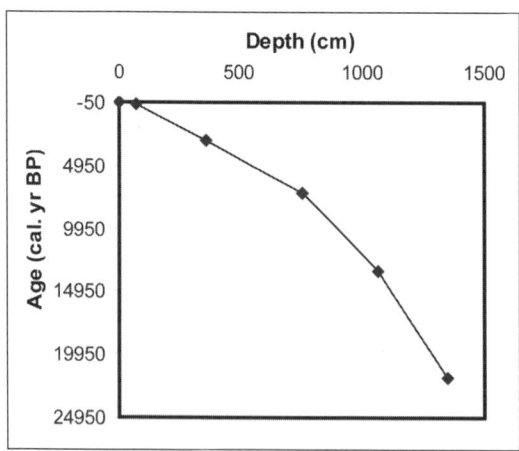

Figure 3. Age–depth curve for the Lake Surprise sediments.

Results

Results of the ROC data are discussed in five time periods, which were assigned to correspond to (shared) changes in the ROC data. These are: 21 500 to 9750 cal. BP; 9750 to 3750 cal. BP; 3750 to 1500 cal. BP; 1500 to 500 cal. BP; and 500 cal. BP to present. Major features of environmental conditions are included to provide a broader context for evaluating the results of ROC analyses. They include the proportion of planktonic diatoms as an indication of variation in water depth, relative proportions of woody plants (predominantly *Eucalyptus* and Casuarinaceae), woody-herbaceous plants (mainly Asteraceae) and herbs (mainly Poaceae) as an indication of the nature of terrestrial vegetation, and charcoal concentrations as a measure of fire activity.

Period 1: 21 500 to 9750 cal. BP

This period, extending from the Last Glacial Maximum to the very early Holocene, shows an initial dominance of woody-herbaceous (mainly Asteraceae with notable Chenopodicaeae) values indicating a largely treeless steppe landscape existing under much cooler and drier conditions than those of today. The low charcoal values probably reflect the lack of fuel for burning in the open herbaceous landscape. The almost total absence of planktonic diatoms suggests that the lake was shallow, reinforcing the postulation of drier conditions. The subsequent rise in woody-plant pollen, almost totally Casuarinaceae (White unpublished data), together with a gradual reduction in woody-herbaceous pollen, suggests a replacement of steppe by an *Allocasuarina verticillata* woodland under ameliorating climatic conditions. Some indication of, at least sporadic, increase in rainfall is provided by peaks in planktonic diatoms. However, the absence of sustained elevated planktonic values suggests that temperature rather than precipitation was the critical factor in facilitating woodland development. In line with an increasing cover of woody vegetation, charcoal values rise. Towards the end of the period, charcoal values reach highest values for the record, and fire may have played some role in facilitating changes noted at the boundary between periods 1 and 2.

Despite the major changes in vegetation and fire activity and the high degree of variability in planktonic taxa representation, ROC analysis of both the pollen and diatom data indicates that these late-glacial assemblages were relatively stable, with chord distance values generally below 0.05 in the pollen data and 0.15 for the diatoms. There is little overall relationship between patterns of change in the two proxies. Although both analyses from both proxies indicate periods of general stability, where increased variability is recorded patterns are generally asynchronous between the indicators. In the latter part of the period there is a marked decrease in variability in the two indicators. This change is time-transgressive, with reduced variability commencing at 11 500 cal. BP in the diatoms and continuing through to 9750 cal. BP. In the pollen data reduced variability commences 1000 years later, at 10 500 cal. BP, but ceases in concert with the change in the diatom data.

Period 2: 9750 to 3750 cal. BP

This early-to-mid Holocene period is marked by an initial reduction in values of Casuarinaceae and peak in woody-herbaceous taxa, followed by an increase in *Eucalyptus*, which then shared dominance of the canopy layer with Casuarinaceae through the remainder of Period 2 (White unpublished data). Charcoal values indicate relatively constant and low levels of burning throughout. The dominance of planktonic taxa through most of the period indicates highest lake levels and presumably highest rainfall within the record, although there is a notable phase of low planktonic values between about 7000 and 6250 cal. BP.

There are few consistent patterns in the ROC data from the two indicators for much of Period 2. From 9000 to 4250 cal. BP, rates of change for the pollen data are generally elevated, while the diatom rate of change fluctuates from well below to well above average. Near the end of this period there is some correspondence between the two indicators, with environmental stability suggested by lowered values recorded from 4500 cal. BP.

Period 3: 3750 to 1500 cal. BP

Falling values for planktonic diatoms through this period suggest reduction in lake level and therefore decreased effective precipitation, while high charcoal values suggest more frequent or intense fires. However, there is little response in the major vegetation groupings that continue to be dominated by *Eucalyptus* and Casuarinaceae woodland or open forest. In contrast, pollen and diatom compositional data show similar elevated rates of change. In the pollen data, values remain well above average throughout this period. The diatom data values are more variable with one sample, dated around 3000 cal. BP, falling just below the record's average.

Period 4: 1500 to 500 cal. BP

The generally low values for planktonic taxa and charcoal suggest relatively low lake levels and infrequent or low-intensity burning throughout this period. Again there is little response in the vegetation, although the tree canopy may have become a little more open. Rates of change are generally reduced in both indicators, although patterns differ in that pollen rates of change are essentially stable about the long-term mean, while the diatom rates of change remain above the long-term mean.

Period 5: 500 cal. BP to the present

There is little change in the mean value of planktonic diatom taxa or in vegetation structure, although a correspondence between a sharp reduction in planktonic values and in tree-pollen percentages (a result of the virtual elimination of Casuarinaceae) in the top two samples may be significant. By contrast, there are sharp increases in charcoal values, although not to levels recorded in Period 3, and in rates of change for both pollen and diatoms that achieve unprecedented levels, with variability far exceeding that recorded elsewhere in the record.

Discussion

Lake Surprise provides a useful picture of changing lake levels and vegetation since the Last Glacial Maximum (Figure 4). It is consistent with other records from the Western Plains region of Victoria (Kershaw *et al.* 2004) in demonstrating that the height of the last glacial period, extending into the late glacial period, was much cooler than today, somewhat drier, and failed to support woodland or forest vegetation. Furthermore, it supports other evidence that climate became warmer and then wetter in the later part of the late glacial and early Holocene, resulting in the initial development of Casuarinaceae woodland and, about 7500 years ago, the establishment of a *Eucalyptus*-Casuarinaceae open forest. In line with other records, lake levels varied during the Holocene with, in this record, highest levels achieved between about 9000 and 3750 cal. BP, but there was little response in dryland vegetation. Within the record, greatest variability appears to have occurred, in both pollen and diatoms, within the last glacial period. However, this appears to have been a time of relatively low rate of change and there is, through the whole record, little relationship between degree of change and actual rate of change in the proxies.

It is also the case that for much of the Lake Surprise record there is relatively little correspondence between the rate of change registered in the two indicators. This result is perhaps not surprising given that terrestrial vegetation and aquatic algae have fundamentally different life strategies and life spans that differ by up to three orders of magnitude. Importantly, while diatom response to a particular perturbation may be concluded within the temporal confines of a single sediment sample (commonly representing 1–100 years) (*cf.* Anderson 1995), dryland vegetation can take hundreds of years to reach equilibrium with external forcing, e.g. climate (e.g. Walker & Chen 1987). Differences in the responsiveness of the indicators are illustrated by the average chord distance between (smoothed) samples, which is approximately three times greater in the diatoms than in the pollen data.

In assessing the potential contribution of human impact to ROC values, the most recent period is informative. Within the period dated from about 500 cal. BP to present, rate of change values for both indicators are clearly the highest for the record. As there is no evidence to suggest that natural climatic variability has been any greater during this period than previously, it might be considered that human activity was the major influence. The increase in burning around the same time, although appearing to lag the ROC data, may have been an important agent of increased variability. The date of 500 cal. BP is beyond the time of European arrival, and the estimate may be too old. Although it seems to substantially pre-date the first appearance of exotic pollen in the record (at 75 cm), this situation is not uncommon, with marked evidence of impact at many sites before establishment of introduced plants (Tibby 2003). This evidence is mainly in the form of increased native disturbance representation (Leahy et al. 2005) that is not a clear feature of this record (White unpublished data). It is nevertheless intriguing that the period beginning about 500 years ago is precisely a time when increasing intensities of site and regional land use appear to have peaked in south-western Victoria, as in many other parts of Australia (e.g. Lourandos 1983a, 1983b; Barker 2004), and therefore the possibility that the peak environmental ROC values during the last 500 years relate, at least in part, to pre-European impacts should not be discounted. However, it is clear that the high rates of change in the latter part of Period 1 can be attributed to European impact, and emphasise the appropriateness of the indicators and technique for detecting environmental change.

In the pre-500 cal. BP sediments there are perhaps three periods where the variability recorded in both the dryland vegetation and the diatoms follows a similar pattern. Periods of low variability were recorded at the beginning of the Holocene and commencing at 4500 cal. BP. In each of these cases, the period of correspondence in the two indicators is relatively short (a maximum of 1500 years). By contrast, the period of high variability between 3750 and 1500 cal. BP was sustained for a substantially longer time (and was without precedent in the pre-European periods). Within this time period, in the diatom record, a number of 200-year periods experienced rates of change unprecedented in the 20 000 year pre-500 cal. BP record, while in the pollen data, the maintenance values above 0.05 chord distance for more than 1000 years does not occur elsewhere in the pre-contact sediments. It appears, therefore, that this period can be accurately characterised as one of substantial variability in both the terrestrial and aquatic environment. It is this period which forms the major focus of subsequent discussion, since it provides a context for assessment of both regional (Lourandos & David 2002) and local (Lourandos 1983a, 1983b Builth 2004) evidence for 'intensification'.

On the basis of current evidence, it is not possible to unequivocally establish whether increases in environmental rate of change between 3750 and 1500 cal. BP are the result of climate, human agency or a combination of the two. However, it is difficult to envisage a land-management practice that would reduce water levels in Lake Surprise (as suggested by reductions in planktonic diatoms commencing at 3750 cal. BP and evidence from other localities, see below). Hence, it appears most likely that some element of natural climate forcing was involved (though we acknowledge that other possibilities involving human agency may explain the changes in the diatom record). Furthermore, while the precise nature of this variability is not clear, it may well have been associated with reduced resource availability to Indigenous populations (via the inferred decreased effective moisture and, by inference, resource biomass). Additionally, it appears that burning became a more important part of the regional environment at this time, with sustained high microscopic charcoal concentrations observed throughout the period 3750 to 1500 cal. BP. This burning may well have been a response to a more arid and/or variable climate during the period, or a land-use response to changing environmental opportunities.

Given that a regional picture for increased intensities of site and regional land use now exists (Lourandos 1983; Lourandos & David 2002) and that periods of elevated variability at individual sites may result from human activity, it is important to assess the regional extent of the trends observed in the Lake Surprise record. Evidence from Lake Keilambete, arguably the most intensively studied and best-dated site on the Western Plains, suggests that variability observed from 3750 to 1500 cal. BP does have regional expression (Bowler 1982; Chivas *et al.* 1985). Jones *et al.* (1998) indicate that lake-level fluctuations with an inferred amplitude approximating 10 m occurred in less than 200 years during the period 3100 to 2500 (uncalibrated) years BP, indicating substantial medium-term variability in precipitation-evaporation ratios. Our results reinforce this notion of increased variability and tend to support Chivas *et al.*'s (1985) results from the same site, which indicate that the phase of variability was well underway by 3100 ^{14}C years BP (*c.* 3300–3200 cal. BP). Since the variability documented herein is, at least partly, related to reduced effective moisture, it is instructive to examine whether there is any relationship to the record of human occupation in south-west Victoria. This is done by examining any relationship to the eel-harvesting systems of the Mount Eccles flow (which, at present, has relatively poor dating control) and then to the occupation history of the region.

Archaeological research has found that Gunditjmara exploitation of the Mount Eccles lava flow focused on wetland resources prior to the arrival of

Europeans in the nineteenth century. The extent and intensity of this exploitation was such that it should, by all definitions, be termed 'aquaculture'. Based on the growing, trapping and processing of the Shortfin eel (*Anguilla australis*), a land-management regime developed that incorporated large-scale cultural modification to the landscape resulting in the creation of dammed wetlands that provided year-round aquatic conditions for eel and other wetland species (Builth 2000, 2002, 2004). These wetlands were interconnected by natural, modified and/or anthropogenic channels that enabled migrating eels to reach the ocean and travel to distant spawning grounds. Traps were constructed downstream of the dams and along the length of the channels so that people could capture the fatter and oil-rich, mature, silver eels (Lourandos 1980a, 1980b, 1987b). The year-round sustainability and reliability of this economic base, plus the technology to produce resource surplus during the annual migrations, had important socioeconomic consequences for the Gunditjmara (Builth in press).

Although the archaeological sites relating to eel aquaculture are yet to be reliably dated (see Lourandos 1980a for preliminary results elsewhere in the Victorian south-west), based on reconstructions of lake levels at Lake Condah on the lava flow Head (1989) considered that in relation to the heights of associated culturally constructed ponds, dams and fish traps, the traps were capable of becoming operational occasionally from about 4000 years ago, but their regular use would have been restricted to the last 2000 years. Such economic innovations appear to support the general trends and interpretations of Lourandos and David (2002; see below), although refinements in chronology are needed. Interestingly, Head's (1989) suggested timing for the period when fish-trapping operations may have coincided with the onset of heightened environmental variability as observed in the Lake Surprise record.

Indirect archaeological evidence suggests a moderately different antiquity for the eel-harvesting system than for the onset of major environmental change, but a coincidence with the archaeological evidence for intensities of rock-shelter use. Williams (1988) considered the earth mounds of the Toolondo–Caramut–Condah–Bessiebelle area to be residential bases at least partly associated with the systematic extraction of eels. These mounds allowed ongoing exploitation of aquatic resources even during times of flooding (e.g. Downey & Frankel 1992; see David 2002 for a summary of the information). With this notion in mind Williams (1988) aimed to establish the antiquity of systematic eel fishing via an investigation of the antiquity of the mounded residential bases. As she and other researchers have established, earth mounds associated with wetlands in western and northern Victoria begin around 2700 years ago, but the vast majority of investigated earth mound sites date to the last 2000 years (e.g. Bird & Frankel 1991a; Coutts 1982; Coutts *et al.* 1978; Downey &

Frankel 1992; Williams 1988). Hence, although this timing does not match the initiation of the high variability phase in the Lake Surprise record (Period 3: 3750–1500 cal. BP), it certainly falls within it. These data raise the possibility that the environmental changes observed in the Lake Surprise record may have been the catalyst for the observed social changes. Certainly, the development of a robust chronology for eel-harvesting systems in south-west Victoria (via direct comprehensive dating) would provide an enhanced understanding of the sensitivity of the local population to the environmental changes documented from Lake Surprise.

On a regional scale, broad-scale increases in intensities of site and regional land use (as indicated by dated occupied layers in rock shelters) appear to accelerate well into this period (peaking after c. 2000 ^{14}C BP[1]; Lourandos & David 2002), although they may have been initiated between 4000 and 3000 years BP as is more clearly indicated in the regional compilations (Bird & Frankel 1991b; Lourandos & David 2002). These data largely support the earlier observations of Lourandos (1983), based on a smaller data set of nineteen archaeological sites. In addition to this broad-scale evidence, there is much evidence at individual sites that provides evidence for increasing intensities of site and regional land use (e.g. Lourandos 1983; McNiven *et al.* 1999). Lourandos and David (2002), in examining any correspondence with the environmental record from this period, utilise, in many ways, what is a similar data-set to the archaeological data, in that composite lake-level records from (near-coastal) South Australian and Victorian lakes are analysed (Ross *et al.* 1992).

Lourandos and David (2002) argue, in part, that the lack of correspondence between the pattern of occupation (dated rockshelter archaeological levels) and lake-level records (interpreted as an indicator of available biophysical resources) suggests that intensification of occupation is likely to have resulted from cultural and social phenomena, rather than from mechanical and necessary immediate responses to environmental change. However, many of the lakes used in the compilation appear insensitive to climate in regard to lake levels (e.g. Cobrico Swamp and Valley Lake). Such insensitivity (combined with original sampling intervals of often low temporal resolution and averaging lake level at 1000 year time intervals), substantially reduces the potential of this analysis to adequately document variability which may have important consequences for human occupation. The data used in such analyses may reflect long-term trends, but they are not fine-grained enough to address human responses to environmental change, nor the changing limitations and opportunities that changing environmental conditions may offer.

We suggest that climate variability may be an equally, or more important, factor than changes in mean climate in driving the availability of biophysical resources in pre-contact times (*cf.* Rowland 1999b), as it is in the present

Part 4 • Late-Holocene change

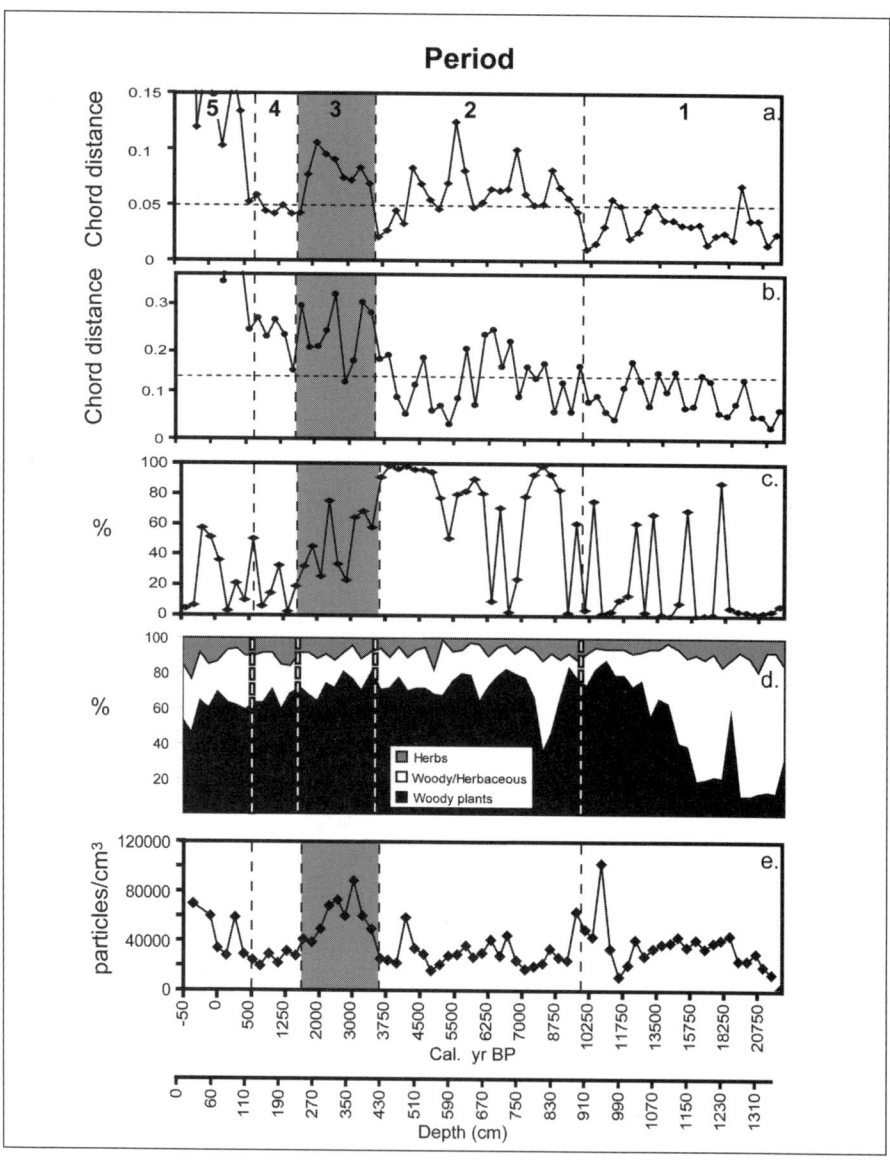

Figure 4. Lake Surprise environmental sequences: (a) rate of change in the dryland pollen assemblages; (b) rate of change in diatom assemblages; (c) proportion of planktonic diatoms; (d) major pollen components of dryland plants; and (e) charcoal concentration. Ages are expressed as calibrated years BP (cal. BP), where BP is before 1950 and ages are rounded to the nearest fifty years. Hence, the surface sediments extracted in 2002 are dated to +50. The average rate of change from the commencement of the records to 500 cal. BP is illustrated by a dashed line in a and b. The shaded section highlights a period characterised by lengthy elevated rates of change in both dryland pollen (i.e. terrestrial) and diatom (i.e. aquatic) indicators.

Australian landscape (Nicholls 1985, 1991). In this context, given the demonstrated variability at Lake Surprise (which may be without precedent post-Last Glacial Maximum), we contend that changes in both economy and nature of occupation (increased intensities of site and regional land use) may have been affected by more variable climate creating a new set of challenges and opportunities for people in the region.

In conclusion, the pollen and diatom records from Lake Surprise have provided a picture of late-Quaternary environmental change in western Victoria which is largely consistent with that observed from other sites. The high-resolution nature of the record has permitted an investigation of environmental variability in the region which has generally been absent from other records. Importantly, in the context of human occupation of the region, a period of high climate variability between 3750 and 1500 cal. BP may have contributed to the change in occupation pattern long documented by Lourandos (e.g. Lourandos 1983, 1997). This preliminary analysis highlights the value of both this site and the ROC approach in providing proxy data with which to assess the interrelationships between people and climate in south-eastern Australia. It is hoped that ongoing and proposed research on the Mount Eccles lava flow (including expansion of the scope of proxy studies and increased resolution of the Lake Surprise palaeoecological record) together with combined palaeoecological and archaeological examination of swamp components of the aquaculture system, will lead to more certain chronological relationships between patterns of environmental and land use changes within the area.

Acknowledgements

We thank the Gunditjmara for their hospitality, informative discussion on the significance of the study site and permission to conduct the study on their traditional lands. We also thank the Victorian Department of Sustainability and Environment for permission for the sediment coring and Paul Leahy, Jim Peterson, Nick Porch, David Tooth and Quaternary Ecology students for field assistance, John Birks for providing a copy of his RATEPOL program, Bruno David for very valuable input into the manuscript and Gary Swinton for preparing Figure 2.

Note

1. Because of the method employed by Lourandos and David (2002), which averages occupation data over 1000 year periods (500 years either 'side' of a given slice), the 2000 14C years BP is a minimum estimate of the date of this increased rockshelter occupation which, statistically, could have begun 500 years earlier.

16.
Landscapes in western Torres Strait history

Cassandra Rowe

Introduction

In his *magnum opus*, *Continent of hunter-gatherers*, Harry Lourandos (1997, p.334) concluded:

> Given the structural similarities between many New Guinean hunter-horticultural and Australia[n] hunter-gatherer economies... together with the Australian archaeological data of the Holocene, it may be argued that both regions appear to have experienced an economic expansion or intensification in the late Holocene, and in particular in the last 2,000–1,000 years or so. In general, the two prehistories are also connected at least in the Torres Strait region and north Australia. The recent (late Holocene), more intensive use of offshore islands (and their marine and terrestrial foods) is common to both southern New Guinea and northern Australian regions.

What Lourandos alludes to here is not only that similar late-Holocene socioeconomic trajectories are evident in these two regions, but more critically that the perceived dichotomy between, on the one hand, 'hunter-gatherer' Australia and, on the other, 'horticultural' New Guinea — each occupying an opposite side of Torres Strait — fades in the geographical and conceptual link that is 'the Strait' (see David & Denham, this volume). When drawing historical links between the two regions, then, Lourandos (1997) was not only writing of contemporaneity in the timing of cultural change — temporal trends in economic production and social practice on both sides of the Strait, for example — but also of changing relationships people had with their surroundings. Thus, Lourandos presents an archaeology of cultural landscapes — not of so-called 'natural' environments, but a history of the way people engaged with their surroundings, and a history that has commonalities across northern Australia, Torres Strait and into New Guinea.

It is often the case that archaeologists use palaeoenvironmental trends to explain cultural or demographic changes, as these are understood from the archaeological record. In such views — and as has been amply critiqued by now (e.g. Barker 2004; Ellen 1982) — people more or less passively react to external forces, and such approaches are most typical of 'hunter-gatherer' archaeology. As such, the environment is examined in terms of the impacts it has or had on human groups; only rarely does archaeology in these scenarios attempt to address the history of those societies and peoples which environmental conditions have purportedly impacted upon.

This paper takes a somewhat different approach to these environmental ones. It is, rather, set within a research framework akin to that other environmental framework, the one that seeks evidence of palaeoenvironmental change to inform us on the role of people in environmental dynamics. I focus on Badu, one of the mid-point islands of Torres Strait, located halfway between New Guinea and mainland Australia. My aim is to further interrogate the Holocene material record — the vegetation record and burning history — as evidence of degrees of human interaction with, and manipulation of, the environment. I ultimately wish to better understand the history of people–land relations in that place which straddles both New Guinea and Australia, or, as some would have it, the horticultural and hunter-gatherer worlds.

Lourandos spoke of increased intensities of regional land use during the late Holocene — including island use — focusing on archaeological sites of residence. However, if an intensification of land use took place, then it is not just the residential places that would provide evidence of increasing land use, but the human impacts on the overall surrounding environments that support the people and that form the landscapes of engagement that would themselves inform us on changing people–land relations. It is this challenge, picking up evidence of changing intensities of land use and forms of landscape engagement, that I explore in this chapter by reference to the island of Badu, where archaeological evidence for temporal trends in regional behaviour and demographic circumstances are presently still largely of a preliminary nature. This chapter examines a recently published report on the Badu 15 rock shelter (David *et al.* 2004b). Badu 15 was selected for its inland position on older landforms as part of the terminal Pleistocene Torres Strait land-bridge phase. Because of its long sedimentary sequence, this site showed good promise to address the timing and pattern of settlement across the region, in particular the western group of Torres Strait islands. The Badu 15 excavation was published without the results of pollen analysis as these were not then available, and thus insight into local inland environments and the possible effect of people on the surrounding landscape were not then presented. One side benefit of this has been that the occupational history of the region has been previously discussed independently of the environmental sequence; this initial decoupling of the cultural and environmental evidence now allows its better merging.

The study area

Torres Strait is a shallow area of submerged continental shelf separating Australia, at Cape York, from south-east New Guinea. The region spans approximately 150 km north–south and contains over 100 islands, coral cays, exposed sandbanks and reefs. Eighteen islands are currently inhabited. Geophysically, Torres Strait can be divided into four main island groups: the high western islands of granitic formation; the north-western islands, which are alluvial in origin; a central group of low-lying coral islands (cays); and an eastern group of basic volcanic origin (Figure 1). Curiously, a similar division can be made following linguistic patterns and pre-European insular allied groups of marriage, raiding and exchange partners (Lawrence 1994). Reef-coring has demonstrated that post-glacial transgression of the shelf commenced *c.* 8500 years BP, with present high sea levels and insular geography attained by approximately 6500 years BP (Torgersen *et al.* 1988; Barham 1999). Rates of sea-level change prior to the attainment of modern levels are still open to debate, although recent assessment of microatolls on the island of Iama/Yam indicates sea level was at least 0.8–1 m higher than present around 5800 years BP, falling gradually until at least 2300 years BP (Woodroffe *et al.* 2000). Island formation is still ongoing today.

Badu is the third-largest island in Torres Strait, following Murulag and Mua. It is located some 70 km north of the Australian mainland, and separated from Mua to the east by a narrow, 2 km-wide passage (Figure 1). The island is 14 km by 13 km in size and consists of eroded remnants of volcanic rocks, chiefly granites and tuffs, forming a prominent east–west-oriented network of hills and ridges rising to 372 m above sea level (ASL) (Mulgrave Peak). The higher peaks are separated by broad, low-lying (10–20 m ASL) sand plains which essentially form a north–south corridor across the island. The hill slopes, extending to the majority of summits, support open forest dominated by *Eucalyptus polycarpa* and *E. alba*. Occupying the lowland plains, where the soil is finer and water may remain on the surface or in the soil for more than half the year, is woodland dominated by several species of *Melaleuca*, including *M. viridiflora* and *M. saligna*. Both the hill slopes and lowland plains incorporate a mosaic of local habitats that includes gallery forest, scattered vine thickets, *Melaleuca* swamp forest, sedgeland, and dune grassland. Mangroves dominate the northern, and

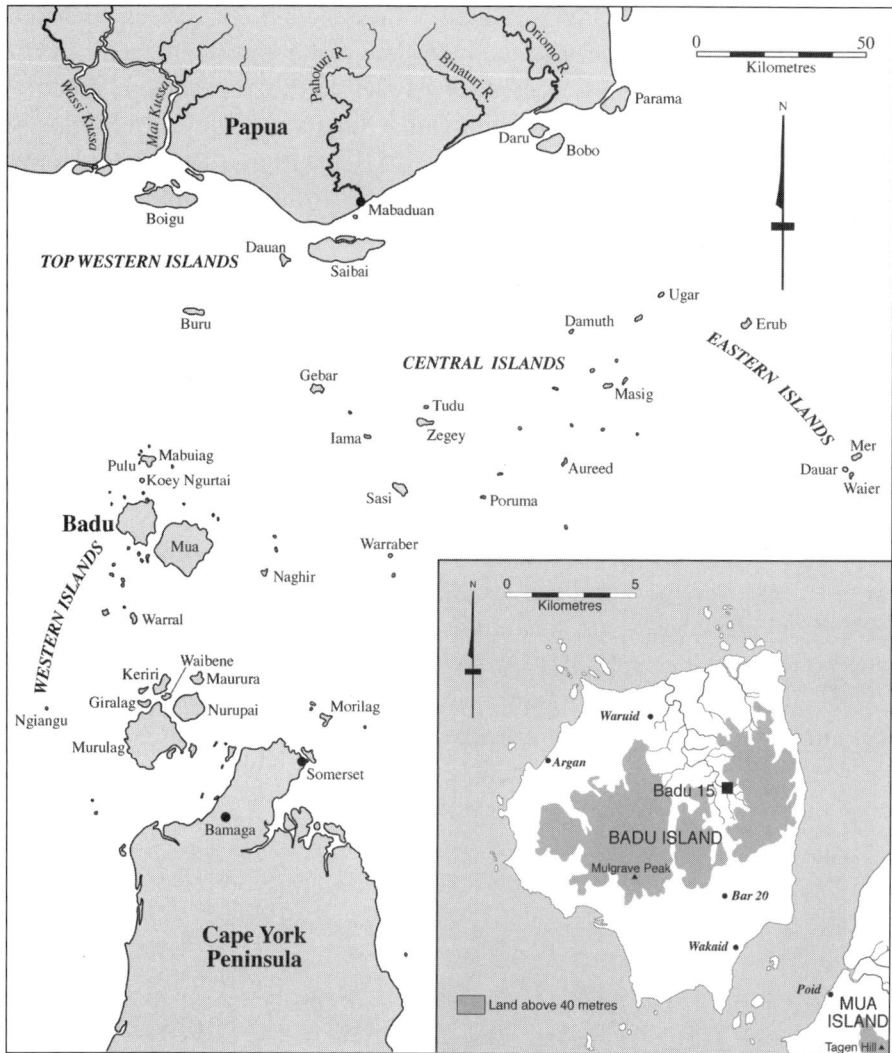

Figure 1. Torres Strait showing major island groups. Inset: Badu, highlighting Badu 15 and sites of environmental study.

to a lesser extent southern, coastlines (Garnett & Jackes 1983). Ecologically, the plant communities of the island resemble, on a smaller scale, the dry seasonal and coastal communities of Cape York Peninsula (Mackey *et al.* 2001). Climate is tropical and seasonal with a pronounced wet season from December to April. A climate station located on Thursday Island, 50 km to the south, records a mean annual rainfall of around 1730 mm, and a mean annual temperature of 26.5°C at sea level (Bureau of Meteorology 2000).

The Badu 15 rock shelter is located 3 km inland of the eastern coastline, positioned at the junction of a sandy lowland plain and steep rocky incline (10°06'S; 142°09'E). The site consists of a series of large overhanging boulders perched slightly above the surrounding plain (Figure 2). The sheltered area is approximately 6 m from dripline to back wall, 11 m wide at the dripline, and a maximum 3 m high inside the dripline. Soft ashy sediments dominate much of the 25 m^2 of floor surface area (David *et al.* 2004b). Badu 15 is located at an ecotone between the vine thickets occupying the rocky incline, and the eucalypt woodland of the plain, 100 m north-east of a seasonal creek. The vine-thicket presents a dense tangle of vegetation, with a low canopy only 2–3 m in height. Vines are abundant and include a number of species, notably *Capparis* spp. and *Smilax australis*. Growing across the thin soils, between borders and in fissures in the rock, the unidentified tree canopy is predominantly deciduous. Downslope and common on the large boulders of the study site is the rock fern *Drynaria quercifolia*. The open-canopy woodland is dominated by *Eucalyptus* spp. with occasional *Melaleuca, Banksia denatata* and *Cycas media*. Recent fire had removed the woodland groundcover at the time of study. On either side of the creek bed, extending out a short distance, there is an area of alluvial sandy soil which supports a woodland mosaic of creekside trees, shrubs, vines, grasses and sedges. Along the banks of the creek itself a mixed plant community exists, containing species such as *Dillenia alata* and *Melastoma polyanthum*.

Figure 2. Badu 15.

Badu 15 Archaeology

A detailed account of the archaeology of Badu 15 can be found in David *et al.* (2004b). Badu 15 was excavated to a maximum depth of 126 cm below ground surface. The consolidated sediments in the lower section, from 126 cm to 57 cm, were primarily inorganic clayey loams with coarse granitic rock material encountered throughout. At 57 cm depth there is a marked transition to a gravelly-loam with sand, characterised as a less compact layer that grades upwards to an ashy loam above 13 cm depth. The site's chronology is based on seven radiocarbon ages, which are reported with sample depths and calibrated ages in Table 1. Unless otherwise stated, the dates given in the text are uncalibrated radiocarbon years before present (years BP). The age distribution of the sequence indicates significant variation in sedimentation rates, with an accelerated period of accumulation, in the upper 50 cm of the excavation.

The only cultural materials recovered from Badu 15 were stone artefacts. Although charcoal was found in each excavation unit (XU) except for the lower XU28 of square J20, particles were attributed to bushfire occurrence (natural or anthropogenic) given the absence of structural evidence for hearths in the excavation. Definite stone artefacts were found in relatively high numbers from XU26 to XU24, including seven in XU24. Above this, artefacts are absent through to XU13 and then occur only sporadically to XU6. Definite artefacts are then found in all excavation units from XU6 and above, increasing to eleven in XU3 (Figure 3).

The Badu 15 archaeological data indicate definitive and sustained human presence between 8000 to 6000 years BP. David *et al.* (2004b) suggest that this early Holocene signature indicates the presence of permanent populations in the region at a time when the island was separating from the mainland as postglacial sea levels rose. The lack of sustained stone-artefact discard after 6000 years BP implies an absence of resident populations soon after Badu became an island. Occasional artefacts are, nevertheless, present in sediments dating between 6000 and 3500 years BP, indicating the sporadic presence of people at this time and low-level site use (likely short-duration visitation). After 3500–3000 years BP the use of Badu 15 once again became more intensive, as indicated by the sustained presence of cultural deposits and heightened sedimentation rates. Beginning sometime between 3500 and 3000 years BP, Badu once again became permanently occupied, for the first time as an island (David *et al.* 2004b). These three phases of occupation and island use are now examined through a consideration of past vegetation and burning events, using pollen, charcoal and sediment analyses.

Table 1. Badu 15 radiocarbon dating results (adapted from David et al. 2004b).

Depth (cm)	XU	Radiocarbon age (years BP)	$\delta^{13}C$ value	Calibrated age* 2 σ (probability)	Laboratory number
11.0–14.1	5	2999±44	−29.4	2964–3264; 3310–3317	Wk-12956
21.9–24.8	9	3470±73	−26.4	3474–3541; 3546–3842 3850–3864	Wk-11496
48.0–52.2	15	3390±40‡	−26.4	3471–3643; 3657–3687	Wk-12900
49.7–55.3	16	3505±79	−27.3	3480–3518; 3549–3925 3950–3959	Wk-9676
68.8–73.7	19	5163±80	−26.3	5656–5998; 6076–6092 6097–6107; 6149–6167	Wk-12901
99.7	24	5966±39	−26.6	6660–6804; 6820–6854	Wk-11946
109.1–115.5	27	8053±42	−26.7	8659–8666; 8702–8709 8717–8742; 8746–9024	Wk-11947

* Calib 4.4
‡ Not referred to in text because of slight date reversal.

Badu 15 pollen and charcoal analysis

In his survey of archaeological pollen analysis, Dimbleby (1985) contrasts soil pollen analysis and the analysis of soil from archaeological sites with traditional stratigraphic palynology, which focuses on stratified waterlogged deposits. Because pollen is deposited and distributed in these contrasting situations in different ways, understanding the distinctive mechanisms of pollen deposition, movement, and destruction is vital to interpretation of fossil assemblages (Pearsall 2000). Dimbleby (1985) discusses these issues in detail and surveys types of depositional environments encountered at archaeological sites. A number of studies in the volume edited by Owen Davis, *Aspects of archaeological palynology: methodology and applications* (1994), also address one or more of these issues through case studies. Common themes appear to be that much pollen in archaeological sites is local, rather than regional, in origin; sedimentation processes are episodic, rather than continuous, on sites;

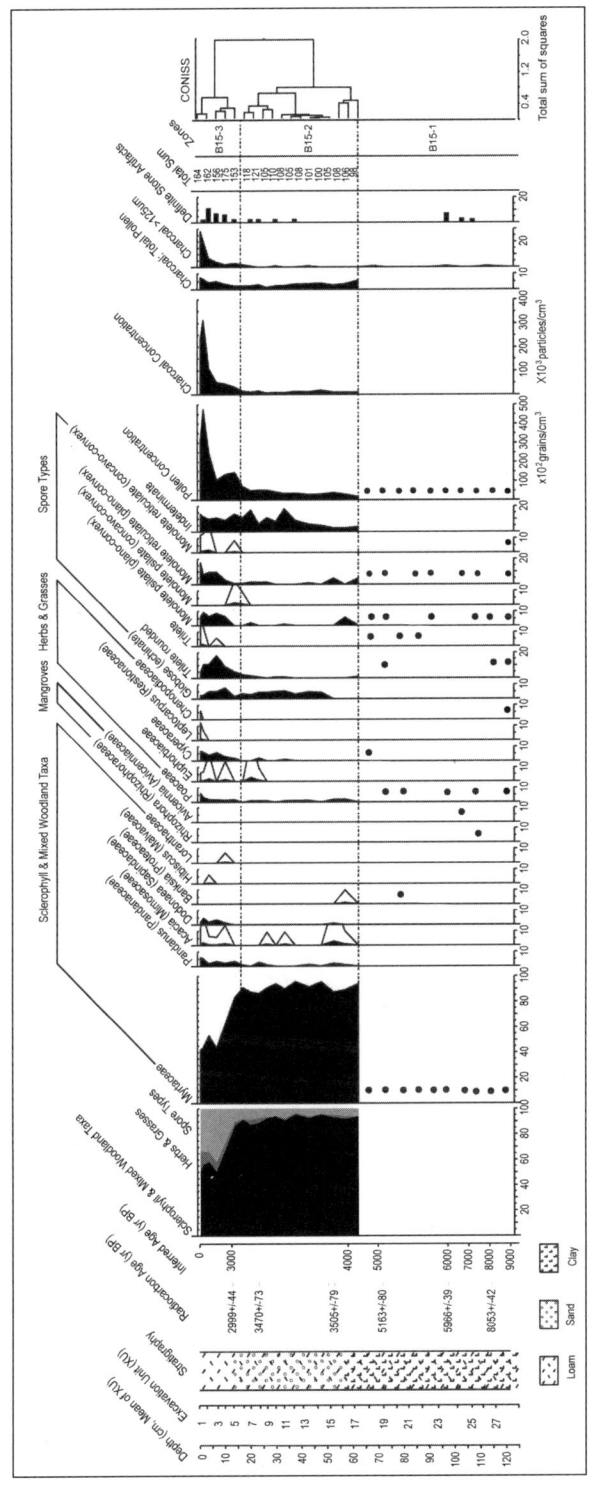

Figure 3. Archaeological site Badu 15 pollen percentage diagram plotted against depth and age. Percentages are derived from the total pollen and spore sum. Exaggeration values are x10. • = Presence in samples with insufficient pollen to generate an adequate sum.

Part 4 • Late-Holocene change

and post-depositional movement of pollen is common (Pearsall 2000; Davis 1994). Although general, each observation serves to caution the interpretation of Badu 15.

Three major pollen zones occur at Badu 15 (see below). The pollen and spore data, along with features of sediment stratigraphy and radiocarbon ages are shown in Figure 3. The age–depth model for the pollen diagram is based on linear interpolation between dated samples.

Zone B15-1 (126–62cm), c. 8500–4300 years BP

Within this zone, no counts reached the desired pollen sum. In a simple record of presence/absence, Myrtaceae is recorded throughout and Poaceae is the most important herbaceous type. In the only appearance of mangrove taxa for the entire sequence, *Rhizophora* and *Avicennia* are present between 105 cm and 95 cm depth. Spore types are diverse in comparison with the pollen. Common monolete-reticulate (plano-convex) and monolete-psilate (plano-convex) types coincide with trilete, trilete-rounded and monolete-reticulate (concavo-convex) categories. Microcharcoal is present in all samples.

Low pollen concentrations in this zone are viewed as a consequence of the dry, consolidated basal clay-loam unit. The pollen and spore assemblage broadly suggests that Myrtaceae dominated the local vegetation, and the ground component was dominated by grasses. Ferns, indicated by spores, are locally present around the rockshelter, but they are also suggestive of wider vegetation disturbance, just as charcoal particles throughout the sediment imply that fires were present. The presence of mangrove taxa may point to the inland migration of mangrove forest during the closing stages of Holocene sea-level rise. The presence of *Rhizophora* and *Avicennia* pollen, together with Chenopodiaceae, suggests that the landward fringe of the mangrove forest was nearer the site than present, and nearer than at any other time covered by the Badu 15 sequence.

Zone B15-2 (62–17 cm), c. 4300–3000 years BP

With an increase in pollen concentration, this zone is characterised by Myrtaceae at or above 85%. *Pandanus* maintains a consistent presence below 5% coinciding with occasional grains of *Acacia*. *Banksia* is a minor component at 57 cm. Among the herbaceous taxa, Poaceae are recorded at 2% or less, and it is not until 23 cm depth that Euphorbiaceae is present in the record and Cyperaceae values expand slightly. Spore types are comparatively common, ranging between 3–8.5%; monolete-psilate (plano-convex) and monolete-reticulate (plano-convex) show greater representation at first, replaced through the zone by globose (echinate). As samples with an increased pollen count, both total pollen and charcoal concentrations are the lowest for the diagram.

These pollen spectra suggest that Myrtaceae forest was locally extensive by 4300 years BP. *Pandanus* and *Acacia* were present in the region and may have been important taxa near the forest limit, restricted at this time to local areas of disturbance and more open canopy. Similarly, the area local to Badu 15 also appears to have been marginal for herbaceous taxa. The minor amounts of preserved charcoal imply that fire was part of the environment at this time, but most likely infrequently and of low intensities. Environmental stability is further implied through reduced ferns (spores), in both diversity and abundance.

Zone B15-3 (17–0cm), c. 3000 years BP to present

This zone is marked by a decline in Myrtaceae from 85% at the start of the unit to 42% at the surface. *Pandanus* increases to a peak of 7% and *Acacia* becomes consistently present after 10 cm depth. *Dodonaea* is introduced to the record, rising through upper levels to 5%. Occasional grains of *Hibiscus* and Loranthaceae are noted. All herbaceous taxa increase on previous averages; Poaceae and Cyperaceae dominate this assemblage. Spore taxa increase up to 41%. Triletrounded, monolete-psilate (plano-convex) and monolete-reticulate (plano-convex) become prominent as a decrease in globose (echinate) type is observed. Monolete-psilate (concavo-convex) and monolete-reticulate (concavo-convex) maintain low percentages and the trilete type records its first appearance. Macroscopic and microscopic charcoal shows an initial increase between 13.5 cm and 3.5 cm but a marked rise in concentration toward the surface. Highest average charcoal/pollen ratios for the record are also achieved. Pollen concentration values increase on the previous zone but are generally low until 3.5 cm depth, at which point values rise sharply.

Although Myrtaceae continues to dominate the Badu 15 landscape, a less continuous forest cover is suggested. The Zone 3 pollen assemblage points to the establishment of an open woodland canopy, facilitating the expansion of *Pandanus* and *Acacia*. This is associated with an increase in both local and regional burning, indicated by high macroscopic and microscopic charcoal densities. The rise in herbaceous pollen, particularly Poaceae, toward the top of this zone lends support to the establishment of a more open vegetation community under a regime of more frequent burning episodes. Disturbance is further reflected through the presence of *Dodonaea* and increased spore concentrations. Owing to greater light penetration, fern growth local to the rockshelter site may be particularly encouraged.

MDS analysis

Figure 4a shows the multi-dimensional scaling (MDS) ordination of excavation units according to presence/absence pollen and spore data. A stress value of 0.2 reflects an adequate representation of the relationship between these twenty-eight samples in two dimensions. The plot depicts two different vegetation community compositions. The spread of samples from XUs 28–7 contrasts with the more tightly clustered grouping of pollen Zone 3 (XUs 6–1), following the transition from Myrtaceae forest dominance to open vegetation. The association between samples with low pollen concentration (XUs 28–18) and samples of Zone 2 (XUs 17–7) supports the interpretation of low counts as a result of soil conditions and not as a result of any significant shift in the vegetation of this earliest period to that subsequently displayed. In Figure 4b the relationship between pollen and spore taxa, charcoal accumulation and human site use is depicted. The differentiation between forest and open vegetation is clearer in this analysis. Changes in composition appear to reflect vegetation responses to the combined effects of increased burning and greater use of the site, from 3500–3000 years BP onwards. Early-Holocene samples of permanent regional land use are clearly separated from those of the late-Holocene permanent island occupation.

In summary, the site of Badu 15 provides evidence for increasing disturbance of the vegetation resulting in the loss of continuous forest cover from approximately 3500–3000 years BP to the present. The pre-3000 years BP record indicates that the surrounding Badu 15 sand plain maintained a Myrtaceae-rich forest cover, the canopy restricting intermediate tree and shrub layers and the dense growth of annual and perennial herbs and grasses. Disturbance, including burning, was minimal. After 3000 years BP, as burning episodes became more frequent, a decline in Myrtaceae encouraged an increase in floristic diversity, incorporating a more prominent understorey and ground cover within an open-woodland structure approaching that of today. Ferns are locally well represented over the last 3000 years, but in view of the increase in archaeological artefacts, may also reflect human transport into the site. Argant (2001), for example, concludes that natural spore dispersion is not the reason for high spore percentages in archaeological sites, citing food and litter (bedding) as possible avenues of introduction.

Pollen from creekside vegetation has not been incorporated into the Badu 15 sediments, and it is unclear whether changes occurred within the vine-thicket community during the recorded period. Pollen transport of most rainforest-associated taxa is notoriously limited and typically under-represented in pollen diagrams (Kershaw & Strickland 1990). Lack of representation at Badu 15 may also be a result of the south-west orientation of the rock-shelter entrance.

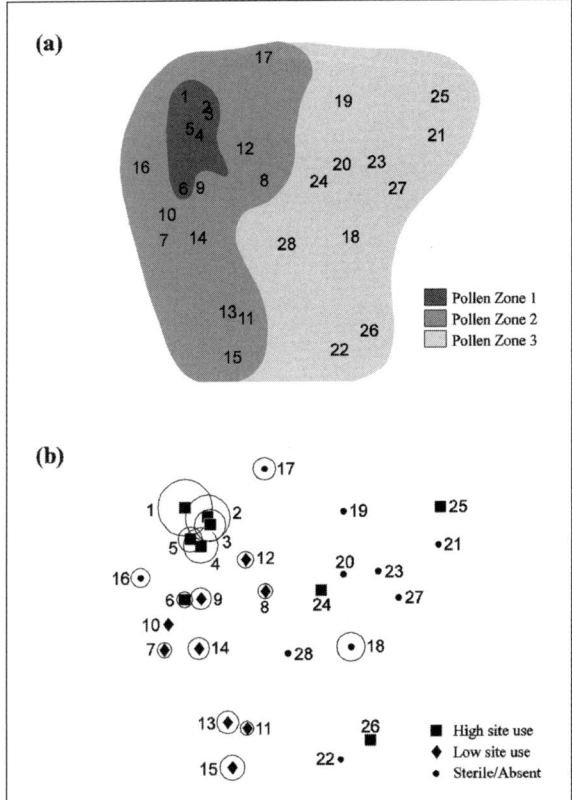

Figure 4. Multi-dimensional Scaling (MDS) ordination in two dimensions for combined pollen and spore presence/absence data set (stress = 0.2): (a) the twenty-eight excavation units with superimposed pollen zones from Figure 2; and (b) the trend in pollen data with human site use and charcoal accumulation (size of circle proportional to the microcharcoal particle value).

The overhang and position of surrounding rocks would only serve to shield the excavated sediments from direct, downslope deposition of vine-thicket pollen. Increased sedimentation rates, coincident with the onset of intensive burning of the Badu 15 landscape, would suggest the expansion of fire onto surrounding slopes, a loss of vine-thicket cover in this instance possibly contributing to soil instability and run-off.

Discussion

The pollen diagram presented here is the first from the western Torres Strait islands and provides a reconstruction of local vegetation history in relation to a known occupation site on Badu. Reconstruction spans a period from before 8000 years BP through to the present and provides information concerning environments older than any of the 'off-site' palaeoenvironmental studies within the island interior (Rowe forthcoming). This chapter further represents a significant attempt at integrating palaeoecological and archaeological research through the marriage of pollen analysis and artefact studies in order to comprehend the full spectrum of human–landscape interrelationships within Torres Strait. The Badu 15 site presents an opportunity to help document the physical nature and ecology of landscape change in the face of a growing interest in landscape as a dimension of human engagement, cultural interaction and development (Harris 1979).

Vegetation changes over the last 3500–3000 years at Badu 15 are interpreted here to be the result of human activity. The upper sediments present a number of important features that point to an anthropogenic explanation for landscape change: increasing sedimentation and charcoal accumulation rates; a trend toward more open vegetation cover; and archaeological evidence consistent with the pollen records. The record as a whole, however, can only be said to indicate a certain higher degree of human activity and occupation, and results pertaining to 8000–6000 years BP are discussed below with a view to refining David *et al*.'s (2004b) description of Badu as 'permanently occupied'. In the absence of sustained human occupation, or in the event of sporadic visits from 6000–3500 years BP, the vegetation can be interpreted in terms of the regional climate record, as indicated through comparisons with other palaeoenvironmental studies.

A feature of Holocene records based on pollen studies across northern Australia is evidence for the so-called mid-Holocene climatic optimum when annual precipitation values and perhaps average temperatures are thought to have been greater than at present (Genever *et al*. 2003). The most detailed Holocene climate and vegetation record for north Queensland centres on a suite of pollen studies on the Atherton Tablelands (Kershaw 1970, 1971, 1983). Indications are that climate became more humid between 10 000 years BP and 7000 years BP. This is based on evidence for the beginning of organic sedimentation at Lake Euramoo and Bromfield Swamp, evidence for more permanent lake conditions at Lake Barrine, and a surge in swamp growth at Lynchs Crater. Swamp became established on Quincan Crater around 7000 years BP (Hiscock & Kershaw 1992). The Atherton dryland vegetation shows encroachment of rainforest over the tableland during this period, with attainment of maximum Holocene development between 6500 and 5000 years BP, from which a warmer and moister climate is also inferred. Results of bioclimatic analysis of plant taxa from Euramoo support these aspects of climatic reconstruction and indicate more specifically that temperatures were more uniform year-round while rainfall was higher during winter (that is, a less pronounced dry season) than today (Hiscock & Kershaw 1992; Genever et al. 2003). This claim is in keeping with the findings of other palaeoclimatic studies for far northern and southern regions of Australia (e.g. Schulmeister 1999; Kershaw 1995). The indication that maximum forest development and higher rainfall were regional phenomena is further supported by evidence for the development of fluvial activity in the Carpentaria Basin (Kershaw 1995) and New Guinea pollen records, showing maximum rainforest extent between 8600 and 5000 years BP (Harrison & Dodson 1993). Against such regional evidence, and against a background of marine transgression, a humid early-to-mid Holocene climate may be surmised for Badu. Under these conditions, a forest environment, dominated by *Eucalyptus*, would be favoured. This is consistent with the record from Groote Eylandt where Schulmeister (1992) argued for the arrival of 'Holocene' vegetation from c. 7500 to 5000 years BP. Through this phase, grass pollen types collapsed in view of highest values for all forest palynomorphs, including both eucalypt open forest and vine-thicket types (Schulmeister 1992).

At Badu 15 the dominance of Myrtaceae forest was maintained from at least 8000 to 3500–3000 years BP. Reduction of forest cover occurred from c. 3500 years BP and, although this appears to have been caused by fire, a change to drier conditions may have also had an influence, perhaps through facilitated burning. However, it is unlikely that naturally occurring fires could have had such a marked impact; an anthropogenic cause is more likely, especially given that figures 3 and 4 indicate major changes in vegetation at a time when change is demonstrated archaeologically. A general increase in human activity around 3500 to 3000 years BP signifies most change is attributable to greater levels of disturbance rather than climatic change. The return to sustained human occupation 3500–3000 years BP has been traced to an influx of people from the north or north-east of Badu by David et al. (2004b). This is the time when occupation becomes intense enough to be archaeologically evident in the northern (Saibai) and eastern (Dauar) ends of Torres Strait and when many islands in the western Pacific first became occupied, at least in part as a direct result of Austronesian expansions (islands off eastern New Guinea to Tonga and Samoa further east, for example; see Smith 2002) (David et al. 2004b; Barham et al. 2004; Barham 2000). The synchronicity of the archaeological visibility of the onset of late Holocene, sustained occupation across the length and width of Torres Strait and beyond implies a single process of colonisation by a fleet, or by an archaeologically rapid sequence of island-hopping colonisers (David et al. 2004b). Austronesian influences are hinted at through rock art (Brady forthcoming) and linguistic evidence, and oral traditions also point to contacts of various types between all groups in the region and with eastern and western Austronesian speakers. Laade (1968; see also David et al. 2004b) in particular quotes 'light skinned Pacific men' coming as traders, settling on Parema (south-west Fly Delta), marrying there, then colonising Torres Strait and marr-ying local women. Red-slipped ceramics on a number of islands — in the western and in the eastern groups — are further testimony for direct or indirect Austronesian influences in the past (David & McNiven 2004; David et al. 2004b).

Importantly for the landscape, Badu 15 demonstrates that the colonisation of Badu 3500 to 3000 years BP incorporated what are today inland island environments and not simply the coastal margins and related back-beach dune complexes, as documented ethnohistorically and thus much assumed in earlier archaeological studies (e.g. Barham & Harris 1983; Moore 1979; Rowland 1985). Thus, the assumptions derived from the ethnohistoric evidence regarding human–environment interactions as being essentially coastal has potentially limited a deeper understanding of settlement patterns and long-term change in Torres Strait. As well, a European preoccupation with collecting/recording material culture and artefacts has also resulted in a lack of documentation relating to the use of fire, disregarding the phenomenon of burning as a social symbol, or the resulting landscape as artefact, similar to terms discussed by Rowntree (1996) and Head (1994). The Badu 15 pollen and charcoal records demonstrate that landscape burning was a component of post-transgression settlement strategies for Badu. Given the evidence presented of sustained occupation and use of Badu 15 and its district after 3500–3000 years BP, it is likely that most, if not all, terrestrial environments of Badu have been modified as a result of such practices.

In view of the discussions surrounding the last c. 3500 years, what of the period from 8000–6000 years BP? David et al. (2004b, p.74) tied the archaeology of this earlier residency to that of the last 3500–3000 years BP — not only through the sustained presence of stone artefacts, but reinforced also through the use of the same descriptive phrase 'permanently occupied' (although they do not envisage comparable patterns of 'permanent occupation'; Bruno David, personal communication 2004). Do the pollen and charcoal results support such a conclusion? From the combined MDS analysis (Figure 4a, b), the post-3500 to 3000 years BP period of occupation has a different pollen and charcoal signal to the 8000–6000 years BP signal. The presence of artefacts in XUs 26–24 may be read as suggesting a resident Badu population, but when combined with their MDS ordination an occupation more akin to sporadic visits, even prolonged absence, and not one of concentrated rock-shelter use is indicated. Occupation at 8000–6000 years BP appears to be of a lower order of intensity to that indicated from the evidence from after 3500 years BP. This difference between, on the one hand, relatively low environmental impact before 6000 years BP and, on the other, relatively high impacts after 3500–3000 years BP, is consistent with the presence of non-village-based ('hunter-gatherer') permanent land use during the early Holocene, and village-based permanent island use during the late Holocene. Similarities, including the diversity of spore types and the common Poaceae record between the two periods support the archaeological evidence relating to the continuous, albeit relatively ephemeral, presence of people within the site. As well, continuous Myrtaceae tree cover is maintained, indicating that the forest was not entirely modified, and thus supporting the evidence of generally low-level human impacts on the environment.

From the data presented here it is clear that there is a close correlation between changes in the archaeological record relating to intensity of site use and the pollen record. Similarly, the charcoal signature indicates a level of burning beyond what would be expected of natural and occasional burning between XUs 5–1 on the MDS map.

I suggest, therefore, that the Badu 15 palaeoenvironmental record at 8000–6000 years BP indicates a pattern of dispersed residence in which Badu 15 is but a small component of a larger landscape and wider human territory, within the vast land bridge connecting New Guinea and Australia. Once Badu became isolated as an island it also became part of a much smaller landscape in which people could live. Archaeological evidence for greater human use of Badu from 3500–3000 years BP onwards closely correlates with evidence of increased environmental impacts as vegetation communities changed and landscape firing increased. The pollen record suggests that this post-3000 years BP environmental and archaeological signal indicates for the first time a settled residence, consistent with what we now know as island 'village life'.

These notions build on Lourandos' (1983b, 1997) concept of varying intensities of land use for Australian archaeology, refining them somewhat by paying close attention to types of residence and intensities of impact. Specifically, the Badu 15 pollen and charcoal can be seen to distinguish between, on the one hand, more mobile 'residential' settlement strategies (where hunter-gatherers moved themselves to spatially dispersed resources) and, on the other hand, more sedentary 'logistical' strategies (where resources were obtained and brought back to a central base camp) (Binford 1980; Lourandos 1997). Lourandos (1997) does link increased sedentism to typically heterogenous environments, which is arguable here: heterogenous perhaps in terms of seasonality of climate, but not in terms of vegetation structure, where the implied permanency of logistical settlement is more likely to produce uniform, constructed surroundings. Lourandos (1997) informs us that residential and logistical strategies can be hypothesised as ends of a spectrum of possible economic settlements and that we might expect hunter-gatherer societies to move back and forth along this spectrum. Residential models present fluid, open group organisation with emphasis on 'immediate-return' economic strategies. In contrast, logistical behaviour is associated with bounded, closed groups demonstrating 'delayed-return' economic practices incorporating fixed facilities. Sedentary logistical behaviour carries implications regarding more intensive physical investment in the landscape, be that through the spiritscapes of McNiven and Feldman (2003), the agricultural practices of interest to Harris (1995), or the manipulation of vegetation through fire (this study). Only within the last 3500 to 3000 years do we see intensive investments of landscapes come into play on Badu. What I suggest, therefore, is that Lourandos' notions of differential intensities of land use, as variously evident across Australia before and after the commencement of the late Holocene, can be rethought as residential-logistical investment involving varying degrees of settlement permanency. On Badu, at least, what is seen in the environmental record is a shift not simply from 'less intensive' to 'more intensive' occupation, but rather one from a 'residential' strategy of relatively mobile occupation to a 'logistical' strategy of greater settlement permanency. That this conclusion has been largely derived from the pollen record signals a new approach to landscape archaeology — one that incorporates the palaeoenvironmental record not only to detail landscape as physical environment, but as a strategised social dwelling.

As a consequence of this study's interest in the environmental landscape of Torres Strait, a unique insight has been gained into the nature of human occupation and activity within western Torres Strait, an insight achieved through the integration of palaeoecological and archaeological evidence. The Badu 15 record now provides baseline data for assessment of the impact of people on the wider landscape of Badu. Pollen and charcoal records provide an indication of the timing and nature of disturbance brought about by human occupation and have been used to infer the extent and type of occupation through time. Such baseline data are important owing to ongoing difficulties associated with separating human and natural processes of disturbance in the palaeoenvironmental and archaeological records (Kirch 1997b). Future research is now directed towards other parts of Badu to document the history of each major vegetation group in order to investigate the archaeological history of individual villages (David & McNiven 2004), and to examine the regional significance of the patterns of change recorded at Badu 15.

Acknowledgements

I wish to thank Bruno David for the opportunity to contribute to this volume, and for the encouragement and constructive discussions surrounding the ideas expressed in this chapter. Thanks also to Bryce Barker, Peter Kershaw and Simon Haberle for helpful comments on earlier drafts, and to Gary Swinton for assistance with the figures.

17.
North of the Cape and south of the Fly: discovering the archaeology of social complexity in Torres Strait

Melissa Carter

Introduction

At a time when the intensification debate was being fuelled by the outcomes of numerous and widespread archaeological fieldwork programs on the Australian mainland and Tasmania (Beaton 1977; Bowdler 1979; Jones 1971; Lourandos 1980a), archaeological research in the Torres Strait islands had barely commenced (Moore 1979; Harris 1975; Vanderwal 1973). Located in an intriguing geographical niche between the Aboriginal cultures of Australia and the Melanesian cultures of New Guinea, throughout most of the twentieth century the Torres Strait islands surprisingly failed to capture the interest and enthusiasm that archaeologists evidently held for its larger neighbouring landmasses. Viewed within the history of anthropological research that has been undertaken in the Torres Strait, this situation becomes all the more remarkable.

In 1898 distinguished natural scientist and ethnologist Alfred Cort Haddon led the Cambridge Anthropological Expedition to Torres Straits, with a goal of undertaking an unprecedented comprehensive anthropological study including ethnology, physical anthropology, psychology, sociology, ethnomusicology and linguistics (Herle & Rouse 1998). The enormous corpus of information recorded by Haddon and his colleagues was compiled into the six volumes of the *Reports of the Cambridge Anthropological Institute to Torres Straits* (published between 1901 and 1935), which continue today to be an important documentary source for researchers in the area. Consequently, it is surprising that the Cambridge-trained archaeologists who paved the way for academic archaeology in Australia during the 1960s did not target the Torres Strait for investigation, instead focusing their interest on the Australian and New Guinea mainlands (McBryde 1986; Murray & White 1981).

The aim of this paper is to provide a brief account of the history of archaeological research in the Torres Strait, from the preliminary investigations undertaken in the 1970s to the long term research projects that have commenced since 2000. This chapter will demonstrate the changing nature of the intent and outcomes of research, which include a shift from a focus on ecological aspects of human antiquity and subsistence to a recognition of how the archaeology informs on the social complexities and dynamics involved in human settlement, economic development and trade and exchange systems. This recent advance in interpreting the archaeology of Torres Strait both reflects the lateness of investigation in the region and, more importantly, lays testimony to the influence of Lourandos' contributions on the social archaeology of Indigenous societies, and of its greater impact on Australian archaeological practice (Lourandos 1977b, 1980b, 1983b).

The Torres Strait islands

Located in the sub-humid tropical environment between Australia's Cape York Peninsula and the south-western coast of Papua New Guinea, the Torres Strait is scattered with over 100 islands, coral reefs, sandbanks and cays. The islands represent a diversity of physical environments, based on their geology and relief, floral and faunal distributions, geography and distance to the adjacent mainlands, as well as the nature and extent of surrounding marine habitats.

The islands of Torres Strait are commonly divided into four biogeographic groups (Figure 1). The mostly large and high granitic Western Islands are located closest to Cape York Peninsula, with which they share similar characteristics in woodland and open forest vegetation. These islands are surrounded by mudflats, mangroves and fringing reefs, providing a variety of marine life, including turtle and dugong. The Northern Islands are located adjacent to the southwestern coast of Papua New Guinea and mostly comprise low formations of estuarine and mangrove sediments derived from the rivers of the southern Papuan coast. These islands are surrounded by mangroves and have large interior brackish and freshwater swamp systems, and although fish and crabs are plentiful, turtles and dugongs are less abundant due to the muddier waters. The Central Islands are predominantly low sandy cays formed by wave action over reef limestone. On these islands water is scarce and vegetation is sparse, although extensive fringing reefs support an abundance of marine life. The high Eastern Islands are located closest to the Great Barrier Reef and are composed of volcanic tuffs and basaltic lavas. These islands have dense vegetation supported by rich, brown soils and fringing reefs that provide a diversity of marine life including sharks, rays, and turtle, although dugongs are rare due to the deeper waters.

This physically diverse island environment was formed sometime between 8500 and 6500 years ago when rising post-glacial seas flooded the Sahul shelf separating the Australian and New Guinean landmasses. By around 5000 to

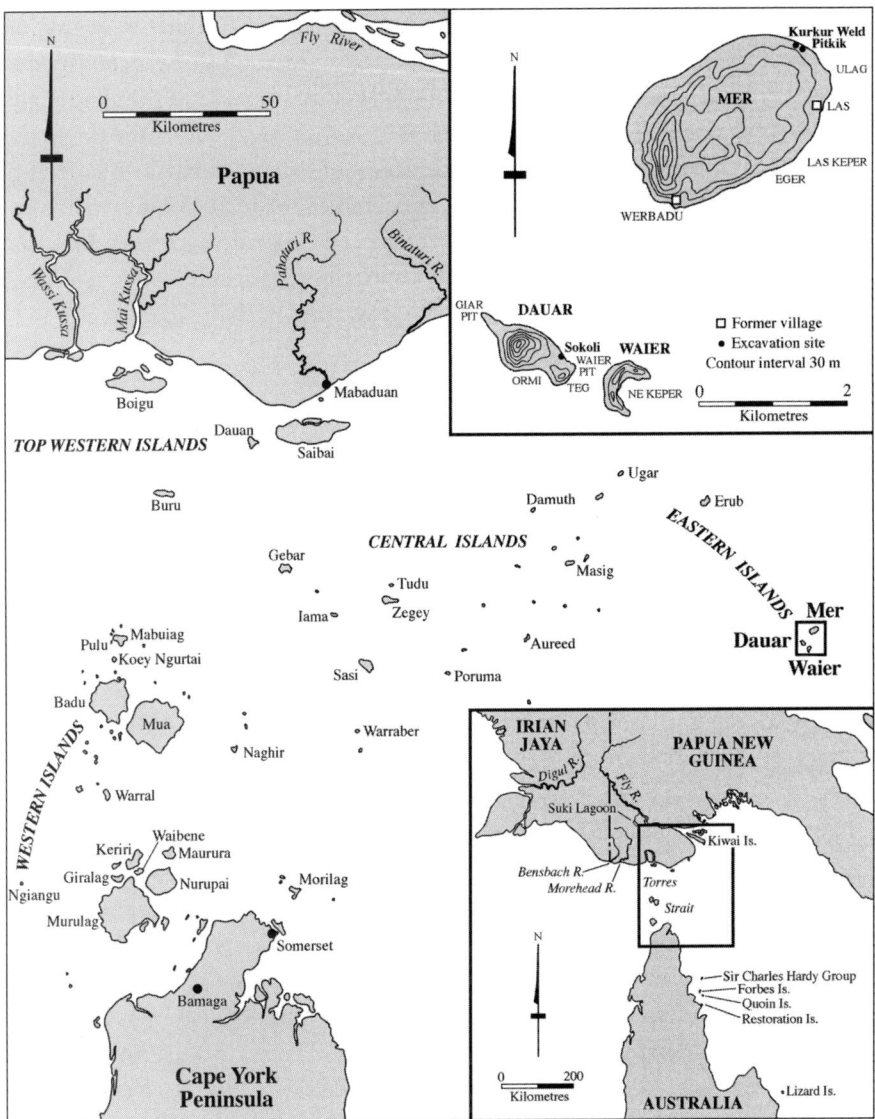

Figure 1. The Torres Strait with, inset, the eastern islands of Mer, Dauar and Waier (after McNiven & Feldman 2003).

4000 years ago the Torres Strait islands had probably reached their present configuration (Barham & Harris 1983). Recent investigations of reef growth in Torres Strait have established that reef colonisation occurred soon after inundation during the Holocene transgression, and that by 5000 years ago the general morphology of reefs was similar to the modern reefs (Barham 2000; Woodroffe et al. 2000). Barham's (2000) investigations on some of the higher

Western and Eastern islands, however, has demonstrated that there was an approximate timelag of at least 2000 to 3000 years after shoreline transgression before the development of fringing island reefs. Barham (2000) has inferred that this timelag resulted not only in limited sediment availability for the formation of near-shore reef flats and reef biotypes, but also a delay in the onset of prograded beach environments. From this data he concluded that the successful maritime exploitation of coastal resources, based on the techniques and strategies documented ethnohistorically in Torres Strait, may only have been feasible from approximately 4500 years BP onwards (Barham 2000, p. 295).

Ethnographic background

Today the unique identity of Torres Strait Islanders as an Indigenous population distinct from both Aboriginal Australians and the Melanesian populations of Papua New Guinea is manifest in several forms. This includes the design and adoption of an official national Torres Strait Islander flag, the promotion of *Ailan Kastom* (Island Custom), and the drive for Indigenous self-determination. This latter resulted in 1994 in the establishment of the Torres Strait Regional Authority (TSRA) as the region's Commonwealth statutory administrative authority. However, there is also important economic, linguistic and traditional variability across the Torres Strait, which remarkably was identified and recorded by some of the first Europeans to venture.

The linguistic divisions were noted in early sources (Sweatman in Allen & Corris 1977, p. 23), and were subsequently recorded in detail during the Cambridge Expedition (Ray 1907). Miriam Mer, the language spoken by the inhabitants of the Eastern Islands, is a Papuan language closely resembling the Bine, Gidra and Gizra languages of the southern New Guinea coast. In contrast it was recognised that the inhabitants of the Northern, Central and Western Islands spoke a dissimilar language that was more comparable to the Aboriginal languages of the Australian mainland (Haddon 1935, p. 289). Known as Kala Lagaw Ya, the language spoken throughout the rest of the Torres Strait has been identified as having a strong Australian language influence (Shnukal & Mitchell 1998; Wurm 1972).

Early observations of subsistence strategies in Torres Strait describe a mixed economy of marine resource procurement and horticulture, combined with limited hunting and gathering of terrestrial resources (Haddon 1912; Jukes 1847, p. 178; MacGillivray 1852, p. 25). Marine subsistence included a number of activities such as the gathering of intertidal shellfish, near-shore and offshore reef fishing, and the hunting of turtle and dugong. However, dependence on marine resource types varied throughout the Strait, largely as a result of the diversity of marine environments and variability in distance to major resource zones, such as Orman reef located north-east of Mabuiag.

Historical records tended to emphasise horticultural practices in the Eastern Islands which, due to their dense vegetation cover, were commonly perceived as the most rich and fertile islands in Torres Strait (MacGillivray, 1852 p. 25; Murray 1874, p. 470; Brockett 1836, p. 11). Cultivated crops observed in Torres Strait included numerous varieties of yams as well as bananas, coconuts and sugar cane (Haddon 1912, pp. 144–51). Recent models of subsistence practices across Torres Strait describe subsistence as varying along a north–south gradient from the Papuan lowlands in the north to the Western Islands in the south:

> In lowland Papua and the northern Torres Strait islands mixed systems existed which blended limited horticulture with foraging; whereas in the southern Torres Strait islands and Cape York Peninsula subsistence was almost completely non-horticultural and a wide range of wild plant and animals resources were exploited. (Harris 1977b, p. 422)

Explanations for this diverse and complex system include the relationship between the location, size and population density of individual islands, inter-island community relations and the availability and size of natural resources on individual islands (Harris 1977b). Ethnohistorical observations shed further light on the relationship between subsistence and traditional patterns of community organisation and socioeconomic structures throughout Torres Strait. For example, in the Western Islands social groups comprised mobile, semipermanent exogamous patriclans and bands (Beckett, 1972), while in the Eastern Islands social organisation existed around exogamous villages and hamlets divided into clan territories (Rivers in Haddon 1908, pp. 169–84).

The broader picture presented by the early Torres Strait ethnographies illustrate that towards the end of the nineteenth century the islands formed the central geographic core of a trans-Strait socioeconomic maritime network. This encompassed the Aboriginal communities of coastal Cape York and the peoples of the southern New Guinea coast, and was made possible by the double-outrigger canoe as the common medium of maritime voyaging (Haddon 1935; Landtman 1927). Island and mainland communities were linked by trade, warfare and intermarriage, while at the periphery Torres Strait Islanders were linked into longer-distance networks of exchange and cultural interaction through trading intermediaries (Barham 2000, p. 228). More recent oral history evidence from both Torres Strait communities and coastal groups from southern Papua provide continuing evidence of these ethnographically documented exchange relationships, kinship connections and population movements (Lawrence 1989, 1994).

After some four centuries of intermittent contact between Torres Strait Islanders and passing European mariners (McNiven 2001), by the 1870s permanent European presence in the Torres Strait was established through the development of pearling and beche-de-mer industries and the arrival of the London Missionary Society (Beckett 1987; Singe 1979). These events had a number of profound effects on traditional ways of life in Torres Strait, such as the relocation of villages and, in some instances, the deaths of large numbers of islanders from disease. However, the ethnographic record reveals that Torres Strait Islanders were not passive victims of European settlement, but incorporated changes, events and interactions into their customs and traditions, simultaneously maintaining and creating a unique cultural identity. It was during this dynamic period in the history of the Torres Strait that Haddon and his colleagues visited the region. Consequently, the information recorded during the Cambridge Expedition portrays a dynamic cultural complex embedded with elaborate ritual, social and economic processes that characterised daily life within Torres Strait, as well as the broader relationships and ties with its Papuan and Australian neighbours.

Early archaeological research: Torres Strait and 'bridge and barrier'

In 1971 the Australian National University hosted the 'Torres Strait Symposium', which represented the first-ever Australian gathering of academics and specialists with knowledge on either the natural or cultural history of Torres Strait (Walker 1972). As a reflection of the lack of archaeological interest the region had received prior to the 1970s, presenters were limited to conceptualising the cultural history of Torres Strait around previously established knowledge about the prehistory of the Australian and New Guinean mainlands (Beckett 2004, p. 7; Golson 1972). It is also clear that there was a broader lack of knowledge about the natural history of Torres Strait, and as pointed out by Walker: 'most authors refer to the dearth of basic information which limits their confidence in their conclusions' (1972, p. vii).

Thus, as a prelude to archaeological research in Torres Strait, the 1971 symposium highlighted the need to address several basic and fundamental questions. These included the antiquity of human occupation of Torres Strait, the nature of traditional subsistence systems (and particularly evidence for the timing and development of the horticultural economy) and the identification of past linkages between Torres Strait Islanders and peoples on the mainlands to the north and south. Determining the degree to which the archaeological evidence corresponded or differed with the documented ethnohistoric record was also viewed as a significant component in developing a greater understanding of the pre–European contact history of Torres Strait (Beckett 1972; Moore 1972). Importantly, however, as a result of the broad knowledge deficiency on both the natural and cultural history of Torres Strait, a theme that was to characterise archaeological research in the region for at least the following two decades had emerged. This theme revolved around the question of whether Torres Strait had acted as either a bridge or a barrier to cultural development on the Papuan and Australian mainlands, with a particular emphasis on determining if Torres Strait had acted as a geographical divide between the emergence of horticulture in the north and hunter-gatherer cultures to the south (Golson 1972; Vanderwal 1973).

The first archaeological investigations undertaken in Torres Strait were conducted in 1971 and 1973 by Moore (1979), with test-pit excavations on Murulag (Prince of Wales Island) and at Evans Bay on the northern coast of Cape York Peninsula. Three radiocarbon dates produced evidence of occupation during the last 700–800 years; Moore (1979, p. 14) concluded that the excavated cultural remains were broadly consistent with the ethnographic record. In 1972 Vanderwal (1973) undertook a six-month-long survey of most of the principal islands of Torres Strait. His aims were to outline the pattern of prehistoric trade relationships throughout Torres Strait and to determine the nature and antiquity of cultural developments in the Eastern and Western islands (Vanderwal 1973). Vanderwal (1973) recorded a variety of site types across the Strait, including a stone quarry on Dauan, dense stone deposits on Mabuiag and occupational shell-midden debris on Saibai, Mer, Iama, Geba and Badu. However, his visits to each island were not much more than fleeting stopovers which collectively resulted in the conclusion that the archaeology of Torres Strait was limited and uninspirational, and could reveal little about deep human antiquity or the historically documented trade networks between the islands and with the adjacent mainland groups (Vanderwal 1973).

David Harris conducted archaeological investigations in Torres Strait from the middle of the 1970s, initially noting the potential of sites on Dauan, Mabuiag and inter-swamp canals on Saibai (Harris 1975). His interest was primarily concerned with combining ecological, ethnohistorical and historical research in order to identify the factors that led to the ethnographically observed variations in horticultural, marine and hunting and gathering economies across Torres Strait (DR Harris 1975, 1976, 1977b, 1979). Using nineteenth century ethnographic accounts he suggested that evidence for early horticultural specialisation would be clearest on the small, high islands of Naghi, Mabuiag and Dauan as the nodal points in the inter-island trade network (DR Harris 1979, p. 105). Harris' research soon led to a program of archaeological and palaeoenvironmental investigation of prehistoric settlement and marine and horticultural subsistence in the Western and Top Western (Northern) Island Groups.

Part 4 • Late-Holocene change

Based at University College London (UCL), this became known as the Torres Strait Research Project and included investigations of Holocene palaeoenvironmental history and coastal archeology by Barham (Barham 1981; Barham & Harris 1983, 1985, 1987), and an archaeological and ethnohistorical examination of coastal resource exploitation on Mabuiag by Ghaleb (1990).

One of the most significant outcomes of Barham's early research was the identification of extensive relict horticultural mound-and-ditch systems and associated well constructions on Saibai, located inland of the canal features recorded by Harris (Barham 1981). From helicopter reconnaissance it was estimated that 5–10% of the 19.9 km^2 area of interior claylands had been cultivated at sometime in the past (Barham & Harris 1985, pp. 253–4). Barham's excavation of one of the mounded features on Saibai revealed three distinct stratigraphic units, which were interpreted as representing both pre- and post-mound construction phases (Barham 1981, p. 18). From these combined results of the 1980 field season on Saibai Barham concluded that construction of the garden systems must have involved considerable organised labour inputs, and that these 'sites represent the most significant evidence for land use prehistory within Torres Strait' (1981, p. 19).

However, the results of radiocarbon dating shell and charcoal remains excavated from depths of 55–60 cm at the site varied in age from approximately 2500 cal. BP to 700 cal. BP (Barham & Harris 1985, p. 264, Appendix 1). Although the broad discrepancy in the dates was attributed to several factors, including a low deposition rate and possible reworking of the archaeological remains due to mound construction, it was concluded that the maximum age for the mound-and-ditch system on Saibai was *c.* 700 cal. BP (Barham & Harris 1985, p. 277). Significantly, Barham's (1999) more recent analyses of cored lithostratigrahic swamp facies on Saibai have led to revisions of the chronological data, with implications for both the antiquity of human occupation of northern Torres Strait and the timing of the development of the horticultural economy. He has recently concluded:

> The combined on-site archaeological radiocarbon dates, and off-site palaeoenvironmental reconstruction, provide sufficient evidence to now model first occupation of the northern Torres Strait islands at some time after 2500 yr BP . . . The development of agricultural mound-and-ditch systems, probably also involving water management and well construction, dates to some time after 1200 yr BP. (Barham 1999, p. 101)

The archaeological research conducted in Torres Strait during the 1980s demonstrated that contrary to Harris' (DR Harris 1979) ecologically focused and ethnohistorically based model, horticulture was not restricted to the small, high rocky islands during the period before the advent of European influence. Inadvertently this result also highlights a failure on Haddon's part to adequately identify the previous widespread distribution of horticultural practices throughout Torres Strait. Importantly, Barham's (1981, 1999) research on Saibai provided the first archeological evidence for horticultural subsistence in Torres Strait, as well as the first evidence to suggest that human occupation of the region was a late-Holocene event. Combined, the results of research conducted throughout the 1980s provided a significant advance in our understanding of the human chronology of Torres Strait Islands and of the links between island ecology and the development of the horticultural subsistence economy.

However, these results were applicable only to northern Torres Strait, where the investigations had primarily been focused, and had also failed to directly address or resolve the bridge-and-barrier debate of the 1970s. It was not until some time after his initial investigations in the Torres Strait that Harris (1995) offered a solution to the long-standing debate. He suggested that as the Torres Strait Islands have existed for around 6000 years, the region has functioned neither as a bridge nor a barrier, particularly to the southward transmission of horticulture, which had emerged in the New Guinea Highlands only several thousand years earlier (Golson 1977). He further claimed that the celebrated subsistence divide or boundary at Torres Strait was a product of modern ethnography, which had exaggerated the contrasts in subsistence practices of Australian 'hunter-gatherers' and Papuan 'agriculturists', as well as the extent and intensity of agriculture in New Guinea as a whole (Harris 1995, p. 854; see also David & Denham, this volume). Thus, with intellectual hindsight, towards the start of the twenty-first century the bridge-and-barrier debate had gradually faded from view allowing for a new era in Torres Strait archaeology (see also McNiven, this volume).

A new research era: evidence of social complexity in Torres Strait

In the years since 2000 two major archaeological research projects have commenced in Torres Strait. The Murray Islands Archaeological Project arose from the long-term investigations of American anthropologists Douglas and Rebecca Bird (Bird & Bliege Bird 1997, 2000; Bliege Bird *et al.* 2000, 2002; Bliege Bird & Bird 2002). Their work on the contemporary marine foraging activities of the Meriam formed the basis of their doctoral theses in anthropology (Bird 1996; Bliege Bird 1996). The archaeological investigations were a community-directed initiative to document past marine resource use, and to determine the time-depth of human occupation on the Murray Islands. This study has formed the basis of my own doctoral research at James Cook University (Carter 2004).

Part 4 • Late-Holocene change

The Western Torres Strait Cultural History Project is led by Ian McNiven and Bruno David from Monash University, and is conducted in conjunction with a number of island communities. This project developed out of a local government initiative to document cultural heritage places and their management needs across the region (Fitzpatrick *et al.* 1998; McNiven *et al.* 2004). A major focus of their research is the archaeology of ritual landscapes through incorporation of the ethnographic record and oral history (David *et al.* 2004a, 2004b; David & McNiven 2004; McNiven & Feldman 2003).

The significance of these recent research projects is that they collectively represent not only a broadening of research focus in a geographic sense, but also a significant increase in new archaeological data for the Torres Strait. Consequently the researchers involved are also largely responsible for a new level of interpretation of the archaeology of Torres Strait. This interpretation informs on the past and present social complexity of the region based on examination of the material correlates of various dynamic processes, such as human occupation, the emergence of subsistence systems, trade and exchange and the relaying of oral history. Most significantly, it is also founded on the notion that Torres Strait Islander history is intimately entwined with how people lived their lives not just as subsistence strategies, but through cosmologies that they address through notions of 'spiritscapes' (David *et al.* 2004c; McNiven 2003) and the 'ritual orchestration' of land and seascapes (McNiven & Feldman 2003). It is perhaps not surprising to learn then, that in their varying capacities as undergraduates and postgraduates at the University of Queensland during the 1980s and 1990s, each of these researchers enjoyed the privilege of Lourandos' unique and revolutionary insights into the social archaeology of Indigenous societies.

One of the major outcomes from excavations conducted on the Eastern Islands of Mer and Dauar has been the establishment of initial site use and the procurement of intertidal marine resources in the eastern Torres Strait from before 2600 cal. BP (Wk 7445 and Wk 8918) (see Carter 2002a and Carter *et al.* 2004a and 2004b for more details on radiocarbon dating). These results are generally consistent with Barham's (1999) date for first human occupation of Saibai, and further confirm a considerable cultural time-depth for Torres Strait. The chronology of human occupation in the Western Islands has also recently been established from the radiocarbon dating of deposits from the Badu 15 rock shelter on Badu Island (David *et al.* 2004b). Their results confirm permanent human occupation of the island from 3500–3000 cal. BP, providing a slightly longer radiocarbon-based chronology for Torres Strait.

David *et al.* (2004b) have highlighted that the emerging widespread late-Holocene human occupation of Torres Strait is a trend that parallels two other well-documented events or phenomena to the north and south. These are the expansion of Austronesian-speaking populations into the western Pacific, and the intensification of coastal and island economies on the Australian mainland — particularly Cape York Peninsula and the central Queensland coast. Consequently, the Torres Strait Islands can now be viewed in the broader context of the processes of human expansion and colonisation of western Melanesia and northern Australia, representing an exciting breakthrough in our understanding of the emergence of the social, economic and cultural complexities portrayed in its archaeological record.

Significantly, however, in support of their theory of early Austronesian links in Torres Strait, David *et al.* (2004b) cite the recent recovery of pottery sherds from several of the islands, including Mer and Dauar in the east (Carter 2002a, 2002b) and Pulu in the Western Islands (David & McNiven 2004). These sherds represent the first pottery recovered from *in situ* archaeological contexts within Torres Strait and date at least from *c.* 2000 cal. BP (Carter 2002a). Mineralogical analyses of the pottery recovered from Mer and Dauar has revealed evidence to suggest that the pottery temper may have been sourced from the interior regions of New Guinea (Carter 2002b, 2004). Although further analysis is required to confirm these results, this highlights the possibility of more expansive trade and exchange between Torres Strait and New Guinea than has been previously documented (Beaver 1920; Haddon 1904, 1908, 1935; Moore 1979). Both the chronology of the recovered sherds and the long-distance exchange networks these imply, strongly attest to the existence of social systems in the past beyond those documented from nineteenth century ethnography within Torres Strait. This in turn confirms a significant degree of technological innovation, as represented by outrigger canoes as the medium of trade voyaging, and a level of organisation and specialisation across community, inter-island and trans-Strait levels through which these trade contacts were established and maintained.

As part of the Murray Island investigations, Richardson's (2000) analysis of the excavated shell assemblages from Mer and Dauar has demonstrated remarkable similarities between the composition of the archaeological species and the contemporary ethnographically recorded marine-based diet of the Meriam (see also Bliege Bird *et al.* 2002). However, more recent analysis of the excavated Dauar assemblages has demonstrated comparative differences in the density of shell remains between sites and changes to the marine resource assemblages at both sites from around 2000 cal. BP (Carter 2004).

From the excavation at Ormi on the south-eastern side of Dauar, the total density of excavated shell remains (128.0 kg/m^3) is over twice the density of shell (55.7 kg/m^3) recovered from the excavation at Sokoli on the north-eastern side of Dauar. As both excavation squares were the same size (1 m x 1 m) and excavated to approximately the same depth (220–230 cm), this represents a significant difference in the nature of the archeological marine-shell deposits. A further difference in the assemblage composition is illustrated by changes that occur from approximately 2000 cal. BP. At Ormi there is a considerable increase in the density of marine shell remains, while for Sokoli the density of marine shell significantly decreases after 2000 cal BP. These changes are also contemporaneous with a major stratigraphic transition at each site, from coarse orange-coloured sand to finer-grained brown colluvium. Within the context of both historical and contemporary anthropological observations of social organisation and subsistence on the Murray Islands, an explanation for these archaeological features is evident.

Meriam social organisation was first described in detail by Rivers (in Haddon 1908, pp. 169–84) and has continued to attract interest in a diversity of research contexts including trade and exchange (Laade 1969; Lawrence 1994), subsistence and economy (Laade 1969,1973), cosmology and identity (Sharp 1993), contemporary land and sea tenure (Bliege Bird et al., 2000), as well as the recent political arena of native title (Bartlett 1993). As first illustrated and described by Haddon (1935, p. 160, see Figure 2) the Meriam population is divided into eight clans, each with their own totem and island district. Residential plots (including the foreshore to the edge of the fringing reef) and interior garden plots tend to be owned and managed by individual patrilines, while both fishing and land-use rights within clan boundaries are further divided among patrlineages (Rivers in Haddon 1908; Bird, 1996, p. 40). The large systems of stone-walled fish traps on the northeastern and southeastern side of Mer are also clan owned and managed (Bird 1996, p. 40, see Figure 2).

The central role played by the Komet clan as intermediaries in the inter-island and trans-Strait trade network was recognised in the early ethnographies (Haddon 1935, p. 186) and is supported by more recent anthropological accounts and Meriam oral history (Laade 1969, 1973; Lawrence 1994). Based on accounts given by his Islander informants Laade (1969) also identified a fundamental east–west distinction between the Meriam clans. He suggested that the Meriam Le clans were regarded as 'the people belong garden', while the Komet Le were the 'people belong water' (Laade 1969, p. 36). According to Laade's interpretation the Meriam Le were the gardeners of Mer and owned most of the fertile land on the eastern side of the island. The Komet Le, on the other hand, inhabited Dauar and Waier and the western side of Mer, and did the majority of the fishing, hunting and gathering of resources. Importantly, Laade (1969) identified that clan specialisation did not translate into restrictions on the consumption of either marine or vegetable foods, but encompassed a form of prohibition on the subsistence activities themselves. A comment from one of Laade's (1969, p. 36) informants emphasises this point:

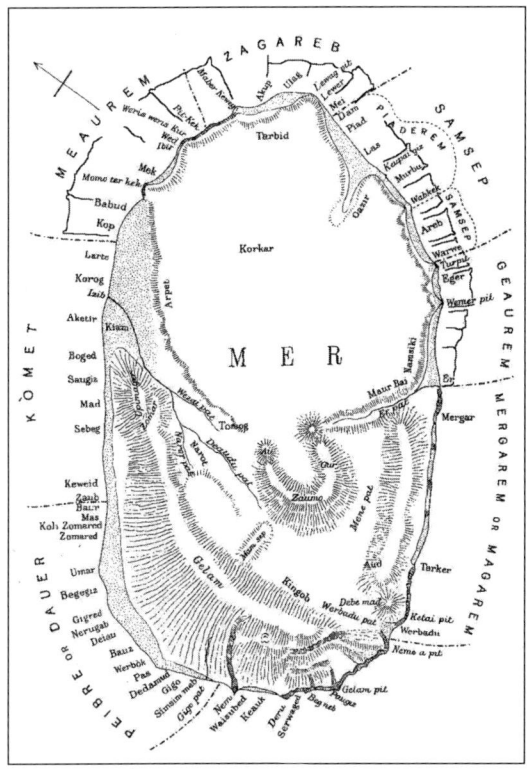

Figure 2. Ethnohistorically recorded clan divisions on Mer Island and the location of stone walled fish traps (after Haddon 1908, p. 170).

When I been young I went for sardines with *weres* [fish scoop]. I fall, got sore leg. My grandfather he take my *weres*, break it, say: 'You never go fishing again'. Bush (gardenland) your fishing ground. You (are a) Samsep.

Similar divisional constructs based on subsistence specialisation and location to resources is characteristic of island Melanesian societies, as illustrated by Roe (2000) for the Solomon Islands. Carter *et al.* (2004b), however, have previously warned against relying on Laade's (1969, 1973) interpretations of clan subsistence specialisation. This warning was largely based on contemporary observations of Meriam intertidal subsistence activities which show that specialisation is the result of male–male competition and social displays of prestige, and that women of all clans fish, garden and collect shellfish for daily household subsistence (Bird & Bliege Bird 1997). As described above, however, results of the analysis of the excavated assemblages have since demonstrated that socially guided restrictions on the production, management and distribution of terrestrial and marine resources may have resulted in spatial and temporal variation in archaeological subsistence remains on the Murray Islands.

The archaeological evidence from Dauar indicates that between initial human occupation of the island and approximately 2000 cal. BP, there existed a broad-ranging subsistence economy based largely on marine resources. After 2000 cal. BP, however, the assemblage from Sokoli illustrates a significant decrease in the deposition of marine remains, while the density of the shell assemblage at Ormi remains constant. The coinciding change in sediment at both sites similarly alludes to a possible change to the nature of subsistence on Dauar around 2000 cal. BP, and more specifically to the development of horticultural practices. This hypothesis has been tested by the analysis of excavated sediment samples for the identification of phytoliths and starch grains at both Sokoli and Ormi (Parr & Carter 2003). The results provided evidence for the presence of common horticultural crops, including banana and coconut, from 2000 cal. BP, as well as shifts in vegetation patterns from this time such as the replacement of the native grass species *Themeda australis* with the more fire-resistant *Imperita cyclindrica* grass species.

I argue that the level of apparent spatial variation in the excavated subsistence remains from 2000 cal. BP testifies to the possible emergence of ethnographically documented forms of social organisation and subsistence specialisation in the eastern Torres Strait shortly after permanent human settlement by 2600 cal. BP. This result is significant for several reasons.

Firstly, it has produced the earliest evidence for the emergence of the horticultural economy in Torres Strait. On Saibai, Barham (1999) established that the construction of horticultural mound-and-ditch systems had commenced by 1200 years BP (based on AMS radiocarbon dates), after tidal inundation of the interior swamp regions ceased due to changing palaeoenvironmental conditions. The earlier development of horticulture in the Eastern Islands provides evidence of the diverse nature of the post-transgression environment of Torres Strait islands, and of the implications this had for the emergence of social organisation in the region.

Secondly, the Murray Islands assemblages illustrate that although contemporary observations of subsistence practices in Torres Strait may provide a point from which to identify continuity in targeted resources and traditional subsistence practices through time (Richardson 2000; Bliege Bird et al. 2002), the archaeological record by its very nature provides a more accurate measure of any changes and developments that may have occurred in these systems, even when such changes are several millennia removed from the ethnographic present. It is through such evidence that the possible emergence of particular forms of social complexity in the Eastern Torres Strait has been established. It is also noted that the presence of extensive systems of stone-walled fish traps mentioned earlier testify to the intensification of marine procurement and management strategies in the Murray Islands, as well as a considerable level of organised labor and skill (see Figure 2).

In dealing with a considerably more-recent period of Torres Strait history, David et al. (2004a) have revealed the ongoing nature of social memorialisation in the western Strait by demonstrating tangible links between archaeology and contemporary oral history. This work concerns the recent results of an excavation of a boulder overhang site called Turao Kula on the large western island of Mua. The boulder is located near a stone-marked grave of a man who was beheaded by raiders from Badu, the attack being watched by his son, Goba, who had escaped and hidden up a nearby tree. After some time Goba climbed down the tree and ran back to the village, where he told what had happened to his father. Goba then led the way to his father's body where the people of Mua then buried it under rocks. The story of Goba was initially recorded by Lawrie (1970, p. 46 cited in David et al. 2004a, p. 161) who was informed that the events had happened not long before the coming of Christianity to Torres Strait in 1871.

On the inside roof of the boulder overhang a number of paintings were recorded and the site displayed evidence of past occupation, including stone artefacts, marine shells, bones, pieces of ochre, charcoal, and also items from the European-contact period such as glass and metal. The excavation continued to a depth of 20–30 cm, at which point bedrock was reached, and revealed two sedimentary layers. Excavated cultural items included stone artefacts, charcoal, burnt earth, marine shell, bone and ochre. Two conventional radiocarbon dates were obtained from excavated charcoal samples. The upper-most sample produced a date of 325±65 years BP (Wk-9943) while the basal sample produced a date of 960±145 years BP (Wk-9944) (David et al. 2004a, p. 166).

From the combined stratigraphic, chronological and cultural data it was concluded that sometime between approximately 500 cal. BP and 100 cal. BP a dramatic change in use of the shelter took place:

> People stopped using the site as intensively as before (as indicated by a sudden drop in numbers of stone artefacts, a cessation of vertebrate faunal remains at the site, and a c. 4-fold slowing down of overall sedimentation rates from 3.8 cm to 1.0 cm/100 years). (David et al., 2004a, p. 167).

However, David et al. (2004a, pp. 167–8) also identified an increase in the deposition of charcoal and ochre in the upper section of the excavation, indicating that the major occupational changes took place around the time of the onset of painting activity at the site. With the aid of digital enhancement the researchers also discovered that one of the paintings at the site depicted an anthropomorphic figure climbing a tree, which has been interpreted as clearly reminiscent of the oral tradition associated with Goba's father's death (David et al. 2004a, p. 168, figures 7 and 8). They surmised that if the powdered ochre recovered from the upper section of the excavation is the by-product of the paintings that illustrate the Goba story, these paintings must post-date the events narrated in the oral tradition (David et al. 2004a, p. 169). Although the painting had been observed during the first half of the twentieth century (Tennant 1959, p. 193 cited in David et al. 2004a, p. 169) the archaeological work at Turao Kula led to a rediscovery of the paintings by the contemporary Kubin community. This was cause for celebration on Mua with a major ceremony held in October 2002 to commemorate these demonstrated links to the past and of a unique opportunity made possible by the merging of oral tradition and archaeology (Brady et al. 2003; David et al. 2004a).

Conclusions

Archaeological investigation of the Torres Strait Islands commenced almost a century after one of the most pivotal anthropological studies in the history of the discipline was undertaken in this region. Instead of the large body of ethnographic data recorded during the Cambridge Expedition inciting archaeological interest in Torres Strait, throughout the majority of the twentieth century the region remained virtually untouched by mainstream archaeological research. When research in Torres Strait commenced during the 1970s the results were generally disappointing and led to largely uninformed conclusions of a recent period of human occupation and an absence or limited diversity in archaeological sites. This period also paved the way for the bridge-and-barrier debate, which resonated throughout the research of the 1980s.

Conducted mostly by the UCL team led by David Harris, the archaeological research conducted in the Torres Strait during the 1980s produced new results that served to disprove a number of previous models as well as establish new theories, particularly concerning the distribution of horticultural subsistence practices across the Strait. Although the antiquity of human occupation had been extended and a clearer understanding of the relationship between island physiography and ecology and human occupation and subsistence established, it was not until Harris' (1995) later insight on the extraneous nature of the bridge-and-barrier debate that it was finally addressed and acquitted.

The most recent research projects are fortunately no longer hindered by the questions of the old, and represent a new level in understanding or the social histories and complexities of Torres Strait culture as they are represented by the archaeological record. Significantly, the results of recent investigations in the Eastern and Western Islands have provided a benchmark for the changing nature of the interpretation of the region's longstanding research questions, such as the origins of human occupation, the development of horticultural subsistence and the nature of trade and exchange systems.

The emerging chronology for permanent human occupation of the Torres Strait islands from around 3500–2500 cal. BP now provides an opportunity to consider Torres Strait from the perspective of patterns of human expansion and sociocultural trends previously established for both western Melanesia and northern tropical Australia. In both of these regions the late Holocene has been identified as a period of population increase with expansion of groups into more marginal environments, such as offshore islands (Barker 1999; Border 1999; Leach 1999; Lourandos 1997; Kirch 1981, 1997a; Rowland 1989, 1996, 1999a; Spriggs 1984, 1997). The period was also a time of intensive cultural, social, economic and technological change, with evidence of such processes appearing in the archaeological record for the first time. In Torres Strait the emergence of subsistence specialisation in the form of combined maritime and horticultural economies from 2000 cal. BP, as well as the presence of pottery sherds and the suspected broad-ranging trade systems they imply, both provide evidence that this region was not peripheral to the dynamic changes experienced by the late-Holocene populations to the north and the south. As this paper has demonstrated, it is only since acknowledging that such social dynamics can indeed be revealed by the archeological record that Torres Strait's cultural past has begun to emerge.

Acknowledgements

To Bruno David, Ian McNiven and Bryce Barker I wish to extend sincere thanks for the invitation to contribute to this book. Harry Lourandos is kindly acknowledged as the inspiration for this paper and as an illuminating and inspiring figure during my undergraduate degree at the University of Queensland. To the communities and families of the Torres Strait who provide support, assistance, and enthusiasm for the archaeological work described in this paper I hold a sincere debt of gratitude and privilege. Martin Gibbs provided comments and suggestions on earlier drafts of this paper and assisted in the production of figures.

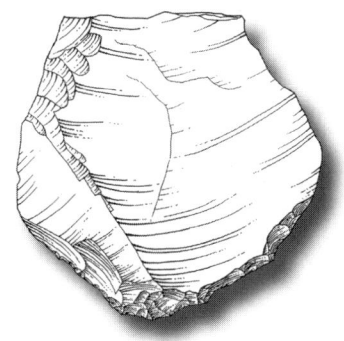

Part 5
Extending the boundaries

Thumbnail scraper dating to sometime between 14 500 and 16 000 BP. It was found in Bone Cave, and was used by Ice Age Tasmanians as they travelled between valleys on wallaby hunting expeditions.

18.
Destabilising how we view the past: Harry Lourandos and the archaeology of Bodmin Moor, south-west England

Barbara Bender

Rewind

1986: a vintage year. The year when, following the African National Congress (ANC) appeal for an international boycott of South African academics, a splinter group from the International Union of Prehistoric and Protohistoric Sciences (IUPPS) decided to hold a meeting to which South African delegates were not invited (Ucko 1987, Chapter 3).

It was not an easy decision, and it split the archaeological establishment down the middle. There were many archaeologists who, though they might be sympathetic to the ANC, felt that academic freedom took precedence, that international networking was more — not less — important in times of political stress, and that, if South Africa were boycotted, why not X or Y or any of the many other tyrannical regimes? On the other hand, there were those who, while recognising the strengths of these arguments, insisted that the work of academics was always reflexive (though the word wasn't bandied about quite as freely in those days), that people worked within historically specific contexts and their work always had political dimensions, and that it was time to abandon the myth of sacrosanct 'ivory towers' and express solidarity with the anti-apartheid cause. Thus, in the summer of 1986 the first meeting of the breakaway group, the World Archaeological Congress (WAC), was held at Southampton, UK, full of clamour and excitement, and attended by many academics from the developing world.

Another conference was held back-to-back with WAC, the Fourth International Conference on Hunting and Gathering Societies. There was no academic boycott, there were South African delegates, and there was a palpable feeling of unease. I had been quite heavily involved in the WAC conference, and yet was on the Hunter-Gatherer committee. Was it a sell-out to go along with the decision not to boycott? If not exactly a sell-out, it was certainly a contradiction.

I had been bowled over by WAC, but I was equally excited by the Hunter-Gatherer conference, mainly because I had helped organise a session on Marxist approaches to gatherer-hunter societies. The word 'Marxist' appeared in the conference handout, but by the time the proceedings were published it was replaced by the more neutral title of 'Historical and evolutionary transformations'. At the top of the list of people to be invited to this session was Harry Lourandos.

I had first met Harry before at an international conference in Vancouver, and had been very curious to see what he was like. He slipped into the conference: very thin, rather dark looking — or was it the fact that he was dressed from head to toe in black that made him seem dark? He appeared rather reserved, introverted. I didn't get to talk to him much.

I don't know to what extent, at that moment in time in the Eighties, the importance of Harry's work had been generally acknowledged. I do know that, for me, perhaps quite selfishly, his 1980 paper published in *World Archaeology* was very significant (Lourandos 1980b). To explain why, I have to go back a little. Five years earlier, I had published a book on the beginnings of farming (Bender 1975). It was a good moment to try and bring things together because, on the one hand, there had been a lot of new research both in the Americas and in the Near East, and, on the other, there had been a flurry of new, 'processual' theorising (Binford 1968; Flannery 1973). Although the 'Processuals' were insisting that now, at last, the focus was on 'The Indian behind the artefact', it turned out (or so it seemed to me) that this Indian was a creature of somewhat economistic habit, whose way of life was all about creating an adaptive equilibrium. The system was constantly fine-tuning itself, but, every now and again, it was battered by forces from outside (environmental, climatic, demographic): forces that required violent adjustments. The move to food production was one such adjustment. Quite apart from the fact that I found Binford's scientific jargon almost impenetrable, this modelling seemed very reductive. But the trouble was that, at the time of writing the book, I couldn't find much to put in its place other than suggesting that there might be many different pathways leading to intensification.

By great good fortune, shortly after finishing the book, I started work in the Department of Anthropology at University College London. It was a wonderfully exciting time because (rather belatedly) French Structural Marxist theorising had arrived. With colleagues like Joel Kahn, John Gledhill, Mike Rowlands and Jonathan Friedman around, the department was buzzing. Without going into the details of the theory, what it did was to question the sharp divide and one-way arrow between 'forces and relations of production' and, instead, emphasised the profoundly two-way movement between the way people relate to each other (the 'social relations of production') and the technologies (the 'forces of production') they deploy. Food is never produced simply to feed faces; it is always produced to feed social relationships. It follows that, in terms of the beginning of food production (i.e. farming, seen as a localisation and, often, an intensification of subsistence strategies), it could be *social* demands that put pressure on subsistence practice, which, in turn, as outputs increased, fuelled changing social relationships.

Pondering these things, I gave a paper at the First International Hunter-Gatherer Conference, held in Paris in 1978. The conference, organised by Maurice Godelier, had an appropriately strong Marxist flavour. I proposed that the intensification of food production was due to internal rather external pressures, and that we needed to look at the particularities of social relations to understand how and why these pressures might occur. The paper was, however, rather short on examples (Bender 1978).

Then came Harry Lourandos' 1980 paper (I had missed his earlier 1977 one published in *Archaeology and Physical Anthropology in Oceania*). Here was not only a discussion along rather similar lines, but also a case study that showed in beautiful and precise detail how the forces and social relations of production worked off each other. I haven't gone back to look at what Harry *really* wrote, but what I *remember* that he wrote was that there were, in parts of Aboriginal Australia, groups of gatherer-hunters whose intense social networks of exchange involved great communal gatherings. The question was how, when people were apparently totally dependent on wild resources, this multitude could be fed? The answer was, first, by ensuring that the feasting occurred at the time of the running of the eels; and second, by digging long channels that deflected the eels towards the meeting grounds (Lourandos 1980b). So simple, so neat, so contrary to Woodburn's notions of systems of immediate return (Woodburn 1972; Bender 1989).

For me, this was an inspirational paper — and a brave one, as it flew in the face of received opinion. No wonder I wanted Harry to come to London; no wonder I wanted to meet this maverick who, in a quite short paper, put question marks around many of the assumptions made about gatherer-hunters, about processes of intensification, about ways in which people might set in motion technological and subsistence changes.

Fast forward

I didn't keep up with Harry, didn't keep up with his work. When, finally, we met up again, nearly twenty years later, in a cafe in a shopping mall in Brisbane, we ruefully (well, I ruefully) noted that we were a lot less slim, we reminisced about our earlier meeting, and Harry kept me amused with stories of his intended retirement, and of his entrepreneurial family. Harry thought that, in retirement, he might have a nice time doing some research on his family history. He was — at least in this respect he hadn't changed — very modest about what he'd been doing in the intervening years and talked very little about how his way of thinking about things had changed over time. He seemed, I thought, fed up with academia: ready to quit and happy to quit.

And myself? Did I, like a good many other people, abandon Marxist theorising, or did it leave an important mark? For a while I went on working on questions about the beginnings of farming. I tried, unsuccessfully, to reverse the term hunter-gatherer to give due weight to the importance of the often predominantly female gathering strategies (Bender 1985) (I now realise that I paid insufficient heed to the fact that, while women's gathering activities are important *economically*, they are often played down in terms of social and cultural relationships. In this respect archaeologists and anthropologists — often male — line up quite tidily alongside *hunter*-gatherers!). I also worked on questions of how and why, in certain contexts, gendered inequalities emerged (Bender 1989); and, looking at developments in North America, tried to unpick the perceived wisdom that farming=sedentism=monumental construction. The Ohio Mound Builders depended on 'wild' resources, moved around, *and* built wonderfully large monumental constructions (Bender 1985).

But, increasingly, I found myself somewhat constrained by the Structural Marxist framework. What was missing in the story was the significance of people's *cultural* perceptions, their understanding of the world around them. Then (and you may note that I am weaving a particular sort of personal narrative; there are many other ways the story could be told), two things happened. First, I became interested in the notion of 'landscape'; more particularly the social construction of, engagement with, and contestation over, landscape. And, second, rather late in the day, I began reading work by Raymond Williams, most particularly *The country and the city* (Williams 1973). Here, for me, was a breakthrough. The Structural Marxists had refused to give causal priority to the forces of production and had forged a two-way interaction with the social relations of production. So, too, with Cultural Marxism, and with Williams' 'structure of feeling' (people's perceptions, their understandings, their world views) were not, as in earlier theorising, the ideological icing on the cake, but were, rather, *integral* to their going-on in the world — to their social relations, economic practices, politics and so on. There was no infrastructure and superstructure, only multiple interactions going every which way.

I've talked about this in a book I wrote on the contested landscapes of Stonehenge (Bender 1998). Talked, too, about the shortcomings in Williams' theorising, and the need to take on board gender as well as class perceptions, a more nuanced understanding of material culture and of *habitus*, a more embodied (phenomenological) understanding of how people engage with the world, and a need to recognise the reflexive nature of our undertakings.

You might say that all this takes one a long way from a Marxist interpretation of history. And, to an extent, you would be right. But, first of all, there is a wide spectrum of Marxist theorising, some of which addresses some of the shortcomings in Williams' approach (Walter Benjamin, for example, cited in David & Denham, this volume, was passionate about the embodied materiality of the world, and his work was deeply reflexive). Second, more generally, amidst the wash of postmodern relativism and reflexivity, and the current emphasis on all things cultural, there is a risk of losing sight of political and economic relations, and of insufficiently focusing upon starkly *real* inequalities. You could say that I am a creature (a gendered creature) of my particular, left-wing, generation, that I can't let go of my hard-earned cultural capital. I wouldn't deny it, but the result is that it still matters to me where and how one positions oneself, matters that one tries to hear and help create spaces for muted or suppressed voices, or, indeed, gets out of the way so that other people can get on with things. It's important to recognise economic and cultural deprivation and that one's work always has political dimensions. I'm not saying that I succeed in doing these things, but I do believe that they should be central to one's concerns.

There's a nice poem by James Fenton that gives voice to such sentiments:

The Ideal
This is where I came from.
I passed this way.
This should not be shameful
Or hard to say.
A self is a self.
It is not a screen.
A person should respect
What he has been.
This is my past
Which I shall not discard.
This is the ideal.
This is hard.

These words serve to underline that, whether we like it or not, where we come from, culturally/socially/politically, affects how we interpret the world. What Harry managed to achieve in his Australian research — and which is often missing in archaeological writing — was a double cultural/political perspective. On the one hand, working with a past in which cultural understanding and sociopolitical and economic relationships went hand in hand, and, on the other, recognising that the past is always filtered through the cultural/ political perspectives of the archaeologist. The past is thus always a *present-past*, and is, by definition, unstable.

It is this double whammy that informs the work that I, as part of a group of archaeologists and anthropologists, undertook on Bodmin Moor. Geographically, the moor — in the furthest south-west corner of England — is a long way from Australia. But perhaps, intellectually, our worlds remained closer than we knew.

Working on Bodmin Moor

In the early 1990s Chris Tilley wrote an important book on phenomenology (Tilley 1994), and then walked and worked on Bodmin Moor in Cornwall, south-west England, trying to understand the changing relationship between Neolithic and Bronze Age ritual places — long mounds, stone rows and circles — and the surrounding landscape, in particular, the high tors, and their social and political implications (Tilley 1995). He left to one side the numerous Bronze Age settlements that are scattered across the moor. This was partly because there were just too many, and they were too complex for one person to survey on his own, but also, I think he would admit, because there was still a lingering distinction being made between ceremonial sites and domestic or settlement sites. The latter were seemingly more mundane, less 'ritual'.

He and I talked about these things and then, in conjunction with Sue Hamilton, decided to attempt an anthropological and archaeological study of one such Bronze Age settlement and its place, and ours, within the landscape ('landscape' here used in the widest sense of the word). We embarked upon a five-year project (from 1995 to 1999) and, over the years, the project went in many different directions.

Stone worlds

The place we chose is called Leskernick. It is a low rounded hill in the north-west part of Bodmin Moor. It is irregularly covered in moorstone (also called clitter): angular rocks, large and small, that have crumbled and tumbled away from the tabular granitic outcrops on the top of the hill. Unlike the other, higher, hills on the moor, there are no dramatic stacked rocks or tors.

On the west and south side of the hill are the footings of about fifty round, stone-built, Bronze Age houses, and spreading out around and beyond these houses are dozens of curvilinear walled enclosures. Houses and enclosures date around the mid-to-late second millennium BC.

On the top of the hill is a large propped stone. The gap created between the two stones forms a peephole which, on the longest day of the year, gathers-in

Part 5 • Extending the boundaries

the last of the sun just before it sinks below the horizon. It seems likely that this propped stone and the ceremonies associated with it predate the settlement, and that it was levered into place by people who moved with their herds between the moors and the surrounding lowland on a seasonal basis. It was perhaps because the hill was already sacred that people chose to settle here, drawing sustenance from the power of the place.

The Bronze Age people who settled on the slopes of the hill also built a large cairn on the hilltop, and on almost every one of the hills that encircle Leskernick there is a similar great cairn (often sited quite close to a tor). It doesn't take much to imagine a sacred time in the year when fires were lit and hilltop answered to hilltop.

Just south of the hill, on the moor, there is a long, stone row made up of very small stones, and also two stone circles, and another (probable) great cairn. Again, the stone row and circles predate the settlement, and again one gets the feeling that the house-builders were engaging with a landscape that was already rich in memories, stories, and ancestral myths.

The archaeologists excavated several of the houses, sections of enclosure walls, and parts of the stone row and one of the stone circles. The anthropologists began by surveying the hillside — the houses, the enclosures, the lobes of clitter – and later moved on to survey (in much less detail) settlements across the moor.

This is not the place to go into any detail; a very large volume will appear in 2005 (Bender *et al.* 2005). Suffice that we can show how people built, rebuilt, and sometimes shut down their houses. And how they built and rebuilt, dismantled, and partially abandoned the surrounding enclosures. They were primarily herds-people, but seem also to have had small garden plots. They lived on the hill for many generations, probably two or three hundred years. While it seems clear to us that an entire community or even, particularly in the earlier stages, two communities, lived on the hill, it is less clear whether they lived there the whole year round. It is possible that they decamped during the winter to an off-moor, somewhat more sheltered settlement. We tend to feel that there is such a deeply *settled* relationship with the hill that it is unlikely that it was abandoned for months on end. But that, perhaps, says more about *our* sense — rather than theirs — of what a strong attachment to place entails.

We have looked at the houses and enclosures, at entrances and exits, and tried to create a landscape not of static places but of movement and footpaths. We can show you the path they took between houses, out through enclosure walls, down to the ford and to the riverine resources. Or the droving road that led up the hill from the moor to the settlement. We think we can show you a processional way leading up the hill between the southern and western settlements to the propped stone. We can walk you along the stone row, and show you where they would have crossed a liminal watery space after which, as they moved towards the higher terminal stones of the row, the fugitive pinnacles of Rough Tor (the most sacred hilltop of the moors) came slowly into view.

We can discuss the places of the living, and of the dead. We think that some of the houses were re-used for small burial cairns; we know that the most peripheral of the enclosures were eventually abandoned, and that, in this liminal space, small burial cairns were built in and alongside the crumbling enclosure walls.

Probably, for nearly all of us, one of the major sources of excitement and wonderment was our ability to track not just their physical but their *metaphysical* relationship to the hill. Here, as elsewhere in our work, it seems likely that Australian Aboriginal peoples, and, indeed, Australian anthropologists, will simply wonder why it has taken European archaeologists so long to recognise the *animate* nature of the Bronze Age world, and the utter foolishness of the divisions that we too often deploy between 'culture' and 'nature'.

We can start with the doorways to the houses. No one in their right minds would locate a doorway on the upslope side of the house where all the wind and rain and mud would enter, but these doorways are not just sited downslope but are systematically orientated towards the high tors on the surrounding hills. On the other hand, often, when you pass through the doorway and enter the house, there is a very large orthostat in the wall directly opposite the doorway. Often this stone is a 'grounder' (one solidly set in the soil) and the house is actually built around this stone-in-place; other times a fine large stone has been brought from higher up the slope and set in place.

At the top of the hill, the enclosure walls approach the great tabular rocks: then stop short. They touch base around the propped stone, and they follow and sometimes scramble through the dense clitter lobes. A wall may loop its way between great grounders and, oftentimes, a pyramidal-shaped rock leans up against the grounder. Sometimes, from a dense pile of clitter, small walls radiate out in all directions. Sometimes the walls enclose tiny — utterly stony — areas seemingly of practical use to neither man nor beast. On the northern and part of the western edge of the settlement the stones that make up the enclosure walls have been chosen, both in terms of shape and size, with most particular care.

In some of the enclosures there are grounders that have had very large (very heavy) stones set atop them; or grounders where the area downslope has been cleared of stones. Some of these we called 'shrine-stones'.

We also found, slightly to our dismay since we began to feel that no one would believe us, that *within* the spreads of clitter, people had continually tinkered with the stones: there might be a short run of wall, or a semicircle of stones, a grounder might be ringed around with small uprights. Discussing these alterations with two geomorphologists, it seems that while some of these stone patternings are fortuitous — the result of periglaciation and downslope slippage — others are quite definitely not (Tilley et al. 2000b).

It seems clear to us that at one and the same moment house-and-enclosure constructions are entirely practical (they do what they have to do: keep out the elements, create spaces for living, for pasturing and so on) *and* utterly cultural. Everything that was done on the hill was done in partnership with the stones. They, the great tabular stones towards the top of the hill, and the clitter that emanated from them, were the ancestral forces. The stones were part of life, they gave life: they had to be nurtured. Sometimes, the patterning of the stone flows was slightly reworked, sometimes some structural feature found in nature was mimicked, oftentimes no such action was required. *All* of the stones formed part of a particular way-of-being in the world; there was no divide between 'nature' and 'culture'.

There are many more aspects to this prehistoric world that we touched upon. We tried to understand changing relationships between house clusters on Leskernick, and beyond Leskernick, and relationships beyond the moor. We are in total agreement with Cornish archaeologists who have long recognised the particularity and significance of these western communities, and have rejected any sort of core–periphery model in which Wessex is the core and Cornwall the benighted edge of Bronze Age developments. A conceptualisation, incidentally, that might owe something to contemporary perceptions of economic and political power relations within southern Britain.

Contemporary landscapes

If we acknowledge that we can only understand the past through the lens of the present — that there is, in fact, only a present past — then we need to know more about how we construct the world around us. Thus, as part of the project Tony Williams (who had been a student at UCL) looked at *our* perceptions of place and of landscape, and how we created pathways, private and public spaces, hierarchically organised and gendered spaces, memory-encompassed places (Bender et al. 2005, chapter 12). Among other things, Williams asked people working on the site to take photographs of places that meant something to them, and then to describe their importance in words. More than anything, these photographs broke along gender lines: the men mainly using landscape format and taking wide-angled shots, the women preferring portrait size, and, very often, photographing more private places of personal experience.

Williams also pulled back to examine alternate landscapes around the campsite that interleaved with the places of excavation and survey. He could, of course, have pulled still further back and opened up towards the places, and the contexts, that people had come from. There is a need to recognise the way in which landscapes — past and present — nest one within the other, and the way in which for some people relationships fan out to far distant places, for others the circumscribed world of everyday living opens towards landscapes told by travellers and myth-makers (Bender *et al.* 1997). Being-in-place is always affected by things out of place.

Contemporary practice

It matters, too, how we go about our business. The making of the project, the moment-to-moment work that takes place, all these things need to be contextualised. There is a hierarchy of knowledge, and a hierarchy of personnel, that needs to be acknowledged. It is deeply unfair that in the end the three directors walk away with most of the kudos, and the dozens of people involved (some not even named) disappear from sight. It is faintly ridiculous that the finished product — the book — eliminates all the hesitations, arguments, false starts and wrong moves that are part of how knowledge is created.

We asked everyone who worked on the project to keep a diary and to make it available to the directors and to Mike Wilmore (at that time a post-graduate student in the anthropology department at UCL, now a lecturer at the University of Adelaide) to work with the diaries, and with people on and off site, to try and reach a better, and perhaps slightly more honest, understanding of how we create knowledge (Bender *et al.* 2005, chapter 11; Wilmore forthcoming). (Though why just the directors? Why just Mike Wilmore?)

As those who read Wilmore's extended account will discover, the project was not exactly tensionless, and one fault-line was between the seeming pragmatism of the excavators and the seeming theory-driven approach of the anthropologists. 'Seeming' is the operative word, and Wilmore demonstrates very clearly how the pragmatics of excavation hinge on historically contingent and changing theoretical understandings, while anthropological theorising is constantly nudging and being nudged by on-the-ground practice. Not perhaps startling findings, but ones that deserve closer scrutiny.

Art and the re-representation of the past

Early in the project we understood that we wanted to find ways to destabilise our text — both written and illustrative. These forms of presentation (the tools of our trade as much as any trowel or shovel) 'frame' our interpretations and retrieval practices, and, all too often, lend a spurious authority to what can only be tentative. They fail to show how knowledge is created and expunged, how possibilities are ignored. We wanted to find ways to acknowledge how fugitive, how slippery, our interpretations are; we wanted to focus on process as much as on end result, for it's the process which allows an insight into our *present*-ing of the past.

In our text we attempted to undercut the authoritative academic findings by using diaries, dialogues, 'messy' context sheets and so on. It took us longer to find ways to destabilise the figurative representations. We tried various forms of mapping, sketching, drawing, painting and photographic montage. Eventually we became somewhat more adventuresome, trying to bring some life to the Leskernick stone world, trying to make our intercessions on the hill more three-dimensional. We used flags that moved in the wind to demarcate the movement along the stone row or up the processional way; configured spoil heaps to mimic distant tors, photographed our shadows on the rocks (indicating, perhaps, the shadowy presence of those that had come and gone, and our own transient intercession in this place).

In another attempt to create a material — though very ephemeral — dialogue with things-in-place, we wrapped some of the stones in cling-film and then painted them. We chose stones that had been worked upon in prehistoric times — recreating past creations in the present for the present — and, involving ourselves in making as well as seeing, understood at first hand how important the process was, as well as the end result. Wrapping the stones had the additional virtue that it allowed us to highlight the often minute human adjustments that had been made to stones — the little arcs and encirclements, stones placed atop stones — which, grey stone upon grey stone, were almost impossible to catch in photographs (Tilley *et al.* 2000b).

Some of the things we tried to do were less pleasing, but sometimes helpfully so. For example, we found, on the high tors across the moors, beautiful solution hollows carved in the granite by water action. These were, nearly always, in 'secret' places, invisible from below or from any distance. They were filled with rainwater. In an attempt to register their symbolic importance, and the fact that they might have been used for libations, we coloured the water white and red. Later, coming across the writings of the earlier Cornish antiquarian, Borlase, we understood better the importance of the *pure* water falling into the hollows from the sky. We thought again about how the water reflected and drew in the clouds and the changing colours of the sky, how its surface was ruffled by wind and by the birds of prey that came to drink. It seemed then that colouring the water worked against the grain, against the meaning, of these secret places (Bender *et al.* 2005, chapter 20).

Other ways of telling

The Leskernick project involved telling stories. Not, we would maintain, *any* old story, but ones that tried do justice to the evidence that we unearthed. But, of course, there are other ways of telling. There are many people with longer, often more intimate, relationships to the moors: commoners who have rights to run their horses, sheep and cattle on the moors and have a strong sense of place, and of intrusion; local people (some who have lived all their lives close to the moors, others that arrived more recently); Cornish archaeologists, and — sometimes one and the same — Cornish nationalists with strong reservations about the rightfulness of a bunch of 'foreigners' descending on 'their' moor. It seemed important that we should not just explain what we were doing, but also allow or recognise a legitimate space for them to react to our work, and to express their own feelings.

We created a travelling exhibition and, in the first instance, set it up in a local church hall. The exhibition discussed the idea of landscape as an engagement, past and present, with place, and went on to detail our own thoughts and practices around Leskernick.

Sitting in on the exhibition for most of one summer allowed a much better understanding of how people reacted to our work and, perhaps more importantly, to the moor. Often, turning their backs on the exhibition, they talked local politics, discussed changing subsistence practices, worried over the effects of global warming. There were very interesting gendered and generational responses, and differences between incomers and older inhabitants. People brought objects that they had found on the moor, exchanging their intimate local knowledge for our more academic understandings of technologies and chronologies (Bender *et al.* 2005, chapter 14).

Conclusions

This seems a good place to pause: with the recognition that archaeologists and anthropologists have a responsibility to disseminate their findings in ways that open towards debate, not just with fellow academics, but with as many people as possible who care about, want to understand more about, want to discuss — sometimes critically — their own and our understanding of the making of place and landscape. It is important to show that the past is never over and done with, that it is always a *present*-past, and that, since it informs both the present and future, it *matters*.

People have always engaged with the land, and have always brought their own understandings to that engagement. In that sense there are underlying structural similarities between 'us' (a multiple 'us') and 'them' (a multiple 'them'). At the same time, the fact that people engage in very different ways has to be understood in terms of interleaving historically contingent social relations, economic and political structures, and cultural perceptions. In terms, too, of interwoven macro- and micro-scales (or nestings) of such embodied and cognised encounters.

Archaeological and anthropological understandings have changed quite dramatically in the last twenty years or so. The boundaries between disciplines have become more fluid, we're more aware of the reflexive and subjective nature of our work, we recognise that we are telling stories, and that it is alright — necessary, actually — that we acknowledge our own presence and use our own imaginings. These ways of going about things destabilise any notion of a fixed or unitary past, they work with an understanding that there are always multiple pasts, and that, in some measure, they are always *our* pasts. The sort of questions that Harry was posing, those long years ago, are embedded in, and remain germane to, our present day preoccupations.

Acknowledgements

It is important to stress that the work done on Bodmin Moor was jointly organised by Chris Tilley, Sue Hamilton and myself. What I have written here is entirely based on our joint work and observations, not to mention the work and observations of dozens of other people who worked with us.

We owe a huge debt to the Cornish Archaeological Unit who, with the Royal Commission, had produced an amazing overview of the moor, complete with detailed survey maps (Johnson & Rose 1994). And to Pete Herring, from the unit, and Dave Hooley from English Heritage.

Publications by Harry Lourandos

Lourandos, H 2004, 'Foreword', in B Barker, *The sea people: late-Holocene maritime hunter-gatherers on the tropical Queensland coast*, pp. ix–x, Terra Australis 20, Pandanus Press, Canberra.

Lourandos, H 2002, 'The archaeology of hunter-gatherer society', in *The international encyclopedia of the social and behavioural sciences*, Elsevier Sciences Limited, Oxford.

Lourandos, H & David, B 2002, 'Long-term archaeological and environmental trends: a comparison from late-Pleistocene–Holocene Australia', in P Kershaw, B David, N Tapper, D Penny & J Brown (eds), *Bridging Wallace's Line: the environmental and cultural history and dynamics of the Australian–South-East Asian region*, pp. 307–38, Advances in geo-ecology 34, Catena Verlag GMBH, Reiskirchen.

Rowe, C, David, B, Stanisic, J & **Lourandos, H** 2001, 'The helicinid land snail *Pleuropoma extincta* (Odhner, 1917) as an environmental indicator in archaeology', *Memoirs of the Queensland Museum*, vol. 46, pp. 741–70.

David, B, Lecole, M, **Lourandos, H**, Baglioni, AJ Jnr & Flood, J 1999, 'Investigating relationships between motif forms, techniques and rock surfaces in north Australian rock art', *Australian Archaeology*, vol. 48, pp. 16–22.

McNiven, IJ, David, B & **Lourandos, H** 1999, 'Long-term Aboriginal use of western Victoria: reconsidering the significance of recent Pleistocene dates for the Grampians–Gariwerd region', *Archaeology in Oceania*, vol. 34, no. 2, pp. 83–5.

David, B & **Lourandos, H** 1999, 'Landscape as mind: land use, cultural space and change in north Queensland prehistory', *Quaternary International*, vol. 59, pp. 107–23.

David, B & **Lourandos, H** 1998, 'Rock art and socio-demography in north-eastern Australian prehistory', *World Archaeology*, vol. 30, no. 2, pp. 193–219.

Lourandos, H & David, B 1998, 'Comparing long-term archaeological and environmental trends: north Queensland, arid and semi-arid Australia', *The Artefact*, vol. 21, pp. 105–14.

Lourandos, H 1997, *Continent of hunter-gatherers*, Cambridge University Press, Cambridge.

David, B & **Lourandos, H** 1997, '37,000 years and more in tropical Australia: investigating long-term archaeological trends in Cape York Peninsula', *Proceedings of the Prehistoric Society*, vol. 63, pp. 1–23.

David, B, Walt, H, **Lourandos, H**, Rowe, M, Brayer, J & Tuniz, C 1997, 'Ordering the rock paintings of the Mitchell–Palmer limestone zone (Australia) for AMS dating', *The Artefact*, vol. 20, pp. 57–72.

Lourandos, H 1996, 'Change in Australian prehistory: scale, trends and frameworks of interpretation', in I Lilley, A Ross & S Ulm (eds), *Proceedings of the 1995 Australian Archaeological Association Conference*, Tempus 6, pp. 15–21, University of Queensland, St Lucia.

David, B, Barbetti, M, Bekessy, R, Bekessy, L, Bultitude, R, Butler, D, Clarkson, C, Clarkson, J, Conn, C, Dredge, M, Eyre, T, Fullagar, R, Goodall, R, Hall, L, Head, J, Hua, Q, Ingram, G, Jones, R, Lawson, E, **Lourandos, H**, Loy, T, Macrokanis, C, McNiven, I, Murray, C, Ogleby, C, Osborne, M, Pole, M, Roberts, R, Schulz, M, Spate, A, Stanisic, J, Summerhayes, G, Taylor, C, Tuniz, C & Whittier, J 1996, 'The Ngarrabullgan Homeland Project: current research in Kuku Djungan country, north Queensland', *Australian Archaeology*, vol. 43, pp. 32–6.

Lourandos, H & Ross, A 1994, 'The great "intensification debate": its history and place in Australian archaeology', *Australian Archaeology*, vol. 39, pp. 54–63

Lourandos, H 1993, 'Hunter-gatherer cultural dynamics: long-and short-term trends in Australian prehistory', *Journal of Archaeological Research*, vol. 1, no. 1, pp. 67–88.

Lourandos, H 1988, 'Seals, sedentism and change in the Bass Strait', in B Meehan & R Jones (eds) *Archaeology with ethnography: an Australian perspective*, pp. 277–85, Australian National University, Canberra.

Lourandos, H 1988, 'Palaeopolitics: resource intensification in Aboriginal Australia', in T Ingold, D Riches & J Woodburn (eds), *Hunters and gatherers: history, evolution and social change*, pp.148–60, Berg, New York.

Lourandos, H 1987, 'Pliestocene Australia: peopling a continent', in O Soffer (ed.), *The Pleistocene Old World: regional perspectives*, pp. 147–65, Plenum, New York.

Lourandos, H 1987, 'Swamp managers of south-western Victoria', in DJ Mulvaney & JP White (eds), *Australians to 1788*, pp. 293–307, Fairfax, Syme & Weldon, Sydney.

Lourandos, H 1985, 'Intensification and Australian prehistory', in TD Price & JA Brown (eds), *Prehistoric hunter-gatherers: the emergence of cultural complexity*, pp. 385–432, Academic Press, Orlando.

Lourandos, H 1985, 'Problems with the interpretation of late-Holocene changes in Australian prehistory', *Archaeology in Oceania*, vol. 10, pp. 37–9.

Lourandos, H 1985, 'Review of J Dawson's *Australian Aborigines*, in *Aboriginal History*, AIAS, Canberra.

Lourandos, H 1984, 'Changing perspectives in Australian prehistory: a reply to Beaton', *Archaeology in Oceania*, vol. 19, pp. 29–33.

Lourandos, H 1983 'Intensification: a late-Pleistocene–Holocene archaeological sequence from south-western Victoria', *Archaeology in Oceania*, vol. 18, pp. 81–94.

Lourandos, H 1983, '10,000 years in the Tasmanian highlands', *Australian Archaeology*, vol. 16, pp. 39–47.

Bowdler, S & **Lourandos, H** 1982, 'Both sides of Bass Strait', in S Bowdler (ed.), *Coastal archaeology in eastern Australia: proceedings of the 1980 Valla Conference on Australian Prehistory*, pp. 121–32, ANU, Canberra.

Lourandos, H 1982, 'Comment on DG Sutton, "Towards the recognition of convergent cultural adaptation in the subantarctic zone"', *Current Anthropology*, vol. 23, no. 1, pp. 77–97, 89–90.

Lourandos, H 1981, 'Comment on B Hayden, "Research and development in the stone age: technological transitions among hunter-gatherers"', *Current Anthropology*, vol. 22, no. 5, pp. 519–48, 536–7.

Lourandos, H 1980, 'Change or stability? Hydraulics, hunter-gatherers and population in temperate Australia', *World Archaeology*, vol. 11, pp. 245–66.

Lourandos, H 1980, 'Forces of change: Aboriginal technology and population in south-western Victoria', unpublished PhD thesis, The University of Sydney, Sydney.

Lourandos, H 1977, 'Aboriginal spatial organization and population: south-western Victoria reconsidered', *Archaeology and Physical Anthropology in Oceania*, vol. 12, pp. 202–25.

Lourandos, H 1977, 'Stone tools, settlement, adaptation: a Tasmanian example', in RVS Wright (ed.), *Stone tools as cultural markers*, pp. 219–24, Australian Institute of Aboriginal Studies, Canberra.

Lourandos, H 1977, 'Review of S Polgar (ed.), *Population, ecology and social evolution*, in *Mankind*, vol. 11, no. 1, pp. 72–3.

Lourandos, H 1976, 'Archaeological fieldwork in south-western Victoria', *Australian Archaeology*, vol. 4, pp. 9–10.

Lourandos, H 1976, 'Aboriginal settlement and land use in south-western Victoria: a report on current field work', *The Artefact*, vol. 1, no. 4, pp. 174–93.

Lourandos, H 1970, 'Coast and hinterland: the archaeological sites of eastern Tasmania', unpublished MA thesis, Australian National University, Canberra.

Lourandos, H 1970, 'A description of the Aboriginal Archaeological sites in Tasmania', in FD McCarthy (ed.), *Aboriginal antiquities in Australia*, pp. 35–8, Australian Institute of Aboriginal Studies, Canberra.

Lourandos, H 1969, 'The study of the Tasmanian Aborigine', *Tasmanian year book*, vol. 3, pp. 69–72.

Lourandos, H 1968, 'Dispersal of activities: the east Tasmanian sites', *Papers and Proceedings of the Royal Society of Tasmania*, vol. 102, pp. 41–6.

References

Please note that the following abbreviations have been used:
AIAS   Australian Institute of Aboriginal Studies
AIATSIS   Australian Institute of Aboriginal and Torres Strait Islander Studies
ANU   Australian National University
NARU   North Australia Research Unit

Australian Broadcasting Corporation 2000, 'Ruddock in hot water over wheel comments', *ABC News Online*, 4 October 2000, at URL: http://www.abc.net.au/news/2000/10/item20001003180316_1.htm

Aboriginal Land Tribunal 1994, 'In the matter of Aboriginal land claims to: Lakefield and Cliff Islands National Parks. Recorded at Cooktown, Bizant, Brisbane and various sites, June to November', transcript of proceedings held by M Langton.

Adams, WY 1998, *The philosophical roots of anthropology*, Center for the Study of Language and Information, Stanford University Press, California.

Allen, H 1979, 'Left out in the cold: why the Tasmanians stopped eating fish', *The Artefact*, 4, pp. 1–10.

Allen, H 1997, 'The distribution of large blades (leilira): evidence for recent changes in Aboriginal ceremonial exchange network', in P McConvell & N Evans (eds), *Archaeology and linguistics: Aboriginal Australia in a global perspective*, Oxford University Press, Melbourne.

Allen, H & Barton G 1989, *Ngarradj Warde Djobkeng: White cockatoo dreaming and the prehistory of Kakadu*, Oceania Monograph 37, Oceania Publications, Sydney.

Allen, J & Corris P (eds) 1977, *The journal of John Sweatman: a nineteenth century surveying voyage in north Australia and Torres Strait*, University of Queensland Press, St Lucia.

Allen, J & Kershaw P 1996, 'The Pleistocene–Holocene transition in Greater Australia', in LG Straus, BV Eriksen, JM Erlandson & DR Yesner (eds), *Humans at the end of the Ice Age: the archaeology of the Pleistocene–Holocene transition*, pp. 175–99, Plenum, New York.

Amis, K 1983, *Selected short stories*, Penguin, Harmondsworth.

Anderson, A, Lilley, I, & O'Connor, S (eds) 2001, *Histories of old ages: essays in honour of Rhys Jones*, Pandanus Books, Research School of Pacific and Asian Studies, ANU, Canberra.

Anderson, NJ 1995, 'Temporal scale, phytoplankton ecology and palaeolimnology', *Freshwater Biology*, 34, pp. 367–78.

Andrefsky, W 1998, *Lithics: macroscopic approaches to analysis*, Cambridge University Press, Cambridge.

Argant, J 2001, 'What is the meaning of the high percentages of fern spores in archaeological sediment palynological analyses?', in DK Goodman & R Clarke (eds), *Proceedings of the IX International Palynological Congress, Houston, Texas, USA, 1996*, pp. 339–45, American Association of Stratigraphic Palynologists Foundation, Dallas.

Angas, GF, 1847, *Savage Life and Scenes in Australia and New Zealand: Being an Artist's Impressions of Countries and People at the Antipodes*, 2 vols, Smith, Elder & Co. London.

Asad, T 1973, *Anthropology and the colonial encounter*, Ithaca Press, London.

Attenbrow, V, David, B & Flood, J 1995 'Mennge-ya and the origins of points: new insights into the appearance of points in the semi-arid zone of the Northern Territory', *Archaeology in Oceania*, 30, pp. 105–20.

Attwood, B 2003, *Rights for Aborigines*, Allen & Unwin, St Leonards, NSW.

Attwood, B & Arnold, J (eds) 1992, 'Power, knowledge and Aborigines', *Journal of Australian Studies*, no. 35.

Avery, J 1985, 'The Law People: history, society and initiation in the Borroloola area of the Northern Territory', unpublished PhD thesis, The University of Sydney.

Baker, R 1989a, 'Land is life: continuity through change for the Yanyuwa from the Northern Territory of Australia', unpublished PhD thesis, University of Adelaide.

Baker, R 1989b, 'Yanyuwa contact history: the value of oral sources', *Oral History Association of Australia Journal*, 11, pp. 30–41.

Baker, R 1990, 'Coming in: the Yanyuwa as a case study in the geography of contact history', in V Chapman & P Read (eds), *Terrible hard biscuits*, pp.123–66, Allen & Unwin, St Leonards, NSW.

Baker, R 1999, *Land is life: from bush to town: the story of the Yanyuwa people*, Allen & Unwin, St Leonards, NSW.

Ballard, C 2001, 'Wetland drainage and agricultural transformations in the Southern Highlands of Papua New Guinea', *Asia Pacific Viewpoint*, vol. 42, nos. 2–3, pp. 287–304.

Balme, J & Wilson, M 2004, 'Perceptions of archaeology in Australia amongst educated young Australians', *Australian Archaeology*, 58, pp. 19–24.

Bapty, I & Yates, T (eds) 1990, *Archaeology after structuralism*, Routledge, London.

Barham, AJ 1981, 'Land use and environmental change in the Western Torres Strait Islands, North Queensland', unpublished fieldwork report held by M Carter.

Barham, AJ 1999, 'The local environmental impact of prehistoric populations on Saibai Island, northern Torres Strait, Australia: enigmatic evidence from Holocene swamp lithostratigraphic records', *Quaternary International*, 59, pp. 71–105.

Barham, AJ 2000, 'Late-Holocene maritime societies in the Torres Strait Islands, northern Australia: cultural arrival or cultural emergence?', *East of Wallace's Line: studies of past and present maritime cultures of the Indo-Pacific region*, pp. 223–314, Modern quaternary research in South-East Asia series 16, AA Balkema Press, Rotterdam.

Barham, AJ & Harris, DR 1983, 'Prehistory and palaeoecology of Torres Strait', in PM Masters & NC Flemming (eds), *Quaternary Coastlines and Marine Archaeology: towards the prehistory of land bridges and continental shelves*, pp. 529–57, Academic Press, London.

Barham, AJ & Harris, DR, 1985, 'Relict field systems in the Torres Strait Region', *Prehistoric intensive agriculture in the tropics*, pp. 247–83, British archaeological reports: international series 232 (vol. 1), Oxford.

Barham, AJ & Harris, DR (eds) 1987, 'Archaeological and palaeoenvironmental investigations in Western Torres Strait, Northern Australia. Final Report to the Research and Exploration Committee of the National Geographic Society on the Torres Strait Research Project Part IIB: July–October 1985', unpublished report, Institute of Archaeology, University of London & Department of Geography, University College London, London.

Barham, AJ, Rowland, MJ & Hitchcock, G 2004, 'Torres Strait *Bepotaim*: an overview of archaeological and ethnoarchaeological investigations', *Torres Strait archaeology and material culture: Memoirs of the Queensland Museum*, Cultural heritage series, vol. 3, no. 1, pp. 1–72.

Barker, B 1999, 'Coastal occupation in the Holocene: environment, resource use and resource continuity', in J Hall & I McNiven (eds), *Australian coastal archaeology*, pp. 119–28, ANH Publications, Canberra.

Barker, B 2004, *The sea people: late-Holocene maritime specialisation in the Whitsunday Islands, central Queensland*, Terra Australis 20, Pandanus Books, Canberra.

Barker, B & Schon, R 1994, 'A preliminary assessment of the spatial distribution of stone artefacts from the South Molle Island Aboriginal Quarry, Whitsunday Islands, central Queensland coast', *Memoirs of the Queensland Museum*, vol. 37, no. 1, pp. 5–12.

Barker, B in press, 'Text as archaeological data: Walter E Roth and Queensland archaeology', in R McDougall & I Davidson (eds), *The Roth family, anthropology and colonial administration*, University College of London Press, London.

Barker, BCW & Macintosh, A 1979, The dingo: a review, *Collected papers in memoriam: NWG Macintosh*, Oceania Monographs 22, pp. 177–203, The University of Sydney.

Barrett, J 2001, Archaeology, the duality of structure and the problem of the archaeological record, in I Hodder (ed.), *Archaeological theory today*, pp. 141–64, Polity Press, Cambridge, UK.

Bartlett, RH 1993, *The Mabo decision, and the full text of the decision in Mabo and Others v. the State of Queensland*, Butterworths, Sydney.

Basso, K 1996, 'Wisdom sits in places: notes on a Western Apache landscape', in S Feld & K Basso (eds), *Senses of place*, pp. 53–70, School of American Research Press, Santa Fe.

Bauer, WE 1958 Letter to Mr Ken J Morris, Deputy Premier and Minister for Labour and Industry, Office of the Minister for Labour and Industry, held by Queensland National Parks & Wildlife Service, Airlie Beach, Queensland.

Beaton, JM 1977, 'Dangerous harvest: investigations in the late prehistoric occupation of upland southeast central Queensland', unpublished PhD thesis, ANU, Canberra.

Beaton, JM 1979, 'Report on Archaeological Fieldwork in the Flinders Island–Bathurst Heads–Princess Charlotte Bay Area, North Queensland', unpublished manuscript Ms 1375, held at the AIATSIS library, Canberra.

Beaton, JM, 1982, 'Fire and water: aspects of Australian Aboriginal management of cycads', *Archaeology in Oceania*, 17, pp. 51–58

Beaton, JM 1983, 'Does intensification account for changes in the Australian Holocene archaeological record?', *Archaeology in Oceania*, 18, pp. 94–7.

Beaton, JM 1985, 'Evidence for a coastal occupation time-lag at Princess Charlotte Bay (North Queensland) and implications for coastal colonization and population growth theories for Aboriginal Australia', *Archaeology in Oceania*, 20, pp. 1–20.

Beaton, JM 1990, 'The importance of past population for prehistory', *Hunter-gatherer demography: past and present*, pp. 23–40, Oceania monograph 39, University of Sydney.

Beaver, WN 1920, *Unexplored New Guinea*, Seeley, Service & Co, London.

Beck, L (ed.) 1995, *Regional approaches to mortuary analysis*, Plenum, New York.

Beck, W, Fullagar, R & White, N 1988, 'Archaeology from ethnography: the Aboriginal use of the cycad as an example', in B Meehan & R Jones (eds), *Archaeology with ethnography: an Australian perspective*, Research School of Pacific Studies, ANU, Canberra.

Beckett, J 1972, 'The Torres Strait Islanders', in D Walker (ed.), *Bridge and barrier: the natural and cultural history of Torres Strait*, pp. 307–26, Research School of Pacific Studies, ANU, Canberra.

Beckett, J 1987, *Torres Strait Islanders: custom and colonialism*, Cambridge University Press, Cambridge, UK.

Beckett, JR (ed.) 1988, *Past and present: the construction of Aboriginality*, Aboriginal Studies Press, Canberra.

Beckett, J 1995, 'The Murray Island land case', *The Australian Journal of Anthropology*, vol. 6, no. 1; 6, no. 2, pp. 15–31.

Beckett, J 2004, 'Writing about Islanders: recent research and future directions', in R Davis (ed.), *Woven histories dancing lives: Torres Strait Islander identity, culture and history*, pp. 2–14, Aboriginal Studies Press, Canberra.

Bell, D 1998, *Ngarrindjeri Wurruwarrin: a world that is, was, and will be*, Spinifex Press, Melbourne.

Bell, D 2001 'The word of a woman: Ngarrindjeri stories and a bridge to Hindmarsh Island', in P Brock (ed.), *Words and silences: Aboriginal women, politics and land*, pp. 117–38, Allen & Unwin, St Leonards.

Bellwood, P 1985, 'Holocene flake and blade industries of Wallacea and their predecessors', in VN Misra & P Bellwood (eds), *Recent advances in Indo-Pacific prehistory: proceedings of the international symposium held at Poona, December 19–21 1978*, pp. 197–205, EJ Brill, Leiden.

Bender, B 1975, *Farming in prehistory*, J Baker, London.

Bender, B 1978, 'Gatherer-hunter to farmer: a social perspective', *World Archaeology*, vol. 10, no. 2, pp. 204–22.

Bender, B 1981 'Gatherer-hunter intensification', in A Sheridan & G Bailey (eds), *Economic Archaeology*, pp. 149–57, British Archaeological Reports, International Series 96, Oxford.

References

Bender, B 1985, 'Emergent tribal formations in the American mid-continent', *American Antiquity*, vol. 50, no. 1, pp. 52–62.

Bender, B 1989 'The roots of inequality', in D Miller, M Rowlands & C Tilley (eds), *Domination and resistance*, pp. 83–95, Unwin Hyman, London.

Bender, B 1998, *Stonehenge: making space*, Berg, Oxford.

Bender, B, Hamilton, S & Tilley, C 1997, 'Leskernick: stone worlds; alternative narratives; nested landscapes', in *Proceedings of the Prehistoric Society*, 63, pp. 147–78.

Bender, B, Hamilton, S & Tilley, C 2005, *Stone worlds: prehistoric and contemporary landscapes of Leskernick on Bodmin Moor*, University College London Press, London.

Benjamin, W 1969, 'Unpacking my library', in H Arendt (ed.), *Illuminations: Walter Benjamin — essays and reflections*, Schocken Books, New York.

Berndt, RM & Berndt, CH 1964, *The World of the First Australians*, Ure Smith, Sydney.

Berndt, R 1970, 'The sacred site: the Western Arnhem Land example', *Australian Aboriginal Studies*, 29.

Berndt, R & Berndt, C 1993, *A world that was: the Yaraldi of the Murray River and the lakes, South Australia*, Melbourne University Press.

Bhabha, H 1994, *The location of culture*, Routledge, London.

Bicchieri, G (ed.) 1972, *Hunters and gatherers today: a socioeconomic study of eleven such cultures in the twentieth century*, Holt, Rinehart & Winston, New York.

Biernoff, D 1974, 'Safe and dangerous places', in LR Hiatt (ed.), *Australian Aboriginal concepts*, pp. 93–105, AIAS, Canberra.

Binford, LR 1962, 'Archaeology as anthropology', *American Antiquity*, 28, pp. 217–35.

Binford, LR 1968, 'Post-Pleistocene adaptations', in SR Binford & L Binford (eds), *New perspectives in archaeology*, pp. 314–41. Aldine, Chicago.

Binford, LR 1971, 'Mortuary practices: their study and their potential', in JA Brown (ed.), *Approaches to the social dimensions of mortuary practices: memoirs society for American archaeology*, 25, pp. 6–29.

Binford, LR 1982, 'The archaeology of place', *Journal of Anthropological Archaeology*, 1, pp. 5–31.

Binford, LR 1980, 'Willow smoke and dogs' tails: hunter-gatherer settlement systems and archaeological site formation', *American Antiquity*, vol. 45, no. 1, pp. 4–20.

Binford, LR 1983, *In pursuit of the past: decoding the archaeological record*, Thames & Hudson, Berlin.

Binford, LR 2001, *Constructing frames of reference: an analytical method for archaeological theory building using hunting and gathering and environmental data sets*, The University of California Press, Berkeley.

Binford, LR & Binford SR (eds) 1968, *New perspectives in archaeology*, Aldine, Chicago.

Binford, SR 1968, 'Variability and change in the near-eastern Mousterian of Levallois facies', in LR Binford & SR Binford (eds), *New perspectives in archaeology*, pp. 49–60, Aldine, Chicago.

Bird, BF & Monahan, CM 1995, 'Death, mortuary ritual, and Natufian social structure', *Journal of Anthropological Archaeology*, 14, pp. 251–87.

Bird, C & Frankel, D 1991a, 'Chronology and explanation in western Victoria and south-east South Australia', *Archaeology in Oceania*, 26, pp. 1–16.

Bird, CFM & Frankel, D 1991b, 'Problems in constructing a prehistoric regional sequence: Holocene south-east Australia', *World Archaeology*, vol. 23, no. 2, pp. 179–92.

Bird, DW 1996, 'Intertidal foraging strategies among the Meriam of the Torres Strait Islands, Australia: an evolutionary ecological approach to the ethnoarchaeology of tropical marine subsistence', unpublished PhD thesis, University of California, Davis.

Bird, DW & Bliege Bird, RB 1997, 'Contemporary shellfish gathering among the Meriam of the Torres Strait Islands, Australia: testing of a central place foraging model', *Journal of Archaeological Science*, 24, pp. 39–63.

Bird, DW & Bliege Bird, RB 2000, 'The ethnoarchaeology of juvenile foraging: shellfishing strategies among Meriam children', *Journal of Anthropological Archaeology*, 19, pp. 461–76.

Bird, DW & Bliege Bird, R in press, 'Mardu children's hunting strategies in the Western Desert, Australia', in BS Hewlett & ME Lamb (eds), *Culture, ecology and psychology of hunter-gatherer children*, Aldine de Gruyter, New York.

Birdsell, JB 1953, 'Some environmental and cultural factors influencing the structuring of Australian Aboriginal populations', *American Naturalist*, 87, pp. 171–207.

Birdsell, JB 1957, 'Some population problems involving Pleistocene man, *Cold Spring Harbor Symposia on Quantitative Biology*, 22, pp. 47–69.

Birdsell, JB 1977, 'The recalibration of a paradigm for the first peopling of Greater Australia', in J Allen, J Golson & R Jones (eds), *Sunda and Sahul: prehistoric studies in South-East Asia, Melanesia and Australia*, pp. 113–67, Academic Press, London.

Birdsell, JB 1993, *Microevolutionary patterns in Aboriginal Australia: a gradient analysis of clines*, Oxford University Press, Oxford.

Black, L 1942, 'Cylcons: mystery stones of the Darling River Valley, unpublished document held by J Bradley.

Blackwood, R & Simpson, KNG 1973, 'Attitudes of Aboriginal skeletons excavated in the Murray Valley region between Mildura and Renmark', *Memoirs of the National Museum of Victoria*, 34, pp. 99–150.

Blainey, G 1983, *Triumph of the nomads: a history of ancient Australia*, Sun Books, Melbourne.

Blaut, JM 1993, *The colonizer's model of the world*, Guilford, New York.

Bliege Bird, R & Bird, DW 2002, 'Constraints of knowing or constraints on growing? Fishing and collecting among the children of Mer', *Human Nature*, 13, pp. 239–68.

Bliege Bird, R, Bird, D & Smith, EA 2000 'A report by the Meriam Ethnographic Research Project in ecological anthropology: the social, cultural, ecological and economic significance of Meriam traditional marine subsistence: implications for an indigenous sea rights claim', unpublished report to the Mer Island Community Council, Mer, Qld.

Bliege Bird, R, Bird, DW, Smith, EA & Kushnick, G 2002, 'Risk and reciprocity in Meriam food sharing', *Evolution and Human Behavior*, 23, pp. 297–321.

Bliege Bird, RB 1996, 'The behavioral ecology of the sexual division of labor among the Meriam of the Torres Strait: gathering, fishing and hunting in a marine ecosystem', unpublished PhD Thesis, University of California, Davis.

Boado, FC & Vazquez, VV 2000, 'Monumentalizing landscape: from present perception to the past meaning of Galician megalithism (north-west Iberian Peninsula)', *European Journal of Archaeology*, 3, pp. 188–216.

Bond, GC & Gilliam, A (eds) 1994, *Social construction of the past: representation as power*, Routledge, London.

Border, A 1999, 'Aboriginal settlement of offshore islands in the southern Great Barrier Reef province, central Queensland', *Australian coastal archaeology*, pp. 129–39, Research papers in archaeology and natural history 31, ANH Publications, Canberra.

Boserup, E 1965, *The conditions of agricultural growth: the economics of agrarian change under population pressure*, Aldine, Chicago.

Bowdler, S 1979, 'Hunter Hill, Hunter Island', unpublished PhD thesis, ANU, Canberra.

Bowdler, S 1981 'Hunters in the highlands: Aboriginal adaptations in the Eastern Australian Uplands', *Archaeology in Oceania*, vol. 16, no. 2, pp. 99–111.

Bowdler, S 1993, 'Views of the past in Australian prehistory', *A community of culture: the people and prehistory of the Pacific*, pp. 123–38, Occasional papers in prehistory 21, ANU, Canberra.

Bowdler, S 1994, 'Permeating the bamboo curtain: Fred McCarthy's interesting questions', in M Sullivan, S Brockwell & A Webb (eds), *Archaeology in the north: proceedings of the 1993 Australian Archaeological Association Conference*, pp. 30–9, NARU, Darwin.

Bowdler, S 1997, 'Building on each other's myths: archaeology and linguistics in Australia', in P McConvell & N Evans (eds), *Archaeology and linguistics: Aboriginal Australia in a global perspective*, pp. 17–26, Oxford University Press, Melbourne.

Bowdler, S & Lourandos, H 1982, 'Both sides of Bass Strait', in S Bowdler (ed.), *Coastal archaeology in eastern Australia*, pp. 16–28, ANU, Canberra.

Bowdler, S & O'Connor, S 1991, 'The dating of the Australian Small Tool Tradition, with new evidence from the Kimberley, WA', *Australian Aboriginal Studies*, 1, pp. 53–62.

Bowler, J 1982, 'Australian salt lakes: a palaeohydrological approach', *Hydrobiologia*, 82, pp. 431–44.

Bowler, JM, Thorne, AG & Polach, H 1972, 'Pleistocene man in Australia: age and significance of the Mungo skeleton', *Nature*, 240, pp. 48–50.

Bowler, JM, Jones, R, Allen, HH, Thorne, AG 1970, 'Pleistocene human remains from Australia: a living site and human cremation from Lake Mungo, western New South Wales', *World Archaeology*, 2, pp. 39–60.

Bowler, PJ 1992, 'From "savage" to "primitive": Victorian evolutionism and the interpretation of marginalised peoples', *Antiquity*, 66, pp. 721–9.

Bowman, DM 1998, 'Tansley Review 101: The impact of Aboriginal landscape burning on the Australian biota', *New Phytologist*, 140, pp. 385–410.

Bradley, JJ 1980–98, 'Field notes: includes translations (by the author) of texts and recordings of Yanyuwa and Garrwa speakers', unpublished field notes held by JJ Bradley.

Bradley, J 1988, *Yanyuwa country: the Yanyuwa people of Borroloola tell the history of their land*, Greenhouse Publications, Richmond.
Bradley, J 1991, '"Li-Maramaranja": The Yanyuwa hunters of marine animals in the Sir Edward Pellew Group, NT', *Records of the South Australia Museum*, vol.25, no. 1, 91–110.
Bradley, J 1997, '*Li-anthawirriyarra*, people of the sea: Yanyuwa relations with their maritime environment', unpublished PhD thesis, Northern Territory University, Darwin.
Bradley, J, Harvey, R, & Norman, D 1997 'Burning for the ancestors, burning for us: a case study from the south west Gulf of Carpentaria', in B Mcaige, R Williams & W Waggit (eds), *Bushfire '97: proceedings of the Australian Bushfire Conference 8–10 July 1997*, CSRIO Tropical Ecosystems, Darwin.
Bradley, J, with Kirton, J and the Yanyuwa Community 1992, 'Yanyuwa Wuka: language from Yanyuwa country, a Yanyuwa dictionary and cultural resource', unpublished document held by JJ Bradley.
Bradley, R 2003, 'Seeing things: perception, experience and the constraints of excavation', *Journal of Social Archaeology*, 3, pp. 151–68.
Brady, L forthcoming, 'The rock art of Torres Strait', unpublished PhD thesis, Monash University, Clayton.
Brady, LM, David, B, Manas, L and the Mualgal (Torres Strait Islanders) Corporation 2003, 'Community archaeology and oral tradition: commemorating and teaching cultural awareness on Mua Island, Torres Strait', *The Australian Journal of Indigenous Education*, 31, pp. 41–9.
Breen, S 2003, 'Re-inventing social evolution', in R Manne (ed.), *Whitewash: on Keith Windschuttle's fabrication of Aboriginal history*, pp. 139–59, Black Inc, Melbourne.
Brisbin, IL, Coppinger, RP, Feinstein, MH, Austad, S & Mayer, JJ 1994, 'The New Guinea singing dog: taxonomy, captive studies and conservation priorities', *Science in New Guinea*, vol. 20, no. 1, pp. 27–38.
Brock, J 1988 *Top End native plants*, J Brock, Darwin.
Brockett, WE 1836, *Narrative of a voyage from Sydney to Torres Straits, in search of the survivors of the Charles Eaton in his Majesty's Colonial Schooner Isabella, CM Lewis Commander*, Henry Bull, Sydney.
Builth, H 2000, 'The connection between the Gunditjmara Aboriginal people and their environment: the case for complex hunter-gatherers in Australia', in G Moore, J Hunt & L Trevillion (eds), *Environment-behaviour research on the Pacific Rim*, pp. 197–212, Faculty of Architecture, The University of Sydney.
Builth, H 2002, 'The archaeology and socioeconomy of the Gunditjmara: a landscape analysis from south-west Victoria, Australia', unpublished PhD thesis, Flinders University, Adelaide.
Builth, H, 2004, 'Mt Eccles lava flow and the Gunditjamara connection: a landform for all seasons', *Proceedings of the Royal Society of Victoria*, 116, pp. 165–84.
Builth, H in press, 'Gunditjmara environmental management: the development of a fisher-gatherer-hunter society in temperate Australia', in J Kim, C Grier & J Uchiyama (eds), *Beyond affluent foragers*, Oxbow Books, Oxford.
Buku-Larrngay Mulka Centre 1999, *Saltwater: Yirrkala bark paintings of sea country – recognising indigenous sea rights*, Buku-Larrngay Mulka Centre in association with Jennifer Isaacs Publishing, Neutral Bay.

References

Bulmer, S 2001, 'Lapita dogs and singing dogs and the history of the dog in New Guinea', in GR Clarke, AJ Anderson & T Vunidilo (eds), *The archaeology of lapita dispersal in Oceania*, pp. 183–201, Terra Australis 17, Pandanus Books, Canberra.

Bureau of Meteorology 2000, *Climate data: Australia*, Climate Services, Bureau of Meteorology, Kent Town.

Busby, JR, 1991, 'BIOCLIM-a bioclimatic analysis and prediction system', in CR Margules & MP Austin (eds), *Nature conservation: cost-effective biological surveys and data analysis*, pp. 64–8, CSIRO, Melbourne.

Byrne, D 1996, 'Deep nation: Australia's acquisition of an indigenous past', *Aboriginal History*, 20, pp. 82–107.

Campbell, J 1984, 'Extending the archaeological frontier: a review of work on the prehistory of north Queensland', *Queensland Archaeological Research*, 1, pp. 173–84.

Cane, S 1989, 'Australian Aboriginal seed grinding and its archaeological record: a case study from the Western Desert', in DR Harris & GC Hillman (eds), *Foraging and farming: the evolution of plant exploitation*, pp. 99–119, Unwin Hyman, London.

Carter, M 2002a, 'Recent results of excavations on the Murray Islands, eastern Torres Strait and implications for early links with New Guinea: bridge and barrier revisited', *Tempus*, 7, pp. 1–10.

Carter, M 2002b, 'The Murray Islands Archaeological Project: results of recent archaeological analyses', *Australian Aboriginal Studies*, 2, pp. 75–7.

Carter, M 2004, 'North of the Cape and south of the Fly: the archaeology of settlement and subsistence on the Murray Islands, eastern Torres Strait', unpublished PhD thesis, James Cook University, Townsville.

Carter, M, Veth, P, Barham, A, Bird, D, O'Connor, S & Bird, R 2004a, 'Archaeology of the Murray Islands, Torres Strait: implications for a regional prehistory', in R Davis (ed.), *Woven histories, dancing lives: Torres Strait Islander identity, culture and history*, pp. 234–58, Aboriginal Studies Press, Canberra.

Carter, M, Barham, A, Veth, P, Bird, D, O'Connor, S & Bird, R 2004b, 'The Meriam Islands Archaeological Project: excavations on Mer and Dauar, eastern Torres Strait', *Torres Strait archaeology and material culture*: Memoirs of the Queensland Museum,: Cultural heritage series, vol. 3, no. 1, pp. 163–82.

Casey, E 1993, *Getting back into place: toward a renewed understanding of the place-world*, Indiana University Press, Bloomington.

Casey, E 1996, 'How to get from space to place in a fairly short stretch of time: phenomenological prolegomena', in S Feld & K Basso (eds), *Senses of place*, pp. 13–52, School of American Research Press, Santa Fe.

Casti, JL 1995, *Complexification: explaining a paradoxical world through the science of surprise*, Harper Collins, New York.

Chandarasekaran, R 2000, 'Australia's "Stolen Generation" seeks payback: Aborigines want apology for kidnappings, *The Washington Post* (6 July), p. A01.

Chapman, R, Kinnes, I & Randsborg, K (eds) 1981, *The archaeology of death*, Cambridge University Press, Cambridge.

Chapman, V 1986, 'Inter-site variability in south-west Sulawesi: results of the 1969 Australian–Indonesian Archaeological Expedition', *Archaeology in Oceania*, 21, pp. 76–84.

Chase, A 1989a, 'Domestication and domiculture in northern Australia: a social perspective', in DR Harris & GC Hillman (eds), *Foraging and farming: the evolution of plant exploitation*, pp. 42–54, Unwin Hyman, London.

Chase, A 1989b, 'Perceptions of the past among north Queensland Aboriginal people: the intrusion of Europeans and consequent social change', in R Layton (ed), *Who needs the past: indigenous values and archaeology*, Unwin, London.

Chase, AK & Sutton, PJ 1981, 'Hunter-gatherers in a rich environment: Aboriginal coastal exploitation in Cape York Peninsula', in A Keast (ed.), *Ecological biogeography of Australia*, pp. 1817–52, W Junk, The Hague.

Chatters, JC 1987, 'Hunter-gatherer adaptations and assemblage structure', *Journal of Anthropological Archaeology*, 6, pp. 336–75.

Childe, VG 1925, *The dawn of European civilisation*, Routledge, London.

Chippindale, C 1989, 'The invention of words for the idea of prehistory', *Proceedings of the Prehistoric Society*, 54, pp. 303–14.

Chivas AR, DeDeckker, P & Shelley, PMG 1985, 'Strontium content of ostracods indicates lacustrine palaeosalinity', *Nature*, 316, pp. 251–3.

Clark, RL 1982, 'Point count estimation of charcoal in pollen preparations and thin sections of sediments', *Pollen et Spores*, 24, pp. 523–35.

Clarke, DL 1978 (1968), *Analytical archaeology*, Methuen & Co Ltd, London.

Clarke, WC 1971, *Place and people: an ecology of a New Guinea community*, University of California Press, Berkeley.

Cohen, MN & Armelagos, GJ (eds) 1984a, *Paleopathology at the origins of agriculture*, Academic Press, New York.

Cohen, MN & Armelagos, GJ 1984b, 'Disease and death at Dr Dickson's mounds', *Natural History*, 9, pp. 12–18.

Colfelt, D 1995, *The Whitsundays book*, Windward Publications Pty Ltd, Sydney.

Conkey, MW 1980, 'The identification of hunter-gatherer aggregation sites: the case of Altimira', *Current Anthropology*, vol. 21, no. 5, pp. 609–30.

Conkey, MW 1990, 'Experimenting with style in archaeology: some historical and theoretical issues', in MW Conkey & CA Hastorf (eds), *The uses of style in Archaeology*, pp. 5–17, Cambridge University Press, Cambridge.

Conkey, MW & Spector, J 1984, 'Archaeology and the study of gender', in M Schiffer (ed.), *Advances in archaeological method and theory* 7, pp.1–38, Academic Press, London.

Corbett, L 1995, *The dingo in Australia and Asia*, University of New South Wales Press, Sydney.

Cosgrove, R 1995, 'The illusion of riches: scale, resolution and explanation in Tasmanian Pleistocene human behaviour', *Tempus Reparatum*, BAR international series 608, Oxford.

Cosgrove, R, Allen, J & Marshall, B 1990, 'Palaeo-ecology and Pleistocene human occupation in south central Tasmania', *Antiquity*, 64, pp. 59–78.

Coutts, PJF 1982, 'Victoria archaeological survey activities report 1979–80', *Records of the Victorian Archaeological Survey*, 13, pp. 1–28, (Melbourne).

Coutts, PJF, Frank, RK & Hughes, PJ 1978, 'Aboriginal engineers of the Western District, Victoria', *Records of the Victorian Archaeological Survey* 7, (Melbourne).

References

Coutts, PJF, Henderson, P & Fullagar, RLK 1979, 'A preliminary investigation of Aboriginal mounds in north-western Victoria', *Records of the Victorian Archaeological Survey* 9, (Melbourne).

Creamer, H 1990, 'Aboriginal perceptions of the past: the implications for cultural heritage management in Australia', in P Gathercole & D Lowenthal (eds), *The politics of the past*, pp. 130–4, Routledge, London.

Cribb, R no date, 'Mounds for the ancestors: the ontology of shell mound accumulation in northern Australia', unpublished manuscript held by L Godwin.

Crowley, GM, Grindrod, J & Kershaw, AP 1994 'Modern pollen deposition in the tropical lowlands of northeast Queensland, Australia', *Review of Palaeobotany and Palynology*, 83, pp. 299–327.

Cundy, B 1985, 'The secondary use and reduction of cylindro-conical stone artefacts from the Northern Territory', *The Beagle*: Occasional papers of the Northern Territory Museum of Arts and Sciences, vol. 2, no. 1, pp. 115–27.

Curr, EM 1886, *The Australian race: its origin, languages, customs, place of landing in Australia, and the routes by which it spread itself over that continent*, in four volumes, John Ferres, Government Printer, Melbourne.

Dams, L 1985, 'Palaeolithic lithophones: descriptions and comparison', *Oxford Journal of Archaeology*, 4, pp. 31–46.

Daniel, G 1962, *The idea of prehistory*, Watts, London.

Darvill, T 2002, *The concise Oxford dictionary of archaeology*, Oxford University Press, Oxford.

Darvill, T & Malone, C 2003, *Megaliths from antiquity*, Antiquity, Cambridge.

David, B 1991, 'Fern Cave, rock art and social formations: rock art regionalisation and demographic changes in south-eastern Cape York Peninsula', *Archaeology in Oceania*, 26, pp. 41–57.

David, B 2002, *Landscapes, rock art and the Dreaming: an archaeology of preunderstanding*, Leicester University Press, London.

David, B, Barbetti, M, Bekessy, R, Bekessy, L, Bultitude, R, Butler, D, Clarkson, C, Clarkson, J, Conn, C, Dredge, M, Eyre, T, Fullagar, R, Goodall, R, Hall, L, Head, J, Hua, Q, Ingram, G, Jones, R, Lawson, E, Lourandos, H, Loy, T, Macrokanis, C, McNiven, I, Murray, C, Ogleby, C, Osborne, M, Pole, M, Roberts, R, Schulz, M, Spate, A, Stanisic, J, Summerhayes, G, Taylor, C, Tuniz, C & Whittier, J 1996, 'The Ngarrabullgan Homeland Project: current research in Kuku Djungan country, north Queensland, *Australian Archaeology*, 43, pp. 32–6.

David, B & Chant, D 1995, 'Rock art and regionalisation in north Queensland prehistory', *Memoirs of the Queensland Museum*, vol. 37, no. 2, pp. 357–528.

David, B, Chant, D & Flood, J 1992, 'Jalijbang 2 and the distribution of pecked faces in Australia', *Memoirs of the Queensland Museum*, vol. 32, no. 1, pp. 61–77.

David, B & Cordell, J 1993, 'Cultural site mapping in the Mitchell River delta: stage 1', unpublished report to the Kowanyama Aboriginal Land and Resources Management Office, Kowanyama, undertaken through the Ethnographic Institute, Berkeley, USA.

David, B, Langton, M & McNiven, I 2002, 'Re-inventing the wheel: indigenous peoples and the master race in Philip Ruddock's "wheel" comments', *PAN: Philosophy, Activism, Nature*, 2, pp. 31–46.

David, B, Lecole, M, Lourandos, H, Baglioni Jnr, AJ & Flood, J 1999, 'Investigating relationships between motif forms, techniques and rock surfaces in north Australian rock art', *Australian Archaeology*, 48, pp. 16–22.

David, B & Lourandos, H 1997, '37,000 years and more in tropical Australia: investigating long-term archaeological trends in Cape York Peninsula', *Proceedings of the Prehistoric Society*, 63, pp. 1–23.

David, B & Lourandos, H 1998, 'Rock art and socio-demography in north-eastern Australian prehistory', *World Archaeology*, vol. 30, no. 2, pp. 193–219.

David, B & Lourandos, H 1999, 'Landscape as mind: land use, cultural space and change in north Queensland prehistory', *Quaternary International*, 59, pp. 107–23.

David, B & McNiven, IJ 2004, 'Western Torres Strait Cultural History Project: research design and initial results', *Torres Strait archaeology and material culture: Memoirs of the Queensland Museum*, Cultural heritage series, vol. 3, no. 1, pp. 199–208.

David, B, McNiven, I, Attenbrow, V, Flood, J & Collins, J 1994, 'Of Lightning Brothers and White Cockatoos: dating the antiquity of signifying systems in the Northern Territory, Australia', *Antiquity*, 68, pp. 241–51.

David, B, McNiven, I, Manas, L, Manas, J, Savage, S, Crouch, J, Neliman, G & Brady, L 2004a, 'Goba of Mua: archaeology working with oral tradition', *Antiquity*, 78, pp. 158–72.

David, B, McNiven, IJ, Mitchell, R, Orr, M, Haberle, S, Brady, L & Crouch, J 2004b, 'Badu 15 and the Papuan–Austronesian settlement of Torres Strait', *Archaeology in Oceania*, 39, pp. 65–78.

David, B, McNiven, I, Mura Badulgal (Torres Strait Islanders) Corporation Committee, Crouch, J & Brady, L 2004c, 'The Argan stone arrangement complex, Badu Island: initial results from Torres Strait', *Australian Archaeology*, 58, pp. 1–6.

David, B & Wilson, M 1999, 'Re-reading the landscape: place and identity in NE Australia during the late Holocene', *Cambridge Archaeological Journal*, vol. 9, no. 2, pp. 163–88.

David, B & Wilson, M (eds) 2002, *Inscribed landscapes: marking and making place*, University of Hawai'i Press, Honolulu.

Davidson, DS 1935, 'The chronology of Australian watercraft', *Journal of the Polynesian Society*, 44, pp. 1–16; 69–84; 137–52; 193–207.

Davidson, DS 1938, 'North-western Australia and the question of influence from the East Indies', *Journal of the American Oriental Society*, vol, 58, no. 1, pp. 61–80.

Davidson, I 1989, 'Is intensification a condition of the fisher-hunter-gatherer way of life?', *Archaeology in Oceania*, 24, pp. 75–8.

Davis, OK 1994, *Aspects of Archaeological Palynology: Methodology and Applications*, AASP contribution series 29, American Association of Stratigraphic Palynologists Foundation, Dallas.

Dawson, J 1881, *Australian Aborigines: the languages and customs of several tribes of Aborigines in the western district of Victoria, Australia*, George Robertson, Melbourne.

D'Costa, DM & Kershaw, AP 1997, 'An expanded pollen data base from south-eastern Australia and its potential for refinement of palaeoclimatic estimates', *Australian Journal of Botany*, 45, pp. 583–605.

de Latour, G 1876, *Brisbane Courier*, 29 November, no pages.

References

DeLyser, D 2001, 'When Less is More: Absence and Social Memory in a California Ghost Town', in P Adams, S Hoelscher and K Till (eds), *Textures of Place: Exploring Humanist Geographies*, pp. 24–40, University of Minnesota Press.

Denham, TP & Barton, H in press, 'The emergence of agriculture in New Guinea: continuity from pre-existing foraging practices' in DJ Kennett & B Winterhalder (eds), *Human behavioralecology and the origins of food production*, Smithsonian Institution Press, Washington.

Dimbleby, GW 1985, *The palynology of archaeological sites*, Academic Press, New York.

Dix, W 1977, 'Facial representations in Pilbara rock engravings' in PJ Ucko (ed.), *Form in indigenous art*, pp. 277–85, AIAS, Canberra.

Dodson, JR & Mooney, SD 2002, 'An assessment of historic human impact on south-eastern Australian environmental systems, using late Holocene rates of environmental change', *Australian Journal of Botany*, 50, pp. 455–64

Dodson, J, Fullagar, R & Head, L 1992, 'Dynamics of environment and people in the forested crescents of temperate Australia', in J Dodson (ed.), *The naive lands: prehistory and environmental change in Australia and the southwest Pacific*, pp. 115–59, Longman Cheshire, Melbourne.

Dortch, CE 1977, 'Early and late stone industrial phases in Western Australia', in RVS Wright (ed.), *Stone tools as cultural markers: change, evolution and complexity*, pp. 104–32, AIAS, Canberra.

Dortch, CE 1981, 'Recognition of indigenous development and external diffusion in Australian prehistory', *Australian Archaeology*, 12, pp. 27–31.

Downey, B & Frankel, D 1992, 'Radiocarbon and thermoluminescence dating of a central Murray mound', *The Artefact*, 15, pp. 31–5.

Dwyer, PD & Minnegal, M 1991, 'Hunting in lowland, tropical rain forest: towards a model of non-agricultural subsistence', *Human Ecology*, 19, pp. 187–212.

Edwards, R 1966, 'Comparative study of rock engravings in south and central Australia', *Proceedings of the Royal Society of South Australia*, 90, pp. 33–8.

Elkin, AP 1938–40, 'Kinship in South Australia', *Oceania*, vol. 8, no. 4, pp. 419–52; vol. 9, no. 1, pp. 41–78; vol. 10, no. 2, pp. 196–234; vol. 10, no. 3, pp. 295–349; vol. 10, no. 4, pp. 369–88.

Elkin, AP 1945, *Aboriginal men of high degree: initiation and sorcery in the world's oldest tradition*, Australasian Publishing Company, Sydney.

Ellen, RF 1982, *Environment, subsistence, and system: the ecology of small-scale social formations*, Cambridge University Press, Cambridge.

Elliot Smith, G 1930, *Human history*, Jonathon Cape, London.

Etheridge, R 1916, 'The cylindro-conical and cornute stone implements of western New South Wales and their significance', *Memoirs of the Geological Society of New South Wales*, Ethnological series 2, Government Printers, Sydney.

Eyre, JE 1845, *Journal of expeditions of discovery into central Australia and overland from Adelaide to King George's Sound*, vol. II, Boone, London.

Eze, EC (ed) 1997, *Race and the enlightenment: a reader*, Blackwell, Oxford.

Fabian, J 1983, *Time and the other: how anthropology makes its object*, Columbia University Press, New York.

Fagan, B 1995, *Ancient North America: the archaeology of a continent*, Thames & Hudson, London.

Fagan, B 1999, *Floods, famines, and emperors: El Niño and the fate of civilizations*, Basic Books, New York.

Faris, JC 1975, 'Social evolution, population and production', in S Polgar (ed), *Population, ecology and social evolution*, pp. 235–71. Mouton, The Hague.

Feld, S 1996, 'Waterfalls of song: an acoustemology of place resounding in Bosavi, Papua New Guinea', in S Feld & K Basso (eds), *Senses of place*, pp. 91–137, School of American Research Press, Santa Fe.

Finlayson, J 2001, 'Anthropology's contribution to public policy formulation: the imagined other?', *Australian Aboriginal Studies*, 2, pp. 18–26.

Fisher, G & Loren, D 2003, 'Embodying identity in archaeology', *Cambridge Archaeological Journal*, 13, pp. 225–30.

Fitzpatrick, J, Cordell, J & McNiven, IJ 1998, 'Torres Strait Culture Site Documentation Project: final draft report', unpublished report prepared for the Island Coordinating Council, Thursday Island.

Flannery, KV 1973, 'The origins of agriculture', *Annual Review of Anthropology*, 2, pp. 271–310.

Flannery, TF 1994, *The future eaters: an ecological history of the Australasian lands and people*, Reed Books, Chatswood.

Flenniken, JJ & White, JP 1985, 'Australian flaked stone tools: a technological perspective', *Records of the Australian Museum*, 36, pp. 131–51.

Flinders, M 1814, *A voyage to Terra Australis, undertaken for the purpose of completing the discovery of that vast country, and prosecuted in the years 1802, 1802 and 1803 in His Majesty's Ship the Investigator etc.*, G & W Nicol, London.

Flood, J 1983, *Archaeology of the Dreamtime: the story of Australia and her people*, Collins, Sydney.

Flood, JM 1989, *Archaeology of the Dreamtime*, 2nd edn, rev., Collins, Sydney.

Flood, JM 1995, *Archaeology of the Dreamtime*, 3rd edn, rev., Harper Collins, Sydney.

Flood, JM 1999, *Archaeology of the Dreamtime*, 4th edn, rev., Harper Collins, Sydney.

Ford, RI 1985, 'The processes of plant production in prehistoric North America', *Prehistoric Plant Production in North America*, pp. 1–18. Anthropological paper 75, Museum of Anthropology, University of Michigan, Ann Arbor.

Frankel, D 1993, 'Pleistocene chronological structures and explanations: a challenge', in MA Smith, M Spriggs & B Fankhauser (eds), *Sahul in review: Pleistocene archaeology in Australia, New Guinea and Island Melanesia*, pp. 24–33, Research School of Pacific Studies, ANU, Canberra.

Frankel, D 1995, 'The Australian transition: real and perceived boundaries', *Antiquity*, vol. 69, special no. 265, pp. 649–55.

Franklin, N 1991, 'Rock art and prehistory: explorations of the Panaramitee style', in P Bahn & A Rosenfeld (eds), *Rock art and prehistory*, pp. 120–35, Oxbow Monograph 10, Oxbow Books, Oxford.

Frederick, U 1997, 'Drawing in differences: changing social context of rock art production in Watarrka (Kings Canyon) National Park, central Australia', unpublished MA thesis, ANU, Canberra.

Frederick, U 1999, 'At the centre of it all: constructing contact through the rock art of Watarrka National Park, central Australia', *Archaeology in Oceania*, vol. 34, no. 3, pp. 132–44.

Frederick, U 2000, 'Keeping the land alive: changing social contexts of landscape and rock art production', in R Torrence & A Clarke (eds), *The archaeology of difference: negotiating cross-cultural engagements in Oceania*, pp. 300–30, Routledge, London.

Friedman, J 1974, 'Marxism, structuralism and vulgar materialism', *Man*, 9, pp. 444–69.

Frith, DW & Frith, CB 1995, *Cape York Peninsula: a natural history*, Reed Books, Chatswood.

Fullagar, R 1994, 'Traces of times past: stone artefacts into prehistory', *Australian Archaeology*, 39, pp. 63–73.

Fullagar, R 2004, 'Australian prehistoric archaeology: the last few years', *Before Farming*, 2004, no. 2, article 1.

Gadamer, H-G 1976, *Philosophical hermeneutics*, D Linge, ed. and trans, University of California Press, Berkeley.

Gadamer, H-G 1988, 'The problem of historical consciousness', in P Rabinow & WM Sullivan (eds), *Interpretive social science: a second look*, University of California Press, Berkeley.

Galloway, P 1992,'The unexamined habitus: direct historic analogy and the archaeology of the text', in JC Gardin & CS Peebles (eds), *Representations in archaeology*, pp. 178–95, Indiana University Press, Bloomington.

Galt-Smith, B 1997, 'Motives for motifs: identifying aggregation and dispersion settlement patterns in the rock art assemblages of Central Australia', unpublished BA (Hons) thesis, University of New England, Armidale.

Garnett, ST & Jackes, BR 1983, 'Vegetation of Badu Island, Torres Strait', *Queensland Naturalist*, 24, pp. 40–52.

Gathercole, P & Lowenthal, D (eds) 1990, *The politics of the past*, Routledge, London

Gelder, K & JM Jacobs 1998, *Uncanny Australia: sacredness and identity in a postcolonial nation*, Melbourne University Press, Carlton.

Gell-Mann, M 1994, *The quark and the jaguar: adventures in the simple and the complex*, Little, Brown & Co, London.

Genever, M, Grindrod, J & Barker, B 2003, 'Holocene palynology of Whitehaven Swamp, Whitsunday Island, Queensland, and implications for the regional archaeological record', *Palaeogeography, Palaeoclimatology, Palaeoecology*, 201, pp. 141–56.

Gero JM 1995, 'Railroading epistemology, palaeoindians and women', in I Hodder, M Shanks, A Alexandri, V Buchli, J Carman, J Last & G Lucas (eds), *Interpreting archaeology*, pp. 175–8, Routledge, London.

Ghaleb, B 1990, 'An ethnographic study of Mabuiag Island, Torres Strait, northern Queensland', unpublished PhD thesis, Institute of Archaeology, University College London, London.

Gibbs, M & Veth, P 2002, 'Ritual engines and the archaeology of territorial ascendancy', in S. Ulm, C. Westcott, J. Reid, A. Ross, I. Lilley, J. Pragnell and L. Kirkwood (eds) Barriers, Borders, Boundaries: Proceedings of the 2001 Australian Archaeological Association Annual Conference, pp. 11–19, *Tempus* 7, Anthropology Museum, the University of Queensland, Brisbane.

Gilchrist, R 1994, *Gender and material culture: the archaeology of religious women*, Routledge, London.

Glover, I 1976, 'Ulu Leang Cave, Maros: a preliminary sequence of post-Pleistocene cultural development in south Sulawesi', *Archipel*, 11, pp. 113–54.

Glover, I 1978, 'Survey and excavation in the Maros district, south Sulawesi, Indonesia: the 1975 field season', *Indo-Pacific Prehistory Association Bulletin*, 1, pp. 60–103.

Glover, IC & Presland, G 1985, 'Microliths in Indonesian flaked stone industries', in VN Misra & P Bellwood (eds), *Recent advances in Indo-Pacific prehistory: proceedings of the international symposium held at Poona, December 19–21, 1978*, pp. 185–95, EJ Brill, Leiden.

Godelier, M 1975 'Modes of production, kinship and demographic structure', in M Bloch (ed), *Marxist analyses and social anthropology*, pp. 3–27, Malaby Press, London.

Godelier, M 1977, *Perspectives in Marxist anthropology*, Cambridge University Press, Cambridge.

Godfrey, M 1983 'Historical sources as aids to archaeological interpretation: examples from Discovery Bay, Victoria', *The Artefact*, vol. 8, nos. 1–2, pp. 55–60.

Godfrey, MCS 1989, 'Shell midden chronology in south-western Victoria: reflections on change in prehistoric population and subsistence', *Archaeology in Oceania*, 24, pp. 65–9.

Gollan, K 1984, 'The Australian dingo: in the shadow of man', in M Archer & G Clayton (eds), *Vertebrate zoogeography and evolution in Australasia*, pp. 921–7, Hesperian Press, Perth.

Gollan, K 1985, 'Prehistoric dogs in Australia: an Indian origin?', in VN Misra & P Bellwood (eds), *Recent advances in Indo-Pacific prehistory: proceedings of the international symposium held at Poona, December 19–21, 1978*, pp. 439–43. EJ Brill, Leiden.

Golson, J 1972, 'Land connections, sea barriers and the relationship of Australian and New Guinea prehistory', in D Walker (ed.), *Bridge and barrier: the natural and cultural history of Torres Strait*, pp. 375–98 ANU, Canberra.

Golson, J 1977, 'No room at the top: agricultural intensification in the New Guinea highlands', in J Allen, J Golson & R Jones (eds), *Sunda and Sahul: prehistoric studies in South-East Asia, Melanesia and Australia*, pp. 601–38, Academic Press, London.

Golson, J 1977, *The ladder of social evolution: archaeology and the bottom rungs*, The University of Sydney Press.

Golson, J & Gardner, D 1990, 'Agriculture and sociopolitical organisation in New Guinea Highlands prehistory', *Annual Review of Anthropology*, 19, pp. 395–417.

Gorecki, P 1986, 'Human occupation and agricultural development in the Papua New Guinea Highlands', *Mountain Research and Development*, 6, pp. 159–66.

Gorecki, P, Grant, M, O'Connor, S & Veth, P 1997, 'The morphology, function and antiquity of grinding implements in Northern Australia', *Archaeology in Oceania*, 32, pp. 141–50.

Gosden, C 1994, *Social being and time*, Blackwell, Oxford.

Gosden, C & Head, L 1999, 'Different histories: a common inheritance for Papua New Guinea and Australia?', in C Gosden & J Hather (eds), *The prehistory of food: appetites for change*, pp. 232–51, Routledge, London.

Gould, RA 1969a 'Puntutjarpa Rockshelter: a reply to Messrs Glover and Lampert', *Archaeology and Physical Anthropology in Oceania*, 4, pp. 229–37.

Gould, RA 1969b, *Yiwara: foragers of the Australian desert*, Collins, London.

Gould, RA 1977, 'Puntutjarpa Rockshelter and the Australian desert culture', *Anthropological Papers of the American Museum of Natural History*, 54.

Gould, RA 1980, *Living archaeology*, Cambridge University Press, Cambridge.

Gould, RA 1991, Arid land foraging as seen from Australia: adaptive models and behavioural realities. *Oceania* 62, pp. 12–33.

Gould, RA, O'Connor, S & Veth, P 2002, 'Bones of contention: a reply to Walshe', *Archaeology in Oceania*, 37, pp. 96–101.

Graves-Brown, P, Jones, S & Gamble, C (eds) 1996, *Cultural identity and archaeology: the construction of European communities*, Routledge, London.

Grayson, DK 1983, *The establishment of human antiquity*, Academic Press, New York.

Grimm EC & Jacobson, GL 1992, 'Fossil-pollen evidence for abrupt climate changes during the past 18,000 years in eastern North America', *Climate Dynamics*, 6, pp. 179–84

Grindrod, J, Moss, P & van der Kaars, S 1999, 'Late Quaternary cycles of mangrove development and decline on the north Australian continental shelf', *Journal of Quaternary Science*, 14, pp. 465–70.

Groube, LM 1993, 'Contradictions and malaria in Melanesian and Australian prehistory', *A Community of Culture: The People and Prehistory of the Pacific*, pp. 164–86, Occasional papers in prehistory 21, ANU, Canberra.

Guddemi, P 1992, 'When horticulturalists are like hunter-gatherers: the Sawiyano of Papua New Guinea', *Ethnology*, 31, pp. 303–14.

Gunn, RG 1995, 'Regional patterning in the Aboriginal rock art of central Australia: a preliminary report', *Rock Art Research*, 12, pp. 117–27.

Gunn, RG 2000, 'Spencer and Gillen's contribution to Australian rock art studies', *Rock Art Research*, vol. 17, no. 1, pp. 56–64.

Haberle, SG 2003, 'The emergence of an agricultural landscape in the highlands of New Guinea', *Archaeology in Oceania*, 38, pp. 149–58.

Haberle, SG & Chepstow-Lusty, A 2000 '*Can climate influence cultural development? A view through time*', Environment and History, 6, pp. 349–69.

Haberle, SG & David, B 2004 'Climates of change: human dimensions of Holocene environmental change in low latitudes of the PEPII transect', *Quaternary International*, 118–19, pp. 165–79.

Haberle, SG, Hope, GS & van der Kaars, S 2001, 'Biomass burning in Indonesia and Papua New Guinea: natural and human induced fire events in the fossil record', *Palaeogeography, Palaeoclimatology, Palaeoecology*, 171, pp. 259–68.

Habu, J & Fitzhugh, B (eds) 2002, *Beyond foraging and collecting: evolutionary change in hunter-gatherer settlement systems*, Kluwer Academic/Plenum, New York.

Haddon, AC 1890, 'The ethnography of the Western Tribe of Torres Strait', *Journal of the Anthropological Institute of Great Britain and Ireland*, 19, pp. 297–440.

Haddon, AC 1900, 'A classification of the stone clubs of British New Guinea', *Journal of the Anthropological Institute of Great Britain and Ireland*, 30, pp. 221–50.

Haddon, AC 1901, *Reports on the Cambridge Anthropological Expedition to Torres Straits: vol. 2, physiology and psychology*, Cambridge University Press, Cambridge.

Haddon, AC 1904, *Reports on the Cambridge Anthropological Expedition to Torres Straits: col. 5, sociology and magic of the Western Islanders*, Cambridge University Press, Cambridge.

Haddon, AC 1908, *Reports on the Cambridge Anthropological Expedition to Torres Straits: vol. 6, sociology and magic of the Eastern Islanders*, Cambridge University Press, Cambridge.

Haddon, AC 1912, *Reports on the Cambridge Anthropological Expedition to Torres Straits: vol. 4, arts and crafts*, Cambridge University Press, Cambridge.

Haddon, AC 1935, *Reports on the Cambridge Anthropological Expedition to Torres Straits: vol. 1, general ethnography*, Cambridge University Press, Cambridge.

Hafner, D 1999, 'Feelings in the heart: Aboriginal experience of land, emotion, and kinship in Cape York Peninsula', unpublished PhD thesis, University of Queensland, St Lucia.

Haglund, L 1976, *The Broadbeach Aboriginal burial ground: an archaeological analysis*, University of Queensland Press, St Lucia.

Hale, HM & Tindale, NB 1930, 'Notes on some human remains in the lower Murray Valley, South Australia', *Records of the South Australian Museum*, 4, pp. 145–218.

Hallam, S 1975 *Fire and hearth: a study of Aboriginal usage and European usurpation in south-western Australia*, AIAS, Canberra.

Hallam, S 1977, 'Topographic archaeology and artefactual evidence', in RVS Wright (ed), *Stone tools as cultural markers: change, evolution and complexity*, pp. 169–77, AIAS, Canberra.

Hallam, S 1985, 'Microlithic industries in Western Australia: some aspects', in VN Misra & P Bellwood(eds), *Recent advances in Indo-Pacific prehistory*, pp. 219–29, Oxford & IBH Publishing, New Dehli.

Hamilakis, Y 2002, 'Experience and corporeality: introduction', in Y Hamilakis, M Pluciennik & S Tarlow (eds), *Thinking through the body: archaeologies of corporeality*, pp 99–103, Kluwer Academic/Plenum Publishers, New York.

Hamilakis, Y, Pluciennik, M & Tarlow, S (eds) 2002, *Thinking through the body: archaeologies of corporeality*, Kluwer Academic/Plenum Publishers, New York.

Hamilton, A 1980, 'Dual social systems: technology, labour and women's secret rites in the eastern Western Desert of Australia', *Oceania*, 51, pp. 4–19.

Harney, W 1953, 'The munja palm', *Walkabout*, January 1953, pp. 42–4.

Harney, W 1959, *Tales from the Aborigines*, Robert Male, London.

Harney, W 1971, *Content to lie in the sun*, Rigby, Sydney.

Harris, DR 1975, 'Traditional patterns of plant-food procurement in the Cape York Peninsula and Torres Strait islands', unpublished fieldwork report, AIAS, Canberra.

Harris, DR 1976, 'Aboriginal use of plant foods in the Cape York Peninsula and Torres Strait Islands', *Newsletter*, 6, pp. 21–2, AIAS, Canberra.

Harris, DR 1977a, 'Alternative pathways towards agriculture', in CA Reed (ed.), *The origins of agriculture*, pp.179–243, Mouton, The Hague.

Harris, DR 1977b, 'Subsistence strategies across Torres Strait', in J Allen, J Golson & R Jones (eds), *Sunda and Sahul: prehistoric studies in South-East Asia, Melanesia and Australia*, pp. 421–63, Academic Press, London.

References

Harris, DR 1979, 'Foragers and farmers in the western Torres Strait Islands: an historical analysis of economic and spatial differentiation', in P Burnham & R Ellen (eds), *Social and economic systems*, pp. 75–109, Academic Press, London.

Harris, DR 1989, 'An evolutionary continuum of people–plant interaction', in DR Harris & GC Hillman (eds), *Foraging and farming: the evolution of plant exploitation*, pp. 11–26, Unwin Hyman, London.

Harris DR 1995 'Early agriculture in New Guinea and the Torres Strait divide', *Antiquity*, vol. 69, special no. 265, pp. 848–54.

Harris, DR & Hillman, GC (eds) 1989, *Foraging and farming: the evolution of plant exploitation*, Unwin Hyman, London.

Harris, M 1968, *The rise of anthropological theory: a history of theories of culture*, Harper Collins, New York.

Harris, M 1979, *Cultural materialism: the struggle for a science of culture*, Random House, New York.

Harrison, SP & Dodson, J 1993, 'Climates of Australia and New Guinea since 18,000 yr BP', in HE Wright, Kutzbach, JE, Webb, T, Ruddiman, WF, Street-Perrot, FA & Bartlein, PJ (eds), *Global climates since the last glacial maximum*, pp. 294–317, University of Minnesota Press, Minneapolis.

Harvey, A 1945, 'Food preservation among Australian tribes', *Mankind*, 3, pp. 191–2

Hayden, B 1977, *Palaeolithic reflections*, AIAS, Canberra.

Hayden, B 1996a, 'Thresholds of power in emergent complex societies', in J Arnold (ed), *Emergent complexity: the evolution of intermediate societies*, pp. 50–8, International Monographs in Prehistory, Ann Arbor.

Hayden, B 1996b, 'The world's longest-lived corporate group: lithic analysis reveals prehistoric social organization near Lillooet, British Columbia', *American Antiquity*, 61, pp. 341–56.

Head, L 1983, 'Environment as artefact: a geographic perspective on the Holocene occupation of south-western Victoria', *Archaeology in Oceania*, 18, pp. 73–80.

Head, L 1986, 'Palaeoecological contributions to Australian prehistory', *Archaeology in Oceania*, vol. 21, no. 2, pp. 121–9.

Head, L 1988, 'Holocene vegetation, fire and environmental history of the Discovery Bay region, south-western Victoria', *Australian Journal of Ecology*, 13, pp. 21–49.

Head, L 1989, 'Using palaeoecology to date Aboriginal fish-traps at Lake Condah, Victoria, *Archaeology in Oceania*, vol. 24, no. 3, pp. 110–15.

Head, L 1994, 'Landscapes socialised by fire: post-contact changes in Aboriginal fire use in northern Australia, and implications for prehistory', *Archaeology in Oceania*, 29, pp. 172–81.

Head, L 2000, *Second nature: the history and implications of Australia as Aboriginal landscape*, Syracuse University Press, Syracuse.

Head, L, D'Costa, DM & Edney, P 1991, 'Pleistocene dates for volcanic activity in western Victoria and implications for Aboriginal occupation', in MAJ Williams, P De Deckker and AP Kershaw (eds), *The Cainozoic in Australia: a reappraisal of the evidence*, pp. 302–8, Geological Society of Australia Special Publication 18.

Herle, A & Rouse, S 1998 (eds), *Cambridge and the Torres Strait: centenary essays on the 1898 anthropological expedition*, pp. 1–22, Cambridge University Press, Cambridge.

Hemming, S (ed.) 1994, *Troddin thru Raukkan, our home: Raukkan re-union 1994*, Raukkan Council & South Australian Museum, Adelaide.

Hemming, S 2000, 'Hindmarsh Island (Kumarangk): challenging Australian mythologies', in S Kleinert & M Neale (eds), *The Oxford companion to Aboriginal art and culture*, pp. 441–4, Oxford University Press, Oxford.

Hemming, S, Jones, PG & Clarke, PA (eds) 1989, Ngurunderi: an Aboriginal Dreaming, South Australian Museum, Adelaide.

Hiatt, B 1967, 'The food quest and the economy of the Tasmanian Aborigines', *Oceania*, 38, pp. 99–133; 190–219.

Hiatt, LR 1986, 'Aboriginal political life', paper presented at the Wentworth lecture, AIATSIS, Canberra.

Hiscock, P 1988, 'Prehistoric settlement patterns and artefact manufacture at Lawn Hill, north-west Queensland', unpublished PhD thesis, University of Queensland, St Lucia.

Hiscock, P 1994a, 'Technological responses to risk in Holocene Australia', *Journal of World Prehistory*, vol. 8, no. 3, pp. 267–92.

Hiscock, P 1994b, 'The end of points', in M Sullivan, S Brockwell & A Webb (eds), *Archaeology in the north: proceedings of the 1993 Australian Archaeological Association conference*, pp. 72–83, NARU, Darwin.

Hiscock, P 1998, 'Revitalising artefact analysis', in Murray (ed.), *Archaeology of Aboriginal Australia: a reader*, pp. 257–65, Allen & Unwin, St Leonards.

Hiscock, P & Attenbrow, V 1998, 'Early Holocene backed artefacts from Australia', *Archaeology in Oceania*, 33, pp. 49–62.

Hiscock, P & Attenbrow, V 2002, 'Morphological and reduction continuums in eastern Australia: measurement and implications at Capertee 3', Tempus, 7, pp. 167–74.

Hiscock, P & Clarkson, C 2000, 'Analysing Australian stone artefacts: an agenda for the twenty first century', *Australian Archaeology*, 50, pp. 98–108.

Hiscock, P & Kershaw, AP 1992, 'Palaeoenvironments and prehistory of Australia's tropical Top End', in J Dodson (ed.), *Palaeoenvironments and prehistory of Australia's tropical Top End*, pp. 43–75, Longman Cheshire, Melbourne.

Hiscock, P & Veth, P 1991, 'Change in the Australian desert culture: a reanalysis of tulas from Puntutjarpa Rockshelter', *World Archaeology*, 22, pp. 332–45.

Hitchcock, G 2004, 'Torres Strait origin of some stone-headed clubs from the Torassi or Bensbach River area, south-west Papua New Guinea', *Torres Strait archaeology and material culture: Memoirs of the Queensland Museum* Cultural heritage series, vol. 3, no. 1, pp. 305–15.

Hobson, KA & Collier, J 1984, 'Marine and terrestrial protein in Australian Aboriginal diets', *Current Anthropology*, 25, pp. 238–40.

Hodder, I (ed.) 1982, *Symbols in action: ethnoarchaeological studies of material culture*, Cambridge University Press, Cambridge.

Hodder, I 1985, 'Postprocessual archaeology', in M Schiffer (ed.), *Advances in archaeological method and theory* 8, pp. 1–26, Academic Press, New York.

Hodder, I (ed.) 1989, *The meanings of things: material culture and symbolic expression*, Unwin Hyman, London.

Hodder, I 1991, *Reading the past: current approaches to interpretation in archaeology*, Cambridge University Press, Cambridge.

References

Hodder, I, Shanks, M, Alexandri, A, Buchli, V, Carman, J, Last, J & Lucas, G 1995, *Interpreting archaeology*, Routledge, London.
Holdaway, S 1995, 'Stone artefacts and the transition', *Antiquity*, 69, pp. 784–97.
Holdaway, S & Porch, N 1995, 'Cyclical patterns in the Pleistocene human occupation of south-west Tasmania', *Archaeology in Oceania*, 30, pp. 74–82.
Hooper, P 1978, 'Cycad poisoning in Australia: etiology and pathology', in RF Keeler, KR van Kampen & LF James (eds), *Effects of poisonous lants on livestock*, pp. 337–47, Academic Press, New York.
Horsfall, N 1987, 'Living in rainforest: the prehistoric occupation of north Queensland's humid tropics', unpublished PhD thesis, James Cook University, Townsville.
Horton, D 1979, 'Tasmanian adaptation', *Mankind*, 12, pp. 28–34.
Horton, D 1982, 'The burning question: Aborigines, fire and Australian ecosystems', *Mankind*, 13, pp. 237–51.
Horton, DR 1993, 'Here be dragons: a view of Australian archaeology', *Sahul in Review: Pleistocene archaeology in Australia, New Guinea and Island Melanesia*, pp. 11–16, Occasional papers in prehistory, 24, ANU, Canberra.
Houston, S & Taube, K 2000, 'An archaeology of the senses: perception and cultural expression in ancient Mesoamerica', *Cambridge Archaeological Journal*, 10, pp. 261–94.
Howchin, W 1934, *The stone implements of the Adelaide tribe of Aborigines now extinct*, Gillingham & Co Ltd, Adelaide.
Howitt, AW 1904, *The native tribes of south-east Australia*, Macmillan, London.
Huchet, BMJ 1991 'Theories and Australian prehistory: the last three decades', *Australian Archaeology*, 33, pp. 44–51.
Hughes, PJ & Lampert, RJ 1982, 'Prehistoric population change in southern coastal New South Wales', in S Bowdler (ed.), *Coastal archaeology in eastern Australia*, pp. 16–28, ANU, Canberra.
Hughes, PJ & Djohadze, V 1980, *Radiocarbon dates from archaeological sites on the south coast of New South Wales and the use of depth/age curves*, Occasional papers in prehistory 1, ANU: Canberra.
Hynes, R & Chase, AK 1982, 'Plants, sites and domiculture: Aboriginal influence on plant communities', *Archaeology in Oceania*, 17, pp. 138–50.
Ingold, T 1979, 'Social and ecological relations of culture-bearing organisms: an essay in evolutionary dynamics', in PC Burnham & RF Ellen (eds), *Social and ecological systems*, pp. 271–91, Academic Press, London.
Ingold, T 1980, *Hunters, pastoralists and ranchers: reindeer economies and their transformations*, Cambridge University Press, Cambridge.
Ingold, T 1993, 'The temporality of the landscape', *World Archaeology*, vol. 25, no. 2, pp. 152–74.
Ingold, T 2000 (1993), 'The temporality of the landscape', in J Thomas (ed.), *Interpretive archaeology: a reader*, pp. 510–30, Leicester University Press, London.
Ingold, T, Riches, D & Woodburn, J (eds) 1988, *Hunters and gatherers: history evolution and social change*, Berg, New York.
Insoll, T 2004, *Archaeology, ritual, religion*, Routledge, London.
Jenkin, G 1979, *Conquest of the Ngarrindjeri: the story of the lower Murray Lakes tribes*, Rigby Publishers, Adelaide.

Johnson, N & Rose, P 1994, *Bodmin Moor: an archaeological survey, vol. 1: the human landscape to c. 1800*, English Heritage and RCHME, London.

Johnson, BJ, Miller, GH, Fogel, ML, Magee, JW, Gagan, MK & Chivas, AR 1999, '65,000 years of vegetation change in central Australia and the Australian summer monsoon', *Science*, 284, pp. 1150–2.

Jones, R 1965a, 'Excavations on a stone arrangement in Tasmania', *Man*, 65, pp. 78–9.

Jones, R 1965b, 'Archaeological reconnaissance in Tasmania, summer 1963/1964', *Oceania*, 35, pp. 191–201.

Jones, R 1966, 'A speculative archaeological sequence for north-west Tasmania', *Records of the Queen Victoria Museum*, 25, pp. 1–12

Jones, R 1967, 'Middens and man in Tasmania', *Australian Natural History*, 18, pp. 359–64.

Jones, R 1968, 'The geographical background to the arrival of man in Australia and Tasmania', *Archaeology and Physical Anthropology in Oceania*, 3, pp. 186–215.

Jones, R 1969, 'Fire-stick farming', *Australian Natural History*, 16, pp. 224–8.

Jones, R 1971, 'Rocky Cape and the problem of the Tasmanians', unpublished PhD thesis, The University of Sydney.

Jones, R 1973, 'Emerging picture of Pleistocene Australians', *Nature*, 246, pp. 278–81.

Jones, R 1977a, 'Man as an element of a continental fauna: the case of the sundering of the Bassian bridge', in J Allen, J Golson & R Jones (eds), *Sunda and Sahul*, pp. 317–86, Academic Press, London.

Jones, R 1977b, 'The Tasmanian paradox', in RVS Wright (ed.), *Stone tools as cultural markers: change, evolution and complexity*, pp. 189–204, AIAS, Canberra.

Jones, R 1978, 'Why did the Tasmanians stop eating fish?', in RA Gould (ed.) *Explorations in ethno-archaeology*, pp. 11–48, School of American Research & University of New Mexico Press, Albuquerque.

Jones, R 1979, 'The fifth continent: problems concerning the human colonization of Australia', *Annual Review of Anthropology*, 8, pp. 445–66.

Jones, R – Bowler, J 1980, 'Struggle for the savanna: northern Australia in ecological and prehistoric perspective', in R Jones (ed.), *Northern Australia: options and implications*, pp.3–31, ANU, Canberra.

Jones, R & Meehan, B 1989, 'Plant foods of the Gidjingali: ethnographic and archaeological perspectives from northern Australia on tuber and seed exploitation', in DR Harris & GC Hillman (eds), *Foraging and farming: the evolution of plant exploitation*, pp. 120–35, Unwin Hyman, London.

Jones, R & White, N 1988, 'Point blank: stone tool manufacture at the Ngilipitji Quarry, Arnhem Land, 1981', in B Meehan & R Jones (eds), *Archaeology with ethnography: an Australian perspective*, pp. 51–88, ANU, Canberra.

Jones RN, McMahon, TA & Bowler, JM 1998 'A high resolution Holocene record of P/E ratio from closed lakes, western Victoria', *Palaeoclimates*, 3, pp. 51–82.

Jones, S & Graves-Brown, P 1996, 'Introduction: archaeology and cultural identity in Europe' in P Graves-Brown, S Jones & C Gamble (eds), *Cultural identity and archaeology: the construction of European communities*, pp. 1–24, Routledge, London.

Jordan, P 2001, 'Ideology, material culture and Khanty ritual landscapes in western Siberia', in K Fewster & M Zvelebil (eds), *Ethnoarchaeology of hunter-gatherers: pictures at an exhibition*, pp. 25–42, Oxford University Press, Oxford.

References

Jukes, JB 1847, *Narrative of the surveying voyage of HMS Fly during the years 1842–46*, T & W Boone, London.

Kamminga, J & Allen, H 1973, *Report of the archaeological survey: Alligator Rivers environmental fact-finding study*, Australian Government, Darwin.

Kearney, A 2000, unpublished field notes held by A Kearney.

Kearney, A 2003, unpublished field notes held by A Kearney.

Keen, I 1994,. *Knowledge and secrecy in an Aboriginal religion: Yolngu of north-east Arnhem Land*, Oxford University Press, Oxford.

Keen, I 1995, 'Metaphor and the metalanguage: "groups" in north-east Arnhem Land, *American Ethnologist*, vol. 22, no. 3, pp. 502–27.

Kenyon, AS & Mahony, DJ 1914, *Stone implements of the Australian Aboroigine: guide*, British Association for the Advancement of Science, Melbourne.

Kershaw, AP 1970, 'A pollen diagram from Lake Euramoo, north-eastern Australia', *New Phytologist*, 69, pp. 785–805.

Kershaw, AP 1971, 'A pollen diagram from Quincan Crater', *New Phytologist*, 70, pp. 669–81.

Kershaw, AP 1983, 'A Holocene pollen diagram from Lynch's Crater, north-eastern Queensland, Australia', *New Phytologist*, 75, pp. 173–91.

Kershaw, AP 1995, 'Environmental change in greater Australia', *Antiquity*, 69, pp. 656–75.

Kershaw, AP 1997, 'A modification of the Troels-Smith system of sediment description and portrayal', *Quaternary Australasia*, 15, pp. 63–8.

Kershaw, AP & Strickland, KM 1990, 'A 10-year pollen trapping record from rainforest in north-eastern Australia', *Review of Palaeobotany and Palynology*, 64, pp. 281–8.

Kershaw, AP, Tibby, J, Penny, D, Yezdani, H, Walkley, R, Cook, E & Johnston, R 2004, 'Latest Pleistocene and Holocene vegetation and environmental history of the Western Plains of Victoria, Australia', *Proceedings of the Royal Society of Victoria*, 116, pp. 141–63.

Kimber, RG & Smith, MA 1987, 'An Aranda ceremony', in DJ Mulvaney & JP White (eds), *Australians to 1788*, pp. 221–37, Fairfax, Syme & Weldon Associates, Broadway.

King, TF 1978, 'Don't that beat the band? Non-egalitarian political organization in prehistoric central California', in C Redman (ed.), *Social archaeology: beyond subsistence and dating*, pp. 225–48, Academic Press, New York.

Kirch, PV (ed.) 1981, *Island societies: archaeological approaches to evolution and transformation*, Cambridge University Press, Cambridge.

Kirch, PV 1997a, *The Lapita peoples: ancestors of the Oceanic world*, Blackwell Publishers, Cambridge.

Kirch, PV 1997b, 'Introduction: the environmental history of Oceanic Islands', in PV Kirch & TL Hunt (eds), *Historical ecology in the Pacific Islands: prehistoric environmental and landscape change*, pp. 1–21, Yale University Press, New Haven.

Laade, W 1968, 'The Torres Strait Islanders' own traditions about their origin', *Ethnos*, 33, pp. 141–58.

Laade, W 1969, 'Ethnographic notes on the Murray Islanders, Torres Strait', *Zeitschrift für Ethnologie*, 94, pp. 33–46.

Laade, W 1973, 'Notes on the clans, economy, trade and traditional law of the Murray Islanders, Torres Straits', *Journal de la Société des Océanistes*, 39, pp. 151–67.

Lamb, L 1996, 'A methodology for the analysis of backed artefact production on the South Molle Island Quarry, Whitsunday Islands', *Tempus*, 6, pp. 151–9.

Lambeck, K & Chappell, J 2001, 'Sea level change through the Last Glacial Cycle', *Science*, 292, pp. 679–86.

Lambeck, K, Yokoyama, Y and Purcell, 2002, Into and out of the Last Glacial Maximum: sea level change during Oxygen Isotope Stages 3 and 2, *Quaternary Science Reviews*, 21, pp.343–60.

Lamond, HG 1960, 'An island tribe', *North Queensland Monthly*, vol. 7, no. 5, pp. 35–40.

Landtman, G 1927, *The Kiwai Papuans of British New Guinea*, Macmillan & Co, London.

Langton, M 1993, 'Transcripts of proceedings of the Cape York Land Summit, held at Port Stewart', held by M Langton.

Langton, M 1998, *Burning questions: emerging environmental issues for indigenous peoples in northern Australia*, Centre for Indigenous Natural and Cultural Resource Management, Northern Territory University, Darwin.

Langton, M 2001, 'Taped interviews with Elders of the Laura Basin area on Aboriginal traditions of burning', transcripts held by M Langton.

Langton, M 2002a, 'Freshwater', unpublished background briefing papers: water rights discussion booklet, Lingiari Foundation, Broome.

Langton, M 2002b, 'The edge of the sacred, the edge of death: sensual inscriptions', in B David & M Wilson (eds), *Inscribed landscapes: marking and making place*, pp. 253–69, University of Hawai'i Press, Honolulu.

Langton, M & David, B 2003, 'William Ricketts Sanctuary, Victoria (Australia): sculpting nature and culture in a primitivist theme park', *Journal of Material Culture*, vol. 8, no. 2, pp. 145–68.

Lansing, JS, Redd, AJ, Karafet, TM, Watkins, J, Ardika, IW, Surata, SPK, Schoenfelder, JS, Campbell, M, Merriwether, AM & Hammer, MF 2004, 'An Indian trader in ancient Bali?', *Antiquity*, 78, pp. 287–93.

Larnach, SL 1978, *Australian Aboriginal Craniology*, Oceania Monographs 21, The University of Sydney.

Law, WB 2003, 'Chipping away in the past: stone artefact reduction and Holocene systems of land use in arid central Australia', unpublished MA thesis, ANU, Canberra.

Lawrence, D 1989, 'From the other side: recently collected oral evidence of contracts between the Torres Strait Islanders and the Papuan peoples of the south-western coast', *Aboriginal History*, 13, pp. 95–123.

Lawrence, D 1994, 'Customary exchange across Torres Strait', *Memoirs of the Queensland Museum*, vol. 34, no. 2, pp. 214–446.

Lawrence, R 1968, *Aboriginal habitat and economy*, Occasional paper of the Department of Geography 6, ANU, Canberra.

Layton, R (ed.) 1989, *Who needs the past? Indigenous values and archaeology*, Unwin Hyman, London.

Layton, R (ed.) 1994, *Conflict in the archaeology of living traditions*, Routledge, London.

Leach, HM 1999, 'Intensification in the Pacific', *Current Anthropology*, vol. 40, no. 3, pp. 311–39.

References

Leahy, PJ, Tibby, J, Kershaw, AP, Heijnis, H & Kershaw, JS in press, 'The impact of European settlement on Bolin Billabong, a Yarra River floodplain lake, Melbourne, Australia', *River research and applications*.

Lee, RB & DeVore, I 1968 (eds), *Man the hunter*, pp. 3–12, Aldine, Chicago.

Leichhardt, L 1847, *Journal of an overland expedition in Australia from Moreton Bay to Port Essington, a distance of upwards of 3000 miles, during the years 1844–45*, T & W Boone, London.

Lévinas, E 1987, *Collected philosophical papers*, Nijhoff, Dordrecht.

Levitt, D 1981, *Plants and people: Aboriginal uses of plants on Groote Eylandt*, AIAS, Canberra.

Lilley, I 2000, 'So near and yet so far: reflections on archaeology in Australia and Papua New Guinea, intensification and culture contact', *Australian Archaeology*, 50, pp. 36–44.

Lilley, I 2001, 'Of cowboys and core-tools: revisionist reflections on Rhys Jones and "The Great Intensification Debate"', in A Anderson, I Lilley & S O'Connor (eds), *Histories of old Aages: essays in honour of Rhys Jones*, pp. 79–88, Pandanus Books, ANU, Canberra.

Littleton, J 1999, 'East and west: burial practices along the Murray River', *Archaeology in Oceania*, 34, pp. 1–14.

Llobera, M 2001, 'Building past landscape perception with GIS: understanding topographic prominence', *Journal of Archaeological Science*, 28, pp. 1005–14.

Lotter, AF 1998, 'The recent eutrophication of Baldeggersee (Switzerland) as assessed by fossil diatom assemblages', *Holocene*, 8, pp. 395–405.

Lourandos, H 1968, 'Dispersal of activities: the east Tasmanian Aboriginal sites', *Papers and Proceedings of the Royal Society of Tasmania*, 102, pp. 41–6.

Lourandos, H 1970 'Coast and hinterland: the archaeological sites of eastern Tasmania', unpublished MA thesis, ANU, Canberra.

Lourandos, H 1976, 'Aboriginal settlement and land use in south-western Victoria: a report on current field work', *The Artefact*, vol. 1, no. 4, pp. 174–93.

Lourandos, H 1977a, 'Stone tools, settlement, adaptation: a Tasmanian example', in R Wright (ed.), *Stone tools as cultural markers: change, evolution and complexity*, pp. 219–24, AIAS, Canberra.

Lourandos, H 1977b, 'Aboriginal spatial organisation and population: south-western Victoria reconsidered', *Archaeology and Physical Anthropology in Oceania*, 12, pp. 202–25.

Lourandos, H 1980a, 'Forces of change: Aboriginal technology and population in south-western Victoria', unpublished PhD thesis, The University of Sydney.

Lourandos, H 1980b, 'Change or stability?: hydraulics, hunter-gatherers and population in temperate Australia', *World Archaeology*, 11, pp. 245–64.

Lourandos, H 1983a, '10,000 years in the Tasmanian highlands', *Australian Archaeology*, 16, pp. 39–47.

Lourandos, H 1983b, 'Intensification: a late Pleistocene–Holocene archaeological sequence from south-western Victoria', *Archaeology in Oceania*, 18, pp. 81–94.

Lourandos, H 1984, 'Changing perspectives in Australian prehistory: a reply to Beaton', *Archaeology in Oceania*, 19, pp. 29–33.

Lourandos, H 1985a, 'Intensification and Australian prehistory', in TD Price & JA Brown (eds), *Prehistoric hunter-gatherers: the emergence of cultural complexity*, pp. 385–423, Academic Press, Orlando, Florida.

Lourandos, H 1985b, 'Problems with the interpretation of late-Holocene changes in Australian prehistory', *Archaeology in Oceania*, 20, pp. 37–9.

Lourandos, H 1987a, 'Pleistocene Australia: peopling a continent', in O Soffer (ed.), *The Pleistocene Old World: regional perspectives*, pp. 147–65, Plenum, New York.

Lourandos, H 1987b, 'Swamp managers of south-western Victoria', in DJ Mulvaney & JP White (eds), *Australians to 1788*, pp. 292–307, Fairfax, Syme & Weldon, Sydney.

Lourandos, H 1988a, 'Palaeopolitics: resource intensification in Aboriginal Australia and Papua New Guinea', in T Ingold, D Riches & J Woodburn (eds), *Hunters and gatherers: history, evolution and social change*, vol. 1, pp. 148–60, Berg, Oxford.

Lourandos, H 1988b, 'Seals, sedentism and change in the Bass Strait', in B Meehan & R Jones (eds), *Archaeology with ethnography: an Australian perspective*, pp. 277–85, ANU, Canberra.

Lourandos, H 1993, 'Hunter-gatherer cultural dynamics: long- and short-term trends in Australian prehistory', *Journal of Archaeological Research*, 1, pp. 67–88.

Lourandos, H 1996, 'Change in Australian prehistory: scale, trends and frameworks of interpretation', in I Lilley, A Ross & S Ulm (eds), *Proceedings of the 1995 Australian Archaeological Association annual conference*, pp. 15–21, University of Queensland, St Lucia.

Lourandos, H 1997 *Continent of hunter-gatherers: new perspectives in Australian prehistory*, Cambridge University Press, Cambridge.

Lourandos, H & David, B 1998, 'Comparing long-term archaeological and environmental trends: north Queensland, arid and semi-arid Australia', *The Artefact*, 21, pp. 105–14

Lourandos, H & David, B 2002, 'Long-term archaeological and environmental trends: a comparison from late Pleistocene–Holocene Australia', in P Kershaw, B David, N Tapper, D Penny & J Brown (eds), *Bridging Wallace's Line: the environmental and cultural history and dynamics of the SE Asian-Australian region*, pp. 307–38, Catena Verlag, Reiskirchen.

Lourandos, H & Ross, A 1994, 'The great "intensification debate": its history and place in Australian archaeology', *Australian Archaeology*, 39, pp. 54–63.

Low, T 2002, *Feral future: the untold story of Australia's exotic invaders*, The University of Chicago Press, Chicago.

Lowie, RH 1937, *The history of ethnological thought*, Farrar & Rinehart Inc, New York.

Lubbock, J 1865, *Pre-historic times: as illustrated by ancient remains, and the manners and customs of modern savages*, Williams & Norgate, London.

Lubbock, J 1870, *The origin of civilisation and the primitive condition of man: mental and social conditions of savages*, Williams & Norgate, London.

MacGillivray, J 1852, *Narrative of the voyage of the HMS Rattlesnake, commanded by the late Captain Owen Stanley, RN, FRS, during the years 1846–1850*, T & W Boone, London.

MacGregor, G 1999 'Making sense of the past in the present: a sensory analysis of carved stone balls', *World Archaeology*, 31, pp. 258–71.

Macintosh, NWG 1971, 'Analysis of an Aboriginal skeleton and a pierced tooth necklace from Lake Nitchie, Australia', *Anthropologie*, vol. 9, no. 1, pp. 49–62.

Macintosh, NWG, Smith, KN & Bailey, AB 1970, 'Lake Nitchie skeleton: unique Aboriginal burial', *Archaeology and Physical Anthropology in Oceania*, vol. 5, no. 2, pp. 85–101.

Mackey, BG, Nix, H & Hitchcock, P 2001, 'The natural heritage significance of Cape York Peninsula', unpublished report, ANUTECH Pty Ltd, Canberra.

Manne, R (ed.) 2003, *Whitewash: on Keith Windschuttle's fabrication of Aboriginal history*, Black Inc, Melbourne.

Marika, R, Ngurruwutthun, D & White, L 1989, 'Always together, *yaka gana*: participatory research at Yirrikala as part of the development of a Yolngu education', unpublished paper presented at the Participatory Research Conference at the University of Calgary, July 1989, manuscript held by M Langton.

Marshall, B 2003, 'An analysis of the archaeological findings of the Kangerung cemetery and Ngarrindjeri social systems', unpublished BA (Hons) thesis, Flinders University, Adelaide.

Marwick, B 2002, 'Inland Pilbara archaeology: a study of the variation in Aboriginal occupation over time and space in the Hamersley Plateau', unpublished MA thesis, The University of Western Australia, Perth.

Mathew, J 1889, 'The Aborigines of Australia', *Journal and Proceedings of the Royal Society of New South Wales*, 23, pp. 335–449.

Maynard, L 1976, 'An archaeological approach to the study of rock art', unpublished MA thesis, The University of Sydney.

McBryde, I 1978, '"Wil-im-ee Moor-ing" or, where do the axes come from?', *Mankind*, 11, pp. 354–82.

McBryde, I 1979, 'Ethnohistory in an Australian context: independent discipline or convenient data quarry?', *Aboriginal History*, 3, pp. 128–51.

McBryde, I 1982, *Coast and estuary: archaeological investigations on the north coast of New South Wales at Wombah and Schnapper Point*, AIAS, Canberra.

McBryde, I 1984, 'Kulin greenstone quarries: social contexts of production and distribution for the Mt William site', *World Archaeology*, 16, pp. 267–85.

McBryde, I 1986, 'Australia's once and future archaeology', *Archaeology in Oceania*, 21, pp. 13–28.

McBryde, I 1987, 'Goods from another country: exchange networks and the people of the Lake Eyre Basin', in DJ Mulvaney & JP White (eds), *Australians to 1788*, pp. 252–73, Fairfax, Syme & Weldon, Sydney.

McCarthy, FD 1936, 'The geographical distribution theory and Australian material culture', *Mankind*, vol. 2, no. 1, pp. 12–16.

McCarthy, FD 1938, 'A comparison of the prehistory of Australia with that of Indo-China, the Malay Peninsula and the Netherlands East Indies', *Proceedings of the Third Congress of Prehistorians of the Far East*, Government Printing Office, Singapore.

McCarthy, FD 1939–40, '"Trade" in Aboriginal Australia, and "trade" relationships with Torres Strait, New Guinea and Malaya', *Oceania*, vol. 9, no. 4, pp. 405–39; vol. 10, no.1, pp. 80–104; vol. 10, no. 2, pp. 171–95.

McCarthy, FD 1940, 'Aboriginal Australian material culture: causative factors in its composition', *Mankind*, vol. 2, no. 8, pp. 241–69; vol. 2, no. 9, pp. 294–320.

McCarthy, FD 1943, 'An analysis of the knapped implements from eight eloura industry stations on the south coast of New South Wales', *Records of the Australian Museum*, vol. 21, no. 3, pp. 127–53.

McCarthy, FD 1953, 'The Oceanic and Indonesian affiliations of Australian Aboriginal culture', *Journal of the Polynesian Society*, vol. 62, no. 3, pp. 243–61.

McCarthy, FD 1957, *Australia's Aborigines: their life and culture*, Colourgravure, Melbourne.

McCarthy, FD 1963, 'Ecology, equipment, economy and trade', in H Sheils (ed.), *Australian Aboriginal studies*, pp. 171–91, Oxford University Press, Melbourne.

McCarthy, FD 1964 'The archaeology of the Capertee Valley, New South Wales', *Records of the Australian Museum*, 26, pp. 197–246.

McCarthy, FD 1966, 'The prehistory of Australia', *Australian Territories*, vol. 6, no. 1, pp. 2–12.

McCarthy, FD 1967, *Australian Aboriginal stone implements*, Trustees of the Australian Museum, Sydney.

McCarthy, FD 1970, 'Prehistoric and recent change in Australian Aboriginal culture', in AR Pilling & RA Waterman (eds), *Diprotodon to detribalisation: studies of change among Australian aborigines*, pp. 142–60, Michigan University Press, East Lansing.

McCarthy, FD 1974, 'Relationships between Australian Aboriginal material culture, and South-East Asia and Melanesia', in AP Elkin & NWG Macintosh (eds), *Grafton Elliot Smith: the man and his work*, pp. 210–26, The University Sydney Press, Sydney.

McCarthy, FD 1976, *Australian Aboriginal stone implements: including bone, shell and tooth implements*, 2nd edn, rev., The Australian Museum Trust, Sydney.

McCarthy, FD 1977, 'The use of stone tools to map patterns of diffusion', in RVS Wright (ed.), *Stone tools as cultural markers: change, evolution and complexity*, pp. 251–62, AIAS, Canberra.

McCarthy, FD, Bramell, E & Noone, HVV 1946, 'The stone implements of Australia', *Australian Museum Memoir* IX, Sydney.

McConvell, P 1996, 'Backtracking to Babel: the chronology of Pama–Nyungan expansion in Australia', *Archaeology in Oceania*, 31, pp. 125–44.

McCourt, T 1975, *Aboriginal Artefacts*, Rigby, Adelaide.

McDonald, JJ 1994, 'Dreamtime superhighway: an analysis of Sydney basin rock art and prehistoric information exchange', unpublished PhD thesis, ANU, Canberra.

McDonald, JJ 1999, 'Bedrock notions and isochrestic choice: evidence for localised stylistic patterning in the engravings of the Sydney region', *Archaeology in Oceania*, vol. 34, no. 3, pp. 145–60.

McDonald, JJ in press, 'Archaic faces to headdresses: the changing role of the rock art across the arid zone', in P Veth, M Smith & P Hiscock (eds), *Desert people: archaeological perspectives*, Blackwell, Oxford.

McDonald, JJ & Veth, P in press, 'Rock art and social identity: a comparison of graphic systems operating in arid and fertile environments in the Holocene', in I Lilley (ed.), *Archaeology of Oceania: Australia and the Pacific slands*, Blackwell, Oxford.

McGlone, MS, Kershaw, AP & Markgraf, V 1992, 'El Niño/southern oscillation climatic variability in Australasian and South American paleoenvironmental records', in HF Diaz & V Markgraf (eds), *El Niño: historical and paleoclimatic aspects of the southern oscillation*, pp. 435–62, Cambridge University Press, Cambridge.

References

McKenzie, K 1983, *The spear in the stone*, (film), AIAS, Canberra.

McLaughlin, D 1977, 'Submission to the Joint Selection Committee on Aboriginal Land Rights in the Northern Territory, 24 June 1977', in *Australian Parliament Joint Selection Committee on Aboriginal Land Rights in the Northern Territory*, pp.1268–1316A, Commonwealth of Australia Publishers, Canberra.

McLaughlin, D with Diridiylma, P 1974, 'Site record sheet: *Upindjauwa*; site number: 6265/0007 (recorded 30 November 1974)', copy held at the Aboriginal Areas Protection Authority, Darwin.

McNamara, K 2000, 'The daily grind: gender in archaeology and the Western Desert phenomena', unpublished BA (Hons) thesis, James Cook University, Townsville.

McNiven, I 1998a, 'Shipwreck saga as archaeological text: reconstructing Fraser Island's Aboriginal past', in I McNiven, L Russell & K Schaffer (eds), *Constructions of colonialism: perspectives on Eliza Fraser's shipwreck*, pp. 37–50, Leicester University Press, London.

McNiven, IJ 1998b, 'Enmity and amity: reconsidering stone-headed club (*gabagaba*) procurement and trade in Torres Strait', *Oceania*, vol. 69, no. 2, pp. 94–115.

McNiven, IJ 1993, 'Tula adzes and bifacial points on the east coast of Australia', *Australian Archaeology*, 36, pp. 22–33.

McNiven, IJ 1999, 'Fissioning and regionalisation: the social dimensions of change in Aboriginal use of the Great Sandy region, south-east Queensland', in J Hall & IJ McNiven (eds), *Australian coastal archaeology*, pp. 157–68. Research Papers in Archaeology and Natural History 31, ANU, Canberra.

McNiven, IJ 2000, 'Backed to the Pleistocene', *Archaeology in Oceania*, 35, pp. 48–52.

McNiven, IJ 2001, 'Torres Strait Islanders and the maritime frontier in early colonial Australia', in L Russell (ed.), *Colonial frontiers: Indigenous–European encounters in early settler societies*, pp. 175–97, Manchester University Press, Manchester.

McNiven, IJ 2003, 'Saltwater People: spiritscapes, maritime rituals and the archaeology of Australian indigenous seascapes', *World Archaeology*, vol. 35, no. 3, pp. 329–49.

McNiven, I, David, B & Lourandos, H 1999, 'Long-term Aboriginal use of western Victoria: reconsidering the significance of recent Pleistocene dates for the Grampians–Gariwerd region', *Archaeology in Oceania* vol. 34, no. 2, pp. 83–5.

McNiven, IJ & Dickinson, WR, David, B, Weisler, M, von Grielinski, F, Carter, M, & Zuppi, U, 2005, Mask Cave: Red-Slipped Pottery and the Australian-Papuan Settlement of Torres Strait, Ms submitted for publication.

McNiven, IJ & Feldman, R 2003, 'Ritually orchestrated seascapes: hunting magic and dugong bone mounds in Torres Strait, NE Australia', *Cambridge Archaeological Journal*, vol. 13, no. 2, pp. 169–94.

McNiven, IJ, Fitzpatrick, J & Cordell, J 2004, 'An Islander world: new approaches to managing the archaeological heritage of Torres Strait, north-east Australia', *Torres Strait archaeology and material culture: Memoirs of the Queensland Museum*, Cultural heritage series, vol. 3, no. 1, pp. 73–91.

McNiven, IJ & von Gnielinski, F 2004, 'Stone club head manufacture on Dauan Island, Torres Strait', *Torres Strait archaeology and material culture: Memoirs of the Queensland Museum*, Cultural heritage series, vol. 3, no. 1, pp. 291–304.

McNiven, IJ & Hitchcock, G 2004, 'Torres Strait Islander marine subsistence specialisation and terrestrial animal translocation', *Torres Strait archaeology and material culture: Memoirs of the Queensland Museum*, Cultural heritage series, vol. 3, no. 1, pp. 105–62.

McNiven, IJ & Russell, L 1997, '"Strange paintings" and "mystery races": Kimberley rock art, diffusionism and colonialist constructions of Australia's Aboriginal past', *Antiquity*, 71, pp. 801–9.

McNiven, IJ & Russell, L 2005, *Appropriated pasts: Indigenous peoples and the colonial culture of archaeology*, AltaMira Press, Walnut Creek.

McNiven, IJ & Russell, L in press, 'Towards a decolonisation of Australian Indigenous archaeology', in H Maschner & RA Bentley (eds), *Handbook of archaeological theory*, AltaMira Press, Walnut Creek.

Meehan, B & Jones, R 1977, 'Preliminary comments on the preparation of *Cycas media* by the Gidjingali of coastal Arnhem Land', in J Beaton, 'Dangerous harvest: appendix IV', unpublished PhD thesis, ANU, Canberra.

Meehan, B, Jones, R, Vincent, A 1999, 'Gulu-kula: dogs in Anbarra society, Arnhem Land', *Aboriginal History*, 23, pp. 83–106.

Meehan, B & White, N (eds) 1990, *Hunting and gathering demography: past and present*, Oceania Monograph, University of Sydney, Sydney.

Meggit, MJ 1964, 'Indigenous forms of government among the Australian Aborigines', *Bijdragen tvt de Taal: Land-en Volken kunde*, 120, pp. 163–78.

Merlan, F 1998, *Caging the rainbow: places, politics, and Aborigines in a north Australian town*, University of Hawai'i Press, Honolulu.

Merleau-Ponty, M 1962, *The phenomenology of perception*, Routledge & Kegan Paul, London.

Meskell, L (ed.). 1998, *Archaeology under fire: nationalism, politics and heritage in the eastern Mediterranean and Middle East*, Routledge, London.

Meskell, L 2002, 'The intersections of identity and politics in archaeology', *Annual Review of Anthropology*, 31, pp. 279–301.

Milham, P & Thompson, P 1976, 'Relative antiquity of human occupation and extinct fauna at Madura Cave, south-eastern Western Australia', *Mankind*, vol. 10, no. 3, pp. 175–80.

Miller, O. 1998 'K'gari, Mrs Fraser and Butchulla oral tradition', in Ian J McNiven, Lynette Russell and Kay Schaffer (eds), *Constructions of Colonialism: Perspectives on Eliza Fraser's Shipwreck*, pp. 28–36, Leicester University Press, London.

Misra, VN & Bellwood, P (eds) 1985, *Recent advances in Indo-Pacific prehistory: proceedings of the international symposium held at Poona, December 19–21, 1978*, EJ Brill, Leiden.

Modjeska, CM 1982, 'Production and inequality: perspectives from central New Guinea', in A Strathern (ed.), *Inequality in New Guinea Highland societies*, pp. 50–108, Cambridge University Press, Cambridge.

Mohen, J-P 1990, *The world of megaliths*, trans H McPhail, Facts on File, New York.

Mohen, J-P 1999a, *Standing stones*, Thames & Hudson, London.

Mohen, J-P 1999b, *Megaliths: stones of memory*, Abrams, New York.

Moore, DR 1972, 'Cape York Aborigines and Islanders of the western Torres Strait', in D Walker (ed.), *Bridge and barrier: the natural and cultural history of Torres Strait*, pp. 327–44, ANU, Canberra.

References

Moore, DR 1979, *Islanders and Aborigines at Cape York: an ethnographic reconstruction based on the 1848–50 'Rattlesnake' journals of OW Brierly and information he obtained from Barbara Thompson*, AIAS, Canberra.

Morgan, LH 1963 (1877), *Ancient society or researches in the lines of human progress from savagery through to barbarism to civilization*, Meridian Books, Cleveland.

Morphy, H 1984, *Journey to the crocodile's nest*, monograph accompanying the film *Madarrpa funeral at Gurka'wuy*, AIAS, Canberra.

Morphy, H 1991, *Ancestral connections: art and an Aboriginal system of knowledge*, The University of Chicago Press, Chicago.

Morphy, H 1996, 'Landscape and the reproduction of the ancestral past', in E Hirsch & M O'Hanlon (eds), *The anthropology of landscape: perspectives on place and space*, pp. 184–209, Clarendon Press, Oxford.

Morwood, MJ & Hobbs, DR 1995, 'Themes in the prehistory of tropical Australia', *Antiquity*, 69, pp. 747–68.

Moser, S 1994, 'Building the discipline of Australian archaeology: Fred McCarthy at the Australian Institute of Aboriginal Studies', in M Sullivan, S Brockwell and A Webb (eds), *Archaeology in the north: proceedings of the 1993 Australian Archaeological Association conference*, pp. 17–29, NARU, Darwin.

Mulvaney, DJ 1960, 'Archaeological excavations at Fromm's Landing on the lower Murray River, South Australia', *Proceedings of the Royal Society of Victoria*, 72, pp. 53–85.

Mulvaney, DJ 1961, 'The Stone Age of Australia', *Proceedings of the Prehistoric Society*, 4, pp. 56–107.

Mulvaney, DJ 1962, 'Advancing frontiers in Australian archaeology', *Oceania*, vol. 33, no. 2, pp. 135–38.

Mulvaney, DJ 1963, 'Prehistory', in H Sheils (ed.), *Australian Aboriginal studies: a symposium of papers presented at the 1961 research conference*, pp. 33–51, Oxford University Press, Melbourne.

Mulvaney, DJ 1966, 'The prehistory of the Australian Aborigines', *Scientific American*, vol. 214, no. 3, pp. 84–93.

Mulvaney, DJ 1969, *The prehistory of Australia*, Frederick A Praeger, New York.

Mulvaney, DJ 1971, 'Aboriginal social evolution: a retrospective view', in DJ Mulvaney & J Golson (eds), *Aboriginal man and environment in Australia*, pp. 368–80, ANU Press, Canberra.

Mulvaney, DJ 1975, *The prehistory of Australia*, Penguin, Harmondsworth.

Mulvaney, DJ 1977, 'Classification and typology in Australia', in RVS Wright (ed.), *Stone tools as cultural markers: change, evolution and complexity*, pp. 262–8, AIAS, Canberra.

Mulvaney, DJ 1985, 'Australian backed blade industries in perspective', in VN Misra & P Bellwood (eds), *Recent advances in Indo-Pacific prehistory: proceedings of the international symposium held at Poona, December 19–21, 1978*, pp. 211–17, EJ Brill, Leiden.

Mulvaney, DJ 1990, 'Introduction to Section 1', *Prehistory and heritage: the writings of John Mulvaney*, pp. 1–2, Occasional papers in prehistory 17, ANU, Canberra.

Mulvaney, DJ 1993, 'Sesqui-centenary to bicentenary: reflections on a museologist', *Records of the Australian Museum*, supplement 17, pp. 17–24.

Mulvaney, DJ & Joyce, EB 1965, 'Archaeological and geomorphological investigations on Mt Moffatt Station, Queensland, Australia', *Proceedings of the Prehistoric Society*, 31, pp. 147–212.

Mulvaney, DJ & Kamminga, J 1999, *Prehistory of Australia*, Allen & Unwin, St Leonards.

Mulvaney, DJ, Lawton, GH & Twidale, CR 1964, 'Archaeological excavation of rockshelter no. 6, Fromm's Landing, South Australia', *Proceedings of the Royal Society of Victoria*, 77, pp. 479–516.

Mulvaney, DJ & Soejono, RP 1971, 'Archaeology in Sulawesi', *Antiquity*, 45, pp. 26–33.

Munn, N 1973, *Walbiri iconography: graphic representation and cultural symbolism in a central Australian society*, Cornell University Press, Ithaca.

Munn, N 1996, 'Excluded spaces: the figure in the Australian Aboriginal landscape', *Critical Inquiry*, 22, pp. 446–65.

Murray, AW 1874, *Wanders in the Western Isles: being a narrative of the commencement and progress of mission work in Western Polynesia*, Yates & Alexander, London.

Murray, T 1988, 'Ethnoarchaeology or palaeoethnology?', *Archaeology with ethnography: an Australian perspective*, pp 1–16, ANU, Canberra.

Murray, T 1992, 'Aboriginal (pre)history and Australian archaeology: the discourse of Australian prehistoric archaeology', *Power, knowledge and Aborigines: Journal of Australian Studies*, pecial edition 35, pp. 1–19.

Murray, T 1998, 'The changing contexts of the archaeology of Aboriginal Australia', in T Murray (ed.), *Archaeology of Aboriginal Australia: a reader*, pp. 1–12, Allen & Unwin, St Leonards.

Murray, T & Williamson, C 2003, 'Archaeology and history', in R Manne (ed.), *Whitewash: on Keith Windschuttle's fabrication of Aboriginal History*, pp. 311–33, Black Inc, Melbourne.

Murray, T & White, JP 1981, 'Cambridge in the bush? Archaeology in Australia and New Guinea', *World Archaeology*, 13, pp. 255–63

Myers, F 1980a, 'The cultural basis of politics in Pintupi life', *Mankind*, vol. 12, no. 3, pp. 197–214.

Myers, F 1980b, 'A broken code: Pintupi political theory and contemporary social life', *Mankind*, vol. 12, no. 4, pp. 311–26.

Myers, F 1986a, 'Always ask: resource use and ownership among Pintupi Aborigines of the Australian western desert', in N Williams & E Hunn (eds), *Resource managers: North American and Australian hunter-gatherers*, pp. 173–96, AIAS, Canberra.

Myers, F 1986b, *Pintupi country, Pintupi self: sentiment, place and politics among Western Desert Aborigines*, Smithsonian Institute Press, Washington DC.

Myers, F 2002, 'Ways of place-making', *La Ricerca Folklorica*, 45, pp. 101–19.

Myers, LD 2004, 'Subtle shifts and radical transformations in hunter-gatherer research in American anthropology: Julian Steward's contributions and achievements', in A Barnard (ed.), *Hunter-gatherers in history, archaeology and anthropology*, pp. 175–86, Berg, Oxford.

Nicholas, D & Kramer, C (eds) 2001, *Ethnoarchaeology in action*, Cambridge University Press, Cambridge.

Nicholls, N 1985, 'Impact of the southern oscillation on Australian crops', *Journal of Climatology*, 5, pp. 553–60.

Nicholls, N 1991, 'The El Niño–southern oscillation and Australian vegetation', *Vegetation*, 91, pp. 23–6.

Noone, HVV 1943, 'Some Aboriginal stone implements of western Australia', *Records of the Australian Museum*, vol. 7, no. 3, pp. 271–80.

O'Connell, JF & Allen, J 1995, 'Human reactions to the Pleistocene–Holocene transition in greater Australia: a summary', *Antiquity*, vol. 69, no. 265, pp. 855–62.

O'Connor, S & Veth, P 1996, 'A preliminary report on recent archaeological research in the semi-arid/arid belt of Western Australia', *Australian Aboriginal Studies*, 2, pp. 42–50.

O'Connor, S, Veth, P & Barham, A 1999, 'Cultural versus natural explanations for lacunae in Aboriginal occupation deposits in northern Australia', *Quaternary International*, 59, pp. 61–70.

O'Connor, S, Veth, P & Campbell, C 1998, 'Serpent's Glen rockshelter: report of the first Pleistocene-aged occupation sequence from the Western Desert', *Australian Archaeology*, 46, pp. 12–21.

O'Shea, JM 1984, *Mortuary variability: an archaeological investigation*, Academic Press, New York.

Oates WJ & Oates, LF (eds) 1970, 'A revised linguistic survey of Australia', *Australian Aboriginal Studies* 33.

Owen, TD 2004, '"Of more than usual interest": A bioarchaeological analysis of ancient Aboriginal skeletal material from south-eastern South Australia', unpublished PhD thesis, Flinders University, Adelaide.

Pardoe, C 1988, 'The cemetery as symbol: the distribution of prehistoric Aboriginal burial grounds in south-eastern Australia', *Archaeology in Oceania*, vol. 23, no. 1, pp. 1–16.

Pardoe, C 1994, 'Bioscapes: the evolutionary landscape of Australia', *Archaeology in Oceania*, 29, 182–90.

Pardoe, C 1995, 'Riverine, biological and cultural evolution in south-eastern Australia', *Antiquity*, 69, pp. 696–713.

Parr, JF & Carter, M 2003, 'Phytolith and starch analysis of sediment samples from two archaeological sites on Dauar Island, Torres Strait, north-eastern Australia', *Vegetation History and Archaeobotany*, vol. 12, no. 2, pp. 131–41.

Parry, WJ 1981, 'Fear of fish and forests: food taboos and diet optimisation in western Tasmania', *Michigan Discussions in Anthropology*, vol. 6, no. 2, pp. 80–101.

Pate, FD 1984, 'Mortuary practices and paleodiet as archaeological signatures of social organization and status at Roonka on the Lower Murray River of South Australia', unpublished MA thesis, Brown University, Providence.

Pate, FD 1995, 'Stable carbon isotope assessment of hunter-gatherer mobility in prehistoric South Australia', *Journal of Archaeological Science*, 22, pp. 81–7.

Pate, FD 1997, 'Bone chemistry and paleodiet: Reconstructing prehistoric subsistence-settlement systems in Australia', *Journal of Anthropological Archaeology*, 16, pp. 103–20.

Pate, FD 1998a, 'Bone collagen stable nitrogen and carbon isotopes as indicators of prehistoric diet and landscape use in south-eastern South Australia', *Australian Archaeology*, 46, pp. 23–9.

Pate, FD 1998b, 'Stable carbon and nitrogen isotope evidence for prehistoric hunter-gatherer diet in the lower Murray River Basin, South Australia', *Archaeology in Oceania*, 33, pp. 92–9.

Pate, FD 1998c, 'Bone collagen preservation at the Roonka Flat Aboriginal burial ground: a natural laboratory', *Journal of Field Archaeology*, 25, pp. 203–17.

Pate, FD 2000, 'Bone chemistry and palaeodiet: bioarchaeological research at Roonka Flat, lower Murray River, South Australia 1983–99', *Australian Archaeology*, 50, pp. 67–74.

Pate, FD, Brodie, R & Owen, TD 2002, 'Determination of geographic origin of unprovenanced Aboriginal skeletal remains in South Australia employing stable isotope analysis', *Australian Archaeology*, 55, pp. 1–7.

Pate, FD, Owen, TD & Lawson, E 2003, 'AMS radiocarbon dating of bone collagen: establishing a chronology for the Swanport Aboriginal burial ground, South Australia', *Australian Archaeology*, 56, pp. 8–11.

Pearce, RH 1974, 'Spatial and temporal distribution of Australian backed blades', *Mankind*, 9, pp. 300–9.

Pearsall, DM 2000, *Paleoethnobotany: a handbook of procedures*, Academic Press, New York.

Pearsall, J & Trumble, B (eds) 1996, *The Oxford English Reference Dictionary* (2nd Ed), Oxford University Press, Oxford.

Peebles, CS & Kus, SM 1977, 'Some archaeological correlates of ranked societies', *American Antiquity*, 42, pp. 421–48.

Perry, WJ 1923, *The children of the sun: a study in the early history of civilisation*, Methuen & Co Ltd, London.

Peterson, N, 1969, 'Secular and ritual links: tow basic and opposed principles of Australian social organisation as illustrated by Walbiri ethnography' *Mankind*, 7, pp. 27–35.

Philip, B 2000, 'Philip Ruddock, ministre Australien de l'immigration et de la réconciliation: "Nous refusons d'être tenus pour responsables"', Le Monde: édition électronique (1 September), at URL: http://www.lemonde.fr/article/0,2320,90746,00.html

Plomley, NJB 1966, *Friendly mission: the Tasmanian journals and papers of George Augustus Robinson 1829–1834*, Tasmanian Historical Research Association, Hobart.

Plomley, NJB 1987, *Weep in silence: a history of the Flinders Island Aboriginal settlement with the Flinders Island journal of George Augustus Robinson 1835–1839*, Blubber Head Press, Hobart.

Povinelli, EA 1993, *Labor's lot: the power, history and culture of Aboriginal action*, The University of Chicago Press, Chicago.

Powell, JM, Kulunga, A, Moge, R, Pono, C, Zimike, F & Golson, J 1975, *Agricultural Traditions in the Mount Hagen Area*, Department of Geography, University of Papua New Guinea, Occasional paper 12, Port Moresby.

Presland, G 1980, 'Continuity in Indonesian lithic traditions', *The Artefact*, vol. 5, no. 1; vol. 5, no. 2, pp. 19–46.

Pretty, GL 1977, 'The cultural chronology of the Roonka Flat', in RVS Wright (ed.), *Stone tools as cultural markers*, pp. 288–331, AIAS, Canberra.

References

Pretty, GL 1986, 'Australian history at Roonka', *Journal of the Historical Society of South Australia*, 14, pp. 107–22.

Pretty, GL & Kricun, ME 1989, 'Prehistoric health status of the Roonka population', *World Archaeology*, 21, pp. 198–224.

Preucel, RW & Hodder, I (eds) 1996, *Contemporary archaeology in theory: a reader*, Blackwell, London.

Price, TD & Brown, JA (eds) 1985, *Prehistoric hunter-gatherers: the emergence of cultural complexity*, Academic Press, New York.

Prokopec, M 1979, 'Demographical and morphological aspects of the Roonka population', *Archaeology and Physical Anthropology in Oceania*, 14, pp. 11–26.

Rainbird, P 2002, 'Making sense of petroglyphs: the sound of rock art', in B David & M Wilson (eds), *Inscribed landscapes: marking and making place*, pp. 93–103, University of Hawaii Press, Honolulu.

Ray, SH 1907, *Reports of the Cambridge Anthropological Expedition to Torres Straits, vol. 3: linguistics*, Cambridge University Press, Cambridge.

Redmond, A 2002, '"Alien abductions", Kimberley Aboriginal rock-paintings, and the speculation about human origins: on some investments in cultural tourism in the northern Kimberley', *Australian Aboriginal Studies*, 2, pp. 54–64.

Reed, CA (ed.) 1977, *Origins of agriculture*, Mouton, The Hague.

Renfrew, C 1973, *Before civilization: the radiocarbon revolution and prehistoric Europe*, Penguin, Harmondsworth.

Renfrew, C & Bahn, P 2000, *Archaeology: theories methods and practice*, Thames & Hudson, London.

Richardson, J 2000, 'Explaining shellfish variability in the Meriam Islands, Australia', unpublished MA thesis, University of Arkansas.

Rick, JW 1987, 'Dates as data: an examination of the Peruvian Preceramic radiocarbon record', *American Antiquity*, 52, pp. 55–73.

Ricks, T 1999, 'Memories of Palestine: uses of oral history and archaeology in recovering a Palestinian past', in T Kapitan (ed.), *Archaeology, history and culture in Palestine and the Near East: essays in memory of Albert E Glock*, pp. 23–46, Scholars Press, Atlanta.

Ridpath, MG & Corbett, LK (eds) 1985, *Ecology of the wet–dry tropics: proceedings of a joint symposium with the Australian Mammal Society in association with the Darwin Institute of Technology*, Darwin, 15–17 May 1983, The Ecological Society of Australia, Melbourne.

Rigsby, B 1980, 'Land, language and people in the Princess Charlotte Bay area', *Contemporary Cape York Peninsula: Proceedings of the Royal Society of Queensland*, pp. 89–90.

Rigsby, B 1981, 'Aboriginal people, land rights, and wilderness on Cape York Peninsula', *Proceedings of the Royal Society of Queensland*, 92, pp. 1–10.

Rigsby, B 1992, 'The languages of the Princess Charlotte Bay region', *The Language Game: papers in memory of Donald C. Laycock, Pacific Linguistics*, series C-110, pp. 353–60.

Rigsby, B 1995, 'Tribes, diaspora people and the vitality of law and custom: some comments', in J Fingleton & J Finlayson (eds), *Anthropology in the native title era*, pp. 25–7, AIATSIS, Canberra.

Rigsby, B 1998, 'A survey of property theory and tenure types', in N Peterson & B Rigsby (eds), *Customary marine tenure in Australia*, pp. 22–46, Oceania monograph 48, The University of Sydney, Sydney.

Rigsby, B & Hafner, D 1992, 'Anthropological report for transfer of public purposes reserve (R11) at Port Stewart to the Port Stewart Lamalama people', unpublished consultants' report prepared for Moomba Aboriginal Corporation, manuscript held by M Langton.

Rigsby, B & Hafner, D 1994, 'Lakefield National Park land claim: claim book, part A', unpublished restricted manuscript, Cape York Land Council, Cairns.

Rigsby, B & Williams, N 1991, 'Reestablishing a home on eastern Cape York Peninsula', *Cultural Survival Quarterly*, vol. 15, no. 2, pp. 11–15.

Rindos, D 1983, *Origins of agriculture: an evolutionary perspective*, Academic Press, New York.

Robins, R & Trigger, D 1989, 'A recent phase of Aboriginal occupation in Lawn Hill Gorge: a case study in ethnoarchaeology', *Australian Archaeology*, 29, pp. 39–51.

Robinson, GA 1839–49, *Manuscript and papers: Port Phillip protectorate*, Mitchell Library, Sydney.

Rodbell, DT, Seltzer, GO, Anderson, DM, Abbott, MB, Enfield, DB & Newman, JH 1999, '~15,000-year record of El Niño-driven alluviation in south-western Ecuador', *Science*, 283, pp. 516–20.

Roe, D 2000, 'Maritime, coastal and inland societies in Island Melanesia: the bush–saltwater divide in Solomon Islands and Vanuatu', *East of Wallace's Line: studies of past and present maritime cultures of the Indo-Pacific region*, pp. 197–222, Modern Quaternary research in South-East Asia series 16, AA Balkema Press, Rotterdam.

Roscoe, P 2002, 'The hunters and gatherers of New Guinea', *Current Anthropology*, vol. 43, no. 1, pp. 153–62.

Rose, DR 2004, 'Freshwater rights and biophilia: Indigenous Australian perspectives', *Dialogue*, vol. 23, no. 3.

Rosenfeld, A 1993, 'A review of the evidence for the emergence of rock art in Australia', *Sahul in review: Pleistocene archaeology in Australia, New Guinea and Island Melanesia*, pp. 71–80, Occasional papers in prehistory 24, ANU, Canberra.

Rosenfeld, A 2002, 'Rock art as an indicator of changing social geographies in central Australia', in B David & M Wilson (eds), *Inscribed landscapes: marking and making place*, pp. 61–78, University of Hawai'i Press, Honolulu.

Rosenfeld, A & Smith, MA 2002, 'Rock art and the history of Puritjarra Rock Shelter, Cleland Hills, central Australia', *Proceedings of the Prehistoric Society*, 68, pp. 103–24.

Ross, A 1985, 'Archaeological evidence for population change in the middle to late Holocene in south-eastern Australia', *Archaeology in Oceania*, 20, pp. 81–9.

Ross A, Donnelly, T & Wasson, R 1992, 'The peopling of the arid zone: human-environment interactions', in JR Dodson (ed.), *The naive lands: prehistory and environmental change in Australia and the southwest Pacific*, pp. 76–114, Longman Cheshire, Melbourne.

Roth WE 1901–06, 'North Queensland ethnography, bulletins 1 to 8', in KF McIntyre (ed.), *The Queensland Aborigines*, vol. 2, facsimile edn, 1984, Hesperian Press, Victoria Park.

Roth. WE 1908–10, 'North Queensland ethnography, bulletins 9 to 18', in KF McIntyre (ed.), *The Queensland Aborigines*, vol. 3, facsimile edn, 1984, Hesperian Press, Victoria Park.

Rothschild, NA 1979, 'Mortuary behavior and social organization', *American Antiquity*, 44, pp. 658–75.

Rowe, C forthcoming, 'Patterns of Holocene environmental change and human impact in western Torres Strait' unpublished PhD thesis, Monash University, Clayton.

Rowland, MJ 1985, 'Archaeological investigations on Moa and Naghi Islands, western Torres Strait', *Australian Archaeology*, 21, pp. 119–32.

Rowland, MJ 1986, 'The Whitsunday Islands: initial historical and archaeological observations and implications for future work', *Queensland Archaeological Research*, 3, pp. 72–87.

Rowland, MJ 1987, 'The distribution of Aboriginal watercraft on the east coast of Queensland: implications for culture contact', *Australian Aboriginal Studies*, 2, pp. 38–45.

Rowland, MJ 1989, 'Population increase, intensification or a result of preservation? explaining site distribution patterns on the coast of Queensland', *Australian Aboriginal Studies*, 2, pp. 32–41.

Rowland, MJ 1996, 'Prehistoric archaeology of the Great Barrier Reef Province: retrospect and prospect', *Tempus*, 4, pp. 191–212.

Rowland, MJ 1999a, 'The Keppel Islands: a "3000 year" event revisited', in J Hall & IJ McNiven (eds), *Australian coastal archaeology*, pp. 141–56, ANH Publications, Canberra.

Rowland, MJ 1999b, 'Holocene environmental variability; have its impacts been underestimated in Australian pre-history?', *The Artefact*, 22, pp. 11–48.

Rowley-Conwy, P 2001, 'Time, change and the archaeology of hunter-gatherers: how original is the "Original Affluent Society"?', in C Panter-Brick, RH Layton & P Rowley-Conwy (eds), *Hunter-gatherers: an interdisciplinary perspective*, pp. 39–72, Cambridge University Press, Cambridge.

Rowntree, LB 1996, 'The cultural landscape concept in American human geography', in C Earle, K Mathewson & MS Kenzer (eds), *The cultural landscape concept in American human geography*, pp. 127–60, Rowman & Littlefield Publishers, Maryland.

Rudder, J 1993, 'Yolngu cosmology: an unchanging cosmos incorporating a rapidly changing world?', unpublished PhD thesis, ANU, Canberra.

Rumsey, A 1994, 'The Dreaming, human agency and inscriptive practice', *Oceania*, 65, pp. 116–30.

Russell, L & McNiven. IJ 1998, 'Monumental colonialism: megaliths and the appropriation of Australia's Aboriginal past', *Journal of Material Culture*, vol. 3, no. 3, pp. 283–99.

Russell-Smith, J, Whitehead, PJ, Williams, RJ & Flannigan, M 2003, 'Fire and savanna landscapes in northern Australia: regional lessons and global challenges', *International Journal of Wildland Fire*, 12, pp. v–ix.

Salgado, B 1994, *Murrundi voices: Ngarrindjeri people's stories from the lower Murray*, Rural City of Murray Bridge, Murray Bridge.

Sansom, B 1980, *Camp at Wallaby Cross: Aboriginal fringe dwellers in Darwin*, AIAS, Canberra.

Saxe, AA 1970, 'Social dimensions of mortuary practices', unpublished PhD thesis, University of Michigan, Ann Arbor.

Saxe, AA 1971, 'Social dimensions of mortuary practices in a Mesolithic population from Wadi Halfa, Sudan', *Memoirs Society for American Archaeology*, 25, pp. 39–71.

Schiffer, M 1976, *Behavioural archaeology*, Academic Press, New York.

Schiffer, M 1987, *Formation processes of the archaeological record*, University of New Mexico Press, Albuquerque.

Service, A & Bradbery, J 1997, *Standing stones of Europe: a guide to the great megalithic monuments*, Trafalgar Square Publishers, London.

Shanks, M & Tilley, C 1987a, *Re-constructing archaeology: theory and practice*, Routledge, London.

Shanks, M & Tilley, C 1987b, *Social theory and archaeology*, Polity Press, Cambridge.

Sharp, N 1993, *Stars of Tagai: the Torres Strait Islanders*, AIAS, Canberra.

Sharp, N 1996, *Re-imagining sea space in history and contemporary life: pulling up some old anchors*, NARU, ANU, Darwin.

Sharp, N 1997, 'Handing on the right to fish: the law of the land and cross-cultural co-operation in a Gulf community in Australia', unpublished NARU seminar paper, 1 December.

Sharp, N 2000, 'Following in the seamarks? The saltwater peoples of tropical Australia', *Indigenous Law Bulletin*, vol. 4, no. 29, pp. 4–7.

Sharp, N 2002, *Saltwater people: the waves of memory*, Allen & Unwin, Crows Nest.

Shennan, S (ed.) 1989, *Archaeological approaches to cultural identity*, Unwin Hyman, London.

Shnukal, A & Mitchell, R 1998, 'Eseli's notebook', *Aboriginal and Torres Strait Islander Studies Unit Research Report Series*, 3, (University of Queensland, St Lucia).

Shulmeister, J 1992, 'A Holocene pollen record from lowland tropical Australia', *Holocene*, vol. 2, no. 2, pp. 107–16.

Shulmeister, J & Lees, BG 1995, 'Pollen evidence from tropical Australia for the onset of an ENSO dominated climate at c.4000 BP', *Holocene*, 5, pp. 10–18.

Simms, SR 1992, 'Ethnoarchaeology: obnoxious spectator, trivial pursuit, or the keys to a time machine?', in L Wandsnider (ed.), *Quandaries and quests: visions of archaeology's future*, pp. 186–98, Center for Archaeological Investigations, Occasional paper 20, Southern Illinois University, Carbondale.

Singe, J 1979, *The Torres Straits: people and history*, University of Queensland Press, St Lucia.

Slack, MJ, Fullagar, RLK, Field, JH & Border, A 2004, 'New Pleistocene ages for backed artefact technology in Australia', *Archaeology in Oceania*, vol. 39, no. 3, pp. 131–7.

Smart, B 1996, 'Postmodern social theory', in B Turner (ed.), *The Blackwell companion to social theory*, pp. 396–428, Blackwell, Oxford.

Smith, A 2002, *An archaeology of West Polynesian prehistory*, Terra Australis 18, Pandanus Books, Canberra.

Smith, BD 2001, 'Low-level food production', *Journal of Archaeological Research*, 9, pp. 1–43.

Smith, M 1982, 'Late Pleistocene Zamia exploitation in southern western Australia', *Archaeology in Oceania*, 17, pp. 109–16.

Smith, MA 1989, 'The case for a resident human population in the central Australian Ranges during full glacial aridity', *Archaeology in Oceania*, 24, pp. 93–105.

Smith, MA, Vellen, I and Pask, J 1995, Vegetation history from archaeological charcoals in central Australia, the late Quaternary record from Puritjarra rockshelter, *Vegetation History and Archaeobotany*, 4, pp. 171–7.

Smith, MA 1996, 'Prehistory and human ecology in central Australia: an archaeological perspective', in SR Morton & DJ Mulvaney (eds), *Exploring central Australia: society, environment and the 1894 Horn Expedition*, pp. 61–73, Surry Beatty & Sons, Chipping Norton.

Smith, MA, Fankhauser, B & Jercher, M 1998, 'The changing provenance of red ochre at Puritjarra rock shelter, Central Australia: late Pleistocene to present', *Proceedings of the Prehistoric Society*, 64, pp. 275–92.

Smith, MA, Prescott, JR & Head, MJ 1997, 'Comparison of ^{14}C and luminescence chronologies at Puritjarra rock shelter, Central Australia', *Quaternary Science Reviews*, 16, pp. 299–320.

Smith, MA & Veth, P in press, 'Radiocarbon dates for baler shell in the Great Sandy Desert', *Australian Archaeology*.

Smyth, RB 1878, *The Aborigines of Victoria: with notes relating to the habits of the natives of other parts of Australia and Tasmania*, John Ferres, Government Printer, Melbourne.

Sollas, WJ 1911, *Ancient hunters and their modern representatives*, Macmillan, London.

Sorensen, M 2000, *Gender archaeology*, Polity Press, Cambridge.

Specht, J 2003, 'On New Guinea hunters and gatherers', *Current Anthropology*, 44, p. 269.

Spencer, WB 1901, *Guide to the Australian ethnographical collection in the National Museum of Victoria*, Government Printer, Melbourne.

Spencer, WB 1921, 'Presidential address: the Aborigines of Australia', in G Sweet & ACD Rivett (eds), *Report of the fifteenth meeting of the Australasian Association for the Advancement of Science*, pp. 53–89. AAAS, Sydney.

Spencer, WB & Gillen, FJ 1904, *The northern tribes of Central Australia*, McMillan, London.

Spencer, WB & Gillen, FJ 1938, *The Native Tribes of Central Australia*, MacMillan, London.

Spivak, G 1988, 'Can the subaltern speak?', in C Nelson & L Grossberg (eds), *Marxism and the interpretation of culture*, pp. 271–313, University of Illinois Press, Urbana.

Spriggs, M 1984, 'The lapita cultural complex: origins, distribution, contemporaries and successors', *Journal of Pacific History*, 19, pp. 202–23.

Spriggs, M 1996, 'Early agriculture and what went before in Island Melanesia: continuity or intrusion?', in DR Harris (ed.), *The origins and spread of agriculture and pastoralism in Eurasia*, pp. 524–37, University College London Press, London.

Spriggs, M 1997, *The island Melanesians*, Blackwell, Oxford.

Stanner, WEH 1979, 'Religion, totemism and symbolism', in WEH Stanner, *White man got no Dreaming: essays 1938–73*, pp. 106–43, ANU Press, Canberra.

Steward, JH 1955 (1977), *The theory of culture change: the methodology of multilinear evolution*, University of Illinois Press, Urbana.
Stirling, EC 1911, 'Preliminary report on the discovery of native remains at Swanport, River Murray; with an inquiry into the alleged occurrence of a pandemic among the Australian Aboriginals', *Transactions of the Royal Society of South Australia*, 35, pp. 4–46.
Stocking, GW jr 1987, *Victorian anthropology*, Macmillan Free Press, New York.
Stockton, ED 1981, 'Reflections around the campfire', *The Artefact*, 2, pp. 3–16.
Stone, J, Peterson, JA, Fifield, LK & Cresswell, RG 1997, 'Cosmogenic chlorine-36 exposure ages for two basalt flows in the Newer Volcanics Province: western Victoria', *Proceedings of the Royal Society of Victoria*, 109, pp. 121–31.
Stone, T & Cupper, ML, 2003, 'Last Glacial Maximum ages for robust humans at Kow Swamp, Southern Australia', *Journal of Human Evolution*, 45, pp. 99–111.
Strang, V 1997, *Uncommon ground: cultural landscapes and environmental values*, Berg, Oxford.
Strehlow, TGH 1947, *Aranda traditions*, Melbourne University Press, Melbourne.
Strehlow, TGH 1970, 'Geography and the totemic landscape in Central Australia: a functional study', in RM Berndt (ed.), *Australian Aboriginal anthropology*, pp. 92–140, University of Western Australia Press, Perth.
Struever, S 1968, 'Woodland subsistence systems in the lower Illinois Valley', in SR Binford & LR Binford (eds), *New perspectives in archaeology*, pp. 285–312, Aldine, Chicago.
Stuiver, M & Reimer, PJ 1993, 'Extended ^{14}C database and revised CALIB radiocarbon calibration program', *Radiocarbon*, 35, pp. 215–30.
Stuiver, M, Reimer, PJ, Bard, E, Beck, JW, Burr, GS, Hughen, KA, Kromer, B, McCormac, FG, van der Plicht, J & Spurk, M 1998, 'INTCAL98 Radiocarbon age calibration 24,000–0 cal BP', *Radiocarbon*, 40, pp. 1041–83.
Sunderland, S & Ray, LJ 1959, 'A note on the Murray Black collection of aboriginal skeletons', *Proceedings Royal Society Victoria*, 71, pp. 45–8.
Taçon, P, Wilson, M & Chippindale, C 1996, 'Birth of the Rainbow Serpent in Arnhem Land rock art and oral history', *Archaeology in Oceania*, vol. 31, no. 3, pp. 103–24.
Tamisari, F 1998, 'Body, vision and movement: in the footprints of the ancestors', *Oceania*, 68, pp. 249–70.
Tamisari, F 2002, 'Names and naming: speaking forms into place', in L Hercus, F Hodges & J Simpson (eds), *The land is map: placenames of indigenous origin in Australia*, pp. 87–102, Pandanus Press, Canberra.
Tamisari, F 2006, 'Personal Acquaintance: Essential Individuality and the Possibilities of Encounters', in T Lea, E Kowal and G Cowlishaw (eds) *Moving Anthropology*, Charles Darwin University Press, Darwin.
Taplin, G 1874, *The Narrinyeri: an account of the tribes of South Australian aborigines inhabiting the country around the Lakes of Alexandrina, Albert, and Coorong, and the lower part of the River Murray*, JT Shawyer, Adelaide.
Taplin, G 1879, *The folklore, manners, customs, and languages of the South Australian Aborigines*, E Spiller, Government Printer, Adelaide.
Tarlow, S 1999 *Bereavement and commemoration: an archaeology of mortality*, Blackwell, Oxford.

References

Tarlow, S 2000, 'Emotion in archaeology', *Current Anthropology*, 41, pp. 713–46.

Taylor, K 2000, 'New pressure on Ruddock', *The Age*, 5 October.

Taylor, L 1996, *Seeing the inside: bark painting in Western Arnhem Land*, Clarendon Press, Oxford.

Terrell, JE 1993, 'Regional studies in anthropology: a Melanesian prospectus', *Current Anthropology*, 34, pp. 177–9.

Terrell, JE 2002, 'Tropical agroforestry, coastal lagoons, and Holocene prehistory in Greater Near Oceania', in S Yoshida & PJ Matthews (eds), *Vegeculture in Eastern Asia and Oceania*, pp. 195–216, JCAS symposium series 16, Japan Centre for Area Studies, National Museum of Ethnology, Osaka.

Terrell, JE, Hart, JP, Barut, S, Cellinese, N, Curet, A, Denham, TP, Haines, H, Kusimba, CM, Latinis, K, Oka, R, Palka, J, Pohl, MED, Pope, KO, Staller, JE & Williams, PR 2003, 'Domesticated landscapes: the subsistence ecology of plant and animal domestication', *Journal of Archaeological Method and Theory*, vol. 10, no. 4, pp. 323–68.

Terrill, A 1998, 'Biri', *Languages of the world*, Lincom Europa, Munich.

Thomas, J 1996, *Time, culture and identity: an interpretive archaeology*, Routledge, London.

Thomas, J 1999, *Understanding the Neolithic*, Routledge, London.

Thomas, J, 2001, 'Archaeologies of place and landscape', in I Hodder (ed.), *Archaeological theory today*, pp. 165–86, Polity Press, Cambridge.

Thomas, J 2002, 'Archaeology, humanism and the materiality of the body', in Y Hamilakis, M Pluciennik & S Tarlow (eds), *Thinking through the body: archaeologies of corporeality*, pp. 29–45, Kluwer Academic/Plenum Publishers, New York.

Thomas, N 1994, *Colonialism's culture: anthropology, travel and government*, Polity Press, Cambridge.

Thomas, N 1981, 'Social theory, ecology and epistemology: theoretical issues in Australian prehistory', *Mankind*, 13, pp. 165–77.

Thomas, N 1990, 'Partial texts: representation, colonialism and agency in Pacific history', *The Journal of Pacific History*, vol. 25, no. 2, pp. 139–58.

Thomson, DF 1939, 'The seasonal factor in human culture: illustrated from the life of a contemporary nomadic group', *Proceedings of the Prehistoric Society*, vol. 5, no. 2, pp. 209–21.

Thomson, DF 1949, 'Arnhem Land: explorations among an unknown people, II', *Geographical Journal*, 113, pp. 1–8.

Thorley, PB 1998, 'Shifting location, shifting scale: a regional landscape approach to the prehistoric archaeology of the Palmer River Catchment, central Australia', unpublished PhD thesis, Northern Territory University, Darwin.

Thorley, P & Gunn, B 1996, 'Archaeological research from the eastern border lands of the Western Desert', unpublished paper for the Western Desert Origins workshop, Australian Linguistic Institute, Canberra.

Thorne, AG 1971a, 'Mungo and Kow Swamp: morphological variation in Pleistocene Australians', *Mankind*, 8, pp. 85–9.

Thorne, AG 1971b, 'The racial affinities and origins of the Australian Aborigines', in DJ Mulvaney & J Golson (eds), *Aboriginal man and environment in Australia*, pp. 316–25, ANU Press, Canberra.

Thorne, AG, Grün, R, Mortimer, G, Spooner, NA, Simpson, JJ, McCulloch, MT, Taylor, L & Curnoe, D 1999, 'Australia's oldest human remains: age of the Lake Mungo 3 skeleton', *Journal of Human Evolution*, 36, pp. 591–612.
Thorne, AG & Macumber, PG 1972, 'Discoveries of late Pleistocene man at Kow Swamp, Australia', *Nature*, 238, pp. 316–19.
Tibby, J 2003, 'Explaining lake and catchment change using sediment derived and written histories: an Australian perspective', *The Science of the Total Environment*, vol. 310, nos. 1–3, pp. 61–71.
Tilley, C (ed.) 1990, *Reading material culture: structuralism, hermeneutics and post-structuralism*, Basil Blackwell, Oxford.
Tilley, C 1994, *A phenomenology of landscape: places, paths and monuments*, Berg, Oxford.
Tilley, C 1995, 'Rocks as resources: landscapes and power', *Cornish Archaeology*, 34, pp. 5–57.
Tilley, C, Hamilton, S & Bender, B 2000a, 'Art and the re-presentation of the past', *The Journal of the Royal Anthropological Institute*, vol. 6, no. 1, pp. 35–62.
Tilley, C, Hamilton, S, Harrison, S & Anderson, E 2000b,' Nature, culture, clitter. Distinguishing between cultural and geomorphological landscapes; the case for hilltop tors in south-west England', *Journal of Material Culture*, vol. 5, no. 2, pp. 197–224.
Tindale NB 1940, 'Results of the Harvard–Adelaide Universities Anthropological Expedition, 1938–39: distribution of Australian Aboriginal tribes; a field survey', *Transactions of the Royal Society of South Australia*, vol. 64, no. 1, pp. 140–231.
Tindale NB 1974, *Aboriginal tribes of Australia*, University of California Press, Berkeley.
Tonkinson, R 1991, *The Mardu Aborigines: living the dream in Australia's desert*, Holt, Rinehart & Winston, Fort Worth.
Torgersen, T, Luly, J, De Deckker, P, Jones, MR, Searle, DE, Chivas, AR & Ullman, WJ 1988, 'Late Quaternary environments of the Carpentaria Basin, Australia', *Palaeogeography, Palaeoclimatology, Palaeoecology*, 67, pp. 245–61.
Torrence, R & Clarke, A (eds) 2000, *The archaeology of different: negotiating cross-cultural engagements in Oceania*, Routledge, London.
Tournal, P 1833, 'Considérations générales sur le phénomène des cavernes à ossemens', *Annales de Chimie et de Physique*, 52, pp. 161–81.
Trezise, P 1993, *Dream road: a journey of discovery*, Allen & Unwin, St Leonards.
Trigger, BG 1984, 'Alternative archaeologies: nationalist, colonialist and imperialist', *Man*, 19, pp. 355–70.
Trigger, BG 1989, *A history of archaeological thought*, Cambridge University Press, Cambridge.
Trigger, D 1989, *Mugularrangu (Garawa) land claim*, Northern Land Council, Darwin.
Tylor, EB 1865, *Researches into the early history of mankind and the development of civilisation*, John Murray, London.
Tylor, EB 1871, *Primitive culture*, John Murray, London.
Tylor, EB 1884, 'How the problems of American anthropology present themselves to the English mind', *Science*, vol. 4, no. 98, pp. 545–51.

Ucko, P 1987, *Academic freedom and apartheid*, Duckworth, London.
Ucko, P & Dimbleby, GW (eds) 1969, *The domestication and exploitation of plants and animals*, Duckworth, London.
Ulm, S in press, 'Themes in the archaeology of mid-to-late Holocene Australia', in T Murray (ed.), *Archaeology from Australia*, Australian Scholarly Publications, Melbourne.
van Dyke, R & Alcock, S 2003, *Archaeologies of memory*, Blackwell Publishers, Melbourne.
Vanderwal, RL 1973, 'The Torres Strait: protohistory and beyond', *Occasional Papers in Anthropology*, 2, pp. 157-94, (University of Queensland).
Veth, P 1989, 'Islands in the interior: a model for the colonisation of Australia's arid zone', *Archaeology in Oceania*, 24, pp. 81–92.
Veth, P 1993, *Islands in the interior: the dynamics of prehistoric adaptations within the arid zone of Australia*, International Monographs in Prehistory, Ann Arbor.
Veth, P 1995, 'Aridity and settlement in north-west Australia', *Antiquity*, 69, pp. 733–46.
Veth, P 1999, 'The occupation of arid coastlines during the terminal Pleistocene of Australia', in J Hall & IJ McNiven (eds), *Australian coastal archaeology*, pp. 65–72, ANU Press, Canberra.
Veth, P 2000, 'Origins of the Western Desert language: convergence in linguistic and archaeological space and time models', *Archaeology in Oceania*, 35, pp. 11–19.
Veth, P in press, 'Cycles of aridity and human mobility: risk-minimization amongst late Pleistocene foragers of the Western Desert, Australia', *Desert people: archaeological perspectives*, Blackwell, Oxford.
Veth, P, Hiscock, P, O'Connor, S & Spriggs, M 1998, 'Gallus at the crossroads: diffusionist models for Asian artefact "traditions" in Australia and the lust hurrah for cultural evolutionism', *Artefact*, 21, pp. 14–18.
Veth, P & McDonald, J 2002, 'Can archaeology be used to address the principle of exclusive possession in native title?', in R Harrison & C Williamson (eds), *After Captain Cook: the archaeology of the recent indigenous past in Australia*, pp. 121–9, The University of Sydney Archaeological Methods Series 8, Sydney.
Veth, P & O'Connor, S 1996, 'A preliminary analysis of basal grindstones from the Carnarvon Range, Little Sandy Desert', *Australian Archaeology*, 43, pp. 20–2.
Veth, PM, O'Connor, S & Wallis, L 2000, 'Perspectives on ecological approaches in Australian archaeology', *Australian Archaeology*, 50, pp. 54–66.
Veth, P, Smith, M & Haley, M 2001, 'Kaalpi: the archaeology of a sandstone outlier in the Western Desert', *Australian Archaeology*, 52, pp. 9–17.
Veth, PM & Walsh, F 1988, 'The concept of "staple" plant foods in the Western Desert region of Western Australia', *Australian Aboriginal Studies*, 2, pp. 19–25.
Waddell, E 1972, *The mound builders: agricultural practices, environment and society in the Central Highlands of New Guinea*, University of Washingon Press, Seattle.
Wagner, R 1986, *Symbols that stand for themselves*, University of Chicago Press, Chicago.
Walker, D (ed.) 1972, *Bridge and barrier: the natural and cultural history of the Torres Strait*, Research School of Pacific Studies, ANU, Canberra.
Walker D & Chen, Y 1987, 'Palynological light on tropical rainforest dynamics', *Quaternary Science Reviews*, 6, pp. 77–92.

Wallace, JS 2002, 'An archaeology of place: an investigation into the experiential nature of place as an alternative to the notion of landscape for archaeology', unpublished BA (Hons) thesis, University of Queensland, St Lucia.

Walsh, K 1990, 'The post-modern threat to the past', in I Bapty & T Yates (ed.), *Archaeology after structuralism*, pp. 278–93, Routledge, London.

Walters, I 1988, 'Fish hooks: evidence for dual social systems in south-eastern Australia'. *Australian Archaeology*, 27, pp. 98–114.

Warner, WL, 1958, *A Black Civilisation*, Harper, Chicago.

Watchman, A 1992, 'Doubtful dates for Karolta engravings', *Australian Aboriginal Studies*, 92, pp. 51–5.

Watchman, A 1993, 'Evidence of a 25,000-year-old pictograph in northern Australia', *Geoarchaeology*, vol. 8, no. 6, pp. 465–73.

Watson, A & Keating, D 1999, 'Architecture and sound: an acoustic analysis of megalithic monuments in prehistoric Britain', *Antiquity*, 73, pp. 325–34.

Watson, H with the Yolngu community at Yirrkala and David Wade Chambers 1989, *Singing the land, signing the land: a portfolio of exhibits*, Deakin University Press, Geelong.

Webb, SG 1989, *The Willandra Lakes hominids*, Research School of Pacific Studies, ANU, Canberra.

Webb, SG 1995, *Palaeopathology of Aboriginal Australians: health and disease across a hunter-gatherer continent*, Cambridge University Press, Cambridge.

Weiner, J, Godwin, L & L'Oste-Brown, S 2002, 'Australian Aboriginal heritage and native title: an example of contemporary Indigenous connection to country in central Queensland', *National Native Title Tribunal Occasional Papers Series*, 1/2002.

Whallon, R 1971, 'Spatial analysis of Palaeolithic occupation areas', in C Renfrew (ed.), *The explanation of culture change: models in prehistory*, pp. 115–30, Duckworth, Surrey.

Whallon, R 1973, 'Spatial analysis of occupation floors I: application of dimensional analysis of variance', *American Antiquity*, 38, pp. 266–78.

White, C 1967, 'Early stone axes in Arnhem Land', *Antiquity*, 41, pp. 149–52.

White, C 1971, 'Man and environment in north-west Arnhem Land', in DJ Mulvaney & J Golson (eds), *Aboriginal man and environment in Australia*, pp. 141–57, ANU Press, Canberra.

White, JP 1971, 'New Guinea and Australian prehistory: the "Neolithic problem"', in DJ Mulvaney & J Golson (eds), *Aboriginal man and environment in Australia*, pp. 182–95, ANU Press, Canberra.

White, JP 1994, 'Australia: the different continent', in G Burenhult (ed.), *People of the Stone Age: hunter-gatherers and early farmers*, pp. 206–25, University of Queensland Press, St Lucia.

White, JP & O'Connell, JF 1979, 'Australian prehistory: new aspects on antiquity', *Science*, 203, pp. 21–8.

White, JP & O'Connell, JF 1982, *A prehistory of Australia, New Guinea and Sahul*, Academic Press, New York.

Whitehead, PJ, Bowman, DMJS, Preece, N, Fraser, F & Cooke, P 2003, 'Customary use of fire by indigenous peoples in northern Australia: its contemporary role in savanna management', *International Journal of Wildland Fire*, 12, pp. 415–25.

Whiting, M 1963, 'Toxicity of cycads', *Economic Botany*, 17, pp. 271–301.
Whitley, GP 1936, 'Aboriginal names mostly of marine animals from north Queensland', *Mankind*, 2, pp. 42–4.
Widlok, T in press, 'Theoretical shifts in the anthropology of desert hunter-gatherers', in P Veth, MA Smith & P Hiscock (eds), *Desert people: archaeological perspectives*, Blackwell, Oxford.
Wiessner, P 1983, 'Style and social information in Kalahari San projectile points', *American Antiquity*, 48, pp. 253–76.
Williams, E 1987, 'Complex hunter-gatherers: a view from Australia', *Antiquity*, 61, pp. 310–21.
Williams, E 1988, *Complex hunter-gatherers: a late-Holocene example from temperate Australia*, British Archaeological Reports, Oxford.
Williams, G 1988, *The standing stones of Wales and south-west England*, British Archaeological Reports, Oxford.
Williams, J, Hook, R & Hamblin, A 2002, *Agro-ecological regions of Australia: methodologies for their derivation and key issues in resource management*, CSIRO Land & Water, Canberra.
Williams, NM 1982, 'A boundary is to cross: observations on Yolngu boundaries and permission', in NM Williams & ES Hunn (eds), *Resource managers: North American and Australian hunter-gatherers*, pp. 131–53, Westview Press, Boulder.
Williams, NM 1986, *The Yolngu and their land: a system of land tenure and the fight for its recognition*, AIAS, Canberra.
Williams, NM & Baines, G (eds) 1993, *Traditional ecological knowledge: wisdom for sustainable development*, Centre for Resource and Environmental Studies, ANU, Canberra.
Williams, NM and ES Hunn (eds) 1982. *Resource Managers: North American and Australian hunter-gatherers*. Westview Press, Boulder.
Williams, NM & Mununggurr D 1989, 'Understanding Yolngu signs of the past', in Layton (ed.), *Who needs the past: indigenous values and archaeology*, Unwin, London.
Williams, R 1973, *The country and the city*, Chatto & Windus, London.
Williamson, C 1998, 'Late-Holocene Australia and the writing of Aboriginal history', in T Murray (ed.), *Archaeology of Aboriginal Australia: a reader*, pp. 141–8, Allen & Unwin, St Leonards.
Wilmore, M forthcoming, 'The book and the trowel: archaeological practice and authority at the Leskernick project', in B Bender (ed.), *The Leskernick project*, Berg, London.
Wilson, D 1851, *The archaeology and prehistoric annals of Scotland*, Sutherland & Knox, Edinburgh.
Winant, H 1990, 'Gayatri Spivak and the politics of the subaltern', *Socialist Review*, vol. 20, no. 3, pp. 81–97.
Windschuttle, K 2001, 'History, anthropology and the politics of Aboriginal society', paper to Samuel Griffith Society annual conference, Melbourne, 1 September 2001, at URL: http://www.sydneyline.com/Land_Rights_SGS.htm
Windschuttle, K 2002, *The fabrication of Aboriginal history 1: Van Diemen's Land 1803–47*, Macleay Press, Sydney.

Winterhalder, B & Smith, EA (eds) 1981, *Hunter-gatherer foraging strategies: ethnographic and archaeological analyses*, University of Chicago Press, Chicago.

Wobst, MH 1977, 'Stylistic behavior and information exchange', in CE Cleland (ed.), *For the director: research essays in honor of James B Griffin*, pp. 317–42, Anthropological papers 61, University of Michigan, Ann Arbor.

Wolfe, P 1999, *Settler colonialism and the transformation of anthropology: the politics and poetics of an ethnographic event*, Cassell, London.

Wolski, N 1995, 'From dry sanctuary to social markers: towards a phenomenology of Aboriginal earthen mounds in Western Victoria', unpublished BA (Hons) thesis, The University of Melbourne, Australia.

Woodburn, J 1972, 'Ecology, nomadic movement and the composition of the local group among hunters and gatherers: an East African example and its implications', in PJ Ucko, R Tringham & G Dimbleby (eds), *Man, settlement and urbanism*, pp. 194–206, Duckworth, London.

Woodroffe, CD & Grindrod, J 1991, 'Mangrove biogeography: the role of Quaternary environmental and sea-level change', *Journal of Biogeography*, 18, pp. 479–92.

Woodroffe, CD, Kennedy, DM, Hopley, D, Rasmussen, C & Smithers, SG 2000, 'Holocene reef growth in Torres Strait', *Marine Geology*, 170, pp. 331–46.

Wright, H jr 1976, 'The environmental setting for plant domestication in the near east', *Science*, 194, pp. 385–9.

Wurm, SA 1972, 'Torres Strait: a linguistic barrier?', in D Walker (ed.), *Bridge and barrier: the natural and cultural history of Torres Strait*, pp. 345–66, Research School of Pacific Studies, ANU, Canberra.

Yen, DE 1989, 'The domestication of environment', in DR Harris & GC Hillman (eds), *Foraging and farming: the evolution of plant exploitation*, pp. 55–75, Unwin Hyman, London.

Yen, DE 1995, 'The development of Sahul agriculture with Australia as bystander', *Antiquity*, 69, special no. 265, pp. 831–47.

Yengoyan, AA 1968,' Demographic and ecological influences on Australian Aboriginal marriage sections', in RB Lee & I DeVore (eds), *Man the hunter*, pp. 185–99, Aldine, Chicago.

Yengoyan, AA 1976, 'Structure, event and ecology in Aboriginal Australia: a comparative viewpoint', in N Peterson (ed.), *Tribes and boundaries in Australia*, pp. 121–32, AIAS, Canberra.

Yoffee, N & Sherratt, A 1993, 'Introduction: the sources of archaeological theory', in N Yoffee & A Sherratt (eds), *Archaeological theory: who sets the agenda?*, pp. 1–9, Cambridge University Press, Cambridge.

Zvelebil, M 1986, *Hunters in transition: Mesolithic societies of temperate Eurasia and the transition to farming*, Cambridge University Press, Cambridge.

Index

abandonment of places 214, 312–13
Aboriginal elders 76, 82, 134, 141–60, 189, 196–203, 239
Aboriginality 16, 68, 70–1
Aboriginal Cultural Heritage Act 137
Aboriginal Land Tribunal 153
Absence, of evidence 82, 109, 184, 257, 275; of occupation 70, 102, 128, 275, 282, 284, 302
academia 3, 20, 22, 25, 30, 35–8, 40, 48, 54, 58, 67–68, 73, 74, 120, 125, 287, 292, 306, 309, 316–17
academic activism 67, 316
academic responsibility 35–7, 316
accumulation 26, 140, 185, 221, 228, 275, 280, 281, 282
accuracy 56, 58–9, 73, 77, 84, 118, 157, 300
action archaeology 38
activity areas 204–6, 209–13, 221, 223, 243
adaptive thinking 3, 7–13, 15, 53, 60, 61, 88, 94, 96, 98–9, 103, 104, 113, 114, 120, 205–14, 227, 253, 307
Adelaide 231
adzes 95; burren 100; tula 87, 97, 98, 99, 100, 243, 245
affiliation to country 130, 142, 144
Africa 5, 89, 306
African National Congress (ANC) 306
age 10, 130, 158, 217, 232, 236, 238, 240; of objects 170, 197
age-depth curves 260, 278
agency 8, 9, 15, 16–19, 23, 92, 111, 113–14, 118, 139, 191, 195, 198, 201, 219–22, 264, 265
aggregation locales 232, 242, 245–50, 252, 253
agreements 132
agriculture 12, 23–5, 31, 46, 54–71, 91, 226, 228, 232, 286, 295; origins of 28, 30, 52, 53, 58, 60–3, 65, 109, 115–6, 254, 257, 294
ahistoricism 9, 23, 89
Ailan Kastom 290
Alaska 14
Alice River 144
Allen, H 28

Allen, J 29
alliances 11, 151, 229, 249, 250, 253
Alu Aya 141
Aluwanja 175
a-Manankurrmara, EM 167
ambivalence 95, 96, 120
Amis, K 46
Anaktuvuk Pass 14
anaemia 232
analogy 10, 43, 49, 73–4, 76, 78, 98, 131, 152, 181, 205, 229
ancestors 13, 15–18, 37, 43, 57, 125–8, 130–2, 134–5, 142, 144–5, 148–50, 154–5, 165, 168, 175, 179, 184, 185, 189–94, 196–97, 199, 202, 216–21
ancestral connections 13, 16, 127, 130–1, 133, 134, 149, 154, 168, 179, 183, 185, 189–91, 193–4, 196, 201–2, 216–8
ancestral journeys 125, 126, 130–1, 148, 165, 189–90, 197, 216–21; and 'strings' 218
Angas, GF 237
animal kill sites 14
appropriation 31, 118; of Indigenous land 5
aquaculture 256, 266, 269
archaeological survey 41, 42, 75, 78, 125, 132–5, 199, 293, 311–2, 314
archaeology and material culture 2, 90, 92–4, 103, 125, 132, 136, 140, 182–202, 233, 243, 284, 309
archaeology as anthropology 25–6, 38, 47, 124–5, 129, 183–4, 205
archaeology as history 25–6, 57
archaeology as science 20–1, 24–5, 37–38, 55–6, 72–3, 79, 83, 90, 114, 119
archaic faces petroglyphs 247
Archer River 142, 153
archival records 18, 28, 43, 45
Argant, J 280
arid zones 27, 58, 211, 232, 243, 244–5, 247–53
Arnhem Land 94, 95, 97, 98, 100, 124, 126, 147, 170, 188, 216, 217
Arrernte (Aranda) 126, 227

368

Index

Asia 67, 92, 93, 94, 95, 97, 98, 99, 100, 102, 105, 254; *see also* Near East, Middle East
assemblage variability 43, 209, 226, 228, 236–9, 240, 247, 250
assimilation 4; of ideas 110, 114
Atherton Tablelands 282
Australian Archaeological Association 38
Australian–Indonesian archaeological expedition to Sulawesi Selatan of 1969 97
Austronesian 283–4, 297
authenticity 73, 78
authoritarianism 227, 240
authority 14, 18, 37, 43, 217, 79, 84, 133, 149, 164, 177, 191, 193, 200, 203, 206, 226, 227, 228, 290, 301
Avery, J 165
avoidance 133, 147; and conflict 175; and representation 37, 44, 202, 213; in debate 29, 102; of wildfires 157
Ayapathu 151

'baby' sites 149
backed artefacts 26, 87–8, 95, 98–102
Badu 15 rock shelter 271, 273–86, 296
Badu island 271–86, 293, 296, 301
Bahn, P 4
baking 172, 238
Balnauran of Clava 221
bananas 291, 300
bands 33, 228, 291
baobab, spread of 58
baptism 150
Barham, AJ 289–91, 294–6, 300
bari bari 133–4
Barngalinyi 133
Barrow Point 141, 151
barter 94
base camps 285
Bathurst Range 142
Bauer, WE 77
bays 153; *see also specific bay names*
beaches 143, 145, 152, 154, 186, 196, 284, 290
beads 228
Beaton, JM 29, 46, 101, 142, 172
beche-de-mer 292
behavioural archaeology 209–10
Bell, D 239
Bellwood, P 100
Benjamin, W 52, 71, 310
Berndt, C 188, 239
Berndt, R 126, 138, 188, 239
Bhabha, H 54
binary oppositions 55, 80, 150
Bindal 76, 78
Bine 290
Binford, LR 14, 23, 42–3, 205, 206, 209–10, 223
Binford, S 43

Bing Bong 168
bioclimatic modelling 257, 282
biography, of objects 185; of place 164
biomass 265
Bird, CFM 29
Bird, DW 295, 298, 299
Birdsell, JB 6, 25, 117–18
Birri Gubba 76
birthplace 129, 130, 132
birthrights 180, 217
Black, GM 234
Blackwater 134
Blackwood, R 234
Blanchetown 226, 228, 235
Blaut, JM 89–90
Bliege Bird, RB 295, 299
blood 131, 138, 170, 191, 202
Bodmin Moor 311
body, the 134, 176, 188, 189, 195, 205, 215–22, 236, 240, 301; *see also* embodiment
body language 197
bone arrangements 13, 197
boomerangs 98, 99, 167, 193
Borlase, W 316
Borroloola 165, 166–7, 173, 177–8, 192
boundaries 74–6, 78, 150, 152–5, 208, 229, 231, 233, 240, 242, 248, 295, 298; disciplinary 12, 26, 184, 205, 222, 318; *see also* frontiers
Bowler, PJ 89
Bowen Basin 134
boycotts 306
Bradley, R 221
Bradshaw rock art 85
Brady, L 283
Brakeman River 157
Bramell, E 95
'bridge and barrier' 103, 292, 295, 302
Brisbane 47, 308
Bromfield Swamp 282
Bronze Age 25, 311–14
Brown, A 126–7
Budjimala 133
burials 14, 15, 18, 93, 129, 130, 149, 188, 197, 199, 226–41, 313
Burketown 166
burning, of the landscape 58, 143, 147–8, 155–9, 178, 180, 255, 261, 262, 264, 265, 271, 275, 279–85
burnt earth 15, 301
Busby, JR 257
butchering sites 14, 206, 210
Butterworth, I 82
buttons 237

Calvert Range 248, 249, 250
Calvert River 162

369

Index

Cambridge Anthropological Expedition to Torres Straits 287
camping 15, 82, 126, 143, 145, 149, 150, 151, 154, 158, 160, 175, 206, 218, 219, 237–8, 285, 312
Canada 68
Canals, *see* drainage systems
Canning Stock Route 251
canoes 75, 93–4, 146, 238; outrigger 92, 102, 104–5, 291, 297
Cape Conway 75
Cape Otway 210
Cape Vanderlin 189
Cape York Land Summit of 1993 153
Cape York Peninsula 27, 81, 94, 105, 135, 139, 141–60, 272–3, 288, 291, 293, 297
Carnarvon Ranges 246, 248
Carpentaria Basin 283
carrying capacity 44
carved trees 132
Casey, E 206, 215, 217, 218, 219, 221, 222
cattle–grazing 139, 145, 146, 147, 155, 157–8, 317
causality 8, 110, 111, 114
cemeteries 14, 28, 221, 226, 228, 230–41
central Australia 99, 126, 227, 242–53
Central Australian Ranges 244, 250
Centre Island 168, 173
Century Mine 132
ceremonial grounds 128, 172
ceremony, *see* ritual
change, *see* social change
channels, *see* drainage systems
charcoal 15, 186, 203, 235, 294, 301; records 256, 259, 261–3, 265, 268, 275, 276–86
Chase, AK 65, 81, 142
Chepstow-Lusty, A 255
chiefdoms 228, 240; hereditary 240
China 4, 53
Chippindale, C 55–6
Chivas AR 265
choice 18, 23, 62, 68, 112, 113, 132, 133
Christianity 301
circumcision 173
citizenship 54, 70
civilization 43, 53, 56, 67–9, 90, 254
clans 130, 148, 150, 154, 193, 238, 239, 248, 291; clan boundaries 149, 298–9
Clarke, DL 2, 23
Clarke, J 149
Clarke Range 76
classical archaeology 20
classification 53–4, 64, 186, 188, 193, 194, 200, 245
Cleland Hills 244, 247, 249
'clever' men 133–4
climate 2, 67, 142, 143, 158, 213, 252, 267, 273, 307; change 15, 45, 109, 113, 244, 254–65, 269, 282–283; warming 254, 260

closed systems 23–4, 27, 32–3, 214, 285–6
clothing pins 236
coasts 27, 41, 42, 43, 45, 72, 74, 76, 77, 78, 81, 94, 100, 102, 103, 104, 139, 141, 142–4, 150, 151, 152, 153, 154, 168, 171, 174, 175, 192, 203, 218, 231–2, 238–9, 247, 273, 274, 284, 288, 290, 291, 293, 294, 297
Cobrico Swamp 267
coconuts 291, 300
cognition 119, 139, 140, 183, 185, 201, 215
Coleman River 144
Colfelt, D 77
collectivity 10, 113
Collinsville 76
colonial diffusionism 88–92, 103, 104
colonialism 4, 5, 9, 11, 16–17, 18, 37, 73, 85, 88, 89, 91, 110, 119, 120, 121, 127, 141, 186; *see also* colonial diffusionism
colonialist discourses 9, 11, 16, 17, 25, 85, 87–9, 91; *see also* colonial diffusionism
colonisation 14, 26, 28, 44, 89, 91, 105, 147, 252, 254, 283–4, 297
Colosseum 3
colour, significance of 202, 221, 316
communion foods 172
community-based archaeology 73, 295
competition 14, 30, 32–3, 60, 62, 229, 240, 299
complexification 32–3, 61, 229, 240
complexity, sociocultural 4, 14, 17, 24–5, 27–34, 36, 38, 46, 48, 53, 60, 61, 63, 64, 83, 94, 108, 110, 111, 114–15, 122, 141, 179, 182, 198–200, 206–8, 226, 228–40, 242, 250, 288, 295–302
conception site 130
Conkey, MW 248, 250
connectivity 6, 13, 15, 62, 67, 85, 127, 140, 142, 150, 196, 199, 216–20, 250, 270, 291
conservatism 31, 35–6, 92, 108, 113, 118, 120, 227, 242, 243–4
contestation 24–5, 39, 183, 206, 207, 250, 309
contingency 109, 145, 162, 215, 315, 317
control over environment 23, 44, 65, 156, 158, 169
convergence of thought 124–5, 244
cooking facilities 15
Cooktown 76
Coorong 231, 239
Cornwall 311, 314
Cosgrove, R 29, 62
cosmology 14, 87, 105, 125, 126, 127, 130, 135, 136, 137, 138, 139, 162, 169, 175, 176, 180, 190, 208, 216, 296, 298
country 133, 134, 135, 142, 147, 152, 159, 162, 164, 167, 168, 172, 178, 179, 183; attachment to 9, 127, 129–30, 132, 136, 146, 149, 150, 151, 153, 168, 175, 178, 180, 181, 186, 189, 190, 191, 194–6, 198, 200–3, 214; manager of 189; owner of 146, 153, 168, 189, 217; rights to 130, 132, 150, 151, 168, 180, 194, 199

370

'cowboy' archaeology 47
craft specialisation 228, 229, 239, 297
craftspeople 210, 229
cranial analyses 211, non-metric 232–3
Creamer, H 83
Cribb, R 135
cribra orbitalia 232
Croker Island 126
cross-cultural comparisons 4, 7
Crown Lagoon 41
cult lodges 227, 238, 239, 240
cultural change, *see* social change
cultural continuity 47, 74, 82, 127–30, 134, 135, 148, 184, 185, 192, 196, 198, 201, 213, 215, 243, 247, 249, 252–3, 300
cultural core 6–7, 10, 13
cultural ecology 6–7, 112
Cultural Marxism 309
cultural materialism 7–8, 205
Cultural Record (Landscapes Queensland and Queensland Estate) Act 132
cultural *nullius* 70
culture history 67, 96, 112
Cumberland Islands 75
Cundy, B 186, 187–8, 201
custodianship 15, 130, 135, 136
custom 57, 91, 127–8, 129, 130, 136, 148–9, 152–3, 290, 292
customary marine tenure 79
cycads 16, 58, 161–81, 186, 193, 199, 255
Cyclone Kathy 173
cylcons 184–203

dams 238, 266
Dams, L 221
dance 178, 216, 218, 219
Darvill, T 182
Darwin 166
Dauan island 293
Dauar island 283, 289, 296–8, 300
Davidson, DS 91, 92, 93, 94, 95
Davis, OK 276
Dawson, J 208
D'Costa, DM 260
Dead Sea Scrolls 128
death 3, 71, 130, 131, 134, 135, 168, 175, 178, 180, 186, 195, 198, 201, 217, 218, 233, 239, 292, 301, 313
decision-making 18, 112, 132–3
De Latour, G. 166, 172
'delayed-return' economic strategies 286
demands, on the environment 9; socio-economic 10–11, 23, 104, 162, 229, 308
demography 7, 22–3, 27, 44, 45, 60, 103, 109, 205, 213, 214, 222, 227, 242, 244, 252, 253, 271, 307; demographic expansion 11, 105, 122, 254–5, 303
dental enamel hypoplasia 232

Department of Immigration and Multicultural Affairs 68, 70
Department of Immigration and Multicultural and Aboriginal Affairs 70
Department of Reconciliation and Aboriginal and Torres Strait Islander Affairs 70
descent 142, 144, 150, 155, 164; cognatic 151; corporate groups 193, 231; matrilineal 168, 174; patrilineal 168, 193, 217
desecration of cultural sites 132, 145–6, 191
Desert Culture 243, 244, 253
devolution 119
Devon Downs 235
DeVore, I 6, 64
dew 155–7, 158, 171
dialectics 8
diatom analysis 256, 257, 259–65, 268, 269
diet 3, 8, 23, 41, 82, 108, 180, 231–2, 240, 245–6, 255, 297
diffusion 5, 6, 9, 17, 25, 61, 67, 85, 87–106, 245, 251, 253
Dimbleby, GW 276
dingoes 26, 85–6, 96, 97–101, 102, 103, 105–6, 234, 235
diplomacy 207, 210
Dirdiyalma, P 175, 198, 199
disadvantage 17, 68–9, 88
disciplinary expectation 7, 8, 26, 47, 57, 80, 86, 88, 96, 114, 117, 119, 122, 137, 140, 159, 182, 183, 184, 186, 205, 208, 222, 318
diseases 106, 130, 134–5, 175–6, 180, 232, 292
displacement 82, 134
dispossession 5, 134
disputes 64, 79, 102, 210
disrespect 131, 135
diversification 97, 140
diversity, sociocultural 40, 59, 90, 117, 134, 209, 226, 228, 241, 245, 246, 247, 250, 251, 253, 302; environmental 233, 279, 280, 285, 288, 290
division of labor 64, 237
Djungan 214
Dodson, JR 105, 256, 283
dogs 100, 105; swimming dog story 146–8; *see also* dingoes
domestication 57–8, 64
domiculture 65, 246
domus 65, 246
Doomadgee 132
Dortch, CE 99–100
drainage systems, anthropogenic 13, 23, 44, 58, 159, 266, 293, 294, 308
Dreaming, the (Story) 81, 82, 124, 126–7, 130–1, 133, 145–8, 149–50, 154, 163–4, 165, 169, 172, 173, 175, 176, 179, 189, 214, 215
Dreaming tracks 126–7, 130–1, 133, 154, 189
dual signalling 248

371

Index

dugong 82, 143, 154, 164, 168, 175, 189, 193, 194, 288, 290
dunes 152, 189, 196, 230, 234, 235–6, 272, 284
Durba Hills 247
Durba Springs 246, 251
duty of care 136
dwelling 140, 162, 180, 204, 205, 206, 207, 213, 219, 221, 222, 256, 286

ecological niches 24, 151, 232
ecological pressure 250
ecological thinking 65, 66, 105–6, 111, 113, 140, 142, 151, 159, 205, 232, 242, 250, 253, 269, 273, 282, 286, 288, 293, 294
edge-ground axes 15, 77, 82, 90, 91, 93–4, 95, 96, 99
Edwards, R 248
efficiency 11, 101–2, 105, 253
eels harvesting 10, 11, 13, 23, 32, 44, 58, 141, 159, 229, 256, 265–7, 308
egalitarianism 114, 226–7, 240
Egypt 3, 57, 128, 254
Eight-class kin system 253
Elliot Smith, G. 91, 93
El Niño–Southern Oscillation (ENSO) 254, 256
emblatic signalling 246
embodiment 15, 16, 193–4, 199, 201, 204, 206, 217, 218, 220, 222, 249, 309–10, 317
emotions 83, 105, 136, 146, 167, 175, 183–4, 194, 196, 198–202, 217, 220
empiricism 6–7, 8, 36, 48, 56, 83, 85, 104, 110, 111, 112–3, 120, 121, 122
emplacement 14, 129, 205, 215, 219, 220, 222; *see also* place
empowerment 20, 72–3
enclosures 311–4
Encounter Bay 239
energy harnessing 10, 12, 24, 44, 58, 61, 65
England, *see* Great Britain
Enlightenment 67, 89
environmental determinism 6, 7, 9, 11, 46, 112
environmental impacts 12, 53, 106, 140, 254, 271, 284–5
environmental impact studies (EIS) 125, 136, 137
environmental knowledge 65, 155, 246
epistemology 7–9, 18–19, 48, 85, 88, 188, 214, 215, 222
equilibrium 45, 227, 263, 307
essentialism 65, 69, 90, 94, 108, 117, 212, 215–16, 220, 222
estates 144, 148–9, 151, 153–4, 155, 158, 159, 165, 174, 176
estuarine zone 144, 152, 153, 154, 288
ethics 204, 214
ethnocentrism 57, 68, 70
ethology 10
etiquette 148

European-contact 57, 81, 301
Evans Bay 293
evolutionism 5, 11, 14, 53, 62, 97–8, 112, 119; biological 30; linear 17, 24, 28, 56–8, 63, 65, 66, 88–92, 109, 116; social 9, 61, 63, 65, 66, 88–92, 114–16; progressionism 28, 56–8, 63, 65, 66, 68, 88–92, 116
exchange, *see* trade
exclusion, of ideas 80, 115, 119, 128, 137, 184, 232, 246; of people 54, 78, 233
exogamy 193, 291
exotic goods 99, 101, 245, 251
experience 14, 16, 21, 30, 47, 54, 81, 82, 103, 127, 130, 133–4, 136, 150, 158, 159, 164, 183, 194, 200, 201, 202, 204–6, 212, 215–23, 246, 303, 314
extensification 109
external influence 9, 10, 17, 61, 67, 85–106, 117, 205, 210, 211, 253, 263, 271, 308
extinction 105, 233
European impacts on the environment 256, 264
Eyre, JE 237–8

Fabian, J 121
Fagan, B 6, 254
falsification, and Indigenous epistemologies 18–19
Faris, JC 205
farming 11, 24–5, 60, 115–6, 306, 308, 309; *see also* agriculture, horticulture
feasts 23, 308
fecundity 128, 145, 154
Federal Court of Australia 136
feelings 149, 162, 218, 309, 317
Feld, S 218
Feldman, R 13, 286, 296
feminist approaches to archaeology 183
fencing 59
Fenton, J 310
fermentation 165–6, 171–2
figurative designs 247, 316
fire 11, 58, 139, 147, 179, 261, 262, 274, 275, 278, 279, 281, 283, 284, 286, 312; management of 13, 140, 148, 155–8
firebreaks 140, 157–8
fire-stick farming 11
First Contact 67, 71
Fisher, G 204
fishhooks 104
fishing 10, 45, 59, 126, 149, 153–4, 238, 266, 290, 298–9
fish traps 9–10, 266, 298, 299, 300
Fitzhugh, B 13
fixed facilities 13, 15, 229, 286; *see also specific types of fixed facilities*
fixity 54, 137–8, 190, 220–1, 286, 318
flags 290, 316

flake and blade technocomplex 100
Flannery, TF 105
Flenniken, JJ 88
Flinders, M. 186, 188, 203
Flinders Island group 142
Flood, JM 100
floods 15, 55, 58, 142, 144, 237, 266, 288
fluidity 33, 208, 209, 214, 285, 318
Fly River (Papua New Guinea) 92, 284
Foelsche River 165, 166, 174, 176
footprints 18, 129, 130–1, 135, 219–20
foraging 57, 59, 64, 66, 140, 216, 219, 253, 291, 295; *see also* hunting and gathering
Ford, RI 64
forest loss 263, 278–80, 283
forestry 141, 152
forgetting 131, 221
fossils 56, 89–90
foxes 105
Frankel, D 29, 35, 108, 111
Frederick, U 248
Friedman, J 8, 307
Fromm's Landing 97, 235
frontiers 3, 12, 253; violence 131, 147, 155
functional explanations 11, 24–5, 61, 187, 209, 211, 253

Gadamer, H-G 18, 54, 214
Galt-Smith, B 247, 248
Gangalidda 132
Gardner, D 66–7
Garrwa 162–71, 176, 179, 202–3
gardens 59, 66, 79, 115, 173, 294, 298, 299, 312; *see also* agriculture, farming, horticulture
Geba island 293
gender 4, 10, 14, 179, 180, 194, 217, 238, 239, 309–10, 317; and space 314
genealogies 149
gene flow 106, 233
genocide 4
Gero, JM 77
Ghaleb, B 294
Ghungalu 134–5
Gia 76, 78
Gibbs, M 250, 253
Gidra 290
gift exchange 94, 192, 194
giving smell 149–50, 217
Gizra 290
gladiators 3
Glover, IC 100
Goba story 301–2
Godelier, M 32, 205, 308
Golson, J 66, 67
Gorecki, P 67
Gould, RA 95, 242, 243, 244, 246
governance 132, 149

grand narratives 14, 54, 108, 110, 116, 118, 121, 130, 184, 220, 222
graphic systems 242, 249–50, 253
grasslands 58, 155, 272
grave goods 226, 233–7
graveyards, *see* cemeteries
Great Barrier Reef 82, 142, 288
Great Basin (USA) 6, 243
Great Britain 35, 45, 56, 311–14, 316–17
Great Dividing Range 143, 144
Greek philosophers 55, 89
greenstone 15
Greenwool, W 150
grindstones 171, 173–5, 179, 245, 247
Groote Eylandt 161, 283
ground-ovens 15, 173, 232, 235, 238
groves 58, 164, 165–7, 169, 173, 180
Gudanji 166
Guddemi, P 64
Gulf of Carpentaria 132–4, 144, 161–81, 182–203
Gunditjmara 265, 266
guns 152–3
Gunwinggu 126
Guugu Yimithirr 141, 151, 153

Haberle, SG 255, 256
habitus 185, 201, 309
Habu, J 13–14
Haddon, AC 92, 287, 290, 291, 292, 298–9
hafting 96–7, 243
Haglund, L 226
Hale, HM 235
Hallam, S 58, 100–1
Hamilakis, Y 204, 221
Hamilton, S 311
hammer-dressing 95
Hann River 144, 153
Harney (senior), W 166, 169, 188
Harris, DR 45, 46, 57, 64, 65, 286, 291, 293–5, 302
Harris, M 7, 205
Harris lines 232
Harrison, SP 283
Harvard–Adelaide Universities Anthropological Expedition of 1938 75
harvesting 12, 65, 141, 145, 151, 229, 256, 265, 266–7
Harvey, A 167
Hayden, B 67
Hayman Island 75
Head, L 62, 266, 284
headbands 236
healing 176–8, 203
health 133, 136, 168, 178, 195, 232
hearths 65, 133, 210, 219, 223, 235, 243, 275
Hegel, G 89

Index

hegemony 5, 63–4
Hemming, S 239
herding 115, 155, 237, 312
heredity 228, 240
heritage, cultural 17, 72, 73, 116, 132, 134, 183, 199, 201, 202; management and protection 127, 128–9, 135–7, 296
hermeneutics 18, 74
Hiatt, B, *see* Meehan, B
Hiatt, LR 226
hierarchy, evolutionary 57; hereditary 228; of authority 226, 239, 315; of knowledge 79, 82, 315; social 227, 228, 239, 314, 315
High Court of Australia 79, 127
Hiscock, P 87–8, 243, 244, 249
historical accuracy 56–7, 58, 65, 73–4, 77, 84, 118, 300
historical archaeology 38
historical materialism 8
historicism 5, 13, 18, 74, 131, 159, 162
historiography, Aboriginal 18; of archaeology 53, 118, 183, 287
history wars 120
Hitchcock, G 92, 106
Hodder, I 79–80, 184
Holdaway, S 29
Holocene, early 15, 49, 88, 142, 236, 239, 240, 255, 261, 263, 264, 275, 280, 283, 285; late 11, 15, 27–9, 32–5, 63, 85, 86, 94, 102–4, 106, 107–8, 112, 141, 159, 161, 207, 213, 215, 229, 231–41, 242–51, 255–7, 262, 270–1, 280, 283, 285, 286, 295, 296, 303; mid 29, 35, 46, 49, 63, 102, 107–8, 141, 215, 232, 244, 254–6, 262, 282, 283, 289
homeostasis 11, 117, 118, 227
Hook Island 82
Horsfall, N 58
horticulture 25, 44–5, 59, 64, 66, 270, 271, 290–1, 292–5, 300, 302–3; *see also* agriculture
Houston, S 223
Huchet, B 7
Hughes, PJ 32, 211, 223
human-environment interaction, *see* people-land relations
human impacts 53, 256, 264, 271, 285
human and social rights 17, 38, 70, 73, 74, 127–8, 130, 148–9, 151, 155, 164, 175, 179, 180, 192, 193–4, 199, 211, 253, 298, 316–17
hunting and gathering
hunting stands 14
huts 238; hut pits 210
hydrologic processes 12
Hynes, R 65

Iama island 272, 293
ice-free corridors 254
identity 4, 37, 70, 72–3, 119, 121, 220, 290, 292, 298; corporate identity 9, 129, 154–5, 164, 179, 180, 183, 198, 217, 219, 220, 246, 247, 249, 250–1, 252; and land 9, 162, 164, 167, 180, 183, 198, 217; symbols of 9, 83, 120, 180, 249, 250, 252
Illinois 228
illness 130, 134, 135, 175, 176–8, 180
imagery, *see* representation
'immediate-return' economic strategies 285, 308
immigrants 70
imperialism, cultural 83
imports 97, 105
incantations 188
inclusiveness 83, 246
increase sites 135, 177–8
independent invention 86, 90
India 93, 95, 98, 100
Indigenous rights, *see* human and social rights
Indonesia 86, 93, 96–8
IndoPacific Prehistory Association (IPPA) 100
Industrial Revolution 35
inequality 309–10
infection 232
infectious disease analyses 232
inference 73–4, 97, 125, 286
information exchange 249–50
ingenuity 69, 94
Ingold, T 8, 139, 140, 158, 212–13
inheritance 5, 16–17, 25, 88, 141, 148, 151–2, 155, 158
inherited friendships 141, 151–2
innovation 6–7, 10, 89, 98, 101, 108, 109, 117, 251–4, 266, 297
insanity 134
inscription 15, 124, 188, 203, 213, 219
Inside-Outside thinking 89–90, 138, 218, 246, 247
Insoll, T 14
intellectual inertia 120–1
intensification 8, 17, 22–3, 27–8, 29–35, 38, 45–8, 60, 62, 87, 98, 101–3, 104, 107–22, 140, 161, 207, 214, 228, 229, 253, 254, 256, 264, 267, 270, 271, 287, 297, 300, 307–8
intensity of occupation 141, 204, 209, 211–12, 223, 251, 252, 255, 284, 285
intentionality 12, 15, 64, 84, 87, 113, 140, 165, 172, 191, 216
interdisciplinary approaches 25–6, 208
intergroup dynamics 11, 12, 14, 60, 229, 240
intergroup relations 10, 11, 162–3, 179, 229
International Conference on Hunting and Gathering Societies 306
International Union of Prehistoric and Protohistoric Sciences (IUPPS) 306
interpretation 2, 8, 10, 12, 22, 27, 28, 29, 34, 42, 46, 48, 53, 59, 60, 63, 66–8, 91, 99, 104, 110, 111, 113–14, 120, 124, 131, 134, 136, 154, 188, 195, 204–5, 206–7, 212, 220, 221–2, 223, 244, 246, 247, 255, 262, 267, 282, 288, 294,

Index

298–9, 301–2, 310, 315; and ethnographic analogy 43–4, 72–5, 125, 182–3, 209, 215; and inclusiveness 16–17, 72–5, 78–80, 83–4, 88, 183; and law 127, 128–9
invasion 116, 156
Ireland 202
irrigation 141
Ithaca (Greece) 40, 43

James Cook University 295
Japan 100
Java 93, 98
Johnson, S 173, 181
Johnson, BJ 255
Jones RN 265
Jones, R 10–11, 20–1, 40–2, 117–20, 124–5
Jones, S 121
Jordan, P 185
Joyce, EB 96–7, 98
juan knives 99
Juru 76, 78

Kaalpi 245, 246–7, 249
Kaanju 149, 153
Kala Lagaw Ya 290
Kalalakinda 165–6, 176
Kalotas, A 244
Kahn, J 307
Kamminga, J 101, 105
Kangoulu 134
Karrakayn, A 180, 197
Keating, D 221
Keen, I 218
Kenniff Cave 96
Keynes, M 49
Kimberleys 93, 94–5, 98–9; rock art 91
King River 144
King, TF 228
Kingston 239
Kin Kopl 150
kinship 79, 148, 149, 155, 167, 168, 177, 178, 188, 189, 190, 195, 199, 200–1, 207; networks 124, 148, 151, 163–4, 168, 179, 192–4, 208, 211, 217, 219, 220, 249, 253, 291
knapping floors 133
knowledge, of the past 17, 19, 22, 23, 56–7, 72–84, 119, 129, 185, 198, 199, 203, 204, 208, 211, 216, 218–9, 292–3, 315; ownership and use 67, 72–84, 137, 149, 151, 199, 200, 203, 204, 216, 218–9, 315, 317
Koko Warra 141–2, 159–60
Koster site 228–9
Kowanyama 149–50
Kow Swamp 14, 226
Kramer, C 182
Kriol 181, 191
Kubin 302
Kuku Thaypan 146–8, 151, 153, 157

Kulinic language group 15
Kuuku Ya'u 81

Laade, W 283, 298–9
labour 192, 213, 294
lagoons 140, 142, 153
Lake Euramoo 282
Lakefield National Park 153
Lake Keilambete 265
Lake Mungo 14
Lake Nitchie 233
Lake Surprise 256–8, 260, 263, 265–9
Lake Victoria 268–9
lakes 140, 144, 226–7
Lamalama 141, 145, 147, 151–3, 156–8
Lamond, HG 77
Lampert, RJ 32, 223
land, colonial appropriation of 4–5, 17, 47, 68, 70, 88–89, 137, 192; and identity 4, 8, 15–16, 18, 66, 73, 89, 108, 113, 125–6, 144–5, 162–4, 180, 183, 185, 189, 195, 199–201, 214–6, 296; inheritance of 144, 148, 151, 180; management and use 10, 14, 104, 148–51, 169, 172, 178–80, 191, 195, 198, 204, 206–10, 212–4, 223, 229, 246, 253–4, 257, 264–7, 269, 271, 280, 285–6, 294, 298; ownership 28, 54, 74, 78–9, 130, 146, 149, 151–3, 164, 168, 192–3, 197, 211, 215, 217, 219, 239, 281; tenure 127–8, 141, 148, 150, 298, 139, 159; *see also* country
landscapes 3, 8, 13–15, 22, 28, 39, 43–4, 49, 64–5, 67, 74, 78, 81, 83, 109, 121, 124–6, 131, 133, 136, 139, 140–2, 144, 147, 149–52, 155, 157–9, 162, 164, 175, 179, 182–5, 190, 195, 198, 202, 212–13, 216–17, 229, 242, 246–7, 253, 256–57, 261, 266, 269, 270–1, 281–2, 284–6, 296, 309, 311–12, 314–15, 317
language 15, 27, 55, 67–8, 76, 78, 122, 139, 141–2, 148, 150–1, 164, 181, 189, 191, 201, 217, 218–19, 242, 245, 248–9, 251–3, 290
Last Glacial Maximum 244, 248–9, 252, 256, 261, 263, 269
Laura Basin 139, 141, 145, 149, 155
lava 256–7, 265–6, 269
Law 127–30, 134, 136, 148, 153–4, 163–4, 172, 178, 185, 191, 193–4, 196–8, 200–1
Lawn Hill Creek 244, 249
leaders, religious 227, 229, 239
Lee, RB 6, 53
Leichhardt, L 165, 166
legislation 127, 136–8
leilira blades 99
Leskernick 311–2, 314, 316–17
Lévinas, E 71
Lilley, I 11, 85, 117–19
Little Sandy Desert 246
Little Swanport 41
Lockhart River 81
Logging 81

Index

'logistical' settlement strategies 41, 141, 285–6
London Missionary Society (LMS) 292
Lowie, RH 91
Lubbock, J 5
lunettes 230
Lynchs Crater 282

Mabo judgement 79, 128
Mabuiag island 290, 293–4
Macassar 102
MacGregor, G 223
Mackay 76
Madura Cave 105
maladaptation 7, 10, 120
malnutrition 232
management of sites 133, 135–7, 139, 296
Manankurra (Manangoora) 165–8, 173–80, 199
Man the Hunter conference 24, 64, 228
mapping 182, 214, 251, 316
Margu 126
maritime trade 86, 105, 291
marking, *see* inscription 124
Marra 167–8
marriage 151, 193, 272, 282
Marrngawi DN 197, 202
Marshall, B 29, 239
Marwick, B. 245
Marxism 309; and forces of production 8, 307–9; and relations of production 8, 22, 87, 229, 307–9
massacres 82, 129, 131
materialism 7–8, 205
mats 235–7
McArthur River 162, 183
McBryde, I 49, 223
McCarthy, FD 91–6, 99, 188
McConvell, P 251
McDonald, JJ 248–9, 251
McLaughlin, D 199
meaning 10, 13, 15, 83, 119, 121, 138, 140, 162, 164, 168, 183–85, 193, 196–9, 202, 215, 218, 220, 222, 316
medicine plants 147
Mediterranean Sea 89, 95
Meehan, B 41, 53
megafauna 26
megaliths 91, 202
Melanesia 94, 98, 105, 297, 303
memory 13, 71, 127, 131, 149, 167, 173, 184, 188–9, 190–2, 194–6, 199–201, 203, 222, 314
Mer island 299
Merlan, F 136
Mersey Valley 145
Meskell, L 119
Mesolithic 95
metaphor 162, 180
method 36, 184, 229, 269
microliths, geometric 87, 95, 99

middens 13, 41, 133, 135, 210, 234
Middle East 52
Middle Range research 23, 35,
migration 26, 100, 254, 278
Mildura 234
Minister Assisting the Prime Minister for Reconciliation 68
Minister for Immigration and Multicultural Affairs 68
misfortune 130, 145
missions 126
mobility 11, 14, 53, 66, 192, 242, 244–6, 248–50, 253
modelling 26, 44, 90, 104, 244, 255, 307
monopolies 227
monsoons 143, 158, 255
monuments 15, 199
Mooney, SD 256
Moore, DR 293
Moorunde 237
Morality, *see* ethics 214
Morehead River 144
Morgan, LH 66, 90
mortar and pestles 187
mortuary differentiation 224, 226, 228, 233, 236, 237, 239–40
mound-and-ditch systems 294, 300
mounds 14–15, 135, 172, 232, 266, 311
mountains 75, 143, 213
Mount Burr 97–8
Mount Cameron West 42
Mount Eccles 256–7, 265, 269
movement, theoretical 6–7 23, 30, 34, 212; socio-cultural 26, 90, 103–4, 127, 141, 178, 217–19, 220–2, 231, 251, 254, 307, 312, 316
Mua island 272, 301–2
Mulgrave Peak 272
multiculturalism 40, 68, 70
multivocality 39
Muluwa 189–90
Mulvaney, DJ 52, 94, 96–101
mummification 91
Munn, N 216
Mununggurr D 80
Murray, T 21
Murray Bridge 234, 238
Murray–Darling river system 230, 226–8, 230–40
Murray Islands 295, 298–300; *see also individual island names*
Murray Islands Archaeological Project 295
Murulag island 272, 293
music 52, 218, 287
Myers, F 126, 213, 226
Myers, LD 7
myth 11, 125–7, 130–1, 133, 136, 138, 152, 169, 201, 241, 251, 306, 312, 315

Index

naming 46, 48, 139, 155, 164
Native Americans 69
native bees 134
native police 147
native title 127–8, 136, 298
Native Title Act 127–8, 136, 298
Nature 60, 63, 66–7, 140, 313–14
Near East 53, 202, 307
necklaces 236
neglect 4
negotiation 16, 72, 163, 173, 179, 194, 196, 198, 200, 206, 208, 219, 222, 241, 250
Neolithic 56, 67, 90, 95 311
netting 93–4
Nevabina Swamp 153
New Archaeology 6, 17, 23–4, 43, 112
New Guinea 10, 12, 23–4, 30–1, 45, 52, 54, 57–63, 65–8, 85–6, 92, 96, 99, 102–6, 141, 151–2, 254–5, 257, 270–2, 283, 285, 287–8, 290–2, 295, 297
New World, the 89, 115, 254
New Zealand 21
Ngarrabullgan 214
Ngaro 75–6, 78, 81–4
Ngarrindjeri 238–9
Ngilipitji quarry 124
Nicholls, N 7
Non-Pama-Nyungan languages 252
Noone, HVV 95
Normanton 76
normative frameworks of thought 12, 96, 115
North America 5, 309
North Island 173, 186, 194
Nunamiut 141
Nyilba, DM 176

Oates, WJ 76
Oates, LF 76
objectivity 35–6, 77–80, 114, 184, 215
obligations 148–9, 152, 228
ochre 191–2, 202, 214, 233, 236, 237, 244, 246, 250, 251, 301–2
O'Connell, JF 99–100, 101, 255
Oenpelli 98
Olduvai Gorge 128
Olkolo 153, 155
Olney, Justice 128, 136
ontology 18–19, 73, 89–90, 139, 144–5, 159, 162, 180, 214–6, 219–20, 222, 223
open systems 23–4, 26, 27, 33, 65, 162, 214, 249, 285–6
oppression 4, 25
optimal foraging theory 32, 140
optimization 32, 66, 140, 151
oral history 18, 79, 84, 174, 185–6, 201, 203, 222, 291, 296, 298, 301; *see also* oral traditions
oral traditions 72–3, 78–9, 82–3, 175, 200, 203, 283–4, 301–2; *see also* oral history

origins of agriculture, *see* agriculture
Orman reef 290
Ormi 297–8, 300
ornamentation 233, 236
orthostats 313
osteoarthritis 232
Otherness 25, 54, 67
Otway Ranges 43
ownership 73, 79, 152–5, 164–5, 179, 192–3, 206, 211, 217, 231; private 175

paintings, *see* pictographs
Palaeolithic 56, 67, 90–1, 95, 209, 250
palaeopathological analyses 231–2
Palm Island 75–6, 81
Pama–Nyungan languages 27, 251, 252
Panaramitee 249
Papua New Guinea 10, 23, 30, 31, 92, 141, 288, 290; *see also* New Guinea
Papuans 30, 94, 104, 290–1, 292–3, 295
paradigm change 108
parallax error 118
parasitism 232
Pardoe, C 28, 230, 232–3
Parr, JF 300
pastoralism 145, 178, 234, 237
patination 249
Pearce, RH 98–9
pearling 292
pearl shells 233, 237
Pearsall, J 184
people-land relations, *see* land
pendants 236
perception 20, 36, 43, 52, 56, 67, 78, 129, 131, 138, 144, 148, 163, 180, 204–5, 215, 219–21, 222, 240, 309, 314, 317
permanence, *see* fixity
Perry, WJ 91, 93
petroglyphs 246–50
phenomenology 15, 39, 183, 219–20, 310, 311
Philip, B 68–9
phytoliths 300
pictographs 214, 216, 218–9, 246–8, 250, 301–2, 316
pigs 23, 59, 106, 152–3
Pilbara–Gascoyne region 244, 247, 251
Pintupi 227
pipes 237
pitfalls 238
plankton 261–3, 265, 268
planting 58, *see also* agriculture, farming, horticulture
plant yields 65, 228
Pleistocene 26, 27, 29, 33, 35, 45, 47, 88, 100, 142, 244, 245, 247, 249, 271
Plomley, NJB 41, 43
pluralism 112

377

Index

points 87, 98, 100, 102, 124–5, 138; bondi 99; harpoon 175; Kimberley 93, 95, 99; pirri 96
politics of archaeology 20, 35–7, 114, 118, 119–21, 317; and political correctness 87
pollen, analysis 256–7, 259–65, 268, 269, 271, 275, 276–286; transport 280
polygyny 32, 62, 229
population, movement 232, 237, 275, 291; density 6, 10, 12, 24, 44–5, 61, 205, 291; pressure 104, 109, 142, 232, 254, 255, 265, 267; size 35, 44–5, 122, 140, 142, 205, 212, 213, 227, 229, 254–5, 275, 284, 303
Porch, N 29
Port Stewart River 153
positivism 33–4, 73, 209, 215, 223
post-colonialism 20, 85, 119, 121, 139, 155
post-modern archaeologies 33–4, 183–4
post-positivist archaeologies 33–4
post-processual thinking 7, 27, 30, 33–4, 38, 67, 111, 112, 204
post-structuralism 112, 183–4
pottery 284, 297, 303
pounding hollows 187
Povinelli, EA 217–8
power 4–5, 18, 25, 31, 67, 70–3, 77, 79, 125, 127, 138, 145, 154, 159, 167, 169, 171–2, 173, 176–7, 180, 190–1, 194–7, 198–200, 203, 221, 222, 227, 312, 314
praxis 36–7
preconceptions 12, 18, 34–5, 38, 52–4, 60, 63, 65, 66, 67, 68, 70, 97, 119; *see also* preunderstanding
predictability 9, 32, 62; of the environment 9, 140
prejudice, *see* preconceptions
Presland, G 100
prestige 32, 62, 177, 191, 194, 196, 299
Pretty, GL 226, 228, 233, 235–7
Preucel, RW 79, 80
preunderstanding 18, 119, 214–15, 223
primitivism 56–7, 60, 61, 63, 68, 89–91, 213
Princess Charlotte Bay 102, 141–2, 144, 148, 150, 160
Prince of Wales Island, *see* Murulag island
privilege 70, 112, 238; and authority 84; and the senses 215, 221
processual archaeology 6, 13, 34, 67, 96, 110, 112, 114–15, 204–7, 210, 307
productivity 9–12, 60, 63, 101, 104, 112, 206
profanation 131
progressivism 5, 28, 31, 53, 55–6, 57, 60, 62, 63, 65, 67–8, 70, 80, 89, 90, 93, 94, 116, 138
Prokopec, M 236
property 132, 138, 141, 148–9, 169, 174–5
proprietary rights, *see* property
Proserpine 75
Protector of Aborigines 43, 76
provisions spreadsheet 64

Pryor, Pat 76
Pryor, Peter 76
public archaeology 22, 34, 38
public narratives 68
Pulu island 297
punishment 130, 135
Puntutjarpa 243
Puritjarra 244, 247, 249–51
purity of race 90

quarries 49, 77, 82, 124–5, 133–4, 138, 206, 246, 293
Quincan Crater 282

race 5, 56, 68, 75, 90, 114
racism 17, 57
radiocarbon dating 14, 29, 105, 233, 255, 259, 260, 275, 278, 293–4, 296, 300–1
rainbow serpent 133
rainfall 6, 141–3, 255, 257, 261–2, 273, 283
rainforest 45, 58, 143, 280, 282–283
rain-making 248
Rakawurlma, JT 178, 180, 194–5
rangelands 139
ranked societies 228
ranking, age, sex 14, 240
Rate-of-Change (ROC) analysis 256–7
Ray, SH 290
reading 18, 44, 74, 112, 125, 127, 157, 221
reciprocity 161, 196, 222, 250
reconciliation 68, 69, 70
Redmond, A 91
Red Point 151
Reed, CA 53
reefs 75, 79, 142, 272, 288, 289, 290
refugia 244
regionalization 212–3, 251, 255
regulations 151, 206–7
reflexivity 34, 37, 310
religion 7, 128, 133, 145, 148, 152, 154–5, 159, 161, 163–4, 167, 177–8, 214, 227, 238–9
religious prohibitions 65
remembrance 19, 190, 192, 200, 218, 221
Renfrew, C 4, 67
repatriation 14
representation 9, 54, 81, 91, 95, 107–8, 112–14, 116–17, 119–22, 184, 192, 208, 315–6
reproduction of knowledge 119, 218
residential patterns 252
'residential' settlement strategies 285
resistance 117
resources, availability of 11, 59, 82, 128, 150, 152–3, 168, 177, 187, 210, 229, 238, 248, 265–7, 291, 308,
resourcing strategies 10–11, 44, 57, 59, 64–6, 79, 108, 113, 141, 149, 151, 154, 158, 164, 169, 177, 179, 208, 212, 228–9, 265, 285, 290, 299

responsibility 37, 152, 180
reverence 154, 195
revisionism 118
rhetoric 114, 116, 119
Richardson, J 297
Riches, D 53
Rick, JW 29
Rick's method 29
Ridgeway, A 70
Rigsby, B 141, 143, 152–3
Rindos, D 53
risk 228
risk-minimisation 105, 242, 253
ritual 13, 32, 62, 102, 105, 132, 148, 155, 165–6, 172, 177–9, 185, 187, 188–94, 200, 209, 215–16, 218, 228–9, 242, 248, 250, 252–3, 292, 311
ritual engines 250
ritual orchestration of landscapes and seascapes 13, 155, 296, 149
rivers 58, 140, 142–4, 149, 153–4, 157, 162, 166, 174, 183, 186, 288
Rivers, WHR 291, 298
Robins, R 182
Robinson, GA 41, 43, 44, 208
Robinson River 162
rock art 14–15, 27–8, 48, 78, 85, 91, 132, 149, 213–14, 221, 244, 246, 247–50, 283; homogeneity of 27, 78, 213, 214, 246–8
Rocky Cape South cave 21, 41
Roe, D 299
Romans, Roman legions 3, 57
Rome (Italy) 3
Roonka 14, 28, 226–9, 231–3, 235–41
Rosenfeld, A 248–50
Ross, A 47
Roth, WE 72, 74–9
Rough Tor 313
Rowland, MJ 77, 87, 101–2, 104
Rowlands, M 307
Rowley-Conwy, P 116
Rowntree, LB 284
Rudder, J 218
Ruddock, P 68–70
Rumsey, A 126
Russell-Smith, J 156

sacred/secret knowledge 199, 172, 188, 190
sacred objects 188, 190, 197–8
sacred sites 137, 188, 190, 316; *see also specific sacred site types*
Sahara Desert 254
Sahul 288
Saibai island 283, 293–6, 300
Salgado, B 239
Saltwater Creek 153
Samoa 283
sampling 78, 259, 267

Sansom, B 218
Santa Fe Institute 61
Savanna 142–3, 174
scale 31, 34, 46, 73, 141, 174, 186, 206–8, 212, 214, 248–9, 251–3, 266–7, 273, 317
scarred trees 132–3
scheduling 246, 248
Schiffer, M 23, 209
science and knowledge 79, 24–5, 37–8, 56, 61, 72–3, 79, 83, 90, 114, 119
scholarship 79, 87–8
Scotland 55, 221
Scottish antiquities 56
Scott River 166
scrapers 234; end 95; thumb-nail 95
sealevel rise 142, 254, 272, 275, 278
Seal Point 43, 209–11
seascapes 13, 104, 149, 163, 202, 296
seasonality 141, 158, 212, 285; of movement 44, 82, 141, 143, 145, 147, 158, 168–9, 212, 237, 285, 312
sedentism 11, 14, 24, 212, 226, 231, 239, 240, 245, 285, 309; semisedentism 229
sedimentation rates 214, 255, 275, 281–2, 301
seed grinding 245–6, 255
senses, the 218, 222
Sepik River 151
Serpents Glen 246, 248
settlement patterns/systems 13–14, 17, 42, 44, 109, 140, 209, 230, 237, 243–4, 250, 254, 271, 284–6, 312
shadows 202, 316
shamanism 14
Shang Dynasty 4
shaping 74, 78, 141, 201
sharing 64, 150–1, 155, 199, 200, 203, 217, 223, 228, 238
Shawcross, W 21
shellfish 131, 232, 234, 290, 299
Shoshonean groups 6
shrines 14
signalling behaviour 251
significance cultural/social 14, 124, 129, 132, 135, 137, 139, 154, 162, 169, 172, 179–80, 182, 184, 188, 192, 199, 209, 216, 220, 286, 309, 314
silencing 10, 13, 54, 118
Simpson, KNG 234
Sir Edward Pellew islands 162, 173–4, 183
site formation processes 15, 41, 46, 214, 235, 271, 275, 280, 300–1
site surveys 41, 42, 75, 78, 125, 132–5, 199, 293, 311–12, 314
skeletal remains 18
Small Tool Tradition 25, 85–7, 95, 100, 102
smelling 217
Smith, A 283
Smith, EA 53

Index

Smith, GE 91, 93
Smith, MA 244, 245, 248, 249, 250
smoking 135
social change, external causality of, 117, 254, 267; internal causality of 8, 9, 105, 244; mechanisms of 15, 59, 62, 117, 204, 215, 226, 254, 267
social control 17, 88, 168, 169
social debate 38, 74
social dynamism 9, 22, 242
social engagement 13, 182, 214–5
social evolution 5, 9, 17, 57, 88–91, 114
social gatherings 10–11, 14
social injustice 38
social interaction 3, 4, 23, 65, 85, 103
social marking; *see also* inscription 15
social networks 26–7, 32–3, 62, 103, 141, 151, 184, 228–9, 248, 249, 252, 308
social organization 4, 10, 127, 155, 185, 201, 228, 249, 291, 298, 300; centralised 231; complex 226
social practice as epiphenomenon 10
social ranking 14, 240
social stasis 8, 48, 66–8, 90, 94, 108, 114, 207, 240, 242
Soejono, RP 97
Sokoli 297–8, 300
Sollas, WJ 5, 60
songs, 81, 165, 171–2, 176, 193, 203, 216, 218–19; song cycles 194–5
sophistication 40, 113
sorcery 174, 188–9, 203.
sorry business 68
sound 221
South Africa 306
Southampton 306
South Australian Museum 203, 226, 228, 234
South–East Asia 99, 100, 102, 105, 254,
South Molle Island 77, 82
South West Island 173
sovereignty 127
space, *see* place
Spain 250
spatial history 214
spearing 135
Spencer, H 66
Spencer, WB 93, 96
spirit mediums 238
spiritscapes 13, 148, 159, 286, 296
spiritual essence 125, 149, 163, 170, 171, 190, 202
spiritual protection 149, 217
springs 155, 246, 251
Sri Lanka 98
stable isotope analyses 231–2, 240; stable carbon 231; protein 231
standardisation 87, 260
Stanner, WEH 217

starch grains 300
stars 163, 218
'starvation tucker' 168
stasis 67, 220, 242
state societies 4
status 4, 10, 14, 32, 62, 132, 190, 191, 197, 198, 199, 229, 233, 240
St. Bees Island 75
stereotyping 87
Steward, JH 6, 7, 9
stewardship 139, 141, 158
Stolen Generation 68
stone arrangements 13, 14
stone artefacts 15, 26, 78, 132, 134, 214, 235, 237, 275, 284, 301
stone artefact scatters 133
stone cairns 221, 313
stone-headed clubs 92
stone markers 196
stone tool manufacture 77, 82, 87, 92, 237, 245
Stonehenge 309
storage sites 14
story-telling 316, 318
stratified societies 25, 228, 240
Strehlow, TGH 227
stress 232, 253, 306
Struever, S 228
subsistence 6–13, 58, 63–4, 66, 81, 108–9, 127, 209–13, 228, 237–9, 288, 290–3, 295–6, 298–300, 302–3, 308, 317
Sulawesi 93, 96–8, 102
Sumarian civilisation 254
Sumatra 93
surplus 32, 60, 62, 228–9, 266
Sutton, PJ 142
Swan Hill 2
Swanport 231, 234, 239
swamps 141, 142, 152, 234, 257, 269, 282, 288, 293, 294, 300
swidden cultivation 59; *see also* agriculture, horticulture
symbolism 162, 165, 188, 201
Syria 89
systems thinking 23

taboos 10
taphonomy 78, 245
Taplin, G 239
Taube, K 223
Tartanga 235
Taskscapes 222
Tasmania 16–17, 21, 23, 29, 40–5, 59, 88, 89, 102, 105, 120, 233, 287; and cessation of fish eating 7, 10, 45
Tasmanian Devil 105, 233
Tasmanian Museum and Art Gallery 21, 40
Tasmanian Tiger 105

380

Index

teaching 20, 36, 43, 47–8
technological change 11, 45, 95, 97–8, 100–2, 104, 108, 122, 159, 208, 214, 251, 303
technological developments 69, 255
technological explanations 7–8, 11, 43, 45, 90, 95, 99–102, 104, 108, 122, 187, 208, 227, 266
tektites 233
temperature 143, 254, 257, 261, 273, 282
temporalities 80, 81, 139, 140, 158–9, 213; *see also* time
temporal trends 33, 35, 140, 255, 270, 271; *see also* historical trajectories
tenure, land 139, 148, 150, 159, 298, sea 79, 141, 298
terra nullius 54, 67
Terrell, JE 12, 64
Terrill, A 76
Territoriality 14, 65, 180, 214, 231, 232, 239–40, 245–6, 250–1, 253
terror 131
text-based studies 34, 53, 73, 77–9, 82–4, 119, 315, 316; *see also* written historical records
Thebes 55
theory, sociocultural 6, 22–4, 27, 32, 34, 43, 46–9, 84, 92, 112, 205, 212, 229, 249, 307, 315
Thieberger, N. 244
Thomas, N 7, 8
Thomson, DF 125, 141
Thorne, AG 98
Three-age system 55
Thursday Island 273
tides 13, 140, 144, 158
Tilley, C 311
time 3, 8, 9, 12,23, 24, 26, 28, 46, 56, 60–2, 65, 127, 129, 175, 178, 185, 192, 196–7; biblical notions of 55; cosmological 125, 130; cyclic 80, 81; linear 55, 80, 81, 114
Timor 102
Tindale, NB 72, 75–6, 78–9, 239
tjurunga 130
Toalian industry 93
Tonkinson, R 244
Toolondo 223, 266
Tonga 283
Torres Strait 12, 58, 86, 92, 103–6, 270–2, 281–4, 286–93, 295–7, 300–3; Islanders 18, 86, 92, 104, 105, 290–2, 296; land-bridge 103, 271, 292
Torres Strait Regional Authority (TSRA) 290
Torres Strait Research Project 294
Tournal, P 55
Townsville 76
toxic foods 161, 171, 176, 179, 255
trade partners 15, 77–8, 86, 93, 166, 171, 207–8, 210, 211, 244, 251, 284, 288, 291, 293, 296–8, 302–3

tradition, Indigenous 18, 41, 47, 72–4, 76, 78–9, 82–3, 87, 125, 127–8, 130, 132–3, 135–6, 139–40, 142, 144–5, 148–55, 163, 175, 185, 190, 198, 200, 203, 269, 283, 290–2, 300–2; archaeological/theoretical 6, 7, 11, 13, 16–18, 22, 27–32, 34, 41, 44–5, 47, 57, 59–61, 64, 68, 85–7, 89, 95, 98, 100, 102, 110, 112–19, 121–2, 182, 184, 204, 222, 227, 240, 276,
traditional law and custom 135, 136, 152, 185, 198, 200
trajectories, historical 12, 20, 28, 31, 34–5, 55, 57, 62, 65, 116, 196, 270; intellectual 46, 204; of ancestral beings 216; *see also* temporal trends
transmission, of disease 106
translocation, of plants 59
trauma 232
treponematoses 232
Trigger, D 182
tropes 9, 121
truth 54, 77–9, 148, 184
Turao Kula 301, 302
turtles 143, 234, 238, 288
Tylor, EB 56, 90
typological approaches 87

Ucko, P 306
uniformitarianism 74, 80
University College London (UCL) 293–4, 302, 307, 314, 315
University of Queensland 20, 36–7, 296
University of New England 45
University of Sydney 20–1, 40, 43
utilitarianism 15, 179, 184, 187–8, 200

validation 83, 228, 229, 231; of knowledge 19, 84
Vanderlin Island 173, 194
Vanderwal, RL 293
vegetation succession 12
views of the past 80, 84, 96, 129
vigilantes 146–8
villages 53, 58, 172, 228, 284–5, 286, 291, 292, 301
vine thickets 272, 274, 280–1, 283
violence, academic 118; adaptive 307; contact 131, 134, 147; frontier 131, 147
vision 219–20, 221, 223
volcanic craters 257, 282
vulgar materialism, *see* cultural materialism

Waanyi 132, 135, 136
Wagner, R 219
Waier island 289, 298
Walker, D 103, 292
Walsh, F 244, 245
Walsh, K 183–4
warfare 291

381

Index

Warragarra rock shelter 45
water management, *see* drainage systems
water content of grass 140, 157, 158; *see also* dew
water eddies 154
waterholes 145–6, 152–4; *see also* lakes
Watson, A 221
ways of knowing, *see* epistemology
wealth 140, 178, 191
Wearyan River 162, 165, 174, 183
weathering 247, 249
Webb, SG 232
Weipa 15
Wenlock River 142
Wessex 314
Western Plains 256, 263, 265
Western Torres Strait Cultural History Project 296
wetland sites 15, 59, 144, 265–6
Whallon, R 209–10
White (Schrire), C 95, 98
White, JP 21, 88, 98, 99–100, 101, 103, 110
White, N 124–5
White Australia Policy 40
Whitehead, PJ 156
Whitsunday Islands 27, 72, 74–8, 81–3
'widow's caps' 234
wildfires, *see* fire
Willandra Lakes 226
Williams, A 314–5

Williams, E 266
Williams, NM 80–1, 143, 150–3
Williams, R 309–10
Williamson, C 115–16
Wilmore, M 315
Wilson, D 55–6
Wilson, M 124
wind 13, 140, 143–4, 155–8, 257, 313, 316
Windschuttle, K 45, 120
Wobst, MH 249
Wolski, N 15–16
Woodburn, J 308
Wood Wood 2
World Archaeological Congress (WAC) 306–7
worship 3
written historical records 72; *see also* text-based studies
Wudalwanga Plain 197
Wulbulinimara, M 168

yams 23, 58, 152, 172, 229, 291
Yanyuwa 161–81, 182–203
Yen, DE 64
Yengoyan, AA 32–3, 253
Yiithuwarra 151
Yolngu 125, 150, 170, 217, 219, 223
Yorta Yorta 127–8, 136, 138

Zeitz, FR 234